The STATS™ 1998 Minor League Scouting Notebook

by John Sickels
and
STATS, Inc.

Edited by Mat Olkin and Jim Callis
Programming by Brent Osland
Statistics by Howe Sportsdata International

STATS
PUBLISHING

Published by STATS Publishing: A division of Sports Team Analysis & Tracking Systems, Inc.

Cover by Ron Freer

Cover photos of Ben Grieve and Todd Helton by Larry Goren

STATS is a trademark of Sports Team Analysis and Tracking Systems, Inc.

First Edition: January, 1998

ISBN 1-884064-48-5

Dedication

This book was written for
Hilda Sickels
Who underwent 36 hours of labor
and loves me anyway;
Thanks for that and so much more.

Acknowledgments

This book could not have been written without the assistance, direct and indirect, of the following people. I would like to thank them.

My beautiful and loving wife, Jeri.

My parents, Joe and Hilda Sickels, and the whole Sickels and Audeh families.

My sister, Lisa Patterson, and her husband Greg.

My in-laws, Marsh and Gwen Jackson, and the entire Jackson family.

Bill James, my former employer, who remains a good friend, and a constant role model.

Eddie Epstein, for his goodwill and sound advice.

Rob Neyer, of ESPN SportsZone; my first editor, and a fine comrade.

Don Zminda, Vice President of Publications for STATS, Inc., who directs the production and editing of the book after I deliver the raw manuscript. He supervises every aspect of the production of this product, and every other STATS book, too. And he does a damn fine job of it.

John Dewan, the President and CEO of STATS, for his steady hand on the helm of this growing company.

Mat Olkin, the co-editor of the book, who also does a damn fine job with the unenviable task of editing my work.

Jim Callis, formerly of *Baseball America,* and the co-editor this year with Mat is a top-notch prospect evaluator in his own right.

Chuck Miller, who did the page layout and spent many long hours producing the final manuscript.

Tony Nistler, Kevin Fullam and Ethan Cooperson, who assisted with editing, stat checking and proofreading.

Brent Osland, who did the programming for this book with assistance from Stefan Kretschmann.

Ron Freer, who designed the cover of the book and Drew Faust, who selected the photos.

Everyone else at STATS who had a hand in getting this book out to you, including: Doug Abel, Art Ashley, Kristen Beauregard, Andrew Bernstein, Grant Blair, Steve Byrd, Mike Canter, Jim Capuano, Dave Carlson, Jeff Chernow, Brian Cousins, Steve "Dick" Drago, Marc Elman, "Not the" Dan Ford, Angela Gabe, Ken Gilbert, Kevin Goldstein, Mike Hammer, Jim Henzler, Mark Hong, Sherlinda Johnson, Antoinette Kelly, Jason Kinsey,

Tracy Lickton, Walter "Joe" Lis, Bob Meyerhoff, Betty Moy, Jim Musso, Jim "Donovan" Osborne, Oscar "Vincente" Palacios, Dean Peterson, Kacey Poulos, Corey "Bip" Roberts, John Sasman, Taasha "Bill" Schroeder, Heather Schwarze, Stephanie Seburn, Matt Senter, Leena Sheth, Lori Smith, Allan Spear, Kevin "Gorman" Thomas, Joseph Weindel, Mike Wenz, Peter Woelflein and Susan Zamechek.

The Public Relations Offices of the Omaha Royals, the Nashville Sounds, the Buffalo Bisons, the Iowa Cubs, the Oklahoma City 89ers, the Wichita Wranglers, the Midland Angels, the El Paso Diablos, and the San Antonio Missions.

John Benson, Josh Boyd, J. J. Cooper, Kimball Crossley, Kevin Culley, Dave Lawson, Daniel Levine, Terry Linhart, Deric McKamey, Ron Shandler, Paul Swanson, Rick Wilton, Craig Wright, and the staff of the *Baseball Prospectus,* are some of the people who contributed information, observations and opinions that were instrumental in the formation of my own evaluations. I regard my peers as colleagues, rather than competitors. Any factual errors, blatant misjudgments, or stupid mistakes in content of the book are, of course, entirely my responsibility.

Derek Botehlo, John Shelby, Ron Swoboda, Mike Jirschele, Al Newman, Mark Shapiro, Marty Esposito, John Leavitt, Bob Hards, Michael Curto and Pat Filippone are some of the baseball people who have communicated with me over the last three years.

Brent Jacobs, John McCartney and Brian Bacher are my friends.

Kirby Puckett, Kent Hrbek, Roger Waters, David Gilmour, Nick Mason, Rick Wright, Syd Barrett, Gene Roddenberry, Thomas Cranmer, Thomas Merton, Aldous Huxley, Noam Chomsky, Evelyn Underhill, Matthew Fox, R. H. Tawney, Gustav Mahler, W. A. Mozart, Susie Robinson, Dr. Richard C. Frucht, Dr. Joel Benson, Dr. John Hopper, Dr. Victor Bailey, Everett Craft, Brien Murphy, Jennifer Van Wiel, B.S., A.B., L.B., Jacinda, Dave, Sunil, Jo Ellen, my friends at Microtech Computers, and my cats Toonces and Spot have been or are playing important parts in the life known as John Sickels.

—John Sickels

Table of Contents

Introduction

Submitted for your approval: the box score of the August 15th, 1997 game between the Iowa Cubs and the Oklahoma City 89ers, as published in the *Des Moines Register* the following morning.

Oklahoma City	AB	R	H	BI		Iowa	AB	R	H	BI
Little CF	5	0	0	0		Cairo 2B	5	1	1	1
Diaz 2B	3	0	1	1		Jennings CF	5	2	4	5
Ortiz 1B	4	0	0	0		Brown LF	5	1	2	2
Simms LF	3	0	0	0		Kieschnick DH	4	1	1	1
Murphy LF	0	0	0	0		Valdes RF	4	0	1	0
Smith DH	4	0	1	1		McCall 1B	4	1	1	1
Sagmoen RF	3	0	0	0		Dalesandro C	4	0	1	0
Silvestri 3B	3	0	0	0		Wilson 3B	4	1	2	0
Brown C	3	0	0	0		Peterson SS	3	3	1	0
Frias SS	4	2	2	0						
TOTAL	31	2	5	2		TOTAL	38	10	14	10

OKLAHOMA CITY	0	0	0		0	0	1		0	1	0	2
IOWA	0	1	3		2	0	0		2	2	X	10

E-Silvestri (21), Wood (1). DP-Oklahoma City 1, Iowa 2. LOB-Oklahoma City 8, Iowa 5. 2B-Frias (17), Cairo (31), Jennings (22), Brown (18). 3B-Jennings (4). HR- Jennings (19), Brown (15), Kieschnick (19), McCall (14). SB-Valdes (8).

OKLAHOMA CITY	IP	H	R	ER	BB	SO
Moody L, 0-1	6.0	11	7	5	0	2
Kell	2.0	3	3	3	1	2
IOWA	IP	H	R	ER	BB	SO
Wood W, 3-2	7.2	4	2	2	5	8
Heredia	1.1	1	0	0	1	0

WP-Kell, Wood 2. U-Schrieber, Simonides, Kowalczyk. T-2:31. A-6,644.

Just looking at the box score, you can see why this game was fun to watch. There was a solid pitching performance from hot prospect Kerry Wood, Robin Jennings hit for the cycle, and several other guys had good games. It wasn't a close game, a pitching duel, or a slugfest; indeed, the score was one-sided, but it was very entertaining.

Kerry Wood struck out eight in seven-plus innings, and the way he did it was very impressive. The radar guns clocked him at a consistent 96 MPH, and no one on the Oklahoma City team could catch up with him. Early in the game he had great command, hitting the corners with the fastball and a nasty breaking pitch. He looked unhittable, and indeed he had a perfect game until the sixth inning, when

Hanley Frias doubled. After that, Wood's command wobbled as he tried to over-throw, but anybody who saw him that night knows what a tremendous young tal-ent he is.

The game had a good mix of minor league veterans like Bubba Smith, Dave Sil-vestri, Mike Simms, and Rod McCall, along with prospects like Wood, Jennings, Frias, and Kevin Brown. The thing I enjoyed most about this game wasn't in the box score. As I sat in General Admission watching the pitchers, the hitters, the fielders, the benches, and the crowd, I remembered exactly how much I love base-ball.

This might be because I was sitting in GA, rather than the press box. I've been go-ing to minor league games for three years now in an "official" capacity as the writer of this book. I usually sit in the press box. This is good because it gives you access to people who see the team every day and have inside information that can be useful. Also, when it is 105 degrees in Wichita in July, the air conditioning is a welcome luxury. Free food is nice, too.

In Des Moines on August 15th, I forgot to arrange press credentials, so I decided to get a GA seat. The weather was warm but not uncomfortable. Bill James once wrote about how the atmosphere of the press box isolates writers from the general public. Based on my experience in this game, I believe that Bill was completely right.

On the drive up to Des Moines that afternoon, I listened to a radio program with some music expert talking about how you can follow "threads" of melody or har-mony through a good piece of music. It can be classical or blues or jazz or rock. Just listen to a piece by Mozart, or Beethoven, or B. B. King, or Pink Floyd, and follow the woodwinds or the strings or the bass guitar, or whatever, through the composition. It enhances the listening experience, and makes any piece of music more enjoyable.

You can do the same thing with a baseball game. You can watch the pitcher, or the center fielder, or the third base umpire, or the reactions of the fans in the first base box seats. You can just take in the totality of the game. The thing is, it's hard to do any of this from the press box. You only have one perspective up there. You can't really watch the crowd or the dugouts. My advice to all baseball writers: get out of the press box more often. Maybe it will help you remember what a wonder-ful game baseball still is.

Player Evaluation

Is evaluating baseball players an art or a science?

A bit of both, perhaps. Over the last 150 years, human beings have made massive strides in understanding causation in the natural world. We can make accurate predictions of natural phenomena much of the time. Our understanding of the laws of gravity and motion enable us to predict the future location of planetary bodies and successfully send spacecraft to Mars and Saturn, for example. Once you get past the physical sciences and into the human sciences of psychology and sociology, however, things become less certain.

Baseball players, being human, have an X factor of uncertainty. We can, using objective statistical measures, figure out which players have the *best* chance to develop, but it is never more than a *probability*. There is, in essence, no such thing as a can't-miss prospect. Even if a guy has a 90 percent chance to develop into a star, like Ben Grieve or Adrian Beltre, there is still a chance he won't make it, due to injury, a crisis of confidence, or some other factor that we can't predict.

Evaluating A Position Player

Scouts traditionally judge position players on their physical "tools," their basic athletic ability in other words. Can he run? Throw? Is he strong? etc. This is understandable, since the quality of competition at the amateur level is too erratic for statistical performace to be reliable. The problem is, scouts make mistakes when they judge players already in professional baseball by this criteria. Having good physical tools doesn't mean much when you're hitting .220.

How a player hits in the minor leagues is a very good indicator of how he will hit in the majors, provided that appropriate adjustments are made regarding age, level of competition, and park factors.

Age is critical. An 18 year old playing anywhere above the Rookie level is impressive; if he's in Double-A, he's incredible. A 20 year old is doing just fine if he is in A-ball; if he's at Double-A or higher, he's damn good. A 24 year old in A-ball probably isn't much of a prospect; by that age, he should be in Double-A at least.

Park factors are very important. Some minor league stadiums, like Lancaster in the California League or Albuquerque in the Pacific Coast League, can increase offensive production by greater than 10 percent. Other parks, like New Britain in the Eastern League, are renowned for their ability to help pitchers. If a guy hits .300 at Albuquerque, that's about equal to .250 or so in Dodger Stadium. If a guy hits .300 at New Britain, that's about .280 or .290 in most major league parks.

What stats should we use when looking for prospects? I look at OPS, also known as OBP+SLUG, which combines two stats that are very valuable for determining offensive production. Comparing this to league averages, we get an idea how good the hitter is compared to his competition. I also look at SEC, secondary average, devised by Bill James. This gauges offensive contributions that other stats like batting average ignore: power, walks, stolen bases. It gives you an idea how broad a player's skills are, and how well a guy helps his team score runs. A guy with a .250 batting average but a .400 secondary average is helping his team score runs more than a guy with a .300 average but a .200 secondary.

As previous readers of this book know, I am a fanatic when it comes to strike-zone judgment. *Hitters must know how to control the strike zone.* Almost all good major league hitters control the strike zone. Frank Thomas controls the strike zone. Chuck Knoblauch controls the strike zone. Larry Walker controls the strike zone. Mike Piazza controls the strike zone. Strike-zone judgment is best measured by the number of walks drawn by the hitter. Generally, a hitter should have a walk total equal to at least 10 percent of his at-bats. If he has 500 at-bats, he needs to have at least 50 walks.

The ratio of walks to strikeouts is also important. If a hitter has 30 walks but just 50 strikeouts, that's acceptable. It means he swings at too many pitches, but at least he is making contact. If a guy has 30 walks but 100 strikeouts, that's bad. It means he doesn't really know what he is doing. On the other hand, if a guy has 80 walks and 100 strikeouts, that's okay. It means he probably takes too many pitches, but taking too many pitches isn't as bad as swinging at too many. It is easier to help a hitter who isn't aggressive enough than a hitter who is too aggressive. Speed is a useful tool, on both offense and defense, but it is often overrated, especially in relation to scoring runs. As the old cliché goes, you can't steal first base. Ask anyone, even an advocate of speed, "Would you rather have a guy hit 50 homers or steal 50 bases?" Unless they are totally insane, they will want the homers. This is not to say that a team of slow-footed sluggers will run away with the pennant. Speed is a useful commodity, but it is just one among many.

Defense is notoriously difficult to measure for minor league players. Field conditions vary widely from park to park and league to league, and lighting is often substandard. We can look to fielding percentage as a measure of reliability, range factor (the number of total chances per nine innings) as an indicator of range afield, and assist totals to help determine arm strength and accuracy for outfielders. Range afield is the most valuable of these attributes. A youngster with good range but a high error rate is more likely to develop into a useful defensive player than a guy with poor range but a low error rate.

Putting it all together, I look for what I have dubbed the *Seven Skills*: strike-zone judgment, hitting for power, hitting for average, offensive speed, range afield, reliability, and throwing arm. My approach is similar to the Five Tools used by scouts, but I believe it is more nuanced.

Evaluating A Pitcher

A method for evaluating pitchers accurately is the Holy Grail of Prospectametrics. There are statistical measures that are useful in predicting the future of pitching prospects, but in general, forecasts regarding pitchers are less accurate than those for hitters. There isn't much we can do about that, until somebody invents a way to prevent young pitchers from getting hurt. Maybe cloning Leo Mazzone would help.

The best indicator for future success we have is strikeout/walk ratio (K/BB). A hurler who strikes out a lot more guys than he walks is a good bet to continue pitching well as he moves up the ladder. Also look at strikeout/innings (K/IP), and hits/innings (H/IP) ratios. A guy with good numbers in those categories probably has good stuff.

Sometimes you will see a pitcher with good K/IP and H/IP marks, but a bad K/BB ratio. Kerry Wood is a current example; Jaret Wright was like that last year. That means he has a good arm, but doesn't quite know how to use it. Sometimes you will see a guy with good K/BB but bad K/IP or H/IP. That means he is likely a finesse guy who relies on control to survive. In general, the guy with the good arm has a better future than the guy who relies on finesse. Most soft-tossers hit the wall in Double-A or Triple-A, although there are always exceptions.

Beyond The Numbers

Looking at the numbers and evaluating them within league and park context is the science part of prospecting. Looking at the so-called "intangibles" is the art part. Many sabermatricians deride traditionalists who talk about a "makeup" and "game face" when describing prospects. This is understandable, since traditionalists often use vague terms to justify capricious decisions. "I don't like Tom Williams' makeup, so let's play Rob Carter instead," says the old manager. You would think Tom Williams was Ru Paul.

On the other hand, it is naive to assume that things like personality and work ethic *don't* count. They damn well do count. Professional athletes are in a race against the clock. They race against time to get a job when they are young. Once they get a job, they contest the decline of their skills as they age. Any player, young or old, needs emotional and mental maturity to get the maximum out of his ability.

It is difficult of course to measure something like personality and work ethic. Some teams use so-called "personality inventories," standardized psychological tests given to potential draftees each spring. Many psychologists discount the validity of such tests, and the results are confidential in any event. On the other hand, simple word of mouth can be inaccurate, too, since players sometimes develop reputations they do not deserve.

Essentially, the intangibles are the X factor of human uncertainty. Some players, like Paul Molitor, Mo Vaughn, or Greg Maddux, have a positive X factor due to their drive, willpower, or intelligence. Others don't. It is hard to separate fact from rumor about player makeup, especially for minor leaguers, but it is still an important ingredient to consider.

Grades

For each player, I will assign a letter grade.

An **A-level** prospect has a very good chance to develop into a high-quality major league player, with stardom quite possible or highly likely in some cases.

A **B-level** prospect should develop into a pretty good player, with some sort of stardom not out of the question.

A **C-level** prospect could develop into a role player, a platoon player, or a mediocre regular. Some C prospects do become stars, but it is uncommon.

There are variations in each category: A C- prospect is quite marginal, but a C+ prospect could develop into a very useful player. A B- prospect is less impressive than a B+ prospect.

Be aware that the grades for pitchers do not correspond directly to the grades for position players. A Grade A shortstop has a much better chance to develop than a Grade A pitcher. On the other hand, a Grade C pitcher has a better shot than a Grade C shortstop. Many excellent major league pitchers were Grade C prospects in the minors.

I don't look too much at guys at the lowest level of the minors, the Rookie leagues and the short-season A leagues. The quality of competition is too inconsistent at those levels. I am also uncomfortable giving a letter grade to any prospect without a full season of experience. Still, there are some guys at those levels that I will discuss in the book, because they were recent first-round draft picks like Dermal Brown, or because people have expressed an interest in them, like Jackson Melian.

Sources

It would be impossible to write a book like this without good sources, both well-known and obscure.

I go to as many minor league games as I can, and watch the players, the coaches, the pregame, and the field contest itself. I'll watch the action from the press box, from behind home plate, and from the foul lines, to get various angles, especially on the pitchers. I talk to baseball people when I can, scouts especially. Most of them are very helpful, once they understand that you sort of know what you are talking about. Sometimes you have to take what baseball people tell you with a grain of salt, especially about players in their own organization. It is also important to talk with other people who study minor league baseball.

Finally, material in the press is extremely helpful. The premiere publication about minor league baseball is *Baseball America*, of course. I don't always agree with their evaluations, but it is an extraordinary source of data about players in all organizations. It is indispensible. *Baseball Weekly* is a good source of info, too, and the combination of those two publications, along with statistical updates and information packets from Howe Sportsdata, serves to keep the avid fan or the book author well-informed.

Spring In The Autumn: The Arizona Fall League

One good place to study prospects is the Arizona Fall League. If you live near the Phoenix area, or can afford to take a junket there for a few days, you can see a lot of minor league players, well-known and unsung, play competitive games in October and November.

I had the pleasure of speaking at a scouting symposium organized by Rick Wilton and Ron Shandler of *Baseball HQ* during the 1997 Arizona Fall League season. It was a great opportunity to meet fellow diamond fanatics, take in the warm desert air, and watch some good baseball. I would highly recommend the experience for anybody interested in the minors. Watch for info on their website about the symposium in 1998.

Last Year's Top 50: In Review

Here is last year's list of Top 50 prospects. I hold myself accountable for what I write, so here goes.

1) Andruw Jones, OF, Atlanta Braves—Should get better and better. Superstar in the making.

2) Vladimir Guerrero, OF, Montreal Expos—Played great when healthy. Will be a star.

3) Nomar Garciaparra, SS, Boston Red Sox—1997 American League Rookie of the Year.

4) Scott Rolen, 3B, Philadelphia Phillies—1997 National League Rookie of the Year.

5) Paul Konerko, 3B, Los Angeles Dodgers—1998 Rookie of the Year Candidate.

6) Ruben Rivera, OF, New York Yankees—Shoulder surgery sidelined him most of season. Traded to Padres, could still be a star.

7) Edgard Velazquez, OF, Colorado Rockies—Moved up to Triple-A, lost command of strike zone. Still a good prospect but needs to rebound.

8) Todd Walker, 3B, Minnesota Twins—Got off to slow start, demoted to Triple-A, rebounded, hit well in September. He should still be good.

9) Todd Helton, 1B, Colorado Rockies—1998 Rookie of the Year Candidate.

10) Mike Sweeney, C, Kansas City Royals—Finally got a shot in the majors, wasn't terrible but a bit of a disappointment.

11) Jaret Wright, RHP, Cleveland Indians—Promoted ahead of schedule, held his own in the majors, World Series hero. Future star if he stays healthy.

12) Kerry Wood, RHP, Chicago Cubs—Awesome arm, promoted to Triple-A too quickly and struggled. Still an excellent prospect, but injuries and control a worry.

13) Miguel Tejada, SS, Oakland Athletics—1998 Rookie of the Year Candidate.

14) Adrian Beltre, 3B, Los Angeles Dodgers—1999 Rookie of the Year Candidate, currently the best prospect in baseball.

15) Dmitri Young, 1B, St. Louis Cardinals—Did okay in majors, but lost job to Mark McGwire. Young needs to do better, and will have his chance in Cincinnati.

16) Karim Garcia, OF, Los Angeles Dodgers—Hard to believe he is still just 22. And he's still a very good prospect. 1998 Rookie of the Year Candidate for the Diamondbacks.

17) Jose Cruz, Jr., OF, Seattle Mariners—Victim, or beneficiary, of one of the worst trades in baseball history. Better than I thought he would be; could hit 400 homers.

18) Ben Grieve, OF, Oakland Athletics—Monster season. 1998 Rookie of the Year Candidate.

19) Ron Wright, 1B, Pittsburgh Pirates—Lost much of season to broken wrist, but hit when healthy. 1998 or 1999 Rookie of the Year Candidate.

20) Hiram Bocachica, SS-2B, Montreal Expos—Struggling to find a position, but he will hit.

21) Jeff Suppan, RHP, Boston Red Sox—Overcame arm woes to earn rotation spot. Should improve; could be the Diamondbacks' ace.

22) Chad Hermanson, 2B, Pittsburgh Pirates—Outstanding young power hitter, trying to learn to play second base.

23) Bob Abreu, OF, Houston Astros—Lost much of season to injury, should still be an effective hitter but star potential is less than it appeared two years ago. Chosen by Tampa Bay in the expansion draft, then traded immediately to the Phillies.

24) Mike Cameron, OF, Chicago White Sox—Showed his broad base of skills in the majors. Power, speed, defense, may have some All-Star seasons.

25) Enrique Wilson, 2B-SS, Cleveland Indians—1998 Rookie of the Year Candidate.

26) Carl Pavano, RHP, Boston Red Sox—1998 Rookie of the Year Candidate.

27) Sidney Ponson, RHP, Baltimore Orioles—Struggled in Double-A, then got hurt. No way to predict his future.

28) Tom Evans, 3B, Toronto Blue Jays—Slowed by rotator cuff surgery, but did okay in Triple-A. Should be a productive player if given the chance.

29) Shannon Stewart, OF, Toronto Blue Jays—Looks like he will be a terrific leadoff man.

30) Neifi Perez, SS, Colorado Rockies—Earned job in the majors, will keep it for some time.

31) Roy Halladay, RHP, Toronto Blue Jays—Struggled in Triple-A after rapid promotion.

32) Wes Helms, 3B, Atlanta Braves—Lost command of the strike zone in Triple-A.

33) Matt Morris, RHP, St. Louis Cardinals—Excellent rookie season, will be a great one if health allows.

34) Jose Guillen, OF, Pittsburgh Pirates—Promoted to majors *way* ahead of schedule, but did OK. Has a chance to be the next Clemente.

35) Kelvim Escobar, RHP, Toronto Blue Jays—Surprise pick by Cito Gaston as Blue Jays closer, and held the job.

36) Livan Hernandez, RHP, Florida Marlins—Livan lived up to the press clippings. World Series MVP.

37) Javier Valentin, C, Minnesota Twins—Offense is stagnating, defense didn't improve. Losing his luster but still young enough to rebound.

38) Donnie Sadler, 2B, Boston Red Sox—Struggled in Triple-A, but still quite young.

39) Pat Cline, C, Chicago Cubs—Offense is stagnating. Still the Catcher-of-the-Future in Wrigley, but that future isn't 1998.

40) Todd Dunwoody, OF, Florida Marlins—Continued broad-based performance, 1998 Rookie of the Year Candidate.

41) Bret Tomko, RHP, Cincinnati Reds—Promoted ahead of schedule, did extremely well in the majors. Could develop into an ace.

42) Wilton Guerrero, 2B, Los Angeles Dodgers—Lost his job due to an inability to turn the double play.

43) Ricky Ledee, OF, New York Yankees—Hit well when healthy, but missed much of year with a hamstring problem.

44) Derrek Lee, 1B, San Diego Padres—Erratic at Las Vegas, but still has star potential. Traded to Florida.

45) Richard Hidalgo, OF, Houston Astros—Held his own in Triple-A. 1998 Rookie of the Year Candidate.

46) Jimmy Anderson, LHP, Pittsburgh Pirates—Promoted too quickly, lost command in Triple-A.

47) Bartolo Colon, RHP, Cleveland Indians—Erratic but promising young pitcher.

48) Eric Ludwick, RHP, St. Louis Cardinals—Traded to Oakland, should be on their staff in 1998. I still like him a lot.

49) T.J. Staton, OF, Pittsburgh Pirates—Command of the strike zone collapsed in Triple-A.

50) Billy McMillon, OF, Florida Marlins—Traded to Philadelphia, should start in 1998.

I don't lose too much sleep over being wrong about pitchers. They are so damn unpredictable that when one has a lousy year (Ponson, Anderson), it's hard to place blame. Conversely, when one has a terrific year (Morris, Tomko), it's hard to take credit.

On the other hand, I *do* lose sleep when I miss a hitter. Sometimes injuries intervene, like for Ruben Rivera, but other times you just plain miss one. I spent quite a bit of time thinking about the disappointing hitters on this list, and placed them in three categories:

1) **Stagnating Young Catchers:** Sweeney, Valentin, Cline. All three of these guys have failed to develop in the way anticipated. We can probably guess why; catching is a tough business.

2) **Strike Zone Failures:** Velazquez, Helms, Staton. I was very high on these guys last year, particularly Velazquez and Staton. They moved up to Triple-A in 1997, and all of them lost track of the strike zone. I can't predict when or if they will get it back, although all three are still prospects at this point.

3) **Todd Walker:** He got off to a slow start, got down on himself to the point where he couldn't sleep, then ended up back in Salt Lake. All the objective evidence says this guy will hit if given the chance. In my opinion, he is not Dave McCarty.

The list for 1998 is on page 331.

This book isn't just about the future stars of baseball. It's also about the future utility infielders, the future middle relievers, and the future pinch runners. Just as a good orchestra needs a third-chair viola, baseball needs platoon players and staff fillers.

It is for this reason that I don't like the philosophy of "Greatest Hits" albums. Does anybody else find something like "Mozart's Greatest Hits" sort of offensive? How do you take "excerpts" from the *Requiem Mass* seriously? That's probably my favorite piece of music right now, but if all I had ever heard of it were excerpts, I doubt I would appreciate it as much. It may have been completed by Sussmayr, but it still still stirs the soul.

The same principle holds for rock music. Take The Doors. Everybody knows about "Light My Fire," but most people my age have never heard intriguing songs like "Peace Frog" because they have never listened to *Morrison Hotel*. All they know are the "Greatest Hits" that some record company executive decided to stick on an album, or that some classic rock station plays occasionally.

Of course, I'm as guilty as anyone. . . I only know Neil Young's work, for example, from *Decade,* a greatest hits album. Ideally speaking, a greatest hits album can serve as an introduction to a musician's body of work. Likewise, an interest in the top prospects serves as an introduction to the study of prospects in general. This book isn't just about the greatest hits of the minor leagues. There are reports on more than 600 players in this book. Don't just look at the Paul Konerkos and the Ben Grieves. Take a look at the Bubba Dixons and the Garrick Haltiwangers. They might not help your roto team or your baseball card investments, but they make the experience complete.

—John Sickels

November 1997

The 1997 Amateur Draft

The 1997 draft class was deep in position players, particularly high school short-stops with offensive potential. The emerging bonus structure forced many teams to make signability, rather than talent, the primary factor in their selections.

As usual, I will avoid granting 1997 picks letter grades. First-year pro performance is not a good predictor of future success, due to the adjustments players have to make to pro playing conditions. I cover the first round, which lasted 31 picks, two supplemental first-round picks of note, and some sleepers.

#1 Matt Anderson, RHP, Detroit Tigers

With the first pick in the draft, the Tigers took Rice University closer Matt Anderson. This marks the third year in a row that Detroit took a college pitcher in the first round, following Mike Drumright in 1995 and Seth Greisinger in 1996. That pair has yet to contribute in the majors, but historically the Tigers are on sound footing. The return rate for college pitchers is considerably higher than the return rate for high school pitchers, as many studies show.

Anderson has an outstanding fastball, clocked in the mid-90s; some reports have him hitting 98 on occasion. He has a wicked knuckle-curve and the attitude that scouts like in a closer. That said, there was risk in picking Anderson. His mechanics look awkward to the eye, and there is concern about how his arm will hold up under pro usage. Additionally, while college pitchers in general have a good track record in the pros, college *closers* do not.

Anderson signed in mid-December for $2.505 million plus incentives.

#2 J. D. Drew, OF, Philadelphia Phillies

Florida State outfielder J.D. Drew was the best position player in the draft. He can do it all: hit for average, hit for power, get on base, and run. He was college baseball's first 30-30 man. Drew's defense is pretty good, too, and he is a clear Seven Skill talent.

He fell to second in the draft because the Tigers wanted a pitcher. They were also concerned about Drew's bonus demands and the fact that Scott Boras was his agent. The Phillies drafted Drew, and offered him a $2 million bonus, which Drew's camp derided as "insulting." A war of words ensued, with Boras claiming that because the Phillies had sent the contract offer to Drew's parents' house, rather than his college apartment, he should be a free agent. Major League Baseball denied the appeal. Drew ended up playing in the independent Northern League, and he played very well, although he had to dodge some chin music from pitchers who don't regard $2 million as an insult. Boras and Drew claim that he has turned pro and should be declared a free agent, and have filed another grievance.

#3 Troy Glaus, 3B, Anaheim Angels

Glaus has been a favorite of scouts since the Padres drafted him out of high school in the second round in 1994. They failed to sign him, so he went to UCLA. His first two collegiate seasons were marred by inconsistency, but he put it all together in 1997, showing outstanding power, the ability to hit for average, and improving defensive skills to go with a cannon arm. His work ethic had been questioned, but is said to have improved greatly this past year, although some insiders say that is propaganda. Glaus did not play pro ball in 1997, but he did sign, and could be a Mike Schmidt-Matt Williams type.

#4 Jason Grilli, RHP, San Francisco Giants

Seton Hall righthander Jason Grilli, whose father Steve pitched in the majors 20 years ago, was the first starting pitcher chosen in the draft. Tall and lanky, Grilli throws in the low 90s, has good breaking stuff, and excellent command at times. He can be erratic, and how good you think he is depends on what day you see him. His ERA in college was not impressive, but his K/BB was great, and that is a better predictor of future success. Grilli is more projectable than most college pitchers, and he may pick up additional velocity as he fills out his 6-5, 180 frame. He needs to get some pro innings in before we make a judgment.

#5 Vernon Wells, OF, Toronto Blue Jays

The Blue Jays love tool-laden young outfielders, though they haven't had a lot of luck in developing them into actual baseball players. A product of Bowie High School in Arlington, Texas, Wells has tremendous tools as you would expect. His power potential is extremely impressive. Most observers didn't think Wells would go this high in the draft, and Toronto's selection of him with the fifth pick may have had more to do with signability than anything else: Wells signed immediately. He then went to the New York-Penn League and tore the place up, hitting over .300 with good power, and showing decent command of the strike zone. We will know more in a year, but right now it looks like the selection of Wells was justified.

#6 Geoff Goetz, LHP, New York Mets

Signability was a clear factor in the Mets' selection of Geoff Goetz, a lefty from Jesuit High School in Tampa. Goetz let it be known before the draft that he wasn't looking for a market-breaking bonus. Scouts love his arm: he hits 93 MPH and throws strikes, but he isn't physically imposing on the mound, standing just 6-0, 165, so few observers thought he would go as high as the sixth pick. He went to the Rookie-level Gulf Coast League, and pitched well in limited action. The Mets need to avoid overworking him, and he is probably at least four years from the majors.

#7 Dan Reichert, RHP, Kansas City Royals

University of the Pacific pitcher Dan Reichert went to the Royals with the seventh pick. This was clearly another signability selection. Reichert has a good fastball in the low-90s and a vicious slider that kills righthanders, but his performance in college was undistinguised. Most teams saw him as a second-rounder. He signed quickly and went to Spokane in the Northwest League, where he pitched decently but was not outstanding. Reichert's mechanics look like they put stress on his elbow, and he may be an above-average injury risk.

#8 J. J. Davis, 1B-RHP, Pittsburgh Pirates

Like the Blue Jays, the Pirates like to draft raw young position players, and J.J. Davis is the latest example. From Baldwin Park High School in Pomona, California, Davis attracts interest as both a hitter and a pitcher, although the Pirates have decided to use him in the field. He stands 6-6 and is quite muscular at 230 pounds. He runs well, has a strong arm, and reminds some scouts of Dave Winfield. Davis is quite raw and will need time to develop; don't look for him before 2001.

#9 Michael Cuddyer, SS, Minnesota Twins

Following the Travis Lee disaster of 1996, the Twins needed to make a big splash with their 1997 selection. It went down to the wire, but they managed to sign high school shortstop Michael Cuddyer just before classes started at Florida State, where he had a scholarship waiting. Cuddyer, from Great Bridge High School in Cheasapeake, Virginia, has been compared to Chipper Jones. Although he does not run as well as Jones and is not a switch-hitter, Cuddyer has excellent power and should hit for average. He has a very strong arm, but may move to third base if his range at short proves inadequate for pro ball. Scouts love his work ethic and intelligence on the field, and he is very polished for a high school player.

#10 Jon Garland, RHP, Chicago Cubs

For the third year in a row, the Cubs selected a high school pitcher. This time it was Jon Garland, a righthander from Kennedy High School in Granada Hills, California. Scouts compare him to Brett Saberhagen at a similar age, and it is easy to see why. Like Sabes, Garland is lean, lose, intelligent, has good mechanics, and throws strikes with a 90-MPH fastball and sharp breaking stuff. He still has projection in his body, meaning he could add velocity. He pitched well in the Arizona League, with great K/BB numbers. The problem for Garland, like all young pitchers, will be staying healthy. Saberhagen was a great pitcher but can't stay off the DL for very long, and unless the Cubs want the same thing to happen to Garland, they need to handle him very carefully. Even if they baby him, he could still get hurt. That's the risk you take when you draft young pitchers.

#11 Chris Enochs, RHP, Oakland Athletics

The Athletics have some really good young position players in their system, but are thin on pitchers, so they addressed that need by picking West Virginia righthander Chris Enochs with the first of two first-round picks. Enochs has a sound pitcher's body at 6-3, 210. His fastball hits 90-92 MPH, he has a good power curve, and a very refined changeup. His control isn't bad, but isn't terrific either. Enochs signed early and went to Modesto in the California League, where he held his own against pro hitters. He should see some Double-A time in 1998, and could reach Oakland in 1999.

#12 Aaron Akin, RHP, Florida Marlins

Although the Marlins would probably deny it, their selection of Aaron Akin with the 12th pick in the draft may have been another signability selection. Akin has a quality fastball timed as high as 95 MPH, but he doesn't have a reliable breaking ball and his command is irregular. He attended the University of Missouri for his freshman year, but dropped out to move on to Cowley County Community College in Kansas. Akin is basically a thrower with a great arm. Whether he develops into a pitcher or not cannot be foreseen at this stage. He missed time after signing with a herniated disk, then had bone chips removed from his elbow, but is supposed to be OK for 1998.

#13 Kyle Peterson, RHP, Milwaukee Brewers

Kyle Peterson is as refined as Aaron Akin is raw. The Stanford product always impressed scouts with his command, his breaking stuff, and his changeup, but was not a consensus first-round talent until he showed he could keep his velocity around 90 MPH consistently. His agent is Scott Boras, but Peterson made it clear that he wanted to sign, and the Brewers didn't have much trouble getting him into pro ball. While Peterson's ceiling is not as high as raw throwers like Akin or high schoolers like Garland, the chance that Peterson will make the majors and have a career there is higher.

#14 Brandon Larson, SS, Cincinnati Reds

Cincinnati's selection of LSU shortstop Brandon Larson is an extremely interesting one. Many baseball people didn't think Larson was worthy of a first-round pick, though he set a record for college shortstops by hitting 40 homers. He was projected as a third-rounder. Questions exist about how much power he will show with wood, and his defensive skills are not spectacular. The Reds sent him directly to Double-A after he signed, something of a gamble even with a successful college hitter. Larson didn't embarrass himself, which is good, but his overall performance was not outstanding and his walk rate was poor, which is not good. He needs time to adjust to the wood bat, but I worry about his command of the strike zone.

#15 Jason Dellaero, SS, Chicago White Sox

The White Sox chose Jason Dellaero, a shortstop from the University of South Florida, with their first-round pick. A switch-hitter, Dellaero has above-average power for an infielder and a strong arm. He didn't hit for average in college, which isn't a good sign since almost everybody hits for average in college, and he didn't overwhelm the South Atlantic League in his pro debut. It is too early to tell at this point, but some scouts think this pick was a stretch.

#16 Lance Berkman, 1B, Houston Astros

Lance Berkman had an outstanding year for Rice University. His selection by the Astros was more than just a Texas publicity stunt: this guy can hit. Berkman, a switch-hitter, has plus power, patience, and will hit for average. He didn't have much trouble adjusting to the wood bat, whacking 11 homers in the tough Florida State League after signing. He will play Double-A and Triple-A in 1998, and should be ready for the majors in 1999. The problem will be finding him a place to play. Jeff Bagwell blocks him at first base, so the Astros will move Berkman to the outfield. He is athletic enough to handle left field.

#17 John Curtice, LHP, Boston Red Sox

Boston draft pick John Curtice was a teammate of Twins pick Mike Cuddyer at Great Bridge High in Cheasapeake, Virginia. Scouts have no questions about Curtice's physical ability. He is a hard-throwing lefthander with good breaking stuff, who was not abused by his high school coach. This makes him a valuable commodity. On the other hand, his mechanics need work, and scouts have serious questions about his personality and work ethic. He got a few innings in in the Gulf Coast League and did well.

#18 Mark Mangum, RHP, Colorado Rockies

Mark Mangum was drafted by Colorado out of Kingwood High School in Kingwood, Texas. The 6-1, 175-pound righthander is an excellent athlete with a 90 MPH fastball and good control. I understand why the Rockies want to draft pitchers, but they concentrate on high school guys, and as we all should know by now, high school pitchers are terrible risks. What is truly amazing is that high school pitchers from Texas are *really* terrible risks.

Here is a complete list of all Texas high school pitchers drafted in the first round of the June draft from 1965 until 1990: Mike Biko, Balor Moore, Ron Broaddus, Roger Quiroga, Larry Payne, David Clyde, Doug Heinhold, Tommy Boggs, Sam Welborn, Andy Hawkins, Rickey Barlow, Jimmy Jones, Jackie Davidson, Wayne Dotson, Scott Scudder, Brian Bohanon, Todd Ritchie, Todd Van Poppel, and Robbie Beckett.

Andy Hawkins was the best first-round high school pitcher drafted from Texas over a 25-year period. Doesn't that tell you something? Now, this doesn't mean that Mangum will fail, but it does tell you what kind of history he is fighting.

#19 Ryan Anderson, LHP, Seattle Mariners

Before the draft, many onlookers thought Ryan Anderson might be the first player picked. From a high school in suburban Detroit, he would have been a natural fit for the Tigers, but serious concerns about his personality arose before the draft, and scared Detroit and a lot of other teams off. On sheer physical talent alone, Anderson is the best high school pitching prospect to come along in years. Nicknamed "Young Unit," Anderson looks very much like Randy Johnson, a huge 6-10 lefthander with blazing stuff. Anderson has been described as flaky, immature, infantile, and just a plain jerk. No one says he has to be a nice guy, of course, but even pitchers with great stuff need some level of intelligence and maturity to succeed in pro ball.

Anderson signed late and didn't get any pro innings in. After signing, he told the press he was going to be the best pitcher in baseball history. No one questions his talent, but he has a lot of work to do if he wants to be a major league pitcher, let alone the best in history. Bluster alone won't cut it.

#20 Adam Kennedy, SS, St. Louis Cardinals

The Cardinals usually draft a college pitcher in the first round, but surprised everyone and changed tacks in 1997, going for Cal State Northridge shortstop Adam Kennedy. Most experts had Kennedy pegged as a third-round pick. His selection in the first round may have been influenced by, you guessed it, signability. Kennedy was an excellent hitter in college, but there was doubt whether his offense would carry over to the wood bat. He works hard at defense, but scouts don't think he will remain at shortstop in the long run. Kennedy did well in his pro debut, and should play in Double-A in 1998.

The Cardinals actually made a bigger splash in the second round by drafting, and signing, Florida prep lefty Rick Ankiel, a Scott Boras client. It took a huge $2.5 million bonus to sign Ankiel, with unknown but probably deleterious effects on the bonus structure next year.

#21 Eric DuBose, LHP, Oakland Athletics

Before the 1997 college baseball season began, Mississippi State southpaw Eric DuBose was at the top of most collegiate prospect lists. An inconsistent junior season hurt his stock, but he was still regarded highly enough to be selected 21st overall by the Athletics. DuBose has a pretty good fastball that gets close to 90 MPH, but his out pitch is a nasty curve. He will need to work on a change. His control is inconsistent, but his mechanics are reasonably smooth, and when everything is clicking he is a tough customer.

#22 Jayson Werth, C, Baltimore Orioles

Jayson Werth played well in the Gulf Coast League after signing out of an Illinois high school, but as most you reading this book know, high school catchers have horrendous track records. Werth is compared to Dale Murphy due to his physical tools, but the fact that Murphy flowered as a player *after* giving up catching is illustrative. Most high school catchers fail to develop beyond a certain point with the bat, for reasons which should be obvious to anyone who has ever squatted behind home plate. Hitting is tough. Hitting when your back is sore and your knees are throbbing is even tougher. It should make us appreciate guys like Ivan Rodriguez and Mike Piazza even more than we do, but it should also make us wary of hyping young catchers unrealistically. Paul Konerko blossomed as a hitter after giving up catching. Javier Valentin, Mike Sweeney, and many others have stagnated.

#23 Donnie Bridges, RHP, Montreal Expos

Hailing from Oak Grove High School in Hattesburg, Mississippi, Donnie Bridges excites scouts with his 92-MPH fastball, his hard slider, his good control, and his lean 6-3, 190 build. There were questions before the draft about his health, since he missed time in April with a sore elbow, but the Expos were convinced he was physically sound and snared him with the 23rd pick. History says the arm problem will likely reoccur. You can draw your own conclusions here.

#24 Tyrell Godwin, OF, New York Yankees

The Yankees picked Tyrell Godwin out of a New Jersey high school, but lost him to a prestigious academic scholarship to the University of North Carolina, where he will play football and baseball. Godwin has exceptional speed and athletic ability, and could develop power as he matures. He is also very intelligent and is an excellent student.

What does it say about George Steinbrenner that an apparently classy person like Tyrell Godwin turns him down, but that a guy like Hideki Irobyou refuses to play for anyone else?

#25 Glenn Davis, 1B, Los Angeles Dodgers

I know you aren't supposed to draft for need, but the Dodgers' selection of Vanderbilt first baseman Glenn Davis is inexplicable. Davis is a first baseman with line-drive power who had a mediocre junior season and was not projected as a first-rounder by most teams. Even if the Dodgers thought Davis was a solid first-round pick, the decision still makes no sense, given the presence of Paul Konerko and Adrian Beltre in the system. For his part, Davis went to the California League after signing and did well, but I still have to wonder what the hell they were thinking about when they chose him.

#26 Darnell McDonald, OF, Baltimore Orioles

If signability had not been an issue, Darnell McDonald would have been one of the first three players picked in the draft. As it was, the outfielder from Englewood, Colorado, had a football scholarship to the University of Texas waiting for him, and it took the deep pockets of the Orioles to convince him to join pro baseball. McDonald has outstanding potential in every category: speed, strength, power arm. He needs to play before we know how the physical tools translate to diamond performance.

#27 Kevin Nicholson, SS, San Diego Padres

The first Canadian ever drafted in the first round, Stetson shortstop Kevin Nicholson is a switch-hitter with some power for someone just 5-9. Despite his stature, scouts think he will continue to produce power and average in the pros, and indeed he hit well in the California League after signing. He broke his wrist in August, but should be fine for spring training. Defensively, his range at shortstop is average, but he has a strong arm and good hands. He may move to second eventually.

#28 Tim Drew, RHP, Cleveland Indians

Tim Drew was an easier sign than his brother J.D., turning down a Florida State scholarship to sign with the Indians out of high school in Georgia. Drew has what it takes to be a workhorse starter: strong legs, and a strong arm. His fastball exceeds 90 MPH, and he also has a hard slider. Drew missed time with a back injury before the draft; otherwise, he could have gone in the first 10 picks. Like all high school pitchers, it's wait and see.

#29 Troy Cameron, SS, Atlanta Braves

A few years ago, the Braves drafted a high school shortstop from Florida named Chipper Jones. That worked out pretty well, so they had no hesitation in selecting another Florida prep shortstop, Troy Cameron, in 1997. Cameron is thought to be an excellent hitter, although questions about his speed and defense kept him out of the upper half of the first round. He didn't hit well in Rookie ball, but that doesn't mean anything yet. Jones didn't either

#30 Jack Cust, 1B, Arizona Diamondbacks

The Diamondbacks' selection of Jack Cust, a high school power hitter from New Jersey, was puzzling, since they already have their first baseman for the next 10 years in Travis Lee. Because of Lee, the Diamondbacks will move Cust to the outfield. How he adjusts is anyone's guess at this point, but he wasn't a good defensive first baseman to begin with. At least Cust can hit, showing excellent power potential from the left side. He hit well in Rookie ball, but will need to adapt defensively.

#31 Jason Standridge, RHP, Tampa Bay Devil Rays

Jason Standridge, a high school pitcher from Alabama, was a third-round candidate on most teams' draft lists. This is the second year in a row that Tampa Bay made a surprising pick: 1996 selection Paul Wilder wasn't a consensus top talent, either. Standridge, who turned down an Auburn football scholarship to sign, is a good athlete with a 90-MPH fastball, but is quite raw otherwise.

#39 Jason Romano, 3B, Texas Rangers

Since they sent their first-round slot to the Yankees for John Wetteland, the Rangers didn't pick until 39th overall, a supplemental pick they received for losing Mike Stanton to free agency. At 39th, they chose Jason Romano, a shortstop from famous Hillsborough High School in Tampa. It must have been one heck of a year for Florida shortstops. Scouts say Romano will hit for average, but question his power and defensive skills. He did not hit well in Rookie ball.

#40 Ryan Bradley, RHP, New York Yankees

Since the Yankees failed to sign Tyrell Godwin with the 24th pick, Ryan Bradley became the highest Yankee draft choice. Bradley has a low-90s fastball and was successful as a closer for Arizona State. He did decently in the New York-Penn League, and the Yanks will groom him for the bullpen.

Some Sleepers To Watch:

Angels	16th round	Casey Child, OF	University of Utah
Red Sox	19th round	David Eckstein, 2B	University of Florida
Rockies	3rd round	Todd Sears, 1B	University of Nebraska
Royals	15th round	Justin Pederson, RHP	University of Minnesota
Yankees	6th round	Jeremy Morris, OF	Florida State
Giants	5th round	Giuseppe Chiaramonte, C	Fresno State

Prospect Reports

A Note On Grades

Here is the heart of the book: prospect reports on 674 players, graded from A to C–.

It isn't wise to compare the grades of two different players and conclude that they are of equal value. Steve Hacker and Christian Guzman, for example, are both Grade C prospects, but for different reasons, and with different potential outcomes. Hacker had a great season, but he was old for the league, isn't good defensively, and must continue to hit at a higher level. Guzman, by comparison, is a Grade C because while he didn't have a good season by my measures, he is very young and could get much better with experience.

If Christian Guzman was Steve Hacker's age, he would be no prospect at all. Conversely, if Hacker was Guzman's age, he would be a Grade A prospect.

I resist giving players at the short-season leagues letter grades, because at any level below full-season A-ball, it is very difficult to predict how players will develop based on their statistical performance. Some guys who tear up the Gulf Coast League flounder at higher levels, but some guys who struggle there blossom into stars. I also don't like giving a grade to anyone who has less than a full season of experience. Nevertheless, there are many intriguing prospects at the lower levels, and while I won't give them letter grades, I will write about some of them. For eligibility, as a loose guideline, I use a maximum of 50 games played in the majors for position players and 50 innings for pitchers. I will break the rule occasionally if there is a player I find particularly interesting, or if a player has exceeded those limits, but hasn't established a level of performance in the majors yet.

The book is designed to be read in several ways. You can open it up to a page at random and read, or you can look up the players for your favorite team, or you can start at the beginning and peruse. I enjoyed writing it, and I hope it is both informative and fun to read. Thanks for your interest.

Chuck Abbott
Anaheim Angels

Pos: 2B **Bats:** Both **Ht:** 6'1" **Wt:** 180 **Age:** 23

Yr Team	Lg	G	AB	R	H	2B	3B	HR	RBI	BB	SO	SB	CS	Avg	OBP	Slg
96 Boise	A	70	268	41	53	9	2	0	20	24	59	11	5	.198	.272	.246
97 Cedar Rapds	A	133	520	86	120	21	5	7	54	62	170	31	12	.231	.315	.331
2 Minor League Yrs		203	788	127	173	30	7	7	74	86	229	42	17	.220	.301	.302

Abbott was Anaheim's first pick in the 1996 draft, a second-rounder from Austin Peay State University. He hit very well in college, but many people thought he would struggle with the wood bat, and he has. He had extreme problems making contact at Cedar Rapids, and while he did draw some walks, 170 strikeouts is about 100 too many for an infielder without power. He can run, for what that is worth, and doesn't have trouble with defense at second base, but right now he looks like a failed pick. **Grade C-**

Jeff Abbott
Chicago White Sox

Pos: OF **Bats:** Right **Ht:** 6'2" **Wt:** 190 **Age:** 25

Yr Team	Lg	G	AB	R	H	2B	3B	HR	RBI	BB	SO	SB	CS	Avg	OBP	Slg
96 Nashville	AAA	113	440	64	143	27	1	14	60	32	50	12	4	.325	.373	.486
97 Nashville	AAA	118	465	88	152	35	3	11	63	41	52	12	7	.327	.385	.486
Chicago	AL	19	38	8	10	1	0	1	2	0	6	0	0	.263	.263	.368
4 Minor League Yrs		423	1605	269	545	106	11	39	249	160	180	36	17	.340	.401	.492

Jeff Abbott got off to a slow start at Nashville, hitting around .270 for most of the first half, but he rallied to finish well above .300, as he always does. His batting average in two Triple-A seasons is .326, in a league not particularly conducive to offense. He can handle both righties and lefties, has power into the gaps, and hits both fastballs and breaking stuff. His swing looks like it was drawn with a straightedge: it is extremely level. Abbott doesn't have great home-run power, and his average is his main offensive contribution. His glove has been knocked in the past, but he has worked hard at defense and led the American Association in fielding percentage. He deserves a chance to play. **Grade B**

Brent Abernathy
Toronto Blue Jays

Pos: 2B **Bats:** Right **Ht:** 6'1" **Wt:** 185 **Age:** 20

Yr Team	Lg	G	AB	R	H	2B	3B	HR	RBI	BB	SO	SB	CS	Avg	OBP	Slg
97 Hagerstown	A	99	379	69	117	27	2	1	26	30	32	22	13	.309	.367	.398
1 Minor League Yr		99	379	69	117	27	2	1	26	30	32	22	13	.309	.367	.398

Toronto drafted Brent Abernathy in the second round in 1996, with the pick acquired from the Marlins as compensation for the signing of Devon White. Abernathy doesn't have much power yet, but he projects as a .300 threat all the way up the ladder. I would like to see him develop a bit more patience, but I'm a walk maniac. He doesn't strike out much, and it would be no surprise if he develops power as he matures. A shortstop in high school, Abernathy moved to second base at Hagerstown and didn't embarrass himself. He has good range and is fairly reliable, but needs experience turning the double play. Overall, it was a promising debut. **Grade B**

Dennis Abreu
Chicago Cubs
Pos: SS **Bats:** Right **Ht:** 6'0" **Wt:** 165 **Age:** 19

Yr Team	Lg	G	AB	R	H	2B	3B	HR	RBI	BB	SO	SB	CS	Avg	OBP	Slg
96 Cubs	R	56	192	32	60	5	0	0	15	21	20	35	9	.313	.384	.339
97 Rockford	A	126	483	71	155	19	3	1	37	45	99	36	26	.321	.386	.379
2 Minor League Yrs		182	675	103	215	24	3	1	52	66	119	71	35	.319	.386	.367

The Cubs signed Dennis Abreu out of Venezuela in 1994; his brother Bob plays for the Phillies. Dennis has an extremely quick bat, and ranked fifth in the Midwest League in hitting. He does not have a great deal of power, but is young enough to develop it. His command of the strike zone is adequate, but needs tightening. Statistically, his season was mixed; his OPS was all right at plus-six, but his SEC was well below average. This means that his base of offensive skills is narrow at this point. Scouts say he has the natural ability to play shortstop, but needs refinement, and the numbers confirm this. His range factor was passable, but he made 37 errors in 95 games. Abreu could be very, very good if he continues to hit for average, develops some power, and improves the glove work. He won't be ready soon, but I like his upside. **Grade B**

Carlos Adolfo
Montreal Expos
Pos: OF **Bats:** Right **Ht:** 5'11" **Wt:** 160 **Age:** 21

Yr Team	Lg	G	AB	R	H	2B	3B	HR	RBI	BB	SO	SB	CS	Avg	OBP	Slg
96 Delmarva	A	132	492	82	134	20	8	10	71	47	106	18	6	.272	.333	.407
97 Wst Plm Bch	A	120	448	62	101	15	2	11	50	38	91	9	18	.225	.289	.342
4 Minor League Yrs		404	1487	222	369	59	18	32	194	135	344	44	37	.248	.311	.377

Adolfo's name is occasionally dropped by prospect watchers, but another season like this one will stop that. He has the physical tools that scouts look for: power, speed, etc., but his performance is less than average. His OPS was well below average at -12 percent. His defense is like his offense: irregular. He has a strong arm and great range, but makes far too many errors. Adolfo is still young enough to improve, but he needs to do it soon. **Grade C-**

Benny Agbayani
New York Mets
Pos: OF **Bats:** Right **Ht:** 5'11" **Wt:** 175 **Age:** 26

Yr Team	Lg	G	AB	R	H	2B	3B	HR	RBI	BB	SO	SB	CS	Avg	OBP	Slg
96 Binghamton	AA	21	53	7	9	1	0	2	8	11	13	1	0	.170	.318	.302
Norfolk	AAA	99	331	43	92	13	9	7	56	30	57	14	5	.278	.339	.435
97 Norfolk	AAA	127	468	90	145	24	2	11	51	67	106	29	14	.310	.401	.440
5 Minor League Yrs		549	1880	300	532	77	24	30	255	251	364	79	33	.283	.373	.397

Ben Agbayani entered pro ball as a 30th-round draft pick in 1993, from Hawaii Pacific University—a roster filler, in other words. He does not excite scouts, but works hard and has turned himself into a player with some value. He lacks natural power and speed, but can drive the ball occasionally and knows how to run the bases. His OPS at Norfolk was good, but not spectacular, at +10 percent. His glove is similar to his bat: he lacks organic tools, but uses what he does have (a decent arm, average range) quite well. Agbayani would be just an average offensive player in the majors and will never start, but you could do worse for a bench guy. Mets manager Bobby Valentine is reportedly quite impressed with him. **Grade C-**

Stevenson Agosto
San Diego Padres

Pos: P Throws: Left Ht: 5'10" Wt: 175 Age: 22

Yr Team	Lg	G	GS	IP	H	R	ER	HR	BB	SO	SV	W	L	Pct.	ERA
96 Cedar Rapds	A	28	28	156.2	143	91	77	12	86	121	0	8	10	.444	4.42
97 Lk Elsinore	A	24	21	137.0	155	91	81	23	50	91	0	5	8	.385	5.32
Rancho Cuca	A	3	3	22.0	18	7	7	2	6	18	0	2	0	1.000	2.86
4 Minor League Yrs		82	65	399.1	385	232	198	39	188	292	1	21	23	.477	4.46

The Padres picked up Stevenson Agosto, a Puerto Rican lefty, from the Angels as part of the Rickey Henderson trade. His stats aren't much to look at, and his fastball isn't over-powering, but when he throws strikes with his breaking stuff, he can be effective. The phrase "when he throws strikes, he can be very effective" will be repeated in various in-carnations throughout this book. Cliches are usually true. As for Agosto, if he improves his command, he could emerge quickly as a real prospect. Another cliche, but equally true. **Grade C-**

Paul Ah Yat
Pittsburgh Pirates

Pos: P Throws: Left Ht: 6'1" Wt: 196 Age: 24

Yr Team	Lg	G	GS	IP	H	R	ER	HR	BB	SO	SV	W	L	Pct.	ERA
96 Erie	A	26	0	27.2	24	15	10	1	6	34	1	1	1	.500	3.25
97 Augusta	A	29	9	90.0	82	34	29	7	16	119	0	5	1	.833	2.90
Lynchburg	A	6	6	48.0	37	8	7	2	4	38	0	5	1	.833	1.31
2 Minor League Yrs		61	15	165.2	143	57	46	10	26	191	1	11	3	.786	2.50

The Pirates drafted Paul Ah Yat from the University of Hawaii in the 21st round in 1996. He spent most of the year as a swingman in the South Atlantic League, posting a ridiculously good K/BB ratio of +233 percent. A late promotion to the Carolina League also went well, and he will likely pitch Double-A in 1998. Ah Yat does not have a big-time fastball, but he throws strikes with his breaking stuff and is intelligent. He needs to prove himself in Double-A before we get excited. **Grade C**

Jose Alberro
New York Yankees

Pos: P Throws: Right Ht: 6'2" Wt: 190 Age: 28

Yr Team	Lg	G	GS	IP	H	R	ER	HR	BB	SO	SV	W	L	Pct.	ERA
96 Okla City	AAA	29	27	171.0	154	73	66	12	57	140	0	9	9	.500	3.47
Texas	AL	5	1	9.1	14	6	6	1	7	2	0	0	1	.000	5.79
97 Okla City	AAA	16	16	91.2	90	48	43	6	29	59	0	5	6	.455	4.22
Columbus	AAA	1	1	8.0	5	4	3	1	1	6	0	0	1	.000	3.38
Texas	AL	10	4	28.1	37	33	25	4	17	11	0	0	3	.000	7.94
7 Minor League Yrs		216	54	555.2	517	249	216	36	198	446	38	26	23	.531	3.50

The Yankees acquired Alberro from the Rangers in July, after Texas put him on waivers. He has not been impressive in his major league exposure, but he has very good control and decent stuff. I think he can be a better-than-adequate pitcher, if given time to settle into a job. In Triple-A, he backs guys off the plate, hits the corners with his slider, then nails the fastball on the inner half. In the majors, he looks intimidated and pitches unassertively. He could get over that with experience, coaching, and time, but he isn't working for a patient employer right now. **Grade C-**

Chad Alexander

Houston Astros

Pos: OF **Bats:** Right **Ht:** 6'0" **Wt:** 190 **Age:** 23

Yr Team	Lg	G	AB	R	H	2B	3B	HR	RBI	BB	SO	SB	CS	Avg	OBP	Slg
96 Quad City	A	118	435	68	115	25	4	13	69	57	108	16	11	.264	.350	.430
97 Kissimmee	A	129	469	67	127	31	6	4	46	56	91	11	8	.271	.352	.388
3 Minor League Yrs		320	1189	182	325	71	15	22	159	138	236	34	20	.273	.352	.414

The Houston system is fairly thin in position players, so Chad Alexander could advance quickly if he plays well. Scouts have liked his tools since his college days at Texas A&M, but like fellow Aggie product Chad Allen of the Twins system, Alexander has never played as well as his tools indicate he should. He is athletic, fast, and strong. His command of the strike zone isn't terrible, but his production is never more than slightly above-average, basically because his power hasn't developed. Alexander is a very good defensive outfielder, for what that is worth. Double-A should tell the tale for him. **Grade C**

Chad Allen

Minnesota Twins

Pos: OF **Bats:** Right **Ht:** 6'1" **Wt:** 190 **Age:** 23

Yr Team	Lg	G	AB	R	H	2B	3B	HR	RBI	BB	SO	SB	CS	Avg	OBP	Slg
96 Ft. Wayne	A	7	21	2	9	0	0	0	2	3	2	1	1	.429	.480	.429
97 Ft. Myers	A	105	401	66	124	18	4	3	45	40	51	27	15	.309	.373	.397
New Britain	AA	30	115	20	29	9	1	4	18	9	21	2	0	.252	.304	.452
2 Minor League Yrs		142	537	88	162	27	5	7	65	52	74	30	16	.302	.363	.410

Allen was drafted in the fourth round in 1996, out of Texas A&M. Scouts liked his tools, but believed that Allen never played up to his ability as a collegian. Fast and strong, Allen steals bases, but hasn't hit for much power. His first pro season was reasonably successful: he hit adequately in the difficult Florida State League, with an OPS of plus-eight percent and a SEC of plus-six. He struggled after being promoted to Double-A, but didn't play there long enough for it to mean anything. Allen is a good defensive outfielder with a strong arm and above-average range. We need to see him hit in Double-A for a full season, and he needs to develop some power if he wants a shot as a regular. **Grade C**

Dusty Allen

San Diego Padres

Pos: 1B-OF   **Bats:** Right   **Ht:** 6'4"   **Wt:** 215   **Age:** 25

Yr Team	Lg	G	AB	R	H	2B	3B	HR	RBI	BB	SO	SB	CS	Avg	OBP	Slg
96 Clinton	A	77	243	46	65	10	3	10	46	67	59	4	7	.267	.429	.457
Rancho Cuca	A	55	208	41	62	15	1	10	45	38	65	3	2	.298	.406	.524
97 Mobile	AA	131	475	85	120	28	4	17	75	81	116	1	4	.253	.360	.436
3 Minor League Yrs		328	1169	218	318	72	9	46	221	219	288	10	15	.272	.387	.467

Stanford product Dusty Allen was San Diego's 30th-round pick in 1995. He is blocked in the Padres system by Wally Joyner, but Allen has some ability and may break through somewhere. He did decently for Mobile in the Southern League last year, showing excellent patience and above-average power. He was steady rather than spectacular, and his OPS was only adequate at plus-five percent, not thrilling for a corner player. Mobile is a good place for homers, but was negative for offense overall. If Allen gets a full season in hitter-haven Las Vegas, he could put up some big numbers and gain additional respect as a prospect. **Grade C**

Marlon Allen

Cincinnati Reds

Pos: 1B   **Bats:** Right   **Ht:** 6'6"   **Wt:** 228   **Age:** 25

Yr Team	Lg	G	AB	R	H	2B	3B	HR	RBI	BB	SO	SB	CS	Avg	OBP	Slg
96 Winston-Sal	A	121	426	57	101	19	1	17	82	32	133	8	2	.237	.291	.406
97 Burlington	A	69	242	42	75	20	1	12	52	36	61	5	3	.310	.403	.550
Chattanooga	AA	62	196	27	50	15	2	4	23	26	39	0	1	.255	.345	.413
4 Minor League Yrs		389	1324	188	349	82	4	48	250	145	362	15	8	.264	.342	.440

In most organizations, Marlon Allen would attract little attention, but the Reds system is quite thin, and he did have a good year. Allen was a 40th-round draft pick in 1994 from Columbus College in Georgia. He was drafted on the off chance that he might be able to turn his huge wingspan into power at the plate. Strike-zone judgment has been a big problem, but he made some progress with that in 1997. He hit very well at Burlington (the Reds lacked a high-level Class-A team), and wasn't awful at Double-A Chattanooga. Allen is a long shot, but that's a better shot than he had a year ago. **Grade C-**

Armando Almanza

St. Louis Cardinals

Pos: P   **Throws:** Left   **Ht:** 6'3"   **Wt:** 205   **Age:** 25

Yr Team	Lg	G	GS	IP	H	R	ER	HR	BB	SO	SV	W	L	Pct.	ERA
96 Peoria	A	52	1	62.0	50	27	19	2	32	67	0	8	6	.571	2.76
97 Pr William	A	58	0	64.2	38	18	12	3	32	83	36	2	3	.400	1.67
4 Minor League Yrs		153	25	281.0	240	128	95	21	121	282	36	18	20	.474	3.04

The Cardinals drafted Armando Almanza in 1993, as a 21st-rounder out of New Mexico Junior College. He has been staff-filler primarily, but did well enough in the closer role at Prince William that he is starting to be referred to as a prospect. Almanza has very good arm strength: a low-90s fastball and a sharp-breaking pitch. He was more aggressive in his approach last year, and many scouts said he should have been in Triple-A by the end of the season. He probably won't close in the majors, but Almanza should be a useful bull-pen lefty. **Grade C+**

Carlos Almanzar   *Toronto Blue Jays*

Pos: P   **Throws:** Right   **Ht:** 6'2"   **Wt:** 166   **Age:** 24

Yr Team	Lg	G	GS	IP	H	R	ER	HR	BB	SO	SV	W	L	Pct.	ERA
96 Knoxville	AA	54	0	94.2	106	58	51	13	33	105	9	7	8	.467	4.85
97 Knoxville	AA	21	0	25.2	30	14	14	2	5	25	8	1	1	.500	4.91
Syracuse	AAA	32	0	51.0	30	9	8	2	8	47	3	5	1	.833	1.41
Toronto	AL	4	0	3.1	1	1	1	1	1	4	0	0	1	.000	2.70
4 Minor League Yrs		156	33	382.1	392	196	156	29	97	347	22	23	26	.469	3.67

A Dominican signed in 1993, Almanzar emerged as a prospect with a fine performance at Syracuse last year. He is not a hard thrower; his fastball is average, but his curveball and changeup are quite competent. Throwing strikes is a habit for him, which makes all of his offerings more effective, of course. Almanzar impressed the Blue Jays in his limited September major league action, and will have a shot at a bullpen job for 1998. He won't close, but he could be quite good as a middle reliever. **Grade C**

Richard Almanzar   *Detroit Tigers*

Pos: 2B   **Bats:** Right   **Ht:** 5'10"   **Wt:** 155   **Age:** 21

Yr Team	Lg	G	AB	R	H	2B	3B	HR	RBI	BB	SO	SB	CS	Avg	OBP	Slg
96 Lakeland	A	124	471	81	144	22	2	1	36	49	49	53	19	.306	.379	.367
97 Jacksnville	AA	103	387	55	94	20	2	5	35	37	43	20	6	.243	.314	.344
3 Minor League Yrs		349	1306	212	357	63	5	7	101	133	144	123	49	.273	.350	.345

I have been commending Almanzar as a fine prospect for two years, so I was a bit disappointed in his performance at Double-A Jacksonville. He wasn't dreadful, but his speed numbers were down, he didn't hit for average, and his defensive reputation was questioned for the first time. On the other hand, I still like him. He was young for the league, there was little deterioration in his strike-zone judgment, he hit better in the second half after a slow start, and he still had a very high range factor at second base. He may have been playing hurt for much or all of the season: he underwent knee surgery in late August. We need to gauge his recovery from the knee problem, but I think he is a good bet to re-coup his lost stock. **Grade B-**

Gabe Alvarez   *Detroit Tigers*

Pos: 3B   **Bats:** Right   **Ht:** 6'1"   **Wt:** 185   **Age:** 24

Yr Team	Lg	G	AB	R	H	2B	3B	HR	RBI	BB	SO	SB	CS	Avg	OBP	Slg
96 Memphis	AA	104	368	58	91	23	1	8	40	64	87	2	3	.247	.361	.380
97 Mobile	AA	114	427	71	128	28	2	14	78	51	64	1	1	.300	.376	.473
3 Minor League Yrs		279	1016	170	297	69	5	28	158	145	182	4	4	.292	.384	.453

A broken foot ruined Gabe Alvarez's 1996 season and oxidized his veneer as a prospect. He returned to Double-A in 1997, and had a fine season, showing a sharp line-drive stroke, good punch to all fields, and solid strike-zone judgment. It was his second year at the level, so his stats have to be discounted somewhat. Most scouts think he will hit, though, and I agree. The glove is more problematic. A shortstop in college, Alvarez was converted to third base due to range limitations, but continues to struggle at the hot corner, fielding just .892 there last year. He needs another year in the high minors to get that under control. Alvarez remains a fine offensive prospect, but his position is a serious question mark. Arizona took him in the expansion draft, then traded him to Detroit in a deal for Travis Fryman. **Grade B**

Jose Amado   *Kansas City Royals*

Pos: 3B   **Bats:** Right   **Ht:** 6'1"   **Wt:** 194   **Age:** 23

Yr Team	Lg	G	AB	R	H	2B	3B	HR	RBI	BB	SO	SB	CS	Avg	OBP	Slg
96 Wisconsin	A	61	232	43	67	13	0	5	36	20	20	6	5	.289	.361	.409
Lansing	A	57	212	39	74	18	1	5	47	17	17	8	4	.349	.414	.514
97 Lansing	A	61	234	49	80	25	1	4	45	24	18	10	2	.342	.403	.509
3 Minor League Yrs		236	893	164	278	71	3	22	161	85	74	39	16	.311	.381	.471

Amado's season was cut in half due to spring shoulder surgery, but when he came off the disabled list, he was unstoppable at Lansing. His OPS was near the top of the league at +26 percent. He showed a great contact swing, with excellent gap power. His batting average would have led the league, had he enough at-bats to qualify. Amado is also a solid defensive third baseman, with very nice range. He needs to prove himself at a higher level, but with the shoulder healed, he could be poised for a breakout. If I were the Royals, I would move him to Double-A in 1998, avoiding the difficult hitting environment at Class-A Wilmington, and giving Amado a chance to advance quickly. **Grade B-**

Manny Amador   *Philadelphia Phillies*

Pos: 3B   **Bats:** Both   **Ht:** 6'0"   **Wt:** 165   **Age:** 22

Yr Team	Lg	G	AB	R	H	2B	3B	HR	RBI	BB	SO	SB	CS	Avg	OBP	Slg
96 Reading	AA	10	18	5	5	2	0	1	3	5	4	0	0	.278	.435	.556
Clearwater	A	52	172	24	47	10	0	5	21	19	46	1	1	.273	.351	.419
97 Scranton-WB	AAA	23	70	12	24	5	0	1	9	6	11	0	0	.343	.392	.457
Reading	AA	63	169	17	41	9	1	2	22	20	29	0	0	.243	.333	.343
5 Minor League Yrs		397	1338	195	349	66	9	30	179	128	242	16	8	.261	.334	.391

With the outstanding Scott Rolen at third base, and prospect Marlon Anderson waiting for the second-base job at the Vet, there isn't a place for Manny Amador to play. So, the Phils are grooming him for a utility role. He could be pretty good at it; he has the physical tools to play either position, and he is not an automatic out. Amador is young, has bat speed, and decent command of the strike zone. He has a lot of problems staying healthy, so he would fit in well with the major league club. **Grade C**

Jimmy Anderson
Pittsburgh Pirates

Pos: P **Throws:** Left **Ht:** 6'1" **Wt:** 180 **Age:** 22

Yr Team	Lg	G	GS	IP	H	R	ER	HR	BB	SO	SV	W	L	Pct.	ERA
96 Lynchburg	A	11	11	65.1	51	25	14	2	21	56	0	5	3	.625	1.93
Carolina	AA	17	16	97.0	92	40	36	3	44	79	0	8	3	.727	3.34
97 Carolina	AA	4	4	24.2	16	6	4	1	9	23	0	2	1	.667	1.46
Calgary	AAA	21	21	103.0	124	78	65	9	64	71	0	7	6	.538	5.68
4 Minor League Yrs		87	85	475.1	425	214	166	18	217	402	0	32	21	.604	3.14

I rated Jimmy Anderson very highly in 1997, but for 1998, his grade has to be cut back. He still has a live arm, especially for a lefty, with a 92-MPH fastball and a nasty slider. He struggles with the changeup, and his lack of an effective offspeed pitch really showed up when he was promoted to the Pacific Coast League after a quick start at Carolina: he got his butt kicked at Calgary. His K/BB ratio was particularly disappointing at -29 percent. Anderson is still a fine prospect, but needs to keep his health, develop an offspeed pitch, and prove that the negative Calgary experience won't hurt his development. **Grade B-**

Marlon Anderson
Philadelphia Phillies

Pos: 2B **Bats:** Left **Ht:** 5'10" **Wt:** 190 **Age:** 24

Yr Team	Lg	G	AB	R	H	2B	3B	HR	RBI	BB	SO	SB	CS	Avg	OBP	Slg
96 Clearwater	A	60	257	37	70	10	3	2	22	14	18	26	1	.272	.315	.358
Reading	AA	75	314	38	86	14	3	3	28	26	44	17	9	.274	.330	.366
97 Reading	AA	137	553	88	147	18	6	10	62	42	77	27	15	.266	.328	.374
3 Minor League Yrs		346	1436	215	395	55	16	18	152	97	159	92	33	.275	.327	.373

Marlon Anderson, Philadelphia's second-round pick out of South Alabama in 1995, is not a superstar in the making, but he should be a solid player. He has a line-drive swing, good control of the strike zone, and fine speed on the bases. He did hit 10 home runs last year, but most evaluators don't think he will hit more than five or six per season in the majors. Anderson is a bit error-prone at the keystone, but he has phenomenal range around the bag, and annually leads his leagues in range factor. I like him, but he may need a year of Triple-A to cut down on his error rate. **Grade B-**

Tony Armas Jr.
Montreal Expos

Pos: P **Throws:** Right **Ht:** 6'4" **Wt:** 175 **Age:** 19

Yr Team	Lg	G	GS	IP	H	R	ER	HR	BB	SO	SV	W	L	Pct.	ERA
96 Oneonta	A	3	3	15.2	14	12	10	1	11	14	0	1	1	.500	5.74
Yankees	R	8	7	45.2	41	18	16	1	13	45	1	4	1	.800	3.15
97 Greensboro	A	9	9	51.2	36	13	6	3	13	64	0	5	2	.714	1.05
Tampa	A	9	9	46.0	43	23	17	1	16	26	0	3	1	.750	3.33
Sarasota	A	3	3	17.2	18	13	13	2	12	9	0	2	1	.667	6.62
3 Minor League Yrs		37	35	190.2	164	88	63	9	71	171	1	15	7	.682	2.97

Tony Armas Jr., the son of the slugger of the same name, was the key prospect in the deal that sent Mike Stanley to New York last summer. He has been touted as a coming star, but the hype is premature. Then he was traded to Montreal as the player to be named in the Pedro Martinez trade. He was superb in the South Atlantic League, but had problems in the more advanced Florida State League. Armas' fastball is just average right now, but his curve and change are highly advanced, he can throw all of his pitches for strikes, and he has a reputation as an intelligent pitcher. Armas hasn't finished growing, and if he adds velocity as his frame fills out, he could be outstanding. As it is for all young pitchers, health is the key for Armas. If he doesn't get hurt, he could be a good one, but his velocity was down at the end of the season, a sign of fatigue. **Grade C+**

Rolando Arrojo   *Tampa Bay Devil Rays*

Pos: P   **Throws:** Right   **Ht:** 6'4"   **Wt:** 210   **Age:** 29

Yr Team	Lg	G	GS	IP	H	R	ER	HR	BB	SO	SV	W	L	Pct.	ERA
97 St. Pete	A	16	16	89.1	73	40	34	6	13	73	0	5	6	.455	3.43
1 Minor League Yr		16	16	89.1	73	40	34	6	13	73	0	5	6	.455	3.43

Arrojo was the ace of the Cuban national team; he defected in 1996, and got a $7 million bonus from the Devil Rays last year. There is no question about his talent; there is serious doubt about his true age. Arrojo took time to work himself into shape in 1997, and his first few outings in the Florida State League did not go well, but he finished strongly, and will pitch for the major league team in 1998. Arrojo has a 92-94 MPH fastball, a nasty slider, and a good splitter. His control is sharp, and he is intelligent and aggressive. Josh Boyd and Mike Mittleman, a fine pair of prospect evaluators, were very impressed with his performance in the Arizona Fall League. Grading Arrojo as a prospect is nearly impossible, because no one knows how old he really is. He and his agent say he was born in July 1968, making him 29, but other people say he may be as old as 33 or 34. The big-name Cuban defectors (Osvaldo Fernandez, Livan Hernandez, Ariel Prieto) have a mixed track record, and it will be a while before we know where Arrojo ranks. I won't give him a letter grade, due to the uncertainty regarding his age, but he should be a very fine pitcher.

Bronson Arroyo   *Pittsburgh Pirates*

Pos: P   **Throws:** Right   **Ht:** 6'5"   **Wt:** 165   **Age:** 21

Yr Team	Lg	G	GS	IP	H	R	ER	HR	BB	SO	SV	W	L	Pct.	ERA
96 Augusta	A	26	26	135.2	123	64	53	11	36	107	0	8	6	.571	3.52
97 Lynchburg	A	24	24	160.1	154	69	59	17	33	121	0	12	4	.750	3.31
3 Minor League Yrs		63	59	357.1	349	172	141	32	78	276	1	25	14	.641	3.55

Arroyo is the classic projectable young pitcher who picks up velocity and emerges as a fine prospect. A third-round draft in 1995 from a Florida high school, Arroyo is tall, thin, and lanky. His velocity has picked up into the low 90s, which, combined with his good curveball, excellent changeup, and pinpoint control, makes him a tough customer. His K/BB was snazzy at +91 percent, but his K/IP and H/IP marks were less impressive. Arroyo is a lithe athlete, and will be a fine fielder with more experience. He needs to stay healthy, and could be inhabiting the Pittsburgh rotation in 1999 if he does well in the high minors. **Grade B**

Mike Asche
Pittsburgh Pirates

Pos: OF **Bats:** Right **Ht:** 6'2" **Wt:** 190 **Age:** 26

Yr Team	Lg	G	AB	R	H	2B	3B	HR	RBI	BB	SO	SB	CS	Avg	OBP	Slg
96 Lynchburg	A	129	498	79	147	25	6	7	54	38	92	26	5	.295	.343	.412
97 Carolina	AA	15	42	2	9	1	1	0	2	4	6	0	0	.214	.283	.286
Lynchburg	A	107	409	70	125	34	4	11	70	41	77	33	3	.306	.368	.489
4 Minor League Yrs		412	1529	235	430	82	18	28	210	131	265	86	16	.281	.339	.413

Mike Asche was drafted in the sixth round in 1994, from Kearney State College in Nebraska. He had the best season of his career at Lynchburg in the Carolina League in 1997, and should move to Double-A in 1998. Asche's best attribute is speed, but he also has a bit of power, and usually makes contact. He is not a terrific defensive player, so if he advances, it will be because he hits. Asche was old for the Carolina League, and needs to establish himself at a higher level. **Grade C**

Chris Ashby
New York Yankees

Pos: 1B **Bats:** Right **Ht:** 6'3" **Wt:** 185 **Age:** 23

Yr Team	Lg	G	AB	R	H	2B	3B	HR	RBI	BB	SO	SB	CS	Avg	OBP	Slg
96 Tampa	A	100	325	55	80	28	0	6	46	71	78	16	4	.246	.388	.388
97 Norwich	AA	136	457	92	114	20	1	24	82	80	95	10	7	.249	.366	.455
5 Minor League Yrs		425	1428	246	370	92	3	44	236	267	312	36	17	.259	.382	.420

Ashby gets little attention as a prospect, but he does two things I like a lot: draw walks and hit for power. He is not a contact hitter, but he takes pitches looking for one to drive, and when he gets it, he can bang it a long way. His OPS was adequate at seven percent above league, but his SEC was excellent at +40 percent, demonstrating that he helps his team score runs despite his low average. Ashby used to be a catcher and would have a better future if he had remained one, but poor defense moved him to first base last year, where he showed decent mobility but made too many errors. I don't think he fits into the Yankees' plans, but I think he will play in the majors, perhaps as a Jim Leyritz-type super-utility bat off the bench. **Grade C+**

Bruce Aven
Cleveland Indians

Pos: OF **Bats:** Right **Ht:** 5'9" **Wt:** 180 **Age:** 26

Yr Team	Lg	G	AB	R	H	2B	3B	HR	RBI	BB	SO	SB	CS	Avg	OBP	Slg
96 Canton-Akrn	AA	131	481	91	143	31	4	23	79	43	101	22	6	.297	.373	.522
Buffalo	AAA	3	9	5	6	0	0	1	2	1	1	0	1	.667	.727	1.000
97 Buffalo	AAA	121	432	69	124	27	3	17	77	50	99	10	3	.287	.371	.481
Cleveland	AL	13	19	4	4	1	0	0	2	1	5	0	1	.211	.250	.263
4 Minor League Yrs		446	1621	284	471	95	17	69	260	155	355	59	22	.291	.369	.498

Bruce Aven has always fought the skeptics. He's a short, balding guy who isn't intimidating in the batter's box, but has above-average power and has hit well at every level, including last year at Triple-A Buffalo. His OPS and SEC marks are always good, and were again in the American Association at +13 percent and +19 percent. His strike-zone judgment is not wonderful; he will chase bad pitches at times, especially inside, but his strikeout rate is okay and he does make contact when down in the count. Aven played center field in 1996, but moved to left last year. He has very good range, but his arm isn't strong. The Indians say he works hard. Aven is one of my favorites, and although he isn't a top-caliber prospect, I wouldn't be afraid to put him in the lineup. **Grade B**

Rolo Avila   *Los Angeles Dodgers*

Pos: OF **Bats:** Right **Ht:** 5'8" **Wt:** 170 **Age:** 24

Yr Team	Lg	G	AB	R	H	2B	3B	HR	RBI	BB	SO	SB	CS	Avg	OBP	Slg
96 High Desert	A	68	296	54	98	17	2	4	33	22	32	15	7	.331	.381	.443
Bowie	AA	60	233	31	62	12	1	2	17	19	34	8	5	.266	.340	.352
Rochester	AAA	12	47	7	14	2	1	0	6	3	4	2	0	.298	.353	.383
97 San Berndno	A	134	507	94	147	25	3	6	47	63	63	52	24	.290	.369	.387
4 Minor League Yrs		450	1681	287	475	90	10	16	147	184	224	141	58	.283	.361	.377

What a wonderful name for a baseball player. Avila led the Big West Conference in stolen bases at Long Beach State in 1994, but despite his speed was just a 20th-round pick, by the Orioles. He did a lot of bench-warming, but managed to avoid getting released, and when he got a chance to play in 1996, he did well. He was traded to the Dodgers over the offseason, then put in another very good season. Avila is not an imposing field presence, but manages to avoid getting the bat knocked out of his hands by working the count and making contact. He is obviously dangerous on the bases, and he is a good defensive out-fielder. Avila needs to play in Double-A; if he succeeds, he could have use as a reserve. **Grade C**

Corey Avrard   *St. Louis Cardinals*

Pos: P **Throws:** Right **Ht:** 6'3" **Wt:** 185 **Age:** 21

Yr Team	Lg	G	GS	IP	H	R	ER	HR	BB	SO	SV	W	L	Pct.	ERA
96 Peoria	A	21	21	110.1	105	73	52	6	58	103	0	5	9	.357	4.24
97 Peoria	A	20	20	93.1	97	76	66	5	69	94	0	4	5	.444	6.36
Pr William	A	8	8	40.1	30	28	24	1	44	50	0	0	3	.000	5.36
3 Minor League Yrs		62	62	298.1	270	202	166	16	204	298	0	10	23	.303	5.01

No one doubts Corey Avrard's physical ability. He can strike anybody out with his 92-MPH fastball and big-bending curve. He can also walk anyone; his command is very erratic, and as long as he has problems throwing strikes, his advancement will be slow. Avrard isn't a dumb fellow; he knows what he has to do to succeed, but like many hard-throwing young pitchers, he has problems keeping his mechanics consistent. He has had injury trouble in the past, and there is a reasonable chance he will get hurt again before he figures out what he is doing. **Grade C-**

Manny Aybar

St. Louis Cardinals

Pos: P **Throws:** Right **Ht:** 6'1" **Wt:** 165 **Age:** 23

Yr Team	Lg	G	GS	IP	H	R	ER	HR	BB	SO	SV	W	L	Pct.	ERA
96 Arkansas	AA	20	20	121.0	120	53	41	10	34	83	0	8	6	.571	3.05
Louisville	AAA	5	5	30.2	26	12	11	1	7	25	0	2	2	.500	3.23
97 Louisville	AAA	22	22	137.0	131	60	53	10	45	114	0	5	8	.385	3.48
St. Louis	NL	12	12	68.0	66	33	32	8	29	41	0	2	4	.333	4.24
4 Minor League Yrs		87	87	522.0	470	223	178	33	147	443	0	26	30	.464	3.07

Converted shortstop Manny Aybar got an early major league call last year, and pitched better than his 2-4 record would indicate. He will probably be in the rotation in 1998, although there are rumors he may be converted to relief. He works with a 92-MPH fastball, a hard slider, and an inconsistent, but promising, changeup. Throwing strikes is usually not a problem, although hitting spots within the strike zone sometimes is. He had a reputation as being overly emotional in the past, but it didn't seem to be much of a problem last year. I don't think Aybar will be a potential ace like Matt Morris, but he should be a good pitcher, as a starter or reliever. **Grade B**

Jason Baker

Montreal Expos

Pos: P **Throws:** Right **Ht:** 6'4" **Wt:** 195 **Age:** 23

Yr Team	Lg	G	GS	IP	H	R	ER	HR	BB	SO	SV	W	L	Pct.	ERA
96 Delmarva	A	27	27	160.1	127	70	50	6	77	147	0	9	7	.563	2.81
97 Expos	R	2	2	7.0	4	0	0	0	3	8	0	0	0	—	0.00
Wst Plm Bch	A	15	14	72.0	90	55	48	10	31	47	0	3	4	.429	6.00
5 Minor League Yrs		78	77	405.0	361	223	172	22	209	304	0	25	22	.532	3.82

Baker is a tall righthander with a terrific arm. His fastball is the best in the Expos system: he can hit 97 MPH. He was quite effective for Delmarva in 1996, but found the Florida State League more difficult in 1997. He had trouble throwing the heater for strikes, didn't make much progress developing his breaking stuff, and spent part of the season on the disabled list with shoulder trouble. If Baker is healthy, and if he improves his command, he could be an excellent pitcher, but those "ifs" are bigger than his fastball. **Grade C**

Paul Bako

Detroit Tigers

Pos: C **Bats:** Left **Ht:** 6'2" **Wt:** 205 **Age:** 25

Yr Team	Lg	G	AB	R	H	2B	3B	HR	RBI	BB	SO	SB	CS	Avg	OBP	Slg
96 Chattanooga	AA	110	360	53	106	27	0	8	48	48	93	1	0	.294	.381	.436
97 Indianapols	AAA	104	321	34	78	14	1	8	43	34	81	0	5	.243	.316	.368
5 Minor League Yrs		443	1413	179	375	72	4	30	174	181	358	11	9	.265	.351	.386

The Reds were hoping that Paul Bako could compete for a major league job in 1998, but his 1997 season at Indianapolis was disappointing. He didn't show as much patience as he did at Chattanooga, and his batting average dropped a good 50 points. He isn't worth much if he doesn't draw walks or hit for average, since he lacks power, despite his size. His OPS was poor at -10 percent. Bako is a fine defensive catcher, having thrown out 42 percent of runners for two consecutive seasons. He calls a good game, and moves well behind the plate for a big guy. Right now, Bako looks like a reserve catcher, although he could get beyond that if the offense returns. He was traded to Detroit in a deal for Mel Nieves. **Grade C**

John Bale   *Toronto Blue Jays*

Pos: P **Throws:** Left **Ht:** 6'4" **Wt:** 195 **Age:** 23

Yr Team	Lg	G	GS	IP	H	R	ER	HR	BB	SO	SV	W	L	Pct.	ERA
96 St. Cathrns	A	8	8	33.1	39	21	18	2	11	35	0	3	2	.600	4.86
97 Hagerstown	A	25	25	140.1	130	83	67	11	63	155	0	7	7	.500	4.30
2 Minor League Yrs		33	33	173.2	169	104	85	13	74	190	0	10	9	.526	4.40

Drafted in the fifth round in 1996, from the University of Southern Mississippi, Bale has good velocity for a lefthander and nice movement on his curve, but has command problems and can be erratic. His K/BB was just four percent above league, but his K/IP was great at +28 percent. Bale is not very good at holding runners, especially for a lefthander, and needs polish fielding his position. For a guy who was a college senior, he needs quite a bit of refinement, but he does have a nice upside. **Grade C**

Ryan Balfe   *San Diego Padres*

Pos: 3B **Bats:** Both **Ht:** 6'1" **Wt:** 180 **Age:** 22

Yr Team	Lg	G	AB	R	H	2B	3B	HR	RBI	BB	SO	SB	CS	Avg	OBP	Slg
96 Lakeland	A	92	347	48	97	21	1	11	66	24	66	3	0	.280	.332	.441
97 Tigers	R	2	7	2	4	0	0	1	1	1	1	0	0	.571	.625	1.000
Lakeland	A	86	312	40	84	13	2	13	48	24	75	1	1	.269	.322	.449
4 Minor League Yrs		336	1185	155	315	57	5	36	175	120	265	7	6	.266	.340	.414

Balfe, drafted out of a New York high school in the eighth round by the Tigers in 1994, has switch-hitting power potential, but his development has been slowed by a series of injuries. He had shoulder problems in 1996; last year, a succession of muscle cramps and pulls in his legs kept him out of the lineup for a month. When he did play, he continued to show the ability to drive the ball out of the park, but his command of the strike zone is marginal, and he needs to succeed at a higher level. Balfe has the athletic ability to be a good defensive player, but like most young infielders, he needs cultivation. The Tigers traded him to San Diego in the offseason. **Grade C+**

Brian Banks   *Milwaukee Brewers*

Pos: OF **Bats:** Both **Ht:** 6'3" **Wt:** 200 **Age:** 27

Yr Team	Lg	G	AB	R	H	2B	3B	HR	RBI	BB	SO	SB	CS	Avg	OBP	Slg
96 New Orleans	AAA	137	487	71	132	29	7	16	64	66	105	17	8	.271	.356	.458
Milwaukee	AL	4	7	2	4	2	0	1	2	1	2	0	0	.571	.625	1.286
97 Tucson	AAA	98	378	53	112	26	3	10	63	35	83	7	3	.296	.353	.460
Milwaukee	AL	28	68	9	14	1	0	1	8	6	17	0	1	.206	.267	.265
5 Minor League Yrs		545	1984	304	564	122	24	57	307	267	429	49	33	.284	.368	.456

Brian Banks returned to Triple-A for another season, and didn't improve over what he did in 1996. In some ways, he was worse. One of his best attributes was an ability to draw walks, but he was less patient in 1997, perhaps in an attempt to hit for more power. It didn't work; his OPS was two percent below league, after being +10 percent the year before. His batting average was higher, but much of that was just the difference between hitting in Tucson and hitting at New Orleans. Banks is an adequate defensive outfielder, and also serves as an emergency catcher. He isn't young anymore, and his chance to earn a real job is fading. **Grade C**

Lorenzo Barcelo　　　　　　　　　　　　　　　　　　*Chicago White Sox*

Pos: P　**Throws:** Right　**Ht:** 6'4"　**Wt:** 205　**Age:** 20

Yr Team	Lg	G	GS	IP	H	R	ER	HR	BB	SO	SV	W	L	Pct.	ERA
96 Burlington	A	26	26	152.2	138	70	60	19	46	139	0	12	10	.545	3.54
97 San Jose	A	16	16	89.0	91	45	39	13	30	89	0	5	4	.556	3.94
Shreveport	AA	5	5	31.1	30	19	14	4	8	20	0	2	0	1.000	4.02
Birmingham	AA	6	6	33.1	36	20	18	2	9	29	0	2	1	.667	4.86
3 Minor League Yrs		65	64	353.1	338	177	149	41	112	311	0	24	17	.585	3.80

Lorenzo Barcelo came to the White Sox as part of the big debacle. . . er, trade. . . with the Giants last summer. He was one of the best pitching prospects in the San Francisco system. A Dominican, Barcelo is quite tall and has yet to completely fill out. His velocity is already very good, and could get better as he matures. He throws strikes with the regularity of an atomic clock, and is said to be bright and coachable. The main concern I have about him is durability. Although he ended last year healthy, it remains to be seen if he will stay that way. **Grade C+**

Andy Barkett　　　　　　　　　　　　　　　　　　　　*Texas Rangers*

Pos: 1B　**Bats:** Left　**Ht:** 6'1"　**Wt:** 205　**Age:** 23

Yr Team	Lg	G	AB	R	H	2B	3B	HR	RBI	BB	SO	SB	CS	Avg	OBP	Slg
96 Charlotte	A	115	392	57	112	22	3	6	54	57	59	3	1	.286	.380	.403
97 Tulsa	AA	130	471	82	141	34	8	8	65	63	86	1	3	.299	.386	.456
3 Minor League Yrs		311	1103	179	324	73	16	19	182	163	211	5	7	.294	.387	.441

The Rangers signed Andy Barkett as an undrafted free agent after his college career at North Carolina State. He does not have the power that teams like in a first baseman, but he draws walks and has a good on-base percentage. It would help him if his glove work were good, but he struggles defensively. Barkett has a sound work ethic, and if hustle and effort earn extra points, he is your man. Unless he develops some power or starts hitting .330, his chance to advance is limited. **Grade C-**

John Barnes　　　　　　　　　　　　　　　　　　　　*Boston Red Sox*

Pos: OF　**Bats:** Right　**Ht:** 6'2"　**Wt:** 205　**Age:** 21

Yr Team	Lg	G	AB	R	H	2B	3B	HR	RBI	BB	SO	SB	CS	Avg	OBP	Slg
96 Red Sox	R	30	101	9	28	4	0	1	17	5	17	4	0	.277	.333	.347
97 Michigan	A	130	490	80	149	19	5	6	73	65	42	19	5	.304	.387	.400
2 Minor League Yrs		160	591	89	177	23	5	7	90	70	59	23	5	.299	.378	.391

Barnes, a fourth-rounder in 1996 from Grossmont Community College in California, had a very nice first full season at Michigan. He doesn't have much power, but is a superior contact hitter with fine command of the strike zone, and good speed on the basepaths. He needs to refine his baserunning. Barnes would have more value if he could develop some power, but the size and strength are present for him to do so, and his ability to make contact will only help him. In the outfield, he is adequate in center and pretty good in left or right. I want to see some power from Barnes, although it might not come for another year or so. **Grade C**

Larry Barnes
Anaheim Angels

Pos: 1B **Bats:** Left **Ht:** 6'1" **Wt:** 195 **Age:** 23

Yr Team	Lg	G	AB	R	H	2B	3B	HR	RBI	BB	SO	SB	CS	Avg	OBP	Slg
96 Cedar Rapds	A	131	489	84	155	36	5	27	112	58	101	9	6	.317	.392	.577
97 Lk Elsinore	A	115	446	68	128	32	2	13	71	43	84	3	4	.287	.353	.455
3 Minor League Yrs		302	1132	194	344	76	10	43	220	128	225	24	15	.304	.379	.503

Barnes destroyed Midwest League pitching in 1996, after signing as an undrafted free agent from Fresno State in 1995. His performance in the 1997 California League was something of a disappointment, however. He continued to show fairly good strike-zone judgment, but his OPS was just six percent above league, and his power production dropped substantially, despite a big hitting season in the Cal League. Although Barnes is not a good athlete to the naked eye, he led the California League in fielding percentage at first base, and shows some mobility. Last year, I compared Barnes to fellow first-base prospect Jesse Ibarra, who tore up the Midwest League in 1995, but wasn't hot in the Cal League in 1996. Ibarra went on to have a very good Double-A season in 1997, and it wouldn't surprise me if Barnes does the same thing. Midland will be a good environment for him. **Grade C**

Michael Barrett
Montreal Expos

Pos: C **Bats:** Right **Ht:** 6'3" **Wt:** 185 **Age:** 21

Yr Team	Lg	G	AB	R	H	2B	3B	HR	RBI	BB	SO	SB	CS	Avg	OBP	Slg
96 Delmarva	A	129	474	57	113	29	4	4	62	18	42	5	11	.238	.277	.342
97 Wst Plm Bch	A	119	423	52	120	30	0	8	61	36	49	7	4	.284	.340	.411
3 Minor League Yrs		301	1090	131	291	72	8	12	143	70	111	19	21	.267	.315	.381

Barrett was an outstanding high school hitter, leading to his selection in the first round in 1995. An infielder as a prep, he moved to catcher in the pros and hasn't been awful. He threw out 33 percent of stealers in 1997, the league average being 36 percent. This was a considerable improvement over the previous season, when he threw out only 23 percent. He has a very strong arm, but needs to iron out his footwork and release. Barrett does call a good game for an inexperienced catcher, and no one questions his work ethic. For a guy who was drafted for his bat, Barrett hasn't hit that well, although he did better last year than the year before. He makes contact, shows doubles power, and should hit some home runs as he matures. The biggest barrier for Barrett will be the fact that catching can stunt the development of young hitters. **Grade C+**

Manuel Barrios

Florida Marlins

Pos: P   **Throws:** Right   **Ht:** 6'0"   **Wt:** 145   **Age:** 23

Yr Team	Lg	G	GS	IP	H	R	ER	HR	BB	SO	SV	W	L	Pct.	ERA
96 Jackson	AA	60	0	68.1	60	29	18	4	29	69	23	6	4	.600	2.37
97 New Orleans	AAA	57	0	82.2	70	32	30	5	34	77	0	4	8	.333	3.27
Houston	NL	2	0	3.0	6	4	4	0	3	3	0	0	0	—	12.00
4 Minor League Yrs		210	0	268.0	247	121	104	14	103	264	50	11	23	.324	3.49

The Astros don't do particularly well with the amateur draft, but they have a strong resource base in Latin America, and Manny Barrios, from Panama, is one of their finds. Barrios has a solid low-90s fastball, a hard slider, decent control, and a bulldog attitude on the mound. He pitched well at New Orleans last year, setting up closer prospect Oscar Henriquez; both could see considerable action now that they have been traded to Florida in the Moises Alou deal. **Grade C+**

Jayson Bass

Seattle Mariners

Pos: OF   **Bats:** Left   **Ht:** 6'3"   **Wt:** 212   **Age:** 23

Yr Team	Lg	G	AB	R	H	2B	3B	HR	RBI	BB	SO	SB	CS	Avg	OBP	Slg
96 Fayettevlle	A	104	295	44	68	12	3	11	43	54	118	19	10	.231	.351	.403
97 Lakeland	A	108	376	58	97	18	4	13	53	41	130	17	7	.258	.331	.431
5 Minor League Yrs		403	1320	193	313	60	19	43	175	168	453	56	25	.237	.327	.409

Bass was drafted in the fifth round, from a high school in Seattle, in 1993. He has all the athletic ability in the world, but it has taken him a long time to learn how to play baseball. Bass had the best season of his career at Lakeland last year, showing his power and speed potentialities, but his command of the strike zone remains a serious problem, as demonstrated by his high strikeout rate. He isn't much of a defensive player. It isn't too late for Bass to develop, but there is no reason to be optimistic that I can see. Seattle took him in the Triple-A Rule 5 draft. **Grade C-**

Fletcher Bates

Florida Marlins

Pos: OF   **Bats:** Both   **Ht:** 6'1"   **Wt:** 193   **Age:** 24

Yr Team	Lg	G	AB	R	H	2B	3B	HR	RBI	BB	SO	SB	CS	Avg	OBP	Slg
96 Capital City	A	132	491	84	127	21	13	15	72	64	162	16	6	.259	.346	.446
97 St. Lucie	A	70	253	49	76	19	11	11	38	33	66	7	6	.300	.387	.593
Binghamton	AA	68	245	44	63	14	2	12	34	26	71	9	3	.257	.328	.478
4 Minor League Yrs		406	1480	255	401	74	39	50	214	199	431	53	27	.271	.359	.475

Secondary average has always been a strength of Fletcher Bates, a toolsy, switch-hitting outfielder. He struggles making contact at times and his batting average fluctuates wildly, but he has power, speed, and draws walks. His SEC in the Eastern League was very good at +27 percent. His defense is nothing terrific, and he would probably be best off in left field in the majors. Bates is not that young anymore, and his strikeout rate remains fearsome, but I still like his broad base of skills. He is a sleeper and he went to Florida in a deal for Dennis Cook. **Grade C+**

Justin Baughman
Anaheim Angels

Pos: SS **Bats:** Right **Ht:** 5'11" **Wt:** 175 **Age:** 23

Yr Team	Lg	G	AB	R	H	2B	3B	HR	RBI	BB	SO	SB	CS	Avg	OBP	Slg
96 Cedar Rapds	A	127	464	78	115	17	8	5	48	45	78	50	17	.248	.322	.351
97 Lk Elsinore	A	134	478	71	131	14	3	2	48	40	79	68	15	.274	.343	.328
3 Minor League Yrs		319	1157	175	296	35	14	8	116	103	195	137	36	.256	.326	.331

Baughman was picked in the fifth round in 1995 from Lewis & Clark College in Oregon. His best offensive attribute is speed; his command of the strike zone is OK, but he doesn't have much punch. Glove work is a strength for him. He has above-average range and doesn't make too many errors. Baughman needs to prove himself in Double-A, and his future, if he has one, is as a utility guy. **Grade C-**

Tim Belk
Cincinnati Reds

Pos: 1B **Bats:** Right **Ht:** 6'3" **Wt:** 200 **Age:** 27

Yr Team	Lg	G	AB	R	H	2B	3B	HR	RBI	BB	SO	SB	CS	Avg	OBP	Slg
96 Indianapols	AAA	120	436	63	125	27	3	15	63	27	72	5	2	.287	.327	.466
Cincinnati	NL	7	15	2	3	0	0	0	0	1	2	0	0	.200	.250	.200
97 Indianapols	AAA	90	255	37	74	18	1	8	38	26	45	5	3	.290	.353	.463
6 Minor League Yrs		598	2095	344	620	128	10	63	326	213	302	49	28	.296	.361	.457

Poor Tim Belk. He has played well in Triple-A for three years in a row, and he didn't deserve to lose his job at Indianapolis to Brian Hunter (yes, *that* Brian Hunter) in June last year. Belk was hitting over .290 at the time. No, Belk is not a bad fielder, and, no, there isn't supposed to be a personality problem. He has a reputation as a hard worker. Obviously, the Reds just don't think he can hit for enough power. Belk isn't wonderful, but if he gets liberated from the Cincinnati organization, he could break out and have a nice season somewhere. He would be decent as part of a platoon combo. **Grade C-**

Jason Bell
Minnesota Twins

Pos: P **Throws:** Right **Ht:** 6'3" **Wt:** 208 **Age:** 23

Yr Team	Lg	G	GS	IP	H	R	ER	HR	BB	SO	SV	W	L	Pct.	ERA
96 Ft. Myers	A	13	13	90.1	61	20	17	1	22	83	0	6	3	.667	1.69
Hardware City	AA	16	16	94.0	93	54	46	13	38	94	0	2	6	.250	4.40
97 New Britain	AA	28	28	164.2	163	71	62	19	64	142	0	11	9	.550	3.39
3 Minor League Yrs		66	63	383.1	343	156	130	33	130	359	0	22	19	.537	3.05

Jason Bell is a big guy, and looks like he should throw harder than he does. His fastball runs 89-90 MPH, but coaches are always trying to get a little more out of him due to his size. His best pitch is a barbed slider, and he also has a decent changeup. His command is good, as reflected in his fine K/BB ratio of +20 percent, but his K/IP was only at plus-nine, and his H/IP was a shade worse than league. He gets the ball up sometimes and can be vulnerable to the gopher ball. Bell is quick to the plate and holds runners well for a righthander. The challenge of the Pacific Coast League will be a difficult one for him, but if he does well, there's plenty of room in the Twins rotation. **Grade B-**

Mike Bell   *Arizona Diamondbacks*

Pos: 3B-2B   **Bats:** Right   **Ht:** 6'2"   **Wt:** 185   **Age:** 23

Yr Team	Lg	G	AB	R	H	2B	3B	HR	RBI	BB	SO	SB	CS	Avg	OBP	Slg
96 Tulsa	AA	128	484	62	129	31	3	16	59	42	75	3	1	.267	.329	.442
97 Okla City	AAA	93	328	35	77	18	2	5	38	29	78	4	2	.235	.302	.348
Tulsa	AA	33	123	17	35	11	0	8	23	15	28	0	1	.285	.375	.569
5 Minor League Yrs		563	2110	269	561	115	18	43	264	208	352	41	26	.266	.335	.399

Two years ago, Mike Bell was thought to be Texas' third baseman of the future, but he was left in the dust by Fernando Tatis, traded to Anaheim, then selected in the expansion draft. Bell's main problem is his bat. He *looks* like a hitter if you watch him, with a nice level swing, but while he will whack the occasional long drive, he has never been as productive as expected. His OPS in the American Association was lower than those posted by famous sluggers like Eric Owens, Frankie Menechino, and Scott Leius. Bell is a good defensive third baseman, and is spending time at second and first to prepare him for a utility job. He is athletic enough to play the outfield if they want to try him there. Bell must hit to get beyond a bench role in the majors. **Grade C**

Rob Bell   *Atlanta Braves*

Pos: P   **Throws:** Right   **Ht:** 6'5"   **Wt:** 225   **Age:** 21

Yr Team	Lg	G	GS	IP	H	R	ER	HR	BB	SO	SV	W	L	Pct.	ERA
96 Eugene	A	16	16	81.0	89	49	46	5	29	74	0	5	6	.455	5.11
97 Macon	A	27	27	146.2	144	72	60	15	41	140	0	14	7	.667	3.68
3 Minor League Yrs		53	51	261.2	271	150	132	22	84	247	0	20	19	.513	4.54

Most of Atlanta's good young pitching prospects are at the lower levels. This is good, because they are young, promising, and projectable, but it is also bad, because it means they are probably a long way from helping the team, and have yet to run the injury gauntlet all young hurlers must survive. The Braves had a solid group of these guys at Macon in the South Atlantic League, including Rob Bell. A third-round pick in 1995 from a high school in New York, Bell is an imposing presence. His fastball hits 93 MPH, and his curve has great rotation; his change is rudimentary at this point. Control isn't a problem for him, and his K/BB was very good at +45 percent. His K/IP was +10 percent, but his H/IP was just a notch above average, so he does have work to do. Bell holds runners very well for a righthander, and scouts are impressed with his pitching instincts and assertiveness. Basically, Bell has everything he needs to succeed, and if he doesn't get hurt, he could be an excellent pitcher. **Grade B**

Ronnie Belliard
Milwaukee Brewers

Pos: 2B **Bats:** Right **Ht:** 5'9" **Wt:** 176 **Age:** 22

Yr Team	Lg	G	AB	R	H	2B	3B	HR	RBI	BB	SO	SB	CS	Avg	OBP	Slg
96 El Paso	AA	109	416	73	116	20	8	3	57	60	51	26	10	.279	.373	.387
97 Tucson	AAA	118	443	80	125	35	4	4	55	61	69	10	7	.282	.379	.406
4 Minor League Yrs		396	1463	261	420	90	20	20	215	171	212	59	29	.287	.369	.417

Yes, he is related to Rafael; they are cousins. Ronnie isn't as good defensively as Raffy, but he is a much better hitter, and his glove at second isn't shabby. Ronnie got off to a very slow start in his first Triple-A season. His batting average hovered around .220 for much of the season, but when the Brewers fired Tucson manager Tim Ireland in late July, Belliard went on a tear, finishing the season with good overall numbers. Ireland was apparently something of a tyrant; Belliard is a sensitive sort, and did not respond to being ridden hard psychologically by his manager. Some people react better to carrots than sticks. He has patience at the plate, good strength for a small guy, and a reliable glove. I think Belliard will be a good player, although he isn't quite ready for a major league job. **Grade B-**

Carlos Beltran
Kansas City Royals

Pos: OF **Bats:** Both **Ht:** 6'1" **Wt:** 175 **Age:** 20

Yr Team	Lg	G	AB	R	H	2B	3B	HR	RBI	BB	SO	SB	CS	Avg	OBP	Slg
96 Lansing	A	11	42	3	6	2	0	0	0	1	11	1	0	.143	.163	.190
Spokane	A	59	215	29	58	8	3	7	29	31	65	10	2	.270	.359	.433
97 Wilmington	A	120	419	57	96	15	4	11	46	46	96	17	7	.229	.311	.363
3 Minor League Yrs		242	856	118	210	34	7	18	98	91	202	33	12	.245	.321	.364

The Royals took multi-tooled Carlos Beltran in the second round in 1995, out of Puerto Rico. Scouts project him as a very good power hitter, which combined with his speed and defense, would make him very valuable. Beltran is still quite raw, and has lots of work to do. His performance at Wilmington was not respectable from a numbers standpoint. . . an OPS six percent below league average won't win a player sabermetric praise. On the other hand, he was playing in a difficult stadium for offense, and was one of the youngest regulars in the circuit, so the season wasn't a complete disaster. Beltran has solid defensive skills in center field, although he makes mistakes of inexperience. It isn't too late by any means for Beltran to have a good career; let's wait and see. **Grade C**

Adrian Beltre
Los Angeles Dodgers

Pos: 3B **Bats:** Right **Ht:** 5'11" **Wt:** 200 **Age:** 19

Yr Team	Lg	G	AB	R	H	2B	3B	HR	RBI	BB	SO	SB	CS	Avg	OBP	Slg
96 Savannah	A	68	244	48	75	14	3	16	59	35	46	4	3	.307	.406	.586
San Berndno	A	63	238	40	62	13	1	10	40	19	44	3	4	.261	.322	.450
97 Vero Beach	A	123	435	95	138	24	2	26	104	67	66	25	9	.317	.407	.561
2 Minor League Yrs		254	917	183	275	51	6	52	203	121	156	32	16	.300	.385	.539

Adrian Beltre is the best prospect in baseball. Ben Grieve and Paul Konerko are closer to the majors, but Beltre will be a great hitter in his own right, and will probably contribute more defensively. Beltre was unstoppable in the difficult Florida State League, with excellent standard stats, plus exquisite marks in the factors I look at. His OPS was outstanding at +38 percent, and he had the second-best SEC in the circuit. He has tremendous power, hits for average, and has notable command of the strike zone for one so young. He even runs well. He should be a Pedro Guerrero-type hitter in the majors, and Pedro, for all his flaws, was one hell of a hitter. Beltre's defense is rough at this point. He has the arm and range to be an excellent defensive third baseman, but needs experience and repetition. That is true for almost every player his age. The only things that could derail Beltre are injuries, immaturity, or criminal organizational mishandling. The first two haven't been a problem yet, but the third might be if the Dodgers don't get over their California addiction to veterans. "You smash hits with your steely bat but you just can't make the team." In Beltre and Konerko, the Dodgers have two of the best three prospects in baseball. Let's hope they know how to use them. **Grade A**

Kris Benson   *Pittsburgh Pirates*

Pos: P **Throws:** Right **Ht:** 6'4" **Wt:** 190 **Age:** 23

Yr Team	Lg	G	GS	IP	H	R	ER	HR	BB	SO	SV	W	L	Pct.	ERA
97 Lynchburg	A	10	10	59.1	49	20	17	1	13	72	0	5	2	.714	2.58
Carolina	AA	14	14	68.2	81	49	38	11	32	66	0	3	5	.375	4.98
1 Minor League Yr		24	24	128.0	130	69	55	12	45	138	0	8	7	.533	3.87

Kris Benson was the first player picked in the 1996 draft, out of Clemson University. He pitched for the U.S. Olympic Team, and didn't begin his pro career until 1997. The Carolina League was not much of a challenge for him (he had the best K/BB mark in the league), but he struggled after a midseason promotion to Double-A. He continued to strike people out at a good pace, but his H/IP shot up and his command fluctuated. The dropoff was attributed mainly to nagging hamstring and ankle injuries, and everyone still expects him to be a star. Benson has a crisp 93-MPH fastball, an excellent curve, and an excellent changeup. His control is precise, and he has made progress in smoothing his mechanics and holding baserunners. Benson is also intelligent, and has a fine work ethic. The main question I have about him is his health. Although he has never had an arm injury, his velocity was down at the end of the college season in 1996, and again at the end of the pro season in 1997. That's a sign of fatigue, and while tiredness is nothing unusual in a young pitcher, it gives me a nagging doubt about his durability. **Grade B+**

Jeff Berblinger   *St. Louis Cardinals*

Pos: 2B **Bats:** Right **Ht:** 6'0" **Wt:** 190 **Age:** 27

Yr Team	Lg	G	AB	R	H	2B	3B	HR	RBI	BB	SO	SB	CS	Avg	OBP	Slg
96 Arkansas	AA	134	500	78	144	32	7	11	53	52	66	23	10	.288	.360	.446
97 Louisville	AAA	133	513	63	135	19	7	11	58	55	98	24	12	.263	.339	.392
St. Louis	NL	7	5	1	0	0	0	0	0	0	1	0	0	.000	.000	.000
5 Minor League Yrs		543	2032	326	583	103	25	37	233	223	313	99	48	.287	.368	.417

Berblinger had good 1995 and 1996 seasons in the Texas League. The Tigers picked him in the major league Rule 5 draft, then traded his rights to the Dodgers. He didn't stick, and ended up back with the Cardinals for 1997. Berblinger has some punch in his bat, especially for an infielder, adequate command of the strike zone, and some speed on the bases. He does better against lefties than righties. It would be a stretch for him to start in the majors, although his bat would have some use off the bench. Berblinger had the highest range factor among American Association regular second basemen last year, and he doesn't commit tons of errors. He can't play shortstop, and doesn't have the arm for third, which limits his appeal as a utility guy. **Grade C**

Brandon Berger
Kansas City Royals

Pos: OF **Bats:** Right **Ht:** 6'0" **Wt:** 205 **Age:** 23

Yr Team	Lg	G	AB	R	H	2B	3B	HR	RBI	BB	SO	SB	CS	Avg	OBP	Slg
96 Spokane	A	71	283	46	87	12	1	13	58	31	64	17	5	.307	.376	.495
97 Lansing	A	107	393	64	115	22	6	12	73	42	79	13	1	.293	.368	.471
2 Minor League Yrs		178	676	110	202	34	7	25	131	73	143	30	6	.299	.371	.481

Berger, from Eastern Kentucky University, was a 14th-round pick in 1996. He showed a potentially broad base of skills at Lansing last year, with a fine SEC of +21 percent. He has some power and some speed, hits for a good average, and makes contact. His defense isn't spectacular, and reporters aren't exactly breaking his door down looking for the scoop on the next big prospect. Berger needs to do well against better competition. He is worth keeping an eye on, in case he does. **Grade C**

Peter Bergeron
Los Angeles Dodgers

Pos: OF **Bats:** Left **Ht:** 6'1" **Wt:** 185 **Age:** 20

Yr Team	Lg	G	AB	R	H	2B	3B	HR	RBI	BB	SO	SB	CS	Avg	OBP	Slg
96 Yakima	A	61	232	36	59	5	3	5	21	28	59	13	9	.254	.335	.366
97 Savannah	A	131	492	89	138	18	5	5	36	67	110	32	21	.280	.367	.368
San Berndno	A	2	8	1	2	0	0	0	1	0	2	2	0	.250	.250	.250
2 Minor League Yrs		194	732	126	199	23	8	10	58	95	171	47	30	.272	.356	.366

Bergeron, picked in the fourth round in 1996 from a Massachusetts high school, had a fruitful full-season debut for Savannah in the South Atlantic League. His best tool is speed, and he is learning the skills necessary to make his tool useful by learning how to take pitches and maximize his on-base percentage. He doesn't have power yet, but some scouts think he might develop it as he matures. If that happens, he could be a Seven Skill talent, although that is just supposition at this point. He does have the work ethic and intelligence necessary to improve. Bergeron is quite a distance from the majors, but his career is off to a good start, and as speed players go, I like him. **Grade C+**

Rafael Betancourt
Boston Red Sox

Pos: P **Throws:** Right **Ht:** 6'1" **Wt:** 187 **Age:** 22

Yr Team	Lg	G	GS	IP	H	R	ER	HR	BB	SO	SV	W	L	Pct.	ERA
97 Michigan	A	27	0	32.1	26	9	7	2	2	52	11	0	3	.000	1.95
1 Minor League Yr		27	0	32.1	26	9	7	2	2	52	11	0	3	.000	1.95

Betancourt, a Venezuelan signed as a shortstop in 1994, converted to the tossing box in 1997 after hitting .167 in 1996. He didn't get much attention from the sporting press in

1997, but check out those numbers: two walks. In 32 innings. With *52* strikeouts. No, that's not a misprint. He really did have a K/BB ratio of 26 to one. Best of all, he's not a soft tosser: he has legitimate major league velocity. It is beyond obvious to say he throws strikes. If he keeps this up, he could spend part of 1998 in the majors. He needs to prove himself at higher levels, but keep a close eye on this guy—he could be a major revelation. It makes me wonder why more teams don't make conversions like this, when a guy with a strong arm proves he can't hit. **Grade B**

Jim Betzsold · Cleveland Indians

Pos: OF **Bats:** Right **Ht:** 6'3" **Wt:** 210 **Age:** 25

Yr Team	Lg	G	AB	R	H	2B	3B	HR	RBI	BB	SO	SB	CS	Avg	OBP	Slg
96 Canton-Akrn	AA	84	268	35	64	11	5	3	35	30	74	4	1	.239	.328	.351
97 Akron	AA	118	434	76	115	21	5	19	79	60	119	4	5	.265	.366	.468
4 Minor League Yrs		394	1369	236	362	72	12	59	231	198	398	14	14	.264	.372	.464

Just what the Indians need—a power-hitting rightfielder. Jim Betzsold, a 20th-round pick in 1994 from Cal State Fullerton, lost most of 1996 to a shoulder injury, but recovered fully and did fairly well in 1997. His OPS was acceptable at plus-eight percent; his SEC was very good at +22 percent. Betzsold has a great arm in right field, leading the Eastern League in assists with 17, and his range isn't that bad, but he does make errors. Although he won't be a star, Betzsold will probably hit enough to be useful in the majors. It won't do him much good with Manny Ramirez around. **Grade C**

Brian Bevil · Kansas City Royals

Pos: P **Throws:** Right **Ht:** 6'3" **Wt:** 190 **Age:** 26

Yr Team	Lg	G	GS	IP	H	R	ER	HR	BB	SO	SV	W	L	Pct.	ERA
96 Wichita	AA	13	13	75.2	56	22	17	4	26	74	0	9	2	.818	2.02
Omaha	AAA	12	12	67.2	62	36	31	10	19	73	0	7	5	.583	4.12
Kansas City	AL	3	1	11.0	9	7	7	2	5	7	0	1	0	1.000	5.73
97 Wichita	AA	4	2	8.0	11	8	5	0	4	10	0	0	0	—	5.63
Omaha	AAA	26	3	39.0	34	22	19	8	22	47	1	2	1	.667	4.38
Kansas City	AL	18	0	16.1	16	13	12	1	9	13	1	1	2	.333	6.61
7 Minor League Yrs		150	124	715.0	630	337	290	65	279	674	1	53	36	.596	3.65

Bevil was excellent in 1996, and after a fine spring training, he opened 1997 with the major league club. He got pounded around, so he went back to Omaha to get his game together, and ended up on the disabled list with a sore elbow. By the end of the season, the soreness had cleared up, and he was throwing free and easy. When healthy, Bevil has a 90-MPH fastball, a crisp slider, and good control. His K/BB ratios are usually admirable. Bevil has had serious arm problems before, so the elbow difficulty is not a good sign. I think he could be a very good pitcher, but fret over his health. **Grade C+**

Nick Bierbrodt

Arizona Diamondbacks

Pos: P **Throws:** Left **Ht:** 6'5" **Wt:** 180 **Age:** 19

Yr Team	Lg	G	GS	IP	H	R	ER	HR	BB	SO	SV	W	L	Pct.	ERA
96 Diamondback	R	8	8	38.0	25	9	7	1	13	46	0	1	1	.500	1.66
Lethbridge	R	3	3	18.0	12	4	1	0	5	23	0	2	0	1.000	0.50
97 South Bend	A	15	15	75.2	77	43	34	4	37	64	0	2	4	.333	4.04
2 Minor League Yrs		26	26	131.2	114	56	42	5	55	133	0	5	5	.500	2.87

Bierbrodt was Arizona's first-round pick in 1996, out of a California high school. He is the classic projectable high school pitching prospect: very tall, very lanky, throws hard and should get even faster as he matures into his body. He spent the second half of 1997 in the Midwest League, and was impressive enough that he was named the league's No. 8 prospect in the *Baseball America* poll of managers. Because he has only half a year in a full-season league, I won't give him a letter grade, but he is a fine young pitching prospect. Understand, though, that the label, "fine young pitching prospect" is hardly a guarantee of success.

Kurt Bierek

New York Yankees

Pos: OF **Bats:** Left **Ht:** 6'4" **Wt:** 200 **Age:** 25

Yr Team	Lg	G	AB	R	H	2B	3B	HR	RBI	BB	SO	SB	CS	Avg	OBP	Slg
96 Tampa	A	88	320	48	97	14	2	11	55	41	40	6	3	.303	.389	.463
97 Norwich	AA	133	473	77	128	32	2	18	78	56	89	4	4	.271	.355	.461
5 Minor League Yrs		550	1981	299	518	92	18	52	296	246	352	25	16	.261	.350	.405

Bierek was drafted out of Southern Cal in 1993, a sixth-rounder. The Yankees move all but their very best prospects through the system very slowly, which has advantages as well as drawbacks. For a raw kid who needs time to develop, moving slowly is advisable, but for a fairly polished player like Bierek, it puts a damper on his career. Bierek has reasonable skills in all the offensive areas except speed, but nothing he does really stands him out of the pack. He has some power, but not tons of it; hits for a good average, though not an outstanding one; and has a decent but not excellent walk rate. It would help him if he had a good glove, but he doesn't. Bierek is likely to wear the Triple-A tag like a forehead tattoo. **Grade C-**

Brent Billingsley

Florida Marlins

Pos: P **Throws:** Left **Ht:** 6'2" **Wt:** 200 **Age:** 22

Yr Team	Lg	G	GS	IP	H	R	ER	HR	BB	SO	SV	W	L	Pct.	ERA
96 Utica	A	15	15	89.2	83	46	40	6	28	82	0	4	5	.444	4.01
97 Kane County	A	26	26	170.2	146	67	57	9	50	175	0	14	7	.667	3.01
2 Minor League Yrs		41	41	260.1	229	113	97	15	78	257	0	18	12	.600	3.35

Billingsley was drafted in the fifth round out of Cal State Fullerton in 1996. His fastball has hit 90 MPH, although 86-88 is his usual figure. His curveball is decent, but what makes him a difficult opponent is his changeup, which borders on unhittable and which he will throw for a strike at any point in the count. All of his ratios were excellent by Midwest League standards: K/BB +75 percent, K/IP +22 percent, H/IP +10 percent. League observers say he is bright and knows how to pitch. Billingsley must avoid injuries, demonstrate that the change will work at higher levels, and prove his immunity to *Leave it to Beaver* jokes. **Grade C+**

Casey Blake   *Toronto Blue Jays*

Pos: 3B **Bats:** Right **Ht:** 6'2" **Wt:** 195 **Age:** 24

Yr Team	Lg	G	AB	R	H	2B	3B	HR	RBI	BB	SO	SB	CS	Avg	OBP	Slg
96 Hagerstown	A	48	172	29	43	13	1	2	18	11	40	5	3	.250	.318	.372
97 Dunedin	A	129	449	56	107	21	0	7	39	48	91	19	9	.238	.319	.332
2 Minor League Yrs		177	621	85	150	34	1	9	57	59	131	24	12	.242	.319	.343

Blake was a college star at Wichita State, hitting .360 with 22 home runs his senior year, but scouts wondered if he would hit with wood, and he fell to the seventh round in the 1996 draft. He struggled at Dunedin in 1997, and it looks like the scouts may have been right. Blake didn't show much pop with natural timber. He did show some speed on the bases, but his glove work at third was inconsistent. He has good range and can make a spectacular play, but makes far too many errors. With a year in pro ball under his belt, there is a chance that Blake could start to hit, but right now it looks like a longshot. **Grade C-**

Alberto Blanco   *Houston Astros*

Pos: P **Throws:** Left **Ht:** 6'1" **Wt:** 170 **Age:** 21

Yr Team	Lg	G	GS	IP	H	R	ER	HR	BB	SO	SV	W	L	Pct.	ERA
96 Quad City	A	11	11	46.2	42	25	18	3	15	58	0	2	2	.500	3.47
97 Jackson	AA	1	1	7.0	5	2	2	1	3	4	0	1	0	1.000	2.57
Astros	R	2	2	5.0	1	0	0	0	1	11	0	0	0	—	0.00
Kissimmee	A	19	19	114.1	83	45	36	4	45	95	0	7	4	.636	2.83
5 Minor League Yrs		80	64	362.2	311	168	140	23	160	359	1	20	19	.513	3.47

A Venezuelan southpaw signed in 1993, Alberto Blanco has one of the better arms in the Houston system. His fastball runs 92 MPH, and his slider is potentially excellent. His control is unsteady, but he strikes people out at a good rate, and is tough to hit. Blanco was very impressive for Kissimmee in the Florida State League last year, but he spent part of the season on the disabled list with a sore shoulder. He had serious elbow problems in 1995 and 1996, so the fact that his shoulder is acting up now is not a good sign. If healthy, he is a fine prospect, but pitchers who are injury-prone when young tend to be injury-prone throughout their careers. **Grade C+**

Paul Blandford   *Montreal Expos*

Pos: 2B **Bats:** Right **Ht:** 5'10" **Wt:** 175 **Age:** 24

Yr Team	Lg	G	AB	R	H	2B	3B	HR	RBI	BB	SO	SB	CS	Avg	OBP	Slg
96 Vermont	A	64	231	39	57	11	7	1	39	34	37	11	9	.247	.342	.368
97 Cape Fear	A	113	398	63	115	23	4	5	40	40	50	20	13	.289	.354	.405
2 Minor League Yrs		177	629	102	172	34	11	6	79	74	87	31	22	.273	.350	.391

Here is a name you won't see in any other book. Blandford was drafted in 1996, a 10th-rounder from the University of Kentucky. He hit .403 with 11 homers and 30 stolen bases during his last collegiate season, but no one considered him a real prospect because he lacked size and athleticism. Blandford was not awesome at Cape Fear, but he held his own, showing an aptitude for contact hitting and demonstrating some value on the bases and in the field. He had the second-best range factor among league regulars. Blandford is borderline as prospects go, but borderline is better than zero. **Grade C-**

Darin Blood
San Francisco Giants

Pos: P   **Throws:** Right   **Ht:** 6'2"   **Wt:** 205   **Age:** 23

Yr Team	Lg	G	GS	IP	H	R	ER	HR	BB	SO	SV	W	L	Pct.	ERA
96 San Jose	A	27	25	170.0	140	59	50	4	71	193	0	17	6	.739	2.65
97 Shreveport	AA	27	27	156.0	152	89	75	12	83	90	0	8	10	.444	4.33
3 Minor League Yrs		68	65	400.1	355	174	146	18	186	361	0	31	19	.620	3.28

A year ago, I was very impressed by Darin Blood, but his 1997 campaign leaves doubts in my mind. He stayed in the rotation at Shreveport all season, pitched many good games, and continued to impress those who saw him as a fine prospect. His numbers should give some pause, however. I'm not talking about his ERA—4.33 isn't bad for the Texas League—but rather his K/BB ratio. It was terrible at -38 percent, a huge drop from the excellent +45 percent mark of 1996. What happened? I'm not sure. His walk rate didn't increase much, but his strikeouts dropped by more than half. There didn't seem to be an injury or loss of velocity. He still throws 89-91 MPH, and his curve, slider, and change remain good pitches. I still believe Blood is a prospect, but until his strikeout rate goes back up, I have reservations about his potential for immediate success. **Grade C+**

Geoff Blum
Montreal Expos

Pos: 2B   **Bats:** Both   **Ht:** 6'3"   **Wt:** 193   **Age:** 24

Yr Team	Lg	G	AB	R	H	2B	3B	HR	RBI	BB	SO	SB	CS	Avg	OBP	Slg
96 Harrisburg	AA	120	396	47	95	22	2	1	41	59	51	6	7	.240	.341	.313
97 Ottawa	AAA	118	407	59	101	21	2	3	35	52	73	14	6	.248	.333	.332
4 Minor League Yrs		426	1501	208	399	78	7	8	176	178	206	31	23	.266	.345	.343

Blum was picked in the seventh round of the 1994 draft, out of the University of California. He isn't a scalding-hot prospect, but has made steady progress up the ladder, and the Expos seem to like him as a candidate for a utility job. They sent him to the Arizona Fall League. Blum is a switch-hitter with patience and a bit of speed, but will never scare anyone with the bat. His main appeal is defensive. He has very good range, especially at second base, and is also capable at third and short. Blum could spend the next 10 years in Triple-A, but he could also spend them in the majors as a bench guy, if some manager takes a liking to him and gives him a chance to get established. **Grade C-**

Hiram Bocachica
Montreal Expos

Pos: SS **Bats:** Right **Ht:** 5'11" **Wt:** 165 **Age:** 22

Yr Team	Lg	G	AB	R	H	2B	3B	HR	RBI	BB	SO	SB	CS	Avg	OBP	Slg
96 Expos	R	9	32	11	8	3	0	0	2	5	3	2	1	.250	.368	.344
Wst Plm Bch	A	71	267	50	90	17	5	2	26	34	47	21	3	.337	.419	.461
97 Harrisburg	AA	119	443	82	123	19	3	11	35	41	98	29	12	.278	.354	.409
4 Minor League Yrs		338	1290	239	376	68	18	20	109	147	268	110	37	.291	.375	.419

Heralded prospect Hiram Bocachica's Double-A debut was disappointing. His overall performance wasn't terrible, but it wasn't up to his previous standards, either. His OPS was league average, and while he started to show some power, his batting average dropped substantially. More disturbing was his defense. He was supposed to move to second base in 1997, but ended up playing much of the year at shortstop. This didn't go well; he fielded .876. Bocachica is still quite young, and I continue to affirm that he will hit, but Montreal needs to settle on a position for him soon, to avoid Wil Cordero-like fielding problems. **Grade B**

Rob Bonanno
Anaheim Angels

Pos: P **Throws:** Right **Ht:** 6'0" **Wt:** 195 **Age:** 27

Yr Team	Lg	G	GS	IP	H	R	ER	HR	BB	SO	SV	W	L	Pct.	ERA
96 Midland	AA	23	6	64.1	79	44	38	8	23	52	2	1	2	.333	5.32
Lk Elsinore	A	13	2	32.2	34	11	8	0	10	34	1	3	2	.600	2.20
97 Midland	AA	21	21	125.1	125	83	64	9	34	64	0	5	10	.333	4.60
4 Minor League Yrs		92	64	438.1	453	239	193	37	115	309	3	26	21	.553	3.96

Rob Bonanno is the fringiest of fringe prospects, but it will not surprise me to see him in the majors someday, at least for a few innings. A 10th-round pick in 1994 from the University of Florida, Bonanno can be very effective when he throws his fine curveball for strikes. Texas League observers were impressed with his ability to nick corners. Bonanno will never get a chance unless he can post some excellent stats somewhere, but that isn't likely as long as he works for the Angels, whose upper-level teams play in horrible leagues for pitchers. **Grade C-**

Bobby Bonds Jr.
San Francisco Giants

Pos: DH-OF **Bats:** Right **Ht:** 6'4" **Wt:** 180 **Age:** 28

Yr Team	Lg	G	AB	R	H	2B	3B	HR	RBI	BB	SO	SB	CS	Avg	OBP	Slg
96 San Jose	A	110	420	65	104	16	5	11	51	43	126	21	5	.248	.318	.388
97 San Jose	A	79	268	46	85	12	3	5	44	48	55	17	10	.317	.427	.440
Phoenix	AAA	1	1	0	0	0	0	0	0	0	0	0	0	.000	.000	.000
6 Minor League Yrs		525	1816	285	452	69	28	34	196	216	550	127	43	.249	.333	.374

Hey, if Pete Rose Jr. can make the majors, Bobby Bonds Jr. can certainly do the same. Bonds has great athletic ability, but his career has been damaged by a cornucopia of injuries, defensive inadequacies, and severe difficulties controlling the strike zone. Bobby doesn't have as much power as his brother, but has more speed. He played well in the California League last year, but he was much older than most of the competition. Does he have a future? Sure. . . he will probably play a few games in the majors, at least as a publicity stunt. And to be honest, it wouldn't be *that* much of a travesty. There have been worse guys in the majors for worse reasons. **Grade C-**

Aaron Boone   *Cincinnati Reds*

Pos: 3B **Bats:** Right **Ht:** 6'2" **Wt:** 190 **Age:** 25

Yr Team	Lg	G	AB	R	H	2B	3B	HR	RBI	BB	SO	SB	CS	Avg	OBP	Slg
96 Chattanooga	AA	136	548	86	158	44	7	17	95	38	77	21	10	.288	.338	.487
97 Indianapolis	AAA	131	476	79	138	30	4	22	75	40	81	12	4	.290	.344	.508
Cincinnati	NL	16	49	5	12	1	0	0	5	2	5	1	0	.245	.275	.265
4 Minor League Yrs		465	1741	280	484	111	17	60	278	162	282	52	24	.278	.343	.465

Aaron Boone may start at third for the Reds in 1998, and if he does, will have an outside chance at Rookie of the Year. He is not a diamond-shattering talent, and I'll be surprised if he makes more than a couple of All-Star teams in his career, but he *will* have a career, probably a long and productive one. None of his tools or skills are well above-average, but he does a lot of things reasonably well. Boone has some power, some speed, and some plate discipline. He is still a gap hitter at this point, although his over-the-fence power is improving. His OPS was good at +12 percent in the American Association. Defensively, Boone has slightly above-average tools across the board. His range, hands, and arm are all pretty good, and should only improve with experience. Boone, as his bloodlines imply, is intelligent and works hard at his game. His career could look a lot like his grandfather's, and Ray Boone was a very solid player. **Grade B**

Josh Booty   *Florida Marlins*

Pos: 3B **Bats:** Right **Ht:** 6'3" **Wt:** 210 **Age:** 22

Yr Team	Lg	G	AB	R	H	2B	3B	HR	RBI	BB	SO	SB	CS	Avg	OBP	Slg
96 Kane County	A	128	475	62	98	25	1	21	87	46	195	2	3	.206	.275	.396
Florida	NL	2	2	1	1	0	0	0	0	0	0	0	0	.500	.500	.500
97 Portland	AA	122	448	42	94	19	2	20	69	27	166	2	2	.210	.254	.395
Florida	NL	4	5	2	3	0	0	0	1	1	1	0	0	.600	.667	.600
4 Minor League Yrs		369	1371	149	278	65	4	49	202	108	503	10	9	.203	.262	.363

First, the good news. Josh Booty has developed into a very good defensive third baseman. His range is excellent and he has cut his error rate drastically. Now, the bad news. He still can't hit, and to be honest, I don't see any reason to think he ever will. Sure, he has power, but he has no clue about the strike zone. His strikeout rate is terrible, he never walks, he is helpless against breaking stuff, or fastballs anywhere but down the middle. Recently, some observers have begun comparing him to Graig Nettles, due to his power and defensive ability. I think that's about right. Josh Booty today is as good as Graig Nettles is. Graig Nettles is 53 years old. **Grade C-**

Dave Borkowski   *Detroit Tigers*

Pos: P **Throws:** Right **Ht:** 6'1" **Wt:** 200 **Age:** 21

Yr Team	Lg	G	GS	IP	H	R	ER	HR	BB	SO	SV	W	L	Pct.	ERA
96 Fayettevlle	A	27	27	178.1	158	85	66	7	54	117	0	10	10	.500	3.33
97 W Michigan	A	25	25	164.0	143	79	63	15	31	104	0	15	3	.833	3.46
3 Minor League Yrs		63	63	399.0	348	188	146	24	94	260	0	29	15	.659	3.29

The Tigers have a nice group of young pitchers in the lower levels of their system, headed by David Borkowski. An 11th-round pick in 1995 from a Detroit suburb, Borkowski's fastball is a consistent 92 MPH, with steep sinking action. His slider and changeup need work, but he throws strikes and is a fierce competitor. Borkowski's ratios fit the scouting reports like a glove. His K/BB was excellent at +67 percent, showing his good command. His H/IP was good at plus-eight percent, showing that he is tough to hit. But his K/IP was poor at -24 percent, showing that he doesn't strike people out. Hitters make contact off of Borkowski because he doesn't change speeds well, but they don't get base hits off him due to the sinking movement on his pitches. Intriguing, and an example of why you shouldn't look only at one indicator when judging a prospect. There is no such thing as a magic stat. **Grade B-**

Heath Bost   *Colorado Rockies*

Pos: P **Throws:** Right **Ht:** 6'4" **Wt:** 200 **Age:** 23

Yr Team	Lg	G	GS	IP	H	R	ER	HR	BB	SO	SV	W	L	Pct.	ERA
96 New Haven	AA	4	0	6.0	5	1	1	0	2	7	0	1	0	1.000	1.50
Asheville	A	41	0	76.0	45	13	11	3	19	102	15	5	2	.714	1.30
97 Salem	A	13	0	15.0	9	4	4	1	2	9	3	1	0	1.000	2.40
Colo Sprngs	AAA	2	0	3.0	10	8	7	1	1	3	0	0	1	.000	21.00
New Haven	AA	38	0	43.0	44	18	17	3	10	45	20	2	2	.500	3.56
3 Minor League Yrs		117	2	182.2	148	56	50	10	37	208	38	14	6	.700	2.46

Bost, an 18th-round selection in 1995 from Catawba College in North Carolina, has been quite effective as a closer so far in the pros. He projects as a middle reliever in the majors, mainly due to his lack of outstanding velocity. His fastball/slider combination is OK, but his pitches have good sink, and he is quite impressive when he throws strikes, which he usually does. Bost has to keep his pitches down to survive, especially given the horrible environments in which he will be asked to pitch over the next year or so. **Grade C**

Mike Bovee   *Anaheim Angels*

Pos: P **Throws:** Right **Ht:** 5'10" **Wt:** 200 **Age:** 24

Yr Team	Lg	G	GS	IP	H	R	ER	HR	BB	SO	SV	W	L	Pct.	ERA
96 Wichita	AA	27	27	176.2	223	113	95	21	40	102	0	10	11	.476	4.84
97 Midland	AA	20	13	102.0	117	53	48	7	23	61	0	8	2	.800	4.24
Vancouver	AAA	12	12	89.0	92	38	34	7	25	71	0	4	3	.571	3.44
Anaheim	AL	3	0	3.1	3	2	2	1	1	5	0	0	0	—	5.40
7 Minor League Yrs		166	153	971.1	1012	484	404	67	246	767	0	60	46	.566	3.74

Acquired in the Chili Davis trade with the Royals, Bovee has pretty good stuff, very good control, and performed well at two levels last year, after several inconsistent seasons in the Royals system. In 12 starts in the strenuous Pacific Coast League, Bovee posted an excellent K/BB ratio of +58 percent. His K/IP and H/IP marks were not as impressive, but were still slightly better than league standards. While he doesn't project as a star, Bovee should develop into a useful major league pitcher. **Grade C+**

Cedrick Bowers
Tampa Bay Devil Rays

Pos: P **Throws:** Left **Ht:** 6'2" **Wt:** 210 **Age:** 20

Yr Team	Lg	G	GS	IP	H	R	ER	HR	BB	SO	SV	W	L	Pct.	ERA
96 Devil Rays	R	13	13	60.1	50	39	36	2	39	85	0	3	5	.375	5.37
97 Chston-SC	A	28	28	157.0	119	74	56	11	78	164	0	8	10	.444	3.21
2 Minor League Yrs		41	41	217.1	169	113	92	13	117	249	0	11	15	.423	3.81

Bowers was a fourth-round pick in 1996, out of high school in Chiefland, Florida. He is a big thrower with good arm strength, but is raw, needs to improve his breaking stuff, and has a lot to learn about pitching. His ratios show this explicitly: his K/IP and H/IP marks were very good at +19 percent and +23 percent, respectively, but his K/BB score was weak at -10 percent. Bottom line: Bowers strikes people out and is hard to hit, but he doesn't have command of his pitches yet. He is young enough to get it if he stays healthy. **Grade C**

Shane Bowers
Minnesota Twins

Pos: P **Throws:** Right **Ht:** 6'6" **Wt:** 215 **Age:** 26

Yr Team	Lg	G	GS	IP	H	R	ER	HR	BB	SO	SV	W	L	Pct.	ERA
96 Hardware City	AA	27	22	131.0	134	71	61	15	42	96	0	6	8	.429	4.19
97 New Britain	AA	14	13	71.1	65	29	27	6	22	59	0	7	2	.778	3.41
Salt Lake	AAA	9	9	56.1	64	35	30	12	14	46	0	6	2	.750	4.79
Minnesota	AL	5	5	19.0	27	20	17	2	8	7	0	0	3	.000	8.05
5 Minor League Yrs		120	79	515.0	499	224	196	43	133	408	5	40	21	.656	3.43

Shane Bowers employs a sneaky fastball, a good curve, and a solid changeup to get hitters out. He is durable, has good mechanics, works quickly, throws strikes, and relies on his defense to help him out. Sounds a lot like Bob Tewksbury, and indeed, it was Tewks' sore shoulder that enabled Bowers to get a few innings in the majors last summer. He didn't pitch particularly well, but the Twins' coaching staff was reportedly impressed with his work habits, and may be inclined to give him another chance. He needs exposure in the majors to get his footing, and it wouldn't surprise me if he had a good year or two at some point. Pitchers are unpredictable. . . **Grade C**

Justin Bowles — Oakland Athletics

Pos: OF   Bats: Left   Ht: 6'0"   Wt: 195   Age: 24

Yr Team	Lg	G	AB	R	H	2B	3B	HR	RBI	BB	SO	SB	CS	Avg	OBP	Slg
96 Sou. Oregon	A	56	214	41	61	20	1	11	45	31	53	8	3	.285	.378	.542
Huntsville	AA	3	12	1	4	0	0	0	2	0	5	0	0	.333	.385	.333
97 Modesto	A	107	394	66	129	39	9	7	51	56	85	6	3	.327	.413	.525
2 Minor League Yrs		166	620	108	194	59	10	18	98	87	143	14	6	.313	.401	.527

A member of the 1996 College World Series champion LSU Tigers, Justin Bowles went in the 16th round of the draft. You can guess why: scouts didn't like his tools, weren't crazy about his defense, and weren't sure he would hit with wood. His season in the California League dispelled the latter doubt. He showed gap power, control of the strike zone, and makes solid contact. He was eighth in the league in hitting. His defense in left field, however, is substandard, so Bowles will have to keep hitting as he moves up. It would be nice if he could add more power, too. **Grade C**

Jason Boyd — Arizona Diamondbacks

Pos: P   Throws: Right   Ht: 6'2"   Wt: 165   Age: 25

Yr Team	Lg	G	GS	IP	H	R	ER	HR	BB	SO	SV	W	L	Pct.	ERA
96 Clearwater	A	26	26	161.2	160	75	70	12	49	120	0	11	8	.579	3.90
97 Reading	AA	48	7	115.2	113	65	62	16	64	98	0	10	6	.625	4.82
4 Minor League Yrs		114	70	497.1	489	263	224	42	189	392	0	30	29	.508	4.05

Boyd was an eighth-round pick of the Phillies in 1994, from John A. Logan (Illinois) Junior College. He performed adequately in his first Double-A exposure last year, and is the kind of guy who can skulk his way into the majors, even if he doesn't pitch that well, especially after being picked in the expansion draft. Boyd has a good 93-MPH fastball and a nice slider, but doesn't change speeds well, and is probably best suited for a relief role. He has a good opportunity to advance with Arizona, but I see no reason to expect immediate success. **Grade C**

Milton Bradley — Montreal Expos

Pos: OF   Bats: Both   Ht: 6'0"   Wt: 170   Age: 19

Yr Team	Lg	G	AB	R	H	2B	3B	HR	RBI	BB	SO	SB	CS	Avg	OBP	Slg
96 Expos	R	31	109	18	27	7	1	1	12	13	14	7	4	.248	.328	.358
97 Vermont	A	50	200	29	60	7	5	3	30	17	34	7	7	.300	.352	.430
Expos	R	9	25	6	5	2	0	1	2	4	4	2	2	.200	.333	.400
2 Minor League Yrs		90	334	53	92	16	6	5	44	34	52	16	13	.275	.342	.404

This writer is in accordance with United Nations Security Council Resolution 779, banning the use of jokes, puns, or word games regarding this player. Bradley was Montreal's first signee in 1996, a second-rounder from a Long Beach high school. He is a switch-hitter with a quick bat and great tools, and he played well against older players in the New York-Penn League in 1997. He will move to full-season ball in 1998. If his strike-zone judgment improves, he could be really good, but we'll have to wait and see. The proof is in the pudding, or rather, in the South Atlantic League.

Terry Bradshaw
St. Louis Cardinals

Pos: OF   Bats: Left   Ht: 6'0"   Wt: 180   Age: 29

Yr Team	Lg	G	AB	R	H	2B	3B	HR	RBI	BB	SO	SB	CS	Avg	OBP	Slg
96 Louisville	AAA	102	389	56	118	23	1	12	44	42	64	21	9	.303	.372	.460
St. Louis	NL	15	21	4	7	1	0	0	3	3	2	0	1	.333	.417	.381
97 Louisville	AAA	130	453	79	113	17	6	8	43	61	79	26	10	.249	.350	.366
7 Minor League Yrs		804	2876	492	774	140	31	57	295	417	519	207	72	.269	.368	.399

The Cardinals have decided that Terry Bradshaw can't play, so no matter what he does at Louisville, his chance for promotion is nil. He seems to realize this, and I think he is suffering from "Discouraged Worker Syndrome," also known as Brooks Kieschnick Disease, or Rich Rowlanditis. Someone who needs a utility outfielder should take a look at Bradshaw; he has the skills for the job. He has doubles power, draws a lot of walks, can steal a base, and isn't shabby in the field. He is too old to be a prospect, but deserves a major league bench job more than some guys who have them. **Grade C-**

Ryan Brannan
Philadelphia Phillies

Pos: P   Throws: Right   Ht: 6'3"   Wt: 210   Age: 22

Yr Team	Lg	G	GS	IP	H	R	ER	HR	BB	SO	SV	W	L	Pct.	ERA
97 Clearwater	A	21	0	27.1	20	2	1	0	8	25	10	0	0	—	0.33
Reading	AA	45	0	52.1	52	18	18	2	20	39	20	4	2	.667	3.10
1 Minor League Yr		66	0	79.2	72	20	19	2	28	64	30	4	2	.667	2.15

Ricky Bottalico, Part Two. Ryan Brannan was a fourth-round draft pick in 1996, from Long Beach State. He has a 95-MPH fastball, and a promising, but inconsistent, slider. His command needs a bit more work, as shown by the drop in his K/IP rate at Reading, but he has the stuff and demeanor to be a dominant bullpen force. Brannan needs to improve his control and develop the slider more, but he could see action in the major league bullpen in 1998, if he develops as quickly as the Phillies expect. **Grade B-**

Russ Branyan
Cleveland Indians

Pos: 3B   Bats: Left   Ht: 6'3"   Wt: 195   Age: 22

Yr Team	Lg	G	AB	R	H	2B	3B	HR	RBI	BB	SO	SB	CS	Avg	OBP	Slg
96 Columbus	A	130	482	102	129	20	4	40	106	62	166	7	4	.268	.355	.575
97 Kinston	A	83	297	59	86	26	2	27	75	52	94	3	1	.290	.398	.663
Akron	AA	41	137	26	32	4	0	12	30	28	56	0	0	.234	.369	.526
4 Minor League Yrs		385	1364	254	354	68	12	103	279	194	500	15	8	.260	.357	.554

Russ Branyan has more power than General Electric, more muscle than Mr. Brawn, more domination over fastballs than. . . well, I can't think of another cliche. Branyan made major progress in 1997, closing some of the holes in his forceful swing and making improvements against breaking stuff. Scouts who saw him say his swing is surprisingly compact; he just needs to learn more about hitting. He was a monster in the Carolina League, although his low average and very high strikeout rate in Double-A show there is still work to do. His OPS at Akron was still good at +17 percent, and he finished the season on a hot streak, slamming 12 homers in August. At the hot corner, Branyan still makes too many errors, but his range factors at both stops were well above average. He should be an acceptable defensive player if he keeps working at it. His work ethic has been criticized in the past, but is reportedly much improved over the last year and a half. Branyan isn't ready yet, and may need another two years before he is prepared for a major league job, but he should develop into a premier power hitter. **Grade B+**

Jason Brester   San Francisco Giants

Pos: P   **Throws:** Left   **Ht:** 6'3"   **Wt:** 190   **Age:** 21

Yr Team	Lg	G	GS	IP	H	R	ER	HR	BB	SO	SV	W	L	Pct.	ERA
96 Burlington	A	27	27	157.0	139	78	69	14	64	143	0	10	9	.526	3.96
97 San Jose	A	26	26	142.1	164	80	67	4	52	172	0	9	9	.500	4.24
3 Minor League Yrs		61	59	323.1	326	169	147	21	128	332	0	20	18	.526	4.09

Jason Brester is possibly the best pitching prospect left in the Giants system. The lefty was drafted in the second round in 1995, out of high school in Burlington, Washington. He throws quite hard for a young southpaw, with a fastball that will hit 90 MPH, and he complements it with a curve, slider, and changeup. He is intelligent, and his command is sharp; his K/BB mark in the California League was aesthetically pleasing at +62 percent. Brester is error-prone with the glove, and needs to improve against the running game, but he is athletic enough to handle the position. He just needs experience. Brester must make the troublesome transition to Double-A, but if he stays healthy, he should be a fine pitcher in the long run. **Grade B-**

Tarrik Brock   Seattle Mariners

Pos: OF   **Bats:** Left   **Ht:** 6'3"   **Wt:** 170   **Age:** 24

Yr Team	Lg	G	AB	R	H	2B	3B	HR	RBI	BB	SO	SB	CS	Avg	OBP	Slg
96 Lakeland	A	53	212	42	59	11	4	5	27	17	61	9	2	.278	.342	.439
Jacksnville	AA	37	102	14	13	2	0	0	6	10	36	3	3	.127	.212	.147
Fayettevlle	A	32	119	21	35	5	2	1	11	14	31	4	5	.294	.384	.395
97 Lancaster	A	132	402	88	108	21	12	7	47	78	106	40	8	.269	.395	.433
7 Minor League Yrs		736	2442	382	565	86	49	22	233	311	700	148	65	.231	.326	.334

A long time ago, in a baseball world far, far away, the Detroit Tigers made raw California high school outfielder Tarrik Brock their second-round pick. That was 1991. Brock did little in the Tigers system except frustrate people. He was released in 1996, then signed on with the Mariners for 1997. Brock responded to the change of organizations, and had the best season of his career. He was considerably more patient at the plate than in the past, and he stole a lot of bases. On the other hand, his OPS was just plus-nine percent, not a good mark considering that Lancaster is the best park for offense in the California League. His defense in right is adequate. Brock is a fringe prospect, but he was no prospect a year ago. **Grade C-**

Troy Brohawn
San Francisco Giants

Pos: P **Throws:** Left **Ht:** 6'1" **Wt:** 190 **Age:** 25

Yr Team	Lg	G	GS	IP	H	R	ER	HR	BB	SO	SV	W	L	Pct.	ERA
96 Shreveport	AA	28	28	156.2	163	99	80	30	49	82	0	9	10	.474	4.60
97 Shreveport	AA	26	26	169.0	148	57	48	10	64	98	0	13	5	.722	2.56
4 Minor League Yrs		69	68	407.2	383	185	153	46	138	250	0	29	20	.592	3.38

Brohawn was a fourth-round pick in 1994, from the University of Nebraska. He had injury problems in 1995, then a mediocre season in 1996. In 1997, he was one of the best pitchers in the Texas League, leading the league in ERA, winning 13 games, and being named to the All-Star team. He was left off most prospect lists, however, because he was repeating the league, and because he is a soft tosser. His fastball is mediocre; he gets people out with a slider, a change, and good control. Brohawn should move to Triple-A in 1998. He will probably struggle at first, and I would have more confidence in him if his strikeout rate was higher. Still, anyone who leads the Texas League in ERA deserves a good shot in Triple-A. **Grade C**

Adrian Brown
Pittsburgh Pirates

Pos: OF **Bats:** Both **Ht:** 6'0" **Wt:** 185 **Age:** 24

Yr Team	Lg	G	AB	R	H	2B	3B	HR	RBI	BB	SO	SB	CS	Avg	OBP	Slg
96 Lynchburg	A	52	215	39	69	9	3	4	25	14	24	18	9	.321	.368	.447
Carolina	AA	84	341	48	101	11	3	3	25	25	40	27	11	.296	.345	.372
97 Carolina	AA	37	145	29	44	4	4	2	15	18	12	9	5	.303	.388	.428
Calgary	AAA	62	248	53	79	10	1	1	19	27	38	20	4	.319	.383	.379
Pittsburgh	NL	48	147	17	28	6	0	1	10	13	18	8	4	.190	.273	.252
6 Minor League Yrs		552	2162	362	617	85	29	19	186	160	241	159	72	.285	.338	.378

I described Adrian Brown last year as "a switch-hitting Jermaine Allensworth," and I think the analogy is still apt. Brown has excellent physical tools, especially speed, and his offense has improved as he has learned the strike zone. He won't be a big power hitter, and looked overwhelmed in his major league time last year, but I think he should be able to hit .260-.280 in the majors eventually. His defense in center field is excellent. I doubt Brown will hit enough to be a regular, but he would make a good reserve outfielder. Come to think of it, that is how I would use Jermaine Allensworth, too. **Grade C**

Dermal Brown
Kansas City Royals

Pos: OF **Bats:** Left **Ht:** 6'1" **Wt:** 210 **Age:** 20

Yr Team	Lg	G	AB	R	H	2B	3B	HR	RBI	BB	SO	SB	CS	Avg	OBP	Slg
96 Royals	R	7	20	1	1	1	0	0	1	0	6	0	2	.050	.095	.100
97 Spokane	A	73	298	67	97	20	6	13	73	38	65	17	4	.326	.404	.564
2 Minor League Yrs		80	318	68	98	21	6	13	74	38	71	17	6	.308	.386	.535

Brown was the Royals' first-round pick in 1996, from a New York high school. He was supposedly a raw tools outfielder, but he didn't look too raw at Spokane last year, battering Northwest League pitching for power and average, and impressing observers with his intelligence and work ethic. His fielding isn't very good, but if he hits like this, it doesn't matter. Because he was just in short-season ball, I won't give him a letter grade, but Dermal Brown could be at the very top of the prospect lists next year.

Kevin L. Brown — Texas Rangers

Pos: C **Bats:** Right **Ht:** 6'2" **Wt:** 200 **Age:** 24

Yr Team	Lg	G	AB	R	H	2B	3B	HR	RBI	BB	SO	SB	CS	Avg	OBP	Slg
96 Tulsa	AA	128	460	77	121	27	1	26	86	73	150	0	3	.263	.373	.496
Texas	AL	3	4	1	0	0	0	0	1	2	2	0	0	.000	.375	.000
97 Okla City	AAA	116	403	56	97	18	2	19	50	38	111	2	2	.241	.313	.437
Texas	AL	4	5	1	2	0	0	1	1	0	0	0	0	.400	.400	1.000
4 Minor League Yrs		422	1460	215	373	90	5	62	225	186	447	4	9	.255	.347	.451

Being a catcher in the Rangers' farm system is somewhat like it was to be Franklin Delano Roosevelt's vice president. Unless something drastic happens, you just sit and wait. Kevin Brown has excellent power potential, and he is a pretty decent defensive catcher, but with Ivan Rodriguez ahead of him and Cesar King behind him, he will never catch more than a handful of games for the Rangers. His swing is too long and he can look bad at times, but he can also hit tape-measure shots. He needs to improve his plate discipline to get the most out of his bat. Brown is more effective against lefthanded pitchers, and his best role in the majors may be as a platoon player. **Grade C**

Mark Brownson — Colorado Rockies

Pos: P **Throws:** Right **Ht:** 6'2" **Wt:** 175 **Age:** 22

Yr Team	Lg	G	GS	IP	H	R	ER	HR	BB	SO	SV	W	L	Pct.	ERA
96 New Haven	AA	37	19	144.0	141	73	56	10	43	155	3	8	13	.381	3.50
97 New Haven	AA	29	29	184.2	172	101	86	24	55	170	0	10	9	.526	4.19
4 Minor League Yrs		118	66	503.1	487	254	204	49	144	504	8	30	31	.492	3.65

Brownson had a good year as a swingman for New Haven in 1996, but was sent back there in 1997; perhaps the Rockies felt he wasn't ready for the challenge of Colorado Springs. Brownson has a fastball in the low 90s, a very good curve, and an adequate slider and change. His control is sharp, his K/BB was particularly good at +67 percent, and he is quite durable, especially considering his build. His move to first is just average, and he needs to polish his fielding, but he is a good athlete and just needs more experience. I would like Brownson more if he weren't pitching for the Rockies, but I would also have doubts about Lefty Grove in his prime if they had him. **Grade C+**

Cliff Brumbaugh — Texas Rangers

Pos: 3B **Bats:** Right **Ht:** 6'2" **Wt:** 205 **Age:** 23

Yr Team	Lg	G	AB	R	H	2B	3B	HR	RBI	BB	SO	SB	CS	Avg	OBP	Slg
96 Chston-SC	A	132	458	70	111	23	7	6	45	72	103	20	7	.242	.345	.362
97 Charlotte	A	139	522	78	136	27	4	15	70	47	99	13	11	.261	.326	.414
3 Minor League Yrs		345	1262	192	348	69	15	23	160	158	253	48	21	.276	.358	.409

Brumbaugh was drafted in the 13th round in 1995, out of the University of Delaware. He started to show some power in the Florida State League last year, which isn't easy. His OPS was five percent above league, which is better than five percent below league, but obviously isn't terrific. Brumbaugh is a very good defensive player. He led the league in fielding at third base, and his range factor was above average. I like his glove, and if he continues to develop his power, he could be a property with some value. **Grade C**

Clayton Bruner   *Detroit Tigers*

Pos: P   **Throws:** Right   **Ht:** 6'3"   **Wt:** 190   **Age:** 21

Yr Team	Lg	G	GS	IP	H	R	ER	HR	BB	SO	SV	W	L	Pct.	ERA
96 Fayettevlle	A	27	26	156.2	124	64	45	6	77	152	0	14	5	.737	2.59
97 W Michigan	A	24	24	166.1	134	52	44	11	48	135	0	15	3	.833	2.38
3 Minor League Yrs		56	54	339.0	273	128	96	18	135	302	0	29	9	.763	2.55

Bruner, a fourth-round pick in 1995 from an Oklahoma high school, made significant progress last year. He has major league stuff; his fastball, curve, and change should all be adequate against major league hitters, but the big improvement last year was in his control. His K/BB ratio was below average in the South Atlantic League in 1996, but last year he cut his walk rate nearly in half, without losing strikeouts, resulting in a fine ratio of +40 percent. Like all young pitchers, the main thing he must do is stay healthy. **Grade C+**

Brian Buchanan   *New York Yankees*

Pos: OF   **Bats:** Right   **Ht:** 6'4"   **Wt:** 220   **Age:** 24

Yr Team	Lg	G	AB	R	H	2B	3B	HR	RBI	BB	SO	SB	CS	Avg	OBP	Slg
96 Tampa	A	131	526	65	137	22	4	10	58	37	108	23	8	.260	.321	.375
97 Columbus	AAA	18	61	8	17	1	0	4	7	4	11	2	1	.279	.348	.492
Norwich	AA	116	470	75	145	25	2	10	69	32	85	11	9	.309	.362	.434
4 Minor League Yrs		338	1330	195	368	60	8	31	172	106	274	48	22	.277	.342	.404

Brian Buchanan put a horrendous 1995 career-threatening ankle injury behind him, and played quite well in his first Double-A season, showing an improved ability to make contact by shortening his swing a little. The batting average was the highest of his professional career. All is not ideal, however; he still doesn't walk enough to satisfy me, and hasn't hit for the power that scouts expect given his musculature. He runs well for a big guy, although I think it is likely he will lose most of the speed over the next two or three years, especially if he bulks up more to increase his power production. He has a strong arm in right field and good range, but makes too many mistakes. Buchanan is a hard worker, and has made progress converting his tools to skills. He did well last year, but I want to see continued improvement in his walk rate before I get excited about him. **Grade C+**

Mike Buddie
New York Yankees
Pos: P **Throws:** Right **Ht:** 6'3" **Wt:** 210 **Age:** 27

Yr Team	Lg	G	GS	IP	H	R	ER	HR	BB	SO	SV	W	L	Pct.	ERA
96 Norwich	AA	29	26	159.2	176	101	79	10	71	103	0	7	12	.368	4.45
97 Norwich	AA	1	0	1.0	0	0	0	0	0	3	0	0	0	—	0.00
Columbus	AAA	53	0	75.0	85	24	22	4	25	67	2	6	6	.500	2.64
6 Minor League Yrs		177	116	758.1	766	442	361	47	366	622	3	49	49	.500	4.28

Buddie throws hard, 90-92 MPH, but he can't change speeds. He struggled as a starter from 1992 to 1996: 682 innings, 681 hits, 4.47 ERA, 43-43 record, lots of walks. The Yankees finally thought, "hey, maybe this guy isn't cut out for the rotation," moved him to the bullpen in 1997, and *voila*, he had a good year. Buddie's control and ERA improved, but he still gives up too many hits for a pitcher with good stuff. He remains a marginal prospect, but marginal is better than released. **Grade C-**

Rob Burger
Philadelphia Phillies
Pos: P **Throws:** Right **Ht:** 6'1" **Wt:** 190 **Age:** 22

Yr Team	Lg	G	GS	IP	H	R	ER	HR	BB	SO	SV	W	L	Pct.	ERA
96 Piedmont	A	27	26	160.0	129	74	60	9	61	171	0	10	12	.455	3.38
97 Clearwater	A	28	27	160.2	131	79	64	8	93	154	0	11	9	.550	3.59
4 Minor League Yrs		71	67	380.1	327	191	157	21	185	409	0	24	26	.480	3.72

Burger was drafted in the 10th round in 1994, from a Pennsylvania high school. He is making steady progress up the ladder; his season in the Florida State League last year was very similar to his 1996 campaign at Piedmont. Burger has a 92-MPH fastball, a solid curve, and an immature, but encouraging, changeup. He has problems keeping his mechanics consistent, which accounts for his control trouble, but when he has everything in synch, he can overpower people. Some observers think he would be better off as a relief pitcher, but he has stayed healthy in the rotation, and could have a future as a durable, inning-devouring starter. Burger needs to improve his control, but he is very young, and has plenty of time to do so, if his arm doesn't fall off from overuse. **Grade C+**

Kevin Burns
Houston Astros
Pos: 1B **Bats:** Left **Ht:** 6'5" **Wt:** 210 **Age:** 22

Yr Team	Lg	G	AB	R	H	2B	3B	HR	RBI	BB	SO	SB	CS	Avg	OBP	Slg
96 Auburn	A	71	269	27	71	19	3	11	55	15	77	2	1	.264	.307	.480
97 Quad City	A	131	477	72	129	28	1	20	86	53	114	1	2	.270	.348	.459
3 Minor League Yrs		244	882	116	234	51	5	34	164	80	215	11	6	.265	.330	.450

Burns was a 34th-round pick in 1994, out of Texarkana Community College in Texas. He is a huge man with a big swing; when he makes contact, the ball will go a long way. He has had problems with the strike zone, but started to get that under control last year at Quad City. His OPS was OK, but not outstanding, for a corner player at +12 percent. Burns is just a name for now, but if he makes more progress with the strike zone, he could attract interest because of his power. **Grade C-**

Brent Butler
St. Louis Cardinals

Pos: SS **Bats:** Right **Ht:** 6'0" **Wt:** 180 **Age:** 20

Yr Team	Lg	G	AB	R	H	2B	3B	HR	RBI	BB	SO	SB	CS	Avg	OBP	Slg
96 Johnson Cty	R	62	248	45	85	21	1	8	50	25	29	8	1	.343	.404	.532
97 Peoria	A	129	480	81	147	37	2	15	71	63	69	6	4	.306	.388	.485
2 Minor League Yrs		191	728	126	232	58	3	23	121	88	98	14	5	.319	.393	.501

Brent Butler was drafted in the third round in 1996, from a North Carolina high school. He looks like an excellent hitter: balanced stance, great bat speed, disciplined, can drive it into the gaps or over the fence, hits to all fields. His OPS was +21 percent, outstanding for an infielder, and his SEC was +23 percent, showing a broad base of skills. No one doubts he will hit; the question is his position. He is a smart, intense, aggressive fielder, but may not have the range to play shortstop in the majors. He may not have the arm for third, so second may be his destination. How good of a player will Butler be? Names like Craig Biggio and Chuck Knoblauch come to mind. This guy is a jewel. **Grade B+**

Rich Butler
Tampa Bay Devil Rays

Pos: OF **Bats:** Left **Ht:** 6'1" **Wt:** 180 **Age:** 24

Yr Team	Lg	G	AB	R	H	2B	3B	HR	RBI	BB	SO	SB	CS	Avg	OBP	Slg
96 Dunedin	A	10	28	1	2	0	0	0	0	5	9	4	1	.071	.212	.071
97 Syracuse	AAA	137	537	93	161	30	9	24	87	60	107	20	7	.300	.373	.523
Toronto	AL	7	14	3	4	1	0	0	2	2	3	0	1	.286	.375	.357
7 Minor League Yrs		726	2594	348	676	98	37	49	304	245	503	84	60	.261	.328	.384

Rich Butler's career had stalled due to injuries and problems with the strike zone, but he turned it around dramatically in 1997. He stayed healthy for a change, but more importantly, he was much more patient at the plate. His walk rate rose radically, with a concurrent increase in production. His OPS was sound at +16 percent; his SEC was very good at +30 percent. You might hear stories about a restructured swing or something, but I would be very surprised if the real reason for his improvement was something other than his improved patience. Butler isn't extremely young, and his defense doesn't draw raves, so he must continue to hit to have value. The Devil Rays picked him in the expansion draft, and if Butler stays healthy and patient, I think he'll be fine. He could hit .270-.290, with lots of doubles and some homers. **Grade B-**

Danny Buxbaum
Anaheim Angels

Pos: 1B **Bats:** Right **Ht:** 6'4" **Wt:** 217 **Age:** 25

Yr Team	Lg	G	AB	R	H	2B	3B	HR	RBI	BB	SO	SB	CS	Avg	OBP	Slg
96 Lk Elsinore	A	74	298	53	87	17	2	14	60	31	41	1	0	.292	.360	.503
97 Midland	AA	130	514	78	148	42	2	10	70	51	91	1	1	.288	.353	.436
3 Minor League Yrs		272	1043	177	311	74	4	32	181	131	163	3	1	.298	.378	.469

A year ago, I had Danny Buxbaum pegged as a breakthrough candidate for 1997, and after his hot start (.391 through May) it looked like I was right. But he fell into a deep slump about the halfway mark, and finished with stats that were very disappointing considering league and park context. The 44 doubles were great, but his home-run total was limited for a man of his size and strength, and his final batting average was not impressive. What happened? When I saw him in mid-June, his swing looked great: short for a big guy, quick, good drive to all fields. When I saw him again in late August, his swing looked much longer. He kept swinging at sliders away, trying to pull them—unsuccessfully, of course. Buxbaum is said to be a nice guy and a hard worker, so effort doesn't seem to be the problem. If anything, Buxbaum may be trying too hard. He may lose his prospect status unless he boosts his power. **Grade C**

Orlando Cabrera   *Montreal Expos*

Pos: SS   **Bats:** Right   **Ht:** 5'11"   **Wt:** 165   **Age:** 23

Yr Team	Lg	G	AB	R	H	2B	3B	HR	RBI	BB	SO	SB	CS	Avg	OBP	Slg
96 Delmarva	A	134	512	86	129	28	4	14	65	54	63	51	18	.252	.327	.404
97 Wst Plm Bch	A	69	279	56	77	19	2	5	26	27	33	32	12	.276	.340	.412
Harrisburg	AA	35	133	34	41	13	2	5	20	15	18	7	2	.308	.378	.549
Ottawa	AAA	31	122	17	32	5	2	2	14	7	16	8	1	.262	.306	.385
Montreal	NL	16	18	4	4	0	0	0	2	1	3	1	2	.222	.263	.222
5 Minor League Yrs		370	1372	243	373	81	16	29	169	124	167	118	41	.272	.333	.418

Unheralded Orlando Cabrera showed a broad base of abilities in 1996, hitting for power and stealing bases, piquing my interest. He continued playing well in 1997 and is now considered one of the best prospects in the Expos system, with a shot at a major league job coming soon. Cabrera has juice in his bat, especially for a player his size, and while he isn't blazing fast, he knows how to steal a base. His command of the strike zone has been good at every level except Triple-A. The fact that his walk rate dropped off at Ottawa indicates he may not be ready for a major league job yet, but I still like his chances. Although Cabrera played mostly shortstop in 1997, his range there is barely average, and he would be better off at second, in my opinion. Cabrera has a good work ethic and a reputation as an intelligent player. I like him. **Grade B**

Enrique Calero   *Kansas City Royals*

Pos: P   **Throws:** Right   **Ht:** 6'2"   **Wt:** 175   **Age:** 23

Yr Team	Lg	G	GS	IP	H	R	ER	HR	BB	SO	SV	W	L	Pct.	ERA
96 Spokane	A	17	11	75.0	77	34	21	5	18	61	1	4	2	.667	2.52
97 Wichita	AA	23	22	127.2	120	78	63	15	44	100	0	11	9	.550	4.44
2 Minor League Yrs		40	33	202.2	197	112	84	20	62	161	1	15	11	.577	3.73

For an organization historically based on pitching, the Royals are curiously short on top-notch mound prospects. Enrique Calero is probably the best one they have; he's good, but not really in the elite class. Calero was drafted in the 27th round in 1996 from St. Thomas University in Florida. He was quite impressive in the Texas League, certainly a big jump to make in one pro season. His fastball is in the low 90s, he has a very sharp slider, good control, smooth mechanics and a bulldog attitude. He is athletic, polished and works hard. I have some concerns about his durability; he has a slight frame and spent two weeks on the disabled list with a sore shoulder. If his arm doesn't disintegrate, Calero should be a very good major league pitcher, although I don't think he projects as a staff anchor. **Grade B-**

Aaron Cames
Florida Marlins

Pos: P **Throws**: Right **Ht**: 6'1" **Wt**: 192 **Age**: 22

Yr Team	Lg	G	GS	IP	H	R	ER	HR	BB	SO	SV	W	L	Pct.	ERA
96 Utica	A	18	9	73.2	60	28	23	2	18	77	0	6	2	.750	2.81
97 Kane County	A	26	26	149.2	143	67	65	11	43	157	0	8	10	.444	3.91
2 Minor League Yrs		44	35	223.1	203	95	88	13	61	234	0	14	12	.538	3.55

Cames was a draft-and-follow, a 1995 51st-rounder from Sacramento City College. The Marlins got his signature on a contract, and sent him to the New York-Penn League in 1996, where he was very effective. His full-season debut in 1997 was respectable, though not outstanding. The ERA was high by Midwest League standards, but his K/BB was admirable at +82 percent. Cames isn't a hard thrower, but he throws strikes and hits spots. He is just a name at this point, but he has potential. **Grade C**

Jason Camilli
Montreal Expos

Pos: SS **Bats**: Right **Ht**: 6'0" **Wt**: 178 **Age**: 22

Yr Team	Lg	G	AB	R	H	2B	3B	HR	RBI	BB	SO	SB	CS	Avg	OBP	Slg
96 Delmarva	A	119	426	53	95	13	2	3	36	63	89	26	17	.223	.329	.284
97 Cape Fear	A	98	396	57	118	35	2	3	43	31	64	22	11	.298	.355	.419
Wst Plm Bch	A	15	47	1	6	3	0	0	1	2	12	0	1	.128	.163	.191
4 Minor League Yrs		401	1505	209	366	70	9	10	130	195	311	83	55	.243	.334	.322

Camilli was picked in the second round in 1994, from high school in Phoenix. He has had difficulty getting out of low A-ball, but did enough last year to revive a bit of optimism about his chances. Camilli showed he could line balls into the gaps at Cape Fear, while improving his ability to make contact. His strike-zone judgment still needs improvement, however. The glove is a potential asset. . . his range factor was good for the South Atlantic League. . . but he still makes too many errors. That phrase, "makes too many errors," boy, I've written that a lot already. Camilli is young enough to progress quickly, but don't make any reservations on his bandwagon. **Grade C-**

Wylie Campbell
Cincinnati Reds

Pos: 3B **Bats**: Both **Ht**: 5'11" **Wt**: 170 **Age**: 23

Yr Team	Lg	G	AB	R	H	2B	3B	HR	RBI	BB	SO	SB	CS	Avg	OBP	Slg
96 Billings	R	70	259	69	96	15	7	0	30	45	29	24	6	.371	.473	.483
97 Chston-WV	A	121	453	73	123	18	4	0	36	41	80	34	12	.272	.341	.329
2 Minor League Yrs		191	712	142	219	33	11	0	66	86	109	58	18	.308	.391	.385

Campbell was a seventh-round pick in 1996, from the University of Texas. During his career with the Longhorns, he showed good speed and patience at the plate, but little power, even with aluminium. In the pros, he has continued to demonstrate his wheels, but has lost some of his patience, and still doesn't drive the ball. Campbell was primarily a second baseman in college, and had trouble with the glove at third last year. He is borderline, but I liked him in college, and I think there is still a chance he could develop into a useful player. **Grade C-**

Ben Candelaria
Toronto Blue Jays

Pos: OF **Bats:** Left **Ht:** 5'11" **Wt:** 167 **Age:** 23

Yr Team	Lg	G	AB	R	H	2B	3B	HR	RBI	BB	SO	SB	CS	Avg	OBP	Slg
96 Knoxville	AA	55	162	16	45	11	2	3	14	18	40	3	3	.278	.357	.426
Dunedin	A	39	125	13	25	5	0	1	6	12	25	1	4	.200	.270	.264
97 Knoxville	AA	120	472	81	139	32	5	15	67	42	89	4	3	.294	.354	.479
6 Minor League Yrs		504	1778	248	467	93	15	32	213	193	376	34	24	.263	.336	.386

Candelaria was selected in the 20th round in 1992, from Puerto Rico. His progress through the Toronto system has been slow, but he is still young, and a solid season for Double-A Knoxville in 1997 has granted him prospect status. Candelaria has line-drive power, and while he isn't a blazing fast runner and doesn't steal many bases, he is a good athlete with a quick swing. His command of the strike zone is neither outstanding nor terrible; likewise his OPS, at plus-eight percent. Defensively, he has a strong arm and good range in right field, but won't win any Gold Gloves. I don't think Candelaria projects as a starter, but if he carries his success to Triple-A, he would be a fine fourth outfielder. **Grade C+**

Jay Canizaro
San Francisco Giants

Pos: 2B **Bats:** Right **Ht:** 5'10" **Wt:** 175 **Age:** 24

Yr Team	Lg	G	AB	R	H	2B	3B	HR	RBI	BB	SO	SB	CS	Avg	OBP	Slg
96 Phoenix	AAA	102	363	50	95	21	2	7	64	46	77	14	4	.262	.347	.388
San Francisco	NL	43	120	11	24	4	1	2	8	9	38	0	2	.200	.260	.300
97 Phoenix	AAA	23	81	12	16	7	0	2	12	9	24	2	2	.198	.278	.358
Shreveport	AA	50	176	36	45	9	0	11	38	26	44	2	2	.256	.354	.494
5 Minor League Yrs		476	1704	292	449	88	17	50	284	207	381	58	26	.263	.346	.423

A couple of years ago, Jay Canizaro looked like Robby Thompson's successor, but now he's just hoping for a bench job. Command of the strike zone, which used to be a strength, has gotten away from him, and he has been nagged by constant injuries. He puts pressure on himself to make up for lost time, which just makes the situation worse. When healthy, Canizaro shows excellent pop for an infielder, and fine defensive skills. He is young enough to come back, but second basemen are quite vulnerable to injury, and many promising keystone prospects stumble at his age. **Grade C**

Jon Cannon
Chicago Cubs

Pos: P **Throws:** Left **Ht:** 6'3" **Wt:** 185 **Age:** 23

Yr Team	Lg	G	GS	IP	H	R	ER	HR	BB	SO	SV	W	L	Pct.	ERA
96 Williamsprt	A	14	13	83.1	61	31	28	6	26	66	0	6	4	.600	3.02
97 Rockford	A	24	20	129.1	110	53	45	13	50	130	0	9	6	.600	3.13
Daytona	A	2	2	13.2	7	2	2	1	10	13	0	1	0	1.000	1.32
2 Minor League Yrs		40	35	226.1	178	86	75	20	86	209	0	16	10	.615	2.98

Jon Cannon, a Quinn Martin production, put together a nice set of numbers last year. Act One: He came out of Canada Junior College in California in the seventh round in 1996. He is tall and thin, and while he doesn't throw extremely hard, he has good control and hits his spots. Act Two: Given his height/weight listing, it would be no surprise if he picked up some additional velocity as he matures. Act Three: Cannon's ratios were very good across the board at Rockford: H/IP +13 percent, K/IP +19 percent, and the all-important K/BB, also +19 percent. Epilogue: He's just a name to be aware of for now, but watch for Cannon. **Grade C+**

Dan Carlson   Tampa Bay Devil Rays

Pos: P **Throws:** Right **Ht:** 6'1" **Wt:** 185 **Age:** 28

Yr Team	Lg	G	GS	IP	H	R	ER	HR	BB	SO	SV	W	L	Pct.	ERA
96 Phoenix	AAA	33	15	146.2	135	61	56	18	46	123	1	13	6	.684	3.44
San Francisco	NL	5	0	10.0	13	6	3	2	2	4	0	1	0	1.000	2.70
97 Bakersfield	A	2	2	6.0	3	0	0	0	1	7	0	0	0	—	0.00
Phoenix	AAA	29	14	109.0	102	53	47	12	36	108	3	13	3	.813	3.88
San Francisco	NL	6	0	15.1	20	14	13	5	8	14	0	0	0	—	7.63
8 Minor League Yrs		217	167	1145.2	1091	541	485	114	431	975	5	93	52	.641	3.81

What did Dan Carlson have to do to get a chance with San Francisco? Take out Giants manager Dusty Baker's garbage? Hold a second job as a janitor for 3Com? Carlson has pitched very well in the Pacific Coast League for *four years,* but the Giants treated him like dog droppings on a Bruno Mali. The problem, as you may have guessed, is that Carlson doesn't light up the radar guns. He relies on excellent control, a fine curveball, cunning, and basic mound intelligence to get hitters out. If it works in the Pacific Coast League, for *four years,* mind you, you figure it might work in the majors, too. The fact that he struck out 14 guys in 15 major league innings is more important than his high ERA in those innings. After Tampa Bay took him in the expansion draft, he could do for the Devil Rays what Rick Reed did for the Mets last year. **Grade C**

Buddy Carlyle   Cincinnati Reds

Pos: P **Throws:** Right **Ht:** 6'2" **Wt:** 175 **Age:** 20

Yr Team	Lg	G	GS	IP	H	R	ER	HR	BB	SO	SV	W	L	Pct.	ERA
96 Princeton	R	10	9	46.1	47	33	24	4	16	42	0	2	4	.333	4.66
97 Chston-WV	A	23	23	143.0	130	51	44	9	27	111	0	14	5	.737	2.77
2 Minor League Yrs		33	32	189.1	177	84	68	13	43	153	0	16	9	.640	3.23

Carlyle was the Reds' second-round pick in 1996, from high school near Omaha, and established himself as Cincinnati's best pitching prospect with a superb 1997 performance. Carlyle has yet to reach physical maturity. He hasn't finished growing, and still has some projection in his arm, which is intriguing because he already throws in the upper 80s consistently, and hits 90 MPH on occasion. His curveball is excellent, and his command is unusually good for a young pitcher. His K/BB was outstanding at +64 percent, but his K/IP rate was eight percent below league. Carlyle needs to improve his changeup, but he holds runners well for a righthander, and is said to be intelligent, if a bit overemotional at times. The main thing Carlyle needs to do is stay healthy. He has the command to be a fine pitcher, and if his velocity picks up a little more, he could be outstanding. **Grade B**

Mike Caruso
Chicago White Sox

Pos: SS **Bats:** Both **Ht:** 6'1" **Wt:** 172 **Age:** 20

Yr Team	Lg	G	AB	R	H	2B	3B	HR	RBI	BB	SO	SB	CS	Avg	OBP	Slg
96 Bellingham	A	73	312	48	91	13	1	2	24	16	23	24	10	.292	.324	.359
97 San Jose	A	108	441	76	147	24	11	2	50	38	19	11	16	.333	.391	.451
Winston-Sal	A	28	119	12	27	3	2	0	14	4	8	3	0	.227	.264	.286
2 Minor League Yrs		209	872	136	265	40	14	4	88	58	50	38	26	.304	.351	.396

From a talent exchange standpoint, the White Sox didn't get totally ripped off in the big trade last summer with the Giants, but there is more to any transaction than just talent exchange. I'm not a White Sox fan, but as a baseball fan, I was insulted by the trade. To dump salaries when you are out of the race is one thing. To dump salaries when you are *three games back,* well, let's just say that shows a certain lack of faith. It is true that the White Sox hung in the race for awhile after the trade, but that isn't the point. Well-heeled big wheel Jerry Reinsdorf certainly showed his credentials as a creep. What kind of person makes Yankees owner George Steinbrenner look good? Jerry Reinsdorf. Who was Lenin referring to when he said that capitalists would barter over the price of the rope by which they would hang themselves? Jerry Reinsdorf. Charade you are, Jerry. Anyhow, in Caruso the Sox did get a very good prospect. He came into the Giants system as a second-round pick in 1996, and is quite advanced for a high school product, having hit very well in the California League, no small feat for a player his age. He is an extreme contact hitter who doesn't have power yet, but should develop some as he fills out. Caruso's glove work is neither terrible nor stellar. He should develop into a decent shortstop in time, or perhaps an above-average second baseman. I'm disturbed by how poorly he hit in the Carolina League after the trade, but the at-bat total is too low to get paranoid about. Basically, Caruso is a top prospect, but needs more punch to go with his contact ability. **Grade B+**

Steve Carver
Philadelphia Phillies

Pos: OF **Bats:** Left **Ht:** 6'3" **Wt:** 215 **Age:** 25

Yr Team	Lg	G	AB	R	H	2B	3B	HR	RBI	BB	SO	SB	CS	Avg	OBP	Slg
96 Clearwater	A	117	436	59	121	32	0	17	79	52	89	1	1	.278	.353	.468
97 Reading	AA	79	282	41	74	11	3	15	43	36	69	2	2	.262	.351	.482
3 Minor League Yrs		252	935	135	261	56	5	39	163	105	187	5	4	.279	.352	.475

Carver is one of the more interesting prospects in the Philadelphia system, although no one but fanatical Phillies fans, front office people, and prospect geeks like me has heard of him. He missed half of the 1997 season due to a shoulder injury, but showed enough in 282 at-bats to give hope that he can hit at the higher levels. Carver has a solid swing, good hitting instincts, and the ability to read breaking pitches. The park at Reading did help his power output. Carver is not a good defensive outfielder, and would be better off at first base. Although his production wasn't spectacular, I think Carver can hit. I am probably too optimistic about him; he wasn't young for the level. I will give him a conservative grade, but I do think he could be a player. **Grade C**

Sean Casey — Cleveland Indians

Pos: 1B **Bats:** Left **Ht:** 6'4" **Wt:** 215 **Age:** 23

Yr Team	Lg	G	AB	R	H	2B	3B	HR	RBI	BB	SO	SB	CS	Avg	OBP	Slg
96 Kinston	A	92	344	62	114	31	3	12	57	36	47	1	1	.331	.402	.544
97 Akron	AA	62	241	38	93	19	1	10	66	23	34	0	1	.386	.448	.598
Buffalo	AAA	20	72	12	26	7	0	5	18	9	11	0	0	.361	.439	.667
Cleveland	AL	6	10	1	2	0	0	0	1	1	2	0	0	.200	.333	.200
3 Minor League Yrs		229	864	138	301	75	4	29	178	86	113	4	2	.348	.413	.545

Scouts always knew Sean Casey could hit, but not many people expected the numbers he put up at Akron and Buffalo last year. He continued to hit for average, as he did in college and the low minors, but the power inherent in his physique manifested itself with a vengeance, especially at Buffalo. Although he missed the first 50 games of the season with torn wrist cartilage, Casey led the Eastern League in OPS at +38 percent; his MLE projects him as a .300 hitter in the majors, with 20-homer power. The improvement in his power stats is attributed to physical maturity and some adjustments in his batting stance. His defense isn't wonderful, but if he hits like this, it doesn't have to be. It will be interesting to see what the Indians do with him. Casey is ready for the majors, but the Cleveland infield is not exactly overfilled with vacancies right now. **Grade A-**

Carlos Casimiro — Baltimore Orioles

Pos: 2B **Bats:** Right **Ht:** 6'0" **Wt:** 155 **Age:** 21

Yr Team	Lg	G	AB	R	H	2B	3B	HR	RBI	BB	SO	SB	CS	Avg	OBP	Slg
96 Bluefield	R	62	239	51	66	16	0	10	33	20	52	22	9	.276	.335	.469
97 Delmarva	A	122	457	54	111	21	8	9	51	26	108	20	13	.243	.290	.383
3 Minor League Yrs		216	803	119	204	41	10	21	95	56	182	43	25	.254	.307	.408

The Orioles signed Casimiro out of the Dominican Republic in 1994. He has drawn interest as a prospect due to his speed and athletic ability, but his command of the strike zone is very poor, and until that improves, it is hard for me to project great success for him in the future. He does have bat speed, but is simply too undisciplined. With the glove, the story is the same: the physical ability is there, but the refinement isn't. He is very young and has time to improve, but I want to see it in the numbers. **Grade C-**

Ramon Castro — Houston Astros

Pos: C **Bats:** Right **Ht:** 6'3" **Wt:** 195 **Age:** 22

Yr Team	Lg	G	AB	R	H	2B	3B	HR	RBI	BB	SO	SB	CS	Avg	OBP	Slg
96 Quad City	A	96	314	38	78	15	0	7	43	31	61	2	0	.248	.317	.363
97 Kissimmee	A	115	410	53	115	22	1	8	65	53	73	1	0	.280	.357	.398
4 Minor League Yrs		347	1191	154	319	66	1	27	179	131	196	8	6	.268	.339	.393

Castro is starting to show why he was a first-round pick out of Puerto Rico in 1994. He had difficulty tailoring a swing that could turn his strength into power, but hit well in a difficult environment last year, and appears to have turned the corner. He is gaining command of the strike zone, and his OPS of plus-seven percent is pretty good, considering park and league context. Castro still has some rough spots defensively, but his throwing has improved greatly. He threw out 45 percent of stealers last year, 10 percent above league average. Castro needs to keep up the good strike-zone judgment. Watch him carefully in Double-A; he could be poised for a major step forward. **Grade B-**

Frank Catalanotto — Detroit Tigers

Pos: 2B **Bats:** Left **Ht:** 6'0" **Wt:** 170 **Age:** 23

Yr Team	Lg	G	AB	R	H	2B	3B	HR	RBI	BB	SO	SB	CS	Avg	OBP	Slg
96 Jacksnville	AA	132	497	105	148	34	6	17	67	74	69	15	14	.298	.398	.493
97 Toledo	AAA	134	500	75	150	32	3	16	68	47	80	12	11	.300	.368	.472
Detroit	AL	13	26	2	8	2	0	0	3	3	7	0	0	.308	.379	.385
6 Minor League Yrs		595	2195	361	629	120	27	47	265	230	286	47	45	.287	.362	.430

Frank Catalanotto is a favorite of prospect analysts everywhere, and was recently named Centerfold of the Year by *Sabermetric Monthly*. The question isn't what can Catalanotto do, but rather, what *can't* he do? Let's see. He hits for power, hits for average, gets on base, runs well, fields well, and hustles. I think that just about covers it. (His choice of reading material reflects his innate intelligence.—Ed.) He led the International League in fielding. He hit at home and on the road. He wasn't too old for the league. What's the problem? Why doesn't he get respect from the professional baseball community? Catalanotto does have problems hitting lefthanders, so it would be a stretch for him to play every day against all pitchers, but as part of a platoon combo, he would be excellent. There is absolutely no reason in the world why Catalanotto needs to spend another year in Triple-A. The signing of Damion Easley to a large contract means the Tigers won't give Catalanotto a chance any time soon, and both the Diamondbacks and Devil Rays passed him up. I just don't get it. He's one fine player, certainly better than any of the players likely to start at second for the expansion clubs. **Grade B**

Dan Cey — Minnesota Twins

Pos: SS-DH **Bats:** Right **Ht:** 6'1" **Wt:** 175 **Age:** 22

Yr Team	Lg	G	AB	R	H	2B	3B	HR	RBI	BB	SO	SB	CS	Avg	OBP	Slg
96 Ft. Wayne	A	27	85	8	22	4	0	0	6	8	11	2	1	.259	.323	.306
97 Ft. Myers	A	127	521	84	148	34	5	7	60	34	85	23	9	.284	.332	.409
2 Minor League Yrs		154	606	92	170	38	5	7	66	42	96	25	10	.281	.330	.394

Is it just me, or are there more sons of major leaguers around these days than there used to be? That would be an interesting study. Dan Cey, offspring of Ron Cey, of course, was a third-round choice in 1996, from the University of California. He does not look like a penguin, or any other waterfowl, and he doesn't resemble his father as a player. Dan is quick and fast, but doesn't have much power. He hit acceptably in the Florida State League last year, although he needs to be more patient and get on base more to maximize the value of his speed. His range at shortstop isn't very good, so he faces a move to second, which reduces his value as a prospect. **Grade C**

Shawn Chacon   *Colorado Rockies*

Pos: P **Throws:** Right **Ht:** 6'3" **Wt:** 195 **Age:** 20

Yr Team	Lg	G	GS	IP	H	R	ER	HR	BB	SO	SV	W	L	Pct.	ERA
96 Rockies	R	11	11	56.1	46	17	10	1	15	64	0	1	2	.333	1.60
Portland	A	4	4	19.2	24	18	15	2	9	17	0	0	2	.000	6.86
97 Asheville	A	28	27	162.0	155	80	70	13	63	149	0	11	7	.611	3.89
2 Minor League Yrs		43	42	238.0	225	115	95	16	87	230	0	12	11	.522	3.59

The Rockies had quite a rotation at Asheville in the South Atlantic League. Shawn Chacon, John Nicholson, and Jake Westbrook are all fine prospects. Chacon probably has the highest ceiling of the group, and the other two have been traded to Montreal. A native Coloradan drafted out of high school in the third round in 1996, Chacon's best pitch is a 93-MPH fastball. He also has a power curve, and while his changeup is just adequate at this stage, he is willing to use it, a good sign for an inexperienced pitcher. His K/BB, K/IP, and H/IP ratios were all just barely above the league average last year. Chacon is bright, but has a tendency to nibble and occasionally lacks concentration. I see no reason to think he won't be a fine pitcher, if he stays healthy. I know I put a health warning on almost every pitcher report; it's like the Surgeon General's label on cigarettes. **Grade B**

Jim Chamblee   *Boston Red Sox*

Pos: 2B **Bats:** Right **Ht:** 6'4" **Wt:** 175 **Age:** 22

Yr Team	Lg	G	AB	R	H	2B	3B	HR	RBI	BB	SO	SB	CS	Avg	OBP	Slg
96 Michigan	A	100	303	31	66	15	2	1	39	16	75	2	2	.218	.270	.290
97 Michigan	A	133	487	112	146	29	5	22	73	53	107	18	4	.300	.384	.515
3 Minor League Yrs		295	990	179	263	53	8	25	128	92	227	29	13	.266	.343	.411

Chamblee, a 12th-rounder drafted in 1995 from Odessa Junior College in Texas, had a terrible season in the Midwest League in 1996. He returned there in 1997 and was outstanding, hitting for power and average, stealing bases, scoring tons of runs, and showing some ability with the glove. No holes in his numbers: OPS +25 percent, SEC +38 percent. Chamblee is adequate in all phases of the defensive game: his range, hands, and arm all rank in the middle of the pack. If he keeps hitting like this, that will be good enough. Will he keep hitting? It's possible. His strike-zone judgment was passable, but could have been better, and he *was* repeating the league. On the other hand, he's not that old, and Michigan isn't great for offense overall. I'm cautiously optimistic. **Grade B-**

Carlos Chantres   *Chicago White Sox*

Pos: P **Throws:** Right **Ht:** 6'3" **Wt:** 175 **Age:** 21

Yr Team	Lg	G	GS	IP	H	R	ER	HR	BB	SO	SV	W	L	Pct.	ERA
96 Hickory	A	18	18	119.2	108	63	50	10	38	93	0	6	7	.462	3.76
South Bend	A	10	9	65.0	61	31	26	3	19	41	0	4	5	.444	3.60
97 Winston-Sal	A	26	26	164.2	152	94	86	21	71	158	0	9	11	.450	4.70
4 Minor League Yrs		81	66	446.0	414	241	198	38	155	368	1	21	27	.438	4.00

Chantres was drafted in the 12th round in 1994, from a Miami high school. He is seldom mentioned as a prospect, and while his ERA at Winston-Salem wasn't too pretty, it's a hitters' haven and he did lead the Carolina League in strikeouts. His control isn't terrible, and his K/BB was pretty good at +17 percent. Chantres does not have outstanding velocity, but he is young enough to pick more up as he develops, and since he already strikes people out, increased velocity could make him a solid talent. **Grade C-**

Anthony Chavez   Anaheim Angels

Pos: P   **Throws:** Right   **Ht:** 5'11"   **Wt:** 180   **Age:** 27

Yr Team	Lg	G	GS	IP	H	R	ER	HR	BB	SO	SV	W	L	Pct.	ERA
96 Lk Elsinore	A	10	0	13.2	8	4	3	0	3	16	4	3	0	1.000	1.98
Midland	AA	31	0	72.2	81	40	34	4	24	55	1	2	4	.333	4.21
97 Midland	AA	33	1	47.0	53	23	22	1	15	35	6	1	2	.333	4.21
Vancouver	AAA	28	0	28.1	21	8	8	2	6	22	15	4	1	.800	2.54
Anaheim	AL	7	0	9.2	7	1	1	1	5	10	0	0	0	—	0.93
6 Minor League Yrs		261	2	374.2	380	203	158	12	143	370	63	25	24	.510	3.80

Anthony Chavez was a 50th-round pick in 1992, from San Jose State University. Although he was a successful college pitcher, he didn't throw hard, and his career expectancy was scant. He refused to give up, pitched well in middle relief for several years, and was rewarded with some Show time in 1997. He did very well in his major league trial, and will have a shot at the bullpen in 1998. Chavez gets people out by throwing strikes with his breaking stuff and by being aggressive. I don't know about you, but I always root for 50th-round draft picks. **Grade C**

Eric Chavez   Oakland Athletics

Pos: 3B   **Bats:** Left   **Ht:** 6'1"   **Wt:** 190   **Age:** 20

Yr Team	Lg	G	AB	R	H	2B	3B	HR	RBI	BB	SO	SB	CS	Avg	OBP	Slg
97 Visalia	A	134	520	67	141	30	3	18	100	37	91	13	7	.271	.321	.444
1 Minor League Yr		134	520	67	141	30	3	18	100	37	91	13	7	.271	.321	.444

Chavez was Oakland's first-round pick in 1996, out of a San Diego high school. Although drafting high school position players can be dangerous, drafting them from populous states with good levels of competition may help limit the risk. If I were a scouting director, I wouldn't have too many qualms about drafting a high school position player from a state with 20 or more electoral votes, unless he was a catcher, of course. Eric Chavez was considered to be the best high school hitter in the 1996 draft, and he didn't do anything to dispel this notion in 1997, hitting very well in the advanced California League. He has a picture-perfect swing that should produce power and average as he moves up. He needs to improve his walk rate to get the most out of his ability, but the Athletics emphasize the strike zone in their hitting instruction, so it shouldn't be a problem for him. He was named Best Defensive Third Baseman by the league managers, but the A's admit he has got a long way to go with the glove. Chavez looks like a great prospect to me. **Grade A-**

Robinson Checo
Boston Red Sox

Pos: P **Throws:** Right **Ht:** 6'1" **Wt:** 165 **Age:** 26

Yr Team	Lg	G	GS	IP	H	R	ER	HR	BB	SO	SV	W	L	Pct.	ERA
97 Sarasota	A	11	11	56.0	54	37	33	9	27	63	0	1	4	.200	5.30
Trenton	AA	1	1	7.2	6	3	2	0	1	9	0	1	0	1.000	2.35
Pawtucket	AAA	9	9	55.1	41	22	21	8	16	56	0	4	2	.667	3.42
Boston	AL	5	2	13.1	12	5	5	0	3	14	0	1	1	.500	3.38
1 Minor League Yr		21	21	119.0	101	62	56	17	44	128	0	6	6	.500	4.24

A Dominican righthander who began his career in Japan, Robinson Checo signed a high-dollar contract with the Red Sox before the 1997 season, and was expected to spend at least part of the season in the major league rotation. It didn't work out that way, but the investment is not a bust, yet. Robinson was slowed by a sore shoulder, a sore elbow, and a sore back at various stages of the season, but he finished healthy and should be fine for 1998. He has a 95-MPH fastball and a hard slider, and when he throws strikes he is extremely tough. His performance at Pawtucket was particularly good, with a K/BB of +82 percent, and he was great for the Red Sox in September. If he stays healthy, Checo should be excellent, but I do have concerns about his durability. **Grade B+**

Bruce Chen
Atlanta Braves

Pos: P **Throws:** Left **Ht:** 6'2" **Wt:** 180 **Age:** 20

Yr Team	Lg	G	GS	IP	H	R	ER	HR	BB	SO	SV	W	L	Pct.	ERA
96 Eugene	A	11	8	35.2	23	13	9	1	14	55	0	4	1	.800	2.27
97 Macon	A	28	28	146.1	120	67	57	19	44	182	0	12	7	.632	3.51
4 Minor League Yrs		62	56	295.0	263	143	115	25	80	319	1	21	16	.568	3.51

Signed as a free agent from Panama in 1993, Bruce Chen was slowed early in his career by nagging injuries, but he was completely healthy in 1997 and ate up the Sally League. His fastball hits 90 MPH, and could get faster as he matures physically, but what makes him special are his outstanding changeup and very good, though inconsistent, curveball. His control is terrific, and there wasn't anything wrong with any of his ratios last year: K/BB +75 percent, K/IP +45 percent, H/IP +18 percent, all excellent by league standards. He even has a nasty move to first base. There is no reason to think that Chen won't have a superb career, except for the fact that he is a young pitcher, and is thus by nature prone to prove prognosticators wrong. At this point, though, Chen is one of the best pitching prospects around. **Grade B+**

McKay Christensen
Chicago White Sox

Pos: OF **Bats:** Left **Ht:** 5'11" **Wt:** 178 **Age:** 22

Yr Team	Lg	G	AB	R	H	2B	3B	HR	RBI	BB	SO	SB	CS	Avg	OBP	Slg
96 White Sox	R	35	133	17	35	7	5	1	16	10	23	10	3	.263	.327	.414
Hickory	A	6	11	0	0	0	0	0	0	1	4	0	0	.000	.083	.000
97 Hickory	A	127	503	95	141	12	12	5	47	52	61	28	20	.280	.357	.382
2 Minor League Yrs		168	647	112	176	19	17	6	63	63	88	38	23	.272	.346	.382

With his tour of duty as a Mormon missionary over, McKay Christensen got down to some baseball in 1997. He signed with the Angels after being drafted in the first round in

1994, on the condition that he be allowed to fulfill his mission obligation. He was traded to the White Sox in 1995, and showed enough to re-establish his credentials as a prospect last year. Christensen's best skill right now is range in the outfield; he runs very well and can track balls with the best of them, although he makes mistakes of inexperience and his throwing isn't great. With the bat, he has some line-drive zip into the gaps, but doesn't have over-the-fence power. His command of the strike zone is good and should improve. He needs to make up for lost time and advance in 1998. At least he's no longer a man on a mission. **Grade C**

Ryan Christenson — *Oakland Athletics*

Pos: OF   **Bats:** Right   **Ht:** 5'11"   **Wt:** 175   **Age:** 24

Yr Team	Lg	G	AB	R	H	2B	3B	HR	RBI	BB	SO	SB	CS	Avg	OBP	Slg
96 Sou. Oregon	A	36	136	31	39	11	0	5	21	19	21	8	6	.287	.376	.478
W Michigan	A	33	122	21	38	2	2	2	18	13	22	2	4	.311	.387	.410
97 Visalia	A	83	308	69	90	18	8	13	54	70	72	20	11	.292	.425	.529
Huntsville	AA	29	120	39	44	9	3	2	18	24	23	5	4	.367	.469	.542
Edmonton	AAA	16	49	12	14	2	2	2	5	11	11	2	0	.286	.435	.531
3 Minor League Yrs		246	893	186	255	46	16	25	132	159	182	42	30	.286	.396	.457

Christenson was drafted in the 10th round in 1995, out of Pepperdine. He was having a nice little season at Class-A Visalia, showing dashes of power and speed, was promoted to Huntsville, tore through the Southern League, got promoted again to Edmonton, and continued to play well. He doesn't have outstanding tools or skills in any one category, but he can do a lot of things pretty well: steal a base, hit a homer, draw a walk. His outfield range is good, although his arm is not strong. Oakland loves his hustle and will give him a shot to win its center-field job in spring training. **Grade C+**

Brady Clark — *Cincinnati Reds*

Pos: OF   **Bats:** Right   **Ht:** 6'2"   **Wt:** 195   **Age:** 24

Yr Team	Lg	G	AB	R	H	2B	3B	HR	RBI	BB	SO	SB	CS	Avg	OBP	Slg
97 Burlington	A	126	459	108	149	29	7	11	63	76	71	31	18	.325	.423	.490
1 Minor League Yr		126	459	108	149	29	7	11	63	76	71	31	18	.325	.423	.490

Clark was signed as an undrafted free agent in 1996, out of the University of San Diego. He received a chance to play every day in 1997, and made the most of it, leading the Midwest League in runs scored, ranking fourth in batting average, and posting an excellent SEC of +53 percent. Clark is also a fine defensive outfielder with very good range, and is reportedly a very hard worker. Clark's main problem from an analytical perspective is his age: he was too old for the league. He needs to do well in Double-A and higher, but I think there is a good chance he will do so. **Grade C**

Matt Clement
San Diego Padres

Pos: P **Throws:** Right **Ht:** 6'3" **Wt:** 190 **Age:** 23

Yr Team	Lg	G	GS	IP	H	R	ER	HR	BB	SO	SV	W	L	Pct.	ERA
96 Clinton	A	16	16	96.1	66	31	30	3	52	109	0	8	3	.727	2.80
Rancho Cuca	A	11	11	56.1	61	40	35	8	26	75	0	4	5	.444	5.59
97 Rancho Cuca	A	14	14	101.0	74	30	18	3	31	109	0	6	3	.667	1.60
Mobile	AA	13	13	88.0	83	37	25	4	32	92	0	6	5	.545	2.56
4 Minor League Yrs		95	95	554.1	479	273	212	22	260	563	0	42	29	.592	3.44

A case can be made that Matt Clement, a relatively obscure farmhand a year ago, is now the best pitching prospect in baseball. I don't think he is the *best,* but he is in the top three. Clement was a third-round pick in 1993, from a Pennsylvania high school. Over the last two years, his velocity has increased from the upper 80s well into the 90s. At the same time, he has increased the sharpness of his curve and slider, shown a willingness to use the changeup, and has improved his command from good to excellent. All of his statistical ratios were outstanding last year; he was named the No. 2 prospect in the California League and the No. 7 prospect in the Southern League. Managers in both circuits praised his pitching knowledge, intelligence, and durability. Clement needs a year in the high minors to consolidate his progress, but if he stays healthy, he should have a spot in the San Diego rotation by 1999. He doesn't get the press clippings of Carl Pavano or Kerry Wood, but he is in their class as a prospect. **Grade A-**

Chris Clemons
Arizona Diamondbacks

Pos: P **Throws:** Right **Ht:** 6'4" **Wt:** 220 **Age:** 25

Yr Team	Lg	G	GS	IP	H	R	ER	HR	BB	SO	SV	W	L	Pct.	ERA
96 Pr William	A	6	6	36.0	36	16	9	6	8	26	0	1	4	.200	2.25
Birmingham	AA	19	16	94.1	91	39	33	7	40	69	0	5	2	.714	3.15
97 Nashville	AAA	22	21	124.2	115	73	63	15	65	70	0	5	5	.500	4.55
Chicago	AL	5	2	12.2	19	13	12	4	11	8	0	0	2	.000	8.53
4 Minor League Yrs		88	84	468.1	457	246	214	51	196	304	0	22	26	.458	4.11

Chris Clemons is living proof that velocity isn't everything. He has a hard sinking fastball, a nasty slider, and can throw strikes with both, but has difficulty with offspeed pitches. He has worked on a curveball and a changeup, and although he uses them well periodically, when he gets into a rough spot he reaches back for the hard stuff. Sometimes this works, and sometimes it doesn't. Clemons can be tough to hit, as his good H/IP of plus-eight shows, but his strikeout ratios were ghastly: K/BB -45 percent, K/IP -26 percent. He throws hard, but not hard enough to get away with *that.* Unless he comes up with something offspeed, he will have a troublesome time in the majors. **Grade C**

Pat Cline
Chicago Cubs
Pos: C   **Bats:** Right   **Ht:** 6'3"   **Wt:** 220   **Age:** 23

Yr Team	Lg	G	AB	R	H	2B	3B	HR	RBI	BB	SO	SB	CS	Avg	OBP	Slg
96 Daytona	A	124	434	75	121	30	2	17	76	54	79	10	2	.279	.373	.475
97 Iowa	AAA	27	95	6	21	2	0	3	10	10	24	0	1	.221	.292	.337
Orlando	AA	78	271	39	69	19	0	7	37	27	78	2	2	.255	.331	.402
5 Minor League Yrs		377	1286	202	335	83	2	42	213	166	302	18	6	.260	.355	.426

A year ago, Pat Cline was a top prospect as a power-hitting young catcher with improving defensive skills, but his 1997 season was a major disappointment. He missed much of the season with nagging injuries, and when he did play was not particularly impressive, with an OPS nearly eight percent below league average and an even worse SEC at -13 percent. His defense regressed too, as he caught just 27 percent of runners; the league average was 38 percent. What happened? He's a catcher. . . injuries and offensive stagnation are two sides of the same backstop coin. Will he come back? Maybe. Maybe not. Cline is still young, and my guess is that he will still have a good career, but he may also fade into the mists of prospect history along with Derek Parks and Steve Decker. **Grade C+**

Ken Cloude
Seattle Mariners
Pos: P   **Throws:** Right   **Ht:** 6'1"   **Wt:** 200   **Age:** 23

Yr Team	Lg	G	GS	IP	H	R	ER	HR	BB	SO	SV	W	L	Pct.	ERA
96 Lancaster	A	28	28	168.1	167	94	79	15	60	161	0	15	4	.789	4.22
97 Memphis	AA	22	22	132.2	131	62	57	15	48	124	0	11	7	.611	3.87
Seattle	AL	10	9	51.0	41	32	29	8	26	46	0	4	2	.667	5.12
4 Minor League Yrs		87	82	514.1	471	242	206	39	190	486	0	38	23	.623	3.60

Ken Cloude was a sixth-round draft pick in 1993, from Baltimore. He was a projectable kid who knew how to pitch, but didn't throw hard. Velocity has come with physical maturity, and he now gets his fastball into the low 90s regularly. His curveball, slider, and changeup are all good pitches, his mechanics are smooth, he stays healthy, and his control and composure on the mound are unwavering. He is intelligent, intense, and competitive. Cloude had a fine season through 22 starts at Memphis, his K/BB ratio ranking very high at +42 percent. He did fairly well in his major league time, and should have a lock on a rotation spot in 1998, or at least he would for my team. Seattle manager Lou Piniella tends to give up on guys if they have a bad inning, let alone a bad outing. Cloude will be a very good pitcher, assuming he stays healthy, which I think he will. **Grade B+**

Danny Clyburn
Baltimore Orioles
Pos: OF   **Bats:** Right   **Ht:** 6'3"   **Wt:** 217   **Age:** 23

Yr Team	Lg	G	AB	R	H	2B	3B	HR	RBI	BB	SO	SB	CS	Avg	OBP	Slg
96 Bowie	AA	95	365	51	92	14	5	18	55	17	88	4	3	.252	.290	.466
97 Rochester	AAA	137	520	91	156	33	5	20	76	53	107	14	4	.300	.372	.498
Baltimore	AL	2	3	0	0	0	0	0	0	0	2	0	0	.000	.000	.000
6 Minor League Yrs		635	2384	331	659	113	17	96	394	166	526	39	26	.276	.329	.459

I mentioned last year that Danny Clyburn needed to improve his strike-zone judgment, in order to get full use of his enormous strength at the plate. Somebody got him the message;

his walk rate shot up last year, his strikeouts were down, and what do you know—his production numbers were up across the board. His batting average jumped 50 points, at a higher level of competition, and he continued to hit for power. Some caution is still warranted: he did much of his damage in his offense-friendly home park, he was less patient at the plate later in the year, and his defense remains substandard. Nevertheless, I think Clyburn turned the corner in 1997, and should be a productive major league hitter, although he won't hit .300 all the time. The main problem will be finding him a place to play. There isn't an obvious spot in Baltimore, and if he doesn't get a chance soon, he might get buried in Triple-A, like Jose Malave and many other guys. **Grade B**

Jason Coble

New York Yankees

Pos: P   Throws: Left   Ht: 6'3"   Wt: 185   Age: 20

Yr Team	Lg	G	GS	IP	H	R	ER	HR	BB	SO	SV	W	L	Pct.	ERA
96 Yankees	R	9	9	32.2	23	11	9	0	20	40	0	1	1	.500	2.48
97 Greensboro	A	24	23	120.1	93	84	66	6	96	99	0	2	11	.154	4.94
2 Minor League Yrs		33	32	153.0	116	95	75	6	116	139	0	3	12	.200	4.41

Coble was a second-round pick in 1996, from a rural Tennessee high school. He has a very live arm, with a fastball clocked as high as 93 MPH and a sharp curve, but his command is weak and he doesn't know how to pitch yet. His H/IP was quite good at +23 percent in the Sally League, an indicator of his good stuff, but his K/IP was below average, and his K/BB was the worst mark in the league at -57 percent. Coble could learn something about pitching and advance quickly, or he could languish for years. There is no way to know which will happen yet. **Grade C**

Gary Coffee

Kansas City Royals

Pos: 1B   Bats: Right   Ht: 6'3"   Wt: 235   Age: 23

Yr Team	Lg	G	AB	R	H	2B	3B	HR	RBI	BB	SO	SB	CS	Avg	OBP	Slg
96 Lansing	A	105	393	52	91	17	2	11	59	53	141	6	1	.232	.328	.369
97 Wilmington	A	120	427	58	95	11	1	11	56	55	157	6	4	.222	.318	.330
4 Minor League Yrs		321	1123	154	276	41	8	34	177	154	368	14	5	.246	.343	.387

Gary Coffee is a huge guy who looks like a cross between Dave Parker and Cecil Fielder. He has excellent power potential and draws some walks, but he strikes out way too much, and struggles to make contact against anything offspeed. A shortstop in high school, he has surprising mobility for a man his size, but makes lots of mistakes with the glove. I don't expect Coffee to develop, but I'm keeping an eye on him. I find him interesting, although I'm not sure why. **Grade C-**

Dave Coggin
Philadelphia Phillies

Pos: P **Throws:** Right **Ht:** 6'4" **Wt:** 195 **Age:** 21

Yr Team	Lg	G	GS	IP	H	R	ER	HR	BB	SO	SV	W	L	Pct.	ERA
96 Piedmont	A	28	28	169.1	156	87	81	12	46	129	0	9	12	.429	4.31
97 Clearwater	A	27	27	155.0	160	96	81	12	86	110	0	11	8	.579	4.70
3 Minor League Yrs		66	66	372.1	361	208	178	25	163	276	0	25	23	.521	4.30

Most baseball professionals will tell you that Dave Coggin is the best pitching prospect in the Phillies system. He probably is, but he has a lot of work to do before he is ready for the majors. Coggin, a high school quarterback, is an outstanding athlete with a very live arm. His fastball has been clocked as high as 94 MPH; his problem is lack of control, plus difficulty developing breaking pitches. He won 11 games in the Florida State League last year, but his ERA was high, and all of his ratios were below average. He is intelligent, and most observers think that all he needs to succeed are innings and experience, to get his mechanics consistent and assemble a foundation of pitching knowledge. His ceiling is high, but the scaffolding is still being assembled. **Grade C+**

Michael Coleman
Boston Red Sox

Pos: OF **Bats:** Right **Ht:** 5'11" **Wt:** 180 **Age:** 22

Yr Team	Lg	G	AB	R	H	2B	3B	HR	RBI	BB	SO	SB	CS	Avg	OBP	Slg
96 Sarasota	A	110	407	54	100	20	5	1	36	38	86	24	5	.246	.320	.327
97 Trenton	AA	102	385	56	116	17	8	14	58	41	89	20	7	.301	.372	.496
Pawtucket	AAA	28	113	27	36	9	2	7	19	12	27	4	2	.319	.391	.619
Boston	AL	8	24	2	4	1	0	0	2	0	11	1	0	.167	.167	.208
4 Minor League Yrs		400	1487	238	402	70	18	37	192	155	336	93	23	.270	.346	.416

A year ago, Michael Coleman was just another "tools" player who didn't know how to use his natural abilities on the field. Now, after a wonderful campaign in the Eastern and International Leagues, he is one of the finest prospects in baseball, and shows signs of developing into a Seven Skill player. Coleman was drafted in the 18th round in 1994, not because he lacked talent, but because most teams assumed he would play college football at Alabama. Boston managed to sign him, but until last year he showed little to encourage enthusiasm. He was excellent at Trenton (OPS +17 percent), even better at Pawtucket (OPS +35 percent), and may start 1998 in the majors. Basically, Coleman figured out how to play baseball. He did better against breaking stuff in particular. Defense in the outfield has never been a problem; he has superb range in center field. His command of the strike zone, while adequate, remains a potential weakness, and he looked bad at times in the Arizona Fall League. If the strike zone doesn't go backwards on him, Coleman will emerge as a fine player, perhaps similar to Ellis Burks. **Grade B+**

Lou Collier

Pittsburgh Pirates

Pos: SS **Bats:** Right **Ht:** 5'10" **Wt:** 170 **Age:** 24

Yr Team	Lg	G	AB	R	H	2B	3B	HR	RBI	BB	SO	SB	CS	Avg	OBP	Slg
96 Carolina	AA	119	443	76	124	20	3	3	49	48	73	29	9	.280	.355	.359
97 Calgary	AAA	112	397	65	131	31	5	1	48	37	47	12	7	.330	.393	.441
Pittsburgh	NL	18	37	3	5	0	0	0	3	1	11	1	0	.135	.158	.135
5 Minor League Yrs		523	1916	317	557	97	18	22	210	188	293	117	52	.291	.363	.395

Scouts like Lou Collier's tools, and his performance has come around. The arrival of Abraham Nunez as Pittsburgh's Shortstop of the Future will keep Collier from starting in the long run, but he can hit, and the ability to play the infield adequately should be enough to ensure him a pension. Collier is unlikely to develop home-run power, but he makes contact against most styles of pitching, has doubles pop, and is not helpless against righthanded pitchers. He should be able to hit .280 in the majors eventually. With the glove, Collier can play shortstop or second base without much trouble, and could probably handle third base or the outfield if asked. I'm not sure he will be a long-term regular for the Pirates, or anybody else, but he'd be quite valuable off the bench. **Grade B-**

Luis Colmenares

Colorado Rockies

Pos: P **Throws:** Right **Ht:** 5'11" **Wt:** 189 **Age:** 21

Yr Team	Lg	G	GS	IP	H	R	ER	HR	BB	SO	SV	W	L	Pct.	ERA
96 Salem	A	32	0	32.2	28	21	19	4	22	45	12	4	5	.444	5.23
Asheville	A	12	12	65.0	58	36	32	6	25	56	0	2	6	.250	4.43
97 Salem	A	32	3	66.2	60	34	29	5	30	70	2	6	1	.857	3.92
4 Minor League Yrs		133	15	233.2	199	113	98	17	110	265	40	15	14	.517	3.77

Colmenares has a live arm despite his size, but the Rockies have had a hard time deciding how to use him. He was mostly a reliever in 1997, and that is where his future lies. Colmenares has a 90-MPH fastball, and his breaking ball is promising. His control can be inconsistent, but when he throws strikes, he is tough. He could make a major league appearance in 1998, although 1999 or 2000 is more likely. Middle relief will be his role. **Grade C**

Decomba Conner

Seattle Mariners

Pos: OF **Bats:** Right **Ht:** 5'10" **Wt:** 184 **Age:** 24

Yr Team	Lg	G	AB	R	H	2B	3B	HR	RBI	BB	SO	SB	CS	Avg	OBP	Slg
96 Winston-Sal	A	129	512	77	144	18	5	20	64	43	117	33	11	.281	.337	.453
97 Jacksnville	AA	47	154	22	32	6	3	4	17	30	45	5	1	.208	.342	.364
Lakeland	A	56	201	35	64	7	4	7	29	21	47	9	2	.318	.381	.498
4 Minor League Yrs		375	1349	236	376	50	24	43	174	160	328	101	23	.279	.355	.447

Scouts like Decomba Conner's combination of strength and speed, but his command of the strike zone, while not terrible, is not a strong point for him. After coming over from Cincinnati in the Ruben Sierra deal, Conner started the year in Double-A for the Tigers. He had ankle problems which cut down on his speed, and while he drew a lot of walks, he struck out excessively, and was having serious problems with Double-A breaking stuff. He was demoted to Lakeland and played better, but the Tigers soured on him, and dropped him from the 40-man roster. The Mariners, short of position-player prospects, claimed him on waivers in October. **Grade C**

Brian Cooper

Anaheim Angels

Pos: P   Throws: Right   Ht: 6'1"   Wt: 175   Age: 23

Yr Team	Lg	G	GS	IP	H	R	ER	HR	BB	SO	SV	W	L	Pct.	ERA
96 Lk Elsinore	A	26	23	162.1	177	100	76	17	39	155	0	7	9	.438	4.21
97 Lk Elsinore	A	17	17	117.0	111	56	46	7	27	104	0	7	3	.700	3.54
3 Minor League Yrs		56	51	341.1	348	187	149	29	88	325	1	17	14	.548	3.93

Cooper was a very good college pitcher at Southern California, and was selected by the Angels in the fourth round in 1995. He had a decent season in the California League in 1996, but opened 1997 on the disabled list. When he came off, the Angels sent him back to Lake Elsinore, and he was awesome. Look at that outstanding K/BB mark, +89 percent. Cooper throws four average pitches, the standard fastball, curve, slider, change combo. None of his offerings are great, but when he throws strikes they are effective. He threw strikes last year. The problem is, he was a league repeater. He needs to do it again at the higher levels. **Grade C**

Trace Coquillette

Montreal Expos

Pos: 2B   Bats: Right   Ht: 5'11"   Wt: 165   Age: 23

Yr Team	Lg	G	AB	R	H	2B	3B	HR	RBI	BB	SO	SB	CS	Avg	OBP	Slg
96 Expos	R	7	25	4	4	1	0	0	0	4	6	1	0	.160	.276	.200
Wst Plm Bch	A	72	266	39	67	17	4	1	27	27	72	9	7	.252	.336	.357
97 Wst Plm Bch	A	53	188	34	60	18	2	8	33	27	27	8	7	.319	.419	.564
Harrisburg	AA	81	293	46	76	17	3	10	51	25	40	9	4	.259	.345	.440
5 Minor League Yrs		466	1676	275	455	99	21	33	234	210	313	68	39	.271	.366	.415

Coquillette, who is *not* Canadian, was drafted in the 10th round in 1993, from Sacramento City College in California. He wasn't much of a prospect, until last year, when he had a sudden burst of firepower at West Palm Beach and continued to hit well at Harrisburg. Physical maturity seems to have helped him. Coquillette is average with the glove; his hands, range and arm all rate okay, but don't knock your eyes out. He'll need to keep hitting to see major league time; his glove won't get him there on its own merits. Will he keep hitting? Possibly. . . he isn't old, and his strike-zone judgment isn't Bootyesque, but I want to see more. **Grade C+**

Francisco Cordero

Detroit Tigers

Pos: P   Throws: Right   Ht: 6'2"   Wt: 170   Age: 20

Yr Team	Lg	G	GS	IP	H	R	ER	HR	BB	SO	SV	W	L	Pct.	ERA
96 Fayetteville	A	2	1	7.0	2	2	2	0	6	7	0	0	0	—	2.57
Jamestown	A	2	2	11.0	5	1	1	0	2	10	0	0	0	—	0.82
97 W Michigan	A	50	0	54.1	36	13	6	2	15	67	35	6	1	.857	0.99
3 Minor League Yrs		73	21	180.1	165	94	74	6	72	157	35	10	11	.476	3.69

Uhhmmmmm. . . those are some pretty good stats, there. Great ERA, high strikeout rate, good control, few hits. The most important number about Francisco Cordero, however, is this one: 98, as in 98 MPH. Unlike most minor league closers who post gaudy stats at the lower levels, Cordero has a blistering fastball. He has a pretty good breaking pitch, too, but it is the heater, and his control of it, that made him unhittable last year. A failed starter, Cordero took to the closer role with a vengeance, and pitches well in tight situations. Even hard-throwing minor league closers tend to have problems at higher levels, so I'm not going to put Cordero on my top-prospect list just yet, but keep an eye on this guy. **Grade B**

Chris Corn   *Pittsburgh Pirates*

Pos: P   **Throws:** Right   **Ht:** 6'2"   **Wt:** 170   **Age:** 26

Yr Team	Lg	G	GS	IP	H	R	ER	HR	BB	SO	SV	W	L	Pct.	ERA
96 Tampa	A	26	25	170.1	145	67	55	10	38	109	0	12	4	.750	2.91
97 Lynchburg	A	28	1	64.2	54	30	23	8	23	66	2	3	4	.429	3.20
4 Minor League Yrs		128	28	373.1	305	141	117	25	105	336	27	24	17	.585	2.82

Corn came to the Pirates from the Yankees in exchange for Charlie Hayes in 1996. Despite his solid season at Tampa that year, the Pirates returned him to A-ball in 1997, this time as a middle reliever. Corn had to be disappointed, but he pitched very well in the role assigned to him. His stuff is average to slightly above, and when his control is sharp, which it has been for two years, he is steadfast on the mound. He needs to prove himself at higher levels, but can't do so if they don't give him a chance. **Grade C-**

Steve Cox   *Tampa Bay Devil Rays*

Pos: 1B   **Bats:** Left   **Ht:** 6'4"   **Wt:** 225   **Age:** 23

Yr Team	Lg	G	AB	R	H	2B	3B	HR	RBI	BB	SO	SB	CS	Avg	OBP	Slg
96 Huntsville	AA	104	381	59	107	21	1	12	61	51	65	2	2	.281	.372	.436
97 Edmonton	AAA	131	467	84	128	34	1	15	93	88	90	1	3	.274	.385	.448
6 Minor League Yrs		533	1883	315	515	111	9	66	347	296	404	12	16	.273	.376	.447

The trade of Mark McGwire left a spot open at first base, but the Athletics left Steve Cox unprotected in expansion, and Tampa Bay snagged him. He is a lefthanded hitter with some power and patience, although he has never come close to matching the home-run power he displayed at high Class-A Modesto in 1995. He has been troubled with back problems on and off throughout his career, obstructing his development as a hitter. Cox dealt decently with Triple-A in 1997, although the big offensive year in the Pacific Coast League meant his OPS was actually only league average. He shows few weaknesses against fastballs, but breaking stuff can get him and his swing gets long at times. His defense at first base is quite good. Cox won't make many All-Star teams, but he should be a functional, productive, Paul Sorrento-type player. **Grade B**

Ryan Creek
Houston Astros

Pos: P **Throws:** Right **Ht:** 6'1" **Wt:** 180 **Age:** 25

Yr Team	Lg	G	GS	IP	H	R	ER	HR	BB	SO	SV	W	L	Pct.	ERA
96 Jackson	AA	27	26	142.0	139	95	83	9	121	119	0	7	15	.318	5.26
97 Jackson	AA	19	19	105.0	95	57	48	10	74	88	0	10	5	.667	4.11
5 Minor League Yrs		105	95	534.0	510	310	248	36	330	455	1	36	35	.507	4.18

Creek has major league stuff: 92-MPH fastball, sharp breaking pitches. He was pitching reasonably well for Jackson, although his control did give him some problems, when he went on the disabled list with a sore shoulder in early August. It was allegedly nothing serious, but the Astros held him out the rest of the season. If healthy, Creek definitely has the arm strength to succeed, but his command has never been consistent and he has been in Double-A for three years. He might be better off in the bullpen. **Grade C**

Felipe Crespo
Toronto Blue Jays

Pos: OF-2B **Bats:** Both **Ht:** 5'11" **Wt:** 190 **Age:** 25

Yr Team	Lg	G	AB	R	H	2B	3B	HR	RBI	BB	SO	SB	CS	Avg	OBP	Slg
96 Dunedin	A	9	34	3	11	1	0	2	6	2	3	1	3	.324	.361	.529
Syracuse	AAA	98	355	53	100	25	0	8	58	56	39	10	11	.282	.389	.420
Toronto	AL	22	49	6	9	4	0	0	4	12	13	1	0	.184	.375	.265
97 Syracuse	AAA	80	290	53	75	12	0	12	26	46	38	7	7	.259	.365	.424
Toronto	AL	12	28	3	8	0	1	1	5	2	4	0	0	.286	.333	.464
7 Minor League Yrs		630	2320	373	657	129	24	54	279	332	340	81	52	.283	.377	.429

With manager Cito Gaston deported, maybe Felipe Crespo will finally get a chance. The man can hit. He has power and patience from both sides of the plate, but Crespo always seems to get hurt just as he is about to get a shot in the majors. The injuries are seldom severe, but while they are bad enough to keep him out of the lineup, managers get tired of hearing about pulled hamstrings and tight leg muscles. If it doesn't need a cast or can't be fixed by an operation, it is hard for them to be patient while the damage heals, especially with a rookie. Crespo was limited defensively at second base, so he spent time in the outfield in 1997. The trouble with this is that while Crespo is a good hitter, he isn't a *great* one. You really have to be a great hitter to get a chance in the outfield in the American League these days. Well, that isn't true with the Blue Jays, I suppose, considering the Orlando Merced debacle. Still, a good organization should be able to get something of value out of Crespo, by putting him on the roster as a fourth outfielder/pinch hitter/emergency infielder, or by trading him. **Grade C+**

Jack Cressend
Boston Red Sox

Pos: P **Throws:** Right **Ht:** 6'1" **Wt:** 185 **Age:** 22

Yr Team	Lg	G	GS	IP	H	R	ER	HR	BB	SO	SV	W	L	Pct.	ERA
96 Lowell	A	9	8	45.2	37	15	12	0	17	57	0	3	2	.600	2.36
97 Sarasota	A	28	25	165.2	163	98	70	15	56	149	0	8	11	.421	3.80
2 Minor League Yrs		37	33	211.1	200	113	82	15	73	206	0	11	13	.458	3.49

Jack Cressend was a notable college pitcher for Tulane, but he doesn't throw hard and had a rough junior season, so he went undrafted. He signed with the Red Sox as a free agent in

1996, and has pitched well in the pros. His K/BB was +33 percent at Sarasota last year, and his K/IP was also good at +16 percent; his H/IP was league average. Translated, those numbers confirm his scouting profile: he is hittable, but has good control and can win games. Cressend's main weakness is an absolute inability to hold runners, although he isn't bad as a fielder otherwise. He must brave the Electric Double-A Finesse Pitcher Acid Test, but he might pass it, especially if he does something about those baserunners. **Grade C**

Jim Crowell · *Cincinnati Reds*

Pos: P   **Throws:** Left   **Ht:** 6'4"   **Wt:** 220   **Age:** 23

Yr Team	Lg	G	GS	IP	H	R	ER	HR	BB	SO	SV	W	L	Pct.	ERA
96 Columbus	A	28	28	165.1	163	89	76	16	69	104	0	7	10	.412	4.14
97 Kinston	A	17	17	114.0	96	41	30	4	26	94	0	9	4	.692	2.37
Akron	AA	3	3	18.0	13	12	9	2	11	7	0	1	0	1.000	4.50
Chattanooga	AA	3	3	19.0	19	6	6	2	5	14	0	2	1	.667	2.84
Indianapols	AAA	3	3	19.2	19	7	6	1	8	6	0	1	1	.500	2.75
Cincinnati	NL	2	1	6.1	12	7	7	2	5	3	0	0	1	.000	9.95
3 Minor League Yrs		66	63	392.2	360	177	145	26	146	273	0	25	18	.581	3.32

A case study in the unpredictability of pitchers: Jim Crowell. A year ago, Crowell was an obscure minor league pitcher toiling in the Outer Limits of the Cleveland system. He didn't throw that hard, and his command wasn't terrific. There was no reason to expect or predict success. A year later, he was in the majors. Crowell breezed through the Carolina League (K/BB +26 percent), made three starts in Double-A, was traded to the Reds in the John Smiley deal, made three more Double-A starts, three more in Triple-A, then spent September in the Show. He really racked up the frequent-flier miles. Crowell has the standard four-pitch arsenal. His fastball is up to 92 MPH, and when he throws strikes, he is effective. There is no way to accurately predict what Crowell may do in 1998. If he maintains his velocity and command, he will do quite well, but my guess is he may struggle, at least initially. **Grade C+**

Jacob Cruz · *San Francisco Giants*

Pos: OF   **Bats:** Left   **Ht:** 6'0"   **Wt:** 175   **Age:** 25

Yr Team	Lg	G	AB	R	H	2B	3B	HR	RBI	BB	SO	SB	CS	Avg	OBP	Slg
96 Phoenix	AAA	121	435	60	124	26	4	7	75	62	77	5	9	.285	.378	.411
San Francisco	NL	33	77	10	18	3	0	3	10	12	24	0	1	.234	.352	.390
97 Phoenix	AAA	127	493	97	178	45	3	12	95	64	64	18	3	.361	.434	.538
San Francisco	NL	16	25	3	4	1	0	0	3	3	4	0	0	.160	.241	.200
4 Minor League Yrs		406	1504	259	467	111	8	32	259	192	235	32	22	.311	.392	.459

Baseball men have always been intrigued with Jacob Cruz, due to his beautiful line-drive swing, but until 1997 his production at the plate was only adequate. His second year in the Pacific Coast League was quite special, at least on the surface, as he led the circuit in batting average and doubles. His OPS and SEC marks were very good at +17 percent and +14 percent, but they weren't at the top of the league, so while he was valuable offensively, he wasn't dominant, despite the lofty average. I project him as a .280-.300 hitter, with mediocre power, in the majors. Cruz is one of the better defensive outfielders in baseball. He has wonderful range for a right fielder, and his arm is strong and accurate. All in all, Cruz is a good player and will help his team win, but he isn't in the same class of prospect as Ben Grieve or Paul Konerko. **Grade B**

Kevin Curtis   *Colorado Rockies*

Pos: OF   **Bats:** Right   **Ht:** 6'2"   **Wt:** 210   **Age:** 25

Yr Team	Lg	G	AB	R	H	2B	3B	HR	RBI	BB	SO	SB	CS	Avg	OBP	Slg
96 Bowie	AA	129	460	69	113	21	2	18	58	54	95	2	1	.246	.328	.417
97 Bowie	AA	22	67	7	18	6	0	1	13	7	22	1	1	.269	.333	.403
New Haven	AA	105	362	58	99	24	0	17	69	34	82	0	2	.273	.341	.481
5 Minor League Yrs		459	1573	238	413	92	3	66	248	201	336	16	15	.263	.353	.451

In the Orioles system, Kevin Curtis was a slow, power-hitting outfielder, hoping to sneak his way into the majors, get hot, and earn a job. Traded to the Rockies in 1997, Curtis is now. . . a slow, power-hitting outfielder, hoping to sneak his way into the majors, get hot, and earn a job. The difference is, he has a much better chance to achieve said hot streak in the Rockies system than with the Orioles. His main problem is a fondness for chasing breaking balls, but the Rockies aren't exactly fanatics about plate discipline. **Grade C-**

Matt Curtis   *Anaheim Angels*

Pos: C   **Bats:** Both   **Ht:** 6'0"   **Wt:** 195   **Age:** 23

Yr Team	Lg	G	AB	R	H	2B	3B	HR	RBI	BB	SO	SB	CS	Avg	OBP	Slg
96 Boise	A	75	305	57	93	29	3	12	62	37	47	2	1	.305	.390	.538
97 Cedar Rapds	A	34	113	21	28	8	1	4	18	17	16	0	0	.248	.351	.442
Lk Elsinore	A	74	264	58	87	25	8	17	55	25	54	3	1	.330	.390	.678
2 Minor League Yrs		183	682	136	208	62	12	33	135	79	117	5	2	.305	.383	.576

The Angels drafted Curtis in the 28th round in 1996, from Fresno State. He is not tool-laden, but hit well in college and has continued to do so in the pros. His strike-zone judgment is passable, although his walk rate isn't as high as I would like. He certainly hit well at Lake Elsinore, with the third-best OPS in the league, +29 percent, granted it was a big offensive year in the California League. His defense behind the plate isn't great. . . he threw out just 24 percent of stealers, and has spent time in the outfield. If his strike-zone judgment improves, or at least doesn't get out of hand, I think Curtis will continue to hit. He may not have a position, however. **Grade C+**

Jeff M. D'Amico   *Oakland Athletics*

Pos: P   **Throws:** Right   **Ht:** 6'3"   **Wt:** 200   **Age:** 23

Yr Team	Lg	G	GS	IP	H	R	ER	HR	BB	SO	SV	W	L	Pct.	ERA
96 Athletics	R	8	0	19.0	14	3	3	0	2	15	0	3	0	1.000	1.42
Modesto	A	1	0	1.0	3	3	2	0	0	0	0	0	0	—	18.00
97 Modesto	A	20	13	97.0	115	57	41	5	34	89	1	7	3	.700	3.80
Edmonton	AAA	10	7	30.2	42	29	28	7	6	19	1	1	2	.333	8.22
2 Minor League Yrs		39	20	147.2	174	92	74	12	42	123	2	11	5	.688	4.51

In 1993, the Milwaukee Brewers drafted a Florida high school pitcher named Jeff D'Amico in the first round. That same year, in the third round, Oakland drafted a high school shortstop from Washington also named Jeff D'Amico. By 1996, Jeff D'Amico the pitcher was in the major leagues, but Jeff D'Amico the shortstop was stalled in the California League. The Athletics thought, hey, maybe the Brewers had the right idea, so they decided to convert their version of Jeff D'Amico into a pitcher. Oakland's D'Amico took to the mound well in the California League, but got roughed up when they pushed him to Triple-A, which wasn't a good idea. As you can imagine, he has a strong arm, but needs to learn how to pitch, and the Pacific Coast League isn't the place for that. **Grade C**

Mike Darr Jr.   *San Diego Padres*

Pos: OF   **Bats:** Left   **Ht:** 6'3"   **Wt:** 205   **Age:** 22

Yr Team	Lg	G	AB	R	H	2B	3B	HR	RBI	BB	SO	SB	CS	Avg	OBP	Slg
96 Lakeland	A	85	311	26	77	14	7	0	38	28	64	7	3	.248	.307	.338
97 Rancho Cuca	A	134	521	104	179	32	11	15	94	57	90	23	7	.344	.409	.534
4 Minor League Yrs		375	1376	211	411	73	20	21	216	166	264	39	16	.299	.374	.427

The Tigers drafted Mike Darr in the second round in 1994. In three seasons, he did little except draw walks and get injured, so they were willing to send him to San Diego as part of the trade for Jody Reed last spring. This was a steal for the Padres, as Darr evolved rapidly into a top prospect. He continued to show command of the strike zone, and he hit the snot out of the ball, for average and power. His OPS was +24 percent. It wasn't park effect, as Rancho Cucomonga was negative for offense last year. Defensively, Darr has work to do reading fly balls and learning to use his good arm, but it is the bat that excites people, and it should. Darr is occasionally accused of being immature, but he isn't a bad fellow, and seems to enjoy playing for the Padres. **Grade B+**

David Darwin   *Detroit Tigers*

Pos: P   **Throws:** Left   **Ht:** 6'0"   **Wt:** 185   **Age:** 24

Yr Team	Lg	G	GS	IP	H	R	ER	HR	BB	SO	SV	W	L	Pct.	ERA
96 Fayetteville	A	17	9	59.0	54	22	21	2	12	49	0	5	2	.714	3.20
97 W Michigan	A	21	4	40.1	23	7	4	2	20	31	3	1	0	1.000	0.89
Lakeland	A	12	12	82.2	70	23	23	2	18	41	0	10	1	.909	2.50
2 Minor League Yrs		50	25	182.0	147	52	48	6	50	121	3	16	3	.842	2.37

Darwin was a 26th-round pick in 1996, from Duke University. Although he does not throw hard, he was Duke's closer, and led the ACC in saves. The Tigers started him off in the bullpen at West Michigan, but when Lakeland needed a starter, Darwin was promoted and converted to the rotation. All he did was go 10-1. As a finesse guy, he must prove himself at higher levels, but his career is off to a good start. **Grade C-**

Cleatus Davidson

Minnesota Twins

Pos: 2B Bats: Both Ht: 5'10" Wt: 160 Age: 21

Yr Team	Lg	G	AB	R	H	2B	3B	HR	RBI	BB	SO	SB	CS	Avg	OBP	Slg
96 Ft. Wayne	A	59	203	20	36	8	3	0	30	23	45	2	3	.177	.259	.246
Elizabethtn	R	65	248	53	71	10	6	6	31	39	45	17	6	.286	.386	.448
97 Ft. Wayne	A	124	478	80	122	16	8	6	52	52	100	39	9	.255	.327	.360
4 Minor League Yrs		332	1241	199	304	43	20	15	150	144	257	79	26	.245	.325	.348

When Cleatus Davidson was in high school in Lake Wales, Florida, scouts compared him to a young Ozzie Smith, due to his fluid motions in the infield, and his pop-gun bat. The Twins picked him in the second round in 1994. Davidson's development has been slow; 1997 was the first year he showed any offense in a full-season league. His command of the strike zone is acceptable, and the more optimistic members of the baseball community think he could develop gap power to go with his speed. Davidson's defense is brilliant but inconsistent; his range factor and double play rate were outstanding at second base, but he still makes too many mistakes. The Twins haven't always been happy with his work ethic or attitude, but he seems to have outgrown much of that. Davidson is still a work in progress. **Grade C**

Ben Davis

San Diego Padres

Pos: C Bats: Both Ht: 6'4" Wt: 205 Age: 21

Yr Team	Lg	G	AB	R	H	2B	3B	HR	RBI	BB	SO	SB	CS	Avg	OBP	Slg
96 Rancho Cuca	A	98	353	35	71	10	1	6	41	31	89	1	1	.201	.264	.286
97 Rancho Cuca	A	122	474	67	132	30	1	17	76	28	107	3	1	.278	.320	.454
3 Minor League Yrs		272	1024	138	258	48	5	28	163	76	232	4	2	.252	.304	.391

With Jose Cruz Jr. belting the ball out of American League ballparks in 1997, the Padres received some serious second-guessing regarding their decision to take high school catcher Ben Davis over Cruz in the 1995 draft. I have been among the second-guessers. . . well, actually, I was a first-guesser, since I thought they were making a mistake at the time, and said so. Cruz will be a star, of course, but Davis did better last year after a miserable 1996 campaign, and has re-emerged as a prospect. He is starting to show power. Don't just look at the 17 homers, but notice the 30 doubles. That's a lot for a catcher, and augers well for his power development. On the other hand, his strike-zone judgment remains terrible, and he is impotent against breaking stuff. Davis has the physical and mental ability to be a top-notch defensive catcher. He threw out 37 percent of runners, exactly league average, but he handles the pitching staff well, and moves like a shortstop. It all boils down to his bat. If he hits, he will be a star. If he doesn't hit, he will make the majors anyhow, but will have value mainly as a bench player. Will he hit? The markers are much better than they were a year ago, but they still aren't great. It really could go either way. **Grade C+**

Tommy Davis
Baltimore Orioles

Pos: 1B **Bats:** Right **Ht:** 6'1" **Wt:** 195 **Age:** 24

Yr Team	Lg	G	AB	R	H	2B	3B	HR	RBI	BB	SO	SB	CS	Avg	OBP	Slg
96 Bowie	AA	137	524	75	137	32	2	14	54	41	113	5	8	.261	.325	.410
97 Rochester	AAA	119	438	74	133	22	2	15	62	43	90	6	1	.304	.368	.466
4 Minor League Yrs		456	1706	251	472	93	8	52	218	144	369	20	14	.277	.338	.432

Tommy Davis didn't look like he was going anywhere after several mediocre seasons following his entrance into pro ball as a second-rounder in 1994. That changed to some extent in 1997. After a slow start caused by a shoulder injury, he had a fine season at Rochester, showing improved ability to make contact, and hitting for an average nearly 40 points higher than his career norms. He now looks like a .270-.280 hitter, with moderately good power. He has turned into a good fielder at first base, after failing at third. Davis won't push anyone out of Baltimore, so his chance will have to come with another team. **Grade C**

Francisco de la Cruz
New York Yankees

Pos: P **Throws:** Right **Ht:** 6'2" **Wt:** 175 **Age:** 24

Yr Team	Lg	G	GS	IP	H	R	ER	HR	BB	SO	SV	W	L	Pct.	ERA
97 Norwich	AA	2	2	8.1	8	3	3	0	7	0	0	0	1	.000	3.24
Tampa	A	8	8	36.2	39	30	28	5	29	22	0	0	2	.000	6.87
Greensboro	A	13	13	84.2	71	41	31	6	36	75	0	5	4	.556	3.30
1 Minor League Yr		23	23	129.2	118	74	62	11	72	97	0	5	7	.417	4.30

The Japanese teams have been increasingly aggressive in seeking Latin American talent, and some of these players are making their way to the United States. Francisco de la Cruz, a Nicaraguan, started his pro career in Japan, but entered the Yankees system in 1997, and was impressive at Greensboro in the South Atlantic League. He struggled in the Florida State League, but did enough overall to establish himself as a prospect. De la Cruz throws in the low 90s, but his command wavers at times, and he needs to consolidate his breaking stuff. He isn't close to the majors at this point, but he does have a chance to reach the Bronx, albeit by the circuitous Nicaragua-Japan-North America route. He must have a lot of experience dealing with culture shock. **Grade C**

Roland de la Maza
Kansas City Royals

Pos: P **Throws:** Right **Ht:** 6'2" **Wt:** 195 **Age:** 26

Yr Team	Lg	G	GS	IP	H	R	ER	HR	BB	SO	SV	W	L	Pct.	ERA
96 Canton-Akrn	AA	40	14	139.2	122	75	68	15	49	132	1	9	7	.563	4.38
97 Buffalo	AAA	34	14	115.0	104	42	37	12	43	73	2	9	4	.692	2.90
Kansas City	AL	1	0	2.0	1	1	1	1	1	1	0	0	0	—	4.50
5 Minor League Yrs		143	83	615.0	552	265	216	66	177	510	4	49	17	.742	3.16

If courage and intellect mean anything, Roland de la Maza should get a chance in the majors. Although he is lucky when his fastball hits 87 MPH, he has a great changeup, a pretty good breaking pitch, reliable control, pitching intelligence, and the bearing of a bulldog. He has been an effective pitcher at every level, with a career record of 49-17, and a solid ERA. He'll take the ball in any situation, and doesn't complain. His lack of velocity makes him a marginal prospect, but he's the kind of marginal prospect that some team should be willing to take a chance on eventually. The Royals picked him up from the Indians in September. **Grade C-**

Luis de los Santos — New York Yankees

Pos: P **Throws:** Right **Ht:** 6'2" **Wt:** 187 **Age:** 20

Yr Team	Lg	G	GS	IP	H	R	ER	HR	BB	SO	SV	W	L	Pct.	ERA
96 Greensboro	A	7	6	31.2	39	17	17	4	11	21	0	4	1	.800	4.83
Oneonta	A	10	10	58.0	44	28	24	3	21	62	0	4	4	.500	3.72
97 Greensboro	A	14	14	88.2	91	45	30	3	13	62	0	5	6	.455	3.05
Tampa	A	10	10	61.2	49	19	16	4	8	39	0	5	0	1.000	2.34
Norwich	AA	4	4	25.0	23	9	7	4	7	15	0	1	1	.500	2.52
3 Minor League Yrs		47	44	270.0	251	120	94	18	62	205	0	19	12	.613	3.13

A product of the Dominican, Luis de los Santos (not to be confused with the veteran minor league infielder of the same name) might be the best pitching prospect in the Yankees system. He is not a giant on the mound, and still has growing to do, but he already hits 93 MPH with his fastball, and his breaking pitches show promise. His control is excellent, and he shows a good feel for pitching, especially for a moundsman his age. There was nothing wrong with any of his K/BB ratios last year; even his K/BB ratio in Double-A was well above Eastern League norms. That is unusual: most pitchers take a hit in K/BB when they get to Double-A for the first time. On the other hand, his K/IP ratios were below league averages, which is atypical for a pitcher with good stuff. I want to see de los Santos have a full season in the high minors, and I won't be totally comfortable until his K/IP rate is better, but he did nothing wrong in 1997 and could be a terrific pitcher. **Grade B+**

Valerio de los Santos — Milwaukee Brewers

Pos: P **Throws:** Left **Ht:** 6'4" **Wt:** 185 **Age:** 22

Yr Team	Lg	G	GS	IP	H	R	ER	HR	BB	SO	SV	W	L	Pct.	ERA
96 Beloit	A	33	23	164.2	164	83	65	11	59	137	4	10	8	.556	3.55
97 El Paso	AA	26	16	114.1	146	83	73	6	38	61	2	6	10	.375	5.75
3 Minor League Yrs		73	51	361.0	391	200	158	20	109	255	6	20	24	.455	3.94

The Brewers consider Valerio de los Santos to be one of the best prospects in their system, which tells you more about the condition of their system than it does about de los Santos. He is a young Dominican with a very live arm; his fastball is consistently in the low 90s, and he has a good splitter. What he doesn't have is anything close to resembling stamina; he wears down easily. He would probably be better off in relief, but the Brewers have used him primarily as a starter to try and build his strength. De los Santos missed the first six weeks of the season with a nasty staph infection, which didn't do much for his endurance. He has potential, but it is largely untapped. **Grade C**

Chris Dean
Seattle Mariners

Pos: 2B   Bats: Both   Ht: 5'10"   Wt: 178   Age: 24

Yr Team	Lg	G	AB	R	H	2B	3B	HR	RBI	BB	SO	SB	CS	Avg	OBP	Slg
96 Wisconsin	A	53	210	32	57	8	2	4	32	18	46	11	7	.271	.339	.386
Lancaster	A	48	174	30	48	10	1	5	22	16	31	7	1	.276	.345	.431
97 Lancaster	A	68	263	59	88	23	5	8	38	41	51	15	10	.335	.436	.551
Memphis	AA	67	237	24	60	11	5	3	18	25	37	3	5	.253	.328	.380
4 Minor League Yrs		424	1563	251	434	84	21	35	185	175	328	64	40	.278	.363	.425

The Mariners drafted Chris Dean in the 20th round in 1993, out of Seminole Junior College in Oklahoma. He has progressed slowly, but had a fine 1997 season, split between the California League and the Southern League. Dean is a switch-hitter with patience at the plate and muscle into the gaps. His stats at Lancaster were boosted by park effects, and while he wasn't awesome at Double-A, he wasn't overpowered by Southern League pitching, either. Dean has excellent range at second base and turns the double play with assurance, but does make a few too many errors. His chances are borderline, but the Mariners farm system isn't exactly bursting with talent, and Dean could see some major league action if the need arises. **Grade C-**

Tim DeCinces
Baltimore Orioles

Pos: DH-C   Bats: Left   Ht: 6'2"   Wt: 195   Age: 23

Yr Team	Lg	G	AB	R	H	2B	3B	HR	RBI	BB	SO	SB	CS	Avg	OBP	Slg
96 Bluefield	R	39	128	24	38	8	0	7	32	24	28	3	1	.297	.403	.523
97 Delmarva	A	127	416	65	107	20	0	13	70	97	117	3	4	.257	.395	.399
2 Minor League Yrs		166	544	89	145	28	0	20	102	121	145	6	5	.267	.397	.428

Tim DeCinces, Doug's son, was drafted in the 17th round in 1996, out of UCLA. Scouts like his bat, but his defensive skills are inadequate, and indeed, he was the designated hitter at Delmarva for most of the season. He has power, but the main thing I noticed about him, other than his pedigree, was his high walk rate. Of course, his strikeout rate is high, too. He needs to hit well at higher levels and find a position. **Grade C**

Wilson Delgado
San Francisco Giants

Pos: SS   Bats: Both   Ht: 5'11"   Wt: 165   Age: 22

Yr Team	Lg	G	AB	R	H	2B	3B	HR	RBI	BB	SO	SB	CS	Avg	OBP	Slg
96 San Jose	A	121	462	59	124	19	6	2	54	48	89	8	2	.268	.337	.348
Phoenix	AAA	12	43	1	6	0	1	0	1	3	7	0	1	.140	.196	.186
San Francisco	NL	6	22	3	8	0	0	0	2	1	5	1	0	.364	.440	.364
97 Phoenix	AAA	119	416	47	120	22	4	9	59	24	70	9	3	.288	.326	.425
San Francisco	NL	8	7	1	1	1	0	0	0	0	2	0	0	.143	.143	.286
4 Minor League Yrs		426	1579	208	450	73	18	16	169	131	278	42	20	.285	.340	.384

With the trade of Mike Caruso to the White Sox, Wilson Delgado is the likeliest candidate to be Shortstop of the Future in San Francisco. He is unrefined as a hitter, but has good bat speed and was very young to be in the Pacific Coast League. Unlike many natural righthanded switch-hitters, he actually does better from the left side, hitting .292 that way last season. He has good speed, although he isn't much of a basestealer, and his defense is promising. He had the second-best range factor among PCL regulars, and he doesn't make as many errors as most young infielders. Delgado has been rushed, and while he isn't ready to make a big splash with the bat, he could handle a major league job defensively. **Grade B-**

David Dellucci   *Arizona Diamondbacks*

Pos: OF   **Bats:** Left   **Ht:** 5'10"   **Wt:** 180   **Age:** 24

Yr Team	Lg	G	AB	R	H	2B	3B	HR	RBI	BB	SO	SB	CS	Avg	OBP	Slg
96 Frederick	A	59	185	33	60	11	1	4	28	38	34	5	6	.324	.438	.459
Bowie	AA	66	251	27	73	14	1	2	33	28	56	2	7	.291	.363	.378
97 Bowie	AA	107	385	71	126	29	3	20	55	58	69	11	4	.327	.421	.574
Baltimore	AL	17	27	3	6	1	0	1	3	4	7	0	0	.222	.344	.370
3 Minor League Yrs		280	986	158	309	62	6	29	138	142	176	22	20	.313	.404	.477

David Dellucci was a surprise callup last summer. He was having a terrific season at Bowie, but scouts have never been wild about him, due to his lack of outstanding musculature. What he lacks in noticeable muscles he makes up for in bat quickness: he can drive pitches into the gaps and over the walls, and is a good example of what plate discipline can do for a hitter. He had the third-best OPS in the Eastern League at +30 percent, and his SEC was also very high at +49 percent. Dellucci is acceptable defensively in center field. He doesn't have great range or a cannon arm, but he catches what he gets to and makes accurate throws. Dellucci is something like a cross between Rusty Greer and Dave Martinez, and should make a very fine player for the Diamondbacks. **Grade B**

Ryan Dempster   *Florida Marlins*

Pos: P   **Throws:** Right   **Ht:** 6'2"   **Wt:** 195   **Age:** 20

Yr Team	Lg	G	GS	IP	H	R	ER	HR	BB	SO	SV	W	L	Pct.	ERA
96 Chston-SC	A	23	23	144.1	120	71	53	13	58	141	0	7	11	.389	3.30
Kane County	A	4	4	26.1	18	10	8	0	18	16	0	2	1	.667	2.73
97 Brevard Cty	A	28	26	165.1	190	100	90	19	46	131	0	10	9	.526	4.90
3 Minor League Yrs		64	60	376.0	369	204	162	33	140	331	0	23	22	.511	3.88

Dempster came over from the Rangers in the John Burkett deal late in 1996. He won 10 games at Brevard County in 1997, but he isn't really close to the majors yet. His ERA was high for the Florida State League, and while his K/BB was very good at +42 percent, his poor H/IP ratio shows he has work to do. His stuff is average right now. His fastball, curve, and change are all just adequate, but his control is good, and scouts think he will pick up velocity as he matures. If he stays healthy, he could develop into a valuable property. **Grade C**

Don Denbow
San Francisco Giants

Pos: OF   **Bats:** Right   **Ht:** 6'4"   **Wt:** 215   **Age:** 24

Yr Team	Lg	G	AB	R	H	2B	3B	HR	RBI	BB	SO	SB	CS	Avg	OBP	Slg
96 Burlington	A	92	302	64	84	17	2	21	62	81	123	19	5	.278	.440	.556
San Jose	A	26	97	19	36	8	3	6	19	17	30	1	1	.371	.466	.701
97 San Jose	A	107	339	58	84	20	1	10	50	86	138	19	12	.248	.403	.401
5 Minor League Yrs		432	1421	254	344	64	10	63	222	289	583	60	21	.242	.377	.434

After a lackluster career, Don Denbow got some attention as a prospect with a solid 1996 season, but last year he went back to his humdrum ways. He has some power, runs well for a big guy, and while I like his walk rate, his strikeout totals are scary. His OPS was adequate at plus-six, not a bad total in the San Jose pitchers' park, but even considering park effect, that's not a good mark for a corner player. His defense last year was notable only for its mediocrity. Scouts say he has a long swing, a report which dovetails well with his high fan rate. Denbow isn't finished as a prospect yet, but the burden of proof rests on his shoulders. **Grade C-**

Edwin Diaz
Arizona Diamondbacks

Pos: 2B   **Bats:** Right   **Ht:** 5'11"   **Wt:** 170   **Age:** 23

Yr Team	Lg	G	AB	R	H	2B	3B	HR	RBI	BB	SO	SB	CS	Avg	OBP	Slg
96 Tulsa	AA	121	499	70	132	33	6	16	65	25	122	8	9	.265	.309	.451
97 Okla City	AAA	20	73	6	8	3	1	1	4	2	27	1	1	.110	.156	.219
Tulsa	AA	105	440	65	121	31	1	15	46	33	102	6	9	.275	.335	.452
5 Minor League Yrs		526	2029	268	545	125	25	52	254	134	473	46	51	.269	.323	.432

Strike-zone judgment. . . strike-zone judgment. . . strike-zone judgment. You can have all the physical talent in the world, but if you strike out 27 times in 73 at-bats, with two walks, like Edwin Diaz did last year at Oklahoma City, you ain't gonna make it in the Show. Diaz has all the athletic ability you could hope for, including bat speed and power, but his strike-zone judgment is about like Benji Gil's. Unless he learns to take a pitch, he will never live up to his potential. Diaz has quick reactions in the infield, but he led the Texas League in errors, and his range was limited at times by a sore knee. He is young enough to get better. . . but people have said the same thing about Gil for years. When the Diamondbacks selected Diaz in the expansion draft, every member of the Frank Catalanotto Fan Club let out a groan. **Grade C**

Einar Diaz
Cleveland Indians

Pos: C   **Bats:** Right   **Ht:** 5'10"   **Wt:** 165   **Age:** 25

Yr Team	Lg	G	AB	R	H	2B	3B	HR	RBI	BB	SO	SB	CS	Avg	OBP	Slg
96 Canton-Akrn	AA	104	395	47	111	26	2	3	35	12	22	3	2	.281	.317	.380
Cleveland	AL	4	1	0	0	0	0	0	0	0	0	0	0	.000	.000	.000
97 Buffalo	AAA	109	336	40	86	18	2	3	31	18	34	2	6	.256	.302	.348
Cleveland	AL	5	7	1	1	1	0	0	1	0	2	0	0	.143	.143	.286
6 Minor League Yrs		550	2009	259	538	106	9	34	227	87	136	21	24	.268	.313	.380

Einar Diaz is a preferred choice of some scouts, who admire his defensive skills and see him as a potentially good hitter, but his numbers are not good, and the times I have seen him I haven't been impressed. He has some bat speed, which must be what his advocates are looking at, but Diaz hits too many 300-foot flyballs, is very impatient, and just doesn't give the impression, to me at least, that he will ever be a hitter. I do understand why his defense draws raves. He moves well behind home plate, has good hands, blocks the plate superbly, and has a strong arm. On the other hand, he only threw out 31 percent of runners; the league average was 38 percent. I really don't see Diaz as anything more than a backup, but he could hang around for 10 years in that role. **Grade C-**

R.A. Dickey

Texas Rangers

Pos: P   Throws: Right   Ht: 6'1"   Wt: 205   Age: 23

Yr Team	Lg	G	GS	IP	H	R	ER	HR	BB	SO	SV	W	L	Pct.	ERA
97 Charlotte	A	8	6	35.0	51	32	27	8	12	32	0	1	4	.200	6.94
1 Minor League Yr		8	6	35.0	51	32	27	8	12	32	0	1	4	.200	6.94

Dickey was the Rangers' first-round pick in 1996, from the University of Tennessee. It was discovered after the draft that his throwing elbow was missing a ligament. The Rangers signed him anyway, albeit at a greatly reduced bonus. He got off to a poor start in the Florida State League, then ended up having to have surgery on the elbow. When healthy, Dickey is a gritty pitcher with solid stuff, good control, and a bulldog heart, but at this stage it is pointless to grade him. There is a chance he may never pitch again.

Nate Dishington

St. Louis Cardinals

Pos: 1B   Bats: Left   Ht: 6'3"   Wt: 210   Age: 23

Yr Team	Lg	G	AB	R	H	2B	3B	HR	RBI	BB	SO	SB	CS	Avg	OBP	Slg
96 Peoria	A	75	208	22	47	12	3	3	30	25	73	1	1	.226	.324	.356
97 Pr William	A	133	448	75	122	20	6	28	106	81	121	8	5	.272	.387	.531
5 Minor League Yrs		419	1400	202	334	69	18	47	223	206	458	27	16	.239	.347	.414

The signing of Mark McGwire probably didn't do a whole lot for Nate Dishington's morale, but if he keeps slugging like he did at Prince William, his chance will come eventually. Drafted as a second-round pick in 1993 from a high school in California, Dishington's career went nowhere until 1997. He became more patient at the plate, shortened up his swing a bit, and drove pitches more consistently for power, while increasing his batting average. His OPS was excellent at +26 percent, a very impressive mark at Prince William, which is not a good place for a power hitter. He still strikes out too much, and has problems with the glove, so he must continue hitting for power to get a chance. If he stays patient, he might just do it. **Grade C+**

Bubba Dixon
San Diego Padres

Pos: P **Throws:** Left **Ht:** 5'10" **Wt:** 165 **Age:** 26

Yr Team	Lg	G	GS	IP	H	R	ER	HR	BB	SO	SV	W	L	Pct.	ERA
96 Memphis	AA	42	0	63.1	53	32	29	6	28	77	3	2	3	.400	4.12
Rancho Cuca	A	11	0	16.1	20	16	13	3	4	20	0	0	3	.000	7.16
97 Mobile	AA	56	0	75.2	67	31	29	4	37	88	1	7	2	.778	3.45
4 Minor League Yrs		188	12	342.1	289	148	128	27	139	399	20	21	16	.568	3.37

Bubba Dixon is weird. No, not like Michael Jackson or Sonny Bono, but in baseball terms, his stats and scouting reports are just plain weird. From looking at his numbers, especially his very high strikeout rate, you would think he was a hard thrower. He isn't, not by any means. . . his best fastball is about 84 MPH, and 82 is more usual. He gets by with a curve and changeup, and good control, but still, he strikes out a lot more guys than he should, given his stuff. You might think he was more effective against lefties, but actually, he does better against righties; again, that is strange, considering his lack of stuff. Dixon is very marginal, but if he keeps pitching well, they can't ignore him forever. Well, actually, T.H.E.Y. can. "T.H.E.Y.," as you Pinky and the Brain fans know, is the acronym for The Horde of Ecumenical Yodelers, a secret society bent on global domination. I'm not a member, but most major league GMs are. **Grade C-**

Robert Dodd
Philadelphia Phillies

Pos: P **Throws:** Left **Ht:** 6'3" **Wt:** 195 **Age:** 25

Yr Team	Lg	G	GS	IP	H	R	ER	HR	BB	SO	SV	W	L	Pct.	ERA
96 Reading	AA	18	5	43.0	41	21	17	4	24	35	0	2	3	.400	3.56
Scranton-WB	AAA	8	2	20.0	32	21	18	4	9	12	0	0	0		8.10
97 Reading	AA	63	0	80.1	61	29	29	8	21	94	8	9	4	.692	3.25
4 Minor League Yrs		130	40	347.2	320	151	130	20	128	295	9	21	18	.538	3.37

Dodd, a University of Florida product, was drafted in the 14th round in 1994. He had back surgery in 1996, but came back last year and had a fine season out of the Reading bullpen. Dodd doesn't burn the radar guns, but his fastball has life, and he has good control of his breaking pitch. His strikeout rate at Reading was very high, +49 percent. Dodd won't close in the majors, but he could handle the lefty short-relief role. **Grade C**

David Doster
Philadelphia Phillies

Pos: 2B **Bats:** Right **Ht:** 5'10" **Wt:** 185 **Age:** 27

Yr Team	Lg	G	AB	R	H	2B	3B	HR	RBI	BB	SO	SB	CS	Avg	OBP	Slg
96 Scranton-WB	AAA	88	322	37	83	20	0	7	48	26	54	7	3	.258	.313	.385
Philadelphia	NL	39	105	14	28	8	0	1	8	7	21	0	0	.267	.313	.371
97 Scranton-WB	AAA	108	410	70	129	32	2	16	79	30	60	5	5	.315	.370	.520
5 Minor League Yrs		535	2014	305	564	151	10	60	302	188	284	36	22	.280	.347	.454

Attention Major League Baseball GMs. No one need go without a good second baseman anymore. Don't like Frank Catalanotto? Don't sign Billy Ripken. Don't go after Carlos Garcia. Try David Doster. He can hit and he can field. . . isn't that what baseball is all about? He has very good punch at the plate for an infielder, and while he isn't likely to hit .315 in the majors, he should hit .280. He has good range around the bag at second, and doesn't make tons of errors. One negative is that he has problems turning the double play, or at least his double-play numbers weren't good last year. They were decent in 1996, so one set of numbers or the other might be a statistical illusion of some sort. Even if he does struggle on the double play, Doster has enough punch in his bat to earn a bench job. **Grade C**

Octavio Dotel   *New York Mets*

Pos: P   **Throws:** Right   **Ht:** 6'5"   **Wt:** 160   **Age:** 22

Yr Team	Lg	G	GS	IP	H	R	ER	HR	BB	SO	SV	W	L	Pct.	ERA
96 Capital City	A	22	19	115.1	89	49	46	7	49	142	0	11	3	.786	3.59
97 Mets	R	3	2	9.1	9	1	1	0	2	7	1	0	0	—	0.96
St. Lucie	A	9	8	50.0	44	18	14	2	23	39	0	5	2	.714	2.52
Binghamton	AA	12	12	55.2	66	50	37	5	38	40	0	3	4	.429	5.98
3 Minor League Yrs		62	53	312.2	266	146	121	15	133	323	1	27	13	.675	3.48

Dotel, a Dominican signed by the Mets in 1993, had an excellent season at Class-A Capital City in 1996. He got off to another good start at St. Lucie last year, but struggled when promoted to Double-A. Dotel has a 92-MPH fastball, a hard slurve, and has worked on a changeup. His command and control were great in 1996, but wavered last year. Some people think he might be better off in relief, where he would have to worry less about changing speeds. As a young pitcher, Dotel is inherently unpredictable. He could blossom into a star within the next year. He could struggle for seven years and then blossom. He could wander around for 10 years as a journeyman. He could get hurt. **Grade C**

Kelly Dransfeldt   *Texas Rangers*

Pos: SS   **Bats:** Right   **Ht:** 6'2"   **Wt:** 195   **Age:** 22

Yr Team	Lg	G	AB	R	H	2B	3B	HR	RBI	BB	SO	SB	CS	Avg	OBP	Slg
96 Hudson Vall	A	75	284	42	67	17	1	7	29	27	76	13	4	.236	.308	.377
97 Charlotte	A	135	466	64	106	20	7	6	58	42	115	25	16	.227	.294	.339
2 Minor League Yrs		210	750	106	173	37	8	13	87	69	191	38	20	.231	.299	.353

Dransfeldt was Texas' fourth-round pick in 1996, from the University of Michigan. He is a fine athlete, with power potential and speed, but he is very inconsistent at the plate, due to. . . drumroll please. . . weak command of the strike zone! His defense is like his offense: he looks good at times, but is very raw, and needs a lot of improvement if he is to make it in the bigs. Dransfeldt is quite unrefined for a guy who went to college at a decent baseball school. He still has a chance, but it's a slim one. **Grade C-**

Matt Drews
Detroit Tigers

Pos: P **Throws:** Right **Ht:** 6'8" **Wt:** 205 **Age:** 23

Yr Team	Lg	G	GS	IP	H	R	ER	HR	BB	SO	SV	W	L	Pct.	ERA
96 Columbus	AAA	7	7	20.1	18	27	19	4	27	7	0	0	4	.000	8.41
Tampa	A	4	4	17.2	26	20	14	0	12	12	0	0	3	.000	7.13
Norwich	AA	9	9	46.0	40	26	23	4	33	37	0	1	3	.250	4.50
Jacksnville	AA	6	6	31.0	26	18	15	3	19	40	0	0	4	.000	4.35
97 Jacksnville	AA	24	24	144.1	160	109	88	23	50	85	0	8	11	.421	5.49
Toledo	AAA	3	3	15.0	14	11	11	2	14	7	0	0	2	.000	6.60
4 Minor League Yrs		95	95	546.1	502	315	237	42	232	397	0	31	40	.437	3.90

I hate to say this, but it is possible the Yankees may have done irreparable harm to Matt Drews when they promoted him too quickly to Triple-A in 1996. The psyches of young pitchers can be fragile things. Drews still has the things that made him a top prospect two years ago: above-average fastball, hard slider, good control, intelligence on the mound. But he may not have recovered mentally from his traumatic experience at Columbus; something is sure wrong with him. Oh, sure, you can say, "He needs to be mentally tough and get over it," but that is easier said than done. Developing young pitchers isn't the same as raising fruit flies in high school evolution experiments. You can't just say "Survival of the Fittest." You don't throw young kids, however talented, into situations they aren't prepared to handle, and then sit back and say, "This guy stinks," when they struggle. Drews isn't finished as a prospect yet, but until his strikeout rate rises back to respectable levels, I would be wary of expecting success. **Grade C**

Mike Drumright
Detroit Tigers

Pos: P **Throws:** Right **Ht:** 6'4" **Wt:** 210 **Age:** 23

Yr Team	Lg	G	GS	IP	H	R	ER	HR	BB	SO	SV	W	L	Pct.	ERA
96 Jacksnville	AA	18	18	99.2	80	51	44	11	48	109	0	6	4	.600	3.97
97 Jacksnville	AA	5	5	28.2	16	7	5	0	13	24	0	1	1	.500	1.57
Toledo	AAA	23	23	133.1	134	78	75	22	91	115	0	5	10	.333	5.06
3 Minor League Yrs		56	56	314.1	279	160	147	39	176	301	0	13	17	.433	4.21

A year ago, Mike Drumright was the best pitching prospect in the Tigers system. Drumright still has the power arm that made him a first-round pick from Wichita State in 1995. He has a fine 93-MPH fastball and a nasty hammer curve, but his changeup is not progressing, and command over his two key pitches regressed last year. There didn't seem to be any sort of injury problem; Triple-A hitters just had a better read on his hard stuff than their Double-A counterparts. Drumright was supposed to be ready for the Detroit rotation in 1998, but he needs more time to get the changeup figured out, and to get his command back to previous levels. If he stays healthy, he will probably be okay, but qualms are building among prospect-watchers. **Grade B-**

Courtney Duncan
Chicago Cubs

Pos: P **Throws:** Right **Ht:** 5'11" **Wt:** 175 **Age:** 23

Yr Team	Lg	G	GS	IP	H	R	ER	HR	BB	SO	SV	W	L	Pct.	ERA
96 Williamsprt	A	15	15	90.1	58	28	22	6	34	91	0	11	1	.917	2.19
97 Daytona	A	19	19	121.2	90	35	22	3	35	120	0	8	4	.667	1.63
Orlando	AA	8	8	45.0	37	28	17	2	29	45	0	2	2	.500	3.40
2 Minor League Yrs		42	42	257.0	185	91	61	11	98	256	0	21	7	.750	2.14

In 1996, the Cubs promoted Amaury Telemaco into the major league rotation ahead of schedule. In 1997, it was Jeremi Gonzalez. In 1998, it could be Courtney Duncan. Drafted in the 20th round in 1996 out of Grambling State University, Duncan has been outstanding in his 1½ seasons of professional ball. An intelligent pitcher, he has adapted to pro conditions, responds well to coaching, and uses his fastball, curve, slider, and change to good effect. Although none of his pitches are dominating, they are all solid offerings, and he knows how to use them. His command is excellent. There was certainly nothing wrong with his stats last year. All of his ratios in the Florida State League were better than +20 percent, and he impressed observers in Double-A as well. Duncan is one of the better pitching prospects in baseball, and only his lack of exceptional velocity keeps him from the top echelon. **Grade B**

Todd Dunn
Milwaukee Brewers

Pos: OF **Bats:** Right **Ht:** 6'5" **Wt:** 220 **Age:** 27

Yr Team	Lg	G	AB	R	H	2B	3B	HR	RBI	BB	SO	SB	CS	Avg	OBP	Slg
96 El Paso	AA	98	359	72	122	24	5	19	78	45	84	13	4	.340	.412	.593
Milwaukee	AL	6	10	2	3	1	0	0	1	0	3	0	0	.300	.300	.400
97 Tucson	AAA	93	332	66	101	31	4	18	66	39	83	5	5	.304	.389	.584
Milwaukee	AL	44	118	17	27	5	0	3	9	2	39	3	0	.229	.242	.347
5 Minor League Yrs		430	1519	287	436	99	15	77	289	175	417	55	22	.287	.367	.524

Milwaukee's first-round pick out of the University of North Florida in 1993, Todd Dunn has excellent tools, and he has learned to use them over the last two years. Horrible strike-zone judgment hurt his performance in the low minors, and while it still isn't terrific, he has made enormous strides, and it is now adequate, or at least it was in Triple-A. He did have problems with major league breaking stuff. His swing is more consistent than it used to be, resulting in good power to all fields. Dunn's OPS was +17 percent in the Pacific Coast League: good, though not outstanding. Dunn is adequate in center field and quite good in right; he has a strong arm, in particular. He will need adjustment time to major league conditions, but could be pretty good if his K/BB judgment improves further. **Grade B-**

Todd Dunwoody   *Florida Marlins*

Pos: OF   **Bats:** Left   **Ht:** 6'2"   **Wt:** 185   **Age:** 22

Yr Team	Lg	G	AB	R	H	2B	3B	HR	RBI	BB	SO	SB	CS	Avg	OBP	Slg
96 Portland	AA	138	552	88	153	30	6	24	93	45	149	24	19	.277	.337	.484
97 Charlotte	AAA	107	401	74	105	16	7	23	62	39	129	25	3	.262	.331	.509
Florida	NL	19	50	7	13	2	2	2	7	7	21	2	0	.260	.362	.500
5 Minor League Yrs		469	1770	303	468	74	29	63	277	169	456	105	36	.264	.334	.446

It will be interesting to see who the Marlins pick to play center for them in 1998; both Todd Dunwoody and Mark Kotsay are ready to play. If they are smart, they will find room for both of them; given the salary dump currently under way, they probably will. Dunwoody is more raw than Kotsay at this point, but his ceiling is higher. He has more raw power and speed, but his baseball skills are less refined, particularly his strike-zone judgment. He still chases too many bad pitches. Dunwoody's OPS was good but not spectacular at +11 percent, but his SEC of +42 percent shows he has a broad range of abilities, even if he lacks polish. His defense in center is excellent. Dunwoody is still quite young, and I think he will develop into a classic Seven Skill player, provided he gets command of the strike zone. Right now, I like Kotsay better, but I wouldn't throw either one off the roster. **Grade B**

Roberto Duran   *Detroit Tigers*

Pos: P   **Throws:** Left   **Ht:** 6'0"   **Wt:** 190   **Age:** 25

Yr Team	Lg	G	GS	IP	H	R	ER	HR	BB	SO	SV	W	L	Pct.	ERA
96 Dunedin	A	8	8	48.1	31	9	6	1	19	54	0	3	1	.750	1.12
Knoxville	AA	19	16	80.2	72	52	46	8	61	74	0	4	6	.400	5.13
97 Jacksnville	AA	50	0	60.2	41	19	16	2	39	95	16	4	2	.667	2.37
Detroit	AL	13	0	10.2	7	9	9	0	15	11	0	0	0	—	7.59
6 Minor League Yrs		181	62	449.2	362	225	193	29	322	544	26	31	24	.564	3.86

Duran was originally in the Dodgers system, having signed with them in 1990 out of the Dominican Republic. He was traded to the Blue Jays a few years later, then went to Detroit last spring for minor league outfield suspect Anton French. This may have been a steal for the Tigers; Duran looks like a potential bullpen contributor, whereas French may be working in a hardware store, trying to sell his tools, five years from now. Duran has an excellent 93-MPH fastball and a hard slider. Although his command wanders on him at times, he can strike anybody out. Duran isn't a sure thing, but arms as live as his don't grow on conifers. **Grade C**

Chad Durbin   *Kansas City Royals*

Pos: P   **Throws:** Right   **Ht:** 6'2"   **Wt:** 177   **Age:** 20

Yr Team	Lg	G	GS	IP	H	R	ER	HR	BB	SO	SV	W	L	Pct.	ERA
96 Royals	R	11	8	44.1	34	22	21	3	25	43	0	3	2	.600	4.26
97 Lansing	A	26	26	144.2	157	85	77	15	53	116	0	5	8	.385	4.79
2 Minor League Yrs		37	34	189.0	191	107	98	18	78	159	0	8	10	.444	4.67

Durbin was drafted in the third round in 1996, out of high school in Baton Rouge. He has one of the best arms in the Royals' system, and given their lack of top-notch mound candidates, he could move quickly if he shows signs of developing. He didn't show a whole lot at Lansing; he has a solid 92-MPH fastball, but his breaking stuff needs work, and he must improve his command within the strike zone. Orthodox **Grade C** prospect.

Radhames Dykhoff — Baltimore Orioles

Pos: P   **Throws:** Left   **Ht:** 6'0"   **Wt:** 205   **Age:** 23

Yr Team	Lg	G	GS	IP	H	R	ER	HR	BB	SO	SV	W	L	Pct.	ERA
96 Frederick	A	33	0	62.0	77	45	39	7	22	75	3	2	6	.250	5.66
97 Bowie	AA	7	0	8.2	10	9	8	2	7	7	0	0	0	—	8.31
Delmarva	A	1	0	3.0	3	0	0	0	0	3	1	0	0	—	0.00
Frederick	A	31	0	67.0	48	19	18	4	38	98	5	3	3	.500	2.42
5 Minor League Yrs		132	17	339.1	339	197	154	25	139	367	13	10	22	.313	4.08

The Orioles are grooming Aruba native Radhames Dykhoff as a bullpen lefty, and he was excellent in that role at Frederick. His strikeout rate was outstanding at +67 percent, the third-best mark in the Carolina League. He didn't give up many hits, either, but his control could use some improvement, and he didn't fare well in Double-A. Dykoff has legitimate, though not overwhelming, velocity, and when his control is sharp, he is deadly against lefties. He will need to pitch well at higher levels, of course, to really get a chance at a bullpen job. **Grade C**

Adam Eaton — Philadelphia Phillies

Pos: P   **Throws:** Right   **Ht:** 6'2"   **Wt:** 180   **Age:** 20

Yr Team	Lg	G	GS	IP	H	R	ER	HR	BB	SO	SV	W	L	Pct.	ERA
97 Piedmont	A	14	14	71.1	81	38	33	2	30	57	0	5	6	.455	4.16
1 Minor League Yr		14	14	71.1	81	38	33	2	30	57	0	5	6	.455	4.16

Eaton was Philadelphia's first-round pick in 1996, from high school in Washington. He is the standard high school pitching product, and as such is intrinsically unpredictable. His performance in half a season at Piedmont doesn't tell us much of anything. Eaton has a 92-MPH fastball, and the makings of a curveball and changeup. He has problems keeping his mechanics consistent. With only a half season of pro ball under his belt, I don't have enough information to give Eaton a letter grade.

Derrin Ebert — Atlanta Braves

Pos: P   **Throws:** Left   **Ht:** 6'3"   **Wt:** 175   **Age:** 21

Yr Team	Lg	G	GS	IP	H	R	ER	HR	BB	SO	SV	W	L	Pct.	ERA
96 Durham	A	27	27	166.1	189	102	74	13	37	99	0	12	9	.571	4.00
97 Greenville	AA	27	25	175.2	191	95	80	24	48	101	0	11	8	.579	4.10
4 Minor League Yrs		92	87	567.0	604	302	235	53	139	349	0	38	25	.603	3.73

An 18th-round pick in 1994 from a California high school, Derrin Ebert held his own in his first Double-A campaign, and could see some major league action within the next year. Tall and thin, Ebert does not possess overpowering stuff. His fastball is just average, so he counts on a curveball, a cut fastball, and a changeup to attack hitters. He got off to a great start in the Southern League, with a 3.10 ERA through 10 starts, but he wore down as the season progressed. Only his K/BB ratio ended above league average. Scouts like his intelligence on the mound. If he stays healthy and picks up some additional strength, he could surprise. Please note that I didn't make any Roger Ebert jokes. **Grade C**

Angel Echevarria   *Colorado Rockies*

Pos: OF   **Bats:** Right   **Ht:** 6'4"   **Wt:** 215   **Age:** 26

Yr Team	Lg	G	AB	R	H	2B	3B	HR	RBI	BB	SO	SB	CS	Avg	OBP	Slg
96 Colo Sprngs	AAA	110	415	67	140	19	2	16	74	38	81	4	3	.337	.393	.508
Colorado	NL	26	21	2	6	0	0	0	6	2	5	0	0	.286	.346	.286
97 Colo Sprngs	AAA	77	295	59	95	24	0	13	80	28	47	6	2	.322	.387	.536
Colorado	NL	15	20	4	5	2	0	0	0	2	5	0	0	.250	.318	.350
6 Minor League Yrs		580	2123	326	624	107	7	75	403	209	420	36	20	.294	.362	.457

To some extent, his statistics are a creation of park/league factors, but Angel Echevarria's home/road splits are not extreme, and he does well enough against lefthanded pitching (.371 last year) that I would not hesitate to use him as a platoon outfielder in the majors. Heck, I would use him as a regular if I had to, especially if I were the Rockies. Echevarria is a legitimate .280 hitter, which in Coors Field means he could hit .340. Defensively, he is more than adequate in right field or left field. Of course, he doesn't have the "veteran leadership qualities" of a Dante Bichette or an Ellis Burks or an Otis Nixon or a Ted Uhlaender, so it is hard for him to get a job. **Grade C+**

Geoff Edsell   *Anaheim Angels*

Pos: P   **Throws:** Right   **Ht:** 6'2"   **Wt:** 195   **Age:** 26

Yr Team	Lg	G	GS	IP	H	R	ER	HR	BB	SO	SV	W	L	Pct.	ERA
96 Midland	AA	14	14	88.0	84	53	46	10	47	60	0	5	5	.500	4.70
Vancouver	AAA	15	15	105.0	93	45	40	7	45	48	0	4	6	.400	3.43
97 Vancouver	AAA	30	29	183.1	196	121	105	11	96	95	0	14	11	.560	5.15
5 Minor League Yrs		126	122	777.1	750	453	378	67	400	529	0	50	47	.515	4.38

You may find this hard to believe, but Geoff Edsell's 5.15 ERA was actually good by 1997 Pacific Coast League standards. There was only one pitcher among qualifiers with an ERA less than 4.00, Edwin Hurtado of Tacoma, and only eight pitchers with ERAs less than 5.00. Edsell, at 5.15, ranked 11th, and he was second in the league in wins. Edsell has a major league arm, but as his poor K/BB ratio shows, he nibbles too much. Durability is his main strength; his arm was not abused as an amateur, and he never gets hurt. Given continued good health, there is a decent chance that Edsell could figure something out and develop into a successful pitcher, but a change of scenery may be needed. His name would be a boon to headline writers. **Grade C-**

Scott Elarton

Houston Astros

Pos: P **Throws:** Right **Ht:** 6'8" **Wt:** 225 **Age:** 22

Yr Team	Lg	G	GS	IP	H	R	ER	HR	BB	SO	SV	W	L	Pct.	ERA
96 Kissimmee	A	27	27	172.1	154	67	56	13	54	130	0	12	7	.632	2.92
97 Jackson	AA	20	20	133.1	103	57	48	6	47	141	0	7	4	.636	3.24
New Orleans	AAA	9	9	54.0	51	36	32	5	17	50	0	4	4	.500	5.33
4 Minor League Yrs		96	96	592.0	508	269	230	40	212	503	0	44	23	.657	3.50

Elarton threw very hard in high school, but when he got into pro ball after signing as a sandwich pick in 1994, his velocity dropped off. He wasn't injured, so this was a bit of a puzzle. This type of thing can happen to tall, young pitchers who are trying to straighten their mechanics out. Last year the fastball came back, resulting in a great season. In addition to the heater, Elarton has a curve, a slider, and a changeup. The slider is the best of the group, and although the others need some work, they are promising. He has amazingly good control for such a tall pitcher, and is intelligent and increasingly aggressive. Elarton's ratios were terrific across the board: K/BB +70 percent, K/IP +42 percent, H/IP +16 percent. All these numbers were at or near the top of the Texas League. Elarton may need a year of Triple-A to refine his curve and change, but if he stays healthy, he could be an ace. **Grade A-**

Juan Encarnacion

Detroit Tigers

Pos: OF **Bats:** Right **Ht:** 6'2" **Wt:** 160 **Age:** 22

Yr Team	Lg	G	AB	R	H	2B	3B	HR	RBI	BB	SO	SB	CS	Avg	OBP	Slg
96 Lakeland	A	131	499	54	120	31	2	15	58	24	104	11	5	.240	.290	.401
97 Jacksnville	AA	131	493	91	159	31	4	26	90	43	86	17	3	.323	.394	.560
Detroit	AL	11	33	3	7	1	1	1	5	3	12	3	1	.212	.316	.394
4 Minor League Yrs		467	1735	230	475	101	15	62	255	118	396	43	17	.274	.334	.456

Juan Encarnacion has always interested scouts due to his wondrous physical tools, but he suddenly developed the skills that make those tools meaningful in 1997. The key, as it usually is when a young player makes dramatic improvement, was improved strike-zone judgment. He cut his strikeout rate and raised his walk rate dramatically, resulting in a higher average, more power production, and an all-around terrific season. His OPS was +23 percent, not quite in Ben Grieve territory, but damn good. His defense in right field is excellent, and he has one of the strongest arms in baseball. Some people project him as a starting outfielder as soon as 1998. Will this happen? Maybe, and maybe not. There are two paths that Encarnacion's career could take from this point. One is the Vladimir Guerrero path. The other is the Edgard Velazquez path. If Encarnacion maintains command of the strike zone, he will be similar to Vladimir Guerrero as a player, and will do well in the majors immediately. If Encarnacion loses command of the strike zone, he will be like Edgard Velazquez: immensely talented, but treading water in Triple-A. Which is more likely? You decide, but just be aware that while Encarnacion is a fine, fine prospect, he does come with a warning label. **Grade B+**

Mario Encarnacion   Oakland Athletics

Pos: OF   **Bats**: Right   **Ht**: 6'2"   **Wt**: 187   **Age**: 20

Yr Team	Lg	G	AB	R	H	2B	3B	HR	RBI	BB	SO	SB	CS	Avg	OBP	Slg
96 W Michigan	A	118	401	55	92	14	3	7	43	49	131	23	8	.229	.321	.332
97 Modesto	A	111	364	70	108	17	9	18	78	42	121	14	11	.297	.378	.541
2 Minor League Yrs		229	765	125	200	31	12	25	121	91	252	37	19	.261	.348	.431

The Athletics have really upgraded their Latin American scouting over the last six or seven years; Mario Encarnacion, signed out of the Dominican Republic in 1994, looks like another prodigy. Two things to draw your attention to: his birthday, September 24, 1977, and the dramatic improvement in his numbers between 1996 and 1997. He is strong and fast, and is making progress turning that into production. Command of the strike zone remains a weakness, and he is the sort of player who could regress if rushed too quickly, but he didn't do anything wrong at Modesto. His OPS was excellent at +21 percent. Encarnacion has the tools to be a good defensive outfielder, but he isn't yet. He makes too many silly mistakes and needs assistance learning to read fly balls. He is young enough to develop into a superstar, but he has work to do. **Grade B+**

Todd Erdos   Arizona Diamondbacks

Pos: P   **Throws**: Right   **Ht**: 6'1"   **Wt**: 205   **Age**: 24

Yr Team	Lg	G	GS	IP	H	R	ER	HR	BB	SO	SV	W	L	Pct.	ERA
96 Rancho Cuca	A	55	0	67.1	63	33	28	2	37	82	17	3	3	.500	3.74
97 Mobile	AA	55	0	59.0	45	22	22	4	22	49	27	1	4	.200	3.36
San Diego	NL	11	0	13.2	17	9	8	1	4	13	0	2	0	1.000	5.27
5 Minor League Yrs		189	38	384.0	333	202	167	30	204	347	45	19	29	.396	3.91

Todd Erdos recovered in 1996 from thyroid and pituitary problems that nearly killed him and ruined the early portion of his career, and continued pitching well in 1997, spending the season as the Double-A closer. He has a 90-MPH fastball and a good curve; he isn't particularly overpowering, but he knows what he is doing, and he is steady and reliable when his command is on, which it usually is. Erdos does not project as a major league closer, but should make a fine addition to the Diamondbacks bullpen. **Grade C+**

Josue Espada   Oakland Athletics

Pos: SS   **Bats**: Right   **Ht**: 5'10"   **Wt**: 175   **Age**: 22

Yr Team	Lg	G	AB	R	H	2B	3B	HR	RBI	BB	SO	SB	CS	Avg	OBP	Slg
96 Sou. Oregon	A	15	54	7	12	1	0	1	5	5	10	0	0	.222	.300	.296
W Michigan	A	23	74	9	20	2	0	0	4	13	11	3	1	.270	.393	.297
97 Visalia	A	118	445	90	122	7	3	3	39	72	69	46	17	.274	.384	.324
2 Minor League Yrs		156	573	106	154	10	3	4	48	90	90	49	18	.269	.378	.318

Espada is ignored in the Oakland shortstop pecking order behind Miguel Tejada and Jose Ortiz, but he is a prospect in his own right. He is older than both Tejada and Ortiz, but that is an unfair comparison, as Espada isn't old as most prospects go. He has no punch at the plate, but he draws a lot of walks and can use his speed on the bases. Defensively, he has good range and a strong arm, but needs to cut down on the errors. At this point, he has no chance to advance in the Oakland system, but if he can pick up some strength at the plate and cut down on the fielding miscues, he could have a career. **Grade C**

Bobby Estalella   *Philadelphia Phillies*

Pos: C   **Bats:** Right   **Ht:** 6'1"   **Wt:** 200   **Age:** 23

Yr Team	Lg	G	AB	R	H	2B	3B	HR	RBI	BB	SO	SB	CS	Avg	OBP	Slg
96 Reading	AA	111	365	48	89	14	2	23	72	67	104	2	4	.244	.365	.482
Scranton-WB	AAA	11	36	7	9	3	0	3	8	5	10	0	0	.250	.341	.583
Philadelphia	NL	7	17	5	6	0	0	2	4	1	6	1	0	.353	.389	.706
97 Scranton-WB	AAA	123	433	63	101	32	0	16	65	56	109	3	0	.233	.332	.418
Philadelphia	NL	13	29	9	10	1	0	4	9	7	7	0	0	.345	.472	.793
5 Minor League Yrs		517	1774	239	433	105	4	73	285	238	435	5	9	.244	.338	.431

A 23rd-round draft pick in 1992 from a Florida high school, Bobby Estalella may start for the Phillies in 1998, especially considering how well he performed in his major league trial. Estalella will not be a .300 hitter over a full season; indeed, he is likely to hover around .250. What he does bring to the plate is excellent power to all fields. He could use more patience and is sometimes overly power-conscious, which inhibits his ability to hit for average. He should be good for 20-plus homers annually, however. Estalella has a good defensive reputation. He threw out 31 percent of runners in the International League, below the league average of 34 percent, but scouts say he has a strong arm. He calls a good game behind the plate, and has a solid work ethic. Overall, Estalella should be a solid offensive and defensive performer in the major leagues. At best, he will be a righthanded Darren Daulton. **Grade B**

Horacio Estrada   *Milwaukee Brewers*

Pos: P   **Throws:** Left   **Ht:** 6'1"   **Wt:** 185   **Age:** 22

Yr Team	Lg	G	GS	IP	H	R	ER	HR	BB	SO	SV	W	L	Pct.	ERA
96 Beloit	A	17	0	29.1	21	8	4	2	11	34	1	2	1	.667	1.23
Stockton	A	29	0	51.0	43	29	26	7	21	62	3	1	3	.250	4.59
97 El Paso	AA	29	23	153.2	174	93	81	11	70	127	1	8	10	.444	4.74
4 Minor League Yrs		108	28	312.0	318	197	170	26	153	290	7	12	21	.364	4.90

A Venezuelan lefty signed way back in 1992, Horacio Estrada spent most of his career in middle relief, but converted to the rotation in 1997 and held his own in the difficult Texas League. None of Estrada's pitches are extremely wonderful, but he can spot his fastball, and his curve and slider are tight when thrown well. His K/BB ratio was slightly better than league average, and his K/IP was actually very good at +15 percent. His ERA was not dreadful by Texas League standards. You will never see his name on prospect lists, but he could sneak in some major league action, and given the volatility of pitcher stocks, he could be a surprise. **Grade C**

Keith Evans
Montreal Expos
Pos: P **Throws:** Right **Ht:** 6'5" **Wt:** 200 **Age:** 22

Yr Team	Lg	G	GS	IP	H	R	ER	HR	BB	SO	SV	W	L	Pct.	ERA
97 Cape Fear	A	21	21	138.0	113	56	40	6	18	102	0	12	7	.632	2.61
Wst Plm Bch	A	7	7	43.2	42	23	21	4	11	20	0	2	4	.333	4.33
1 Minor League Yr		28	28	181.2	155	79	61	10	29	122	0	14	11	.560	3.02

Evans, a University of California product, was drafted in the eighth round in 1996. He doesn't throw hard, but his combination of command and control enabled him to dominate the inexperienced hitters of the South Atlantic League in 1997. His K/BB ratio was +140 percent, which isn't too bad, I would say. League managers named him Pitcher with the Best Control. Promoted to the Florida State League, Evans found the hitters less readily fooled, and his stats suffered. He could rebound, he could disappear. **Grade C-**

Tom Evans
Toronto Blue Jays
Pos: 3B **Bats:** Right **Ht:** 6'1" **Wt:** 180 **Age:** 23

Yr Team	Lg	G	AB	R	H	2B	3B	HR	RBI	BB	SO	SB	CS	Avg	OBP	Slg
96 Knoxville	AA	120	394	87	111	27	1	17	65	115	113	4	0	.282	.452	.485
97 Dunedin	A	15	42	8	11	2	0	2	4	11	10	0	0	.262	.448	.452
Syracuse	AAA	107	376	60	99	17	1	15	65	53	104	1	2	.263	.365	.434
Toronto	AL	12	38	7	11	2	0	1	2	2	10	0	1	.289	.341	.421
6 Minor League Yrs		638	2133	334	569	119	8	64	323	367	477	27	10	.267	.380	.420

Evans spent much of the spring recovering from shoulder surgery, but when he was finally healthy, he played well. A September audition in SkyDome was successful, and Evans has a good chance to start 1998 in Toronto. He will be a very fine player. Evans' best offensive skill is his ability to draw walks. He has good power, too, probably more than his 1997 numbers indicate, due to the injury. He projects as a .260-.280 hitter, with double-digit homer power and 70-90 walks. Evans is an excellent defensive player. He led the International League in fielding percentage *and* range factor, a rare and cherished combination. Optimistically, he could develop into a righthanded version of Graig Nettles, but even if he isn't *that* good, he will still be a valuable player. **Grade B**

Scott Eyre
Chicago White Sox
Pos: P **Throws:** Left **Ht:** 6'1" **Wt:** 160 **Age:** 25

Yr Team	Lg	G	GS	IP	H	R	ER	HR	BB	SO	SV	W	L	Pct.	ERA
96 Birmingham	AA	27	27	158.1	170	90	77	12	79	137	0	12	7	.632	4.38
97 Birmingham	AA	22	22	126.2	110	61	54	14	55	127	0	13	5	.722	3.84
Chicago	AL	11	11	60.2	62	36	34	11	31	36	0	4	4	.500	5.04
6 Minor League Yrs		118	116	648.1	590	318	262	45	281	663	0	51	28	.646	3.64

Eyre tore an elbow ligament and had Tommy John surgery in 1995, recovered with an adequate season in 1996, then pitched very well in 1997. His velocity is back to pre-injury levels: above-average fastball, good curve and changeup. Command was a problem at times his first year back, but he regained authority over his pitches in Double-A last year, posting an able K/BB ratio of +28 percent. He did alright in his major league exposure, although his mastery did fail him at times in the Show. That's not unusual the first time

around. Basically, I think Eyre can pitch, but he needs health and a patient manager.
Grade C+

Brian Falkenborg   *Baltimore Orioles*

Pos: P   **Throws:** Right   **Ht:** 6'6"   **Wt:** 187   **Age:** 20

Yr Team	Lg	G	GS	IP	H	R	ER	HR	BB	SO	SV	W	L	Pct.	ERA
96 Orioles	R	8	6	28.0	21	13	8	1	8	36	0	0	3	.000	2.57
High Desert	A	1	0	1.0	1	0	0	0	0	1	0	0	0	—	0.00
97 Bowie	AA	1	1	1.2	3	3	3	0	3	0	0	0	1	.000	16.20
Delmarva	A	25	25	127.0	122	73	63	6	46	107	0	7	9	.438	4.46
2 Minor League Yrs		35	32	157.2	147	89	74	7	57	144	0	7	13	.350	4.22

Falkenborg was Baltimore's first pick in 1996, a second-rounder from high school in Washington. He is very tall, very lanky, and very projectable. His fastball is average right now, but given his height, and the fact that his mechanics are already pretty good, scouts expect his velocity to increase substantially. He will use a curveball and changeup, but both are inconsistent at this stage. Falkenborg is astute and has what it takes between the ears to be a sound pitcher. His stats at Delmarva weren't tremendous, but hot numbers aren't what the Orioles are looking for right now. They want him to get innings in, build arm strength, and refine his breaking stuff. From that perspective, he is doing fine, but he must stay healthy, and I would like to see improvement in his numbers soon. **Grade C+**

Carlos Febles   *Kansas City Royals*

Pos: 2B   **Bats:** Right   **Ht:** 5'11"   **Wt:** 165   **Age:** 21

Yr Team	Lg	G	AB	R	H	2B	3B	HR	RBI	BB	SO	SB	CS	Avg	OBP	Slg
96 Lansing	A	102	363	84	107	23	5	5	43	66	64	30	14	.295	.414	.427
97 Wilmington	A	122	438	78	104	27	6	3	29	51	95	49	11	.237	.333	.347
3 Minor League Yrs		278	989	202	264	63	16	11	92	143	189	95	33	.267	.373	.396

I noticed Carlos Febles after his fine 1996 season at Lansing; I liked his patience at the plate, his speed and his range around the bag at second. He moved up to Wilmington in 1997, and while he continued to steal bases and flash the leather, his batting average dropped off substantially. Wilmington is a rotten place to hit, however, and I think his bat will be OK in the long run. Febles led the league in errors at second base, but his range factor remains very high, and he can turn the double play very well. I'm not as enthusiastic about him as I was a year ago, but I still believe he will be a good player. **Grade B-**

Pedro Felix   *San Francisco Giants*

Pos: 3B   **Bats:** Right   **Ht:** 6'1"   **Wt:** 180   **Age:** 20

Yr Team	Lg	G	AB	R	H	2B	3B	HR	RBI	BB	SO	SB	CS	Avg	OBP	Slg
96 Burlington	A	93	321	36	85	12	2	5	36	18	65	5	2	.265	.303	.361
97 Bakersfield	A	135	515	59	140	25	4	14	56	23	90	5	7	.272	.310	.417
4 Minor League Yrs		309	1068	116	279	39	7	19	111	50	208	13	13	.261	.298	.364

Signed out of the Dominican Republic in 1994, Pedro Felix has attracted little notice as a prospect, but he is quite young and showed some ability in the California League last year. His command of the strike zone is weak, as it is for many young Latin players, but he has bat speed and projects power. Bakersfield is a great home run park, so the 14 homers is not an impressive total; his power remains largely untapped. Defense is another matter. Felix led Cal League third basemen in both fielding percentage and range factor, so he can obviously pick it at the hot corner. I want to see more offensive development, but I like his potential, and I think he could be quite a surprise in the next year or so, especially if he improves his strike-zone discernment. **Grade C+**

Jose Fernandez   *Montreal Expos*

Pos: 3B   **Bats:** Right   **Ht:** 6'2"   **Wt:** 210   **Age:** 23

Yr Team	Lg	G	AB	R	H	2B	3B	HR	RBI	BB	SO	SB	CS	Avg	OBP	Slg
96 Delmarva	A	126	421	72	115	23	6	12	70	50	76	23	13	.273	.358	.442
97 Wst Plm Bch	A	97	350	49	108	21	3	9	58	37	76	22	14	.309	.386	.463
Harrisburg	AA	29	96	10	22	3	1	4	11	11	28	2	0	.229	.315	.406
4 Minor League Yrs		362	1305	196	358	61	17	34	203	124	264	87	32	.274	.344	.425

Montreal signed Fernandez out of the Dominican in 1993. He looks like a power hitter, but his line-drive swing doesn't produce great force. He does make contact, and his command of the strike zone isn't dreadful. He runs well for a big guy. In the Florida State League, his OPS was well above average at +16 percent, and his SEC was also pleasant at +28 percent. Fernandez is adept with the glove, posting the highest range factor among FSL regulars, without committing exorbitant amounts of errors. He will have trouble attracting attention unless his power production picks up, but I think it might. **Grade B-**

Robert Fick   *Detroit Tigers*

Pos: 1B   **Bats:** Left   **Ht:** 6'1"   **Wt:** 195   **Age:** 24

Yr Team	Lg	G	AB	R	H	2B	3B	HR	RBI	BB	SO	SB	CS	Avg	OBP	Slg
96 Jamestown	A	43	133	18	33	6	0	1	14	12	25	3	1	.248	.306	.316
97 W Michigan	A	122	463	100	158	50	3	16	90	75	74	13	4	.341	.429	.566
2 Minor League Yrs		165	596	118	191	56	3	17	104	87	99	16	5	.320	.403	.510

Robert Fick had an awesome 1996 season for Cal State Northridge, hitting .420 with 25 homers, but many scouts scoffed, saying his numbers were a result of aluminum. It looked like they might be right after he struggled in the New York-Penn League, but in 1997 he adjusted to the wood bat, and had a monster season for West Michigan. Moving from catcher to first base helped him concentrate on hitting. There simply aren't any holes in his numbers: .341 average, minor league-leading 50 doubles, 16 homers, 75 walks, OPS +38 percent, SEC +58 percent, 32-game hitting streak. . . in an extreme pitcher's park, no less. He looks like he should also be a good defensive player at first base, given time. My friend Terry Linhart saw him play last year and was very impressed by his poise on the field. Fick was a bit older than most of his competition, and for that reason he is not a top-echelon prospect. . . yet. If I were the Tigers, I would promote him to Double-A in 1998. He has nothing left to learn in A-ball. **Grade B**

Luis Figueroa

Seattle Mariners

Pos: 3B **Bats:** Right **Ht:** 5'11" **Wt:** 177 **Age:** 21

Yr Team	Lg	G	AB	R	H	2B	3B	HR	RBI	BB	SO	SB	CS	Avg	OBP	Slg
96 Lancaster	A	9	31	5	12	4	1	0	6	2	6	0	1	.387	.424	.581
Everett	A	4	13	4	6	1	1	0	3	2	1	0	0	.462	.533	.692
Wisconsin	A	36	137	18	40	9	0	2	19	6	14	1	1	.292	.331	.401
97 Wisconsin	A	125	482	56	138	27	2	3	60	33	21	3	3	.286	.339	.369
3 Minor League Yrs		206	783	97	231	43	4	5	99	55	51	5	7	.295	.348	.379

A Puerto Rican signed as an undrafted free agent in 1995, Luis Figueroa has a steady line-drive swing and makes excellent contact at the plate. His overall production was nothing unique at Wisconsin last year, but his ability to put wood on the ball at a young age is promising. He needs to get stronger, but he may develop into a .300 hitter in time. That's his only hope; his defense at third base is barely ordinary, so he has to hit to advance. **Grade C-**

Nelson Figueroa

New York Mets

Pos: P **Throws:** Right **Ht:** 6'1" **Wt:** 165 **Age:** 23

Yr Team	Lg	G	GS	IP	H	R	ER	HR	BB	SO	SV	W	L	Pct.	ERA
96 Capital City	A	26	25	185.1	119	55	42	10	58	200	0	14	7	.667	2.04
97 Binghamton	AA	33	22	143.0	137	76	69	14	68	116	0	5	11	.313	4.34
3 Minor League Yrs		71	59	404.2	313	162	137	27	148	395	0	26	21	.553	3.05

Figueroa was awesome in the South Atlantic League in 1996, but as a finesse pitcher he faced a tough transition to Double-A in 1997. His season for Binghamton wasn't terrible, but didn't meet the standards he established in the low minors. His control remained very good, but his strikeout rate dropped precipitously, resulting in a weak K/BB ratio of -10 percent. Figueroa's fastball averages 84 MPH. His split-finger, curve, and change are all good pitches, but his command has to be perfect for them to work, since his fastball is assailable by nearly all hitters. I think Figueroa actually has a chance to succeed in the long run, since he is quite intelligent and has a strong competitive streak, but he will need adjustment time at each level, especially the majors. **Grade C**

Ben Fleetham

Montreal Expos

Pos: P **Throws:** Right **Ht:** 6'1" **Wt:** 205 **Age:** 25

Yr Team	Lg	G	GS	IP	H	R	ER	HR	BB	SO	SV	W	L	Pct.	ERA
96 Delmarva	A	16	0	19.2	9	4	3	2	7	34	13	1	0	1.000	1.37
Wst Plm Bch	A	31	0	30.2	15	8	7	0	15	48	17	0	1	.000	2.05
Harrisburg	AA	4	0	6.0	2	0	0	0	5	6	1	0	0	—	0.00
97 Ottawa	AAA	9	0	9.0	2	3	2	1	10	14	1	1	2	.333	2.00
Harrisburg	AA	49	0	50.1	28	21	17	4	33	69	30	2	1	.667	3.04
4 Minor League Yrs		136	0	162.2	87	53	40	8	92	229	65	5	4	.556	2.21

Fleetham was a 36th-round pick in 1994, from Rollins College. The Expos asked him to participate in the replacement-player fiasco of 1995. Fleetham refused, then found himself assigned to the lowest level of the Expos system. Angered, he left the organization, played a few innings in an independent league, then sat out the rest of the campaign. Needless to say, the Expos weren't thrilled. They could have blackballed him, but instead they smoothed things over and Fleetham returned to the fold. Two good seasons later, he is a middle-relief candidate. Fleetham's fastball hits 90 MPH, his breaking pitch is adequate, and he is a tough customer when his command is on. **Grade C**

Ignacio Flores   *Los Angeles Dodgers*

Pos: P   Throws: Right   Ht: 6'2"   Wt: 188   Age: 22

Yr Team	Lg	G	GS	IP	H	R	ER	HR	BB	SO	SV	W	L	Pct.	ERA
97 San Antonio	AA	27	18	133.0	125	59	48	5	39	102	1	10	7	.588	3.25
2 Minor League Yrs		43	30	201.2	191	101	84	8	77	178	1	16	11	.593	3.75

The Dodgers signed Mexican righthander Ignacio Flores in 1995. He pitched in the Pioneer League that year, then spent 1996 on loan with Saltillo in the Mexican League, where he was not particularly effective (5-10, 5.09, 108 walks in 141 innings). The Dodgers brought him back to the U.S. in 1997, and he had a good year for San Antonio. His K/BB was particularly impressive at +49 percent, and was a dramatic improvement over his poor numbers in Mexico. Flores' stuff is not outstanding, but is effective enough to get big-league hitters out, when his control is sharp. If he keeps the command he showed in Double-A last year, he could be a surprise in 1998. **Grade C+**

Joe Fontenot   *Florida Marlins*

Pos: P   Throws: Right   Ht: 6'2"   Wt: 185   Age: 21

Yr Team	Lg	G	GS	IP	H	R	ER	HR	BB	SO	SV	W	L	Pct.	ERA
96 San Jose	A	26	23	144.0	137	87	71	7	74	124	0	9	4	.692	4.44
97 Shreveport	AA	26	26	151.1	171	105	93	12	65	103	0	10	11	.476	5.53
3 Minor League Yrs		58	55	314.0	322	197	168	19	149	241	0	19	18	.514	4.82

Fontenot was selected in the first round out of a Louisiana high school by the Giants in 1995. He was very young to be in Double-A in 1997, and it shows in his numbers. Fontenot has excellent stuff, but he doesn't know how to use it consistently. His fastball hits 93 MPH with ease, and his curveball is amazingly good for such a young pitcher. His changeup is erratic, and while he generally throws strikes, command of his pitches within the strike zone is a serious problem. He gave up a lot of hits for a pitcher with great stuff: his H/IP was very bad at -15 percent. Scouts say his mechanics are inconsistent. Fontenot certainly has the talent to be a fine pitcher, but isn't ready yet. He will probably repeat Double-A, and could do much better with a year under his belt. . . provided he stays healthy, of course. The Giants sent him to the Marlins in the Nen deal. **Grade B-**

Tom Fordham
Chicago White Sox

Pos: P **Throws:** Left **Ht:** 6'2" **Wt:** 210 **Age:** 24

Yr	Team	Lg	G	GS	IP	H	R	ER	HR	BB	SO	SV	W	L	Pct.	ERA
96	Birmingham	AA	6	6	37.1	26	13	11	4	14	37	0	2	1	.667	2.65
	Nashville	AAA	22	22	140.2	117	60	54	15	69	118	0	10	8	.556	3.45
97	Nashville	AAA	21	20	114.0	113	64	60	14	53	90	0	6	7	.462	4.74
	Chicago	AL	7	1	17.1	17	13	12	2	10	10	0	0	1	.000	6.23
	5 Minor League Yrs		117	111	706.0	632	309	272	66	270	597	0	52	32	.619	3.47

I wrote last year that Tom Fordham had had a cancerous tumor removed from his arm. Let me state clearly that *this did not occur*. Tom Fordham *never* had a tumor in his arm, or anywhere else for that matter. The source of my report was an erroneous magazine article, the retraction of which I missed; an inexcusable mistake on my part. My apologies to Tom; the responsibility for the error was mine. Anyhow, false arm tumors aside, Fordham struggled at Nashville, after being considered for the White Sox staff in spring training. He still has good stuff for a lefty: 89-MPH fastball, reliable curve. As long as he stays healthy, I think Fordham is a good bet to rebound. **Grade C**

Jim Foster
Baltimore Orioles

Pos: C **Bats:** Right **Ht:** 6'4" **Wt:** 220 **Age:** 26

Yr	Team	Lg	G	AB	R	H	2B	3B	HR	RBI	BB	SO	SB	CS	Avg	OBP	Slg
96	Frederick	A	82	278	35	70	20	2	7	42	39	32	6	3	.252	.349	.414
	Bowie	AA	9	33	7	10	0	1	2	9	7	6	0	0	.303	.415	.545
97	Rochester	AAA	3	9	4	5	2	0	0	4	3	0	0	1	.556	.667	.778
	Frederick	A	61	200	48	70	12	1	16	65	45	28	8	0	.350	.478	.660
	Bowie	AA	63	211	36	58	12	0	7	41	36	31	1	1	.275	.380	.431
	5 Minor League Yrs		528	1799	294	508	123	11	56	318	277	253	25	12	.282	.384	.456

Foster was a 22nd-round pick in 1993, out of Providence College. His career has been slowed by injuries, inconsistency, and a backlog of catchers in the Baltimore system, but he whaled the Hades out of the ball at Frederick (OPS +57 percent, the best mark in the league), and wasn't bad at Bowie. He has patience at the plate, and some power, although not as much as one would expect from a man his size. Defensively, he is pretty good. Foster moves around well for a big guy, and controls the running game adequately. He isn't young, but if I had a team, I would be willing to take a look at him as a backup or platoon catcher. **Grade C**

Keith Foulke

Chicago White Sox

Pos: P Throws: Right Ht: 6'1" Wt: 195 Age: 25

Yr Team	Lg	G	GS	IP	H	R	ER	HR	BB	SO	SV	W	L	Pct.	ERA
96 Shreveport	AA	27	27	182.2	149	61	56	16	35	129	0	12	7	.632	2.76
97 Phoenix	AAA	12	12	76.0	79	38	38	11	15	54	0	5	4	.556	4.50
Nashville	AAA	1	1	4.2	8	3	3	1	0	4	0	0	0	—	5.79
San Francisco	NL	11	8	44.2	60	41	41	9	18	33	0	1	5	.167	8.26
Chicago	AL	16	0	28.2	28	11	11	4	5	21	3	3	0	1.000	3.45
4 Minor League Yrs		72	70	460.0	419	191	168	44	85	377	0	32	17	.653	3.29

Keith Foulke was the only one of the six players the White Sox received in the big trade with the Giants who was ready for the majors. A starter in the minors, Foulke pitched in relief for the Sox and did well. The phrases "wise move" and "Terry Bevington" seldom belong in the same sentence, but it was a good idea to start Foulke off in the pen. Finesse pitchers often take extra time to get their bearings in the majors. Observing Earl Weaver's dictum about keeping young pitchers in the bullpen is rare nowadays, although I doubt Bevington did it for that reason. He probably just thought Foulke didn't have enough of a fastball to start. Of course, lack of a fastball didn't keep the inert corpse of Doug Drabek off the mound. . . well, never mind. Foulke relies on a mediocre fastball, a good curve, a great changeup, and pinpoint control to get hitters out. It worked in the Pacific Coast League, which means it will probably work in the majors eventually, if he stays healthy and keeps his confidence. **Grade B**

Micah Franklin

St. Louis Cardinals

Pos: OF Bats: Both Ht: 6'0" Wt: 195 Age: 25

Yr Team	Lg	G	AB	R	H	2B	3B	HR	RBI	BB	SO	SB	CS	Avg	OBP	Slg
96 Toledo	AAA	53	179	32	44	10	1	7	21	27	60	3	2	.246	.354	.430
Louisville	AAA	86	289	43	67	18	3	15	53	40	71	2	3	.232	.338	.471
97 Louisville	AAA	99	326	49	72	14	1	12	48	51	74	2	0	.221	.329	.380
St. Louis	NL	17	34	6	11	0	0	2	2	3	10	0	0	.324	.378	.500
8 Minor League Yrs		770	2649	476	705	139	16	126	458	389	719	63	38	.266	.372	.473

To tell you the truth, I was surprised when the Cardinals called up Micah Franklin last year. He's not their type of player. Franklin is a slow, switch-hitting outfielder with power and patience, but a low batting average. Despite what he did with the Cardinals last year, he would struggle to hit .250 in a full season in the majors. On the other hand, he could very well hit 25 homers, and draw 80 walks. His defense in the outfield isn't impressive, so the power production is all he has. He will go through streaks where he does nothing at the plate for several days at a time, but he will also have significant power tears. Whether or not he holds a job depends more on how much his manager is willing to wait through the rough spots than anything else. **Grade C**

Ryan Franklin
Seattle Mariners

Pos: P Throws: Right Ht: 6'3" Wt: 160 Age: 25

Yr Team	Lg	G	GS	IP	H	R	ER	HR	BB	SO	SV	W	L	Pct.	ERA
96 Port City	AA	28	27	182.0	186	99	81	23	37	127	0	6	12	.333	4.01
97 Memphis	AA	11	8	59.1	45	22	20	4	14	49	0	4	2	.667	3.03
Tacoma	AAA	14	14	90.1	97	48	42	11	24	59	0	5	5	.500	4.18
5 Minor League Yrs		126	110	737.0	728	383	304	66	177	531	0	39	40	.494	3.71

Franklin was drafted in the 23rd round in 1992, from Seminole Junior College in Oklahoma. He doesn't throw very hard, but his breaking pitches are effective when mixed well with the fastball. Franklin stalled in Double-A for a couple of years, with uninspired performances, but good K/BB ratios. He got off to a hot start in 1997, then was promoted to Triple-A, where he spent some time on the disabled list with a minor shoulder ailment, but finished the season healthy, and was reasonably successful considering league context. Franklin is the typical **Grade C** prospect. He might turn into a good pitcher, or he might spend the next 10 years as a journeyman in the high minors.

Mike Freehill
Anaheim Angels

Pos: P Throws: Right Ht: 6'3" Wt: 177 Age: 26

Yr Team	Lg	G	GS	IP	H	R	ER	HR	BB	SO	SV	W	L	Pct.	ERA
96 Vancouver	AAA	7	0	10.0	16	11	11	1	8	5	0	1	1	.500	9.90
Midland	AA	47	0	50.0	49	25	19	4	21	48	17	7	6	.538	3.42
97 Midland	AA	35	0	37.0	46	33	29	4	20	32	10	0	7	.000	7.05
Lk Elsinore	A	21	0	22.2	18	7	5	1	8	20	8	0	1	.000	1.99
4 Minor League Yrs		192	0	219.2	220	121	96	16	79	190	71	15	26	.366	3.93

Freehill opened 1997 as Midland's closer and was, in a word, terrible. He was demoted to Lake Elsinore and salvaged his season, but he has a lot to prove in 1998. Freehill, drafted in the 15th round in 1994 from San Diego State, has a low-90s fastball and a sharp slider. His mechanics are awkward, and he sometimes has trouble throwing strikes. If he has a major league future, it is as a middle reliever. **Grade C-**

Ryan Freel
Toronto Blue Jays

Pos: SS Bats: Right Ht: 5'10" Wt: 175 Age: 22

Yr Team	Lg	G	AB	R	H	2B	3B	HR	RBI	BB	SO	SB	CS	Avg	OBP	Slg
96 Dunedin	A	104	381	64	97	23	3	4	41	33	76	19	15	.255	.321	.362
97 Knoxville	AA	33	94	18	19	1	1	0	4	19	13	5	3	.202	.348	.234
Dunedin	A	61	181	42	51	8	2	3	17	46	28	24	5	.282	.447	.398
3 Minor League Yrs		263	899	154	235	42	11	10	91	120	166	60	30	.261	.360	.366

Freel was drafted in the 10th round in 1995, from Tallahassee Community College in Florida. His exceptionally good walk rate caught my attention last year. He is very fast, and the combination of wheels and patience is intriguing. He was a second baseman in college, but the Jays are trying him at shortstop, but he doesn't really have the range for the position, and he makes too many errors. Freel is just a name for now. **Grade C-**

Alejandro Freire
Detroit Tigers

Pos: 1B **Bats:** Right **Ht:** 6'1" **Wt:** 170 **Age:** 23

Yr Team	Lg	G	AB	R	H	2B	3B	HR	RBI	BB	SO	SB	CS	Avg	OBP	Slg
96 Kissimmee	A	115	384	40	98	24	1	12	42	24	66	11	7	.255	.309	.417
97 Lakeland	A	130	477	85	154	30	2	24	92	50	84	13	4	.323	.396	.545
4 Minor League Yrs		399	1361	204	404	81	4	52	212	129	250	38	17	.297	.365	.477

Freire came to the Detroit system as an afterthought in the nine-player trade with Houston last winter. He had some offensive ability, but his defense in the outfield was shaky at best, and scouts didn't like his funky swing. The Tigers moved Freire to first base, and he proceeded to destroy Florida State League pitching, no easy task. His home park at Lakeland is one of the better hitting parks in the circuit, and he was a league repeater, but it was still an excellent season. His OPS was +33 percent. Freire will need to prove that he can do the same at higher levels, and I'm not exactly sure where he fits in Detroit's long-term plans, but I am reasonably confident he will continue to hit. **Grade B-**

Joe Freitas
St. Louis Cardinals

Pos: OF **Bats:** Right **Ht:** 6'3" **Wt:** 195 **Age:** 24

Yr Team	Lg	G	AB	R	H	2B	3B	HR	RBI	BB	SO	SB	CS	Avg	OBP	Slg
96 New Jersey	A	45	163	29	56	10	3	4	37	25	35	0	1	.344	.418	.515
97 Peoria	A	122	436	78	109	16	1	33	86	58	148	6	1	.250	.345	.518
3 Minor League Yrs		181	646	115	174	32	4	37	132	88	201	8	2	.269	.359	.503

If you want power and nothing else, Joe Freitas is your man. A sixth-round pick in 1995 from Fresno State, Freitas is very strong and crushes mediocre fastballs, but is weak against breaking stuff and can be struck out by a sharp pitcher. He draws some walks, but his strikeout rate gives me pause along with his weak defensive skills and the fact that he was old for the Midwest League. He is worth keeping track of, but don't expect a whole lot unless he cuts his strikeouts, raises his walks more, or starts hitting for average at higher levels. **Grade C-**

Hanley Frias
Arizona Diamondbacks

Pos: SS **Bats:** Both **Ht:** 6'0" **Wt:** 160 **Age:** 24

Yr Team	Lg	G	AB	R	H	2B	3B	HR	RBI	BB	SO	SB	CS	Avg	OBP	Slg
96 Tulsa	AA	134	505	73	145	24	12	2	41	30	73	9	9	.287	.325	.394
97 Okla City	AAA	132	484	64	128	17	4	5	46	56	72	35	15	.264	.340	.347
Texas	AL	14	26	4	5	1	0	0	1	1	4	0	0	.192	.222	.231
6 Minor League Yrs		706	2599	372	688	111	35	14	252	254	421	158	74	.265	.330	.351

I have been hyping Hanley Frias as a prospect for two years now, and with Benji Gil finally proving that he can't distinguish between a slider and a sausage, I thought Frias might get a chance in Texas. Instead, he went to Arizona in expansion, where he will be behind Jay Bell. Frias makes contact from both sides of the plate and has adequate plate discipline and blazing speed on the bases. He needs to get stronger, but will never be a power threat. Frias is an excellent defensive shortstop, with great range, soft hands, and a strong arm. He makes spectacular plays look easy, but also botches his share of routine chances. He should get over that in time. Frias is not the kind of guy who will lead your team to a championship, but he won't hurt you if he has to play, and will be useful for Arizona. **Grade C+**

Brad Fullmer   *Montreal Expos*

Pos: 1B **Bats:** Left **Ht:** 6'1" **Wt:** 185 **Age:** 23

Yr Team	Lg	G	AB	R	H	2B	3B	HR	RBI	BB	SO	SB	CS	Avg	OBP	Slg
96 Wst Plm Bch	A	102	380	52	115	29	1	5	63	32	43	4	6	.303	.367	.424
Harrisburg	AA	24	98	11	27	4	1	4	14	3	8	0	0	.276	.311	.459
97 Harrisburg	AA	94	357	60	111	24	2	19	62	30	25	6	4	.311	.372	.549
Ottawa	AAA	24	91	13	27	7	0	3	17	3	10	1	1	.297	.317	.473
Montreal	NL	19	40	4	12	2	0	3	8	2	7	0	0	.300	.349	.575
3 Minor League Yrs		367	1394	205	431	102	8	39	223	104	119	21	21	.309	.368	.478

Scouts have always known that Brad Fullmer could hit, ever since the Expos drafted him in the second round in 1993 from a California high school. The questions for him were health and defense. Shoulder problems dogged him early in his career, but Fullmer has been healthy for three years now. He started his career as a third baseman, but the arm problem and a tendency to make critical errors shifted him to the outfield. He wasn't good as a flycatcher, either, so rather than force the issue, the Expos moved him to first base for 1997. The results were excellent: he has continued to hit and looks like he will be fine defensively. Fullmer has astounding bat speed and a silk-smooth swing. He always hits for average, the power is developing, and while he doesn't walk that much, he seldom strikes out. His OPS was very good at +16 percent. Fullmer has the rare ability to combine high-average contact hitting with power. He will be a stalwart in the Expos' infield, perhaps as early as 1998. **Grade B+**

Joe Funaro   *Florida Marlins*

Pos: SS **Bats:** Right **Ht:** 5'9" **Wt:** 170 **Age:** 25

Yr Team	Lg	G	AB	R	H	2B	3B	HR	RBI	BB	SO	SB	CS	Avg	OBP	Slg
96 Kane County	A	89	291	57	90	20	2	7	43	40	42	5	3	.309	.401	.464
97 Brevard Cty	A	125	470	67	150	16	6	4	53	49	65	9	5	.319	.387	.404
3 Minor League Yrs		270	950	148	290	46	11	13	112	106	128	19	10	.305	.379	.418

Funaro, a 21st-round pick in 1995 from Eastern Connecticut State, is an organization player who has done well so far in A-ball. He is a contact hitter who doesn't drive the ball for power, but is smart enough not to try; he is content to hit the ball where it is pitched and hope for the best. So far, that has been good enough, although Double-A will prove a sterner test. Funaro is just adequate with the glove at shortstop, although it isn't for lack of effort. He isn't a real prospect, but if he hits in Double-A, he could get some Show time as an emergency reserve. **Grade C-**

Chris Fussell
Baltimore Orioles

Pos: P **Throws:** Right **Ht:** 6'2" **Wt:** 185 **Age:** 21

Yr Team	Lg	G	GS	IP	H	R	ER	HR	BB	SO	SV	W	L	Pct.	ERA
96 Frederick	A	15	14	86.1	71	36	27	8	44	94	0	5	2	.714	2.81
97 Bowie	AA	19	18	82.1	102	71	65	12	58	71	0	1	8	.111	7.11
Frederick	A	9	9	50.0	42	23	22	5	31	54	0	3	3	.500	3.96
4 Minor League Yrs		69	61	340.2	305	178	156	31	189	382	0	20	17	.541	4.12

Fussell emerged as a fine pitching prospect in 1996, but he pitched terribly at Bowie in 1997. He did better when demoted to Frederick, but it was still a lousy season. Fussell has one of the best arms in the Orioles system, with a 92-MPH fastball, a power curve, and a hopeful changeup. He can dominate a game when he throws strikes, but he didn't throw many strikes in the Eastern League. His stats were lousy no matter how you slice them, and even in the Carolina League, his control was subpar. Fussell had elbow trouble in 1996, and even though he stayed in the rotation all year in 1997, you have to wonder if there was a physical problem. If his command comes around, he could be good, but you can say that about a lot of guys. **Grade C**

Eddie Gaillard
Detroit Tigers

Pos: P **Throws:** Right **Ht:** 6'1" **Wt:** 180 **Age:** 27

Yr Team	Lg	G	GS	IP	H	R	ER	HR	BB	SO	SV	W	L	Pct.	ERA
96 Jacksnville	AA	56	0	88.0	82	40	33	8	50	76	1	9	6	.600	3.38
97 Toledo	AAA	55	0	53.0	52	27	25	7	24	54	28	1	4	.200	4.25
Detroit	AL	16	0	20.1	16	12	12	2	10	12	1	1	0	1.000	5.31
5 Minor League Yrs		206	23	372.1	354	158	134	27	150	289	56	24	20	.545	3.24

The Tigers selected Eddie Gaillard in the 13th round of the 1993 draft, from Florida Southern University. He has picked up size and strength from his college days, and now gets his fastball into the 92-94 MPH range consistently. He does not have a particularly good breaking pitch, but he generally throws strikes with the sinking heater, and is very aggressive. Gaillard is unlikely to make it as a closer unless he improves his breaking stuff, but he could be a good middle relief guy. **Grade C**

Shawn Gallagher
Texas Rangers

Pos: 1B **Bats:** Right **Ht:** 6'0" **Wt:** 187 **Age:** 21

Yr Team	Lg	G	AB	R	H	2B	3B	HR	RBI	BB	SO	SB	CS	Avg	OBP	Slg
96 Chston-SC	A	88	303	29	68	11	4	7	32	18	104	6	1	.224	.280	.356
Hudson Vall	A	44	176	15	48	10	2	4	29	7	48	8	5	.273	.306	.420
97 Charlotte	A	27	99	7	14	4	0	0	8	5	35	0	0	.141	.189	.182
Pulaski	R	50	199	41	64	13	3	15	52	10	49	2	0	.322	.359	.643
3 Minor League Yrs		272	1007	127	268	53	12	33	165	60	284	33	10	.266	.314	.441

Gallagher was an incredible high school hitter, hitting .591 with 19 homers his senior year at New Hanover High in Wilmington, North Carolina. He smashed five homers in a game and tied the national record with a 51-game hitting streak. He was not a consensus top talent, however, mainly due to his poor defensive skills, and the Rangers picked him up in the fifth round in 1995. His pro career is an instruction in the importance of plate discipline. Gallagher has bat speed, power, and good hitting mechanics. . . but he will swing at anything. As a result, he has struggled every time the Rangers have tried him in full-season ball. Will he ever come around? Chances are against it, unless he improves his strike-zone judgment. **Grade C-**

Amaury Garcia

Florida Marlins

Pos: 2B **Bats:** Right **Ht:** 5'10" **Wt:** 160 **Age:** 22

Yr Team	Lg	G	AB	R	H	2B	3B	HR	RBI	BB	SO	SB	CS	Avg	OBP	Slg
96 Kane County	A	105	391	65	103	19	7	6	36	62	83	37	19	.263	.370	.394
97 Brevard Cty	A	124	479	77	138	30	2	7	44	49	97	45	11	.288	.358	.403
4 Minor League Yrs		375	1367	247	383	69	16	14	127	196	291	138	47	.280	.376	.385

Garcia doesn't get much attention as a prospect, but the Dominican infielder is making progress. He is improving his baserunning skills, and while he will never be a big-time offensive performer, he gets on base enough to make his speed useful. His defense continues to gradually improve. He has good range and makes fewer errors each season. We need to see him hit in Double-A, but if he does well there, he should have a nice career. **Grade C+**

Apostol Garcia

Detroit Tigers

Pos: P **Throws:** Right **Ht:** 6'0" **Wt:** 155 **Age:** 21

Yr Team	Lg	G	GS	IP	H	R	ER	HR	BB	SO	SV	W	L	Pct.	ERA
97 W Michigan	A	33	5	65.2	48	26	22	2	31	52	1	7	2	.778	3.02
1 Minor League Yr		33	5	65.2	48	26	22	2	31	52	1	7	2	.778	3.02

A Dominican signed as a shortstop in 1994, Apostol Garcia hit .194 at Fayetteville in 1996, making it apparent that he would not hit. The Tigers decided to convert him to mound work in 1997, and he shows some promise. Garcia spent the year working out of the West Michigan bullpen, primarily in middle and long relief. He was clocked as high as 93 MPH, but needs to improve his command and his breaking stuff. **Grade C**

Freddy Garcia

Pittsburgh Pirates

Pos: 3B **Bats:** Right **Ht:** 6'2" **Wt:** 186 **Age:** 25

Yr Team	Lg	G	AB	R	H	2B	3B	HR	RBI	BB	SO	SB	CS	Avg	OBP	Slg
96 Lynchburg	A	129	474	79	145	39	3	21	86	44	86	4	2	.306	.358	.534
97 Calgary	AAA	35	121	21	29	6	0	5	17	9	20	0	0	.240	.293	.413
Carolina	AA	73	282	47	82	17	4	19	57	18	56	0	1	.291	.342	.582
Pittsburgh	NL	20	40	4	6	1	0	3	5	2	17	0	0	.150	.190	.400
4 Minor League Yrs		382	1401	240	393	80	11	69	242	135	290	9	11	.281	.343	.501

Freddy Garcia has excellent power, but his command of the strike zone is unsteady, and pitchers in the Pacific Coast League exploited his penchant for chasing breaking balls last year. He did hit very well at Double-A Carolina, but even there his walk rate was low. Defensively, Garcia has the tools to be a fine third baseman, but makes too many wild throws with his strong arm. His development, both offensively and defensively, was probably hindered by spending all of 1995 on the Pirates' bench as a major league Rule 5 pickup from the Blue Jays' system. Garcia isn't that young anymore, and unless he gets the strike zone under control and steadies his glove work, he may be destined for a career as a Triple-A slugger in the Hensley Meulens mode. That said, he could start for Pittsburgh in 1998. **Grade C**

Freddy Garcia — *Houston Astros*

Pos: P   Throws: Right   Ht: 6'3"   Wt: 180   Age: 21

Yr Team	Lg	G	GS	IP	H	R	ER	HR	BB	SO	SV	W	L	Pct.	ERA
96 Quad City	A	13	13	60.2	57	27	21	3	27	50	0	5	4	.556	3.12
97 Kissimmee	A	27	27	179.0	165	63	51	6	49	131	0	10	8	.556	2.56
3 Minor League Yrs		51	51	298.0	282	122	101	11	90	239	0	21	15	.583	3.05

Freddy Garcia is yet another Venezuelan Astros prospect. Maybe Houston should have threatened to move to Caracas when they wanted a new stadium. Garcia was signed in 1994, and 1997 was his first complete campaign in a full-season league. He did very well, ranking fifth in the Florida State League in ERA, and posting a fine K/BB mark of +33 percent. Garcia's velocity has increased from mediocre to excellent over the last year, and his fastball is now clocked at 93 MPH. Both of his secondary pitches, a change and a curve, need work, but his control and mechanics are fine. Garcia needs to prove himself at the higher levels, and given his youth, the Astros should be careful with him. He's had some elbow trouble in the past. **Grade B**

Jose Garcia — *Milwaukee Brewers*

Pos: P   Throws: Right   Ht: 6'4"   Wt: 215   Age: 19

Yr Team	Lg	G	GS	IP	H	R	ER	HR	BB	SO	SV	W	L	Pct.	ERA
96 Helena	R	2	0	1.2	1	3	3	0	3	2	0	0	0	—	16.20
97 Beloit	A	27	26	155.1	145	89	69	9	70	126	0	6	11	.353	4.00
2 Minor League Yrs		29	26	157.0	146	92	72	9	73	128	0	6	11	.353	4.13

Jose Garcia was drafted in the second round by the Brewers in 1996, from a high school in California. He is a big pitcher with a good fastball that could improve further as he matures. His stats at Beloit were not good: K/BB -10 percent, K/IP minus-four, H/IP league average. Garcia has a major league arm, but he needs to refine his breaking pitches, develop a changeup, throw strikes more consistently, and learn more about pitching. He has time to do all that, if he doesn't get hurt. **Grade C**

Karim Garcia — *Arizona Diamondbacks*

Pos: OF   Bats: Left   Ht: 6'0"   Wt: 172   Age: 22

Yr Team	Lg	G	AB	R	H	2B	3B	HR	RBI	BB	SO	SB	CS	Avg	OBP	Slg
96 San Antonio	AA	35	129	21	32	6	1	5	22	9	38	1	1	.248	.297	.426
Albuquerque	AAA	84	327	54	97	17	10	13	58	29	67	6	4	.297	.353	.529
Los Angeles	NL	1	1	0	0	0	0	0	0	0	1	0	0	.000	.000	.000
97 Albuquerque	AAA	71	262	53	80	17	6	20	66	23	70	11	5	.305	.361	.645
Los Angeles	NL	15	39	5	5	0	0	1	8	6	14	0	0	.128	.239	.205
5 Minor League Yrs		558	2104	349	591	114	46	98	375	173	498	43	22	.281	.335	.519

Aren't you getting tired of reading about Karim Garcia in prospect books? I'm getting tired of writing about him, but according to his birth certificate, he is still just a baby in baseball years. He doesn't have much left to prove in Triple-A. . . his OPS was a fine +21 percent, and the attitude problems that clouded his 1996 campaign seem to have subsided. His strikeout rate remains worrisome, and I believe he could have some serious problems adjusting to major league breaking pitches. He could be a very mediocre hitter for 300-400 at-bats, but in the long run he should still have a very good career. Garcia played mostly in left last year after previous seasons in right. His defensive numbers were poor, after being good in the past. This was probably a reflection of the sore shoulder that bothered him all year, resulting in August surgery which ended his season. Assuming the shoulder comes around, he should be a productive slugger for the Diamondbacks. Whether he hits 100 major league home runs or 300 depends on his true age. **Grade B+**

Josh Garrett   Boston Red Sox

Pos: P **Throws:** Right **Ht:** 6'4" **Wt:** 190 **Age:** 20

Yr Team	Lg	G	GS	IP	H	R	ER	HR	BB	SO	SV	W	L	Pct.	ERA
96 Red Sox	R	7	5	27.0	22	8	5	0	5	17	0	1	1	.500	1.67
97 Michigan	A	22	22	138.2	164	94	74	13	35	64	0	8	10	.444	4.80
2 Minor League Yrs		29	27	165.2	186	102	79	13	40	81	0	9	11	.450	4.29

Garrett was Boston's first-round pick in 1996, out of a high school in Indiana. He is tall, thin, lanky, and projectable, but he had problems getting people out in his full-season debut in the Midwest League. His control is very good for a young moundsman, but his command within the strike zone is weak, and he gives up a lot of hits for a guy with a 90-MPH fastball. His H/IP was rotten at -25 percent. Garrett is said to be intelligent and competitive, which is a good thing, because he has a lot of work to do to make himself a successful pro pitcher. **Grade C**

Alberto Garza   Cleveland Indians

Pos: P **Throws:** Right **Ht:** 6'3" **Wt:** 195 **Age:** 20

Yr Team	Lg	G	GS	IP	H	R	ER	HR	BB	SO	SV	W	L	Pct.	ERA
96 Burlington	R	9	9	39.2	34	24	24	5	15	34	0	2	4	.333	5.45
97 Columbus	A	18	18	95.0	72	34	33	7	32	107	0	8	3	.727	3.13
Kinston	A	1	1	8.0	5	3	3	0	4	4	0	1	0	1.000	3.38
2 Minor League Yrs		28	28	142.2	111	61	60	12	51	145	0	11	7	.611	3.79

"Pssstttt. . . hey, buddy." "Who, me?" "Yeah, you. Cm'ere. I got something for ya." "What is it?" "It's a. . . prospect. . . that no one has ever heard of. . ." *"A prospect???"* *"SSSSHHHHHHHHHH!!!!* What's the matter with you, frog, you want everybody to hear?" If you don't know what that is about, ask your children. Anyhow, Alberto Garza *is* a prospect, and no one has ever heard of him. A 44th-round draft pick in 1995, he pitched well in 1996 and excellently in 1997. Check out the great K/BB ratio. Like all young pitchers, he will need to avoid injury, but he has a live arm and good control, and that's the combo you look for. **Grade B-**

Jeremy Giambi
Kansas City Royals

Pos: OF Bats: Left Ht: 6'0" Wt: 185 Age: 23

Yr Team	Lg	G	AB	R	H	2B	3B	HR	RBI	BB	SO	SB	CS	Avg	OBP	Slg
96 Spokane	A	67	231	58	63	17	0	6	39	61	32	22	5	.273	.440	.424
97 Lansing	A	31	116	33	39	11	1	5	21	23	16	5	1	.336	.451	.578
Wichita	AA	74	268	50	86	15	1	11	52	44	47	4	4	.321	.422	.507
2 Minor League Yrs		172	615	141	188	43	2	22	112	128	95	31	10	.306	.435	.489

Jeremy Giambi was a sixth-round pick in 1996, out of Cal State Fullerton. Yes, he is Jason's brother, and like his sibling, he can hit. Jeremy is smaller than Jason and doesn't have as much power, but he has a smooth line-drive swing, excellent plate discipline, and shows few weaknesses as a hitter. He can hit fastballs or breaking stuff, and will pull pitches into the alleys or slap them to the opposite field, depending on how he is pitched. He is a good defensive player, although he would be stretched to play center in the majors due to mediocre range. Giambi is intelligent and works hard; to be honest, I don't understand why he fell to the sixth round in the draft. He looks like a hell of a good player to me. **Grade B+**

Kevin Gibbs
Los Angeles Dodgers

Pos: OF Bats: Both Ht: 6'2" Wt: 182 Age: 23

Yr Team	Lg	G	AB	R	H	2B	3B	HR	RBI	BB	SO	SB	CS	Avg	OBP	Slg
96 Vero Beach	A	118	423	69	114	9	11	0	33	65	80	60	19	.270	.369	.343
97 San Antonio	AA	101	358	89	120	21	6	2	34	72	48	49	19	.335	.451	.444
3 Minor League Yrs		283	996	196	299	38	21	3	87	173	176	149	43	.300	.408	.390

The public-address guys need to get out their old Deep Purple tapes and play "Speed King" when Kevin Gibbs comes to the plate. This guy is a burner. Drafted in the sixth round in 1995 from Old Dominion, Gibbs has drawn interest from scouts because of his running ability, but he started to show life in his bat at San Antonio last year. Yes, it was the Texas League, but San Antonio is actually a pitcher's park, and it was his first year at the level. His OPS was a solid +15 percent, mainly on the strength of his on-base percentage, which increases the utility of his speed, of course. It is possible his patience at the plate is helping him grow as a hitter. He makes contact and might develop some gap power if he picks up a bit more muscle, although he will never hit more than a handful of home runs. The wheels help him in the outfield; he has excellent range in center, although his arm is weak. At the least, Gibbs will be a superior reserve outfielder, but if his offense continues to improve, he could be a Brett Butler-type leadoff man. **Grade C+**

114

Derrick Gibson   Colorado Rockies

Pos: OF **Bats:** Right **Ht:** 6'2" **Wt:** 238 **Age:** 23

Yr Team	Lg	G	AB	R	H	2B	3B	HR	RBI	BB	SO	SB	CS	Avg	OBP	Slg
96 New Haven	AA	122	449	58	115	21	4	15	62	31	125	3	12	.256	.313	.421
97 New Haven	AA	119	461	91	146	24	2	23	75	36	100	20	13	.317	.377	.527
Colo Sprngs	AAA	21	78	14	33	7	0	3	12	5	9	0	2	.423	.458	.628
5 Minor League Yrs		504	1897	314	535	89	23	85	331	135	527	71	44	.282	.343	.488

Gibson's physical tools are outstanding, and it is only natural to salivate over the thought of this man playing in Coors Field. His combination of power and speed is compared to the young Bo Jackson's, and he was ticketed to go to Bo's alma mater, Auburn on a football scholarship (as a linebacker) before he had problems with the entrance exams. Gibson's 1997 was a repeat performance in Double-A, but he was still fairly young for the level, and he sure whacked the ball in his limited Triple-A exposure. His Eastern League OPS was quite good at +21 percent, although he could drive that much higher if he were more patient. Control of the strike zone remains a dangerous problem, and if he struggles at higher levels, it will be for that reason. Gibson has the athletic ability to be a great outfielder, but he has a hard time tracking flyballs, and is just average defensively. His arm is strong but inaccurate. I saw Gibson in the Arizona Fall League, and I didn't like his loopy swing. He needs to prove himself against Triple-A pitchers for a full season. **Grade B**

Tim Giles   Toronto Blue Jays

Pos: DH-1B **Bats:** Left **Ht:** 6'3" **Wt:** 215 **Age:** 22

Yr Team	Lg	G	AB	R	H	2B	3B	HR	RBI	BB	SO	SB	CS	Avg	OBP	Slg
96 Medicne Hat	R	68	258	36	69	17	0	10	45	19	52	5	0	.267	.314	.450
97 Hagerstown	A	112	380	54	127	32	0	12	56	46	95	2	2	.334	.402	.513
2 Minor League Yrs		180	638	90	196	49	0	22	101	65	147	7	2	.307	.368	.487

Giles was a 20th-round pick in 1996, hailing from UNC Greensboro. He led the Big South Conference in home runs while hitting .360, but he was slow and couldn't play defense, so he fell to the lower levels of the draft. Giles is still slow, and spent most of 1997 at designated hitter, but he continues to hit well, even with the wooden bat. His OPS was near the top of the Sally League at +32 percent. Because of his defensive limitations, he must keep hitting to have a chance, but it is possible he will do so. **Grade C**

Eric Gillespie   Anaheim Angels

Pos: 1B **Bats:** Left **Ht:** 5'10" **Wt:** 200 **Age:** 22

Yr Team	Lg	G	AB	R	H	2B	3B	HR	RBI	BB	SO	SB	CS	Avg	OBP	Slg
96 Boise	A	61	192	28	53	11	5	3	38	25	50	0	1	.276	.357	.432
97 Cedar Rapds	A	122	421	78	107	26	7	18	72	55	80	8	0	.254	.343	.477
2 Minor League Yrs		183	613	106	160	37	12	21	110	80	130	8	1	.261	.348	.463

Gillespie, a product of Cal State Northridge, was drafted in the 10th round in 1996. He was a third baseman in college, but moved to first in the pros. He is short and not particularly athletic, but he has some offensive potential, as shown by his acceptable OPS of +14 percent and his excellent SEC of +42 percent. His defense at first is good, but not spectacular. Gillespie needs to keep hitting to establish his credentials and move beyond the status of organization player. **Grade C-**

Chris Gissell

Chicago Cubs

Pos: P **Throws:** Right **Ht:** 6'4" **Wt:** 180 **Age:** 20

Yr Team	Lg	G	GS	IP	H	R	ER	HR	BB	SO	SV	W	L	Pct.	ERA
96 Cubs	R	11	10	61.1	54	23	16	1	8	64	0	4	2	.667	2.35
97 Rockford	A	26	24	143.2	155	89	71	7	62	105	0	6	11	.353	4.45
2 Minor League Yrs		37	34	205.0	209	112	87	8	70	169	0	10	13	.435	3.82

Gissell's 1997 stats aren't much to look at, but scouts say he has the ability to develop into a good pitcher. He was drafted in the fourth round in 1996, from a high school in Washington. Some observers pegged him as a first-round pick, but concerns about his signability dropped him down the list. He signed with the Cubs, pitched terrifically in his debut in the Gulf Coast League, but he was less effective at the full-season level last year. Gissell has a 90-MPH fastball, a curve he can throw for strikes, and an adequate changeup that he needs to improve. He is lanky, projectable, and could pick up more velocity as he develops physically. Gissell was not abused in high school, so if the Cubs are careful with him, he has a good chance to stay healthy. He needs to pitch better, but is capable of doing so. **Grade C**

Mike Glavine

Cleveland Indians

Pos: 1B-DH **Bats:** Left **Ht:** 6'3" **Wt:** 210 **Age:** 25

Yr Team	Lg	G	AB	R	H	2B	3B	HR	RBI	BB	SO	SB	CS	Avg	OBP	Slg
96 Columbus	A	38	119	17	33	5	0	6	16	28	33	0	0	.277	.416	.471
97 Columbus	A	114	397	62	95	16	0	28	75	80	127	0	1	.239	.370	.491
3 Minor League Yrs		198	671	107	166	31	0	45	119	130	197	1	1	.247	.372	.495

Yes, he is Tom's brother. Mike Glavine was selected in the 22nd round in 1995, out of Northeastern University. A broken thumb ruined 1996 for him, and being a first baseman in a system clogged with them, 1997 was a critical season. He showed excellent power at Columbus in the South Atlantic League, and despite his low batting average, he was a valuable offensive player, with an OPS of +25 percent and the best SEC in the circuit at +87 percent. On the other hand, for a 24-year-old to hit just .239 in the Sally League. . . well, that's not too good, to be nice about it. It isn't too late for Glavine to have a career, but he needs to move quickly, and his chance won't come with Cleveland. **Grade C-**

Mike Glendenning
San Francisco Giants

Pos: OF **Bats:** Right **Ht:** 6'0" **Wt:** 210 **Age:** 21

Yr Team	Lg	G	AB	R	H	2B	3B	HR	RBI	BB	SO	SB	CS	Avg	OBP	Slg
96 Bellingham	A	73	265	54	69	19	4	12	48	39	80	4	6	.260	.355	.498
97 Bakersfield	A	134	503	95	130	27	0	33	100	63	150	1	4	.258	.341	.509
2 Minor League Yrs		207	768	149	199	46	4	45	148	102	230	5	10	.259	.346	.505

The Giants drafted Mike Glendenning from Los Angeles Pierce Junior College in 1996, as a 10th-rounder. He is extremely strong and has great power potential, but has difficulty with breaking pitches and strikes out too much. He belted 33 homers in the California League last year, but struck out 150 times and had problems making contact. His home park in Bakersfield is very friendly for power hitters, so even the home-run total must be taken with a grain of salt, or perhaps a dash of pepper. (Maybe some basil, or cumin. Garlic can be good in small quantities, and I've also found that a sprinkle of allspice can enliven most dishes.) Glendenning has a strong arm, but limited range, and is not accomplished defensively. **Grade C**

Rudy Gomez
New York Yankees

Pos: 2B **Bats:** Right **Ht:** 5'11" **Wt:** 180 **Age:** 23

Yr Team	Lg	G	AB	R	H	2B	3B	HR	RBI	BB	SO	SB	CS	Avg	OBP	Slg
96 Yankees	R	16	58	12	16	6	0	0	10	9	7	0	1	.276	.403	.379
Tampa	A	40	130	15	38	9	1	1	24	26	12	4	1	.292	.403	.400
97 Norwich	AA	102	393	65	118	18	7	5	52	61	64	11	7	.300	.405	.420
2 Minor League Yrs		158	581	92	172	33	8	6	86	96	83	15	9	.296	.404	.411

Rudy Gomez hit .420 for the University of Miami in 1996, but went in the 10th round of the draft because, like most college second basemen, he lacks the physical attributes that excite scouts. He is a solid contact hitter, however, and played very well at Double-A Norwich in 1997. He doesn't have great pop at the plate, but Gomez makes contact with regularity and knows how to hit. He has command of the strike zone. With the glove, he has average range and an average arm, but doesn't make large numbers of errors. Gomez is a sleeper, but if he keeps hitting .300, they won't be able to ignore him forever. On the other hand, this is the Yankees. . . I guess they could. **Grade C+**

Alex Gonzalez
Florida Marlins

Pos: SS **Bats:** Right **Ht:** 6'0" **Wt:** 150 **Age:** 21

Yr Team	Lg	G	AB	R	H	2B	3B	HR	RBI	BB	SO	SB	CS	Avg	OBP	Slg
96 Marlins	R	10	41	6	16	3	0	0	6	2	4	1	0	.390	.419	.463
Kane County	A	4	10	2	2	0	0	0	0	2	4	0	0	.200	.385	.200
Portland	AA	11	34	4	8	0	1	0	1	2	10	0	0	.235	.297	.294
97 Portland	AA	133	449	69	114	16	4	19	65	27	83	4	7	.254	.305	.434
3 Minor League Yrs		228	780	117	207	28	10	21	110	53	142	17	10	.265	.319	.408

A year ago, Alex Gonzalez was a skinny kid from Venezuela with a bad shoulder. Scouts said he was a great prospect, but being injured, he never had a chance to prove it. Surgery fixed the shoulder, and he more than held his own in Double-A in 1997. . . at a very young age. Some people think he will be better than Edgar Renteria, which is saying something, since Renteria is going to be a star. Gonzalez is developing power, despite his build. His numbers at Portland last year were respectable, although *everyone* hit at Portland last year, so park effects knock much of the luster off. Still, he is extremely young, and guys who hit in Double-A at his age develop into hitting stars more often than not. His glove work is underdeveloped, but his range is superb, and the Marlins say he may eventually move Renteria to third base, which should also tell us something. I want to see improvement in his strike-zone judgment, but there is plenty of time for that. Score one for the scouts; Gonzalez looks great. **Grade B+**

Lariel Gonzalez   *Colorado Rockies*

Pos: P **Throws:** Right **Ht:** 6'4" **Wt:** 180 **Age:** 21

Yr Team	Lg	G	GS	IP	H	R	ER	HR	BB	SO	SV	W	L	Pct.	ERA
96 Asheville	A	35	0	45.0	37	21	18	2	37	53	4	1	1	.500	3.60
97 Salem	A	44	0	57.0	42	19	16	3	23	79	8	5	0	1.000	2.53
3 Minor League Yrs		94	11	159.2	123	71	60	9	103	180	14	9	5	.643	3.38

A Dominican righthander signed in 1994, Lariel Gonzalez is projected as the Rockies' closer in 2000 or so. It is easy to understand why—he has a 95-MPH fastball, a good slider, and a splitter that is improving. His control, while not perfect, is advancing, and he has the aggressive, assertive comportment that scouts like in a closer. His K/IP for Salem was awesome at +69 percent, second in the league behind teammate Steve Shoemaker. We need to see Gonzalez at higher levels, but he is very young, throws very hard, and hasn't done anything wrong yet. **Grade B**

Raul Gonzalez   *Kansas City Royals*

Pos: OF **Bats:** Right **Ht:** 5'8" **Wt:** 175 **Age:** 24

Yr Team	Lg	G	AB	R	H	2B	3B	HR	RBI	BB	SO	SB	CS	Avg	OBP	Slg
96 Wichita	AA	23	84	17	24	5	1	1	9	5	12	1	2	.286	.333	.405
97 Wichita	AA	129	452	66	129	30	4	13	74	36	52	12	8	.285	.335	.456
7 Minor League Yrs		668	2407	358	660	143	25	56	317	238	298	52	32	.274	.339	.424

Raul Gonzalez looks like he should be a good player, but his actual production, while not terrible, isn't that impressive. He is well-muscled and athletic, and the ball jumps off his bat, but his numbers aren't outstanding considering league and park context. His OPS was only league average. Gonzalez does make contact, and he is young enough that there is still a chance he could break out with the bat. Although he has the physical tools to do well defensively, he has problems reading fly balls and tends to make wild, inaccurate throws. He is a prime example of how tools and skills aren't the same thing. **Grade C**

Arnie Gooch
New York Mets

Pos: P **Throws:** Right **Ht:** 6'2" **Wt:** 195 **Age:** 21

Yr Team	Lg	G	GS	IP	H	R	ER	HR	BB	SO	SV	W	L	Pct.	ERA
96 St. Lucie	A	26	26	167.2	131	74	48	7	51	141	0	12	12	.500	2.58
97 Binghamton	AA	27	27	161.0	179	106	91	12	76	98	0	10	12	.455	5.09
4 Minor League Yrs		95	89	553.2	505	284	217	32	215	456	0	31	39	.443	3.53

Gooch had a fine season at Class-A St. Lucie in 1996, but moving to Double-A exposed his weaknesses as a pitcher. His sinking fastball meets and exceeds the 90-MPH threshold of respectability, but his secondary pitches, a curve and change, have regressed. His ratios, solid across the board in the past, were lousy at Binghamton: K/BB, -32 percent; K/IP, -23 percent; and H/IP, -19 percent. There isn't any good news in those numbers. Gooch is still very young, and could rebound quickly if he keeps his health, but there is no evidence it will happen soon. **Grade C**

Rick Gorecki
Tampa Bay Devil Rays

Pos: P **Throws:** Right **Ht:** 6'3" **Wt:** 167 **Age:** 24

Yr Team	Lg	G	GS	IP	H	R	ER	HR	BB	SO	SV	W	L	Pct.	ERA
97 San Berndno	A	14	14	51.0	38	22	22	4	32	58	0	2	3	.400	3.88
San Antonio	AA	7	7	45.1	26	8	7	3	15	33	0	4	2	.667	1.39
Los Angeles	NL	4	1	6.0	9	10	10	3	6	6	0	1	0	1.000	15.00
6 Minor League Yrs		113	107	562.1	504	279	230	38	295	477	0	32	32	.500	3.68

Rick Gorecki is similar to Bret Saberhagen, Billy Swift, or Mike Grace: a guy with a major league arm, good control, pitching intelligence, and a rotten health record. He is usually effective and scouts have always loved him, but he can't stay off the disabled list. Gorecki lost 1995 to a hernia, and 1996 to shoulder surgery. He came back in 1997 and pitched very well in the Dodgers system, especially towards the end of the season. Gorecki has an 89-MPH moving fastball, and an outstanding curve which he can throw for strikes. He is highly intelligent, and has fine pitching instincts. If he can stay away from the doctors, Gorecki should have a career in the majors, but I sure wouldn't want to bet my pitching staff on his health. **Grade C**

Chad Green
Milwaukee Brewers

Pos: OF **Bats:** Both **Ht:** 5'10" **Wt:** 185 **Age:** 22

Yr Team	Lg	G	AB	R	H	2B	3B	HR	RBI	BB	SO	SB	CS	Avg	OBP	Slg
96 Ogden	R	21	81	22	29	4	1	3	8	15	23	12	3	.358	.455	.543
97 Stockton	A	127	513	78	128	26	14	2	43	37	138	37	16	.250	.300	.366
2 Minor League Yrs		148	594	100	157	30	15	5	51	52	161	49	19	.264	.324	.391

Green was Milwaukee's first-round pick in 1996, from the University of Kentucky. Scouts project Green as a prototype leadoff man, due to his blazing speed, but unless he improves his on-base percentage, Green would be very poor in the role. He had problems making contact against California League pitching in 1997. He didn't draw enough walks, and his strikeout rate was excessive for a guy without much power. His OPS was -13 percent, his SEC minus-nine. Having numbers like that at the top of the lineup is not advised by scientists, philosophers, or theologians. Green is an excellent defensive outfielder with extraordinary range, but unless the Brewers were looking for a defensive sub with that first-round pick, he has to be considered a disappointment. Then again, he was drafted more for signability than anything. **Grade C-**

Scarborough Green   St. Louis Cardinals

Pos: OF **Bats:** Both **Ht:** 5'10" **Wt:** 170 **Age:** 23

Yr Team	Lg	G	AB	R	H	2B	3B	HR	RBI	BB	SO	SB	CS	Avg	OBP	Slg
96 St. Pete	A	36	140	26	41	4	1	1	11	21	22	13	9	.293	.393	.357
Arkansas	AA	92	300	45	60	6	3	3	24	38	58	21	8	.200	.295	.270
97 Arkansas	AA	76	251	45	77	14	4	2	29	36	48	11	5	.307	.397	.418
Louisville	AAA	52	209	26	53	11	2	3	13	22	55	10	7	.254	.325	.368
St. Louis	NL	20	31	5	3	0	0	0	1	2	5	0	0	.097	.152	.097
5 Minor League Yrs		475	1623	238	398	50	17	10	124	204	362	106	47	.245	.333	.315

Also known as Bert Green, Scarborough was drafted in the 10th round in 1992, as a high school shortstop from Missouri. He is fast and quick (they aren't the same thing), and occasionally hits well, but will never produce great power. Sometimes he tries to slap at the ball to use his speed, and sometimes it works. Other times he tries to hit for power, and that doesn't work. Green is a very good athlete, and has developed into a fine defensive outfielder. His arm is surprisingly strong for a guy his size. I doubt he will hit enough to be of much value, but could hang around as a defensive sub/pinch runner/Triple-A roster filler for years. **Grade C-**

Seth Greisinger   Detroit Tigers

Pos: P **Throws:** Right **Ht:** 6'4" **Wt:** 190 **Age:** 22

Yr Team	Lg	G	GS	IP	H	R	ER	HR	BB	SO	SV	W	L	Pct.	ERA
97 Jacksnville	AA	28	28	159.1	194	103	92	29	53	105	0	10	6	.625	5.20
1 Minor League Yr		28	28	159.1	194	103	92	29	53	105	0	10	6	.625	5.20

The Tigers took Seth Greisinger, from the University of Virginia and the U.S. Olympic Team, with their first-round pick in 1996. He was extremely impressive in spring training with the major league club, and word was that he would challenge for a spot in the Detroit rotation as soon as 1998. Plans have changed; Greisinger was disturbingly ineffectual at Double-A Jacksonville. While he showed the sharp control, fine breaking pitches, and effective changeup that had been advertised, the velocity on his fastball was inconsistent. At times, he was in the low 90s, but at other times the heater was tepid. He was healthy and stayed in the rotation all year, but his performance has to be regarded as a disappointment. Greisinger did pitch better in the second half, and no one has given up on him as a prospect, but this isn't the way he wanted to start his career. **Grade C**

Ben Grieve
Oakland Athletics

Pos: OF   **Bats:** Left   **Ht:** 6'4"   **Wt:** 220   **Age:** 21

Yr Team	Lg	G	AB	R	H	2B	3B	HR	RBI	BB	SO	SB	CS	Avg	OBP	Slg
96 Modesto	A	72	281	61	100	20	1	11	51	38	52	8	7	.356	.430	.552
Huntsville	AA	63	232	34	55	8	1	8	32	35	53	0	3	.237	.338	.384
97 Huntsville	AA	100	372	100	122	29	2	24	108	81	75	5	1	.328	.455	.610
Edmonton	AAA	27	108	27	46	11	1	7	28	12	16	0	1	.426	.484	.741
Oakland	AL	24	93	12	29	6	0	3	24	13	25	0	0	.312	.402	.473
4 Minor League Yrs		464	1723	336	531	102	6	63	345	292	341	28	17	.308	.413	.484

I have to admit, I was a bit slow to give Ben Grieve his due. His full-season debut in 1995 wasn't particularly successful, and I rated him as a B- prospect in the 1996 book, a grade that in retrospect looks ridiculous. Even then, he had good command of the strike zone. He started to hit well in 1996, and I boosted him up to A- in the 1997 edition. Now, I rate him as the second-best prospect in baseball, behind Adrian Beltre, and a good case can be made that Grieve should be first. The potential that the scouts saw when he went second overall in the 1994 draft has clearly been realized. His numbers in Double-A are incredible: he led the Southern League in both OPS and SEC. His Triple-A numbers are preposterously good: a .426 average? An OPS of 1.224, +48 percent?? For a 20 year old??? Who is this guy, Robert Redford? Even his defense improved last year. I won't insult your intelligence by telling you that Grieve will be a star. The question now is, will he break any records? And he may very well break records, unless he breaks an ankle or the law or something. **Grade A**

Giomar Guevara
Seattle Mariners

Pos: 2B   **Bats:** Right   **Ht:** 5'9"   **Wt:** 158   **Age:** 25

Yr Team	Lg	G	AB	R	H	2B	3B	HR	RBI	BB	SO	SB	CS	Avg	OBP	Slg
96 Port City	AA	119	414	60	110	18	2	2	41	54	102	21	7	.266	.353	.333
97 Tacoma	AAA	54	176	29	43	5	1	2	13	5	39	3	7	.244	.269	.318
Memphis	AA	65	228	30	60	10	4	4	28	20	42	5	5	.263	.321	.395
Seattle	AL	5	4	0	0	0	0	0	0	0	2	1	0	.000	.000	.000
5 Minor League Yrs		500	1726	262	452	78	16	20	188	187	386	49	46	.262	.335	.360

The Mariners would like Venezuelan Giomar Guevara to take the second-base spot beside Alex Rodriguez one of these days, but I don't think it will happen soon. A converted shortstop, Guevara has the range and athleticism to be a superb defensive player, but he still makes too many errors. With the bat, he lacks patience and power, and hasn't shown the ability to consistently hit for average, either. He is old enough that unless he starts hitting within the next year, he probably never will. Even if he cuts down on the errors, it would be unwise for a major league team to carry his bat. **Grade C**

Aaron Guiel

San Diego Padres

Pos: OF   Bats: Left   Ht: 5'10"   Wt: 190   Age: 25

Yr Team	Lg	G	AB	R	H	2B	3B	HR	RBI	BB	SO	SB	CS	Avg	OBP	Slg
96 Midland	AA	129	439	72	118	29	7	10	48	56	71	11	7	.269	.364	.435
97 Midland	AA	116	419	91	138	37	7	22	85	59	94	14	10	.329	.431	.609
Mobile	AA	8	26	9	10	2	0	1	9	5	4	1	0	.385	.500	.577
5 Minor League Yrs		528	1851	353	529	129	26	60	294	279	379	57	30	.286	.390	.481

Aaron Guiel was a component of the trade that sent Rickey Henderson to Anaheim for the stretch run. He isn't a blazing plasma burst of a prospect, but he has solid secondary offensive skills, and had a very good season in the Texas League. His SEC ranked fourth in the league at +65 percent. On the other hand, he was a league repeater, and Midland is an incredible park for offense of all kinds. Guiel can play second base, third base, or the outfield without causing undue stress to the defense. He won't be a regular, but would make a fine bench player. **Grade C+**

Carlos Guillen

Houston Astros

Pos: SS   Bats: Both   Ht: 6'0"   Wt: 150   Age: 22

Yr Team	Lg	G	AB	R	H	2B	3B	HR	RBI	BB	SO	SB	CS	Avg	OBP	Slg
96 Quad City	A	29	112	23	37	7	1	3	17	16	25	13	6	.330	.405	.491
97 Jackson	AA	115	390	47	99	16	1	10	39	38	78	6	5	.254	.322	.377
New Orleans	AAA	3	13	3	4	1	0	0	0	0	4	0	0	.308	.308	.385
3 Minor League Yrs		177	620	90	171	28	4	15	71	63	124	36	12	.276	.342	.406

Scouts have always said that Carlos Guillen, a Venezuelan signed in 1992, was one of the best prospects in the Houston system. The problem was, he was always on the disabled list, usually with some variety of shoulder injury. He finally managed to stay healthy for most of the season, and did decently at Double-A Jackson. Guillen has good pop from both sides of the plate, and scouts project him hitting for both average and power in the majors. He usually makes contact, but is occasionally impatient, an understandable problem given his lack of experience. Guillen has the tools to be a sharp defensive player, but he makes too many errors at this point. . . again, this is understandable. He is quite young, but needs to refine his skills before he is ready for the majors. If he can stay away from the surgeons, he could be very good. **Grade B**

Lindsay Gulin

New York Mets

Pos: P   Throws: Left   Ht: 6'3"   Wt: 160   Age: 21

Yr Team	Lg	G	GS	IP	H	R	ER	HR	BB	SO	SV	W	L	Pct.	ERA
96 Capital City	A	19	19	112.1	88	40	33	6	57	134	0	7	7	.500	2.64
97 St. Lucie	A	9	6	26.1	36	31	27	2	21	11	0	0	3	.000	9.23
Capital City	A	17	15	99.0	77	37	32	2	60	118	0	8	1	.889	2.91
3 Minor League Yrs		56	45	292.0	241	123	104	15	154	314	0	22	11	.667	3.21

Gulin was selected in the 16th round in 1995, from high school in the metropolis of Issaquah, Washington. He has been a very effective pitcher throughout his brief career, but doesn't get mentioned as a prospect very often because he doesn't throw all that hard. Gulin pitched well at Capital City, but he was helped by a friendly park, and his walk rate was too high. . . 60 walks in 99 innings isn't good. He struggled badly after promotion to St. Lucie. Gulin is very projectable. If he picks up additional velocity to go with his breaking stuff, and improves his control, he could have a career. **Grade C**

Cristian Guzman   *New York Yankees*

Pos: SS **Bats:** Both **Ht:** 6'0" **Wt:** 150 **Age:** 20

Yr Team	Lg	G	AB	R	H	2B	3B	HR	RBI	BB	SO	SB	CS	Avg	OBP	Slg
96 Yankees	R	42	170	37	50	8	2	1	21	10	31	7	6	.294	.341	.382
97 Tampa	A	4	14	4	4	0	0	0	1	1	1	0	1	.286	.333	.286
Greensboro	A	124	495	68	135	21	4	4	52	17	105	23	12	.273	.309	.356
2 Minor League Yrs		170	679	109	189	29	6	5	74	28	137	30	19	.278	.318	.361

Scouts drool over this guy, another bounty of the Yankees' increased presence in Latin America. The scariest thing for the small-market teams shouldn't be the fact that the big boys can sign free agents. It should be that an intelligently run big-market team can spend two or three times as much money on scouting. As for Guzman, he has tools coming out of his ears, but so far he doesn't know how to use them. His walk rate was horrific, his strikeout rate excessive for a guy with limited power. That is not a good combination. Unless he learns the strike zone, his speed will have little value, and his hitting development will be stunted. Guzman has the physical ability to be a great shortstop, and his potential is clear, but right now it is just that: potential. **Grade C**

Domingo Guzman   *San Diego Padres*

Pos: P **Throws:** Right **Ht:** 6'3" **Wt:** 198 **Age:** 22

Yr Team	Lg	G	GS	IP	H	R	ER	HR	BB	SO	SV	W	L	Pct.	ERA
96 Clinton	A	6	5	20.2	32	33	29	2	19	18	0	0	5	.000	12.63
Idaho Falls	R	15	10	65.1	52	41	30	7	29	75	0	4	2	.667	4.13
97 Clinton	A	12	12	79.0	66	36	28	7	25	91	0	4	5	.444	3.19
Rancho Cuca	A	6	6	38.0	42	23	23	6	16	39	0	3	2	.600	5.45
4 Minor League Yrs		79	46	298.2	282	194	161	25	139	311	11	21	19	.525	4.85

A Dominican signed in 1993, Domingo Guzman has one of the better arms in the San Diego system. His fastball runs 92-94 MPH, with movement, and both his curveball and changeup are good pitches when he throws them properly. He telegraphs his offspeed stuff too often, and more experienced hitters can get a read on him after a time through the order. Guzman was excellent at Clinton, but the better hitters in the California League were able to take advantage of this deficiency. He also missed time with a shoulder strain. Guzman's talent is obvious, but he has weaknesses, and he must stay healthy to overcome them. **Grade C**

Edwards Guzman
San Francisco Giants

Pos: 3B **Bats:** Left **Ht:** 5'11" **Wt:** 192 **Age:** 21

Yr Team	Lg	G	AB	R	H	2B	3B	HR	RBI	BB	SO	SB	CS	Avg	OBP	Slg
96 San Jose	A	106	367	41	99	19	5	1	40	39	60	3	5	.270	.344	.357
97 Shreveport	AA	118	380	52	108	15	4	3	42	33	57	3	1	.284	.341	.368
2 Minor League Yrs		224	747	93	207	34	9	4	82	72	117	6	6	.277	.342	.363

This guy is as anonymous as a pothead at a Grateful Dead concert, but he looks like a prospect to me. He is a contact hitter without a lot of power, but he played most of the 1997 season at 20 years of age. Twenty year olds who can hit even adequately in Double-A are fine prospects, as a rule. His defense at third is nothing special, so it is his bat I am watching. He needs to develop some power, but if his birth certificate is close to accurate, he could be a major surprise within the next year or two. Until then, be cautious, but be alert. **Grade C+**

Chris Haas
St. Louis Cardinals

Pos: 3B **Bats:** Left **Ht:** 6'2" **Wt:** 210 **Age:** 21

Yr Team	Lg	G	AB	R	H	2B	3B	HR	RBI	BB	SO	SB	CS	Avg	OBP	Slg
96 Peoria	A	124	421	56	101	19	1	11	65	64	169	3	2	.240	.347	.368
97 Peoria	A	36	115	23	36	11	0	5	22	22	38	3	0	.313	.430	.539
Pr William	A	100	361	58	86	10	2	14	54	42	144	1	1	.238	.323	.393
3 Minor League Yrs		327	1139	180	288	55	6	37	191	180	444	8	6	.253	.360	.409

The Cardinals used a supplemental first-round pick on Chris Haas in 1995. He has excellent power potential from the left side, but struggles to make contact, as his high strikeout rate indicates. On the other hand, he does draw walks, and can occasionally produce a blistering hot streak. He is still young enough to solve his bat problems. After doing very poorly with the glove in 1996, Haas made major strides in 1997, leading the Carolina League in fielding at third base, and showing good range for a big guy. He still has work to do with the bat, but his chances are better than they looked a year ago. **Grade C+**

Steve Hacker
Minnesota Twins

Pos: DH-1B **Bats:** Right **Ht:** 6'5" **Wt:** 240 **Age:** 23

Yr Team	Lg	G	AB	R	H	2B	3B	HR	RBI	BB	SO	SB	CS	Avg	OBP	Slg
96 Eugene	A	75	292	45	73	15	1	21	61	26	64	0	0	.250	.318	.524
97 Macon	A	117	460	80	149	35	1	33	119	34	91	1	0	.324	.370	.620
3 Minor League Yrs		208	809	129	234	53	2	56	189	61	168	1	0	.289	.343	.567

Steve Hacker, who led NCAA Division I in home runs for Southwest Missouri State in 1995, had a dazzling season for Macon, leading the Sally League in OPS at +43 percent, and scaring the hornets out of any pitcher who left a fastball in his wheelhouse. In spite of those accomplishments, he is a good example of why you can't look only at the raw stats, even a good one like OPS. Hacker was a bit old for the league, and his walk rate was low. He is overaggressive, and pitchers at higher levels will take advantage of that unless he makes some adjustments. He is also not much of a defensive player, being relegated to the DH role most of the year. Hacker has had injury problems (a broken finger last year, a broken cheekbone in 1995). I still want to see him at a higher level before I get excited, but the Twins obviously liked him enough to take him as the player to be named for Greg Myers. **Grade C**

John Halama   *Houston Astros*

Pos: P   **Throws:** Left   **Ht:** 6'5"   **Wt:** 195   **Age:** 26

Yr Team	Lg	G	GS	IP	H	R	ER	HR	BB	SO	SV	W	L	Pct.	ERA
96 Jackson	AA	27	27	162.2	151	77	58	10	59	110	0	9	10	.474	3.21
97 New Orleans	AAA	26	24	171.0	150	57	49	9	32	126	0	13	3	.813	2.58
4 Minor League Yrs		123	63	475.1	430	186	151	29	136	356	3	30	20	.600	2.86

Halama was one of the major surprises of 1997. A 23rd-round pick in 1994 from the College of St. Francis in New York, Halama has never received much respect, due to a fastball that is only average on a good day. His curveball, while occasionally erratic, has good movement, and his changeup is excellent. His control is matchless, and scouts compare him to Jimmy Key due to his grace under pressure. Like Key, he will throw inside against righthanded hitters, but can also paint the corners. Halama's K/BB ratio was a wonderful +100 percent in the American Association, and he led the league in ERA. He did have the New Orleans stadium on his side, which reduces the luster of his numbers a bit. Despite the fact that he doesn't throw hard, Halama impressed everyone last year, and most people think he will succeed in the majors, given adjustment time. Watching a finesse pitcher adjust to the majors is like watching a Plymouth Valiant duel a semi. If he is smart, and a little lucky, the guy driving the Valiant can win. **Grade B**

Roy Halladay   *Toronto Blue Jays*

Pos: P   **Throws:** Right   **Ht:** 6'6"   **Wt:** 200   **Age:** 20

Yr Team	Lg	G	GS	IP	H	R	ER	HR	BB	SO	SV	W	L	Pct.	ERA
96 Dunedin	A	27	27	164.2	158	75	50	7	46	109	0	15	7	.682	2.73
97 Knoxville	AA	7	7	36.2	46	26	22	4	11	30	0	2	3	.400	5.40
Syracuse	AAA	22	22	125.2	132	74	64	13	53	64	0	7	10	.412	4.58
3 Minor League Yrs		66	64	377.1	371	200	155	28	126	251	0	27	25	.519	3.70

The Blue Jays are extremely aggressive about promoting pitchers. If a prospect has two or three good games in a row, he is automatically a candidate for promotion. Halladay was not particularly successful at Double-A, but Toronto promoted him anyway, and he struggled at Syracuse. This was not for want of stuff: his fastball hits 96 MPH, his knuckle-curve is awesome when he throws it for strikes, and he has an adequate changeup. His basic problem is command and consistency. Notice that I didn't say control; Halladay doesn't walk that many people, but his command *within* the strike zone needs sharpening, and he has difficulty keeping his mechanics in line. None of that is unusual for a young pitcher, and Halladay certainly has the intellect and work ethic to improve. His ratios weren't good at Syracuse. The K/BB was especially poor at -24 percent, so there is work to do. If health problems do not intervene, Halladay could be a superb pitcher, but he needs a consolidation season. I'm not sure the Blue Jays will give him enough time to ripen, however. He is a candidate for Matt Drews Disease. **Grade B**

Matt Halloran
San Diego Padres
Pos: SS **Bats:** Right **Ht:** 6'2" **Wt:** 185 **Age:** 20

Yr Team	Lg	G	AB	R	H	2B	3B	HR	RBI	BB	SO	SB	CS	Avg	OBP	Slg
96 Padres	R	39	134	22	35	7	4	0	15	10	22	2	1	.261	.322	.373
97 Clinton	A	46	154	19	31	7	0	1	22	8	37	9	3	.201	.256	.266
2 Minor League Yrs		85	288	41	66	14	4	1	37	18	59	11	4	.229	.287	.316

Scratch one first-rounder. The Padres drafted Halloran in the first round in 1996, out of high school in Virginia. He had a reputation as a tough, heady player, but in 1997 he ruined his own prestige. He missed much of the season with injury, didn't hit well when he did take the field, and alienated the front office and the media with his whining. He complained that the press was critical of his play, and refused to talk with them. Halloran also seemed to be less than amenable to instruction or advice. Now, he is young, and immature behavior is quite common among 19 year olds, but even if his attitude were wonderful, his numbers were so bad last year that his prospect status would be marginal. **Grade C-**

Garrick Haltiwanger
New York Mets
Pos: OF **Bats:** Right **Ht:** 6'2" **Wt:** 190 **Age:** 23

Yr Team	Lg	G	AB	R	H	2B	3B	HR	RBI	BB	SO	SB	CS	Avg	OBP	Slg
96 Pittsfield	A	60	203	36	52	9	2	9	37	24	55	9	4	.256	.343	.453
97 Capital City	A	125	441	59	115	19	2	14	73	45	107	20	7	.261	.341	.408
2 Minor League Yrs		185	644	95	167	28	4	23	110	69	162	29	11	.259	.342	.422

An 11th-round pick in 1996 from The Citadel, Garrick Haltiwanger is an athletic outfielder with multiple tools and evolving skills. He has above-average power and speed, but needs to improve his command of the strike zone for his abilities to achieve full fruition. Even so, his performance was very good last year considering league and park context: OPS +11 percent, SEC +20 percent. Scouts say Haltiwanger can go get the ball in the field, but his range factor in left was very low, so his defense is a question mark, at least in my mind. I think Haltiwanger has promise, but he needs to improve his strike-zone judgment at least somewhat. **Grade C**

Joe Hamilton
Boston Red Sox
Pos: OF **Bats:** Left **Ht:** 6'0" **Wt:** 185 **Age:** 23

Yr Team	Lg	G	AB	R	H	2B	3B	HR	RBI	BB	SO	SB	CS	Avg	OBP	Slg
96 Red Sox	R	1	4	1	1	0	0	0	0	0	1	0	0	.250	.250	.250
Michigan	A	108	389	54	102	20	2	13	58	45	117	3	5	.262	.341	.424
97 Sarasota	A	104	317	51	88	17	3	12	52	43	89	14	3	.278	.363	.464
6 Minor League Yrs		422	1393	203	344	61	9	45	198	209	403	30	17	.247	.346	.401

Hamilton was a fourth-round pick in 1992, from a Massachusetts high school. He has made snail-like progress through the system, but had a pretty good year at Sarasota last year, showing some power in a tough environment, and he wasn't too old for the league. His OPS was sound at +17 percent. Hamilton is a weak defensive outfielder, so he has to hit at higher levels to get a chance. He won't be found on many prospects lists, but he might surprise in 1998. He also might vanish. **Grade C**

Mark Hamlin

Montreal Expos

Pos: OF **Bats:** Right **Ht:** 6'3" **Wt:** 220 **Age:** 24

Yr Team	Lg	G	AB	R	H	2B	3B	HR	RBI	BB	SO	SB	CS	Avg	OBP	Slg
96 Portland	A	54	202	22	55	8	2	4	26	16	53	5	3	.272	.335	.391
Salem	A	9	28	1	4	0	0	1	2	4	3	0	0	.143	.273	.250
97 Asheville	A	134	497	79	144	31	0	18	74	55	107	6	3	.290	.372	.461
2 Minor League Yrs		197	727	102	203	39	2	23	102	75	163	11	6	.279	.358	.433

Hamlin was a 24th-round pick in 1996, from Georgia Southern. He hit .370 there as a senior, but he was too old to draw extensive draft interest, and was selected mainly as roster filler. Hamlin had a good season for Asheville in 1997, with a nice OPS of +20 percent. He runs well for a big guy, and has some power potential. His command of the strike zone is adequate, but could be better, and he will need to hit well at higher levels to stay on the radar, given his age and lack of defensive skills. The Rockies traded him to Montreal in the Mike Lansing deal. **Grade C**

Jed Hansen

Kansas City Royals

Pos: 2B **Bats:** Right **Ht:** 6'1" **Wt:** 195 **Age:** 25

Yr Team	Lg	G	AB	R	H	2B	3B	HR	RBI	BB	SO	SB	CS	Avg	OBP	Slg
96 Wichita	AA	99	405	60	116	27	4	12	50	29	72	14	8	.286	.339	.462
Omaha	AAA	29	99	14	23	4	0	3	9	12	22	2	0	.232	.330	.364
97 Omaha	AAA	114	380	43	102	20	2	11	44	32	78	8	1	.268	.327	.418
Kansas City	AL	34	94	11	29	6	1	1	14	13	29	3	2	.309	.394	.426
4 Minor League Yrs		430	1533	229	405	86	15	38	170	175	301	74	23	.264	.347	.414

If the Royals decide to commit to their young players, Jed Hansen is likely to start at second base in 1998, especially considering how well he played in his major league exposure. He shouldn't be expected to hit .300 all the time, but he should be good for a sturdy .260, with doubles power and a reasonable amount of patience. He chases breaking stuff at times, but improved in that department last year. Hansen doesn't have tremendous physical talent, but he plays with intelligence and Chuck Knoblauch-like intensity. Defensively, he has very good range and can turn the double play. Hansen won't be a star, but he will be a steady presence in the infield, and will help his teams win. **Grade B-**

Jason Hardtke

Chicago Cubs

Pos: 2B **Bats:** Both **Ht:** 5'10" **Wt:** 175 **Age:** 26

Yr Team	Lg	G	AB	R	H	2B	3B	HR	RBI	BB	SO	SB	CS	Avg	OBP	Slg
96 Binghamton	AA	35	137	23	36	11	0	3	16	16	16	0	1	.263	.340	.409
Norfolk	AAA	71	257	49	77	17	2	9	35	29	29	4	6	.300	.368	.486
New York	NL	19	57	3	11	5	0	0	6	2	12	0	0	.193	.233	.281
97 Norfolk	AAA	97	388	46	107	23	3	11	45	40	54	3	6	.276	.343	.436
Binghamton	AA	6	26	3	10	2	0	1	4	2	2	0	0	.385	.429	.577
New York	NL	30	56	9	15	2	0	2	8	4	6	1	1	.268	.323	.411
8 Minor League Yrs		847	3208	522	926	210	29	70	419	384	367	65	46	.289	.365	.438

The Cubs claimed Jason Hardtke on waivers at the end of the season, and with Miguel Cairo leaving in expansion and Ryne Sandberg retiring, the opportunity for Hardtke may finally be here. He is a switch-hitter with good command of the strike zone and above-average pop for an infielder. Knee injuries killed his speed, and while he is not a dominant offensive player, he is better with the stick than many major league infielders. Scouts love his hustle. Hardtke is versatile with the glove; he can play second, third or short, although the keystone is his best position. He led International League second basemen in range factor, and was second in fielding percentage. I've been saying it for three years, and I will continue to say it: *Jason Hardtke can play.* A smart manager should be able to get something out of him. **Grade C+**

Adonis Harrison   Seattle Mariners

Pos: 2B   **Bats:** Left   **Ht:** 5'9"   **Wt:** 165   **Age:** 21

Yr Team	Lg	G	AB	R	H	2B	3B	HR	RBI	BB	SO	SB	CS	Avg	OBP	Slg
96 Lancaster	A	16	40	7	14	4	0	0	5	8	13	4	1	.350	.458	.450
Wisconsin	A	54	196	29	52	15	2	1	24	19	36	5	3	.265	.333	.378
97 Wisconsin	A	125	412	61	131	26	6	7	62	55	74	25	18	.318	.403	.461
3 Minor League Yrs		240	803	128	242	52	13	9	105	119	160	41	31	.301	.395	.432

Harrison was a 24th-round pick in 1994, from a high school in California. He is a small guy without a lot of pop at the plate, but he makes contact, works the count, and ranked sixth in the Midwest League in hitting. He needs to show he can hit at higher levels; due to his size, he may get the bat knocked out of his hands. Harrison was a shortstop in high school, and has the physical skills to be a good defensive player, but he really isn't yet. He is a long way from the majors; he's only in the book due to the fact that the Mariners have traded all of their real prospects away. **Grade C-**

Gary Haught   Oakland Athletics

Pos: P   **Throws:** Right   **Ht:** 6'1"   **Wt:** 190   **Age:** 27

Yr Team	Lg	G	GS	IP	H	R	ER	HR	BB	SO	SV	W	L	Pct.	ERA
96 Huntsville	AA	45	0	67.0	67	33	29	4	24	52	4	3	2	.600	3.90
97 Huntsville	AA	6	0	9.2	15	6	6	2	2	6	0	0	1	.000	5.59
Edmonton	AAA	30	2	42.2	37	20	17	7	13	35	11	1	1	.500	3.59
Oakland	AL	6	0	11.1	12	9	9	3	6	11	0	0	0	—	7.15
6 Minor League Yrs		211	26	474.2	429	196	174	49	157	405	23	33	17	.660	3.30

Gary Haught was drafted way back in 1992, from the University of Southwestern Louisiana in the 22nd round. He is an "organization pitcher," meaning he eats innings when the prospects are between starts or on the DL. Like many organization pitchers, he got a chance to close last year, and did a fine job. Haught has good control, a deceptive motion, and a curveball. That's about it, but it is enough to get him a chance with a desperate team, and who knows, he might do something with it. Stranger things have happened. Like a guy named "Newt" rising to a position of authority. **Grade C-**

Wes Helms   Atlanta Braves

Pos: 3B   **Bats:** Right   **Ht:** 6'4"   **Wt:** 210   **Age:** 21

Yr Team	Lg	G	AB	R	H	2B	3B	HR	RBI	BB	SO	SB	CS	Avg	OBP	Slg
96 Durham	A	67	258	40	83	19	2	13	54	12	51	1	1	.322	.367	.562
Greenville	AA	64	231	24	59	13	2	4	22	13	48	2	1	.255	.306	.381
97 Richmond	AAA	32	110	11	21	4	0	3	15	10	34	1	1	.191	.286	.309
Greenville	AA	86	314	50	93	14	1	11	44	33	50	3	4	.296	.371	.452
4 Minor League Yrs		441	1636	236	454	97	7	46	249	140	326	15	10	.278	.346	.430

A year ago, there was talk that Chipper Jones would move to shortstop in 1998, with Wes Helms taking over at third base. That seems less likely now. No one questions Helms' ability to handle third defensively: he has major league range, a major league arm, and doesn't make tons of errors. He has very solid power potential as well, projected to 20-25 homers a year by some scouts, primarily due to his quick wrists. Helms might have the quickest wrists this side of Tony Gwynn, but at Richmond he hit more like Jesse Helms. It doesn't take a baseball scientist to see that his stats there were awful. His walk rate was actually not that bad, but he struck out way too much and looked confused. About like Jesse Helms. Demoted to Greenville, he recovered and salvaged the season. Helms is still very young and remains a fine prospect, but he'll likely need a year of Triple-A. **Grade B**

Todd Helton   Colorado Rockies

Pos: 1B   **Bats:** Left   **Ht:** 6'2"   **Wt:** 195   **Age:** 24

Yr Team	Lg	G	AB	R	H	2B	3B	HR	RBI	BB	SO	SB	CS	Avg	OBP	Slg
96 New Haven	AA	93	319	46	106	24	2	7	51	51	37	2	5	.332	.425	.486
Colo Sprngs	AAA	21	71	13	25	4	1	2	13	11	12	0	0	.352	.439	.521
97 Colo Sprngs	AAA	99	392	87	138	31	2	16	88	61	68	3	1	.352	.434	.564
Colorado	NL	35	93	13	26	2	1	5	11	8	11	0	1	.280	.337	.484
3 Minor League Yrs		267	983	170	320	70	6	26	167	148	149	6	7	.326	.412	.488

Todd Helton is probably the leading candidate for 1998 National League Rookie of the Year. He has nothing left to prove in Triple-A, and now that the Big Cat has gone to Atlanta, Helton will play every day. He has a smooth swing that can drive the ball to all fields, his power is growing, and his plate discipline is very good. Unlike some Rockies hitters, he will remain an above-average hitter even on the road. Scouts liken him to a cross between Mark Grace and Don Mattingly at their peaks. Helton can occasionally be tied up with hard stuff up and in, but most hitters are vulnerable to that, and Helton makes adjustments according to how he is pitched. Defense is another strength, especially at first base, although he is athletic enough to play the outfield fairly well despite a lack of great speed. Helton is a good bet to eventually win a batting title in Coors Field, and if his power escalates further, he could be a Triple Crown threat. **Grade A**

Bret Hemphill — *Anaheim Angels*

Pos: C   **Bats:** Both   **Ht:** 6'3"   **Wt:** 210   **Age:** 26

Yr Team	Lg	G	AB	R	H	2B	3B	HR	RBI	BB	SO	SB	CS	Avg	OBP	Slg
96 Lk Elsinore	A	108	399	64	105	21	3	17	64	52	93	4	3	.263	.353	.459
97 Midland	AA	78	266	46	82	15	2	10	63	47	56	0	2	.308	.417	.492
4 Minor League Yrs		374	1297	202	349	70	7	39	208	178	292	7	9	.269	.360	.424

Scouts have always been champions of Bret Hemphill's defensive abilities; he lasted until the 14th round in the 1994 draft because no one thought he would hit. It didn't look like he would, until 1996, when he had a good half-season at Lake Elsinore. He continued to swing the bat well at El Paso in 1997, although the park and league context were in his favor. He is reasonably patient, and while he can be overpowered, he has learned to drive the ball occasionally with his natural strength. Hemphill has a reputation as an excellent defensive catcher, but he threw out just 29 percent of stealers last year. He does move well behind a good plate, and can call a good game. Hemphill would make a decent second catcher. Now for the bad news: he could miss all of 1998 after reconstructive surgery on his throwing shoulder, which he injured in a collision. **Grade C**

Oscar Henriquez — *Florida Marlins*

Pos: P   **Throws:** Right   **Ht:** 6'6"   **Wt:** 220   **Age:** 24

Yr Team	Lg	G	GS	IP	H	R	ER	HR	BB	SO	SV	W	L	Pct.	ERA
96 Kissimmee	A	37	0	34.0	28	18	15	0	29	40	15	0	4	.000	3.97
97 New Orleans	AAA	60	0	74.0	65	28	23	4	27	80	12	4	5	.444	2.80
Houston	NL	4	0	4.0	2	2	2	0	3	3	0	0	1	.000	4.50
4 Minor League Yrs		144	26	302.2	287	170	137	18	156	273	28	16	23	.410	4.07

Another Venezuelan signed by the Astros, Oscar Henriquez is a huge pitcher with a vicious fastball, often compared to Jose Mesa and Armando Benitez. His heater bores in on hitters at 96 MPH; he has been clocked as high as 98 on occasion. He also has a good curveball. His control is improving, and hitters don't have much of a chance against him when his command of the curve is on. The fastball/curve combo is good enough for him to close in the majors. Henriquez has had health problems, including a rare, and sometimes fatal, neurological disorder called myasthenia gravis, which causes paralysis. He seems to be over that, but there are concerns that he may be too emotional for the closer role. Traded to Florida in the Moises Alou deal, Henriquez may get a chance to close in 1998. **Grade B**

Russ Herbert — *Chicago White Sox*

Pos: P   **Throws:** Right   **Ht:** 6'4"   **Wt:** 200   **Age:** 25

Yr Team	Lg	G	GS	IP	H	R	ER	HR	BB	SO	SV	W	L	Pct.	ERA
96 Pr William	A	25	25	144.0	129	73	54	12	62	148	0	6	10	.375	3.38
97 Birmingham	AA	27	26	158.2	136	72	64	14	80	126	0	13	5	.722	3.63
4 Minor League Yrs		91	87	520.2	433	235	190	41	232	490	0	26	29	.473	3.28

Hardly anyone has heard of Russ Herbert, but he is someone to watch. In his first Double-A season he led the Southern League in ERA, and he is not a soft tosser. His fastball can hit 90 MPH, although 88-89 is more normal. Combined with his slider and change, his stuff can be very effective. Herbert struggles with his control occasionally, a problem reflected in his below-average K/BB of -13 percent. On the other hand, his H/IP was very good at +18 percent, showing his major league stuff. Herbert is durable, and could evolve into an inning-eating workhorse starter. He needs to improve his control a bit first though. **Grade C+**

Brett Herbison
New York Mets

Pos: P **Throws:** Right **Ht:** 6'5" **Wt:** 175 **Age:** 20

Yr Team	Lg	G	GS	IP	H	R	ER	HR	BB	SO	SV	W	L	Pct.	ERA
96 Kingsport	R	13	12	76.2	43	18	11	4	31	86	0	6	2	.750	1.29
Pittsfield	A	1	1	2.0	4	6	5	0	4	1	0	0	1	.000	22.50
97 Capital City	A	28	27	160.0	166	86	71	13	63	146	0	7	14	.333	3.99
3 Minor League Yrs		52	50	284.2	250	127	101	22	116	268	0	17	17	.500	3.19

Herbison was a high school star in Illinois as a shortstop, but when the Mets picked him in the second round in 1995, they saw him as a pitcher. He moved to the mound full-time after signing, and while he was hardly dominant, he did well enough to justify the decision. Herbison's fastball is just average right now, but is expected to improve substantially as he fills out and learns more about pitching. His curveball and changeup are highly advanced for an inexperienced pitcher. Ratio-wise, his performance in the Sally League was mediocre; his K/BB and K/IP were okay at plus-six percent each, but the park helped him out. Still, considering his inexperience and projectability, he deserves substantial slack, and I will give it to him. **Grade C+**

Chad Hermansen
Pittsburgh Pirates

Pos: 2B **Bats:** Right **Ht:** 6'2" **Wt:** 185 **Age:** 20

Yr Team	Lg	G	AB	R	H	2B	3B	HR	RBI	BB	SO	SB	CS	Avg	OBP	Slg
96 Augusta	A	62	226	41	57	11	3	14	41	38	65	11	3	.252	.377	.513
Lynchburg	A	66	251	40	69	11	3	10	46	29	56	5	1	.275	.352	.462
97 Carolina	AA	129	487	87	134	31	4	20	70	69	136	18	6	.275	.373	.478
3 Minor League Yrs		325	1221	212	333	71	14	53	199	163	315	38	12	.273	.366	.484

Pittsburgh's first-round pick in 1995, Chad Hermansen will be one of the leading power hitters of the early 21st century. The question is, what position will he play? Hermansen isn't a great hitter for average at this point, but his power makes up for it, and he was extremely young to be playing in Double-A. He strikes out a bit too much, but he draws his share of walks, can smash the ball out of any park, and runs well. His OPS was +10 percent, which is very good for a very young power hitter in a tough Carolina park, and his fine SEC of +35 percent shows he contributes a great deal to the offense. No one doubts that this guy will hit, but he still doesn't have a position. The Pirates last year tried him at shortstop, then center field, then second base, and he looked pretty bad at all of them. If I were the Pirates, I would stick him in left field and be done with it. Sure, he would be more valuable up the middle. . . if you don't mind your second baseman fielding .920 with limited range. I think Hermansen will be great, wherever he plays. **Grade A-**

Juan Hernaiz
Detroit Tigers

Pos: OF Bats: Right Ht: 5'11" Wt: 185 Age: 23

Yr Team	Lg	G	AB	R	H	2B	3B	HR	RBI	BB	SO	SB	CS	Avg	OBP	Slg
96 Savannah	A	132	492	68	137	19	8	14	73	21	96	42	15	.278	.317	.435
97 Lakeland	A	118	438	58	122	13	6	12	56	22	107	29	13	.279	.317	.418
6 Minor League Yrs		439	1535	200	414	52	19	31	177	65	356	96	39	.270	.305	.389

Hernaiz, a Dodgers farm product, came to Detroit in a minor league deal following the 1996 season. Like most Dodgers merchandise, Hernaiz is toolsy, with above-average power and speed potential, but struggles to control the strike zone. His walk rate was very low at Lakeland, and unless he gets that under control, he won't survive at higher levels. Hernaiz is only adequate with the glove in center field, and would be better off in left or right. He has an outside chance to make it. The Tigers should give him a dose of whatever they gave Juan Encarnacion last year. **Grade C-**

Elvin Hernandez
Pittsburgh Pirates

Pos: P Throws: Right Ht: 6'1" Wt: 165 Age: 20

Yr Team	Lg	G	GS	IP	H	R	ER	HR	BB	SO	SV	W	L	Pct.	ERA
96 Augusta	A	27	27	157.2	140	60	55	13	16	171	0	17	5	.773	3.14
97 Carolina	AA	17	17	92.2	104	67	59	11	26	66	0	2	7	.222	5.73
Lynchburg	A	3	0	5.0	4	1	1	0	1	5	1	0	0	—	1.80
3 Minor League Yrs		61	58	345.2	330	168	144	32	65	296	1	25	13	.658	3.75

Young Dominican Elvin Hernandez was excellent in the South Atlantic League in 1996, but the more experienced hitters of the Southern League found his finesse offerings rather tasty in 1997. His fastball is average on a good day, and while his slider and changeup are pretty decent, he has a tendency to nibble with them. He didn't give up many walks last year, but his H/IP skyrocketed and his strikeout rate plummeted, due to the fact that it is more difficult to trick Double-A hitters. Hernandez is still very young, and has time to pick up some velocity and sharpen his command. He hasn't done it yet, though. **Grade C**

Francis Hernandez
Baltimore Orioles

Pos: P Throws: Right Ht: 6'0" Wt: 160 Age: 21

Yr Team	Lg	G	GS	IP	H	R	ER	HR	BB	SO	SV	W	L	Pct.	ERA
96 Frederick	A	37	0	45.1	44	26	23	6	21	39	12	4	3	.571	4.57
97 Frederick	A	49	0	58.1	51	23	15	8	21	51	24	4	4	.500	2.31
Bowie	AA	6	0	5.2	7	1	1	0	4	2	0	0	0	—	1.59
3 Minor League Yrs		119	0	139.2	123	56	45	16	55	118	48	10	10	.500	2.90

A Dominican relief pitcher signed in 1994, Francis Hernandez has a live arm, but the Orioles have kept him in the bullpen to avoid overworking him due to his small frame. He had a successful year as the closer at Frederick, and should move up to Double-A in 1998. Like almost all minor league closers, his chance to actually close in the majors is limited, but there doesn't seem to be any reason why he can't be a middle reliever if he does well in the high minors. **Grade C-**

Ramon Hernandez
Oakland Athletics

Pos: C   Bats: Right   Ht: 6'0"   Wt: 170   Age: 21

Yr Team	Lg	G	AB	R	H	2B	3B	HR	RBI	BB	SO	SB	CS	Avg	OBP	Slg
96 W Michigan	A	123	447	62	114	26	2	12	68	69	62	2	3	.255	.355	.403
97 Visalia	A	86	332	57	120	21	2	15	85	35	47	2	4	.361	.427	.572
Huntsville	AA	44	161	27	31	3	0	4	24	18	23	0	0	.193	.281	.286
3 Minor League Yrs		301	1083	183	317	59	10	35	214	161	148	10	9	.293	.389	.463

With two teams in the California League, Oakland had a unique opportunity to examine the credentials of top catching prospects Ramon Hernandez and A. J. Hinch in something approaching a controlled experiment. They both excelled. Hernandez showed amazing offensive consistency, battering Cal League pitching for both power and average, and showing good command of the strike zone. His defense also drew positive comment. When Hinch was promoted to Triple-A, Hernandez moved up to Double-A Huntsville, and was terrible. He continued to show power, but the batting average dropped off 150 points. I'm not worried; his command of the strike zone remained intact, which means the batting average should rebound with time. The main significance of his Double-A struggle is that it moves Hinch ahead in the pecking order. Hernandez, however, remains one of the best catching prospects in the game. The Oakland farm system is truly loaded with position-player talent. **Grade B+**

Santos Hernandez
Tampa Bay Devil Rays

Pos: P   Throws: Right   Ht: 6'1"   Wt: 172   Age: 25

Yr Team	Lg	G	GS	IP	H	R	ER	HR	BB	SO	SV	W	L	Pct.	ERA
96 Burlington	A	61	0	66.2	39	15	14	4	13	79	35	3	3	.500	1.89
97 San Jose	A	47	0	57.0	51	26	22	7	14	87	15	2	6	.250	3.47
Shreveport	AA	11	0	15.2	13	4	4	1	3	14	6	1	1	.500	2.30
4 Minor League Yrs		195	0	251.2	204	95	79	20	60	313	69	16	25	.390	2.83

A Panamanian reliever signed in 1994, Santos Hernandez is a numbers guy: he doesn't have great scouting reports, but his statistics are too good to ignore. The Giants let him rot as staff filler in the Midwest League for three seasons, but he always pitched well, and continued to do so when promoted to Double-A near the end of the 1997 season. The problem, of course, is that he doesn't throw very hard, but his control is exceptional and he strikes people out. He has an average fastball, but a good splitter. He will be a middle-relief candidate for the Devil Rays. **Grade C**

Mike Hessman
Atlanta Braves

Pos: 3B   Bats: Right   Ht: 6'5"   Wt: 220   Age: 20

Yr Team	Lg	G	AB	R	H	2B	3B	HR	RBI	BB	SO	SB	CS	Avg	OBP	Slg
96 Braves	R	53	190	13	41	10	1	1	15	12	41	1	1	.216	.277	.295
97 Macon	A	122	459	69	108	25	0	21	74	41	167	0	2	.235	.305	.427
2 Minor League Yrs		175	649	82	149	35	1	22	89	53	208	1	3	.230	.297	.388

A 15th-round pick in 1996 from a California high school, Mike Hessman has two above-average tools in his power and his throwing arm, but has a lot of work to do at the plate.

He is too aggressive, as his high strikeout rate and mediocre walk rate show, and is vulnerable to any pitch with a curl in it. I am including him in the book because I like his power potential. He is young enough to amply improve, but it won't be easy. **Grade C-**

Richard Hidalgo

Houston Astros

Pos: OF　**Bats:** Right　**Ht:** 6'2"　**Wt:** 175　**Age:** 22

Yr Team	Lg	G	AB	R	H	2B	3B	HR	RBI	BB	SO	SB	CS	Avg	OBP	Slg
96 Jackson	AA	130	513	66	151	34	2	14	78	29	55	11	7	.294	.341	.450
97 New Orleans	AAA	134	526	74	147	37	5	11	78	35	57	6	10	.279	.330	.432
Houston	NL	19	62	8	19	5	0	2	6	4	18	1	0	.306	.358	.484
6 Minor League Yrs		683	2591	336	733	176	25	62	373	162	371	72	56	.283	.330	.442

Richard Hidalgo has a good chance to earn an outfield job in 1998. The Venezuelan delights scouts with his tools; he has made slow but steady progress converting them to skills. Hidalgo is very strong for his size, and while his power is mainly to the gaps right now, he projects as a 25-homer guy eventually. His stats last year were hurt by playing in a horrible hitters' park at New Orleans, but he was still named the No. 3 prospect in the American Association by *Baseball America*. He makes contact, but is often impatient, and needs to be more selective. Hidalgo is a solid defensive outfielder, with above-average range and a superb arm, and would be an asset at any outfield position. He played well in a September trial, but he is more likely to hit .270 than .300 in the majors over a full season at this stage. Hidalgo is very young, and is probably four years from his peak. He is already a good player, and could be a Seven Skill player if he continues to develop. **Grade B+**

A.J. Hinch

Oakland Athletics

Pos: C　**Bats:** Right　**Ht:** 6'1"　**Wt:** 195　**Age:** 23

Yr Team	Lg	G	AB	R	H	2B	3B	HR	RBI	BB	SO	SB	CS	Avg	OBP	Slg
97 Modesto	A	95	333	70	103	25	3	20	73	42	68	8	3	.309	.400	.583
Edmonton	AAA	39	125	23	47	7	0	4	24	20	13	2	0	.376	.473	.528
1 Minor League Yr		134	458	93	150	32	3	24	97	62	81	10	3	.328	.420	.568

You're a good one, Mr. Hinch. A.J. Hinch had a long and successful career at Stanford University, but he didn't decide to go with pro ball until his senior year, after playing in the Olympics. Scouts have always adored his glove, but questioned whether he would hit in the pros. A sore shoulder inhibited his throwing at Stanford, and his offense moved ahead of his defense. He was healthy in 1997, tore through the California League, then played even better in six weeks in the PCL. His swing is compact but powerful, and he is an intelligent hitter. Defensively, his arm strength is only average, a result of the shoulder problem, but he has a quick release, calls a good game, and led the Cal League in fielding percentage. With Ben Grieve, Miguel Tejada, Hinch and several other guys, the Athletics have a robust nucleus of young talent. **Grade B+**

Brett Hinchliffe

Seattle Mariners

Pos: P   Throws: Right   Ht: 6'4"   Wt: 205   Age: 23

Yr Team	Lg	G	GS	IP	H	R	ER	HR	BB	SO	SV	W	L	Pct.	ERA
96 Lancaster	A	27	26	163.1	179	105	77	19	64	146	0	11	10	.524	4.24
97 Memphis	AA	24	24	145.2	159	81	72	20	45	107	0	10	10	.500	4.45
6 Minor League Yrs		127	101	639.2	685	383	302	69	208	536	3	40	43	.482	4.25

Hinchcliffe is a spindly presence on the mound. He hasn't picked up a lot of velocity since signing out of high school in 1992, but his control is good, and he survives by not being afraid to throw strikes with average stuff. His transition to Double-A in 1997 was not a terrific success, but he wasn't terrible, and with a year there under his waistband, he could advance in 1998. He could also stagnate. His vignette is similar to that of Ryan Franklin, another Seattle farmhand. **Grade C**

Steve Hoff

Florida Marlins

Pos: P   Throws: Left   Ht: 6'4"   Wt: 205   Age: 20

Yr Team	Lg	G	GS	IP	H	R	ER	HR	BB	SO	SV	W	L	Pct.	ERA
96 Padres	R	16	13	85.1	66	37	27	2	36	104	0	8	2	.800	2.85
97 Clinton	A	12	12	76.1	72	28	23	4	18	78	0	7	1	.875	2.71
Rancho Cuca	A	14	13	66.1	73	56	46	6	48	59	0	4	5	.444	6.24
2 Minor League Yrs		42	38	228.0	211	121	96	12	102	241	0	19	8	.704	3.79

Hoff was a 15th-round pick in 1995, from a California high school. He signed late and didn't begin his career until 1996, but he has moved very quickly. Hoff's fastball is just average right now, but his breaking stuff is very impressive. At Clinton, his control was on, and he pitched excellently. His K/BB was outstanding at +116 percent, his K/IP very good at +21 percent. His H/IP was just league average, and when he was promoted to the California League, his other numbers fell off, too. At the higher level, Hoff was very tentative, afraid to challenge hitters like he did at Clinton. He should be able to correct that with experience, assuming the standard disclaimer: will he stay healthy? He was traded to Florida in the Kevin Brown deal. **Grade C+**

Damon Hollins

Atlanta Braves

Pos: OF   Bats: Right   Ht: 5'11"   Wt: 180   Age: 23

Yr Team	Lg	G	AB	R	H	2B	3B	HR	RBI	BB	SO	SB	CS	Avg	OBP	Slg
96 Richmond	AAA	42	146	16	29	9	0	0	8	16	37	2	3	.199	.278	.260
97 Richmond	AAA	134	498	73	132	31	3	20	63	45	84	7	2	.265	.329	.460
6 Minor League Yrs		547	2014	301	525	121	8	69	302	199	408	52	22	.261	.329	.431

A fourth-round pick in 1992 from a high school in California, Damon Hollins made progress in his first full Triple-A season. 1996 was lost to a broken wrist, but he rebounded in 1997, showing major improvement in strike-zone judgment. He cut his strikeouts substantially. His OPS was only slightly above league at plus-four percent, so he's not ready to make an impact yet. Although Hollins runs well, he has never been a basestealer. His speed does show up in the outfield: he always posts very high range factors in center field. Paired with his strong arm, it makes him an asset on defense. Hollins is still young, and if he builds on the progress he made last year, he could be a valuable player. With the wrist injury a year behind him, a major increase in power is not out of the question. **Grade C+**

David Hooten
Minnesota Twins

Pos: P   Throws: Right   Ht: 6'0"   Wt: 175   Age: 22

Yr Team	Lg	G	GS	IP	H	R	ER	HR	BB	SO	SV	W	L	Pct.	ERA
96 Elizabethtn	R	6	0	8.1	6	4	4	0	5	15	1	1	0	1.000	4.32
Ft. Wayne	A	21	0	37.1	30	11	10	0	13	39	2	4	1	.800	2.41
97 Ft. Wayne	A	28	27	165.2	134	57	48	5	54	138	0	11	8	.579	2.61
2 Minor League Yrs		55	27	211.1	170	72	62	5	72	192	3	16	9	.640	2.64

Hooten, a Mississippi State product, was selected in the 14th round in 1996. He pitched quite well in the Midwest League last year, posting some pretty good ratios: K/BB +27 percent, H/IP +15 percent. His K/IP was right at league average. Hooten works with a fastball just a tick above average, and an excellent curve. His control is good and he knows how to pitch. He needs to face the test of Double-A before we know exactly how good of a prospect he is. **Grade C**

Victor Hurtado
Florida Marlins

Pos: P   Throws: Right   Ht: 6'1"   Wt: 155   Age: 20

Yr Team	Lg	G	GS	IP	H	R	ER	HR	BB	SO	SV	W	L	Pct.	ERA
96 Kane County	A	27	27	176.0	167	79	64	10	56	126	0	15	7	.682	3.27
97 Brevard Cty	A	17	16	92.0	102	54	50	9	34	58	0	4	7	.364	4.89
3 Minor League Yrs		51	50	301.1	283	138	117	19	106	212	0	22	15	.595	3.49

Hurtado was a fine prospect after his 1996 season in the Midwest League, but shoulder problems resulted in a slow start to 1997 and he didn't begin pitching until June. He didn't perform well at Brevard County, and needs to step forward in 1998 to maintain his prospect status. Hurtado's fastball is only average, but when his arm is fit, he gets people out with his curveball, changeup and control. He is very young, and should pick up velocity as he matures, but all of that depends on whether or not he stays healthy. There isn't any way to predict that. **Grade C**

Norm Hutchins
Anaheim Angels

Pos: OF   Bats: Left   Ht: 6'2"   Wt: 185   Age: 22

Yr Team	Lg	G	AB	R	H	2B	3B	HR	RBI	BB	SO	SB	CS	Avg	OBP	Slg
96 Cedar Rapds	A	126	466	59	105	13	16	2	52	28	110	22	8	.225	.277	.335
97 Lk Elsinore	A	132	564	82	163	31	12	15	69	23	147	39	17	.289	.321	.466
4 Minor League Yrs		360	1401	192	354	55	32	19	146	73	355	84	37	.253	.295	.378

Norm Hutchins is on the verge of. . . something. He had the best offensive season of his career in 1997, and will move to Double-A in 1998. The speed and power that made him a second-round pick in 1994 are clearly blossoming. He has made substantial progress tailoring his swing and learning to deal with breaking stuff. His range in center field is superb, and while he still makes too many errors, that should resolve itself with experience. So, why is his future still uncertain? First of all, the old bugaboo of strike-zone judgment remains a problem. . . too many strikeouts, not enough walks. Secondly, a *Baseball America* article quotes Angels roving hitting instructor Gene Richards as saying that Hutchins' outburst of power is "scary." Not scary in a good way, but in a bad way. The Angels are apparently worried that Hutchins may develop too much power and ruin his speed game. You can draw your own conclusions from that, but it will be *very* interesting to see how Hutchins plays in 1998. **Grade C**

Bernard Hutchison   *Colorado Rockies*

Pos: OF   **Bats:** Right   **Ht:** 5'10"   **Wt:** 160   **Age:** 23

Yr Team	Lg	G	AB	R	H	2B	3B	HR	RBI	BB	SO	SB	CS	Avg	OBP	Slg
96 Portland	A	51	192	29	50	6	0	0	13	16	34	20	3	.260	.325	.292
97 Asheville	A	108	419	59	97	10	2	0	30	35	91	81	18	.232	.294	.265
2 Minor League Yrs		159	611	88	147	16	2	0	43	51	125	101	21	.241	.304	.273

Bernard Hutchison isn't really my kind of player, but 81 stolen bases gets my attention. A 22nd-round pick in 1996 from the University of Montevallo (Rusty Greer's alma mater) in Alabama, Hutchison is a slap hitter who relies on the transwarp drive in his legs to give him offensive value. He needs to get stronger to avoid getting the bat knocked out of his hands at higher levels, and it would also help if he were more patient. His range in center is outstanding, of course, but he makes too many errors and has a weak arm. If everything goes right for Hutchison, he could be Vince Coleman, but his chance to hit enough to help is slim. **Grade C-**

Raul Ibanez   *Seattle Mariners*

Pos: OF   **Bats:** Left   **Ht:** 6'2"   **Wt:** 210   **Age:** 25

Yr Team	Lg	G	AB	R	H	2B	3B	HR	RBI	BB	SO	SB	CS	Avg	OBP	Slg
96 Port City	AA	19	76	12	28	8	1	1	13	8	7	3	2	.368	.424	.539
Tacoma	AAA	111	405	59	115	20	3	11	47	44	56	7	7	.284	.353	.430
Seattle	AL	4	5	0	0	0	0	0	0	0	1	0	0	.000	.167	.000
97 Tacoma	AAA	111	438	84	133	30	5	15	84	32	75	7	5	.304	.349	.498
Seattle	AL	11	26	3	4	0	1	1	4	0	6	0	0	.154	.154	.346
6 Minor League Yrs		555	2018	336	616	133	25	60	363	211	296	32	29	.305	.370	.485

With Jose Cruz Jr. out of the Mariners' outfield, Raul Ibanez may receive a chance to play in Seattle in 1998, unless they trade him for Danny Tartabull or Ruben Sierra or Otto Velez or something. Ibanez has a smooth swing that produces hard liners to all fields. He will never be a major power force, but should be good for .270-.290 averages, with double-digit homer production. His OPS was only slightly above league last year, but Tacoma is a very difficult park by Pacific Coast League standards. Ibanez can play a pretty decent right field, and has an accurate if not overly strong arm, but will move to left in the majors. I don't see Ibanez as a coming star, and he certainly doesn't have Cruz's potential, but he would make an adequate regular, and could have some very good years. **Grade B-**

Jesse Ibarra
Detroit Tigers

Pos: 1B **Bats:** Both **Ht:** 6'3" **Wt:** 195 **Age:** 25

Yr Team	Lg	G	AB	R	H	2B	3B	HR	RBI	BB	SO	SB	CS	Avg	OBP	Slg
96 San Jose	A	126	498	74	141	38	0	17	95	63	108	5	1	.283	.366	.462
97 Jacksnville	AA	115	441	73	125	24	1	25	91	55	85	3	2	.283	.363	.512
4 Minor League Yrs		440	1637	252	470	109	3	86	323	230	370	9	5	.287	.377	.515

The Tigers picked up Jesse Ibarra from the Giants last winter; I'm not sure what they wanted with another power-hitting first-base prospect, since they already have several, but Ibarra played well in his Double-A debut, and is a solid prospect. He has good command of the strike zone, and is dangerous from both sides of the plate. He makes contact better than most power hitters, and will go to the opposite field or pull the ball, depending on how he is pitched. His OPS was pleasant at +13 percent. Ibarra needs work with the glove, and may best be cast as a DH. He can hit, but I'm not sure where he fits in in Detroit. **Grade B-**

Jeff Inglin
Chicago White Sox

Pos: OF **Bats:** Right **Ht:** 5'11" **Wt:** 185 **Age:** 22

Yr Team	Lg	G	AB	R	H	2B	3B	HR	RBI	BB	SO	SB	CS	Avg	OBP	Slg
96 Bristol	R	50	193	27	56	10	0	8	24	11	25	9	6	.290	.357	.466
Hickory	A	22	83	12	30	6	2	2	15	4	11	2	1	.361	.393	.554
97 Hickory	A	135	536	100	179	34	6	16	102	49	87	31	8	.334	.388	.509
2 Minor League Yrs		207	812	139	265	50	8	26	141	64	123	42	15	.326	.381	.504

Jeff Inglin was selected in the 16th round in 1996, out of Southern Cal, where he hit .392 with 14 home runs his junior year. Those were better stats than those posted by Trojans teammate Jacque Jones, who went in the second round to Minnesota. Jones has a prettier swing and is better with the glove, so scouts like him better. Inglin has continued to hit in pro ball, ranking third in the Sally League in batting average, and posting a mark of +30 percent in both OPS and SEC. I would like to see him walk more, but he seemed to adjust to the wooden bat quite nicely. Defensively, he is adequate in left field, but will never be a big help with the glove. Inglin is a Bobby Higginson-type prospect: a successful college hitter who went low in the draft because scouts didn't like his tools. Watch for Inglin as he moves up; he could be very good. **Grade C+**

Darron Ingram
Cincinnati Reds

Pos: OF **Bats:** Right **Ht:** 6'3" **Wt:** 225 **Age:** 21

Yr Team	Lg	G	AB	R	H	2B	3B	HR	RBI	BB	SO	SB	CS	Avg	OBP	Slg
96 Chston-WV	A	15	48	5	9	3	0	1	6	8	19	0	0	.188	.298	.313
Billings	R	65	251	49	74	13	0	17	56	34	88	7	3	.295	.382	.550
97 Burlington	A	134	510	74	135	25	4	29	97	46	195	8	5	.265	.324	.500
4 Minor League Yrs		320	1173	178	308	52	8	63	223	118	430	19	13	.263	.330	.482

Aristotle counselled moderation in all things, but there are some things in this world that are best enjoyed in excess. Home-run power is one of them. Strikeouts aren't. Darron Ingram, drafted in the 12th round in 1994 from a high school in Kentucky, has enormous power potential, but an equally enormous inclination to strike out. He will crush fastballs, but struggles against breaking stuff, and is usually fooled by changeups. His OPS was good at +14 percent, but unless he shows better plate discipline, he is unlikely to carry that to higher levels. Ingram is also a poor defensive outfielder. He is still quite young and has time to improve, but right now he is a work in progress. **Grade C+**

Johnny Isom   *Baltimore Orioles*

Pos: OF   **Bats**: Right   **Ht**: 5'11"   **Wt**: 210   **Age**: 24

Yr Team	Lg	G	AB	R	H	2B	3B	HR	RBI	BB	SO	SB	CS	Avg	OBP	Slg
96 Frederick	A	124	486	69	141	27	3	18	104	40	87	8	6	.290	.349	.469
97 Bowie	AA	135	518	70	142	28	4	20	91	44	121	1	5	.274	.341	.459
3 Minor League Yrs		318	1216	186	356	69	11	44	251	109	235	18	13	.293	.356	.476

The Orioles drafted Johnny Isom out of Texas Wesleyan University in 1995. He has hit quite well in pro ball for a 28th-round pick, and made a successful transition to Double-A last year. Isom has above-average power to all fields, and while he can be overpowered by hard stuff inside, or tricked with breaking pitches away, he hits mediocre stuff frequently enough to make a living. He does need to improve his command of the strike zone to maintain his current level of success. Isom was bothered by a shoulder problem most of the season, and did not play particularly well defensively. He is a hard worker, and is quite intelligent. Isom will move to Triple-A in 1998, and could see some major league time if he hits well. **Grade C+**

Damian Jackson   *Cincinnati Reds*

Pos: SS   **Bats**: Right   **Ht**: 5'10"   **Wt**: 160   **Age**: 24

Yr Team	Lg	G	AB	R	H	2B	3B	HR	RBI	BB	SO	SB	CS	Avg	OBP	Slg
96 Buffalo	AAA	133	452	77	116	15	1	12	49	48	78	24	7	.257	.333	.374
97 Buffalo	AAA	73	266	51	78	12	0	4	13	37	45	20	8	.293	.383	.383
Indianapolis	AAA	19	71	12	19	6	1	0	7	10	17	4	1	.268	.361	.380
Cleveland	AL	8	9	2	1	0	0	0	0	0	1	1	0	.111	.200	.111
Cincinnati	NL	12	27	6	6	2	1	1	2	4	7	1	1	.222	.323	.481
6 Minor League Yrs		664	2380	394	626	113	13	30	217	293	456	180	56	.263	.350	.359

The Reds picked up Damian Jackson as part of the John Smiley trade with the Indians. A glut of infielders made Jackson expendable in Cleveland, but with Cincinnati he may get a chance to play. Scouts have always liked Jackson's athletic ability and physical talents, and he has made headway offensively over the last two years. He doesn't have great power, but controls the strike zone, makes contact, and can steal a base. His OPS was league average in the American Association, while his SEC was good for an infielder at nine percent over league. Jackson is still a bit error-prone at shortstop, but he led the AA in range factor, and can also play second base and the outfield if needed. As contact-hitting middle infielders with speed and promising defense go, I like him. **Grade B**

Ryan Jackson

Florida Marlins

Pos: OF **Bats:** Left **Ht:** 6'2" **Wt:** 195 **Age:** 26

Yr Team	Lg	G	AB	R	H	2B	3B	HR	RBI	BB	SO	SB	CS	Avg	OBP	Slg
96 Marlins	R	7	25	5	9	0	0	0	5	1	3	2	0	.360	.407	.360
Brevard Cty	A	6	26	4	8	2	0	1	4	1	7	1	0	.308	.333	.500
97 Portland	AA	134	491	87	153	28	4	26	98	51	85	2	5	.312	.380	.544
4 Minor League Yrs		351	1289	220	388	87	11	43	230	142	209	22	16	.301	.371	.486

Ryan Jackson had a great year in the Midwest League in 1995, but he was too old for the level, so he needed to prove himself in Double-A in 1996. He lost that season to an injured knee, however, and while he played well in 1997, he is still in the position to have to prove himself. He is also buried behind several hotter prospects. Jackson has a good line-drive swing, and is an intelligent hitter with punch to all fields. His OPS was fine at +20 percent, although he did get some help from the park. He is adequate defensively, but nothing special. I like Jackson and I think he can hit, but he is older than most prospects, and it may be hard for him to get a chance to show his ability. Potential openings in the Florida outfield give him a slim chance to get a look this year. **Grade C**

Elinton Jasco

Chicago Cubs

Pos: 2B **Bats:** Right **Ht:** 5'10" **Wt:** 150 **Age:** 22

Yr Team	Lg	G	AB	R	H	2B	3B	HR	RBI	BB	SO	SB	CS	Avg	OBP	Slg
96 Rockford	A	120	464	95	136	11	7	1	43	62	97	48	14	.293	.381	.353
97 Daytona	A	84	281	50	94	10	4	1	22	31	61	32	11	.335	.404	.409
4 Minor League Yrs		310	1135	214	346	38	16	4	96	138	241	147	54	.305	.383	.377

Although he missed much of the season with a finger injury, Elinton Jasco did well enough in the Florida State League to qualify as a prospect. He drew lots of walks, stole tons of bases, and boosted his batting average 40 points while rising a level. Power is not his game, but he gets on base enough and has such good speed that the lack of power hasn't hurt him yet. Jasco's glove work needs improvement. He makes too many errors, and despite his quickness and athletic ability, his range factor is below average. He also has trouble with the double play. I am reasonably certain that Jasco will develop into a good offensive player, but if he doesn't get the defense in order, it won't matter much. He will never hit for the power that teams want in an outfielder, so if he wants a shot, he has to learn to play the infield. **Grade C+**

Corey Jenkins

Boston Red Sox

Pos: OF-DH **Bats:** Right **Ht:** 6'2" **Wt:** 195 **Age:** 21

Yr Team	Lg	G	AB	R	H	2B	3B	HR	RBI	BB	SO	SB	CS	Avg	OBP	Slg
96 Lowell	A	65	228	37	51	7	2	8	29	28	81	5	0	.224	.310	.377
97 Michigan	A	111	426	68	102	17	4	18	62	28	129	5	5	.239	.301	.425
3 Minor League Yrs		211	778	117	171	25	6	27	97	67	253	15	7	.220	.292	.371

Jenkins, drafted in the first round in 1994 from a South Carolina high school, is the best athlete in the Red Sox system this side of Michael Coleman. He isn't a great baseball player, at least not yet, mainly due to weak strike-zone judgment. He also has a lot of problems defensively. Jenkins is still very young, and if he gets a clue about the strike zone, he could develop rapidly, like Coleman did in 1997. But it isn't likely. **Grade C-**

Geoff Jenkins   *Milwaukee Brewers*

Pos: OF   **Bats:** Left   **Ht:** 6'1"   **Wt:** 205   **Age:** 23

Yr Team	Lg	G	AB	R	H	2B	3B	HR	RBI	BB	SO	SB	CS	Avg	OBP	Slg
96 El Paso	AA	22	77	17	22	5	4	1	11	12	21	1	2	.286	.391	.494
Stockton	A	37	138	27	48	8	4	3	25	20	32	3	3	.348	.433	.529
97 Tucson	AAA	93	347	44	82	24	3	10	56	33	87	0	2	.236	.308	.409
3 Minor League Yrs		194	716	115	195	43	14	18	126	86	186	9	10	.272	.353	.447

There must be a voodoo doll somewhere with Geoff Jenkins' name on it, or perhaps Bud Selig's. Like most Milwaukee prospects, Jenkins has been dogged by injuries ever since he signed, in his case as a first-round pick out of the University of Southern California in 1995. He lost much of 1996 to a bad shoulder injury, and wasn't healthy when he did play. Same story in 1997, although this time it was his knee. It bothered him all year, and he finally had surgery to repair damaged cartilage in early August. Because of the injuries, his statistics may not be a reliable barometer of his potential. Scouts say Jenkins has excellent power potential, should hit for a decent average, and is a very hard worker. If his body cooperates, Jenkins should be a fine player. He did do very well in the Arizona Fall League. **Grade B-**

Robin Jennings   *Chicago Cubs*

Pos: OF   **Bats:** Left   **Ht:** 6'2"   **Wt:** 200   **Age:** 25

Yr Team	Lg	G	AB	R	H	2B	3B	HR	RBI	BB	SO	SB	CS	Avg	OBP	Slg
96 Iowa	AAA	86	331	53	94	15	6	18	56	32	53	2	0	.284	.346	.529
Chicago	NL	31	58	7	13	5	0	0	4	3	9	1	0	.224	.274	.310
97 Iowa	AAA	126	464	67	128	25	5	20	71	56	73	5	3	.276	.359	.481
Chicago	NL	9	18	1	3	1	0	0	2	0	2	0	0	.167	.158	.222
6 Minor League Yrs		676	2510	349	728	132	30	73	378	243	357	37	41	.290	.355	.454

The Cubs needed an outfielder. They had four good candidates in Jennings, Brooks Kieschnick, Brant Brown, and Pedro Valdes. They gave chances to Brown and Kieschnick, gave up on both of them too quickly, then settled on Doug Glanville, leaving Jennings and Valdes to rot in Iowa. Now, Glanville had a pretty good year, for Doug Glanville, but he doesn't bring to the table the one thing the Cubs desperately need: POWER. This may seem odd, but if you look at history, the Cubs have seldom had many power hitters in their lineup, despite Wrigley Field. Maybe that is why they always suck. Anyhow, Jennings was stranded in Des Moines all season, and he had another good year, with an OPS of +11 percent and a SEC of +20. These aren't terrific numbers, but they are solid, and that is what Jennings is, a solid hitter. I really like his swing. His defense has improved from passable to above-average in left field. Jennings is not a superstar type to build your team around, but he can get on base and hit for some power, and the Cubs need guys who can do those things. **Grade B-**

Mike Jerzembeck

New York Yankees

Pos: P   Throws: Right   Ht: 6'1"   Wt: 185   Age: 25

Yr Team	Lg	G	GS	IP	H	R	ER	HR	BB	SO	SV	W	L	Pct.	ERA
96 Columbus	AAA	1	0	1.2	1	1	1	0	1	0	0	0	0	—	5.40
Norwich	AA	14	13	69.2	74	38	35	9	26	65	0	3	6	.333	4.52
Tampa	A	12	12	73.1	67	26	24	4	13	60	0	4	2	.667	2.95
97 Norwich	AA	8	8	42.0	21	10	8	1	16	42	0	2	1	.667	1.71
Columbus	AAA	20	20	130.1	125	55	52	14	37	118	0	7	5	.583	3.59
5 Minor League Yrs		87	83	466.0	422	186	170	36	143	407	0	28	22	.560	3.28

Mike Jerzembeck, a son of Queens Village, New York, attended the University of North Carolina and was drafted by the Yankees in the fifth round in 1993. He was a hard thrower in college, but elbow surgery in 1995 cost him both his velocity and his prospect status. He came back in 1996 to pitch decently, but his chances were questioned as long as the fastball was marginal. All that changed in 1997. Another year removed from surgery, Jerzembeck's heater regained its college velocity, consistently in the low 90s. The curve, slider, and change he refined when the fastball was diluted are all good pitches, and he can hit spots with them. His K/BB at Columbus was an excellent +57 percent. There has been no indication that the elbow injury will recur, although that is always a possibility. I like Jerzembeck, and I think he will be a good pitcher if his arm remains healthy. **Grade B**

D'Angelo Jimenez

New York Yankees

Pos: SS   Bats: Both   Ht: 6'0"   Wt: 160   Age: 20

Yr Team	Lg	G	AB	R	H	2B	3B	HR	RBI	BB	SO	SB	CS	Avg	OBP	Slg
96 Greensboro	A	138	537	68	131	25	5	6	48	56	113	15	17	.244	.317	.343
97 Columbus	AAA	2	7	1	1	0	0	0	1	0	1	0	0	.143	.125	.143
Tampa	A	94	352	52	99	14	6	6	48	50	50	8	14	.281	.368	.406
3 Minor League Yrs		291	1110	162	291	53	19	14	125	129	195	29	34	.262	.338	.382

A Dominican shortstop signed in 1995, D'Angelo Jimenez is a favorite of scouts due to his athletic ability, his fluid actions in the field, and quick wrists that promise more offense with physical maturity. He did okay in his full-season debut in 1996, but was much better at Tampa in 1997, cutting his strikeouts dramatically, while keeping his walk rate at a very good level. His OPS was fine for a middle infielder at plus-eight percent, and while he doesn't have tons of power yet, that could appear in time. Jimenez also made great progress defensively. He cut his errors from 50 in 1996 to 21 in 1997, while maintaining an above-average range factor. I like the progress Jimenez made with the bat and glove last year, and further improvement should be expected, given his age. He could be a terrific player, especially if his power develops, which I think it will. **Grade B+**

Jose Jimenez

St. Louis Cardinals

Pos: P **Throws:** Right **Ht:** 6'3" **Wt:** 170 **Age:** 24

Yr Team	Lg	G	GS	IP	H	R	ER	HR	BB	SO	SV	W	L	Pct.	ERA
96 Peoria	A	28	27	172.1	158	75	56	6	53	129	0	12	9	.571	2.92
97 Pr William	A	24	24	145.2	128	73	50	12	42	81	0	9	7	.563	3.09
3 Minor League Yrs		66	65	408.1	367	196	141	21	120	295	0	26	23	.531	3.11

Signed out of the Dominican Republic in 1993, Jose Jimenez isn't particularly young, doesn't have great stuff, and didn't have tremendous statistics at Prince William. So why is he in the book? Basically, because he throws strikes and manages to get people out without awesome stuff. Jimenez has an average fastball, an adequate curve, and a pretty good changeup. His motion is very deceptive, which aids him considerably. Jimenez is the kind of guy that may burst on the scene by learning a new pitch, improving his command from very good to perfect, or by signing a contract with a strange man in a red suit, although that is really more Jerry Reinsdorf's sort of thing. **Grade C-**

Adam Johnson

Atlanta Braves

Pos: OF **Bats:** Left **Ht:** 6'0" **Wt:** 185 **Age:** 22

Yr Team	Lg	G	AB	R	H	2B	3B	HR	RBI	BB	SO	SB	CS	Avg	OBP	Slg
96 Eugene	A	76	318	58	100	22	9	7	56	19	32	4	1	.314	.359	.506
97 Durham	A	133	502	80	141	39	3	26	92	50	94	18	8	.281	.341	.526
2 Minor League Yrs		209	820	138	241	61	12	33	148	69	126	22	9	.294	.348	.518

The Braves signed 33 players from the 1996 draft. Thirty-second on the list was Adam Johnson, an outfielder from the University of Central Florida, selected in the 55th round. He proved he was more than roster filler last year at Durham, and it is conceivable he could be the best player in Atlanta's draft class, despite his lowly standing. He was one of the best offensive players in the Carolina League, posting an OPS of +19 percent and a SEC of +37. Defense was supposed to be a weakness, but he had a very good range factor in right field and showed off a strong arm. He can be impatient at times, and will need to establish himself at higher levels, but I like him. **Grade B-**

Jason Johnson

Tampa Bay Devil Rays

Pos: P **Throws:** Right **Ht:** 6'6" **Wt:** 220 **Age:** 24

Yr Team	Lg	G	GS	IP	H	R	ER	HR	BB	SO	SV	W	L	Pct.	ERA
96 Lynchburg	A	15	5	44.1	56	37	32	6	12	27	0	1	4	.200	6.50
Augusta	A	14	14	84.0	82	40	29	2	25	83	0	4	4	.500	3.11
97 Lynchburg	A	17	17	99.1	98	43	41	4	30	92	0	8	4	.667	3.71
Carolina	AA	9	9	57.1	56	31	26	6	16	63	0	3	3	.500	4.08
Pittsburgh	NL	3	0	6.0	10	4	4	2	1	3	0	0	0	—	6.00
6 Minor League Yrs		116	100	592.2	613	336	265	34	181	478	0	26	45	.366	4.02

A huge righthanded pitcher with a pretty good arm, Jason Johnson turned himself into a prospect last year after several years as a staff filler for the Pirates. Signed as an undrafted free agent in 1992, Johnson was consistently effective for the first time last season, and did particularly well at Carolina. His ratios there ranged from incredible to solid: K/BB +118 percent, K/IP +42 percent, H/IP plus-six percent. Johnson utilizes a fastball/curveball arsenal, and while none of his offerings are outstanding, he learned to challenge hitters last season. He might backslide, but he might not. He is certainly with the right team, having gone to Tampa in expansion. **Grade C+**

Jonathan Johnson   *Texas Rangers*

Pos: P   Throws: Right   Ht: 6'0"   Wt: 180   Age: 23

Yr Team	Lg	G	GS	IP	H	R	ER	HR	BB	SO	SV	W	L	Pct.	ERA
96 Okla City	AAA	1	1	9.0	2	0	0	0	1	6	0	1	0	1.000	0.00
Tulsa	AA	26	25	174.1	176	86	69	15	41	97	0	13	10	.565	3.56
97 Okla City	AAA	13	12	58.0	83	54	47	6	29	33	1	1	8	.111	7.29
Tulsa	AA	10	10	71.2	70	35	28	3	15	47	0	5	4	.556	3.52
3 Minor League Yrs		58	55	356.1	365	189	157	26	102	208	1	21	27	.438	3.97

The Rangers made Johnson their first-round pick in 1995, out of Florida State. They expected him to hold a rotation spot in the majors by 1998, but it won't happen. Johnson's fastball is only average. His best pitch is a wicked curveball. He also has a good changeup, and when his location and control programs are properly initialized, he is a tough customer. Johnson was bothered by a sore back for much of last season, and it showed. He got killed in the American Association because his command was off, and while he did better after going back down to Tulsa, the season was still a grave disappointment. No one has ever questioned Johnson's intelligence or competitive fire, so if he is healthy, there is a reasonable chance he will rebound. He needs to do well for at least half a season in Triple-A before getting a major league chance. **Grade C**

Mark Johnson   *Chicago White Sox*

Pos: C   Bats: Left   Ht: 6'0"   Wt: 185   Age: 22

Yr Team	Lg	G	AB	R	H	2B	3B	HR	RBI	BB	SO	SB	CS	Avg	OBP	Slg
96 South Bend	A	67	214	29	55	14	3	2	27	39	25	3	3	.257	.368	.379
Pr William	A	18	58	9	14	3	0	0	3	13	6	0	0	.241	.389	.293
97 Winston-Sal	A	120	375	59	95	27	4	4	46	106	85	4	2	.253	.420	.379
4 Minor League Yrs		344	1053	138	243	58	7	8	107	231	183	11	11	.231	.372	.322

Johnson, the White Sox' first-round pick as a high school catcher back in 1994, started to show some offensive ability in 1997. Part of the reason was simple maturity, and part of it was the successful resolution of some severe family difficulties, leaving him free to concentrate on baseball. Johnson does not have power or a high batting average, but he has incredible strike-zone judgment and draws truckloads of walks. The on-base percentage is his only contribution with the bat right now, but it is an important one, and command of the strike zone gives him a better chance to develop as a hitter than he would otherwise have. Glove work is an asset for him: he led the Carolina League in fielding percentage, and he threw out 34 percent of runners, a respectable total. Double-A will be a vital test. **Grade C**

Mark Johnson
Florida Marlins

Pos: P **Throws:** Right **Ht:** 6'3" **Wt:** 215 **Age:** 22

Yr Team	Lg	G	GS	IP	H	R	ER	HR	BB	SO	SV	W	L	Pct.	ERA
97 Kissimmee	A	26	26	155.1	150	67	53	8	39	127	0	8	9	.471	3.07
1 Minor League Yr		26	26	155.1	150	67	53	8	39	127	0	8	9	.471	3.07

The Astros drafted Mark Johnson in the first round in 1996, out of the University of Hawaii. He is not the prototype flamethrowing first-round pick, but was a polished college pitcher expected to succeed in the pro ranks quickly. The Astros selected him in part because his bonus demands were reasonable. Johnson works with the standard four-pitch arsenal: fastball, slider, curve, change. His fastball is only average by major league standards, but he spots it in the strike zone well, and his breaking stuff is effective. Johnson did well in his pro debut, with a fine K/BB of +62 percent, but the real test for him will be Double-A. He isn't exactly a soft tosser, but he doesn't overpower people, and needs to prove that he can carry his command to higher levels. He went to Florida as the player to be named in the Moises Alou trade. **Grade C+**

Nick Johnson
New York Yankees

Pos: 1B **Bats:** Left **Ht:** 6'3" **Wt:** 195 **Age:** 19

Yr Team	Lg	G	AB	R	H	2B	3B	HR	RBI	BB	SO	SB	CS	Avg	OBP	Slg
96 Yankees	R	47	157	31	45	11	1	2	33	30	35	0	0	.287	.422	.408
97 Greensboro	A	127	433	77	118	23	1	16	75	76	99	16	3	.273	.398	.441
2 Minor League Yrs		174	590	108	163	34	2	18	108	106	134	16	3	.276	.404	.432

Nick Johnson was New York's third-round pick in 1996, from a California high school. His pro career has gone very well to this point. Johnson combines power potential with patience at the plate, a potent combination that gave him a fine OPS of +21 percent, and a SEC near the top of the Sally League at +54 percent. He makes a few too many errors at first base, but is very mobile and was named the Best Defensive First Baseman in the *Baseball America* poll of managers. Johnson has received little attention as a prospect in the press so far, but I think he will be a solid player, and possibly much more. **Grade B-**

Russ Johnson
Houston Astros

Pos: 3B **Bats:** Right **Ht:** 5'10" **Wt:** 185 **Age:** 25

Yr Team	Lg	G	AB	R	H	2B	3B	HR	RBI	BB	SO	SB	CS	Avg	OBP	Slg
96 Jackson	AA	132	496	86	154	24	5	15	74	56	50	9	4	.310	.382	.470
97 New Orleans	AAA	122	445	72	123	16	6	4	49	66	78	7	4	.276	.370	.366
Houston	NL	21	60	7	18	1	0	2	9	6	14	1	1	.300	.364	.417
3 Minor League Yrs		386	1416	223	395	56	13	28	176	172	188	26	13	.279	.360	.396

Russ Johnson is not overwelmingly talented, but he plays hard and impresses observers with his fervor for baseball and his drive on the field. He will never be a major power hitter and is unlikely to hit for an exceptional average, but he stays within his limits, draws a lot of walks, and is not an easy out. His OPS was just below league average at New Orleans, but that is a tough place to hit, and he was impressive in limited action with Houston. Johnson played mostly third base last year. He has played shortstop in the past, but his best position is probably second. Craig Biggio blocks him there, of course. **Grade B-**

Jacque Jones
Minnesota Twins

Pos: OF **Bats:** Left **Ht:** 5'10" **Wt:** 175 **Age:** 22

Yr Team	Lg	G	AB	R	H	2B	3B	HR	RBI	BB	SO	SB	CS	Avg	OBP	Slg
96 Ft. Myers	A	1	3	0	2	1	0	0	1	0	0	0	1	.667	.667	1.000
97 Ft. Myers	A	131	539	84	160	33	6	15	82	33	110	24	12	.297	.340	.464
2 Minor League Yrs		132	542	84	162	34	6	15	83	33	110	24	13	.299	.341	.467

Minnesota's failure to sign Travis Lee in 1996 draft left Southern Cal outfielder Jacque Jones as its highest signee, from the second round. A college star and member of the 1996 U.S. Olympic Team, Jones strained a medial-collateral knee ligament during his first pro game, but avoided surgery and had a good full-season debut in 1997. He got off to a blistering start, slumped in June and July, then rebounded in August to finish with good overall stats. As expected, he hit for average, but showed more power and speed than scouts expected. On the other hand, he had problems with command of the strike zone. His walk rate was well below the 10 percent threshold of acceptability. He will need to improve that as he moves up the ladder. Jones is a very good defensive outfielder with the range to play center in the majors. Overall, it was a promising debut, but I worry about his command of the strike zone, and about the long-term health of the knee. If he improves his plate discipline, he could be a Seven Skill guy. **Grade B**

Jaime Jones
Florida Marlins

Pos: OF-DH **Bats:** Left **Ht:** 6'3" **Wt:** 190 **Age:** 21

Yr Team	Lg	G	AB	R	H	2B	3B	HR	RBI	BB	SO	SB	CS	Avg	OBP	Slg
96 Kane County	A	62	237	29	59	17	1	8	45	19	74	7	2	.249	.299	.430
97 Brevard Cty	A	95	373	63	101	27	4	10	60	44	86	6	1	.271	.346	.445
3 Minor League Yrs		193	744	115	197	50	7	22	119	77	194	18	7	.265	.331	.440

Jaime Jones, Florida's first-round pick in 1995 out of a California high school, has a handsome swing that should produce both power and average, but his pro career has been marred by injuries and inconsistency. In 1996, a broken wrist derailed his season; last year, it was a stress fracture in his hip. When healthy, Jones displays everything scouts like in a young hitter. He has bat speed, hand-eye coordination, and great hitting mechanics. His production in the difficult Florida State League last year was quite good at +12 percent, and he showed better understanding of the strike zone than in the past. Jones has the tools to do well with the glove, but his range factors and assist totals are low, he makes too many errors, and some scouts say he doesn't try very hard in the field. He is very businesslike and professional when it comes to hitting, however, so if there really is an effort issue on defense, it is likely just a matter of youth. Jones needs a year of complete health. If he gets it, a breakout season is possible. This grade could be too low. **Grade B**

Ryan Jones

Toronto Blue Jays

Pos: 1B **Bats:** Right **Ht:** 6'3" **Wt:** 220 **Age:** 23

Yr Team	Lg	G	AB	R	H	2B	3B	HR	RBI	BB	SO	SB	CS	Avg	OBP	Slg
96 Knoxville	AA	134	506	70	137	26	3	20	97	60	88	2	2	.271	.351	.453
97 Syracuse	AAA	41	123	8	17	5	1	3	16	15	28	0	2	.138	.241	.268
Knoxville	AA	86	328	41	84	19	3	12	51	27	63	0	1	.256	.315	.442
5 Minor League Yrs		550	2008	264	495	112	7	74	341	200	441	5	7	.247	.320	.420

Ryan Jones, a strapping young power hitter with a good 1996 Double-A campaign on his resume, stunk up the International League early in 1997. He was hapless against the more experienced Triple-A moundsmen, and while he hit better after going back to Knoxville, it was a very disappointing season overall. Jones can be vulnerable to breaking stuff away and fastballs in on his fists. He adjusted to this in Double-A, and even at Syracuse his walk rate was good. There is still time for Jones to figure out what he is doing, but the Mark McGwire comparisons sometimes made by scouts aren't appropriate until Jones has some consistent, outstanding success in Triple-A. **Grade C**

Timothy Jorgensen

Cleveland Indians

Pos: 3B-DH **Bats:** Left **Ht:** 6'3" **Wt:** 200 **Age:** 25

Yr Team	Lg	G	AB	R	H	2B	3B	HR	RBI	BB	SO	SB	CS	Avg	OBP	Slg
96 Kinston	A	119	412	56	89	24	0	17	64	41	103	1	2	.216	.294	.398
97 Kinston	A	91	334	49	95	19	2	18	65	28	47	0	1	.284	.336	.515
3 Minor League Yrs		283	1041	149	280	62	11	43	181	101	213	5	4	.269	.336	.474

Tim Jorgensen was the best baseball player in the history of the University of Wisconsin-Oshkosh, being named Small College Player of the Year in 1995. His brother Terry, who played in the majors a few years back, was the second-best player in school history. Tim hit .491, with 39 home runs and 121 RBI, during his last college season, before being drafted by the Indians in the eighth round. After his full-season debut in 1996, it looked like his gaudy college stats were a result of aluminum and weak competition, but he hit much better in 1997, reestablishing his credentials. His OPS was fine at +17 percent, and he is reasonably effective with the glove. Jorgensen needs to prove himself in Double-A, but he is blocked by other players in the Cleveland system, and will have to fight his way up the ladder. **Grade C**

Mike Judd

Los Angeles Dodgers

Pos: P **Throws:** Right **Ht:** 6'2" **Wt:** 200 **Age:** 22

Yr Team	Lg	G	GS	IP	H	R	ER	HR	BB	SO	SV	W	L	Pct.	ERA
96 Greensboro	A	29	0	28.1	22	14	12	2	8	36	10	2	2	.500	3.81
Savannah	A	15	8	55.1	40	21	15	2	15	62	3	4	2	.667	2.44
97 Vero Beach	A	14	14	86.2	67	37	34	4	39	104	0	6	5	.545	3.53
San Antonio	AA	12	12	79.0	69	27	24	0	33	65	0	4	2	.667	2.73
Los Angeles	NL	1	0	2.2	4	0	0	0	0	4	0	0	0	—	0.00
3 Minor League Yrs		92	34	284.1	218	104	89	8	101	298	21	17	12	.586	2.82

Looking for a sleeper? Try Mike Judd. Originally drafted by the Yankees in the ninth round in 1995 from Grossmont Junior College in California, Judd came to the Dodgers in a midseason trade in 1996, and had an excellent 1997 campaign. Yankees owner George Steinbrenner's people were using him in relief, but the Dodgers converted him to starting, and he was excellent, especially at San Antonio. He is a hard thrower: his fastball was voted the best in the Florida State League, and he also has a hard slider. An incredible stat: he gave up no home runs, that's right, *zero* homers, in the Texas League, which is equivalent to not being bitten by a mosquito in the Amazon. Judd needs to improve his control a bit, and of course he faces the Albuquerque Agonizer, but there are 29 other teams out there who would love to have him. **Grade B+**

Gabe Kapler
Detroit Tigers

Pos: OF **Bats**: Right **Ht**: 6'1" **Wt**: 190 **Age**: 22

Yr Team	Lg	G	AB	R	H	2B	3B	HR	RBI	BB	SO	SB	CS	Avg	OBP	Slg
96 Fayetteville	A	138	524	81	157	45	0	26	99	62	73	14	4	.300	.378	.534
97 Lakeland	A	137	519	87	153	40	6	19	87	54	68	8	6	.295	.361	.505
3 Minor League Yrs		338	1279	206	378	104	10	49	220	139	178	23	12	.296	.366	.507

Gabe Kapler is one of my favorite unheralded prospects. He was a 57th-round pick in 1995, from Moorpark Junior College in California, and has played well at every level of pro ball so far. Kapler can hit the stitches off the ball. He has a level swing that generates power to all fields, he hits for average, he controls the strike zone, and makes adjustments in accordance to how he is being pitched. His OPS was excellent in the FSL at +22 percent, likewise his SEC at +32 percent. His glove? That's good too. Kapler is a bit error-prone, but he has above-average range for a right fielder, and has a strong and accurate arm. His personality and work ethic are also positives. He wasn't old for the league. Bottom line: he's a great prospect. **Grade B+**

Jason Kershner
Philadelphia Phillies

Pos: P **Throws**: Left **Ht**: 6'2" **Wt**: 160 **Age**: 21

Yr Team	Lg	G	GS	IP	H	R	ER	HR	BB	SO	SV	W	L	Pct.	ERA
96 Piedmont	A	28	28	168.0	154	81	70	12	59	156	0	11	9	.550	3.75
97 Clearwater	A	22	16	99.1	113	49	43	9	21	51	1	5	10	.333	3.90
3 Minor League Yrs		63	57	330.1	334	172	149	31	109	271	1	20	21	.488	4.06

Jason Kershner had an impressive season at Piedmont in 1996, but had problems staying healthy in 1997, and spent the season swinging between the rotation and the bullpen at Clearwater. He does not throw hard, but is lanky, young, and projectable. If he keeps his health, picks up some arm strength, and maintains his ability to throw strikes, he could have a future, but those are significant question marks. **Grade C-**

Kyle Kessel

New York Mets

Pos: P   Throws: Left   Ht: 6'0"   Wt: 160   Age: 21

Yr Team	Lg	G	GS	IP	H	R	ER	HR	BB	SO	SV	W	L	Pct.	ERA
96 Pittsfield	A	13	13	79.2	80	44	42	6	19	67	0	2	6	.250	4.74
97 Capital City	A	27	27	168.2	131	63	51	8	53	151	0	11	11	.500	2.72
3 Minor League Yrs		52	52	318.1	273	130	107	16	93	288	0	20	17	.541	3.03

Kessel was a 60th-round draft pick in 1994, not because scouts didn't like him, but because he had a basketball scholarship to Texas A&M. He played hoops for the Aggies for two seasons, working in the Mets system during the summers, but for 1997 he dropped the hardwood for the diamond. The results were rewarding, as he posted a solid season for Capital City, with a very good K/BB of +23 percent in particular. Kessel doesn't have blazing stuff, but his offerings have zip, his control is reliable, and he has a feel for pitching. Keep an eye on him. **Grade C+**

Jeff Key

Philadelphia Phillies

Pos: OF   Bats: Left   Ht: 6'1"   Wt: 200   Age: 23

Yr Team	Lg	G	AB	R	H	2B	3B	HR	RBI	BB	SO	SB	CS	Avg	OBP	Slg
96 Clearwater	A	101	348	53	85	15	4	3	34	16	82	15	3	.244	.296	.336
97 Clearwater	A	136	522	85	147	37	11	17	87	29	112	15	9	.282	.325	.492
5 Minor League Yrs		483	1745	262	455	86	30	44	256	118	443	54	25	.261	.317	.420

Key was drafted in the fourth round in 1993, from a Georgia high school. He is a good athlete with power and speed, and posted a solid OPS in the Florida State League of +16 percent, but his strike-zone judgment remains dreadful, and he is unlikely to hit well at higher levels unless he improves it. His defense in the outfield is mediocre, so the bat is all he has. **Grade C**

Brooks Kieschnick

Tampa Bay Devil Rays

Pos: OF-1B   Bats: Left   Ht: 6'4"   Wt: 228   Age: 25

Yr Team	Lg	G	AB	R	H	2B	3B	HR	RBI	BB	SO	SB	CS	Avg	OBP	Slg
96 Iowa	AAA	117	441	47	114	20	1	18	64	37	108	0	1	.259	.315	.431
Chicago	NL	25	29	6	10	2	0	1	6	3	8	0	0	.345	.406	.517
97 Iowa	AAA	97	360	57	93	21	0	21	66	36	89	0	2	.258	.323	.492
Chicago	NL	39	90	9	18	2	0	4	12	12	21	1	0	.200	.294	.356
5 Minor League Yrs		512	1896	235	525	107	5	78	270	172	390	6	14	.277	.338	.462

Have you ever worked for an irrational employer? A boss who is erratic, unpredictable, makes capricious decisions without apparent cause, won't stick to a decision once it is made, does not use the talents of his employees properly, plays favorites, and asks you to do things you aren't capable of doing? Now you know how Brooks Kieschnick feels. He is a victim of the Cubs special brand of Dilbert Baseball, along with Brant Brown, Robin Jennings, and Pedro Valdes. If you watch Kieschnick play, it is clear that he is trying too hard to hit for power. Two years ago, he was willing to go to the opposite field. Now he tries to pull everything, resulting in a longer swing, a lower batting average, but no genuine increase in power production. This is likely a result of his frustration with not getting a chance to earn a job. Kieschnick hit .295 with 23 homers at Iowa in 1995. The Cubs said "nice season," but didn't give him a real shot to prove himself in the majors, instead farting around with Luis Gonzalez. It is easy to say, "Kieschnick should be patient," but patience is only operative if there is hope. The Cubs gave Kieschnick no reason to hope for a better future. They seem to be doing the same thing to Jennings, Brown, and Valdes, and it would be poetic justice if, come 1999, the Cubs sign Ruben Sierra to man their suddenly thin outfield. As for Kieschnick, he could blossom now that he has moved on to Tampa Bay, but it is possible his career is permanently crippled. I think the former is more likely than the latter. **Grade C+**

Cesar King   *Texas Rangers*

Pos: C   **Bats:** Right   **Ht:** 6'0"   **Wt:** 175   **Age:** 20

Yr Team	Lg	G	AB	R	H	2B	3B	HR	RBI	BB	SO	SB	CS	Avg	OBP	Slg
96 Chston-SC	A	84	276	35	69	10	1	7	28	21	58	8	5	.250	.303	.370
97 Charlotte	A	91	307	51	91	14	4	6	37	35	58	8	6	.296	.366	.427
Tulsa	AA	14	45	6	16	1	0	1	8	5	3	0	1	.356	.420	.444
2 Minor League Yrs		189	628	92	176	25	5	14	73	61	119	16	12	.280	.343	.403

A Dominican catcher signed in 1994, Cesar King has the tools to be an awesome defensive player in the Ivan Rodriguez mode, and his offense has promise as well. With the bat, he is mainly a line-drive hitter right now, but he makes contact and should develop more power as he grows. His OPS was very good at +13 percent, and he sparkled in his brief Double-A time. Behind the plate, King has the physical aspects of catching well under control. He threw out an outstanding 53 percent of runners attempting to steal, and has Rodriguez-like quickness around the dish. Observers say he does need help learning to call a game. He has time to learn; Rodriguez isn't going anywhere. Someone will have a job for King by the year 2000. **Grade B+**

Curtis King   *St. Louis Cardinals*

Pos: P   **Throws:** Right   **Ht:** 6'5"   **Wt:** 205   **Age:** 27

Yr Team	Lg	G	GS	IP	H	R	ER	HR	BB	SO	SV	W	L	Pct.	ERA
96 Arkansas	AA	5	0	5.0	15	12	11	1	6	5	1	0	1	.000	19.80
St. Pete	A	48	0	55.2	41	20	17	0	24	27	30	3	3	.500	2.75
97 Arkansas	AA	32	0	36.1	38	19	18	7	10	29	16	2	3	.400	4.46
Louisville	AAA	16	0	22.0	19	5	5	1	6	9	3	2	1	.667	2.05
St. Louis	NL	30	0	29.1	38	14	9	0	11	13	0	4	2	.667	2.76
4 Minor League Yrs		142	33	328.2	286	126	107	16	115	189	50	19	17	.528	2.93

The Cardinals drafted Curtis King in the fifth round in 1994, from the baseball powerhouse Philadelphia College of Textiles. He works well with a low-90s fastball and a power slider, and can make hitters look bad when his command is on. He saw considerable action in the major league bullpen in August and September, and did well enough that a setup role in 1998 is likely, although not guaranteed. He should be good in the part, but isn't likely to be a closer any time this century. **Grade C**

Mike Kinkade
Milwaukee Brewers

Pos: 3B   **Bats:** Right   **Ht:** 6'1"   **Wt:** 210   **Age:** 24

Yr Team	Lg	G	AB	R	H	2B	3B	HR	RBI	BB	SO	SB	CS	Avg	OBP	Slg
96 Beloit	A	135	499	105	151	33	4	15	100	47	69	23	12	.303	.394	.475
97 El Paso	AA	125	468	112	180	35	12	12	109	52	66	17	4	.385	.455	.588
3 Minor League Yrs		329	1233	293	425	87	17	31	248	142	173	66	25	.345	.430	.518

Mike Kinkade had a good season in the Midwest League in 1996, but was old for the competition. The Brewers wisely decided to move him to Double-A in 1997, to find out what he could do against real competition, and the results were spectacular, to say the least. El Paso is an excellent hitters' park, at least for average. It increases batting average by 16 percent compared to the rest of the league, so we can't assume that Kinkade is going to be a batting champ in the majors. He should be able to hit .280-.300 though, and he has command of the strike zone and good gap power. His defense is rotten. He made 60 errors at third base, which is beyond dreadful. Because of his defensive problems and El Paso stat inflation, Kinkade is *not* one of the best prospects in baseball. But he is a good one. **Grade B**

Matt Kinney
Boston Red Sox

Pos: P   **Throws:** Right   **Ht:** 6'4"   **Wt:** 190   **Age:** 21

Yr Team	Lg	G	GS	IP	H	R	ER	HR	BB	SO	SV	W	L	Pct.	ERA
96 Lowell	A	15	15	87.1	68	51	26	0	44	72	0	3	9	.250	2.68
97 Michigan	A	22	22	117.1	93	59	46	4	78	123	0	8	5	.615	3.53
3 Minor League Yrs		45	39	232.1	190	123	81	4	132	206	2	12	17	.414	3.14

Matt Kinney is following in the footsteps of Carl Pavano and Brian Rose, as a fairly raw New England high school pitcher drafted in a middle round by Boston, who adapts well to pro ball and emerges as a prospect. Kinney was drafted in the sixth round in 1995, out of Bangor, Maine. He works with the standard four pitches: fastball, curve, slider, change. The heater is his best offering right now, in the low 90s, but all of them have the potential to be very good. Kinney can overpower people (K/IP +25 percent), but he needs to improve his control, as demonstrated by his K/BB ratio, -22 percent. If he stays healthy and throws strikes more consistently, Kinney could be very good, but those are big ifs for a young pitcher, and he ended the season with a sore shoulder. **Grade C+**

Daron Kirkreit
Cincinnati Reds

Pos: P   **Throws:** Right   **Ht:** 6'6"   **Wt:** 225   **Age:** 25

Yr Team	Lg	G	GS	IP	H	R	ER	HR	BB	SO	SV	W	L	Pct.	ERA
96 Kinston	A	6	6	32.2	23	7	7	3	10	19	0	2	0	1.000	1.93
97 Buffalo	AAA	1	1	7.0	3	0	0	0	1	2	0	1	0	1.000	0.00
Akron	AA	26	20	117.2	131	96	68	15	69	83	0	8	9	.471	5.20
5 Minor League Yrs		86	79	462.0	423	263	214	47	208	399	0	28	32	.467	4.17

Daron Kirkreit was Cleveland's first-round pick in 1993, from UC Riverside. He was supposed to be a 15-20 game winner by now, but a torn rotator cuff in 1995 intervened in his march to the majors. When healthy, Kirkreit has a nasty 93-MPH sinking fastball and a hard slider, and although most of his arm strength is supposedly back, his command isn't, and he got whacked around pretty good in the Eastern League. It can take a couple of years to fully recover from such surgery, and there is a chance that Kirkreit could rebound, but it isn't a bet I would want to take. The Reds are taking that chance after signing Kirkreit to a minor league pact in November. **Grade C-**

Danny Klassen
Arizona Diamondbacks

Pos: SS   **Bats:** Right   **Ht:** 6'0"   **Wt:** 175   **Age:** 22

Yr Team	Lg	G	AB	R	H	2B	3B	HR	RBI	BB	SO	SB	CS	Avg	OBP	Slg
96 Stockton	A	118	432	58	116	22	4	2	46	34	77	14	8	.269	.335	.352
97 El Paso	AA	135	519	112	172	30	6	14	81	48	104	16	9	.331	.396	.493
5 Minor League Yrs		501	1789	292	502	93	15	26	229	187	386	86	39	.281	.361	.393

Klassen was drafted in the second round by the Brewers in 1993, from a Florida high school. A bad knee injury in 1995 cost him considerable development time, but he did well in the Texas League in 1997 at a young age, re-establishing himself as a prospect. Klassen's stats were inflated by El Paso last year. He does not project as a .300 hitter in the majors, but should be able to hit .260-.280, with respectable punch for a shortstop. He does need to improve his strike-zone judgment. With the glove, Klassen shows acceptable range at short, but made 50 errors last year, many on throws. If he can polish up the glove work and carry his offense to Triple-A, Klassen could be an adequate regular. With Jay Bell around, the Diamondbacks don't need him right away. **Grade C+**

Josh Klimek
Milwaukee Brewers

Pos: 3B   **Bats:** Left   **Ht:** 6'1"   **Wt:** 175   **Age:** 24

Yr Team	Lg	G	AB	R	H	2B	3B	HR	RBI	BB	SO	SB	CS	Avg	OBP	Slg
96 Helena	R	67	253	56	75	17	0	6	51	42	39	5	1	.296	.393	.435
97 Beloit	A	121	443	62	118	31	3	12	66	39	56	4	8	.266	.329	.431
2 Minor League Yrs		188	696	118	193	48	3	18	117	81	95	9	9	.277	.353	.432

Klimek was a 10th-round pick in 1996, from the University of Illinois. He had been Big Ten Player of the Year, hitting .400 with 26 homers, and winding up on the *Baseball America* All-America team. Klimek doesn't have the range for shortstop, so the Brewers moved him to third base last year. He made 30 errors, but showed good range, and should be adequate defensively. The question is, will he hit? His OPS was five percent over league, but Beloit is a hitting park, so his performance was mediocre. With a year to adjust to the wood bat, there is a chance that Klimek may start to hit. **Grade C**

Brandon Knight
Texas Rangers

Pos: P   Throws: Right   Ht: 6'0"   Wt: 170   Age: 22

Yr Team	Lg	G	GS	IP	H	R	ER	HR	BB	SO	SV	W	L	Pct.	ERA
96 Hudson Vall	A	9	9	53.0	59	29	26	1	21	52	0	2	2	.500	4.42
Charlotte	A	19	17	102.0	118	65	58	9	45	74	0	4	10	.286	5.12
97 Charlotte	A	14	12	92.2	82	33	23	9	22	91	0	7	4	.636	2.23
Tulsa	AA	14	14	90.0	83	52	45	12	35	84	0	6	4	.600	4.50
3 Minor League Yrs		68	63	404.1	391	208	178	36	150	364	0	25	23	.521	3.96

Knight was drafted in 1995, a 14th-rounder from Ventura Junior College in California. He was awesome in the Florida State League, with wonderful ratios in all categories: K/BB +106 percent, K/IP +28 percent, H/IP +10 percent. He struggled immediately after his promotion to Double-A, but pitched well down the stretch. The Rangers now consider him to be one of their best pitching prospects. Knight has a 90-MPH fastball. His curve, slider, and changeup are all very good, and he throws strikes with ease. He is intelligent, confident, and handles himself well on the mound. Knight had some shoulder trouble at the end of the season, and for that reason I am a bit hesistant to project tremendous success in 1998. He had a great season, and if healthy he should be a fine pitcher, but there are lots of things that can go wrong for him. **Grade B**

Bill Koch
Toronto Blue Jays

Pos: P   Throws: Right   Ht: 6'3"   Wt: 210   Age: 23

Yr Team	Lg	G	GS	IP	H	R	ER	HR	BB	SO	SV	W	L	Pct.	ERA
97 Dunedin	A	3	3	21.2	27	10	5	1	3	20	0	0	1	.000	2.08
1 Minor League Yr		3	3	21.2	27	10	5	1	3	20	0	0	1	.000	2.08

Koch, the Blue Jays' first-round pick in 1996, got off to a great start at Dunedin, showing fine control for a pitcher with a 97-MPH fastball. Unfortunately, his season ended after three starts when he blew out an elbow ligament. He had reconstructive surgery, and while he may return to the mound sometime in 1998, there is no way to tell if he will get the heater and/or his command back.

Ryan Kohlmeier
Baltimore Orioles

Pos: P   Throws: Right   Ht: 6'2"   Wt: 195   Age: 20

Yr Team	Lg	G	GS	IP	H	R	ER	HR	BB	SO	SV	W	L	Pct.	ERA
97 Bowie	AA	2	0	2.2	0	0	0	0	2	5	1	0	0	—	0.00
Delmarva	A	50	0	74.2	48	22	22	8	17	99	24	2	2	.500	2.65
1 Minor League Yr		52	0	77.1	48	22	22	8	19	104	25	2	2	.500	2.56

Baltimore drafted Ryan Kohlmeier in the 14th round in 1996, out of Butler County Community College in Kansas. He signed late and didn't make his debut until 1997, but what a debut it was. He isn't getting any play as a prospect, but his ratios last year were incredible: K/BB +150 percent, K/IP +53 percent, H/IP +37 percent, all right near the top of the Sally League. He has average major league stuff and obviously throws strikes. Kohlmeier may not close in the majors, but if he keeps pitching like that, he would make a fine reliever. **Grade C**

Brandon Kolb   *San Diego Padres*

Pos: P   **Throws:** Right   **Ht:** 6'1"   **Wt:** 190   **Age:** 24

Yr Team	Lg	G	GS	IP	H	R	ER	HR	BB	SO	SV	W	L	Pct.	ERA
96 Clinton	A	27	27	181.1	170	84	69	7	76	138	0	16	9	.640	3.42
97 Rancho Cuca	A	10	10	63.0	60	29	21	0	22	49	0	3	2	.600	3.00
3 Minor League Yrs		50	49	305.2	285	156	123	8	140	229	0	22	15	.595	3.62

Kolb was San Diego's fourth-round pick in 1995, from Texas Tech. He has a live arm and has been effective in the pros, but he made just 10 starts in the California League last year before being disabled with a shoulder injury. As I write this, he hasn't had surgery, and is expected back healthy in 1998, but that can change rapidly. His future is entirely predicated on what happens to his shoulder. **Grade C-**

Danny Kolb   *Texas Rangers*

Pos: P   **Throws:** Right   **Ht:** 6'4"   **Wt:** 190   **Age:** 23

Yr Team	Lg	G	GS	IP	H	R	ER	HR	BB	SO	SV	W	L	Pct.	ERA
96 Chston-SC	A	20	20	126.0	80	50	36	5	60	127	0	8	6	.571	2.57
Charlotte	A	6	6	38.0	38	18	18	1	14	28	0	2	2	.500	4.26
Tulsa	AA	2	2	11.2	5	1	1	0	8	7	0	1	0	1.000	0.77
97 Tulsa	AA	2	2	11.1	7	7	6	1	11	6	0	0	2	.000	4.76
Charlotte	A	24	23	133.0	146	91	72	10	62	83	0	4	10	.286	4.87
3 Minor League Yrs		66	64	373.0	314	189	146	17	183	297	0	16	27	.372	3.52

In terms of pure arm strength, Danny Kolb is probably the best pitching prospect the Rangers have, but there is more to pitching than just taking the mound and throwing hard. Kolb has a 94-MPH fastball and a hard slider, but he doesn't have much in the way of an offspeed pitch, his command isn't great, and he doesn't always show an interest in learning how to pitch. He is young enough to get over all of those problems, but it will require some effort on his part, as well as patient instruction from the coaching staff. Perhaps the Rangers can hire a team of scientists to graft Jonathan Johnson's head onto Danny Kolb's body. **Grade C**

Toby Kominek   *Milwaukee Brewers*

Pos: OF   **Bats:** Right   **Ht:** 6'2"   **Wt:** 205   **Age:** 24

Yr Team	Lg	G	AB	R	H	2B	3B	HR	RBI	BB	SO	SB	CS	Avg	OBP	Slg
96 Stockton	A	100	358	76	106	17	7	7	47	49	97	10	7	.296	.390	.441
97 Stockton	A	128	476	83	143	28	7	15	72	50	107	22	14	.300	.393	.483
3 Minor League Yrs		296	1069	204	317	60	17	32	167	120	269	46	24	.297	.387	.474

I think the Brewers are trying to corner the market on guys whose names begin with the letter K. Kinkade, Krause, Kominek, Klimek. Sounds like some sort of sinister conspiracy to me. Kominek had an acceptable year in the California League in 1996, but a logjam of outfielders forced him back to the same league in 1997, and not surprisingly, he did very well. He has some measure of power and speed, and is an excellent defensive outfielder. He needs a shot at a higher level, but could hit .360 at El Paso. **Grade C**

Paul Konerko
Los Angeles Dodgers

Pos: 3B **Bats:** Right **Ht:** 6'3" **Wt:** 210 **Age:** 22

Yr Team	Lg	G	AB	R	H	2B	3B	HR	RBI	BB	SO	SB	CS	Avg	OBP	Slg
96 San Antonio	AA	133	470	78	141	23	2	29	86	72	85	1	3	.300	.397	.543
Albuquerque	AAA	4	14	2	6	0	0	1	2	1	2	0	1	.429	.467	.643
97 Albuquerque	AAA	130	483	97	156	31	1	37	127	64	61	2	3	.323	.407	.621
Los Angeles	NL	6	7	0	1	0	0	0	0	1	2	0	0	.143	.250	.143
4 Minor League Yrs		452	1672	279	501	90	6	92	350	232	288	7	8	.300	.388	.526

You don't need me to tell you that this guy is a great prospect. As a general rule, 21-year-old players who can mash the ball in Triple-A are tremendous prospects, and Konerko does nothing to dispel this precept. His OPS was near the top of the league at +24 percent, his SEC likewise at +45 percent. His strike-zone judgment is excellent: good walk rate, very few strikeouts, especially for a power hitter. It is true he did this at Albuquerque, in a great hitting year, even for the PCL, and he did a lot of his damage at home. Still, I'm convinced he will hit, and hit well, in the majors. He could be a spectacular power hitter. . . remember, he is probably six years from his prime. He has major league 25 home run power right now, which could project out to 40 at his peak, or more if the hitting boom continues. The only question for Konerko is his defense. The Dodgers tried moving him to third base last year, and while he wasn't a disaster, he was hardly a defensive asset. He fielded .925 and his range factor was average. That's actually not too bad for a former catcher, but his long-term future is at first base, and on numerous All-Star teams. **Grade A**

Corey Koskie
Minnesota Twins

Pos: 3B **Bats:** Left **Ht:** 6'3" **Wt:** 215 **Age:** 24

Yr Team	Lg	G	AB	R	H	2B	3B	HR	RBI	BB	SO	SB	CS	Avg	OBP	Slg
96 Ft. Myers	A	95	338	43	88	19	4	9	55	40	76	1	1	.260	.338	.420
97 New Britain	AA	131	437	88	125	26	6	23	79	90	106	9	5	.286	.414	.531
4 Minor League Yrs		383	1344	208	381	84	16	51	222	186	288	12	10	.283	.376	.484

Double-A is a major stumbling block for many minor league players, but Corey Koskie passed that test gracefully in 1997. A 26th-round pick in 1994, Koskie had a remarkable year in a difficult park, hitting for very good power, drawing a ton of walks, and avoiding excessive strikeouts. His OPS was excellent at +23 percent, his SEC even better at +65 percent, third in the league. As a lefthanded hitter, he has special appeal in the Metrodome. Koskie does have some weaknesses. He can be had by a good breaking pitch or changeup, although he has improved against them, and he is prone to streaks and slumps. Defensively, he is nothing special. He has a strong arm, but most third basemen do, and his range is just average. He could wind up at first base eventually. Koskie will play in the Pacific Coast League in 1998, and could put up some big numbers. **Grade B**

Mark Kotsay

Florida Marlins

Pos: OF   **Bats:** Left   **Ht:** 6'0"   **Wt:** 180   **Age:** 22

Yr Team	Lg	G	AB	R	H	2B	3B	HR	RBI	BB	SO	SB	CS	Avg	OBP	Slg
96 Kane County	A	17	60	16	17	5	0	2	8	16	8	3	0	.283	.436	.467
97 Portland	AA	114	438	103	134	27	2	20	77	75	65	17	5	.306	.405	.514
Florida	NL	14	52	5	10	1	1	0	4	4	7	3	0	.192	.250	.250
2 Minor League Yrs		131	498	119	151	32	2	22	85	91	73	20	5	.303	.409	.508

Since Kirby Puckett's retirement, I haven't had a favorite player, but I'm considering Mark Kotsay. Requirements: must hustle, must play great despite lack of overwhelming physical tools. Kotsay fits the bill. He is not particularly muscular or swift afoot, but this man can play some baseball. He has a beautiful swing, and he knows how to hit, controlling the strike zone and hanging in against both fastballs and breaking pitches. He will pull the ball or go to the opposite field, depending on the situation. He isn't a burner on the bases, but he knows how to run them. Defensively, Kotsay has above-average range, primarily due to effort and positioning, and while his arm is not overly strong, it is extremely accurate. He is quite reliable and led the Eastern League in fielding percentage. Kotsay is ready for the majors now, and there is no doubt in my mind that he will have a long and successful career. **Grade A-**

Scott Krause

Milwaukee Brewers

Pos: OF   **Bats:** Right   **Ht:** 6'1"   **Wt:** 195   **Age:** 24

Yr Team	Lg	G	AB	R	H	2B	3B	HR	RBI	BB	SO	SB	CS	Avg	OBP	Slg
96 El Paso	AA	24	85	16	27	5	2	3	11	2	19	2	0	.318	.341	.529
Stockton	A	108	427	82	128	22	4	19	83	32	101	25	6	.300	.368	.504
97 El Paso	AA	125	474	97	171	33	11	16	88	20	108	13	4	.361	.390	.578
4 Minor League Yrs		454	1719	329	535	108	24	55	310	122	403	77	26	.311	.369	.498

Scott Krause joined Mike Kinkade and Danny Klassen as the Killer K's at El Paso last year. The park helped all of their stats, and of the three, Krause has the weakest command of the strike zone. He does have good power, and when he makes contact he can drive the ball a long way, but he is very vulnerable to stuff on the outer half of the plate, basically because he tries to pull everything. Krause is a sound defensive outfielder, and Texas League observers told me he was a hard worker and a good guy to have around in the clubhouse. Krause needs to be more patient at the plate to get the most out of his considerable ability. **Grade C+**

Marc Kroon

San Diego Padres

Pos: P   **Throws:** Right   **Ht:** 6'2"   **Wt:** 195   **Age:** 25

Yr Team	Lg	G	GS	IP	H	R	ER	HR	BB	SO	SV	W	L	Pct.	ERA
96 Memphis	AA	44	0	46.2	33	19	15	4	28	56	22	2	4	.333	2.89
97 Las Vegas	AAA	46	0	41.2	34	22	21	5	22	53	15	1	3	.250	4.54
San Diego	NL	12	0	11.1	14	9	9	2	5	12	0	0	1	.000	7.62
7 Minor League Yrs		191	86	592	514	315	261	45	341	606	41	28	37	.431	3.97

Padres manager Bruce Bochy likes hard throwers in the bullpen, and Marc Kroon is likely to earn a middle-relief slot in 1998. He has the gas, with a 96-MPH fastball and a mid-80s slider; that's an overpowering combination against most hitters. Kroon's control has improved since he converted to relief, although it still isn't all that terrific. Command and concentration lapses are blamed for his inconsistency, and it would take a stomach of iron for a manager to entrust him with ninth-inning leads at this point. Bochy won't have to do that, and Kroon should be a pretty good middle man, unless he gets hurt or his shaky control completely collapses. **Grade B-**

Jeff Kubenka   *Los Angeles Dodgers*

Pos: P **Throws:** Left **Ht:** 6'0" **Wt:** 195 **Age:** 23

Yr Team	Lg	G	GS	IP	H	R	ER	HR	BB	SO	SV	W	L	Pct.	ERA
96 Yakima	A	28	0	32.1	20	11	9	2	10	61	14	5	1	.833	2.51
97 San Berndno	A	34	0	39.0	24	4	4	1	11	62	19	5	1	.833	0.92
Albuquerque	AAA	8	0	7.1	11	9	7	2	2	10	2	0	2	.000	8.59
San Antonio	AA	19	0	25.2	10	2	2	1	6	38	4	3	0	1.000	0.70
2 Minor League Yrs		89	0	104.1	65	26	22	6	29	171	39	13	4	.765	1.90

Jeff Kubenka put up some ridiculously good numbers last season. A K/BB of +190 percent in the California League? That's better than excellent, and his numbers in the Texas League weren't any worse. Who is this guy, and is he a prospect? Kubenka was drafted in 1996, a 38th-rounder from St. Mary's University in Texas. Whether or not he is a prospect depends on who you ask. Since you are reading this book, I assume that you are asking me, and my opinion is that yes, he is a prospect, although not a terrific one. Kubenka's fastball is well below average. He gets people out with a screwball, and exquisite control. Kubenka's future is in middle relief. He will have to keep pitching well to get a shot at a job, since he's not the sort of guy that teams will be patient with. He could have a 15-year career, bouncing from team to team, pitching very well at times, but getting released as soon as he struggles. **Grade C**

Mike Kusiewicz   *Colorado Rockies*

Pos: P **Throws:** Left **Ht:** 6'2" **Wt:** 185 **Age:** 21

Yr Team	Lg	G	GS	IP	H	R	ER	HR	BB	SO	SV	W	L	Pct.	ERA
96 Salem	A	5	3	23.0	19	15	13	2	12	18	1	0	1	.000	5.09
New Haven	AA	14	14	76.1	83	38	28	4	27	64	0	2	4	.333	3.30
97 New Haven	AA	10	4	28.1	41	28	20	2	10	11	0	2	4	.333	6.35
Salem	A	19	18	117.2	99	44	33	5	32	107	0	8	6	.571	2.52
3 Minor League Yrs		70	61	373.2	341	166	123	19	115	310	1	20	19	.513	2.96

A shoulder problem cost Kusiewicz the first half of 1996, but when he pitched he was quite effective in Double-A. He returned there in 1997, with an eye to a quick promotion if he started well, but he was so ineffective that he ended up being demoted instead. He steered the ship off the shoals at Salem, salvaging his status, but the campaign leaves the Rockies wondering. Kusiewicz works with an average fastball, a sharp curve, and a forkball, and usually locates his pitches well. He still has youth on his side, but will have to prove himself in Double-A all over again. **Grade C+**

Joe LaGarde
Los Angeles Dodgers

Pos: P   **Throws:** Right   **Ht:** 5'9"   **Wt:** 180   **Age:** 23

Yr Team	Lg	G	GS	IP	H	R	ER	HR	BB	SO	SV	W	L	Pct.	ERA
96 Vero Beach	A	14	4	44.1	41	17	12	0	22	46	1	4	3	.571	2.44
San Antonio	AA	24	0	31.0	28	7	6	0	10	22	9	3	1	.750	1.74
Albuquerque	AAA	10	0	12.0	14	7	7	2	9	11	0	0	0	—	5.25
97 San Antonio	AA	53	0	69.1	68	34	29	6	31	65	17	4	4	.500	3.76
5 Minor League Yrs		169	59	478.0	475	241	199	27	222	382	29	28	31	.475	3.75

Los Angeles selected Joe LaGarde in the 18th round in 1993, out of a high school in North Carolina. He bears more than a little resemblance to Tom Gordon: a short righthander with good stuff, although his arms aren't as long as Gordon's. LaGarde works with a 90-MPH fastball and a good curve. His control is usually reliable, and he had a decent year as a closer in Double-A, although he wasn't dominant. LaGarde would be better regarded as a prospect if he played in another organization. With the Athletics, or the Twins, or the Phillies, he would probably have already seen major league action. With the Dodgers, he is just another pitcher. He is still young and has some growing up to do, but he could be an acceptable major league pitcher if given the chance. **Grade C**

Jason Lakman
Chicago White Sox

Pos: P   **Throws:** Right   **Ht:** 6'4"   **Wt:** 220   **Age:** 21

Yr Team	Lg	G	GS	IP	H	R	ER	HR	BB	SO	SV	W	L	Pct.	ERA
96 Hickory	A	13	13	63.2	66	55	48	7	43	43	0	0	6	.000	6.79
Bristol	R	13	13	66.2	70	48	42	5	38	64	0	4	4	.500	5.67
97 Hickory	A	27	27	154.2	139	82	67	11	70	168	0	10	9	.526	3.90
3 Minor League Yrs		62	58	326.1	319	202	172	25	163	298	0	17	19	.472	4.74

Drafted in the seventh round in 1995 from a high school in Washington, Jason Lakman is basically a big kid who throws hard. Command and control problems limited his pro success before last year, but he started to put things together in the Sally League, and had himself a nice season. His K/IP rate was very good at +26 percent, but his K/BB mark was mediocre. Lakman is terrible at holding runners, and needs polish in all aspects of mound work. At this point, his career could follow too many paths to enumerate. **Grade C**

Ryan Lane
Minnesota Twins

Pos: 2B   **Bats:** Right   **Ht:** 6'1"   **Wt:** 185   **Age:** 23

Yr Team	Lg	G	AB	R	H	2B	3B	HR	RBI	BB	SO	SB	CS	Avg	OBP	Slg
96 Ft. Myers	A	106	404	74	110	20	7	9	62	60	96	21	9	.272	.367	.423
Hardware City	AA	33	117	13	26	5	1	2	12	8	29	3	4	.222	.270	.333
97 New Britain	AA	128	444	63	115	26	2	5	56	43	79	18	7	.259	.321	.360
5 Minor League Yrs		484	1737	266	434	104	13	25	209	217	381	66	33	.250	.335	.368

As a second baseman in the Twins organization, Ryan Lane attracts little notice. I've thought of him as a sleeper for several years, however, due to his pop at the plate, his speed, and his walk rate in A-ball. He didn't knock anybody's socks off in Double-A last year, but he wasn't terrible. Defensively, he is very good at second base, ranking second in the Eastern League in range factor, and leading the circuit in double plays per game. I would like to see Lane elevate his walk rate back to the standards he posted in the lower minors. Right now, Lane projects as a very useful utility infielder, at least as long as Chuck Knoblauch is in town. **Grade C**

Nelson Lara   *Florida Marlins*

Pos: P   **Throws: Right**   **Ht: 6'4"**   **Wt: 165**   **Age: 19**

Yr Team	Lg	G	GS	IP	H	R	ER	HR	BB	SO	SV	W	L	Pct.	ERA
96 Marlins	R	7	0	9.2	6	11	6	0	12	3	0	1	2	.333	5.59
97 Kane County	A	29	0	38.1	37	20	17	1	14	43	3	1	2	.333	3.99
3 Minor League Yrs		47	0	69.2	64	44	32	2	37	55	4	3	5	.375	4.13

Lara, a Dominican, is another Florida power arm, with a 98-MPH fastball that can overpower most everyone. He doesn't have much of a breaking pitch, and while the fastball was good enough in a relief role at Kane County last year, he really does need another offering. His fastball can also be quite straight. Lara won't be in the majors soon; he needs to refine his mechanics, learn another pitch, and build stamina. But you have to love the velocity of the heater, especially since he can throw it for strikes. **Grade C+**

Andy Larkin   *Florida Marlins*

Pos: P   **Throws: Right**   **Ht: 6'4"**   **Wt: 181**   **Age: 23**

Yr Team	Lg	G	GS	IP	H	R	ER	HR	BB	SO	SV	W	L	Pct.	ERA
96 Brevard Cty	A	6	6	27.2	34	20	13	0	7	18	0	0	4	.000	4.23
Portland	AA	8	8	49.1	45	18	17	6	10	40	0	4	1	.800	3.10
Florida	NL	1	1	5.0	3	1	1	0	4	2	0	0	0	—	1.80
97 Charlotte	AAA	28	27	144.1	166	109	97	23	76	103	0	6	11	.353	6.05
6 Minor League Yrs		100	89	530.2	514	285	239	41	173	418	2	26	34	.433	4.05

A year ago, Andy Larkin was listed as Florida's No. 3 Prospect in the *Baseball America* Top 10 Organization Prospects list. I like those lists; they aren't gospel, but they are quite interesting, and are generally reliable barometers of how organizations view the relative abilities of their own prospects. Larkin had a terrible year in Triple-A in 1997, and I wonder how the Marlins view him now. Although he stayed in the rotation all year, health problems have been a factor in the past. He has had back and elbow difficulties throughout his career. When everything is right with Larkin, he has a live arm, great control, and impresses scouts with his pitching instincts, but his command was way off last year. Will he get it back? Sure, if he stays healthy. You know what the chances of that are likely to be. **Grade C-**

Stephen Larkin

Cincinnati Reds

Pos: OF **Bats:** Left **Ht:** 6'0" **Wt:** 190 **Age:** 24

Yr Team	Lg	G	AB	R	H	2B	3B	HR	RBI	BB	SO	SB	CS	Avg	OBP	Slg
96 Winston-Sal	A	39	117	13	21	2	0	3	6	14	25	6	1	.179	.265	.274
Chston-WV	A	58	203	30	55	7	2	5	33	35	40	5	4	.271	.387	.399
97 Chston-WV	A	129	464	88	129	23	10	13	79	52	83	28	9	.278	.354	.455
4 Minor League Yrs		418	1440	209	357	62	14	28	189	188	287	69	31	.248	.336	.369

The Reds seem to have adopted some sort of "genetic scouting" approach in recent years, drafting or trading for the sons and brothers of major leaguers. Stephen Larkin, sibling of Barry, was originally in the Rangers system, a 10th-rounder in 1994 from the University of Texas, where he briefly was sidelined with a congenital heart defect. In pro ball, he has never performed well at any stage above the South Atlantic League, and although he had a nice season at Charleston last year, it doesn't mean much, considering his age and experience level. Larkin has some tools. . . power, speed. . . but he has yet to show them at a meaningful tier of competition. That doesn't prove he won't, but it makes it unlikely. **Grade C-**

Tom LaRosa

Minnesota Twins

Pos: P **Throws:** Right **Ht:** 5'10" **Wt:** 180 **Age:** 22

Yr Team	Lg	G	GS	IP	H	R	ER	HR	BB	SO	SV	W	L	Pct.	ERA
96 Ft. Wayne	A	15	13	89.1	77	46	35	7	33	90	0	7	3	.700	3.53
97 Ft. Myers	A	25	23	135.2	120	73	65	10	66	118	0	8	6	.571	4.31
2 Minor League Yrs		40	36	225.0	197	119	100	17	99	208	0	15	9	.625	4.00

Minnesota's sixth round pick in 1996, out of UNLV, Tom LaRosa is a short lefty with zip in his arm that belies his stature. His fastball has velocity and movement, and his breaking pitch is sharp. He did quite well in his pro debut in 1996, but in 1997 he didn't pitch particularly well given the league and park. His K/BB ratio was below average, and his ERA too high. On the other hand, his H/IP was good at +10 percent, and his K/IP even better at +13, both indications of his good stuff. The talent is still there, and LaRosa has the potental to improve dramatically. It might help if he were converted to relief. **Grade C**

Jason LaRue

Cincinnati Reds

Pos: C **Bats:** Right **Ht:** 5'11" **Wt:** 195 **Age:** 24

Yr Team	Lg	G	AB	R	H	2B	3B	HR	RBI	BB	SO	SB	CS	Avg	OBP	Slg
96 Chston-WV	A	37	123	17	26	8	0	2	14	11	28	3	0	.211	.287	.325
97 Chston-WV	A	132	473	78	149	50	3	8	81	47	90	14	4	.315	.377	.484
3 Minor League Yrs		227	779	130	225	66	4	15	126	74	146	20	9	.289	.361	.442

LaRue, a fifth-round pick in 1995 from Dallas Baptist University, got his first opportunity to play every day in 1997, and made the most of it. He ranked fifth in the South Atlantic League in hitting, lined 50 doubles to tie for the minor league lead, and showed unusual speed for a catcher. His OPS was quite good at +24 percent. Defensively, he has some work to do. . . he caught just 28 percent of stealers. LaRue was a bit old for the Sally

League, so he needs to prove himself at higher levels, as well as improve his throwing. **Grade C**

Chris Latham
Minnesota Twins

Pos: OF   **Bats:** Both   **Ht:** 6'0"   **Wt:** 188   **Age:** 24

Yr Team	Lg	G	AB	R	H	2B	3B	HR	RBI	BB	SO	SB	CS	Avg	OBP	Slg
96 Salt Lake	AAA	115	376	59	103	16	6	9	50	36	91	26	9	.274	.338	.420
97 Salt Lake	AAA	118	492	78	152	22	5	8	58	58	110	21	19	.309	.386	.423
Minnesota	AL	15	22	4	4	1	0	0	1	0	8	0	0	.182	.182	.227
7 Minor League Yrs		624	2251	404	639	98	38	43	270	339	561	205	96	.284	.380	.418

Obtained from Los Angeles in the 1995 Kevin Tapani trade, Chris Latham improved slightly in his second season for Salt Lake. He has a burst of speed and some pop in his bat, but his plate discipline still needs improvement, and his overall production was not that good considering context. Latham has worked to revamp his stance at the plate, but with inconclusive results so far. His OPS and SEC were both just under league average. Defensively, he has very good range and a strong arm, but still tends to make careless errors. At this point, Latham has no future as a starter, but he could be a useful reserve if he makes fewer errors and gets on base a bit more. **Grade C**

Joe Lawrence
Toronto Blue Jays

Pos: SS   **Bats:** Right   **Ht:** 6'2"   **Wt:** 190   **Age:** 21

Yr Team	Lg	G	AB	R	H	2B	3B	HR	RBI	BB	SO	SB	CS	Avg	OBP	Slg
96 St. Cathrns	A	27	92	22	20	7	2	0	11	14	16	1	1	.217	.324	.337
97 Hagerstown	A	116	446	63	102	24	1	8	38	49	107	10	12	.229	.311	.341
2 Minor League Yrs		143	538	85	122	31	3	8	49	63	123	11	13	.227	.313	.340

Lawrence, Toronto's first-round pick in 1996 from Louisiana, was a highly advanced high school hitter, but he hasn't done well in the pros so far. He has good bat speed and hitting mechanics, but so far the performance isn't there, primarily due to mediocre command of the strike zone. His OPS was six percent below league. Lawrence needs to hit, because while he is not particularly error-prone, his range at shortstop is limited, and he faces a move to third. He has time and youth on his side. **Grade C-**

Brett Laxton
Oakland Athletics

Pos: P   **Throws:** Right   **Ht:** 6'2"   **Wt:** 205   **Age:** 24

Yr Team	Lg	G	GS	IP	H	R	ER	HR	BB	SO	SV	W	L	Pct.	ERA
96 Sou. Oregon	A	13	8	32.2	39	34	28	4	26	38	0	0	5	.000	7.71
97 Visalia	A	29	22	138.2	141	62	46	7	50	121	0	11	5	.688	2.99
2 Minor League Yrs		42	30	171.1	180	96	74	11	76	159	0	11	10	.524	3.89

As a freshman in 1993, Brett Laxton was the ace of LSU's staff, winning the National Championship game over Wichita State with an incredible 16-strikeout performance that marked him as a top prospect for the 1995 draft. It didn't happen; arm injuries in 1994 and 1995 robbed him of his fastball, costing him his elite-prospect status. He didn't enter pro ball until 1996, when the A's drafted him in the 24th round. This could have been a steal.

Much of his velocity was back in 1997, and he always did know how to pitch. His K/BB was very good at +19 percent, and although his other ratios were around league average, his ERA ranked third in the Carolina League. It was an impressive performance from someone most organizations had written off as a casualty. If he stays healthy, Laxton has the mental and physical equipment to be a very good pitcher. **Grade C+**

Juan LeBron   Kansas City Royals

Pos: OF   **Bats:** Right   **Ht:** 6'4"   **Wt:** 195   **Age:** 20

Yr Team	Lg	G	AB	R	H	2B	3B	HR	RBI	BB	SO	SB	CS	Avg	OBP	Slg
96 Royals	R	58	215	19	62	9	2	3	30	6	34	1	2	.288	.314	.391
97 Lansing	A	35	113	12	24	7	0	3	20	0	32	0	0	.212	.216	.354
Spokane	A	69	288	49	88	27	1	7	45	17	74	8	4	.306	.347	.479
3 Minor League Yrs		209	763	97	200	48	5	15	108	33	178	9	9	.262	.296	.397

LeBron was Kansas City's first-round pick, out of Puerto Rico, in 1995. Scouts love his power potential and compare him to Juan Gonzalez, but LeBron's plate discipline is so disastrous it may qualify for a FEMA loan. You would figure that in 113 at-bats in the Midwest League he could draw at least *one* walk, by accident or something. Unless Le-Bron learns to take a pitch at least once a week, all speculation about his power potential is pointless. **Grade C-**

Ricky Ledee   New York Yankees

Pos: OF   **Bats:** Left   **Ht:** 6'2"   **Wt:** 160   **Age:** 24

Yr Team	Lg	G	AB	R	H	2B	3B	HR	RBI	BB	SO	SB	CS	Avg	OBP	Slg
96 Norwich	AA	39	137	27	50	11	1	8	37	16	25	2	2	.365	.421	.635
Columbus	AAA	96	358	79	101	22	6	21	64	44	95	6	3	.282	.360	.553
97 Yankees	R	7	21	3	7	1	0	0	2	2	4	0	0	.333	.417	.381
Columbus	AAA	43	170	38	52	12	1	10	39	21	49	4	0	.306	.385	.565
8 Minor League Yrs		578	2078	383	559	109	33	85	324	302	517	45	30	.269	.363	.476

The Yankees are high enough on Ledee that they refused to trade him to San Diego in the Hidecki Irabu deal. As I write this, Ledee is projected to start in left field for New York in 1998, although given owner George Steinbrenner's historic lust for veteran free agents, that is hardly a sure thing. If Ledee does play, he will be good. He can hit for power and average, and has a pull swing nicely tailored for the Bronx. His strikeout rate is high, but he draws enough walks to indicate that he knows what he is doing at the plate. Ledee was great at Columbus, but missed much of the season with a severely strained groin muscle. His defense is just adequate, and he will be limited to left in the majors. Assuming he doesn't get brushed aside by Shane Mack or Mike Greenwell or Jim Wohlford, Ledee will have a good career as a Paul O'Neill-type. **Grade B+**

Carlos Lee
Chicago White Sox

Pos: 3B **Bats:** Right **Ht:** 6'2" **Wt:** 202 **Age:** 21

Yr Team	Lg	G	AB	R	H	2B	3B	HR	RBI	BB	SO	SB	CS	Avg	OBP	Slg
96 Hickory	A	119	480	65	150	23	6	8	70	23	50	18	13	.313	.337	.435
97 Winston-Sal	A	139	546	81	173	50	4	17	82	36	65	11	5	.317	.357	.516
4 Minor League Yrs		417	1569	213	477	100	12	36	228	79	191	47	31	.304	.335	.452

Carlos Lee, a young Panamanian, was one of the best offensive players in the Carolina League, with an OPS of +20 percent. His SEC was just three percent above league however, meaning that his skills, while impressive, are a bit narrow. He doesn't walk much and his power is still in the developmental stage. Those 50 doubles sure look great, however, and it is a good bet that many of them will turn into homers in the next year or two. Lee can be too aggressive, but his bat speed is good enough that it hasn't hurt him. League managers tabbed him as the Best Defensive Third Baseman, although he did make 34 errors. He has the tools; he just needs practice to refine the skills. Lee is bright and interested in baseball; he could be a great one if all goes well. **Grade B+**

Corey Lee
Texas Rangers

Pos: P **Throws:** Left **Ht:** 6'2" **Wt:** 180 **Age:** 23

Yr Team	Lg	G	GS	IP	H	R	ER	HR	BB	SO	SV	W	L	Pct.	ERA
96 Hudson Vall	A	9	9	54.2	42	24	20	1	21	59	0	1	4	.200	3.29
97 Charlotte	A	23	23	160.2	132	66	62	9	60	147	0	15	5	.750	3.47
2 Minor League Yrs		32	32	215.1	174	90	82	10	81	206	0	16	9	.640	3.43

The Rangers have showed increasing interest in college pitchers during the 1990s. Although this is the correct approach from an historical standpoint, so far they don't have much to show for their draft efforts. Corey Lee looks very promising, however. A supplemental first-round pick in 1996 from North Carolina State, Lee has been very effective in pro ball. His season for Charlotte was solid in all categories: K/BB +22 percent, K/IP +19 percent, H/IP +16 percent. Lee's fastball is just average, but his slider, curve, and change are all major league caliber, and he obviously throws strikes. He is aggressive, intelligent, and durable. Lee will need to carry his success forward to Double-A and Triple-A, and if he does well there he could challenge for a rotation spot in 2000. He isn't likely to be a dominant pitcher, but he could be a very good one. **Grade B-**

Derrek Lee
Florida Marlins

Pos: 1B **Bats:** Right **Ht:** 6'5" **Wt:** 220 **Age:** 22

Yr Team	Lg	G	AB	R	H	2B	3B	HR	RBI	BB	SO	SB	CS	Avg	OBP	Slg
96 Memphis	AA	134	500	98	140	39	2	34	104	65	170	13	6	.280	.360	.570
97 Las Vegas	AAA	125	472	86	153	29	2	13	64	60	116	17	3	.324	.399	.477
San Diego	NL	22	54	9	14	3	0	1	4	9	24	0	0	.259	.365	.370
5 Minor League Yrs		550	2050	356	600	118	10	81	332	232	540	66	32	.293	.366	.479

Derrek Lee has been on top prospect lists for several years now, and he's still there. His first full Triple-A season was a campaign of contrasts. For much of the season, his power production was disappointing: he had only six home runs by the end of July, a low total obviously, especially considering his past output and the nature of the park in Las Vegas. He was very hot in August, and while his final total of 13 still isn't that good, he still projects as an impressive power hitter. Lee has the bat speed and strength to hit .300, with 25-30 homers, in the majors. At times he is very patient, but he also goes through bouts of anxiousness. Last year wasn't the first time he was streaky. Lee did cut his strikeouts significantly in 1997, a good sign for the future. I doubt he is ready for immediate success, but he is still very young, and most players who hold their own in Triple-A at his age develop into stars. He changed addresses in the offseason, joining the Marlins in a trade for Kevin Brown. **Grade B+**

Travis Lee   *Arizona Diamondbacks*

Pos: 1B   **Bats:** Left   **Ht:** 6'3"   **Wt:** 205   **Age:** 22

Yr Team	Lg	G	AB	R	H	2B	3B	HR	RBI	BB	SO	SB	CS	Avg	OBP	Slg
97 High Desert	A	61	226	63	82	18	1	18	63	47	36	5	1	.363	.473	.690
Tucson	AAA	59	227	42	68	16	2	14	46	31	46	2	0	.300	.387	.573
1 Minor League Yr		120	453	105	150	34	3	32	109	78	82	7	1	.331	.431	.631

Barring injury or unforeseen catastrophe, Travis Lee will be the Diamondbacks' first baseman on Opening Day 1998. . . and maybe Opening Day 2008. When he was in college, scouts compared him to Mark Grace, who like Lee played for San Diego State. The difference is that Lee has legitimate home-run power. He has one of the most beautiful swings around, makes good contact, controls the strike zone, catches up with fastballs, hangs back on breaking stuff, and can pull the ball for power or go with the pitch. He was way ahead of the California League; the Diamondbacks, who didn't have a farm team in a higher classification, loaned him to the Brewers system, and he continued to hit well at Tucson. He was named the Best Prospect in the California League, and the No. 4 prospect in the PCL. Lee runs well for a big guy, is sound defensively, and has a good personality. Does he have any weaknesses? Maybe not. He will battle Todd Helton for Rookie of the Year. **Grade A**

Donny Leon   *New York Yankees*

Pos: 3B   **Bats:** Both   **Ht:** 6'2"   **Wt:** 180   **Age:** 21

Yr Team	Lg	G	AB	R	H	2B	3B	HR	RBI	BB	SO	SB	CS	Avg	OBP	Slg
96 Yankees	R	53	191	30	69	14	4	6	46	9	30	1	2	.361	.394	.571
97 Greensboro	A	137	516	45	131	32	1	12	74	15	106	6	4	.254	.278	.390
3 Minor League Yrs		206	748	78	207	47	5	18	125	27	150	7	7	.277	.306	.425

Leon got some attention as a prospect last year with a fine performance in the Gulf Coast League, but he moved up to Greensboro in 1997 and didn't play well. A non-drafted free agent signed in 1995 from Polk Community College in Florida, Leon intrigues scouts with his bat speed from both sides of the plate, but his discipline is lousy. He'll swing at anything at this point, and his OPS was four percent below average. His glove work needs polish, to say the least: he made 40 errors. Leon may have potential, but unless he learns the strike zone, it will remain untapped. **Grade C-**

Jose Leon
St. Louis Cardinals

Pos: 3B Bats: Right Ht: 6'0" Wt: 160 Age: 21

Yr Team	Lg	G	AB	R	H	2B	3B	HR	RBI	BB	SO	SB	CS	Avg	OBP	Slg
96 Johnson Cty	R	59	222	29	55	9	3	10	36	17	92	5	3	.248	.306	.450
New Jersey	A	7	28	4	8	3	1	1	3	0	7	0	0	.286	.333	.571
97 Peoria	A	118	399	50	92	21	2	20	54	32	122	6	5	.231	.301	.444
4 Minor League Yrs		271	943	114	214	40	9	31	121	70	318	12	13	.227	.290	.387

Leon was drafted out of Puerto Rico in the 22nd round in 1994. He has bat speed and good power potential, but he has problems with the strike zone. He has time to correct that, but if he doesn't, he'll be a Puerto Rican Mike Gulan. Leon needs improvement with the glove as well; he has the tools to play third base, but he makes a lot of errors, and his range factors are low. He is just a name to know for now. **Grade C-**

Brian Lesher
Oakland Athletics

Pos: OF Bats: Right Ht: 6'5" Wt: 205 Age: 27

Yr Team	Lg	G	AB	R	H	2B	3B	HR	RBI	BB	SO	SB	CS	Avg	OBP	Slg
96 Edmonton	AAA	109	414	57	119	29	2	18	75	36	108	6	5	.287	.352	.498
Oakland	AL	26	82	11	19	3	0	5	16	5	17	0	0	.232	.281	.451
97 Edmonton	AAA	110	415	85	134	27	5	21	78	64	86	14	3	.323	.415	.564
Oakland	AL	46	131	17	30	4	1	4	16	9	30	4	1	.229	.275	.366
6 Minor League Yrs		628	2223	380	624	120	15	80	357	303	525	61	43	.281	.372	.456

Is the glass half empty or half full? Brian Lesher has major league power, but before last year strike-zone problems hurt him in Triple-A. He made major strides against breaking stuff and outside pitches at Edmonton in 1997, resulting in a higher average, more walks, and improved overall production, but when he got promoted to the majors he fell back into bad habits, with the usual consequences. He's not young as prospects go, and he needs to adjust quickly to major league conditions to avoid getting buried or labeled as a minor league hitter. His chance of having a Geronimo Berroa-type career is about the same as his chance of having a Brent Cookson-type career. **Grade C**

Marc Lewis
Minnesota Twins

Pos: OF Bats: Right Ht: 6'2" Wt: 175 Age: 22

Yr Team	Lg	G	AB	R	H	2B	3B	HR	RBI	BB	SO	SB	CS	Avg	OBP	Slg
96 Macon	A	66	241	36	76	14	3	5	28	21	31	25	8	.315	.364	.461
Durham	A	68	262	43	78	12	2	6	26	24	37	25	9	.298	.360	.427
97 Greenville	AA	135	512	64	140	17	3	17	67	25	84	21	14	.273	.316	.418
4 Minor League Yrs		432	1608	239	460	74	16	38	202	109	223	121	48	.286	.333	.423

Marc Lewis attracted notice in 1996 by stealing 50 bases at Macon and Durham. His speed numbers were down in 1997, but he improved his power output, the increase attributed to added muscle and physical maturity. He still runs well, too. His OPS was actually a bit below league average, mainly due to a weak on-base percentage. He needs to be more patient, but since his strikeout mark isn't bad, he should be able to do so. That would help him get on base more, making his speed more valuable, and getting him better pitches to hit for power. With the glove, Lewis has above-average range and could play center in the majors. His arm is average or a bit above. Although Lewis needs to be more patient, I like the power he added to his game. He was sent to Minnesota as the player to be named in the Greg Colbrunn trade. **Grade B-**

Jeff Liefer   *Chicago White Sox*

Pos: OF   **Bats:** Left   **Ht:** 6'3"   **Wt:** 195   **Age:** 23

Yr Team	Lg	G	AB	R	H	2B	3B	HR	RBI	BB	SO	SB	CS	Avg	OBP	Slg
96 South Bend	A	74	277	60	90	14	0	15	58	30	62	6	5	.325	.396	.538
Pr William	A	37	147	17	33	6	0	1	13	11	27	0	0	.224	.277	.286
97 Birmingham	AA	119	474	67	113	24	9	15	71	38	115	2	0	.238	.302	.422
2 Minor League Yrs		230	898	144	236	44	9	31	142	79	204	8	5	.263	.328	.435

Liefer looked like the second coming of Robin Ventura in the lower minors, but he has struggled at the plate for the last year and a half. Rotator-cuff problems and a propensity for errors have shifted him from third to the outfield, so if he doesn't get the offense going, his prospect status will dim quickly. He continued to show power at Birmingham, but command of the strike zone got away from him, and he looked weak against breaking stuff. His OPS was infirm at minus-seven percent. Liefer was a horrible third baseman, and he isn't good in the outfield, either. Eight errors, two assists, and a low range factor is a bad blend. It is too early to give up on him, and perhaps the bad shoulder was having some sort of residual effect. If he doesn't hit in 1998, he risks getting buried. **Grade C**

Tal Light   *Colorado Rockies*

Pos: 3B   **Bats:** Right   **Ht:** 6'3"   **Wt:** 205   **Age:** 24

Yr Team	Lg	G	AB	R	H	2B	3B	HR	RBI	BB	SO	SB	CS	Avg	OBP	Slg
96 Asheville	A	52	205	34	67	15	0	12	51	21	58	8	4	.327	.389	.576
Salem	A	64	234	29	55	10	0	13	36	19	59	3	1	.235	.305	.444
97 New Haven	AA	25	83	10	20	6	0	5	11	5	36	0	1	.241	.284	.494
Salem	A	104	373	57	99	19	2	15	65	59	144	0	1	.265	.368	.448
3 Minor League Yrs		268	958	143	258	54	2	49	176	122	314	11	7	.269	.355	.483

Tal Light has excellent power, but he is an all-or-nothing hitter who strikes out extravagantly. He is also a terrible defensive third baseman, and really belongs across the diamond at first, where he played quite a bit at Oklahoma State. Of course, he has no chance to make it at that position, due to the presence of Todd Helton in the organization, so the Coorsies have kept him at third. Light's chance for a career is entirely dependent on his ability to make contact. If he cuts down on the strikeouts and shows some ability to hit for average at the higher levels, he could do some damage in the thin Colorado air, but he needs to do it soon. **Grade C-**

Ted Lilly

Los Angeles Dodgers

Pos: P **Throws:** Left **Ht:** 6'1" **Wt:** 180 **Age:** 22

Yr Team	Lg	G	GS	IP	H	R	ER	HR	BB	SO	SV	W	L	Pct.	ERA
96 Yakima	A	13	8	53.2	25	9	5	0	14	75	0	4	0	1.000	0.84
97 San Berndno	A	23	21	134.2	116	52	42	9	32	158	0	7	8	.467	2.81
2 Minor League Yrs		36	29	188.1	141	61	47	9	46	233	0	11	8	.579	2.25

Lilly was picked in the 23rd round in 1996 out of Fresno Community College. Scouts liked him, but his fastball was fairly ordinary, and most people thought he would attend college, which explains his draft status. He chose the pro route instead, and right now it looks like he made the right decision. Lilly has a lively fastball that is up to 90 MPH, and a decent curveball. His command is outstanding, as indicated by his superb +142 percent K/BB ratio. His K/IP and H/IP marks were also near the top of the league at +36 and +12 percent, respectively. He was voted Pitcher with the Best Control by the league managers, and even threw a no-hitter. Pitchers with 90-MPH fastballs and great control tend to go far, if their arms don't fall off. Injury risk and Albuquerque are the two obstacles Lilly will have to overcome, and he ended the season with elbow trouble. **Grade B**

Mike Lincoln

Minnesota Twins

Pos: P **Throws:** Right **Ht:** 6'2" **Wt:** 200 **Age:** 22

Yr Team	Lg	G	GS	IP	H	R	ER	HR	BB	SO	SV	W	L	Pct.	ERA
96 Ft. Myers	A	12	11	59.2	64	31	27	5	25	24	0	5	2	.714	4.07
97 Ft. Myers	A	20	20	134.0	130	41	34	4	25	75	0	13	4	.765	2.28
2 Minor League Yrs		32	31	193.2	194	72	61	9	50	99	0	18	6	.750	2.83

Mike Lincoln was drafted in the 13th round in 1996, from the University of Tennessee. You won't see him on many prospect lists, and there is reason for that. His control is legitimately outstanding, and you can't argue with his win-loss record or ERA at Fort Myers last year. His K/BB ratio was great at +49 percent. The problem is, control is all he has: he doesn't throw hard at all. His K/IP mark reflects this, at -27 percent; his H/IP was league average. Lincoln's strikeout rate was much higher in college, so there is a chance, albeit an outside one, that he could continue pitching well as he moves up. I won't really believe in him until that K/IP rate rises, but he does deserve a fair hearing. **Grade C-**

Cole Liniak

Boston Red Sox

Pos: 3B Bats: Right Ht: 6'1" Wt: 181 Age: 21

Yr Team	Lg	G	AB	R	H	2B	3B	HR	RBI	BB	SO	SB	CS	Avg	OBP	Slg
96 Michigan	A	121	437	65	115	26	2	3	46	59	59	7	6	.263	.358	.352
97 Sarasota	A	64	217	32	73	16	0	6	42	22	31	1	2	.336	.402	.493
Trenton	AA	53	200	20	56	11	0	2	18	17	29	0	1	.280	.338	.365
3 Minor League Yrs		261	933	126	265	60	2	12	114	102	127	10	9	.284	.360	.391

Liniak was selected in the seventh round in 1995, from a California high school. He is a fine athlete with a sharp line-drive swing, and a knack for contact against all styles of pitching. He has little power at this stage, although that may come with time. His SEC was horrible at Double-A, -40 percent, indicating that despite his decent average, he did little to help the offense at that level. To have real value with the bat, he needs power development, or else he must hit .330 consistently. Liniak is a very promising defensive player, with above-average range and a howitzer arm. Liniak's offensive game is too one-dimensional right now, but he is youthful enough to augment his contact ability with power. **Grade B-**

Mark Little

Texas Rangers

Pos: OF Bats: Right Ht: 6'0" Wt: 200 Age: 25

Yr Team	Lg	G	AB	R	H	2B	3B	HR	RBI	BB	SO	SB	CS	Avg	OBP	Slg
96 Tulsa	AA	101	409	69	119	24	2	13	50	48	88	22	10	.291	.377	.455
97 Okla City	AAA	121	415	72	109	23	4	15	45	39	100	21	9	.263	.338	.446
4 Minor League Yrs		391	1470	249	401	93	19	40	172	160	334	77	38	.273	.355	.444

Little, a product of Memphis University, was selected in the eighth round in 1994. He has very good speed on the bases, and surprising pop in his bat, but needs more patience at the plate in order to get his on-base percentage higher. It would also help him drive more pitches for power. His OPS was only slightly above average, so more power production would help. Little has excellent range in center field, and for that reason the Rangers see him as a future reserve outfielder. So do I. **Grade C**

Claudio Liverziani

Seattle Mariners

Pos: OF Bats: Left Ht: 6'0" Wt: 185 Age: 23

Yr Team	Lg	G	AB	R	H	2B	3B	HR	RBI	BB	SO	SB	CS	Avg	OBP	Slg
97 Wisconsin	A	108	346	73	88	22	4	5	31	68	93	11	4	.254	.381	.384
1 Minor League Yr		108	346	73	88	22	4	5	31	68	93	11	4	.254	.381	.384

The Mariners signed Claudio Liverziani as a free agent in 1996; he had played for the Italian Olympic Baseball Team in Atlanta. Italy has a small but growing baseball culture. Liverziani didn't hit for a high average or great power at Wisconsin, but he works pitchers for walks, is fundamentally sound considering his lack of top-notch amateur experience, and is a solid defensive outfielder. His chance to make the majors is remote, but with a year to adjust to American culture, he could do much better in 1998. **Grade C-**

Paul LoDuca
Los Angeles Dodgers

Pos: C   **Bats:** Right   **Ht:** 5'10"   **Wt:** 193   **Age:** 25

Yr Team	Lg	G	AB	R	H	2B	3B	HR	RBI	BB	SO	SB	CS	Avg	OBP	Slg
96 Vero Beach	A	124	439	54	134	22	0	3	66	70	38	8	2	.305	.400	.376
97 San Antonio	AA	105	385	63	126	28	2	7	69	46	27	16	8	.327	.399	.465
5 Minor League Yrs		452	1612	226	492	96	3	17	224	207	161	45	24	.305	.385	.400

In 1993, his junior year at Arizona State, Paul LoDuca led the Pac-10 South in hitting with a .446 average. That's a tough conference, and although scouts liked his bat, no one was surprised when he fell to the 25th round in the draft. LoDuca was non-athletic, mediocre defensively, and slow as hell, so scouts wrote him off as an "organization player." He filled rosters for four years in the Dodgers organization, but he received significant playing time at Double-A last year, and did enough that people are noticing him again. LoDuca has an extremely quick swing out of a slightly open stance, and can hit the ball hard in any direction. His command of the strike zone is very good, and he even managed to steal some bases last year, despite his lack of foot speed. His defense has improved dramatically since his college days; he threw out 46 percent of runners to lead the Texas League, and was named Best Defensive Catcher. LoDuca can hit, is smart, and works hard. He would make a fine reserve catcher behind Mike Piazza, or anybody else for that matter. **Grade C**

Carlton Loewer
Philadelphia Phillies

Pos: P   **Throws:** Right   **Ht:** 6'6"   **Wt:** 220   **Age:** 24

Yr Team	Lg	G	GS	IP	H	R	ER	HR	BB	SO	SV	W	L	Pct.	ERA
96 Reading	AA	27	27	171.0	191	115	100	24	57	119	0	7	10	.412	5.26
97 Scranton-WB	AAA	29	29	184.0	198	120	94	20	50	152	0	5	13	.278	4.60
3 Minor League Yrs		84	84	519.2	555	311	248	53	174	389	0	23	29	.442	4.30

The Phillies have been very patient with Carlton Loewer since drafting him out of Mississippi State in the first round in 1994. His 5-13 record at Scranton wasn't anything to write home about, but his K/BB ratio was great at +58 percent, and his strikeout rate rose to a respectable level, after being below average in previous seasons. Loewer has a 90-MPH fastball, a very good curve, and a useable changeup. He throws strikes, but still tends to groove pitches when behind in the count. He has proven durable, having never missed a start due to injury in three professional seasons. Loewer is not likely to be a staff ace, but should be a sturdy inning-eater if he can improve his approach to pitching when behind the hitters. **Grade C+**

Steve Lomasney
Boston Red Sox

Pos: C **Bats:** Right **Ht:** 6'0" **Wt:** 185 **Age:** 20

Yr Team	Lg	G	AB	R	H	2B	3B	HR	RBI	BB	SO	SB	CS	Avg	OBP	Slg
96 Lowell	A	59	173	26	24	10	0	4	21	42	63	2	0	.139	.313	.266
97 Michigan	A	102	324	50	89	27	3	12	51	32	98	3	4	.275	.353	.488
3 Minor League Yrs		190	589	86	128	43	3	16	79	82	177	7	5	.217	.328	.382

Lomasney was picked in the fifth round in 1995, out of Peabody, Massachusetts, and was one of several New Englanders selected by Boston in the middle rounds of that draft. He is an excellent athlete, especially for a catcher. Offensively, he is still tailoring his swing, and many scouts think he will hit for average and power as he matures. Behind the plate, he is raw but has great promise. He threw out just 22 percent of runners, despite a strong arm, and needs to improve his footwork. On the other hand, he has great actions behind the plate and pilots pitchers well. At this stage, he is more potential than production. **Grade C**

George Lombard
Atlanta Braves

Pos: OF **Bats:** Left **Ht:** 6'0" **Wt:** 208 **Age:** 22

Yr Team	Lg	G	AB	R	H	2B	3B	HR	RBI	BB	SO	SB	CS	Avg	OBP	Slg
96 Macon	A	116	444	76	109	16	8	15	51	36	122	24	17	.245	.311	.419
97 Durham	A	131	462	65	122	25	7	14	72	66	145	35	7	.264	.365	.439
4 Minor League Yrs		404	1477	221	352	54	19	37	163	170	449	120	45	.238	.328	.376

George Lombard gives tool-loving scouts heart palpitations. Kind of like the way some of us feel about the new ex-Borg character on *Star Trek: Voyager*. Nice wrenches. Anyhow, Lombard has made slow progress converting his athletic ability into performance, but he has made progress. His walk rate has risen substantially, and he continues to gradually increase his power production. On the other hand, his strikeout rate is dangerously high, and he remains unrefined as a hitter and baserunner. Defensively, he has excellent range, but his arm is often inaccurate and he makes errors. Lombard does work hard at his game and has made huge strides considering that he played almost no high school baseball. I am optimistic about Lombard's chance for improvement, but I can't really tell you why because I don't know myself. **Grade C**

Garrett Long
Pittsburgh Pirates

Pos: 1B **Bats:** Right **Ht:** 6'3" **Wt:** 195 **Age:** 21

Yr Team	Lg	G	AB	R	H	2B	3B	HR	RBI	BB	SO	SB	CS	Avg	OBP	Slg
96 Erie	A	20	70	5	20	2	1	0	7	9	17	1	2	.286	.370	.343
97 Augusta	A	83	280	50	84	10	2	7	41	61	78	5	2	.300	.426	.425
Lynchburg	A	9	29	1	6	3	0	1	5	3	10	0	0	.207	.281	.414
3 Minor League Yrs		161	550	86	162	21	4	11	77	105	140	8	7	.295	.408	.407

Long was Pittsburgh's second-round pick in 1995, from high school in Houston. He lost nearly all of 1996 and much of 1997 to shoulder surgery, but came back from rehab to show some offensive potential last year. He is very patient at the plate, perhaps too patient, considering his strikeout rate, and while he doesn't drive the ball over the fences consistently yet, he is quite strong, and should develop power in time. Long is a bright guy, and should be able to make adjustments as he moves up. A sleeper, and while the strikeouts scare me a bit, the walks intrigue me. **Grade C**

Terrence Long   *New York Mets*

Pos: OF   **Bats:** Left   **Ht:** 6'1"   **Wt:** 179   **Age:** 22

Yr Team	Lg	G	AB	R	H	2B	3B	HR	RBI	BB	SO	SB	CS	Avg	OBP	Slg
96 Capital City	A	123	473	66	136	26	9	12	78	36	120	32	7	.288	.342	.457
97 St. Lucie	A	126	470	52	118	29	7	8	61	40	102	24	8	.251	.310	.394
4 Minor League Yrs		415	1523	208	387	74	24	38	222	154	353	84	27	.254	.326	.409

The tools are here, but the performance isn't. Terrence Long, New York's second first-round pick in 1994 behind Paul Wilson, grappled with the Florida State League in 1997 and did not do well. He still has athletic ability, speed, and strength, but his strike-zone judgment remains questionable, and he doesn't drive pitches for power. His OPS was just below league average. Long has good range in center field, but needs more experience tracking fly balls and using his arm strength correctly. I was optimistic about Long's chance to develop last year, but am less sanguine now. **Grade C**

Braden Looper   *St. Louis Cardinals*

Pos: P   **Throws:** Right   **Ht:** 6'5"   **Wt:** 225   **Age:** 23

Yr Team	Lg	G	GS	IP	H	R	ER	HR	BB	SO	SV	W	L	Pct.	ERA
97 Pr William	A	12	12	64.1	71	38	32	6	25	58	0	3	6	.333	4.48
Arkansas	AA	19	0	21.1	24	14	14	2	7	20	5	1	4	.200	5.91
1 Minor League Yr		31	12	85.2	95	52	46	8	32	78	5	4	10	.286	4.83

Looper was the Cardinals first-round pick in 1996, from Wichita State, the third player picked overall. He was a closer in college, and projects into the same role in the majors, but the Cardinals used him as a starter at Prince William to help him work on his breaking pitches. He made progress after a slow start, then was promoted to Arkansas and moved back to the bullpen. He had some trouble in the Texas League, then his season ended early due to a sore shoulder. Allegedly, the injury is nothing serious, but we will have to see. Looper has a blazing 95-MPH fastball with excellent movement. He also has a changeup and a slider, both of which need work, but should be good pitches given time. His control is usually solid, and he has a closer-type attitude. If healthy, he should be a very good pitcher, similar perhaps to Darren Dreifort, another Wichita State product. Dreifort had a lot of arm trouble, and hopefully Looper can avoid the same. **Grade B**

Jose Lopez
New York Mets

Pos: 3B **Bats:** Right **Ht:** 6'1" **Wt:** 175 **Age:** 22

Yr Team	Lg	G	AB	R	H	2B	3B	HR	RBI	BB	SO	SB	CS	Avg	OBP	Slg
96 St. Lucie	A	121	419	63	122	17	5	11	60	39	103	18	10	.291	.362	.434
97 Norfolk	AAA	2	6	1	2	0	0	0	0	0	2	0	0	.333	.333	.333
St. Lucie	A	23	87	14	17	3	1	4	13	3	25	2	0	.195	.231	.391
Binghamton	AA	66	207	31	51	10	1	11	26	13	63	4	2	.246	.290	.464
4 Minor League Yrs		344	1180	181	316	60	12	34	170	105	299	33	15	.268	.331	.425

Lopez has one thing that scouts really like in a hitter: great bat speed. He lacks one thing that I really like in a hitter: strike-zone judgment. He hits the ball hard and projects good power, but at this point he'll swing at anything. This seems to be endemic to the Mets organization. Almost all their hitting prospects strike out too much and don't walk enough. Lopez is young enough to improve, but he needs good coaching. He also needs to recover from a labrum tear in his shoulder. This is most suspicious. Is Dallas Green still in the organization as a hitting instructor? "Be aggressive, swing at anything near the plate, you pansy. And I don't care if your shoulder hurts." **Grade C-**

Luis Lopez
Toronto Blue Jays

Pos: 1B **Bats:** Right **Ht:** 6'0" **Wt:** 200 **Age:** 24

Yr Team	Lg	G	AB	R	H	2B	3B	HR	RBI	BB	SO	SB	CS	Avg	OBP	Slg
96 St. Cathrns	A	74	260	36	74	17	2	7	40	27	31	2	3	.285	.364	.446
97 Hagerstown	A	136	503	96	180	47	4	11	99	60	45	5	8	.358	.430	.533
2 Minor League Yrs		210	763	132	254	64	6	18	139	87	76	7	11	.333	.407	.503

Lopez is an interesting story. He played college ball at Coastal Carolina, but wasn't drafted and ended up in the independent Northern League. He played a few games for the St. Paul Saints in 1995, then was loaned to the Ogden Raptors of the Pioneer League, where he hit .357. He was old for the level, however, so no one thought much of it. The Blue Jays signed him as a free agent in 1996 to help fill out the St. Catharines roster in the New York-Penn League, and he played well enough to avoid getting released. In 1997, his diligence was rewarded. Lopez had the second-best OPS in the Sally League, +39 percent, led the league in hitting, won the MVP Award and established himself as a prospect. Lopez has a nice line-drive swing, and is an intelligent hitter who controls the zone and hits to all fields. He will need to prove himself at higher levels, but I think there is a good chance he will. **Grade C**

Mendy Lopez
Kansas City Royals

Pos: SS **Bats:** Right **Ht:** 6'2" **Wt:** 165 **Age:** 23

Yr Team	Lg	G	AB	R	H	2B	3B	HR	RBI	BB	SO	SB	CS	Avg	OBP	Slg
96 Wichita	AA	93	327	47	92	20	5	6	32	26	67	14	4	.281	.341	.428
97 Omaha	AAA	17	52	6	12	2	0	1	6	8	21	0	0	.231	.333	.327
Wichita	AA	101	357	56	83	16	3	5	42	36	70	7	5	.232	.304	.336
4 Minor League Yrs		400	1399	207	388	86	14	19	166	120	258	58	21	.277	.338	.400

Scouts like Mendy Lopez, and say he has a great deal of offensive potential, but he has yet to show it in Double-A. He can make contact, but flies out a lot. If he gets stronger, some of those flies could get over the fences, but it hasn't happened yet. Defensively, he has very quick reactions, pretty good range, and a cannon arm that occasionally goes wild on him. He can play shortstop or third base, although he won't have the bat to play at the hot corner if he doesn't pick up the hitting. **Grade C**

Pee Wee Lopez   *New York Mets*

Pos: C   **Bats:** Right   **Ht:** 6'0"   **Wt:** 195   **Age:** 21

Yr Team	Lg	G	AB	R	H	2B	3B	HR	RBI	BB	SO	SB	CS	Avg	OBP	Slg
96 Kingsport	R	65	250	53	79	22	4	7	58	31	25	0	1	.316	.397	.520
Pittsfield	A	5	14	2	6	0	1	0	3	1	1	0	0	.429	.467	.571
97 St. Lucie	A	113	375	40	93	19	0	3	30	39	56	3	2	.248	.318	.323
2 Minor League Yrs		183	639	95	178	41	5	10	91	71	82	3	3	.279	.353	.405

Pee Wee Lopez was drafted in the eighth round in 1996, from Miami-Dade Community College South. Scouts like his untapped power potential and quick bat, but his performance at St. Lucie wasn't special at all, granted that it is a tough environment in which to hit. His OPS was well below average. His glove is better: he threw out 42 percent of stealers, the league average being 36 percent, and he didn't make gobs of errors. At this point, the scouting reports and the numbers don't mesh. One reason for optimism may be that his strike-zone judgment is better than most players in the Mets system, although I doubt many scouts have noticed that. **Grade C**

Mike Lowell   *New York Yankees*

Pos: 3B   **Bats:** Right   **Ht:** 6'4"   **Wt:** 195   **Age:** 24

Yr Team	Lg	G	AB	R	H	2B	3B	HR	RBI	BB	SO	SB	CS	Avg	OBP	Slg
96 Greensboro	A	113	433	58	122	33	0	8	64	46	43	10	3	.282	.355	.413
Tampa	A	24	78	8	22	5	0	0	11	3	13	1	1	.282	.298	.346
97 Norwich	AA	78	285	60	98	17	0	15	47	48	30	2	1	.344	.439	.561
Columbus	AAA	57	210	36	58	13	1	15	45	23	34	2	4	.276	.347	.562
3 Minor League Yrs		344	1287	198	373	86	1	39	194	143	154	18	10	.290	.362	.449

Lowell was a 20th-round pick in 1995, from Florida International University. He wasn't a hot prospect by any means, but hey, you need someone to fill those rosters. Lowell had a pretty good year in 1996, but in 1997 he exploded with an offensive outburst that no one expected. He was outstanding in a difficult park at Norwich, with an OPS of +25 percent, showing excellent strike-zone judgment, and the rare ability to combine contact with power. He moved up to Columbus and wasn't quite as good, but his OPS of +19 percent was still sound. He can do the job with the glove, with a strong arm in particular, but isn't likely to win many Gold Gloves. The apparent explanation of Lowell's Great Leap Forward is that he did extensive weight-lifting last season to add needed power; he planned to work on his flexibility and lateral movement to improve his defense this winter. He is a fine prospect; it will be fascinating to see how the Yankees handle him. **Grade B+**

Terrell Lowery
Chicago Cubs

Pos: OF   **Bats:** Right   **Ht:** 6'3"   **Wt:** 175   **Age:** 27

Yr	Team	Lg	G	AB	R	H	2B	3B	HR	RBI	BB	SO	SB	CS	Avg	OBP	Slg
96	Binghamton	AA	62	211	34	58	13	4	7	32	44	44	5	6	.275	.400	.474
	Norfolk	AAA	62	193	25	45	7	2	4	21	22	44	6	3	.233	.312	.352
97	Iowa	AAA	110	386	69	116	28	3	17	71	65	97	9	8	.301	.401	.521
	Chicago	NL	9	14	2	4	0	0	0	0	3	3	1	0	.286	.412	.286
6 Minor League Yrs			569	2084	344	582	109	37	48	272	305	452	102	71	.279	.372	.436

You certainly can't argue with what Terrell Lowery did in Des Moines last year, hitting for average, power, drawing walks, and posting an excellent OPS of +23 percent. The Cubs picked him up in the minor league Rule 5 draft last winter. Scouts have always loved his tools, but last year was the first season he consistently showed solid on-the-field skills and performance. Lowery can field, too, showing superior range in center field; his arm is average, but usually accurate. Injuries and lack of baseball experience held him back in the past, and although he is too old to be a top-notch prospect and is probably at his peak now, it wouldn't surprise me if he ended up having a respectable career. **Grade C+**

Robert Luce
Seattle Mariners

Pos: P   **Throws:** Right   **Ht:** 6'0"   **Wt:** 168   **Age:** 23

Yr	Team	Lg	G	GS	IP	H	R	ER	HR	BB	SO	SV	W	L	Pct.	ERA
96	Everett	A	23	0	41.0	45	26	20	6	16	47	7	3	4	.429	4.39
97	Lancaster	A	14	14	86.1	100	43	27	8	24	57	0	10	1	.909	2.81
	Memphis	AA	13	13	75.2	90	40	33	5	14	41	0	5	2	.714	3.93
2 Minor League Yrs			50	27	203.0	235	109	80	19	54	145	7	18	7	.720	3.55

The Mariners drafted Rob Luce in the ninth round in 1996, out of UNLV. He ended his first full pro season in Double-A, quite an achievement for a pitcher with an 86-MPH fastball. What Luce lacks in velocity, he makes up for in movement: his fastball has excellent sink, and he spots it well in the strike zone. His slider and changeup are acceptable, and he will throw any pitch in any situation. Luce gives up large numbers of hits, but he doesn't walk many guys, and has a gift for getting out of jams. He needs to prove that he can do this in Triple-A, but even if he does that, his role in the majors would probably be as a reliever. **Grade C**

Eric Ludwick
Florida Marlins

Pos: P   **Throws:** Right   **Ht:** 6'5"   **Wt:** 210   **Age:** 26

Yr	Team	Lg	G	GS	IP	H	R	ER	HR	BB	SO	SV	W	L	Pct.	ERA
96	Louisville	AAA	11	11	60.1	55	24	19	4	24	73	0	3	4	.429	2.83
	St. Louis	NL	6	1	10.0	11	11	10	4	3	12	0	0	1	.000	9.00
97	Louisville	AAA	24	11	80.0	67	31	26	7	26	85	4	6	8	.429	2.93
	Edmonton	AAA	6	3	19.0	22	7	7	1	4	20	0	1	1	.500	3.32
	St. Louis	NL	5	0	6.2	12	7	7	1	6	7	0	0	1	.000	9.45
	Oakland	AL	6	5	24.0	32	24	22	7	16	14	0	1	4	.200	8.25
5 Minor League Yrs			105	87	524.0	487	258	206	30	224	435	4	34	36	.486	3.54

Ludwick, acquired from Oakland in the Kurt Abbott trade, has obviously mastered Triple-A hitters, but hasn't gotten his sea legs in the majors yet. I think he will. His stuff is solid:

92-MPH fastball, hard slider, changeup and curve. Control of his stuff has been a strength in the minors, but a major weakness in the Show. This is not unusual, and he will likely overcome that with time. Part of his problem is lack of a defined role: the Cardinals kept switching him between the bullpen and the rotation, and the Athletics didn't make a firm commitment either way. Basically, there is no apparent reason for Eric Ludwick not to be a very successful major league pitcher. . . but the same can be said for Scott Ruffcorn. . .
Grade B

Julio Lugo   *Houston Astros*

Pos: SS **Bats:** Right **Ht:** 5'11" **Wt:** 155 **Age:** 22

Yr Team	Lg	G	AB	R	H	2B	3B	HR	RBI	BB	SO	SB	CS	Avg	OBP	Slg
96 Quad City	A	101	393	60	116	18	2	10	50	32	75	24	11	.295	.350	.427
97 Kissimmee	A	125	505	89	135	22	14	7	61	46	99	35	8	.267	.329	.408
3 Minor League Yrs		285	1128	185	318	46	19	18	127	104	205	76	26	.282	.344	.404

Lugo was a 43rd-round pick in 1994, out of Connors State Junior College in Oklahoma. He gets little attention, but he has good speed and a touch of spark in his bat. Lugo was four percent above league in OPS, not a bad mark for an infielder at Kissimmee, and some of the 14 triples he hit might go for homers next year. Lugo led the Florida State League in errors with 40, but he also had the highest range factor in the circuit. Remember, guys who have great range but make too many errors often settle down as they mature. I like Lugo, but I want to see him make a successful transition to Double-A. **Grade B-**

Curt Lyons   *Cincinnati Reds*

Pos: P **Throws:** Right **Ht:** 6'5" **Wt:** 228 **Age:** 23

Yr Team	Lg	G	GS	IP	H	R	ER	HR	BB	SO	SV	W	L	Pct.	ERA
96 Chattanooga	AA	24	24	141.2	113	48	38	8	52	176	0	13	4	.765	2.41
Cincinnati	NL	3	3	16.0	17	8	8	1	7	14	0	2	0	1.000	4.50
97 Iowa	AAA	8	8	29.2	35	23	21	8	21	26	0	0	2	.000	6.37
Orlando	AA	2	2	6.0	6	5	5	0	2	8	0	0	0	—	7.50
6 Minor League Yrs		102	98	569.2	523	252	196	35	203	512	0	38	28	.576	3.10

A year ago, I considered Curt Lyons one of the top pitching prospects in baseball. When the Reds traded him to the Cubs for Ozzie Timmons, the sabermetric world let loose a hearty guffaw at Cincy GM Jim Bowden's expense. Timmons didn't do anything for the Reds, but Lyons did even less for the Cubs, reporting overweight, spending most of the year on the disabled list with a sore shoulder, and pitching poorly when he did take the mound. Will he recover? Hell, I don't know. History is no guide. . . there are plenty of examples both positive and negative. We'll have to wait and see. The Cubs gave up on him, and the Reds reclaimed him on waivers. **Grade C-**

Katsuhiro Maeda

New York Yankees

Pos: P **Throws:** Right **Ht:** 6'2" **Wt:** 215 **Age:** 26

Yr Team	Lg	G	GS	IP	H	R	ER	HR	BB	SO	SV	W	L	Pct.	ERA
96 Yankees	R	2	2	9.0	4	3	3	1	2	7	0	1	1	.500	3.00
Tampa	A	2	2	10.2	11	5	5	0	6	8	0	0	0	—	4.22
Norwich	AA	9	9	53.1	49	25	24	4	21	30	0	3	2	.600	4.05
97 Norwich	AA	25	21	124.1	117	75	63	14	62	76	0	8	10	.444	4.56
2 Minor League Yrs		38	34	197.1	181	108	95	19	91	121	0	12	13	.480	4.33

Personally, I don't see any reason to get excited about Kat Maeda. The major league arm is there, but the command isn't, and his personality hardly inspires confidence. I'm not talking about the hair-color issue, but rather the fact that he just doesn't give the impression, to me at least, that he really knows how to use his stuff. It is possible of course that he could learn to do so. If Maeda does learn to pitch, the first objective indicator will be an increase in his strikeout rate. Don't trust word-of-mouth press reports in cases like this; look for the statistical evidence. **Grade C**

Jose Malave

Boston Red Sox

Pos: OF **Bats:** Right **Ht:** 6'2" **Wt:** 195 **Age:** 26

Yr Team	Lg	G	AB	R	H	2B	3B	HR	RBI	BB	SO	SB	CS	Avg	OBP	Slg
96 Pawtucket	AAA	41	155	30	42	6	0	8	29	12	37	2	1	.271	.329	.465
Boston	AL	41	102	12	24	3	0	4	17	2	25	0	0	.235	.257	.382
97 Pawtucket	AAA	115	427	87	127	24	2	17	70	55	78	12	4	.297	.376	.482
Boston	AL	4	4	0	0	0	0	0	0	0	2	0	0	.000	.000	.000
8 Minor League Yrs		574	2145	374	630	120	14	94	379	211	411	35	19	.294	.358	.494

I feel sorry for this guy. Malave can hit, but the Red Sox have about as much faith in him as Nietzsche had in the Golden Rule. His OPS was very decent at +13 percent, and he actually hit better on the road than in the Pawtucket bandbox. Given a shot in the majors, Malave could hit .270-.290, with very good power and reasonable strike-zone judgment. That's not awesome, but it could help some teams. Defensively, he is adequate at best in right field, and is probably better suited to left, where his inaccurate arm is less of a liability. It may be hard to believe these days, but there are some teams out there that could use more power, and Malave could provide some, cheaply. **Grade C+**

Randi Mallard

Cincinnati Reds

Pos: P **Throws:** Right **Ht:** 6'1" **Wt:** 185 **Age:** 22

Yr Team	Lg	G	GS	IP	H	R	ER	HR	BB	SO	SV	W	L	Pct.	ERA
96 Princeton	R	13	11	66.0	66	42	27	2	38	72	0	2	7	.222	3.68
97 Chston-WV	A	13	12	56.1	51	25	24	0	23	61	0	3	3	.500	3.83
2 Minor League Yrs		26	23	122.1	117	67	51	2	61	133	0	5	10	.333	3.75

Drafted in the second round in 1996, from Hillsborough Community College in Florida, Randi Mallard is blessed with a fine major league arm, and it looks like he knows how to use it. He has a moving 92-MPH fastball and a good curve. Mallard also has solid control, and his ratios at Charleston were nicely congruous: K/BB +12 percent, H/IP +10 percent, K/IP +25 percent. Mallard missed much of the season with a sore elbow, but he seemed healthy at the end of the campaign. If the arm holds up, I like his chances to surprise us in 1998. **Grade C+**

James Manias
Tampa Bay Devil Rays

Pos: P   Throws: Left   Ht: 6'4"   Wt: 190   Age: 23

Yr Team	Lg	G	GS	IP	H	R	ER	HR	BB	SO	SV	W	L	Pct.	ERA
96 Butte	R	16	13	72.0	98	64	42	8	22	55	0	5	4	.556	5.25
97 St. Pete	A	28	28	171.1	163	84	72	16	40	119	0	13	5	.722	3.78
2 Minor League Yrs		44	41	243.1	261	148	114	24	62	174	0	18	9	.667	4.22

Manias was drafted in the 25th round in 1996, from Fairfield University. He emerged as more than roster filler with a nice little season in the Florida State League. Manias' best fastball is 88 MPH, but he has a sharp slider, and a curve with a nice bend to it. His control is very good, but his strikeout rate at St. Petersburg was low: -10 percent. Like all finesse guys, he must prove he can be effective at the higher levels, but he is a smart guy and might be able to adjust. **Grade C-**

T.R. Marcinczyk
Oakland Athletics

Pos: 1B   Bats: Right   Ht: 6'2"   Wt: 195   Age: 24

Yr Team	Lg	G	AB	R	H	2B	3B	HR	RBI	BB	SO	SB	CS	Avg	OBP	Slg
96 Sou. Oregon	A	63	216	29	48	13	2	7	38	22	57	3	3	.222	.304	.398
97 Modesto	A	133	463	89	128	41	2	23	91	71	107	4	4	.276	.381	.523
2 Minor League Yrs		196	679	118	176	54	4	30	129	93	164	7	7	.259	.357	.483

The Athletics have an interesting farm-system philosophy. On the one hand, they sign lots of raw Latin players, like Miguel Tejada, Tony Batista, Jose Ortiz, Ramon Hernandez, and Mario Encarnacion. They draft the occasional high school sensation like Ben Grieve or Eric Chavez. But they surround the young crude guys with lots of experienced college players, like A. J. Hinch, Justin Bowles, or in this case, T.R. Marcinczyk, drafted in the 28th round from the University of Miami in 1996. I think it is a good philosophy, giving the youngsters experienced players to learn from and bond with. Marcinczyk showed power and patience at Modesto, although scouts question if he will hit for enough of an average at higher levels. He also has problems controlling his temper: he punched out a catcher after getting beaned in one game. Hopefully, the younger guys won't follow his example of what to do when you get hit by a pitch. **Grade C**

Jesus Marquez
Detroit Tigers

Pos: OF   Bats: Left   Ht: 6'0"   Wt: 175   Age: 25

Yr Team	Lg	G	AB	R	H	2B	3B	HR	RBI	BB	SO	SB	CS	Avg	OBP	Slg
96 Lancaster	A	126	490	84	147	31	10	20	106	45	78	19	8	.300	.363	.527
97 Jacksnville	AA	114	465	56	124	24	4	12	74	22	77	9	5	.267	.301	.413
6 Minor League Yrs		524	1978	272	546	86	23	45	299	149	347	60	37	.276	.330	.411

Marquez, a product of the Mariners system signed out of Venezuela, came to the Tigers as a free agent last spring, and had an adequate season in Double-A. He has a nice line-drive swing and can be dangerous, but he is overaggressive at the plate, which keeps his on-base percentage down, and bridles his overall development as a hitter. He is a pretty good defensive player, but his glove won't earn him a job unless he hits. If he learns patience, he has a chance, but he isn't young. **Grade C**

Jason Marquis   *Atlanta Braves*

Pos: P   **Throws:** Right   **Ht:** 6'1"   **Wt:** 185   **Age:** 19

Yr Team	Lg	G	GS	IP	H	R	ER	HR	BB	SO	SV	W	L	Pct.	ERA
96 Danville	R	7	4	23.1	30	18	12	0	7	24	0	1	1	.500	4.63
97 Macon	A	28	28	141.2	156	78	69	10	55	121	0	14	10	.583	4.38
2 Minor League Yrs		35	32	165.0	186	96	81	10	62	145	0	15	11	.577	4.42

Although drafting high school pitchers is riskier than selling pictures of Saddam Hussein in a Kuwaiti bazaar, the Braves have been doing it a lot over the last six or seven years. Expensive signees like Jacob Shumate, Billy Blythe, Jamie Arnold and Jamie Howard have blown up in their face, but 1996 selection Jason Marquis looks like a keeper. Not tall or physically imposing by top-prospect standards, Marquis has an excellent arm and has been clocked as high as 95 MPH. His curve is a potential out pitch, but he doesn't have much of a changeup yet. Marquis got off to a hot start at Macon last year, at one point standing 10-2, 3.08. He slumped in the second half, and I'm a bit concerned that he may have been overworked. Assuming his arm doesn't wear out, he should develop into a fine pitcher. I think it is interesting that of the Atlanta highly-touted high school draftees I mentioned above, only Marquis was *not* drafted from a state south of the Mason-Dixon line. I believe that high school pitchers from the South are both overworked and overexposed. If I were forced by the threat of a tactical nuclear weapon to draft a high school pitcher, I would look first to one from a Northern state. **Grade B**

Eli Marrero   *St. Louis Cardinals*

Pos: C   **Bats:** Right   **Ht:** 6'1"   **Wt:** 180   **Age:** 24

Yr Team	Lg	G	AB	R	H	2B	3B	HR	RBI	BB	SO	SB	CS	Avg	OBP	Slg
96 Arkansas	AA	116	374	65	101	17	3	19	65	32	55	9	6	.270	.336	.484
97 Louisville	AAA	112	395	60	108	21	7	20	68	25	53	4	4	.273	.318	.514
St. Louis	NL	17	45	4	11	2	0	2	7	2	13	4	0	.244	.271	.422
5 Minor League Yrs		469	1634	249	422	78	14	72	281	131	264	28	20	.258	.316	.455

Marrero is getting major play as a prospect, and will probably start 1998 in the St. Louis lineup. I may be in the minority here, but I don't see him as an outstanding prospect or Rookie of the Year contender. Don't get me wrong, he's a good prospect, but there are better ones around, in my opinion. Marrero's offensive production was good at Louisville, +10 percent, although he hit much better in his friendly home park than on the road. Scouts say his swing is more consistent than it used to be, but it still looks awkward to me, and his strike-zone judgment needs work. Defensively, he has all the tools and skills. He can throw bullets down to second base, blocks the plate, moves around well, and has learned to call a good game. I think Marrero will be a good player, but I just can't bring myself to get as wild about him as some people are. **Grade B**

Damaso Marte
Seattle Mariners
Pos: P   Throws: Left   Ht: 6'2"   Wt: 194   Age: 24

Yr Team	Lg	G	GS	IP	H	R	ER	HR	BB	SO	SV	W	L	Pct.	ERA
96 Wisconsin	A	26	26	142.1	134	82	71	8	75	115	0	8	6	.571	4.49
97 Lancaster	A	25	25	139.1	144	75	64	15	62	127	0	8	8	.500	4.13
3 Minor League Yrs		62	56	318.1	303	168	144	25	147	281	0	18	16	.529	4.07

Marte is a hard-throwing lefthander signed out of the Dominican Republic in 1993. His stats at Lancaster in the California League are better than they look considering the context in which they were produced, and he should get a full shot in Double-A in 1998. Given the historic enthusiasm that the Mariners show for young pitchers, he could see action in the majors very quickly. Given the historic impatience that the Mariners show with young pitchers when they struggle, he could get demoted as quickly as he may be promoted. Marte certainly has the arm strength to succeed, but command has been a problem at times. Still, he's one of the better prospects in a weak system. **Grade C+**

Felix Martinez
Kansas City Royals
Pos: SS   Bats: Both   Ht: 6'0"   Wt: 168   Age: 23

Yr Team	Lg	G	AB	R	H	2B	3B	HR	RBI	BB	SO	SB	CS	Avg	OBP	Slg
96 Omaha	AAA	118	395	54	93	13	3	5	35	44	79	18	10	.235	.320	.322
97 Omaha	AAA	112	410	55	104	19	4	2	36	29	86	21	11	.254	.313	.334
Kansas City	AL	16	31	3	7	1	1	0	3	6	8	0	0	.226	.351	.323
5 Minor League Yrs		531	1796	250	458	68	15	12	156	151	353	124	54	.255	.321	.330

When I saw Felix Martinez play in 1996, his swing was long, he swung from the heels, and hit a lot of lazy fly balls. When I saw Felix Martinez play in 1997, he looked totally different. His swing was much shorter, more level, and produced line drives and grounders. The funny thing is, his numbers were almost identical both seasons. . . he is still a .250 hitter, without power. With the glove, he has the actions of an acrobat at shortstop, but he is still very error-prone on routine plays. He has made real progress controlling his temper, which was a serious problem in the past. Martinez is still young, but he needs to do more with the bat and settle down defensively to earn a job. **Grade C**

Willie Martinez
Cleveland Indians
Pos: P   Throws: Right   Ht: 6'2"   Wt: 165   Age: 20

Yr Team	Lg	G	GS	IP	H	R	ER	HR	BB	SO	SV	W	L	Pct.	ERA
96 Watertown	A	14	14	90.0	79	25	24	5	21	92	0	6	5	.545	2.40
97 Kinston	A	23	23	137.0	125	61	47	13	42	120	0	8	2	.800	3.09
3 Minor League Yrs		48	48	267.0	268	136	113	19	88	248	0	14	14	.500	3.81

The Indians have promoted or traded most all of their young pitching prospects over the last year, leaving youthful Venezuelan Willie Martinez as their top mound candidate for the future. His 1997 season got off to a scary start when he had elbow surgery in January, but the procedure wasn't major, and he showed no ill effects when he took to the box. Martinez has great stuff: 92-MPH fastball, sharp breaking stuff, developing a changeup. His control is very good, and he knows how to pitch. His ratios ranged from outstanding to OK last year: K/BB +49 percent, K/IP plus-seven, H/IP plus-three. The main thing Martinez needs is experience, to establish his reservoir of knowledge, and to build his arm strength. The fact that he has already had surgery, however minor, is worrisome. The Tribe needs to be careful with him. **Grade B+**

Onan Masaoka
Los Angeles Dodgers

Pos: P **Throws:** Left **Ht:** 6'0" **Wt:** 188 **Age:** 20

Yr Team	Lg	G	GS	IP	H	R	ER	HR	BB	SO	SV	W	L	Pct.	ERA
96 Savannah	A	13	13	65.0	55	35	31	7	35	80	0	2	5	.286	4.29
97 Vero Beach	A	28	24	148.2	113	72	64	16	55	132	1	6	8	.429	3.87
3 Minor League Yrs		56	44	263.0	196	132	115	25	137	287	4	10	17	.370	3.94

The Dodgers really like this guy, and it is not hard to understand why: 93-MPH lefthanded fastballs are rarer than Old Testament scholars who read minor league baseball books. Masaoka has had trouble developing his promising-but-erratic curveball, and his changeup is inconsistent, but so far the heater has been enough to get people out because he throws strikes with it. His ratios were quite nice across the board: K/BB +19 percent, K/IP +15 percent, H/IP +22 percent, all well above league norms. He holds runners well, but needs polish in other aspects of fielding around the mound. He is not physically impressive size-wise, giving rise to fears of injury, so the Dodgers need to handle him carefully, which they have so far. Masaoka should be very good if he stays healthy, improves the breaking stuff, and isn't abused. **Grade B**

Ruben Mateo
Texas Rangers

Pos: OF **Bats:** Right **Ht:** 6'0" **Wt:** 170 **Age:** 20

Yr Team	Lg	G	AB	R	H	2B	3B	HR	RBI	BB	SO	SB	CS	Avg	OBP	Slg
96 Chston-SC	A	134	496	65	129	30	8	8	58	26	78	30	9	.260	.309	.401
97 Charlotte	A	99	385	63	121	23	8	12	67	22	55	20	5	.314	.359	.509
2 Minor League Yrs		233	881	128	250	53	16	20	125	48	133	50	14	.284	.331	.448

Signed out of the Dominican in 1994, Ruben Mateo has been compared to Jose Guillen and Vladimir Guerrero, due to his multiple offensive skills and physical talent. He already hits for a high average, should develop more power, and while he is not exactly a disciplined hitter, he is not a wild swinger, either. His OPS was excellent by Florida State League standards at +23 percent. Mateo did miss the last portion of the season with a wrist injury, but should be healthy for spring. Defensively, he has the range and arm to shine in center or right. Basically, all Mateo needs is experience, although I would like to see his walk rate move up a bit. He should challenge for an outfield spot in 1999 or 2000, and could develop into a premier Seven Skill guy. **Grade B+**

Troy Mattes
Montreal Expos

Pos: P   **Throws:** Right   **Ht:** 6'7"   **Wt:** 185   **Age:** 22

Yr Team	Lg	G	GS	IP	H	R	ER	HR	BB	SO	SV	W	L	Pct.	ERA
96 Delmarva	A	27	27	173.1	142	77	55	14	50	151	0	10	9	.526	2.86
97 Wst Plm Bch	A	20	16	102.0	123	61	56	8	20	61	1	6	9	.400	4.94
4 Minor League Yrs		75	70	408.2	379	209	162	27	131	309	1	24	26	.480	3.57

Like most tall pitchers, Troy Mattes can scare the wax out of hitters when everything is right, in his case with a vicious slider. But things weren't right too often for Mattes at West Palm Beach. He continued to show good control and his K/BB mark was excellent at +51 percent, but his H/IP was unacceptable at -23 percent. He doesn't throw that hard for a pitcher his size, and while he throws strikes, they aren't always *quality* strikes. When he gets his stuff down the middle, he gets hit. Mattes is young and has plenty of time to rebound if he keeps his health. **Grade C**

Gary Matthews Jr.
San Diego Padres

Pos: OF   **Bats:** Both   **Ht:** 6'3"   **Wt:** 185   **Age:** 23

Yr Team	Lg	G	AB	R	H	2B	3B	HR	RBI	BB	SO	SB	CS	Avg	OBP	Slg
96 Rancho Cuca	A	123	435	65	118	21	11	7	54	60	102	7	8	.271	.366	.418
97 Rancho Cuca	A	69	268	66	81	15	4	8	40	49	57	10	4	.302	.416	.478
Mobile	AA	28	90	14	22	4	1	2	12	15	29	3	1	.244	.352	.378
4 Minor League Yrs		400	1405	225	361	64	21	19	164	211	355	51	26	.257	.359	.373

The Padres drafted Gary Matthews Jr. in the 13th round in 1993, from Mission Junior College in California. The son of the former major league outfielder with the same name, Matthews broke out last year, hitting very well at Rancho Cucamonga, although it was his second year in the league, and he will need to prove himself at a higher level. Matthews is patient at the plate, has gap power, and runs well. He has developed into a good defensive outfielder. I want to see Matthews hit in Double-A for a full season, but I like what he did last year, and I was impressed with him in the Arizona Fall League. **Grade C+**

Jason Maxwell
Chicago Cubs

Pos: SS   **Bats:** Right   **Ht:** 6'0"   **Wt:** 175   **Age:** 26

Yr Team	Lg	G	AB	R	H	2B	3B	HR	RBI	BB	SO	SB	CS	Avg	OBP	Slg
96 Orlando	AA	126	433	64	115	20	1	9	45	56	77	19	4	.266	.355	.379
97 Orlando	AA	122	409	87	114	22	6	14	58	82	72	12	9	.279	.397	.465
5 Minor League Yrs		542	1777	338	468	80	14	50	231	291	352	56	32	.263	.371	.409

Maxwell, a Double-A repeater at age 25, deserves a look by somebody. He has intriguing secondary offensive skills, especially for an infielder, with some power, a touch of speed, and a lot of patience at the plate. His SEC was very high at .411, +45 percent in the Southern League. It wouldn't be that high in the majors, but he's a better offensive player than many of the stiffs inhabiting major league benches. Maxwell is not outstanding with the glove, but he is not terrible, either, and can do a respectable job at second, third or short. He has a reputation as a hard worker, and I, for one, would like to see him get a clean shot at a utility job. **Grade C-**

Rod McCall

Chicago Cubs

Pos: 1B-DH Bats: Left Ht: 6'7" Wt: 235 Age: 26

Yr Team	Lg	G	AB	R	H	2B	3B	HR	RBI	BB	SO	SB	CS	Avg	OBP	Slg
96 Canton-Akrn	AA	120	440	80	132	29	2	27	85	52	118	2	0	.300	.382	.559
97 Buffalo	AAA	36	107	12	25	5	0	6	20	9	37	0	0	.234	.300	.449
Orlando	AA	19	70	11	21	2	0	6	20	10	24	0	0	.300	.398	.586
Iowa	AAA	49	148	26	42	5	0	14	35	22	53	0	0	.284	.382	.601
8 Minor League Yrs		803	2759	420	711	146	4	148	492	369	895	14	13	.258	.352	.474

Rod McCall was in the Indians system, but Cleveland needs another slugging first baseman like Bill Clinton needs another scandal, so they sent him to the Cubs in exchange for minor league infielder Bobby Morris last May. McCall has one skill and one skill only: the ability to hit home runs, but he is damn good at it. His swing is long, and he is vulnerable to breaking stuff, but he will crush anything mediocre. Defensively, he's best suited for DH, which means he isn't likely to get a chance in Chicago, or for any other NL team for that matter. McCall has genuine Show power, and I would like to see what he could do with 500 major league at-bats, but his chance of getting them anytime soon is pretty slim. **Grade C-**

Scott McClain

New York Mets

Pos: 3B Bats: Right Ht: 6'3" Wt: 209 Age: 25

Yr Team	Lg	G	AB	R	H	2B	3B	HR	RBI	BB	SO	SB	CS	Avg	OBP	Slg
96 Rochester	AAA	131	463	76	130	23	4	17	69	61	109	8	6	.281	.361	.458
97 Norfolk	AAA	127	429	71	120	29	2	21	64	64	93	1	3	.280	.370	.503
8 Minor League Yrs		857	2857	444	748	145	13	86	401	416	618	42	31	.262	.357	.412

If my team needed a third baseman, I would not hesitate to try Scott McClain. He played well in the Baltimore system in 1995 and 1996, but found himself blocked by Cal Ripken. The Mets traded for McClain, but with the emergence of Edgardo Alfonzo, there is no room for him at Shea either. McClain is a pretty good offensive player, with above-average power and a proper measure of patience. His OPS was nice at +15 percent, and his SEC was fine at +31 percent. He does not have tremendous pull power, but can hit the ball hard to all fields. McClain is the sort of hitter who would probably struggle in his first major league exposure, but given adjustment time he would hit .270-.280 with 15-20 homers in a full major league season. Those aren't exceptional numbers by today's standards, but they aren't terrible, and considering that his defense is solid, he is a player with value. McClain has excellent range, a strong and accurate arm, and has been voted Best Defensive Third Baseman in the International League for two years in a row. He deserves a job more than some guys who have them. **Grade C+**

Donzell McDonald   New York Yankees

Pos: OF   Bats: Both   Ht: 6'0"   Wt: 165   Age: 23

Yr Team	Lg	G	AB	R	H	2B	3B	HR	RBI	BB	SO	SB	CS	Avg	OBP	Slg
96 Oneonta	A	74	282	57	78	8	10	2	30	43	62	54	4	.277	.374	.397
97 Tampa	A	77	297	69	88	23	8	3	23	48	75	39	18	.296	.400	.458
3 Minor League Yrs		179	689	149	192	36	19	5	62	107	161	104	24	.279	.380	.408

Scouts will tell you that Donzell McDonald, whose brother Darnell was the Orioles' first-round pick in 1997, is a prospect because of his speed and athletic ability. I like his speed, but what attracts my attention is his walk rate. The great walk rate means his on-base percentage is high enough to make his undoubted swiftness very valuable. It also means he has enough command of the strike zone to develop as a hitter, prosper at higher levels, and perhaps develop some power, especially if he can cut the strikeouts a bit. McDonald was a 22nd-round pick in 1995 from Yavapai Junior College in Arizona. His season in the Florida State League was cut short by a broken finger, but he played extremely well when in the lineup. His SEC was particularly excellent at +82 percent, trailing only vet Greg Blosser and superstud Adrian Beltre in that category. McDonald has super range in center field, although his arm isn't strong and he may play left in the majors. He has a reputation as a bright guy and a willing learner. I want to see him in Double-A, but he looks great right now. **Grade B+**

John McDonald   Cleveland Indians

Pos: SS   Bats: Right   Ht: 5'11"   Wt: 175   Age: 23

Yr Team	Lg	G	AB	R	H	2B	3B	HR	RBI	BB	SO	SB	CS	Avg	OBP	Slg
96 Watertown	A	75	278	48	75	11	0	2	26	32	49	11	1	.270	.354	.331
97 Kinston	A	130	541	77	140	27	3	5	53	51	75	6	5	.259	.324	.348
2 Minor League Yrs		205	819	125	215	38	3	7	79	83	124	17	6	.263	.334	.342

Here is someone that I guarantee 99 percent of you have never heard of. McDonald was drafted in the 12th round in 1996, from Providence College. He is not a great hitter by any means, but he can control the strike zone, and with experience he might hold his own at the upper levels. What I noticed about him was his great defensive numbers: he led the Carolina League in both fielding percentage *and* range factor, which is pretty rare. At the lower levels, the guys with high range factors tend to be youngsters with a lot of ability but little polish, while the fellows with good fielding percentages tend to be more refined but have less basic talent. To have range and reliability combined, especially in a shortstop, is special. We need to see if he can hit at higher levels of course, but if his glove is really that good, he will get some major league time eventually. **Grade C-**

Kevin McGlinchy   *Atlanta Braves*

Pos: P   **Throws:** Right   **Ht:** 6'5"   **Wt:** 220   **Age:** 20

Yr Team	Lg	G	GS	IP	H	R	ER	HR	BB	SO	SV	W	L	Pct.	ERA
96 Danville	R	13	13	72.0	52	21	9	2	11	77	0	3	2	.600	1.13
Eugene	A	2	2	6.2	7	5	4	2	1	5	0	0	0	—	5.40
97 Durham	A	26	26	139.2	145	78	76	14	39	113	0	3	7	.300	4.90
2 Minor League Yrs		41	41	218.1	204	104	89	18	51	195	0	6	9	.400	3.67

Kevin McGlinchy was drafted in the fifth round in 1995, and signed after a year at Central Florida Community College. He was terrific in his pro debut in the Appalachian League, and was promoted all the way to Durham for 1997. By most statistical measures, his season was not a success. A 3-7 record with a high ERA was not what the Braves had in mind, and his K/IP and H/IP ratios were worse than league. On the other hand, his K/BB ratio was an outstanding +51 percent, so there is room for hope, especially since he is not a finesse guy. McGlinchy works with a 93-MPH fastball, a curveball, and a changeup. Scouts like his demeanor on the mound, and many of them think he could be an ace. He is very young, and anything can happen to a young pitcher. **Grade B-**

Tony McKnight   *Houston Astros*

Pos: P   **Throws:** Right   **Ht:** 6'5"   **Wt:** 205   **Age:** 20

Yr Team	Lg	G	GS	IP	H	R	ER	HR	BB	SO	SV	W	L	Pct.	ERA
96 Astros	R	8	5	21.2	28	21	15	1	7	15	0	2	1	.667	6.23
97 Quad City	A	20	20	115.1	116	71	60	7	55	92	0	4	9	.308	4.68
3 Minor League Yrs		31	28	148.2	158	97	80	8	64	115	0	7	11	.389	4.84

McKnight was Houston's first-round pick in 1995, from a high school in Arkansas. His arm was abused as an amateur; he once threw more than 200 pitches in a game, and he missed almost all of 1996 with shoulder trouble. He came back in 1997 and made 20 starts in the Midwest League. He wasn't terrible, but he has work to do. McKnight still has good stuff, but needs to improve his command. He might be able to do so, if the arm holds up, but that is an enormous "if." **Grade C**

Billy McMillon   *Philadelphia Phillies*

Pos: OF   **Bats:** Left   **Ht:** 5'11"   **Wt:** 172   **Age:** 26

Yr Team	Lg	G	AB	R	H	2B	3B	HR	RBI	BB	SO	SB	CS	Avg	OBP	Slg
96 Charlotte	AAA	97	347	72	122	32	2	17	70	36	76	5	3	.352	.418	.602
Florida	NL	28	51	4	11	0	0	0	4	5	14	0	0	.216	.286	.216
97 Charlotte	AAA	57	204	34	57	18	0	8	26	32	51	8	0	.279	.378	.485
Scranton-WB	AAA	26	92	18	27	8	1	4	21	12	24	2	0	.293	.375	.533
Philadelphia	NL	24	72	10	21	4	1	2	13	6	17	2	1	.292	.333	.458
Florida	NL	13	18	0	2	1	0	0	1	0	7	0	0	.111	.111	.167
5 Minor League Yrs		515	1884	342	562	126	11	66	346	290	384	42	19	.298	.396	.482

Technically, McMillon violates my 50-game rule, but the Phillies don't have many position-player prospects, so I will put him in the book. He should play every day in 1998, and I am certain he will be a good player. McMillon has been a major league hitter for at least two years. He has a picturesque swing that should produce high batting averages with

184

moderate power. Defensively, he lacks tremendous skills, but hustles and has worked hard to make himself adequate with the glove. McMillon is intelligent, personable, and has the "intangible" personality traits that scouts like. Although he is at his peak now, and won't be a Hall of Fame talent, McMillon will be a fine player. **Grade B**

Brian Meadows   *Florida Marlins*

Pos: P **Throws:** Right **Ht:** 6'4" **Wt:** 210 **Age:** 22

Yr Team	Lg	G	GS	IP	H	R	ER	HR	BB	SO	SV	W	L	Pct.	ERA
96 Brevard Cty	A	24	23	146.0	129	73	58	13	25	69	0	8	7	.533	3.58
Portland	AA	4	4	27.0	26	15	13	1	4	13	0	0	1	.000	4.33
97 Portland	AA	29	29	175.2	204	99	90	23	48	115	0	9	7	.563	4.61
4 Minor League Yrs		91	89	532.2	556	286	238	49	124	333	0	29	24	.547	4.02

Florida has quite a livery of good young position players, but there aren't very many pitching prospects in the system, or at least there weren't before the rash of November trades. Brian Meadows was a third-round pick in 1994, from an Alabama high school. He is a big guy, and while he has not developed excellent velocity yet, he has command of his breaking pitches and knows what he is doing on the mound. The velocity on his fastball has moved into the 90-MPH range, and he could get faster. His K/BB ratio was very good at +29 percent; his other ratios were not impressive. Meadows does two things very well: throw strikes and stay healthy. As long as he can do that, he has a chance. **Grade C+**

Gil Meche   *Seattle Mariners*

Pos: P **Throws:** Right **Ht:** 6'3" **Wt:** 190 **Age:** 19

Yr Team	Lg	G	GS	IP	H	R	ER	HR	BB	SO	SV	W	L	Pct.	ERA
96 Mariners	R	2	0	3.0	4	2	2	0	1	4	0	0	1	.000	6.00
97 Everett	A	12	12	74.2	75	40	33	7	24	62	0	3	4	.429	3.98
Wisconsin	A	2	2	12.0	12	5	4	1	4	14	0	0	2	.000	3.00
2 Minor League Yrs		16	14	89.2	91	47	39	8	29	80	0	3	7	.300	3.91

Meche was Seattle's first-round pick in 1996, from a Louisiana high school. He had injury problems in high school, including a mono-like virus and elbow soreness, but was fine in 1997. He has a 94-MPH fastball, a sharp curve, and a developing changeup. His control is good and getting better, and he has a reputation as a fervent adversary. The only real question about Meche is his health. Elbow problems are like athlete's foot: you think it's gone for good, but it can come back with a vengeance. Meche could be at the top of the prospect lists a year from now, but he might also be buried on the disabled list.

Rafael Medina

Florida Marlins

Pos: P **Throws:** Right **Ht:** 6'3" **Wt:** 194 **Age:** 23

Yr Team	Lg	G	GS	IP	H	R	ER	HR	BB	SO	SV	W	L	Pct.	ERA
96 Norwich	AA	19	19	103.0	78	48	35	7	55	112	0	5	8	.385	3.06
97 Rancho Cuca	A	3	3	18.0	13	4	4	1	5	14	0	2	0	1.000	2.00
Las Vegas	AAA	13	13	66.2	90	60	56	12	39	50	0	4	5	.444	7.56
5 Minor League Yrs		79	79	417.1	379	232	187	35	196	389	0	22	26	.458	4.03

Medina came to the Padres as part of the Hideki Irabu deal, along with top prospect Ruben Rivera. Irabu's struggles aside, this was a good trade for the Padres, receiving two top prospects for an out-of-shape pitcher who wouldn't work for them. It looks even better after San Diego used Medina to get Kevin Brown from the Marlins. Medina pitched very poorly at Las Vegas, but is still well-regarded due to his 95-MPH fastball and hard curve. His problems at Vegas were attributed to a series of severe blisters, as well as a weight problem. Arm troubles that dogged him in the past are supposedly no longer an issue. Medina also pitched very well in the Arizona Fall League. He is inherently unpredictable, but the upside is very high. **Grade B**

Tony Medrano

Kansas City Royals

Pos: 2B **Bats:** Right **Ht:** 5'11" **Wt:** 155 **Age:** 23

Yr Team	Lg	G	AB	R	H	2B	3B	HR	RBI	BB	SO	SB	CS	Avg	OBP	Slg
96 Wichita	AA	125	474	59	130	26	1	8	55	18	36	10	8	.274	.302	.384
97 Wichita	AA	108	349	45	86	9	1	4	42	26	32	8	2	.246	.297	.312
Omaha	AAA	17	59	10	12	0	0	4	9	4	5	0	1	.203	.242	.407
5 Minor League Yrs		479	1726	225	456	74	12	24	184	105	153	38	22	.264	.309	.363

Tony Medrano is very similar to fellow Royals prospect Mendy Lopez. Scouts say both of them will hit, but so far they're 0-for-2. Medrano is a contact hitter, but he doesn't drive the ball, and his production is below average. He used to play shortstop, but a lack of range has forced a shift to second, and and he's done very well there, although he needs to polish up his double-play pivot. Medrano's outlook is just like Lopez': he's young enough to improve, but there's little to get excited about just yet. **Grade C**

Dave Melendez

Detroit Tigers

Pos: P **Throws:** Right **Ht:** 6'0" **Wt:** 168 **Age:** 21

Yr Team	Lg	G	GS	IP	H	R	ER	HR	BB	SO	SV	W	L	Pct.	ERA
96 Fayettevlle	A	27	21	130.2	114	56	38	7	40	121	0	11	4	.733	2.62
97 Lakeland	A	15	15	102.1	70	28	20	5	32	79	0	8	4	.667	1.76
Jacksnville	AA	12	11	72.2	77	47	43	10	24	55	0	6	4	.600	5.33
2 Minor League Yrs		54	47	305.2	261	131	101	22	96	255	0	25	12	.676	2.97

The Tigers signed Dave Melendez as an undrafted free agent out of Puerto Rico in 1996. He has moved up the ladder quickly, pitching extremely well at Lakeland last year. He did tussle with the Southern League, and will probably return to Double-A in 1998. Melendez does not have a blistering fastball, but he throws strikes with his curve, slider, and change, and will use the fastball effectively on the corners. He is quite young, and may pick up some velocity as he matures. Despite his high ERA in Double-A, his K/BB mark was still very good at +27 percent. Melendez has a lot of potential, but he needs at least a year in the high minors before seeing major league action. **Grade C+**

Jackson Melian   *New York Yankees*

Pos: OF   **Bats:** Right   **Ht:** 6'2"   **Wt:** 185   **Age:** 18

Yr Team	Lg	G	AB	R	H	2B	3B	HR	RBI	BB	SO	SB	CS	Avg	OBP	Slg
97 Yankees	R	57	213	32	56	11	2	3	36	20	52	9	1	.263	.323	.376
1 Minor League Yr		57	213	32	56	11	2	3	36	20	52	9	1	.263	.323	.376

Melian was signed with great fanfare out of Venezuela; his $1.6 million bonus was a record for a product of that fine nation. His pro debut in the Gulf Coast League was only a moderate success from a statistical standpoint, but that means nothing, since stats at that level are notoriously unreliable predictors of future success. Scouts give Melian above-average to excellent marks in all the "tool" categories. They also say he is intelligent and works hard. Will he develop all Seven Skills that make the "tools" worthwhile? Probably, although I can't produce any numbers to prove it, and I can't give him a letter grade at this point.

Juan Melo   *San Diego Padres*

Pos: SS   **Bats:** Both   **Ht:** 6'3"   **Wt:** 185   **Age:** 21

Yr Team	Lg	G	AB	R	H	2B	3B	HR	RBI	BB	SO	SB	CS	Avg	OBP	Slg
96 Rancho Cuca	A	128	503	75	153	27	6	8	75	22	102	6	8	.304	.345	.429
97 Las Vegas	AAA	12	48	6	13	4	0	1	6	1	10	0	0	.271	.294	.417
Mobile	AA	113	456	52	131	22	2	7	67	29	90	7	9	.287	.329	.390
4 Minor League Yrs		428	1642	222	477	89	12	22	211	96	329	28	29	.290	.337	.400

Melo, a Dominican signed in 1993, is thought to be the Shortstop of the Future by the Padres, perhaps as soon as 1999. He has a great deal of natural ability, but his offensive production is repressed by that haunting demon of young hitters: command of the strike zone. Melo will swing at anything. He has wiry strength, pleasant bat speed, and can hit for average, but his power totals aren't as good as they could be, and his on-base percentage is low. Melo has shown some improvement as a defensive player, and should be a reliable major league shortstop given time. Whether he becomes a star or just an adequate regular depends on if he learns to take a pitch. Melo is young enough to evolve rapidly. **Grade B-**

Mitch Meluskey   *Houston Astros*

Pos: C   **Bats:** Both   **Ht:** 5'11"   **Wt:** 185   **Age:** 24

Yr Team	Lg	G	AB	R	H	2B	3B	HR	RBI	BB	SO	SB	CS	Avg	OBP	Slg
96 Kissimmee	A	74	231	29	77	19	0	1	31	29	26	1	1	.333	.402	.429
Jackson	AA	38	134	18	42	11	0	0	21	18	24	0	0	.313	.396	.396
97 Jackson	AA	73	241	49	82	18	0	14	46	31	39	1	3	.340	.417	.589
New Orleans	AAA	51	172	22	43	7	0	3	21	25	38	0	0	.250	.347	.343
6 Minor League Yrs		566	1855	241	497	119	5	30	256	245	336	12	9	.268	.353	.386

Meluskey became a prospect in 1996 when he suddenly started hitting for average. I was skeptical, since the season was out of his career context, and wanted to see some power. He provided that in large doses at Jackson last year, and although his production fell off when he moved up to a difficult hitting environment at New Orleans, I am now reasonably certain that he can hit. He has always had command of the strike zone. Meluskey has pretty good defensive tools, and while he won't threaten to win many Gold Gloves, baserunners cannot challenge him without taking a risk. He moves around well and is said to call a good game. If the Astros decide to punt on Brad Ausmus, at the least Meluskey could hold the job without hurting the team. If he keeps hitting .300, he could be quite valuable. **Grade B-**

Carlos Mendoza   *Tampa Bay Devil Rays*

Pos: OF   **Bats:** Left   **Ht:** 5'11"   **Wt:** 160   **Age:** 23

Yr Team	Lg	G	AB	R	H	2B	3B	HR	RBI	BB	SO	SB	CS	Avg	OBP	Slg
96 Capital City	A	85	300	61	101	10	2	0	37	57	46	31	13	.337	.452	.383
97 Binghamton	AA	59	228	36	87	12	2	1	13	14	25	14	12	.382	.427	.465
Devil Rays	R	9	0	0	0	0	0	0	0	0	0	0	0	—	—	—
Norfolk	AAA	10	35	3	5	0	1	0	0	3	4	1	0	.143	.231	.200
New York	NL	15	12	6	3	0	0	0	1	4	2	0	0	.250	.500	.250
3 Minor League Yrs		214	755	156	256	31	5	2	74	101	99	74	31	.339	.426	.401

Carlos Mendoza doesn't have much power and isn't a longball threat, but he is a solid line-drive hitter with good speed, and has hit for average at every level. He will take a walk, unlike most hitters in the Mets system, which makes his speed more valuable. Despite the wheels, he is not a great defensive player, being limited to left field due to a weak arm and average fielding range. If he could field better, Mendoza would be an excellent fourth outfielder. As it stands, he must keep hitting .330 to get a chance to play, but he could very well do so. One of the highlights of the expansion draft TV coverage was Mets manager Bobby Valentine saying that there were some "weird" things about Mendoza. Elaborate, Bobby, please! **Grade C**

Frankie Menechino   *Oakland Athletics*

Pos: 2B   **Bats:** Right   **Ht:** 5'9"   **Wt:** 175   **Age:** 27

Yr Team	Lg	G	AB	R	H	2B	3B	HR	RBI	BB	SO	SB	CS	Avg	OBP	Slg
96 Birmingham	AA	125	415	77	121	25	3	12	62	64	84	7	9	.292	.391	.453
97 Nashville	AAA	37	113	20	26	4	0	4	11	26	31	3	2	.230	.397	.372
Birmingham	AA	90	318	78	95	28	4	12	60	79	77	7	3	.299	.447	.525
5 Minor League Yrs		562	1924	362	540	119	19	44	267	388	369	52	27	.281	.411	.431

A poor man's Frank Catalanotto, which is really funny if you think about it. Menechino is a small guy who has fought his way to Triple-A by working hard, making adjustments, and refusing to give up when he struggled. He is very patient at the plate, and has more power than one expects from a guy his size, in part because he is so selective. His glove work is an asset: he has good range, can turn the double play, and doesn't muff the ball too often. Menechino won't get a chance until he plays well for a full season in Triple-A, and even then it will be a battle for him. He is no worse a player than Mark Lemke. Ironically, the Oakland A's selected Menechino in this year's Triple-A Rule 5 draft. Last year, they took Catalanotto in the major league phase but foolishly returned him to the Tigers. **Grade C**

Hector Mercado
New York Mets

Pos: P **Throws:** Left **Ht:** 6'3" **Wt:** 205 **Age:** 23

Yr Team	Lg	G	GS	IP	H	R	ER	HR	BB	SO	SV	W	L	Pct.	ERA
96 Kissimmee	A	56	0	80.0	78	43	37	4	48	68	3	3	5	.375	4.16
97 Charlotte	AAA	1	1	5.0	5	5	5	2	5	1	0	0	1	.000	9.00
Portland	AA	31	17	129.2	129	66	57	10	54	125	0	11	3	.786	3.96
6 Minor League Yrs		166	83	591.0	547	322	262	29	315	477	3	34	41	.453	3.99

Hector Mercado was picked by the Astros in the 13th round in 1992, out of Puerto Rico. He has a live arm, but never did much in five seasons for Houston and drew his release in 1996. The Marlins picked him up, taught him a splitter to go with his fastball and slider, and boom, had themselves a prospect. His strikeout ratios were fine last year: K/BB +15 percent, K/IP +19 percent. His H/IP mark was league average. This wouldn't be the first time a pitcher got a new life by switching organizations, but we need to see Mercado do it again before we get overly excited. The Phillies selected him in the major league Rule 5 draft, then traded him to the Mets. **Grade C+**

Mike Metcalfe
Los Angeles Dodgers

Pos: 2B **Bats:** Right **Ht:** 5'10" **Wt:** 175 **Age:** 25

Yr Team	Lg	G	AB	R	H	2B	3B	HR	RBI	BB	SO	SB	CS	Avg	OBP	Slg
96 Vero Beach	A	2	5	0	0	0	0	0	0	0	0	0	0	.000	.000	.000
97 San Berndno	A	132	519	83	147	28	7	3	47	55	79	67	32	.283	.356	.382
4 Minor League Yrs		333	1275	223	366	52	10	6	102	150	152	169	74	.287	.363	.358

If speed is what you want, Mike Metcalfe is your man. One of the most dangerous baserunners in the minor leagues, Metcalfe isn't just fast, but he is smart on the bases, too. At the plate, he has little power, but makes contact and doesn't try to do things he isn't capable of doing. He is steady in the field, leading the California League in fielding percentage at second base, but his defensive range isn't great, which just shows that foot speed and glove quickness aren't the same thing. We need to see him at higher levels, and his future is as a utility man. **Grade C-**

Chad Meyers
Chicago Cubs

Pos: 2B **Bats:** Right **Ht:** 6'0" **Wt:** 180 **Age:** 22

Yr Team	Lg	G	AB	R	H	2B	3B	HR	RBI	BB	SO	SB	CS	Avg	OBP	Slg
96 Williamsprt	A	67	230	46	56	9	2	2	26	33	39	27	6	.243	.349	.326
97 Rockford	A	125	439	89	132	28	4	4	58	74	72	54	16	.301	.408	.410
2 Minor League Yrs		192	669	135	188	37	6	6	84	107	111	81	22	.281	.388	.381

Meyers was selected in the fifth round in 1996, out of Creighton University. His full-season debut in 1997 was quite successful, as he showed very good strike-zone judgment, the ability to hit for average, great speed, and a bit of pop in a tough league. His SEC was his best offensive number, a terrific +53 percent. Meyers' defense at second wasn't hot in his first extended trial at the position, and given his lack of size it is unlikely he will develop enough power to return to the outfield, his college position. If he improves his fielding, he has a chance. **Grade C**

Jason Middlebrook
San Diego Padres

Pos: P **Throws**: Right **Ht**: 6'3" **Wt**: 200 **Age**: 22

Yr Team	Lg	G	GS	IP	H	R	ER	HR	BB	SO	SV	W	L	Pct.	ERA
97 Rancho Cuca	A	6	6	22.1	29	15	10	1	12	18	0	0	2	.000	4.03
Clinton	A	14	14	81.1	76	46	36	4	39	86	0	6	4	.600	3.98
1 Minor League Yr		20	20	103.2	105	61	46	5	51	104	0	6	6	.500	3.99

When Jason Middlebrook was a freshman at Stanford in 1994, he threw 96 MPH, with control, and looked to be a first-round pick in 1996, possibly the first player drafted. Instead, he went in the ninth round. His sophomore and junior years were ruined by elbow surgery, lacerating his draft status. The Padres took a flier on him, and it is safe to say they would like to take 10 more just like it, even though he cost them $750,000. Middlebrook's elbow seems fine now, and most of his velocity is back. He always did know how to pitch; he just needs innings to get back in the groove. If Middlebrook does stay healthy, he could develop into a commanding force on the mound. Personally, I need to see more to be sure his arm won't fall off. **Grade C+**

Doug Mientkiewicz
Minnesota Twins

Pos: 1B **Bats**: Left **Ht**: 6'2" **Wt**: 190 **Age**: 23

Yr Team	Lg	G	AB	R	H	2B	3B	HR	RBI	BB	SO	SB	CS	Avg	OBP	Slg
96 Ft. Myers	A	133	492	69	143	36	4	5	79	66	47	12	2	.291	.374	.411
97 New Britain	AA	132	467	87	119	28	2	15	61	98	67	21	8	.255	.390	.420
3 Minor League Yrs		303	1069	165	289	70	7	21	155	182	133	35	12	.270	.380	.408

Doug Mientkiewicz, a fifth-round pick from Florida State in 1995, is the kind of hitter the secondary average method loves. He didn't hit for a terrific average or for tons of power, but his SEC was a sparkling .420, +46 percent compared to league average. This was primarily due to his high walk rate and his good speed, especially for a first baseman. He is an extremely good defensive player, leading the Eastern League in fielding percentage, and impressing scouts with his mobility and alertness on the field. He can also play third base and the outfield reasonably well. The presence of David Ortiz in the Twins organization gives Mientkiewicz little hope of earning a starting job, but his combination of secondary offensive skills and superior defense should earn him a bench job somewhere. **Grade C+**

Kevin Millar
Florida Marlins

Pos: 1B **Bats**: Right **Ht**: 6'1" **Wt**: 195 **Age**: 26

Yr Team	Lg	G	AB	R	H	2B	3B	HR	RBI	BB	SO	SB	CS	Avg	OBP	Slg
96 Portland	AA	130	472	69	150	32	0	18	86	37	53	6	5	.318	.375	.500
97 Portland	AA	135	511	94	175	34	2	32	131	66	53	2	3	.342	.423	.605
4 Minor League Yrs		529	1919	291	601	133	6	82	378	247	260	15	15	.313	.399	.517

Poor Kevin Millar had a solid Double-A season in 1996, but found himself back in Portland for 1997 when the Marlins signed minor league vet Brian Daubach to play first in Triple-A. Millar didn't sulk, and instead had an even better year. People are finally starting to admit that this guy can hit. His OPS was the second-best in the Eastern League, behind Indians prospect Sean Casey. You might be thinking that Millar's defense must be terrible or something, but it isn't. He doesn't make truckloads of errors, and looks fairly mobile around the bag. If Millar were lefthanded, he would have a better chance at a major league job, but even as a righty he deserves an opportunity to show what he can do. **Grade C+**

David Miller   Cleveland Indians

Pos: OF   **Bats:** Left   Ht: 6'4"   **Wt:** 200   Age: 24

Yr Team	Lg	G	AB	R	H	2B	3B	HR	RBI	BB	SO	SB	CS	Avg	OBP	Slg
96 Kinston	A	129	488	71	124	23	1	7	54	38	94	14	7	.254	.305	.348
97 Akron	AA	134	509	84	153	27	9	4	61	48	77	22	11	.301	.361	.413
2 Minor League Yrs		263	997	155	277	50	10	11	115	86	171	36	18	.278	.334	.381

A first-round pick from Clemson in 1995, David Miller looked like a failure after his mediocre performance in 1996 and the first half of 1997. His stats through 250 at-bats at Akron: .256, no homers, 11 steals, 22 walks, 47 strikeouts. Blech. He raised his average nearly 50 points in the second half, however, and started to show a little pop in his bat. He finished with an OPS one percent below league, which isn't good, but is better than 10 percent below league, which is where he was in 1996. Miller, a first baseman in college, has moved to the outfield and spent time in left and center. He's improved substantially with the glove, but needs more experience. Overall, Miller salvaged his career with his blistering second half, but he needs to keep hitting to avoid the "draft bust" label. **Grade C**

Trever Miller   Houston Astros

Pos: P   **Throws:** Left   Ht: 6'3"   **Wt:** 175   Age: 24

Yr Team	Lg	G	GS	IP	H	R	ER	HR	BB	SO	SV	W	L	Pct.	ERA
96 Toledo	AAA	27	27	165.1	167	98	90	19	65	115	0	13	6	.684	4.90
Detroit	AL	5	4	16.2	28	17	17	3	9	8	0	0	4	.000	9.18
97 New Orleans	AAA	29	27	163.2	177	71	60	15	54	99	0	6	7	.462	3.30
7 Minor League Yrs		166	149	910.0	950	498	419	66	327	590	0	47	59	.443	4.14

Trever Miller was part of the big nine-player trade between the Tigers and Astros last winter. He is a soft-tossing lefthanded starter who relies on command and control to survive. Miller stayed in the rotation all season at New Orleans, but his ratios aren't that impressive. His basic problem is that he nibbles too much, which means that he tries to hit spots, but fails to do so. If he actually did hit his spots consistently, he wouldn't be called "a nibbler." Instead, he would be called "crafty." My point here is that the margin between success and failure in baseball is very narrow, especially for a finesse pitcher. You already knew that, of course, but it is interesting the way our expressions change, even if we are describing the same philosophy. **Grade C**

Wade Miller
Houston Astros

Pos: P **Throws:** Right **Ht:** 6'2" **Wt:** 185 **Age:** 21

Yr Team	Lg	G	GS	IP	H	R	ER	HR	BB	SO	SV	W	L	Pct.	ERA
96 Astros	R	11	10	57.0	49	26	24	1	12	53	0	3	4	.429	3.79
Auburn	A	2	2	9.0	8	9	5	0	4	11	0	1	1	.500	5.00
97 Quad City	A	10	8	59.0	45	27	22	7	10	50	0	5	3	.625	3.36
Kissimmee	A	14	14	100.0	79	28	20	3	14	76	0	10	2	.833	1.80
2 Minor League Yrs		37	34	225.0	181	90	71	11	40	190	0	19	10	.655	2.84

Here is an interesting story for you. Wade Miller was drafted in the 20th round out of Topton, Pennsylvania, in 1996. Now, this wasn't Topton High School, nor a college. . . he was just drafted from the town. The fact that he wasn't attending school may explain why no one but the Astros noticed him. Miller has a very strong arm. His sinking fastball is in the low 90s, and he also has a change and a slider. He can throw any of his pitches for strikes at will. Take a gander at his K/BB ratio at Kissemmee: +161 percent, the best mark in the Florida State League. Any pitcher with good stuff and this level of control is a fine prospect, no matter where he was drafted. **Grade B-**

Ralph Milliard
Florida Marlins

Pos: 2B **Bats:** Right **Ht:** 5'10" **Wt:** 160 **Age:** 24

Yr Team	Lg	G	AB	R	H	2B	3B	HR	RBI	BB	SO	SB	CS	Avg	OBP	Slg
96 Charlotte	AAA	69	250	47	69	15	2	6	26	38	43	8	4	.276	.381	.424
Portland	AA	6	20	2	4	0	1	0	2	1	5	1	0	.200	.238	.300
Florida	NL	24	62	7	10	2	0	0	1	14	16	2	0	.161	.312	.194
97 Charlotte	AAA	33	132	19	35	5	1	4	18	9	21	5	3	.265	.326	.409
Portland	AA	19	69	13	19	1	2	0	5	7	8	3	2	.275	.351	.348
Florida	NL	8	30	2	6	0	0	0	2	3	3	1	1	.200	.314	.200
5 Minor League Yrs		441	1642	317	449	92	11	29	183	238	240	60	34	.273	.375	.396

A couple of years ago, Ralph Milliard looked like an excellent prospect, but various injuries as well as alleged discipline problems have knocked him back. I say "alleged" because sometimes it is hard to tell fact from fiction with questions of attitude and personality. Milliard was vocal with his opinion that he wasn't given a fair shot at the second-base job handed to Luis Castillo, but when Castillo failed Milliard didn't play particularly well, got sent back to the minors, then spent much of the season on the disabled list. If healthy, Milliard has above-average pop in his bat for an infielder, as well as fine defensive skills. His chance won't come in Florida. **Grade C+**

Kevin Millwood
Atlanta Braves

Pos: P **Throws:** Right **Ht:** 6'4" **Wt:** 205 **Age:** 23

Yr Team	Lg	G	GS	IP	H	R	ER	HR	BB	SO	SV	W	L	Pct.	ERA
96 Durham	A	33	20	149.1	138	77	71	17	58	139	1	6	9	.400	4.28
97 Greenville	AA	11	11	61.1	59	37	28	8	24	61	0	3	5	.375	4.11
Richmond	AAA	9	9	60.2	38	13	13	2	16	46	0	7	0	1.000	1.93
Atlanta	NL	12	8	51.1	55	26	23	1	21	42	0	5	3	.625	4.03
5 Minor League Yrs		119	70	503.0	430	275	222	48	249	464	3	27	31	.466	3.97

An 11th-round pick in 1993, Kevin Millwood had an acceptable 1996 season at Durham, and opened 1997 in the Double-A Greenville rotation. He pitched satisfactorily through 11 starts, was promoted to Richmond, pitched brilliantly, and ended up seeing considerable time in Atlanta, primarily due to the injury to Terrell Wade. Big, strong, and durable, Millwood has a 92-MPH fastball that keeps gaining velocity. His second-best pitch is probably his slider, and he will also use a curve and a splitter as a change of pace. When he is aggressive and throws strikes, he is very impressive. At the least, Millwood projects as a solid starter, and considering the Mazzone factor, he may have ace potential. **Grade B**

Eric Milton
New York Yankees

Pos: P **Throws:** Left **Ht:** 6'3" **Wt:** 200 **Age:** 22

Yr Team	Lg	G	GS	IP	H	R	ER	HR	BB	SO	SV	W	L	Pct.	ERA
97 Tampa	A	14	14	93.1	78	35	32	8	14	95	0	8	3	.727	3.09
Norwich	AA	14	14	77.2	59	29	27	2	36	67	0	6	3	.667	3.13
1 Minor League Yr		28	28	171.0	137	64	59	10	50	162	0	14	6	.700	3.11

Milton was the Yankees' first-round pick in 1996, from the University of Maryland. He has distinguished arm strength for a lefty, with a fastball topping 90 MPH with movement. He throws strikes with the fastball, a curve, a slider and a changeup, and he knows how to pitch. His ratios in the Florida State League were great, and while there was some slippage in the Eastern League, he was still very impressive. He can field his position and pays attention to runners on base. Milton will pitch Triple-A in 1998, and could see some major league time if he does well and the Yankees need a starter. If Milton stays healthy, he could develop into Andy Pettitte. **Grade B+**

Damon Minor
San Francisco Giants

Pos: 1B **Bats:** Left **Ht:** 6'7" **Wt:** 230 **Age:** 24

Yr Team	Lg	G	AB	R	H	2B	3B	HR	RBI	BB	SO	SB	CS	Avg	OBP	Slg
96 Bellingham	A	75	269	44	65	11	1	12	55	47	86	0	2	.242	.363	.424
97 Bakersfield	A	140	532	98	154	34	1	31	99	87	143	2	1	.289	.391	.532
2 Minor League Yrs		215	801	142	219	45	2	43	154	134	229	2	3	.273	.382	.496

The Giants selected Damon Minor in the 12th round in 1996. He played at the University of Oklahoma, like his twin brother Ryan. Their scouting profiles are similar: huge sluggers with big swings but enormous power. For his part, Damon smashed the ball pretty good in the California League, although his home park in Bakersfield helped out a lot, and his strikeout rate was distressing. He does draw walks, which helped give him a very high

SEC of +42 percent. Minor is mobile for a big guy, but made 22 errors last year. He needs to polish the defense and prove that higher-level breaking stuff won't frustrate his swing. **Grade C+**

Ryan Minor

Baltimore Orioles

Pos: 3B   **Bats:** Right   **Ht:** 6'7"   **Wt:** 225   **Age:** 24

Yr Team	Lg	G	AB	R	H	2B	3B	HR	RBI	BB	SO	SB	CS	Avg	OBP	Slg
96 Bluefield	R	25	87	14	22	6	0	4	9	7	32	1	0	.253	.330	.460
97 Delmarva	A	134	488	83	150	42	1	24	97	51	102	7	3	.307	.387	.545
2 Minor League Yrs		159	575	97	172	48	1	28	106	58	134	8	3	.299	.379	.532

Ryan Minor was a second-round draft pick out of the University of Oklahoma in 1996. . . by the Philadelphia 76ers. In the baseball draft, he went in the 33rd round, not because scouts didn't like him, but because of his standing on the hardwood. He didn't make the 76ers, but may try for the NBA again after his baseball contract expires in 1998. That would be a shame. He has limited baseball experience, but played very well for Delmarva and was named the Top Prospect in the South Atlantic League by *Baseball America*. Minor has excellent power potential, and good command of the strike zone for a player of his height and inexperience. His swing is a bit too long, and that might hurt him at higher levels. Defensively, he shows off a terrific arm at third base and has good range, but he fielded .899. Minor is raw for a college product, and we need to see him at higher levels, but it was a promising debut. **Grade B**

Mike Mitchell

San Diego Padres

Pos: 1B   **Bats:** Left   **Ht:** 6'3"   **Wt:** 205   **Age:** 24

Yr Team	Lg	G	AB	R	H	2B	3B	HR	RBI	BB	SO	SB	CS	Avg	OBP	Slg
97 Rancho Cuca	A	109	440	78	154	36	1	17	106	35	83	2	0	.350	.401	.552
3 Minor League Yrs		286	1069	149	326	65	3	30	200	92	168	3	1	.305	.361	.456

Mitchell was drafted by the Yankees in the ninth round in 1994. He had had a good career at UCLA, but scouts were never wild about his tools, so when he suffered a severe shoulder injury in 1995, the Yankees released him. Hey, they had Don Mattingly; what did they need a first-base prospect for? Mitchell hooked up with the Padres, his shoulder is fine now, and he was awesome in the California League in 1997. Although he doesn't draw enough walks for my taste, he has a sharp swing, makes contact, and can drive fastballs or breaking pitches for power. He did struggle against lefties, so he may be better off as a platoon player. We need to see him in Double-A, but he didn't do anything wrong last year. Watch for him as a sleeper. **Grade C**

Chad Moeller
Minnesota Twins
Pos: C **Bats:** Right **Ht:** 6'3" **Wt:** 210 **Age:** 23

Yr Team	Lg	G	AB	R	H	2B	3B	HR	RBI	BB	SO	SB	CS	Avg	OBP	Slg
96 Elizabethtn	R	17	59	17	21	4	0	4	13	18	9	1	2	.356	.519	.627
97 Ft. Wayne	A	108	384	58	111	18	3	9	39	48	76	11	8	.289	.386	.422
2 Minor League Yrs		125	443	75	132	22	3	13	52	66	85	12	10	.298	.406	.449

Moeller came out of the University of Southern California in the seventh round of the 1996 draft. He is a perfect example of how different people watching the same player can see different things. I have a scouting report from a friend of mine who saw Moeller play a few times last year, and his commentary was that while Moeller could hit, he looked lousy on defense. On the other hand, Midwest League managers named him the Best Defensive Catcher in the league in the *Baseball America* poll. Moeller threw out 34 percent of runners. Guess what the league average was? 34 percent. He did lead the league in errors with 15. Usually, statistical and anecdotal evidence dovetail quite nicely, but they really don't in this case. The numbers and the anecdotes do agree that he can hit, though.
Grade C

Gabe Molina
Baltimore Orioles
Pos: P **Throws:** Right **Ht:** 5'11" **Wt:** 190 **Age:** 22

Yr Team	Lg	G	GS	IP	H	R	ER	HR	BB	SO	SV	W	L	Pct.	ERA
96 Bluefield	R	23	0	30.0	29	12	12	1	13	33	7	4	0	1.000	3.60
97 Delmarva	A	46	0	91.0	59	24	22	3	32	119	7	8	6	.571	2.18
2 Minor League Yrs		69	0	121.0	88	36	34	4	45	152	14	12	6	.667	2.53

Molina, an Arizona State product, was picked in the 21st round in 1996. He is short, doesn't throw hard, and isn't a hot prospect, but he was extremely effective as a swingman in the South Atlantic League. Of course, he was pitching against hitters with little pro experience, so as a college guy, he should have done well. He is just a name for now.
Grade C-

Shane Monahan
Seattle Mariners
Pos: OF **Bats:** Left **Ht:** 6'1" **Wt:** 200 **Age:** 23

Yr Team	Lg	G	AB	R	H	2B	3B	HR	RBI	BB	SO	SB	CS	Avg	OBP	Slg
96 Lancaster	A	132	585	107	164	31	12	14	97	30	124	19	5	.280	.316	.446
97 Memphis	AA	107	401	52	121	24	6	12	76	30	100	14	7	.302	.352	.481
Tacoma	AAA	21	85	15	25	4	0	2	12	5	21	5	1	.294	.341	.412
3 Minor League Yrs		319	1304	208	376	68	24	29	217	76	285	47	15	.288	.329	.444

Shane Monahan is a lot of fun to watch. A second-round pick out of Clemson in 1995, the son of former NHL player Hartland Monahan is a fine athlete who plays baseball with fiery intensity. At times he is too aggressive. . . he will run himself into outs, sacrifice his body to attempt an impossible defensive play, and strikes out too much for a player with mediocre power. He has excellent bat speed and projects as a .280-.300 hitter in the majors, but he is very impatient, which limits his on-base percentage and probably inhibits his power development. Monahan is being groomed to fill the left-field cavern in the

Kingdome, but he may need a year to master Triple-A breaking stuff before he is ready for the job. I like him more than I like most players with weak strike-zone judgment. **Grade B-**

Steve Montgomery — Baltimore Orioles

Pos: P **Throws:** Right **Ht:** 6'7" **Wt:** 230 **Age:** 24

Yr Team	Lg	G	GS	IP	H	R	ER	HR	BB	SO	SV	W	L	Pct.	ERA
96 High Desert	A	44	3	71.2	85	54	42	8	34	79	2	5	6	.455	5.27
97 Bowie	AA	24	23	136.1	116	56	47	15	52	127	0	10	5	.667	3.10
Rochester	AAA	2	1	6.2	15	12	9	1	3	2	0	0	2	.000	12.15
4 Minor League Yrs		115	27	270.2	246	129	101	24	110	272	14	18	14	.563	3.36

Montgomery was originally in the Royals system, signed as an undrafted free agent in 1994. He had a 1.56 ERA in Rookie ball, which wasn't enough to prevent his release, and he drifted to an independent league in 1995. The Orioles picked him up as a staff filler in 1996, but when he received an unexpected chance to start in Double-A in 1997, he took advantage of it and had a fine year. All of his ratios were good. Despite his size, Montgomery doesn't throw hard, which is why scouts don't like him much, and relies on a nasty slider to get people out. He did well last year and deserves a full shot in Triple-A. You never know with pitchers. **Grade C**

Eric Moody — Texas Rangers

Pos: P **Throws:** Right **Ht:** 6'6" **Wt:** 185 **Age:** 27

Yr Team	Lg	G	GS	IP	H	R	ER	HR	BB	SO	SV	W	L	Pct.	ERA
96 Tulsa	AA	44	5	95.2	92	40	38	4	23	80	16	8	4	.667	3.57
97 Okla City	AAA	35	10	112.0	114	49	43	13	21	72	1	5	6	.455	3.46
Texas	AL	10	1	19.0	26	10	9	4	2	12	0	0	1	.000	4.26
5 Minor League Yrs		124	47	439.0	426	181	159	24	88	310	17	28	21	.571	3.26

Eric Moody is a thin, wiry pitcher with surprisingly good velocity. His fastball runs 88-90 MPH, and he throws strikes with it, along with his nice slider. His K/BB ratios are always good, and were again last year at +74 percent. Moody's main problem throughout his career has been a tendency to get hurt, and it happened again late last year, when he came down with a sore shoulder. He will rest it over the winter, and if everything is okay, he could earn a job on somebody's staff in 1998. He isn't a terrific talent, but can contribute to a major league team under the right circumstances. **Grade C**

Trey Moore — Montreal Expos

Pos: P **Throws:** Left **Ht:** 6'1" **Wt:** 200 **Age:** 25

Yr Team	Lg	G	GS	IP	H	R	ER	HR	BB	SO	SV	W	L	Pct.	ERA
96 Port City	AA	11	11	53.2	73	54	46	6	33	42	0	1	6	.143	7.71
Lancaster	A	15	15	94.1	106	57	43	10	31	77	0	7	5	.583	4.10
97 Harrisburg	AA	27	27	162.2	152	91	75	15	66	137	0	11	6	.647	4.15
4 Minor League Yrs		88	87	520.2	501	285	233	41	212	463	0	38	25	.603	4.03

Trey Moore was a decent prospect in the Mariners system in 1995, but his 1996 season was a disaster, and he found himself traded to Montreal in the Jeff Fassero deal. He responded to the change of scenery and pitched decently for Harrisburg. His ratios were all slightly above average: K/BB +12 percent, K/IP plus-seven, H/IP plus-three. Moore works with an 88-MPH fastball, a sharp slider, and an adequate changeup. He can be very impressive at times, but also goes through periods where he loses the touch and can't get anybody out. While Moore isn't exactly a soft tosser, he doesn't overpower people and needs reliable command to succeed. **Grade C**

Julio Moreno   *Baltimore Orioles*

Pos: P   **Throws:** Right   **Ht:** 6'1"   **Wt:** 145   **Age:** 22

Yr Team	Lg	G	GS	IP	H	R	ER	HR	BB	SO	SV	W	L	Pct.	ERA
96 Frederick	A	28	26	162.0	167	80	63	14	38	147	0	9	10	.474	3.50
97 Bowie	AA	27	25	138.2	141	76	59	20	64	106	0	9	6	.600	3.83
4 Minor League Yrs		73	66	392.1	400	210	162	39	122	324	0	25	23	.521	3.72

A Dominican signed in 1993, Julio Moreno is a pretty good pitching prospect, although he isn't in the top echelon. His fastball is about average, 88-90 MPH, and his slider is cruel at times. His changeup isn't good yet, and while he throws strikes, his command within the strike zone is occasionally sloppy, and he gives up too many hits. His H/IP was six percent worse than the Eastern League average. Moreno is very projectable and could increase his velocity. He isn't ready for the majors until that happens, or until he improves his ability to hit spots. **Grade C+**

Orber Moreno   *Kansas City Royals*

Pos: P   **Throws:** Right   **Ht:** 6'1"   **Wt:** 140   **Age:** 20

Yr Team	Lg	G	GS	IP	H	R	ER	HR	BB	SO	SV	W	L	Pct.	ERA
96 Royals	R	12	7	46.1	37	15	7	2	10	50	1	5	1	.833	1.36
97 Lansing	A	27	25	138.1	150	83	74	15	45	128	0	4	8	.333	4.81
3 Minor League Yrs		47	35	206.2	202	107	87	17	62	199	1	10	10	.500	3.79

A Venezuelan signed in 1994, Moreno is a projectable young pitcher who wasn't outstanding, or even average, in the Midwest League last year, but who attracted some notice due to his arm strength. He has a low-90s fastball, the makings of a breaking pitch, and good control, but he needs to learn more about pitching. Like teammate Chad Durbin, Moreno could vault into prominence rather quickly if he figures something out, or he could continue moseying along in the low minors indefinitely. **Grade C**

Scott Morgan   *Cleveland Indians*

Pos: OF   **Bats:** Right   **Ht:** 6'7"   **Wt:** 230   **Age:** 24

Yr Team	Lg	G	AB	R	H	2B	3B	HR	RBI	BB	SO	SB	CS	Avg	OBP	Slg
96 Columbus	A	87	305	62	95	25	1	22	80	46	70	9	5	.311	.415	.616
97 Kinston	A	95	368	86	116	32	3	23	67	47	87	4	2	.315	.396	.606
Akron	AA	21	69	11	12	3	0	2	6	8	20	1	0	.174	.266	.304
3 Minor League Yrs		269	986	201	287	78	4	49	186	127	240	20	12	.291	.381	.527

Scott Morgan was terrific in the Sally League in 1996, but had his share of doubters due to the fact that he was older than most of the competition. He moved up a notch to the Carolina League in 1997, and continued to hit the dickens out of the ball. (Why doesn't anybody ever say, "hit the Shakespeare out of the ball?") His OPS was outstanding at +29 percent. Morgan struggled after being promoted to Double-A, however, so there is still doubt as to the true level of his ability. Defensively, he is nothing special, so he will have to make it on the strength of his offense. Will he make it? Personally, I don't put too much stock in a mere 69 at-bats in Double-A, and I think he will hit in the long run. Morgan has plenty of competition in the Indians system, so he will have to hit soon to avoid getting classified as a "minor league hitter" by the baseball ignorencia. **Grade C+**

Warren Morris   *Texas Rangers*

Pos: 2B   **Bats:** Left   **Ht:** 5'10"   **Wt:** 175   **Age:** 24

Yr Team	Lg	G	AB	R	H	2B	3B	HR	RBI	BB	SO	SB	CS	Avg	OBP	Slg
97 Charlotte	A	128	494	78	151	27	9	12	75	62	100	16	5	.306	.390	.470
Okla City	AAA	8	32	3	7	1	0	1	3	3	5	0	0	.219	.286	.344
1 Minor League Yr		136	526	81	158	28	9	13	78	65	105	16	5	.300	.384	.462

Morris was the big hero for LSU in the 1996 College World Series, winning the championship game with a home run in the bottom of the ninth. The Rangers picked him up in the fifth round, and he was sterling at Charlotte in the Florida State League. Morris is an outstanding hitter for an infielder, with a sharp swing that produces surprising power to all fields. He is reasonably patient, and should continue to hit at higher levels. Morris is just adequate defensively, although the Rangers will take adequate if he keeps hitting like this. He has a fine work ethic, and impresses observers with his intensity. With Edwin Diaz in Arizona, Morris should be the second baseman of the future in Arlington. **Grade B**

Julio Mosquera   *Toronto Blue Jays*

Pos: C   **Bats:** Right   **Ht:** 6'0"   **Wt:** 165   **Age:** 26

Yr Team	Lg	G	AB	R	H	2B	3B	HR	RBI	BB	SO	SB	CS	Avg	OBP	Slg
96 Knoxville	AA	92	318	36	73	17	0	2	31	29	55	6	5	.230	.301	.302
Syracuse	AAA	23	72	6	18	1	0	0	5	6	14	0	0	.250	.316	.264
Toronto	AL	8	22	2	5	2	0	0	2	0	3	0	1	.227	.261	.318
97 Syracuse	AAA	10	35	5	8	1	0	0	1	2	5	0	0	.229	.289	.257
Knoxville	AA	87	309	47	90	23	1	5	50	22	56	3	4	.291	.345	.421
Toronto	AL	3	8	0	2	1	0	0	0	0	2	0	0	.250	.250	.375
5 Minor League Yrs		414	1477	200	413	84	9	12	192	114	234	20	19	.280	.340	.373

Julio Mosquera is said to be the best defensive catcher in the Toronto system, but unless he improves his hitting, he is destined for a backup role. He occasionally hits for a good average, but his power production is restricted, his strike-zone judgment is limited, and, to me at least, he doesn't look like he knows what he is doing at the plate. Behind the plate is another matter. He has excellent defensive reactions, moves like a cat, and calls a good game. On the other hand, while his throwing arm looks strong, he nailed only 26 percent of runners. That number must improve, or else his chance at even a bench job will be slim. **Grade C-**

Damian Moss
Atlanta Braves

Pos: P **Throws:** Left **Ht:** 6'0" **Wt:** 187 **Age:** 21

Yr Team	Lg	G	GS	IP	H	R	ER	HR	BB	SO	SV	W	L	Pct.	ERA
96 Durham	A	14	14	84.0	52	25	21	9	40	89	0	9	1	.900	2.25
Greenville	AA	11	10	58.0	57	41	32	5	35	48	0	2	5	.286	4.97
97 Greenville	AA	21	19	112.2	111	73	67	13	58	116	0	6	8	.429	5.35
4 Minor League Yrs		85	82	464.1	384	240	203	41	258	507	0	28	29	.491	3.93

Australian southpaw Damian Moss has an average fastball, but his sharp curve and his changeup make his heat look quicker. He had a very fine strikeout rate in Double-A last year, but he walked a few too many people, didn't pitch well with runners on base, and ended the year with a sore elbow that eventually required surgery. Any grade we give him is just a guess; we need to see how he recovers from the injury.

Chad Mottola
Cincinnati Reds

Pos: OF **Bats:** Right **Ht:** 6'3" **Wt:** 215 **Age:** 26

Yr Team	Lg	G	AB	R	H	2B	3B	HR	RBI	BB	SO	SB	CS	Avg	OBP	Slg
96 Indianapols	AAA	103	362	45	95	24	3	9	47	21	93	9	6	.262	.307	.420
Cincinnati	NL	35	79	10	17	3	0	3	6	6	16	2	2	.215	.271	.367
97 Chattanooga	AA	46	174	35	63	9	3	5	32	16	23	7	1	.362	.408	.534
Indianapols	AAA	83	284	33	82	10	6	7	45	16	43	12	4	.289	.333	.440
6 Minor League Yrs		664	2348	358	651	119	21	79	369	203	461	71	36	.277	.336	.447

Chad Mottola was the fifth overall pick in the 1992 draft, from Central Florida University. The Reds thought he would have made some All-Star teams by now, but his progress has been sluggish, primarily because he has never learned the strike zone. He has power, but he is overaggressive, does poorly against breaking pitches of all kinds, and has a long swing. Mottola is a solid defensive outfielder and has good speed for a big guy, but time is running out on his bat. **Grade C**

Tony Mounce
Houston Astros

Pos: P **Throws:** Left **Ht:** 6'2" **Wt:** 185 **Age:** 23

Yr Team	Lg	G	GS	IP	H	R	ER	HR	BB	SO	SV	W	L	Pct.	ERA
96 Kissimmee	A	25	25	155.2	139	65	39	7	68	102	0	9	9	.500	2.25
97 New Orleans	AAA	1	1	4.2	2	1	1	1	6	6	0	0	0	—	1.93
Jackson	AA	25	25	145.0	165	91	81	18	66	116	0	8	9	.471	5.03
4 Minor League Yrs		87	87	524.0	480	236	182	33	215	439	0	37	28	.569	3.13

Tony Mounce's career ERA before 1997 was 2.40. As a finesse pitcher, the transition to Double-A was likely to be a difficult one for him, especially the tough Texas League, and it was. He didn't fail the test entirely, but he was hardly outstanding, and will need to make adjustments to thrive at higher levels. Mounce's fastball is average at best. He does have a sharp curve, and his changeup is good when thrown correctly. Because of his pedestrian fastball, his command must be razor-sharp for him to get hitters out. It wasn't last year, but it is too early to give up on him. **Grade C**

Blaine Mull
Florida Marlins

Pos: P   **Throws:** Right   **Ht:** 6'4"   **Wt:** 186   **Age:** 21

Yr Team	Lg	G	GS	IP	H	R	ER	HR	BB	SO	SV	W	L	Pct.	ERA
96 Lansing	A	28	28	174.2	186	91	63	9	40	114	0	15	8	.652	3.25
97 Wichita	AA	8	8	44.2	66	41	33	4	23	16	0	1	2	.333	6.65
Wilmington	A	19	19	111.1	126	55	44	6	33	64	0	8	6	.571	3.56
4 Minor League Yrs		83	83	471.0	528	267	208	31	148	274	0	30	26	.536	3.97

Blaine Mull started the season in Wichita, but was too tentative and got his head handed to him by Texas League hitters. He went back down to Wilmington and did adequately, but the season was an overall disappointment. Mull has a pretty good arm: 90-MPH fastball, good slider and change. His stuff is more than sufficient, but he gets in trouble by nibbling and by not throwing quality strikes. As a result, his strikeout rate is lower than expected from a pitcher with good stuff. He is tall and thin, and still has room to grow, so if his velocity increases, his margin for error may widen. He was traded to Florida for Jeff Conine. **Grade C**

Greg Mullins
Milwaukee Brewers

Pos: P   **Throws:** Left   **Ht:** 6'0"   **Wt:** 160   **Age:** 26

Yr Team	Lg	G	GS	IP	H	R	ER	HR	BB	SO	SV	W	L	Pct.	ERA
96 El Paso	AA	23	1	28.0	30	25	22	7	17	28	2	1	5	.167	7.07
Stockton	A	10	0	11.1	13	5	5	0	4	12	1	0	0	—	3.97
97 Stockton	A	30	0	33.0	22	9	8	2	12	52	19	0	2	.000	2.18
El Paso	AA	25	0	23.1	19	8	7	2	11	21	13	1	1	.500	2.70
3 Minor League Yrs		107	9	155.0	132	70	65	13	64	175	37	9	9	.500	3.77

Mullins was signed as an undrafted free agent in 1995, from the University of North Florida. He doesn't have much of a fastball, but his curveball is very good, and he throws strikes. He did well in both the California and Texas Leagues last year, and could see some bullpen time in 1998. Mullins will never be entrusted with the closer role, but his curve is tough on lefties, and he might have a future as a Tony Fossas-type. **Grade C-**

Peter Munro
Boston Red Sox

Pos: P   **Throws:** Right   **Ht:** 6'2"   **Wt:** 185   **Age:** 22

Yr Team	Lg	G	GS	IP	H	R	ER	HR	BB	SO	SV	W	L	Pct.	ERA
96 Sarasota	A	27	25	155.0	153	76	62	4	62	115	1	11	6	.647	3.60
97 Trenton	AA	22	22	116.1	113	76	64	12	47	109	0	7	10	.412	4.95
3 Minor League Yrs		63	61	361.1	345	190	152	19	142	298	1	23	20	.535	3.79

Peter Munro is a favorite of scouts, and it is easy to discern why. He throws 93 MPH, his pitches have terrific movement, and he is a rugged competitor on the mound. From a numbers standpoint, he is very promising, but still coarse. His strikeout rate in Double-A was high at +19 percent, his K/BB surprisingly good at +25 percent. On the other hand, his ERA was quite elevated considering league and park context. Scouts say Munro needs to change speeds better to get the most out of his considerable ability, and there has been talk of making him a closer if his offspeed stuff doesn't improve. That might be a good idea, especially since Munro has had bouts of shoulder trouble. **Grade B**

Heath Murray

San Diego Padres

Pos: P **Throws:** Left **Ht:** 6'4" **Wt:** 205 **Age:** 24

Yr Team	Lg	G	GS	IP	H	R	ER	HR	BB	SO	SV	W	L	Pct.	ERA
96 Memphis	AA	27	27	174.0	154	83	62	13	60	156	0	13	9	.591	3.21
97 Las Vegas	AAA	19	19	109.0	142	72	66	10	41	99	0	6	8	.429	5.45
San Diego	NL	17	3	33.1	50	25	25	3	21	16	0	1	2	.333	6.75
4 Minor League Yrs		89	89	552.0	560	274	221	35	199	485	0	38	31	.551	3.60

Heath Murray's surface stats at Las Vegas aren't appealing, but considering league and park context, they really aren't that bad. His K/BB and K/IP ratios were still well above league norms. He did give up too many hits, but that is no sin at Vegas; Sandy Koufax would give up a lot of hits in that park. Murray's fastball is average, sometimes slightly above, but his breaking pitches and changeup are good, and when he throws strikes and has a good defense behind him, he can win. Murray is the kind of pitcher who may need time to adjust to major league conditions, but he is smart enough to do so. The question is, will a major league team be patient enough to let him make the transition? **Grade C+**

Bryant Nelson

Chicago Cubs

Pos: 3B **Bats:** Both **Ht:** 5'10" **Wt:** 170 **Age:** 24

Yr Team	Lg	G	AB	R	H	2B	3B	HR	RBI	BB	SO	SB	CS	Avg	OBP	Slg
96 Kissimmee	A	89	345	38	87	21	6	3	52	19	27	8	2	.252	.290	.374
97 Orlando	AA	110	382	51	110	33	2	8	58	45	43	5	7	.288	.359	.448
4 Minor League Yrs		420	1565	210	449	111	20	21	205	106	138	32	25	.287	.330	.424

A couple of years ago, this guy was all the rage as a prospect in the Astros system. A wrist injury crippled him in 1996, and he was traded to the Cubs system last year, where he actually had a pretty decent season with the bat in Double-A. When healthy, he'll hit for a good average with some doubles, and his command of the strike zone has improved to the point where his on-base percentage could become an asset. His defense, on the other hand, is still terrible. He is athletic enough to be a good defensive player, but he makes way too many errors. . . a fielding percentage below .900 is worse than terrible, to be honest. Nelson could see some major league time if he gets hot or develops more power, but he has got to improve the glove work. **Grade C**

David Newhan

San Diego Padres

Pos: 2B **Bats:** Left **Ht:** 5'11" **Wt:** 180 **Age:** 24

Yr Team	Lg	G	AB	R	H	2B	3B	HR	RBI	BB	SO	SB	CS	Avg	OBP	Slg
96 Modesto	A	117	455	96	137	27	3	25	75	62	106	17	8	.301	.386	.538
97 Visalia	A	67	241	52	67	15	2	7	48	44	58	9	3	.278	.389	.444
Huntsville	AA	57	212	40	67	13	2	5	35	28	59	5	5	.316	.398	.467
3 Minor League Yrs		308	1149	222	331	68	8	46	187	176	279	44	23	.288	.383	.481

Newhan opened eyes with his fine offensive season in 1996, but the A's kept him in the California League in 1997 so he could learn to play second base, moving in from the out-field, without having to move up to Double-A. The transition went pretty well, and when he did move up to Huntsville at the halfway mark he played even better. Newhan is a contact hitter with some pop; he works the count and doesn't try to do more than he is capable of. Glove-wise, he looks okay at second base but needs experience and polish. No one sees him as a potential regular, but if he can hack it in the infield, he would be a fine utility guy. He was traded to San Diego in the offseason. **Grade C+**

Eric Newman

San Diego Padres

Pos: P **Throws:** Right Ht: 6'4" **Wt:** 220 Age: 25

Yr Team	Lg	G	GS	IP	H	R	ER	HR	BB	SO	SV	W	L	Pct.	ERA
96 Clinton	A	34	14	113.1	101	71	54	9	67	108	1	5	7	.417	4.29
97 Rancho Cuca	A	35	15	123.2	104	64	57	12	73	141	0	13	6	.684	4.15
3 Minor League Yrs		95	53	361.0	348	225	187	29	213	345	1	27	24	.529	4.66

A fifth-round pick in 1994 out of Texas Tech, Eric Newman has done fairly well as a swingman for two years now, and should see some Double-A action in 1998. His fastball runs 90-92 MPH, and his curveball and changeup have improved. His control still needs work, but he strikes people out at a good rate, and usually does well in pressure situations. We need to see how he does in Double-A; I'd like to see him enhance his control. **Grade C**

John Nicholson

Montreal Expos

Pos: P **Throws:** Right Ht: 6'4" **Wt:** 205 Age: 20

Yr Team	Lg	G	GS	IP	H	R	ER	HR	BB	SO	SV	W	L	Pct.	ERA
96 Rockies	R	11	11	65.2	42	16	12	1	14	65	0	3	5	.375	1.64
Portland	A	3	3	15.0	12	8	7	0	10	11	0	0	1	.000	4.20
97 Asheville	A	25	25	135.2	128	70	57	13	36	115	0	8	9	.471	3.78
2 Minor League Yrs		39	39	216.1	182	94	76	14	60	191	0	11	15	.423	3.16

Nicholson was the Rockies' second-round pick in 1996, from a Houston high school. He could have been a first-round pick, but a severe knee injury suffered while quarterbacking his high school football team scared off most teams. The knee is fine now. He has a 90-MPH fastball, a hammer curve, and good control for a young power pitcher. Nicholson was effective at Asheville in 1997, and teamed with Shawn Chacon and Jake Westbrook to form a promising starting staff. He lost time early in the season to an inflamed rotator cuff, but the Rockies handled him carefully and he seems OK now. He has the physical and mental stuff to be a solid major league pitcher, and while scouts say he has a build that promises durability, I worry about any kid pitcher with any hint of rotator-cuff trouble. Nicholson and Westbrook were traded to Montreal for Mike Lansing. I just don't get it. It was possible for the Rockies to get a good second baseman without giving up their future. . . imagine what Frank Catalanotto could do in Coors Field. Nicholson could be the ace of the Montreal staff in 2001, or just another young pitcher injury casualty. **Grade B-**

Trot Nixon
Boston Red Sox

Pos: OF Bats: Left Ht: 6'1" Wt: 195 Age: 23

Yr Team	Lg	G	AB	R	H	2B	3B	HR	RBI	BB	SO	SB	CS	Avg	OBP	Slg
96 Trenton	AA	123	438	55	110	11	4	11	63	50	65	7	9	.251	.329	.370
Boston	AL	2	4	2	2	1	0	0	0	0	1	1	0	.500	.500	.750
97 Pawtucket	AAA	130	475	80	116	18	3	20	61	63	86	11	4	.244	.331	.421
4 Minor League Yrs		422	1535	220	386	55	12	50	214	209	270	37	22	.251	.341	.401

It has been quite a struggle for Trot Nixon, but he hit well after getting off to a very slow start in Triple-A. Nixon was mired below .200 through late June, but got hot in July and raised his batting average to tolerable levels. I like his patience at the plate, and his SEC of +16 percent shows that he contributed to the offense despite the low average. His OPS was right at league average. Nixon is a great defensive outfielder, with above-average range, a very strong arm, and a "through-the-fences" attitude. Why has his career been a trial to this point? Part of the problem was a bad back injury, which seems to have healed finally, but another aspect is that Nixon may be too intense emotionally. You want guys to hustle, but Nixon tends to get down on himself and press when things don't go well right away. That sort of problem can be overcome with experience and maturity, if the organization and the player approaches it correctly. Still, a guy who tries too hard is much better than a guy who doesn't try hard enough. **Grade C+**

Todd Noel
Chicago Cubs

Pos: P Throws: Right Ht: 6'4" Wt: 185 Age: 19

Yr Team	Lg	G	GS	IP	H	R	ER	HR	BB	SO	SV	W	L	Pct.	ERA
96 Cubs	R	3	0	4.0	4	4	3	0	2	4	0	0	0	—	6.75
97 Cubs	R	12	11	59.0	39	27	13	1	30	63	1	5	1	.833	1.98
2 Minor League Yrs		15	11	63.0	43	31	16	1	32	67	1	5	1	.833	2.29

Noel was the Cubs' first-round pick in 1996, out of high school in Louisiana. He has pitched well in limited action, but was bothered by shoulder and elbow tenderness in 1996. To their credit, the Cubs have been patient and haven't pushed him. Noel should pitch in a full-season league in 1998, and could do very well, but his health is an ardent question.

Greg Norton
Chicago White Sox

Pos: 3B Bats: Both Ht: 6'1" Wt: 182 Age: 25

Yr Team	Lg	G	AB	R	H	2B	3B	HR	RBI	BB	SO	SB	CS	Avg	OBP	Slg
96 Birmingham	AA	76	287	40	81	14	3	8	44	33	55	5	5	.282	.357	.436
Nashville	AAA	43	164	28	47	14	2	7	26	17	42	2	3	.287	.350	.524
Chicago	AL	11	23	4	5	0	0	2	3	4	6	0	1	.217	.333	.478
97 Nashville	AAA	114	414	82	114	27	1	26	76	57	101	3	5	.275	.366	.534
Chicago	AL	18	34	5	9	2	2	0	1	2	8	0	0	.265	.306	.441
5 Minor League Yrs		567	2074	325	560	112	12	57	308	275	404	34	30	.270	.356	.418

Greg Norton finally showed the power scouts expected since his days at the University of Oklahoma. Maturity, a physical strengthening program, and adjustments to his swing are the reasons given for the big homer increase. He was repeating the league, too, which always helps. Norton's OPS was quite nice at +19 percent, and his SEC was near the top of the league at +44 percent, a reflection of his power and good walk rate. He will nail a fastball, but looks vulnerable to changeups, especially when he bats from the left side. Norton played mostly shortstop in 1996, but moved to third in 1997. He was a bad defensive shortstop, so the move made sense, but he is pretty awful at third, too; his .896 fielding percentage was downright horrendous. He does have good range, for what that is worth. Norton could probably hit 20 home runs at the major league level, but at this point he doesn't have a position. **Grade C**

Phillip Norton   *Chicago Cubs*

Pos: P **Throws:** Left **Ht:** 6'1" **Wt:** 180 **Age:** 22

Yr Team	Lg	G	GS	IP	H	R	ER	HR	BB	SO	SV	W	L	Pct.	ERA
96 Cubs	R	1	0	3.0	1	0	0	0	0	6	0	0	0	—	0.00
Williamsprt	A	15	13	85.0	68	33	24	1	33	77	0	7	4	.636	2.54
97 Rockford	A	18	18	109.0	92	51	39	4	44	114	0	9	3	.750	3.22
Daytona	A	7	6	42.1	40	11	11	5	12	44	0	3	2	.600	2.34
Orlando	AA	2	1	7.0	8	2	2	0	2	7	0	1	0	1.000	2.57
2 Minor League Yrs		43	38	246.1	209	97	76	10	91	248	0	20	9	.690	2.78

Norton shot up the ladder in 1997, a year after signing as a 10th-round pick out of Texarkana Junior College in Texas. He was great in 109 innings at Rockford, great in 42 innings at Daytona, and, you guessed it, great in seven innings at Orlando. Although he is not an imposing presence on the field, he has zip in his fastball and isn't afraid to throw strikes. His K/BB at Rockford was impressive at +42 percent, and his ratios did not deteriorate as he moved up, which is a very good sign. It is unusual for a junior college pitcher who was not a high-round draft to end up in Double-A within a year of signing. Watch for him, he could sneak up on us soon. **Grade B-**

Abraham Nunez   *Pittsburgh Pirates*

Pos: SS **Bats:** Both **Ht:** 5'11" **Wt:** 160 **Age:** 22

Yr Team	Lg	G	AB	R	H	2B	3B	HR	RBI	BB	SO	SB	CS	Avg	OBP	Slg
96 St. Cathrns	A	75	297	43	83	6	4	3	26	31	43	37	14	.279	.353	.357
97 Lynchburg	A	78	304	45	79	9	4	3	32	23	47	29	14	.260	.313	.345
Carolina	AA	47	198	31	65	6	1	1	14	20	28	10	5	.328	.385	.384
Pittsburgh	NL	19	40	3	9	2	2	0	6	3	10	1	0	.225	.289	.375
2 Minor League Yrs		200	799	119	227	21	9	7	72	74	118	76	33	.284	.346	.359

Nunez came to Pittsburgh as part of the Carlos Garcia/Orlando Merced trade; the Pirates got a lot of players in that deal, for very little. Nunez is a small guy and will never be a huge offensive threat, but he makes contact, is relatively patient for a young Latin infielder, and has good speed on the bases. He hit surprisingly well at Double-A, granted it was just half a season. Some people think he could be a .300 hitter in the majors, although I doubt it. Nunez is a flashy, talented infielder, with good range, nice hands, and an impressive arm for a small guy. He needs polish, but most infielders his age do. I don't think Nunez is ready to succeed in the majors, at least not with the bat, but given his age and renowned work ethic, he could develop into quite a player. **Grade B**

Sergio Nunez
Chicago White Sox

Pos: 2B **Bats:** Right **Ht:** 5'11" **Wt:** 155 **Age:** 23

Yr Team	Lg	G	AB	R	H	2B	3B	HR	RBI	BB	SO	SB	CS	Avg	OBP	Slg
96 Wilmington	A	105	402	60	109	23	6	3	40	38	54	44	11	.271	.339	.381
97 Royals	R	5	14	3	4	1	1	0	0	0	4	2	0	.286	.333	.500
Wichita	AA	34	137	18	38	1	1	1	11	6	17	12	3	.277	.308	.321
4 Minor League Yrs		327	1245	208	352	44	17	13	100	127	158	128	45	.283	.354	.377

Sergio Nunez has major league ability, but he has been blasted with injuries throughout his career; in 1997 it was an injured thumb ligament. He makes contact and has bat speed, but lacks power. He does run very well, combining speed with aggressiveness on the bases. With the glove, Nunez is smooth but sloppy, if that makes any sense. He has fine range, a strong arm, and quick hands, but he makes silly mistakes. Some people have concerns about his personality, but I spoke with him briefly last year, and he seemed like a bright, personable young man. I have a hard time getting excited about anybody who has just three extra base hits in over 100 at-bats, but I think Nunez has a good chance to be a decent player eventually, despite his mediocre grade. So do the White Sox, who picked him up in an offseason trade. **Grade C**

Vladimir Nunez
Arizona Diamondbacks

Pos: P **Throws:** Right **Ht:** 6'5" **Wt:** 240 **Age:** 23

Yr Team	Lg	G	GS	IP	H	R	ER	HR	BB	SO	SV	W	L	Pct.	ERA
96 Visalia	A	12	10	53.0	64	45	32	10	17	37	0	1	6	.143	5.43
Lethbridge	R	14	13	85.0	78	25	21	4	10	93	0	10	0	1.000	2.22
97 High Desert	A	28	28	158.1	169	102	91	36	40	142	0	8	5	.615	5.17
2 Minor League Yrs		54	51	296.1	311	172	144	50	67	272	0	19	11	.633	4.37

The Diamondbacks signed Cuban defector Vladimir Nunez to a $1.75 million bonus in 1996. His fastball ranges from 92-97 MPH, depending on the state of his mechanics, and he has a powerhouse curveball. He doesn't have much of a changeup, but his control is very good, and his stats last year at High Desert are better than they look on the surface. That stadium is death for pitchers; a 5.17 ERA there isn't bad at all, and his fine K/BB ratio of +74 percent is a strong indicator of future success. Nunez needs polish. He is adjusting to the culture shock of moving to the United States, and while it would be a stretch to project him winning big in the majors in 1998, it isn't impossible that he could repeat what Livan Hernandez did last year. It is also possible he could struggle like Ariel Prieto. **Grade B**

Ryan Nye

Philadelphia Phillies

Pos: P   Throws: Right   Ht: 6'2"   Wt: 195   Age: 24

Yr Team	Lg	G	GS	IP	H	R	ER	HR	BB	SO	SV	W	L	Pct.	ERA
96 Reading	AA	14	14	86.2	76	41	37	9	30	90	0	8	2	.800	3.84
Scranton-WB	AAA	14	14	80.2	97	52	45	10	30	51	0	5	2	.714	5.02
97 Scranton-WB	AAA	17	17	109.1	117	70	67	20	32	85	0	4	10	.286	5.52
Philadelphia	NL	4	2	12.0	20	11	11	2	9	7	0	0	2	.000	8.25
4 Minor League Yrs		85	84	515.1	518	261	233	50	140	413	0	36	23	.610	4.07

Nye was a second-round pick in 1994, out of Texas Tech. He has an adequate fastball, but a nasty slider, and when his command is on, he can be difficult to hit. His control is good, but he gives up a lot of hits, and probably needs another effective pitch to complement the slider. Nye's season at Scranton was ruined by a torn ribcage muscle. He should be healthy in 1998, but it would be a stretch to predict great success. **Grade C-**

Kirt Ojala

Arizona Diamondbacks

Pos: P   Throws: Left   Ht: 6'2"   Wt: 200   Age: 29

Yr Team	Lg	G	GS	IP	H	R	ER	HR	BB	SO	SV	W	L	Pct.	ERA
96 Indianapolis	AAA	22	21	133.2	143	67	56	15	31	92	0	7	7	.500	3.77
97 Charlotte	AAA	25	24	149.0	148	74	58	13	55	119	0	8	7	.533	3.50
Florida	NL	7	5	28.2	28	10	10	4	18	19	0	1	2	.333	3.14
8 Minor League Yrs		199	169	1096.0	1061	529	442	85	443	803	1	70	54	.565	3.63

Ojala had several good seasons for Columbus in the Yankees system, but his salary was too low for owner George Steinbrenner, so he never got a chance in New York. The Reds had him in 1996 and he pitched well for Indianapolis, but he is allergic to dog hair, so he drifted to the Marlins in 1997. Once again, he had a good Triple-A season, but this time the call finally came and he was decent in limited major league action. Ojala has an okay fastball, but his slider is very good and he knows how to pitch. I commend the Marlins for giving him a chance, though they lost him to the Diamondbacks as a free agent. Ojala could easily sink back to Triple-A and never be seen again, or he could end up with 700 major league innings and a pension. It all depends on timing and luck. **Grade C-**

Augie Ojeda

Baltimore Orioles

Pos: SS   Bats: Both   Ht: 5'9"   Wt: 171   Age: 23

Yr Team	Lg	G	AB	R	H	2B	3B	HR	RBI	BB	SO	SB	CS	Avg	OBP	Slg
97 Frederick	A	34	128	25	44	11	1	1	20	18	18	2	5	.344	.429	.469
Bowie	AA	58	204	33	60	9	1	2	23	31	17	7	0	.294	.390	.377
Rochester	AAA	15	47	5	11	3	1	0	6	8	4	1	2	.234	.345	.340
1 Minor League Yr		107	379	63	115	23	3	3	49	57	39	10	7	.303	.397	.404

Augie Ojeda was a defensive star at the University of Tennessee, and a member of the 1996 U.S. Olympic Team as a glove sub. He went in the 13th round because nobody thought he would hit, so his 1997 pro debut is even more amazing than it looks on the surface. He got off to a hot start in the Carolina League, was promoted to Double-A, continued to hit well, then finished the season in Rochester. Although he doesn't have much power, he makes excellent contact and controls the strike zone. Ojeda is a fine defensive shortstop, and is a very heady player. If he continues to hit like this, he could be tremendous. I want to see more, but am cautiously opimistic, especially given his nice walk rate. **Grade B-**

Jason Olsen

Chicago White Sox

Pos: P   Throws: Right   Ht: 6'4"   Wt: 210   Age: 23

Yr Team	Lg	G	GS	IP	H	R	ER	HR	BB	SO	SV	W	L	Pct.	ERA
96 South Bend	A	9	9	56.2	39	16	11	3	13	55	0	4	1	.800	1.75
Hickory	A	4	4	26.1	19	5	4	1	6	32	0	2	1	.667	1.37
Pr William	A	12	12	79.0	74	39	34	5	31	55	0	6	4	.600	3.87
97 Birmingham	AA	28	27	160.1	183	101	87	14	58	121	0	9	14	.391	4.88
2 Minor League Yrs		53	52	322.1	315	161	136	23	108	263	0	21	20	.512	3.80

For a converted third baseman drafted in 1994, Jason Olsen has come a long way, but the winding road ahead has a few more curves in it. His ERA and won-lost record at Birmingham were not attractive and he gave up a lot of hits, but his K/BB was very solid at +15 percent. He has unusual control for a pitcher with limited experience, but the fact that he gives up too many hits indicates he gives batters too much of the plate. His velocity is good, in the low 90s, but his breaking stuff needs work. I think that Olsen probably needs a full season in Double-A, but he is the kind of guy who could come very quickly if he figures something out. **Grade C**

Luis Ordaz

St. Louis Cardinals

Pos: SS   Bats: Right   Ht: 5'11"   Wt: 170   Age: 22

Yr Team	Lg	G	AB	R	H	2B	3B	HR	RBI	BB	SO	SB	CS	Avg	OBP	Slg
96 St. Pete	A	126	423	46	115	13	3	3	49	30	53	10	5	.272	.317	.338
97 Arkansas	AA	115	390	44	112	20	6	4	58	22	39	11	10	.287	.324	.400
St. Louis	NL	12	22	3	6	1	0	0	1	1	2	3	0	.273	.304	.318
5 Minor League Yrs		479	1631	197	434	68	26	11	200	83	202	44	26	.266	.303	.360

Venezuelan shortstop Luis Ordaz handled the transition to Double-A quite well in 1997 and received a brief major league trial, which he also handled well. He will play Triple-A in 1998, and could have a big league job soon. Ordaz has a quick bat, and while I am not enamored of his low walk rate, he does make contact and has hit for a decent average. He isn't a fast baserunner, but can steal a base if called upon to do so. Ordaz's range and reliability numbers were just average last year, but scouts say he will be an excellent defensive shortstop at the major league level. We will have to see about that. **Grade C+**

Magglio Ordonez

Chicago White Sox

Pos: OF **Bats:** Right **Ht:** 5'11" **Wt:** 155 **Age:** 24

Yr Team	Lg	G	AB	R	H	2B	3B	HR	RBI	BB	SO	SB	CS	Avg	OBP	Slg
96 Birmingham	AA	130	479	66	126	41	0	18	67	39	74	9	10	.263	.330	.461
97 Nashville	AAA	135	523	65	172	29	3	14	90	32	61	14	10	.329	.364	.476
Chicago	AL	21	69	12	22	6	0	4	11	2	8	1	2	.319	.338	.580
6 Minor League Yrs		650	2363	327	637	142	16	59	325	196	355	61	41	.270	.328	.418

I wrote in last year's book that Magglio Ordonez "wouldn't surprise me if he had a very good season in 1997," but I sure as hell didn't expect *this*. I thought he might bat .290, not .329, and I certainly didn't expect him to lead the American Association in hitting. Let's just say I was pleasantly surprised. Ordonez, a Venezuelan signed by the White Sox in 1991, matured as a hitter last year when he adopted a consistent batting stance. He used to experiment with different approaches, sometimes during the same at-bat, and ended up confusing himself. He was great at Nashville, winning the batting title, and being named the Best Batting Prospect in the league in the *Baseball America* poll of managers. Ordonez is very muscular, and will whack pitches in the middle or outer half of the plate to the opposite field, hard. I would like to see him develop more plate discipline, but his strikeout rate is good, and he makes contact. Defensively, he has the range to play center and the arm to play right, but needs more experience at one position, since the Sox have moved him around a lot. I don't think Ordonez is going to be a full-scale megastar, but he should have a very rewarding career. **Grade B+**

Eddie Oropesa

San Francisco Giants

Pos: P **Throws:** Left **Ht:** 6'2" **Wt:** 200 **Age:** 26

Yr Team	Lg	G	GS	IP	H	R	ER	HR	BB	SO	SV	W	L	Pct.	ERA
96 San Berndno	A	33	19	156.1	133	74	58	8	77	133	1	11	6	.647	3.34
97 Shreveport	AA	43	9	124.0	122	58	54	7	64	65	0	7	7	.500	3.92
4 Minor League Yrs		131	39	399.0	356	176	147	19	188	304	4	26	18	.591	3.32

Eddie Oropesa really isn't a serious prospect, but he has an interesting background, and should see some major league innings at some point. A Cuban southpaw originally signed by the Dodgers, Oropesa has just average stuff. When his command is sharp, he can get people out, especially with his curveball, but his poor K/BB ratio shows that he is seldom dominant. He is very durable, however, and can pitch in any role. Oropesa also has a wicked move to first base and is very tough on baserunners. Like I said, he isn't a hot prospect by any means, but could sneak a few Show innings in. It isn't impossible he could luck into a real job if his strikeout rate rises. **Grade C-**

Pablo Ortega
Tampa Bay Devil Rays

Pos: P **Throws:** Right **Ht:** 6'2" **Wt:** 170 **Age:** 21

Yr Team	Lg	G	GS	IP	H	R	ER	HR	BB	SO	SV	W	L	Pct.	ERA
96 Devil Rays	R	13	13	82.1	61	24	18	1	12	86	0	4	6	.400	1.97
97 Chston-SC	A	29	29	188.2	173	87	60	10	30	142	0	12	10	.545	2.86
1 Minor League Yr		42	42	271.0	234	111	78	11	42	228	0	16	16	.500	2.59

Ortega was signed as a free agent out of Mexico after he pitched a year for Laredo in the Mexican League. He threw the first pitch in the history of the Devil Rays organization in 1996, and did well in his full-season debut in 1997. Ortega has a decent fastball, 88-90 MPH, an okay slider, and an excellent changeup. His command and control are very good, and his K/BB ratio was outstanding at +100 percent. On the other hand, his H/IP ratio was only adequate, and his K/IP was weak at -13 percent. Ortega needs to maintain his command and show that he can succeed at higher levels. **Grade C+**

David Ortiz
Minnesota Twins

Pos: 1B **Bats:** Left **Ht:** 6'4" **Wt:** 230 **Age:** 22

Yr Team	Lg	G	AB	R	H	2B	3B	HR	RBI	BB	SO	SB	CS	Avg	OBP	Slg
96 Wisconsin	A	130	487	89	156	34	2	18	93	52	108	3	4	.320	.389	.509
97 Ft. Myers	A	61	239	45	79	15	0	13	58	22	53	2	1	.331	.385	.556
New Britain	AA	69	258	40	83	22	2	14	56	21	78	2	6	.322	.379	.585
Salt Lake	AAA	10	42	5	9	1	0	4	10	2	11	0	1	.214	.250	.524
Minnesota	AL	15	49	10	16	3	0	1	6	2	19	0	0	.327	.353	.449
4 Minor League Yrs		371	1377	223	429	100	9	55	274	134	348	10	16	.312	.374	.517

Known as David Arias when he played in the Seattle system, this highly promising slugger changed his name to Ortiz last spring. The Mariners will bitterly regret giving him away for Dave Hollins. Ortiz blasted the ball in the Florida State League and the Eastern League, in home parks not conducive to offense. His marks were outstanding across the board: OPS +33 percent in the FSL, +23 percent in the EL; SEC +31 percent in the FSL, +19 percent in the EL. Although he is not a particularly patient hitter and doesn't walk enough for my taste, it is hard to argue with what he did last year, hitting for power and average and more than holding his own in a September look-see. He doesn't try to pull everything, but gets a good look at the ball with a wide open stance, and will take pitches to the opposite field. He never looks intimidated. Although listed at 6-4, 230, he looks like he's 6-6, 240. There are hints that Ortiz' birth certificate is a little off. However old he really is, he will be a very, very good major league hitter, and possibly a great one. **Grade B+**

Jose Ortiz
Oakland Athletics

Pos: SS **Bats:** Right **Ht:** 5'11" **Wt:** 160 **Age:** 20

Yr Team	Lg	G	AB	R	H	2B	3B	HR	RBI	BB	SO	SB	CS	Avg	OBP	Slg
96 Athletics	R	52	200	43	66	12	8	4	25	20	34	16	5	.330	.392	.530
Modesto	A	1	4	0	1	0	0	0	0	0	1	0	0	.250	.250	.250
97 Modesto	A	128	497	92	122	25	7	16	58	60	107	22	14	.245	.332	.421
2 Minor League Yrs		181	701	135	189	37	15	20	83	80	142	38	19	.270	.348	.451

Jose Ortiz played in the Rookie-level Arizona League in 1996, hit .330, and was named the fourth-best prospect in the circuit by *Baseball America*. Oakland, due to franchise shuffling throughout the minors, ended up without a slow-A full-season team, and was forced to send Ortiz to the tough fast-A California League in 1997. He acquitted himself well against tough competition, and is following in Miguel Tejada's footsteps as a top-notch shortstop prospect. Ortiz's OPS was a notch below average, but no one is complaining about his performance given his age. Ortiz has the physical ability to be a fine glove man, but isn't yet, as 53 errors indicate. That should drop with experience. Ortiz is raw, but the natural gifts for renown are here. **Grade B+**

Ramon Ortiz
Anaheim Angels

Pos: P **Throws:** Right **Ht:** 6'0" **Wt:** 150 **Age:** 21

Yr Team	Lg	G	GS	IP	H	R	ER	HR	BB	SO	SV	W	L	Pct.	ERA
96 Angels	R	16	8	68.0	55	28	16	5	27	78	1	5	4	.556	2.12
Boise	A	3	3	19.2	21	10	8	3	6	18	0	1	1	.500	3.66
97 Cedar Rapds	A	27	27	181.0	156	78	72	22	53	225	0	11	10	.524	3.58
2 Minor League Yrs		46	38	268.2	232	116	96	30	86	321	1	17	15	.531	3.22

Ramon Ortiz, listed at a thin six-feet-even with room to grow, was signed out of the Dominican in 1995. Ortiz throws very hard, 92-94 MPH, and has been compared to Pedro Martinez due to his velocity, his command, and his small build. Ortiz has a great slider to go with the heater, and he can throw both for strikes at will. His strikeout numbers at Cedar Rapids were awesome: K/BB +112 percent, K/IP +48 percent, both near the top of the league. His H/IP was good at plus-nine percent, although not as good as the K numbers. Basically, the only question about Ortiz is health. He threw a lot of innings last year. There are occasionally pitchers like Pedro Martinez, who can hold up to a heavy workload at a young age, but there are many more like Salomon Torres, who break down under heavy physical and psychological burdens imposed too early. I hope the Angels are careful with Ortiz, because he is something special. **Grade B+**

Russ Ortiz

San Francisco Giants

Pos: P   Throws: Right   Ht: 6'1"   Wt: 200   Age: 23

Yr Team	Lg	G	GS	IP	H	R	ER	HR	BB	SO	SV	W	L	Pct.	ERA
96 San Jose	A	34	0	36.2	16	2	1	0	20	63	23	0	0	—	0.25
Shreveport	AA	26	0	26.2	22	14	12	0	21	29	13	1	2	.333	4.05
97 Shreveport	AA	12	12	56.2	52	28	26	3	37	50	0	2	3	.400	4.13
Phoenix	AAA	14	14	85.0	96	57	52	11	34	70	0	4	3	.571	5.51
3 Minor League Yrs		116	26	245.1	209	106	94	15	127	274	47	9	9	.500	3.45

A year ago, it looked like Russ Ortiz was going to make his mark as a reliever, but the Giants decided to convert him to starting work. This brought mixed results. Ortiz, a fourth-rounder in 1995 from the University of Oklahoma, has a nasty 95-MPH fastball with tremendous sinking action. His curveball is very promising, if erratic, and he needs to refine his offspeed stuff if he is to make it as a starter. Control is a problem for him, but he held up well under the load of a starter, and could prove to be quite durable if they keep him in the role. They may not do so; the word is he may move back to relief. The arm strength is certainly there for him to succeed. If he does move back to the bullpen, he could advance quickly. **Grade B-**

Jimmy Osting

Atlanta Braves

Pos: P   Throws: Left   Ht: 6'5"   Wt: 200   Age: 20

Yr Team	Lg	G	GS	IP	H	R	ER	HR	BB	SO	SV	W	L	Pct.	ERA
96 Eugene	A	5	5	24.1	14	11	7	1	13	35	0	2	1	.667	2.59
97 Macon	A	15	15	57.2	54	28	21	3	29	62	0	2	3	.400	3.28
3 Minor League Yrs		31	30	121.0	114	73	59	5	67	140	0	6	11	.353	4.39

Jimmy Osting has a very good arm, a fine work ethic, and firm grasp of how to pitch. He also just had Tommy John surgery, not a good thing for a 21-year-old pitcher to experience. Osting opened the season on the DL with a sore elbow, returned in May and pitched very well, then blew out a ligament after 16 starts and went under the knife. He could come back, but it will be at least a year and probably longer before the full extent of his recovery can be gauged.

Roy Padilla

Boston Red Sox

Pos: OF   Bats: Left   Ht: 6'7"   Wt: 230   Age: 22

Yr Team	Lg	G	AB	R	H	2B	3B	HR	RBI	BB	SO	SB	CS	Avg	OBP	Slg
96 Michigan	A	103	386	58	108	20	6	2	40	34	56	21	8	.280	.340	.378
Sarasota	A	8	27	2	8	2	0	0	2	2	3	4	0	.296	.345	.370
97 Sarasota	A	130	463	66	114	16	4	2	38	41	80	24	19	.246	.314	.311
5 Minor League Yrs		289	877	126	230	38	10	4	80	77	139	49	27	.262	.326	.342

Red Sox partisans in the press occasionally refer to converted pitcher Roy Padilla as a prospect, but personally, I'm skeptical. Padilla has obvious speed, and scouts like his athletic ability, but it doesn't look to me like he is going to hit much. He does have outstanding range in the outfield, although he made more errors (11) than he had assists (nine) last year, which is never a good sign. He is still quite young, and has almost no background as a hitter, so he has potential for development, but I wouldn't count on it. **Grade C-**

211

Jim Parque
Chicago White Sox

Pos: P   **Throws:** Left   **Ht:** 5'10"   **Wt:** 166   **Age:** 22

Yr Team	Lg	G	GS	IP	H	R	ER	HR	BB	SO	SV	W	L	Pct.	ERA
97 Winston-Sal	A	11	11	61.2	29	19	19	3	23	76	0	7	2	.778	2.77
Nashville	AAA	2	2	10.2	9	5	5	0	9	5	0	1	0	1.000	4.22
1 Minor League Yr		13	13	72.1	38	24	24	3	32	81	0	8	2	.800	2.99

I seldom write about guys the year they were drafted unless they were pure first-round picks, or the first player signed by their organization, but when someone just drafted finishes the season in Triple-A, well, you have to make allowances. Parque went in the supplemental portion of the first round. His arm and pitching ability are top-notch, but scouts downgraded him a bit due to his size. Despite his stature, his fastball hits 91 MPH, and he throws it on the corners. He also has a sharp slider and a truly effective changeup, and he is a very intelligent pitcher. His ratios at Winston-Salem were phenomenal, especially his absurdly good H/IP mark of 29 hits in 62 innings. The only real concern about Parque relates to his stature: scouts wonder if he will hold up under pro usage patterns. I want to see him for a full season before I go wacko with the grade, but this guy could be something special, and this grade could be too low. **Grade B**

Jason Parsons
Cincinnati Reds

Pos: 1B   **Bats:** Both   **Ht:** 6'3"   **Wt:** 220   **Age:** 25

Yr Team	Lg	G	AB	R	H	2B	3B	HR	RBI	BB	SO	SB	CS	Avg	OBP	Slg
96 Princeton	R	23	91	22	37	9	0	5	17	5	9	0	2	.407	.439	.670
Chston-WV	A	48	162	18	46	11	0	3	24	15	25	3	1	.284	.352	.407
Winston-Sal	A	14	46	4	16	3	0	0	7	2	5	0	2	.348	.388	.413
97 Chston-WV	A	131	460	87	143	34	0	20	102	62	99	5	1	.311	.405	.515
3 Minor League Yrs		276	981	178	312	77	0	33	198	116	179	11	7	.318	.399	.497

Parsons was a 29th-round pick in 1995, from Dallas Baptist University. He was one of the more threatening hitters in the South Atlantic League in 1997, showing considerable power and a reasonable measure of patience. His OPS was near the top of the league at +33 percent. The problem for Parsons is that he was too old for the league. He needs to keep hitting like that at higher levels. If I were the Reds, I would move him directly to Double-A in 1998, to find out if his bat is for real. **Grade C-**

Mike Pasqualicchio
Milwaukee Brewers

Pos: P   **Throws:** Left   **Ht:** 6'1"   **Wt:** 205   **Age:** 23

Yr Team	Lg	G	GS	IP	H	R	ER	HR	BB	SO	SV	W	L	Pct.	ERA
96 Stockton	A	18	17	71.1	67	35	28	3	36	69	0	3	3	.500	3.53
97 Stockton	A	17	15	85.1	93	67	61	10	44	58	1	1	10	.091	6.43
3 Minor League Yrs		43	39	188.0	190	116	100	15	100	148	1	7	13	.350	4.79

The Brewers' second-round pick in 1995 from Lamar University, Mike Pasqualicchio has a live 92-MPH fastball, a decent curve, and a nice changeup. He also has a very bad back, which cost him much of 1996 and 1997, and eventually resulted in surgery. At this stage, there is no way of knowing if he will stay healthy enough to become an effective pitcher, but his performance in the pros hasn't been great even when healthy, and there are concerns about his work ethic and attitude. On the other hand, he did do well in the Arizona Fall League, and if he is healthy, he could advance quickly. **Grade C**

Brian Passini   *Milwaukee Brewers*

Pos: P   Throws: Left   Ht: 6'3"   Wt: 195   Age: 23

Yr Team	Lg	G	GS	IP	H	R	ER	HR	BB	SO	SV	W	L	Pct.	ERA
96 Helena	R	15	14	77.2	91	37	30	5	27	71	0	7	2	.778	3.48
97 Beloit	A	19	19	123.0	114	48	44	14	35	116	0	9	5	.643	3.22
Stockton	A	8	8	45.1	40	28	24	7	21	34	0	1	5	.167	4.76
2 Minor League Yrs		42	41	246.0	245	113	98	26	83	221	0	17	12	.586	3.59

Brian Passini was drafted in the eighth round in 1996, from Miami University in Ohio. One of my undergraduate professors, Dr. Joel Benson, got his Ph.D. from there. Anyhow, Passini is the archetype lefty starter with average stuff. When his control is sharp, as it was at Beloit, he can get people out, but if he is too tentative, as he was at Stockton, he gets knocked around easily. His K/BB in the Midwest League as solid at +33 percent, but much less impressive in the California League. He isn't a hot prospect, but Passini is worth keeping track of. He could do what Steve Woodard did in 1997, emerging in the majors after improving his command from good to excellent. **Grade C**

John Patterson   *Arizona Diamondbacks*

Pos: P   Throws: Right   Ht: 6'6"   Wt: 200   Age: 20

Yr Team	Lg	G	GS	IP	H	R	ER	HR	BB	SO	SV	W	L	Pct.	ERA
97 South Bend	A	18	18	78.0	63	32	28	3	34	95	0	1	9	.100	3.23
1 Minor League Yr		18	18	78.0	63	32	28	3	34	95	0	1	9	.100	3.23

Patterson was originally drafted by the Expos in the first round in 1996. As they did with Travis Lee, the Diamondbacks signed him on the open market, after he was declared a free agent on a contract technicality. Patterson has a blistering 94-96 MPH fastball, a solid curve, and a good changeup for such a young pitcher. His command is very good, considering his age, and he pitched very well in half a season of Midwest League action. Ignore the 1-9 record; that was caused by poor run support and pitch limits. Basically, the only things that Patterson needs to do are stay healthy, build some stamina, and develop more consistency. With less than 80 Class-A innings under his belt, I won't give him a letter grade, but he could be up near the top of the list next year.

Jeff Patzke
Toronto Blue Jays

Pos: 2B **Bats:** Both **Ht:** 6'0" **Wt:** 170 **Age:** 24

Yr Team	Lg	G	AB	R	H	2B	3B	HR	RBI	BB	SO	SB	CS	Avg	OBP	Slg
96 Knoxville	AA	124	429	70	130	31	4	4	66	80	103	6	5	.303	.418	.422
97 Syracuse	AAA	96	316	38	90	25	2	2	29	51	66	0	3	.285	.384	.396
6 Minor League Yrs		565	1973	286	523	113	15	24	232	306	382	26	23	.265	.366	.374

Well, the Carlos Garcia trade certainly worked out well. Billy Ripken could have played as poorly as Garcia, for less money. Jeff Patzke would have played better than Garcia or Ripken for *a lot* less money, like, say, the minimum salary. Patzke is a switch-hitter who makes contact, can drive the ball into the gaps and is willing to take a walk. He is still young, and it is possible he could hit .300 in the majors one of these days. Patzke can field, too; he has well above-average range, quick hands, and can turn the double play. I don't understand why the Blue Jays have wasted time with guys like Tomas Perez when they had a perfectly good player like Patzke sitting around. Well, actually, the reason is that Patzke doesn't *look* like a player. . . he doesn't have athletic ability oozing out of his pores. Scouts are taught not to look at stat sheets, so they downgrade Patzke and other guys like him. I think that's a mistake. Patzke can play, though he was designated for assignment by Toronto. **Grade B**

Josh Paul
Chicago White Sox

Pos: C **Bats:** Right **Ht:** 6'1" **Wt:** 185 **Age:** 22

Yr Team	Lg	G	AB	R	H	2B	3B	HR	RBI	BB	SO	SB	CS	Avg	OBP	Slg
96 White Sox	R	1	0	0	0	0	0	0	0	1	0	0	0	—	1.000	—
Hickory	A	59	226	41	74	16	0	8	37	21	53	13	4	.327	.386	.504
97 White Sox	R	5	14	3	6	0	1	0	0	1	3	1	0	.429	.467	.571
Birmingham	AA	34	115	18	34	5	0	1	16	12	25	6	2	.296	.367	.365
2 Minor League Yrs		99	355	62	114	21	1	9	53	35	81	20	6	.321	.384	.462

Paul was drafted out of Vanderbilt in the second round in 1996, the highest draftee the White Sox signed that year. I won't grade him since he lost almost all of 1997 after breaking the hamate bone in his left hand, but hit well when he did play. Paul looks like he will have a productive bat, but questions exist about his defense, and we need to see him get a full season. He's very athletic and might be converted to another position to take advantage of his tools.

Carl Pavano
Montreal Expos

Pos: P **Throws:** Right **Ht:** 6'5" **Wt:** 230 **Age:** 22

Yr Team	Lg	G	GS	IP	H	R	ER	HR	BB	SO	SV	W	L	Pct.	ERA
96 Trenton	AA	27	26	185.0	154	66	54	16	47	146	0	16	5	.762	2.63
97 Pawtucket	AAA	23	23	161.2	148	62	56	13	34	147	0	11	6	.647	3.12
4 Minor League Yrs		81	78	532.0	451	205	173	37	140	478	0	37	20	.649	2.93

Carl Pavano is probably the best pitching prospect in baseball, and will earn a rotation spot for the Expos in 1998, having gone north in the Pedro Martinez trade. Pavano has everything you look for in a young pitcher: velocity, control, intelligence, a record of success. He was bothered by biceps tendinitis in spring training, but when he took the mound at Pawtucket, he was outstanding. He was named the Best Prospect in the International League by *Baseball America*. Pavano has a 94-MPH fastball, a very good slider, a good curve and a pretty good changeup. He throws them all for strikes, and there were no dents in his numbers; his K/BB in particular was wonderful at +125 percent. Really, the only worry I have about Pavano is his health. I know I say that about every pitcher, but the last pitcher who seemed to have *everything* going for him to this extent was Paul Wilson, and we know what happened to him. Pavano might be the next Paul Wilson, but he also might be the next Matt Morris. I think the latter is more likely than the former. **Grade A-**

Kit Pellow

Kansas City Royals

Pos: 3B   **Bats:** Right   **Ht:** 6'1"   **Wt:** 200   **Age:** 24

Yr Team	Lg	G	AB	R	H	2B	3B	HR	RBI	BB	SO	SB	CS	Avg	OBP	Slg
96 Spokane	A	71	279	48	80	18	2	18	66	20	52	8	3	.287	.344	.559
97 Lansing	A	65	256	39	76	17	2	11	52	24	74	2	0	.297	.366	.508
Wichita	AA	68	241	40	60	12	1	10	41	21	72	5	2	.249	.311	.432
2 Minor League Yrs		204	776	127	216	47	5	39	159	65	198	15	5	.278	.341	.503

Pellow was a 22nd-rounder in 1996 from the University of Arkansas. He played well in college; I'm not sure why he wasn't more highly regarded. Pellow was excellent at Lansing, and hit well at Wichita immediately after his promotion, but got overly pull-conscious and fell into a slump in July. He does have authentic power, but needs to do a better job against breaking stuff outside the strike zone. Scouts say that Pellow isn't a good defensive player, but he made several impressive plays in games I saw, and his range factor in the Texas League was excellent. He does make too many errors, many on throws. There is talk that the Royals may convert him to catcher; we'll see about that. Pellow needs to cut down on his strikeouts, and tighten up his glove work. He has made quick progress for a 22nd-round pick. **Grade C**

Angel Pena

Los Angeles Dodgers

Pos: C   **Bats:** Right   **Ht:** 6'0"   **Wt:** 220   **Age:** 23

Yr Team	Lg	G	AB	R	H	2B	3B	HR	RBI	BB	SO	SB	CS	Avg	OBP	Slg
96 Savannah	A	36	127	13	26	4	0	6	16	7	37	1	1	.205	.246	.378
97 San Berndno	A	86	322	53	89	22	4	16	64	32	84	3	5	.276	.344	.519
3 Minor League Yrs		171	587	90	155	37	5	26	95	60	153	6	7	.264	.335	.477

A Dominican signed in 1993, Angel Pena got his first chance to play regularly last season and did quite nicely in the California League. His OPS was reasonably good at +13 percent; his SEC was a bit better at +23 percent. Command of the strike zone is neither a strength nor a weakness for him at this point. He threw out 39 percent of runners, one percent above the league average and his fielding percentage was in the middle of the pack, all of which means he is adequate defensively; nothing special, but not bad. He won't be moving in on Mike Piazza anytime soon, but if he continues to develop, Pena could be a good player. **Grade C+**

Juan Pena
Boston Red Sox

Pos: P **Throws:** Right **Ht:** 6'5" **Wt:** 210 **Age:** 20

Yr Team	Lg	G	GS	IP	H	R	ER	HR	BB	SO	SV	W	L	Pct.	ERA
96 Michigan	A	26	26	187.2	149	70	62	16	34	156	0	12	10	.545	2.97
97 Sarasota	A	13	13	91.1	67	39	30	8	23	88	0	4	6	.400	2.96
Trenton	AA	16	14	97.0	98	56	51	13	31	79	0	5	6	.455	4.73
3 Minor League Yrs		70	59	438.2	363	186	159	39	97	375	1	25	25	.500	3.26

Pena had a distinguished season in the Midwest League in 1996, and he continued to do well in the Florida State League in 1997. Promoted to Double-A midway, he struggled. This isn't unusual, especially for a guy who doesn't throw that hard. His fastball is average by major league standards; it is his fine slider that gives him potential. When he throws it and the fastball aggressively for strikes, he is a dangerous competitor, but he was too tentative in Double-A, especially in his first few starts. He might get over that, and if he does he could contribute in 1998, but I am ambivalent about his immediate chances, especially since there are hints of arm trouble. **Grade C**

Tyrone Pendergrass
Atlanta Braves

Pos: OF **Bats:** Both **Ht:** 6'1" **Wt:** 174 **Age:** 21

Yr Team	Lg	G	AB	R	H	2B	3B	HR	RBI	BB	SO	SB	CS	Avg	OBP	Slg
96 Danville	R	54	220	50	68	8	7	3	23	24	39	40	6	.309	.384	.450
Macon	A	12	45	8	12	1	1	1	3	4	12	5	3	.267	.340	.400
97 Macon	A	127	489	81	127	16	5	6	37	60	101	70	15	.260	.344	.350
3 Minor League Yrs		245	942	158	241	29	13	11	70	103	203	123	28	.256	.334	.349

Tyrone Pendergrass sounds like he should be a blues musician. "The three greatest blues musicians in history were Muddy Waters, B.B. King, and Tyrone Pendergrass." Or maybe a Civil War leader. "Brigadier General Tyrone Pendergrass flanked the Union Third Corps at Gettysburg." Signed out of a tryout camp in 1995, he was named the Best Baserunner in the South Atlantic League and is thought to be the fleetest guy in the Braves system. His speed shows up on offense and defense: he steals tons of bases, and has a great range factor in the outfield. Although he strikes out too much for someone with limited power, he demonstrates some selectivity at the plate, and that should help him develop. I like him more than I like most speed guys in the low minors, although it will be some time before Pendergrass is ready to contribute in the majors. **Grade C**

Brad Penny
Arizona Diamondbacks

Pos: P **Throws:** Right **Ht:** 6'4" **Wt:** 195 **Age:** 19

Yr Team	Lg	G	GS	IP	H	R	ER	HR	BB	SO	SV	W	L	Pct.	ERA
96 Diamondback	R	11	8	49.2	36	18	13	1	14	52	0	2	2	.500	2.36
97 South Bend	A	25	25	118.2	91	44	36	4	43	116	0	10	5	.667	2.73
2 Minor League Yrs		36	33	168.1	127	62	49	5	57	168	0	12	7	.632	2.62

Penny was Arizona's fifth-round pick in 1996, out of high school in Broken Arrow, Oklahoma. (Is that where they accidentally drop nuclear missiles?—Ed.) His first full season felt like a dream. Penny impressed Midwest League observers with a solid low-90s fastball, a very good curve, and fine control. He still needs work on the changeup, but he is a bright kid, has good mechanics for a youngster, and could pick up even more velocity as he grows into his body. All of his pitching ratios were superior: K/BB +34 percent, K/IP +16 percent, H/IP +19 percent. Penny has a hard time holding baserunners, and needs to refine his actions around the mound, but there is plenty of time for that. Penny won't be able to afford any black limousines immediately, but if he doesn't get hurt, he should have a fine career. **Grade B**

Danny Peoples   *Cleveland Indians*

Pos: OF-DH **Bats**: Right **Ht**: 6'1" **Wt**: 207 **Age**: 23

Yr Team	Lg	G	AB	R	H	2B	3B	HR	RBI	BB	SO	SB	CS	Avg	OBP	Slg
96 Watertown	A	35	117	20	28	7	0	3	26	28	36	3	1	.239	.392	.376
97 Kinston	A	121	409	82	102	21	1	34	84	84	145	8	1	.249	.380	.555
2 Minor League Yrs		156	526	102	130	28	1	37	110	112	181	11	2	.247	.383	.515

Peoples was drafted out of the University of Texas in the first round in 1996. No one questioned his raw power, but most people thought the pick was a reach, since Peoples lacked all the tools and skills *except* power. He was drafted that high because he agreed to a prearranged $400,000 bonus that was well below market value. He erased at least some of that skepticism by crushing Carolina League pitching in 1997, posting an OPS of +29 percent, and a SEC of +91 percent, both in the top four of the league. Note the high SEC; that means he is a productive offensive player, able to put runs on the board despite his low batting average. Peoples will never be a great defensive player, but he adapted well to left field after playing first base in college. He will never be a Seven Skill player, but the skill he does have is a critical one. I want to see him deal with breaking pitches at the higher levels, and his strikeout rate is scary. **Grade C+**

Jhonny Perez   *Houston Astros*

Pos: OF **Bats**: Right **Ht**: 5'10" **Wt**: 150 **Age**: 21

Yr Team	Lg	G	AB	R	H	2B	3B	HR	RBI	BB	SO	SB	CS	Avg	OBP	Slg
96 Kissimmee	A	90	322	54	87	20	2	12	49	26	70	16	16	.270	.329	.457
97 Kissimmee	A	69	273	40	72	16	5	3	22	12	38	8	6	.264	.294	.392
Jackson	AA	48	154	16	39	7	0	3	17	12	26	4	3	.253	.311	.357
4 Minor League Yrs		308	1107	171	302	67	9	23	146	87	187	69	35	.273	.331	.412

I really liked Jhonny Perez as a sleeper a year ago, but the Astros switched him from shortstop to the outfield in 1997, and he never got on track with the bat. He has been forgotten by most observers. This may be a mistake; he didn't do much last year, but he is still very young, and I still believe he has significant potential as an offensive player. Keep track of him. **Grade C+**

Odaliz Perez
Atlanta Braves
Pos: P Throws: Left Ht: 6'1" Wt: 175 Age: 19

Yr Team	Lg	G	GS	IP	H	R	ER	HR	BB	SO	SV	W	L	Pct.	ERA
96 Eugene	A	10	6	23.2	26	16	10	2	11	38	0	2	1	.667	3.80
97 Macon	A	36	0	87.1	67	31	16	4	27	100	5	4	5	.444	1.65
3 Minor League Yrs		58	18	176.0	141	69	42	6	56	200	5	9	11	.450	2.15

Check out this guy. He's gotten *no* attention, but those numbers really stand out. Perez was signed as a free agent out of the Dominican in 1994. He is very young, and was voted the Best Reliever in the circuit by Sally League managers. He has a 93-MPH fastball, and a sharp breaking pitch. His ratios were great across the line: K/BB +57 percent, K/IP +32 percent, H/IP +23 percent. A word of caution: minor league relievers, even those who are young and throw hard, like Perez, tend to struggle as they advance. **Grade B-**

Matt Perisho
Texas Rangers
Pos: P Throws: Left Ht: 6'0" Wt: 190 Age: 22

Yr Team	Lg	G	GS	IP	H	R	ER	HR	BB	SO	SV	W	L	Pct.	ERA
96 Lk Elsinore	A	21	18	128.2	131	72	60	9	58	97	0	7	5	.583	4.20
Midland	AA	8	8	53.1	48	22	19	4	20	50	0	3	2	.600	3.21
97 Midland	AA	10	10	73.0	60	26	24	5	26	62	0	5	2	.714	2.96
Vancouver	AAA	9	9	52.1	68	42	31	3	29	47	0	4	4	.500	5.33
Anaheim	AL	11	8	45.0	59	34	30	6	28	35	0	0	2	.000	6.00
5 Minor League Yrs		110	105	634.1	667	375	312	43	304	496	0	46	34	.575	4.43

The Angels sung arias about Perisho as a prospect ever since they drafted him out of an Arizona high school in 1993's third round. A 1994 elbow injury set him back, but he has been healthy for two years now. In 1997, he was excellent in the Texas League, less effective but still decent in the Pacific Coast League, then got knocked around in the majors. He was eventually sent to Texas as part of the Ken Hill trade. Perisho works with an 89-MPH fastball, and his curve, slider, and change all offer hope. His command vacillates at times, and when it does he gets blasted. He has to throw strikes to succeed. What happens to him in 1998 depends entirely on his command. If it is great, he could win 15 games for Texas. If it is mediocre, he could win 10. If it is wobbly, he could still win 10. . . for Oklahoma City. **Grade B-**

Brandon Pernell
San Diego Padres
Pos: OF Bats: Right Ht: 6'2" Wt: 180 Age: 20

Yr Team	Lg	G	AB	R	H	2B	3B	HR	RBI	BB	SO	SB	CS	Avg	OBP	Slg
96 Padres	R	53	174	38	58	9	10	1	33	18	30	14	4	.333	.392	.517
97 Clinton	A	95	340	63	96	26	3	12	41	44	77	15	5	.282	.372	.482
3 Minor League Yrs		196	688	123	197	46	14	15	103	78	161	37	11	.286	.361	.459

Hey, you, out there in the cold, here's a prospect for you. I guarantee nobody in your fantasy league has heard of this guy, but you should watch for Brandon Pernell in 1998. He was drafted in the 19th round in 1995, from a California high school, and while he never gets any attention, he has had a good career so far. Pernell has good, and improving, plate discipline, a lanky build that has yet to fill out, and a nice swing. His Clinton stats don't knock your socks off, but that is a tough place to hit, and he was one of the younger regulars in the league. He isn't a good defensive player yet, but may be with time. For me, Pernell fits the profile of a young guy with plate discipline who could surface as a major prospect soon. Stop, look, and listen; his train may be coming. **Grade C+**

Chan Perry   *Cleveland Indians*

Pos: 1B-DH **Bats:** Right **Ht:** 6'2" **Wt:** 200 **Age:** 25

Yr Team	Lg	G	AB	R	H	2B	3B	HR	RBI	BB	SO	SB	CS	Avg	OBP	Slg
96 Kinston	A	96	358	44	104	27	1	10	62	36	33	2	3	.291	.356	.455
97 Akron	AA	119	476	74	150	34	2	20	96	28	61	3	3	.315	.355	.521
4 Minor League Yrs		380	1430	210	429	107	8	44	240	135	171	18	8	.300	.361	.478

Chan Perry is similar to his oft-injured brother Herb: a righthanded first baseman who hits for a good average and some power. Chan, drafted in the 44th round from the University of Florida in 1994, has never excited scouts, but he has hit well enough to be regarded as a candidate for the majors. His OPS was above-average at +13 percent in the Eastern League, and his MLE suggests he could hit .270-.280 in the Show. The main problem for Chan is that he is with the wrong team; the Indians have three guys ahead of him on the depth chart. Chan is pretty good, but he's not *that* good, and there is a good chance he will play the next five years in Triple-A. **Grade C**

Charles Peterson   *Pittsburgh Pirates*

Pos: OF **Bats:** Right **Ht:** 6'3" **Wt:** 200 **Age:** 23

Yr Team	Lg	G	AB	R	H	2B	3B	HR	RBI	BB	SO	SB	CS	Avg	OBP	Slg
96 Carolina	AA	125	462	71	127	24	2	7	63	50	104	33	10	.275	.345	.381
97 Carolina	AA	126	442	59	111	26	4	7	68	40	105	20	11	.251	.318	.376
5 Minor League Yrs		535	1968	287	531	87	20	26	252	199	397	121	63	.270	.339	.374

Peterson has been in Double-A for two years, and there is no evidence he will be able to turn his physical tools into baseball skills. He is strong, but has only mediocre power, since he has never been able to sculpt a swing that can lift the ball. His command of the strike zone is marginal, which doesn't help. Peterson does have a strong arm and good range in right field, but if he doesn't hit, that doesn't matter much. The sands are nearly at the bottom of the hourglass. **Grade C-**

Jay Peterson   *Cincinnati Reds*

Pos: P **Throws:** Right **Ht:** 6'4" **Wt:** 185 **Age:** 22

Yr Team	Lg	G	GS	IP	H	R	ER	HR	BB	SO	SV	W	L	Pct.	ERA
96 Rockford	A	15	15	94.0	82	50	36	8	39	87	0	4	7	.364	3.45
Daytona	A	8	7	27.2	35	29	20	3	21	15	0	0	2	.000	6.51
97 Burlington	A	26	26	144.2	139	88	72	12	79	112	0	14	6	.700	4.48
4 Minor League Yrs		74	72	388.0	383	257	204	31	223	305	0	25	27	.481	4.73

Peterson was a first-round pick out of high school in 1994, but the Cubs gave up on him after three inconsistent seasons and traded him to the Reds. He won 14 games in the Midwest League last year, but pitched at that level before and remains a raw talent. Peterson throws hard, but his command is unsteady, and he has never learned how to change speeds or use his breaking pitches effectively. He could still mature into a useful pitcher, but each year that passes makes it less likely. **Grade C-**

Ben Petrick   *Colorado Rockies*

Pos: C   **Bats:** Right   **Ht:** 6'0"   **Wt:** 195   **Age:** 20

Yr Team	Lg	G	AB	R	H	2B	3B	HR	RBI	BB	SO	SB	CS	Avg	OBP	Slg
96 Asheville	A	122	446	74	105	24	2	14	52	75	98	19	9	.235	.350	.392
97 Salem	A	121	412	68	102	23	3	15	56	62	100	30	11	.248	.347	.427
2 Minor League Yrs		243	858	142	207	47	5	29	108	137	198	49	20	.241	.349	.409

Seven Skill catchers are quite rare, but Ben Petrick could be one soon. He already has six of the seven: he hits for power, controls the strike zone, steals bases, fields well, throws well, and has good mobility for a catcher. All he lacks is the ability to hit for average, but that may come in time. Petrick has excellent secondary offensive skills, as demonstrated by his terrific SEC of +45 percent. He is quite patient and very strong for his size, but his swing still needs some refinement. A running back in high school, Petrick is a fine athlete with outstanding speed for a catcher and good baserunning technique. Petrick has improved greatly as a defensive catcher, and does everything well behind the plate. The main problem for him will be the fact that catching can curtail the development of young hitters. He did miss some time with an abdominal strain last year, but overall he has been very durable. Watch for him in Double-A. **Grade B+**

Jose Pett   *Pittsburgh Pirates*

Pos: P   **Throws:** Right   **Ht:** 6'6"   **Wt:** 190   **Age:** 22

Yr Team	Lg	G	GS	IP	H	R	ER	HR	BB	SO	SV	W	L	Pct.	ERA
96 Knoxville	AA	7	7	44.0	37	20	20	4	10	38	0	4	2	.667	4.09
Syracuse	AAA	20	18	109.2	134	81	71	10	42	50	0	2	9	.182	5.83
97 Carolina	AA	14	14	74.1	76	37	29	5	25	39	0	4	4	.500	3.51
Calgary	AAA	3	3	14.0	25	15	15	4	8	8	0	0	3	.000	9.64
5 Minor League Yrs		89	86	484.1	517	291	244	40	156	280	0	23	36	.390	4.53

A Brazilian pitcher signed for a big bonus by the Blue Jays, Pett came to the Pirates as part of the Carlos Garcia/Orlando Merced trade last winter. He has been dogged by elbow and shoulder problems, but when healthy he has a solid low-90s fastball, favorable breaking stuff, and a very projectable body that promises even more velocity. He finished the 1997 season pitching fairly well in Double-A, but got lit up in Triple-A, and his strikeout rate remains low for a pitcher with good stuff. He is still very young, and could develop if healthy. **Grade C**

Jason Phillips
Pittsburgh Pirates

Pos: P **Throws:** Right **Ht:** 6'6" **Wt:** 215 **Age:** 24

Yr Team	Lg	G	GS	IP	H	R	ER	HR	BB	SO	SV	W	L	Pct.	ERA
96 Augusta	A	14	14	89.2	79	35	24	3	29	75	0	5	4	.556	2.41
Lynchburg	A	13	13	73.2	82	47	37	3	35	63	0	5	6	.455	4.52
97 Lynchburg	A	23	23	138.2	129	66	58	10	35	140	0	11	6	.647	3.76
Carolina	AA	4	4	31.0	21	8	8	1	9	22	0	1	2	.333	2.32
6 Minor League Yrs		125	101	609.2	586	364	284	25	298	549	0	37	41	.474	4.19

Jason Phillips' prospect profile is extremely similar to that of Jason Johnson, a fellow Pittsburgh system pitcher who was lost in the expansion draft. Phillips was drafted in the 14th round in 1992 from a Pennsylvania high school. Like Johnson, he is a very tall pitcher with adequate stuff, who turned the corner in 1997 when he improved his command. His ratios at Lynchburg ranged from excellent to good: K/BB +92 percent, K/IP +16 percent, H/IP plus-six percent. He continued to pitch well after a late promotion to Carolina. Phillips needs a year in the high minors to consolidate his improvement, but he could surprise in 1998. **Grade C+**

Calvin Pickering
Baltimore Orioles

Pos: 1B **Bats:** Left **Ht:** 6'3" **Wt:** 283 **Age:** 21

Yr Team	Lg	G	AB	R	H	2B	3B	HR	RBI	BB	SO	SB	CS	Avg	OBP	Slg
96 Bluefield	R	60	200	45	65	14	1	18	66	28	64	8	2	.325	.411	.675
97 Delmarva	A	122	444	88	138	31	1	25	79	53	139	6	3	.311	.394	.554
3 Minor League Yrs		197	704	141	233	55	2	44	167	83	209	14	5	.331	.408	.602

Pickering, a native of the Virgin Islands, was chosen in the 35th round out of a Tampa high school in 1995. He is enormous, and has weighed 300 pounds at times, but when he makes contact, he can drive balls from coast to coast. The idea of his lefthanded bat hitting in Camden Yards makes Orioles officials salivate. Pickering strikes out too much, but his command of the strike zone isn't bad for an inexperienced player of his size. His defense is very inconsistent. He made 27 errors, but moves decently for such a huge guy. Pickering needs to watch his weight to avoid Cecilitis, and I doubt he will hit for as high an average at higher levels, but he has the best power potential in the Baltimore system. **Grade B-**

A.J. Pierzynski
Minnesota Twins

Pos: C **Bats:** Left **Ht:** 6'3" **Wt:** 202 **Age:** 21

Yr Team	Lg	G	AB	R	H	2B	3B	HR	RBI	BB	SO	SB	CS	Avg	OBP	Slg
96 Ft. Wayne	A	114	431	48	118	30	3	7	70	22	53	0	4	.274	.308	.406
97 Ft. Myers	A	118	412	49	115	23	1	9	64	16	59	2	1	.279	.313	.405
4 Minor League Yrs		353	1284	157	371	79	7	26	212	66	164	2	9	.289	.324	.422

Pierzynski, drafted in the third round from a Florida high school in 1994, is a favorite of scouts due to his commanding physical presence on the field and his lefthanded power potential. The Florida State League is a power hitter's graveyard, and Fort Myers is a particularly difficult place to hit even for the league, so the fact that he was only slightly above league average in OPS isn't too terrible. His command of the strike zone remains a weakness, but he is young enough to improve substantially. He has the tools to be a good defensive catcher, but threw out 33 percent of runners attempting to steal. The league average was 35 percent, so he has work to do there. Overall, Pierzynski has promise, but needs progression on both offense and defense. **Grade C+**

Marc Pisciotta   Chicago Cubs

Pos: P   **Throws:** Right   **Ht:** 6'5"   **Wt:** 240   **Age:** 27

Yr Team	Lg	G	GS	IP	H	R	ER	HR	BB	SO	SV	W	L	Pct.	ERA
96 Calgary	AAA	57	0	65.2	71	38	30	3	46	46	1	2	7	.222	4.11
97 Iowa	AAA	42	0	45.2	29	12	12	2	23	48	22	6	2	.750	2.36
Chicago	NL	24	0	28.1	20	10	10	1	16	21	0	3	1	.750	3.18
7 Minor League Yrs		310	12	411.0	377	208	155	14	235	358	89	28	29	.491	3.39

Pisciotta did little in the Pirates system for six years, after being drafted in the 19th round in 1991. The Cubs claimed him on waivers after the '96 campaign, after his Arizona Fall League coach had made some mechanical adjustments to his delivery, and *BOOM,* they had themselves a prospect. Pisciotta's velocity increased from 90-91 MPH to 95-96 MPH as a result of the adjustment. This made his slider more effective, and his control improved. He pitched well in his major league term, and should have a middle-relief spot locked up for '98. His story is a perfect example of why pitchers are unpredictable, and why players sometimes dramatically improve when they move to a new team. **Grade B-**

Placido Polanco   St. Louis Cardinals

Pos: 2B   **Bats:** Right   **Ht:** 5'10"   **Wt:** 168   **Age:** 22

Yr Team	Lg	G	AB	R	H	2B	3B	HR	RBI	BB	SO	SB	CS	Avg	OBP	Slg
96 St. Pete	A	137	540	65	157	29	5	0	51	24	34	4	4	.291	.323	.363
97 Arkansas	AA	129	508	71	148	16	3	2	51	29	51	19	5	.291	.331	.346
4 Minor League Yrs		401	1536	196	428	56	12	5	153	78	130	34	17	.279	.316	.340

Placido Polanco is similar to his 1997 double-play mate Luis Ordaz: a young infielder with a quick bat, hits for a good average, not much power, weak strike-zone judgment, good glove reputation. Like Ordaz, whether Polanco develops into a regular or just a good bench guy depends on how his offense comes along. Polanco is faster than Ordaz, and his glove work is more refined at this stage. He led the Texas League in fielding, and he matched it with a very high range factor. Of the two, I think Polanco is more likely to emerge as a regular. **Grade B-**

Cliff Politte
St. Louis Cardinals

Pos: P **Throws:** Right **Ht:** 5'11" **Wt:** 185 **Age:** 24

Yr Team	Lg	G	GS	IP	H	R	ER	HR	BB	SO	SV	W	L	Pct.	ERA
96 Peoria	A	25	25	149.2	108	50	43	8	47	151	0	14	6	.700	2.59
97 Pr William	A	19	19	120.1	89	37	30	11	31	118	0	11	1	.917	2.24
Arkansas	AA	6	6	37.2	35	15	9	3	9	26	0	4	1	.800	2.15
2 Minor League Yrs		50	50	307.2	232	102	82	22	87	295	0	29	8	.784	2.40

St. Louis drafted Cliff Politte in the 54th round in 1995, out of Jefferson Junior College in Missouri. This was a steal; he looks like a terrific prospect. Politte was awesome at Prince William, and, if anything, even more impressive at Arkansas. His ratios in Class A were excellent across the board: K/BB +88 percent, K/IP +11 percent, H/IP +17 percent, all safely above league norms. They did not deteriorate in Double-A very much, a token of success for the future. Politte works with a 90-MPH sinking fastball, curve, slider, and change. He can throw any of his pitches for strikes, and is an intelligent pitcher. He probably needs a full year in the high minors, but if he stays healthy, he should challenge for a major league spot in 1999. **Grade B+**

Sidney Ponson
Baltimore Orioles

Pos: P **Throws:** Right **Ht:** 6'1" **Wt:** 200 **Age:** 21

Yr Team	Lg	G	GS	IP	H	R	ER	HR	BB	SO	SV	W	L	Pct.	ERA
96 Frederick	A	18	16	107.0	98	56	41	6	28	110	0	7	6	.538	3.45
97 Bowie	AA	13	13	74.2	77	51	45	11	32	56	0	2	7	.222	5.42
Orioles	R	1	0	2.0	0	0	0	0	0	1	0	1	0	1.000	0.00
4 Minor League Yrs		57	52	334.1	322	181	146	29	93	276	0	20	19	.513	3.93

Sidney Ponson materialized as a great prospect out of nowhere in 1996, but in 1997 the transporter beam malfunctioned, and he disappeared back into subspace. He got off to a good start in Double-A, with 19 strikeouts in 15 innings, but then his velocity started to fall off, his command wavered, and he ended up on the disabled list with a sore elbow and never came off. When healthy, Ponson has a blistering 93-MPH fastball, sharp breaking stuff, and great control, but if his arm is bad, none of that really matters. Watch health reports on him in 1998; if he is OK, he could rebound quickly, but if he goes under the knife, dump your stock. **Grade C**

Dante Powell
San Francisco Giants

Pos: OF **Bats:** Right **Ht:** 6'2" **Wt:** 185 **Age:** 24

Yr Team	Lg	G	AB	R	H	2B	3B	HR	RBI	BB	SO	SB	CS	Avg	OBP	Slg
96 Shreveport	AA	135	508	92	142	27	2	21	78	72	92	43	23	.280	.371	.465
Phoenix	AAA	2	8	0	2	0	1	0	0	2	3	0	1	.250	.400	.500
97 Phoenix	AAA	108	452	91	109	24	4	11	42	52	105	34	10	.241	.323	.385
San Francisco	NL	27	39	8	12	1	0	1	3	4	11	1	1	.308	.372	.410
4 Minor League Yrs		422	1642	288	431	89	17	47	215	191	379	147	47	.262	.343	.423

I have no idea how to evaluate Dante Powell. His physical tools are exceptional, and at times he flashes wonderful baseball skills, but only at times. For much of last year, he was your standard raw "tools" player, struggling to accomplish anything on the field, at least in

Triple-A. When he played in the majors, he looked great. I would caution the Giants not to get too excited about that. Thirty-nine at-bats means as little as a promise from Bill Clinton. Nevertheless, it is quite possible that Powell could continue to play great in the majors. . . he was terrific all year in 1996. Serious questions have been raised regarding his attitude, although that is supposedly less of a problem now than in the past. I'm going to give him a **Grade B**, but to tell you the truth, that's just a wild guess. He could be Rookie of the Year, or he could hit .220 at Triple-A.

Jeremy Powell

Montreal Expos

Pos: P   **Throws:** Right   **Ht:** 6'5"   **Wt:** 230   **Age:** 21

Yr Team	Lg	G	GS	IP	H	R	ER	HR	BB	SO	SV	W	L	Pct.	ERA
96 Delmarva	A	27	27	157.2	127	68	53	9	66	109	0	12	9	.571	3.03
97 Wst Plm Bch	A	26	26	155.0	162	75	52	3	62	121	0	9	10	.474	3.02
4 Minor League Yrs		78	78	448.1	418	208	162	18	177	319	0	29	26	.527	3.25

Jeremy Powell was drafted in the fourth round in 1994, from Sacramento. He is a big guy, but his fastball isn't overwhelming. He gets hitters out by throwing strikes with a very good curve. Powell's numbers in the Florida State League were okay. His ERA ranked ninth in the circuit, which is good, of course, but his ratios were all right around league average. The biggest point in his favor is durability. His arm eats innings without getting indigestion. As long as he stays healthy, there is a satisfactory chance he adjust to each level and emerge as a good pitcher. **Grade C**

Arquimedez Pozo

Boston Red Sox

Pos: 3B   **Bats:** Right   **Ht:** 5'10"   **Wt:** 160   **Age:** 24

Yr Team	Lg	G	AB	R	H	2B	3B	HR	RBI	BB	SO	SB	CS	Avg	OBP	Slg
96 Tacoma	AAA	95	365	55	102	12	5	15	64	39	40	3	3	.279	.352	.463
Pawtucket	AAA	11	37	6	9	1	0	1	3	3	6	0	0	.243	.333	.351
Boston	AL	21	58	4	10	3	1	1	11	2	10	1	0	.172	.210	.310
97 Pawtucket	AAA	101	377	61	107	18	1	22	70	37	55	4	4	.284	.358	.512
Boston	AL	4	15	0	4	1	0	0	3	0	5	0	0	.267	.250	.333
6 Minor League Yrs		668	2539	417	758	145	23	85	376	233	296	53	41	.299	.361	.474

Say what you will about Red Sox GM Dan Duquette, but he is really good at picking up valuable players that other organizations have given up on. Arquimedez Pozo is another one of these guys, stolen from the Mariners in 1996 because Seattle manager Lou Piniella didn't like him. Pozo clearly has nothing left to prove in Triple-A; his numbers at Pawtucket were good both offensively and defensively, and he is still relatively young. I don't know if he is in the Red Sox' plans or not, and maybe there is something about him that rubs managers the wrong way, but on numbers alone, this guy can play. It is high time somebody gave him a real shot, not 50 at-bats here and there, but a real 450 at-bat season. I doubt they would be disappointed. **Grade B**

Jamey Price
Oakland Athletics

Pos: P **Throws:** Right **Ht:** 6'7" **Wt:** 205 **Age:** 26

Yr Team	Lg	G	GS	IP	H	R	ER	HR	BB	SO	SV	W	L	Pct.	ERA
96 W Michigan	A	20	16	89.1	80	22	17	1	19	88	0	6	1	.857	1.71
97 Huntsville	AA	20	20	110.1	153	71	65	16	38	80	0	9	3	.750	5.30
Edmonton	AAA	2	1	11.0	9	3	2	0	1	10	0	2	0	1.000	1.64
2 Minor League Yrs		42	37	210.2	242	96	84	17	58	178	0	17	4	.810	3.59

Price, a tall pitcher with good stuff and fine control, was awesome at Western Michigan in 1996, but scuffled in Double-A in 1997. His season wasn't as bad as it looked on the surface, as there was an explosion of hitting at Huntsville that drove all the ERAs skyward, but it wasn't good no matter how you look at it. His K/BB was nice at +28 percent, but his other marks were lousy, and he ended the year on the disabled list with a sore shoulder. Price had elbow problems in high school and college, so the shoulder trouble gives him The Golden Matched Set of Injuries, which you too can order from the Franklin Mint. Price has ability if healthy, but that's a big if. **Grade C-**

Eddie Priest
Cincinnati Reds

Pos: P **Throws:** Left **Ht:** 6'1" **Wt:** 200 **Age:** 23

Yr Team	Lg	G	GS	IP	H	R	ER	HR	BB	SO	SV	W	L	Pct.	ERA
96 Winston-Sal	A	4	4	12.1	5	2	1	1	6	9	0	1	0	1.000	0.73
97 Chston-WV	A	14	14	77.0	79	38	31	6	10	70	0	5	3	.625	3.62
Chattanooga	AA	14	14	91.2	101	39	35	7	17	63	0	4	6	.400	3.44
4 Minor League Yrs		57	57	333.0	319	142	118	24	69	284	0	22	18	.550	3.19

Priest was a ninth-round selection in 1994, from Southern Union Junior College in Alabama. He lost almost all of 1996 to shoulder surgery, but returned healthy in 1997 and was excellent at two levels. Priest throws an 89-MPH fastball, a sharp breaking pitch, and a decent changeup. His command and control are admirable, and he is reputed to be bright and coachable. Priest's K/BB ratio in Double-A was extraordinary at +172 percent. His other marks were much less impressive, right around league average. If he is healthy, and if he keeps his command superior as he moves up the ladder, Priest should be very good. No pitcher comes with a guarantee, but Priest could be one of the surprises of 1998. **Grade B-**

Steve Prihoda
Kansas City Royals

Pos: P **Throws:** Left **Ht:** 6'6" **Wt:** 220 **Age:** 25

Yr Team	Lg	G	GS	IP	H	R	ER	HR	BB	SO	SV	W	L	Pct.	ERA
96 Wilmington	A	47	0	79.1	50	17	13	1	22	89	25	6	6	.500	1.47
97 Wichita	AA	70	0	89.0	87	34	32	3	40	68	10	0	3	.000	3.24
3 Minor League Yrs		131	13	237.2	202	87	70	11	80	220	35	7	15	.318	2.65

The true test for finesse pitchers is Double-A, and while Steve Prihoda didn't pass it with flying colors, he did well enough to advance to the next level. Prihoda's fastball is below-average, but he has a good curveball and an exquisite changeup which he'll throw at any point in the count. He also has a bizarre arms-and-legs delivery that perplexes lefthanded hitters. It's as a lefty one-out guy that Prihoda hopes to make his mark. **Grade C**

Kenny Pumphrey
New York Mets

Pos: P   **Throws:** Right   **Ht:** 6'6"   **Wt:** 195   **Age:** 21

Yr Team	Lg	G	GS	IP	H	R	ER	HR	BB	SO	SV	W	L	Pct.	ERA
96 Pittsfield	A	14	14	87.0	68	41	31	1	41	61	0	7	2	.778	3.21
97 Capital City	A	27	27	165.2	137	70	57	11	72	133	0	12	6	.667	3.10
4 Minor League Yrs		63	61	375.1	306	170	139	21	171	312	0	27	14	.659	3.33

Pumphrey was selected in the fourth round in 1994, from a Maryland high school. He is intimidating on the mound at 6-6, and has the elevated velocity on his fastball one expects from a pitcher of that height, but his mechanics are erratic and his control needs work. Those problems are to be expected from a tall pitcher, too. Pumphrey pitched decently at Capital City in 1997, his first full-season exposure, although the park helped his raw stats. His K/BB was well below average at -23 percent, meaning he has a lot of work to do. His career could take any number of directions. **Grade C+**

Mark Quinn
Kansas City Royals

Pos: OF   **Bats:** Right   **Ht:** 6'1"   **Wt:** 185   **Age:** 23

Yr Team	Lg	G	AB	R	H	2B	3B	HR	RBI	BB	SO	SB	CS	Avg	OBP	Slg
96 Lansing	A	113	437	63	132	23	3	9	71	43	54	14	8	.302	.367	.430
97 Wilmington	A	87	299	51	92	22	3	16	71	42	47	3	2	.308	.400	.562
Wichita	AA	26	96	26	36	13	0	2	19	15	19	1	1	.375	.474	.573
3 Minor League Yrs		270	994	168	306	70	8	33	198	115	148	18	12	.308	.386	.494

Looking for a hitter that no one has ever heard of? Try Mark Quinn. Drafted in the 11th round in 1995, out of Rice University, Quinn was downgraded by scouts when he was in college because of his unorthodox batting stance. He stands wide open and sort of lunges toward third as he swings, but he still makes contact, even on pitches away. He has bulked up and is showing power to go with the contact; his OPS was the third-best in the Carolina League, and he was playing in a park that cuts run production by 12 percent. Quinn isn't a great defensive outfielder, and probably never will be, but if he keeps hitting .300 with power, it shouldn't matter. He will have to fight the skeptics because of his stance, but I think Quinn will win the argument in the long run. **Grade B**

Rob Radlosky
Minnesota Twins

Pos: P   **Throws:** Right   **Ht:** 6'2"   **Wt:** 200   **Age:** 24

Yr Team	Lg	G	GS	IP	H	R	ER	HR	BB	SO	SV	W	L	Pct.	ERA
96 Ft. Myers	A	28	16	104.0	116	70	63	11	46	80	1	4	6	.400	5.45
97 Ft. Myers	A	23	22	128.1	87	42	37	10	37	109	0	9	5	.643	2.59
4 Minor League Yrs		92	67	409.1	368	204	175	33	157	343	1	27	23	.540	3.85

Rob Radlosky was drafted in the 22nd round in 1993 out of Central Florida Community College. He has always had a good arm, but his pro career was marred by command problems. He took a major step foward at Fort Myers last year, ranking well in all the categories. His H/IP was particularly good at +31 percent. On the other hand, it was his second year at that level. We need to see him in Double-A. **Grade C**

Ryan Radmanovich   *Minnesota Twins*

Pos: OF   **Bats:** Left   **Ht:** 6'2"   **Wt:** 185   **Age:** 26

Yr Team	Lg	G	AB	R	H	2B	3B	HR	RBI	BB	SO	SB	CS	Avg	OBP	Slg
96 Hardware City	AA	125	453	77	127	31	2	25	86	49	122	4	11	.280	.353	.523
97 Salt Lake	AAA	133	485	92	128	25	4	28	78	67	138	11	4	.264	.355	.505
5 Minor League Yrs		459	1651	283	448	89	17	82	285	200	445	45	32	.271	.355	.495

Ryan Radmanovich emerged as a prospect with a fine 1996 season in Double-A. Moving to Triple-A Salt Lake in 1997, he continued to hit for power, but his batting average fell off substantially, and his strikeout rate climbed into the dangerous range. He has a strong pull swing that could do some damage in the Metrodome, but he needs to improve against breaking pitches, or major league pitchers would carve him up. He swings hard at everything. His OPS was just slightly above league at Salt Lake. His range is acceptable and he has a strong arm, but makes too many errors. Radmanovich needs to take a step forward in 1998, or risk being tagged as a "minor league hitter." **Grade C**

Brady Raggio   *St. Louis Cardinals*

Pos: P   **Throws:** Right   **Ht:** 6'4"   **Wt:** 210   **Age:** 25

Yr Team	Lg	G	GS	IP	H	R	ER	HR	BB	SO	SV	W	L	Pct.	ERA
96 Arkansas	AA	26	24	162.1	160	68	58	17	40	123	0	9	10	.474	3.22
97 Louisville	AAA	22	22	138.0	145	68	64	18	32	91	0	8	11	.421	4.17
St. Louis	NL	15	4	31.1	44	24	24	1	16	21	0	1	2	.333	6.89
5 Minor League Yrs		105	78	539.0	532	237	200	47	112	417	1	33	30	.524	3.34

After a fine 1996 season in the Texas League, Brady Raggio moved up to Louisville, hoping to prove that he was a fine prospect, despite his lack of tremendous velocity. He wasn't awesome in the American Association, but he wasn't terrible, and did well enough that he got the call to the majors when the Cardinals needed a pitcher in midsummer. The 6.89 ERA wasn't what St. Louis manager Tony La Russa and pitching coach Dave Duncan were looking for, but it often takes a while for finesse pitchers to adjust to major league conditions. Raggio's fastball is average, and while his curve and slider don't buckle knees, they are effective when thrown to spots. His changeup is pretty good, too. Raggio's K/BB ratio at Louisville was excellent at +44 percent. He will be a competent major league pitcher if they are patient with him. **Grade C**

Steve Rain   *Chicago Cubs*

Pos: P **Throws:** Right **Ht:** 6'6" **Wt:** 225 **Age:** 22

Yr Team	Lg	G	GS	IP	H	R	ER	HR	BB	SO	SV	W	L	Pct.	ERA
96 Orlando	AA	35	0	38.2	32	15	11	4	12	48	10	1	0	1.000	2.56
Iowa	AAA	26	0	26.0	17	9	9	3	8	23	10	2	1	.667	3.12
97 Iowa	AAA	40	0	44.1	51	30	29	8	34	50	1	7	1	.875	5.89
Orlando	AA	14	0	14.2	16	7	5	2	8	11	4	1	2	.333	3.07
5 Minor League Yrs		192	16	288.0	246	119	98	19	121	282	48	20	12	.625	3.06

Rain was awesome at every level of the minor leagues. . . until he got to Triple-A Iowa in 1997. Although he had been the closer in Des Moines for the last six weeks of 1996, the Cubs brass felt he needed more experience, and returned him to Iowa in a middle-relief role, after he showed up in spring training overweight. Supposedly, there was nothing wrong with his arm last year. . . his velocity was normal (88-90 MPH). His slider and splitter were still sharp enough for him to strike out well over a hitter per inning, which is great, but his command and control were off, and he was frequently roughed up. If he is healthy, and loses the extra poundage, I think he will rebound. **Grade C**

Jason Rakers   *Cleveland Indians*

Pos: P **Throws:** Right **Ht:** 6'2" **Wt:** 197 **Age:** 24

Yr Team	Lg	G	GS	IP	H	R	ER	HR	BB	SO	SV	W	L	Pct.	ERA
96 Columbus	A	14	14	77.1	84	37	31	5	17	64	0	5	4	.556	3.61
97 Kinston	A	17	17	102.2	93	41	35	10	18	105	0	8	5	.615	3.07
Buffalo	AAA	1	1	7.0	5	0	0	0	1	3	0	1	0	1.000	0.00
Akron	AA	7	7	41.0	36	21	20	3	11	31	0	1	4	.200	4.39
3 Minor League Yrs		53	53	303.0	290	126	111	21	71	276	0	19	16	.543	3.30

Rakers was a 25th-round pick in 1995, from New Mexico State University. Few people had mentioned Rakers and the word "prospect" in the same sentence, but he had a great year in 1997. He totally dominated the Carolina League, with a ridiculously good K/BB ratio of +142 percent, did not disgrace himself in Double-A, and closed the season with one good Triple-A start. He is not that big, does not throw that hard, and had trouble staying healthy before last year, but obviously he knows how to pitch. If the Indians need pitching help in 1998, Rakers could get a shot. I'd rather take my chances with him than one of those guys teams always drag out of the trash can, like Mark Davis or Mitch Williams or (groan) Rudy Seanez. **Grade C+**

Matt Raleigh   New York Mets

Pos: 3B-1B **Bats:** Right **Ht:** 5'11" **Wt:** 205 **Age:** 27

Yr Team	Lg	G	AB	R	H	2B	3B	HR	RBI	BB	SO	SB	CS	Avg	OBP	Slg
96 Frederick	A	21	57	8	13	0	1	1	8	12	22	3	0	.228	.370	.316
High Desert	A	27	84	17	24	6	0	7	13	14	33	2	0	.286	.384	.607
Bowie	AA	4	8	0	2	1	0	0	2	1	3	0	0	.250	.333	.375
97 Binghamton	AA	122	398	71	78	15	0	37	74	79	169	0	2	.196	.330	.513
6 Minor League Yrs		508	1648	295	382	82	5	107	284	319	629	34	10	.232	.358	.482

"Extremism in defense of liberty is no vice," said Barry Goldwater, but extremism in pursuit of secondary average is another matter. I fully endorse the concept of secondary average. Some players with low batting averages help their team score runs because of their power, their walks or their speed. Some players with high batting averages don't help their teams because they don't hit for power, don't have patience, or are poor on the bases. I use secondary average to help uncover prospects with a broad base of skills, but I have never seen as bizarre a set of numbers as those posted by Matt Raleigh last year. You don't need me to tell you they are weird. The man hit .196 in Double-A, but his OPS was still above-average at +10 percent, and his SEC was downright outstanding at +80 percent, the best mark in the circuit. It would be interesting, just as an experiment, to see what this guy could do in the majors, to see exactly how far the concept of secondary average can be taken, to see if it is possible to be a productive offensive player while hitting .160. It would also be interesting to combine the DNA of humans and artichokes, but that doesn't mean we should do it. **Grade C-**

Alex Ramirez   Cleveland Indians

Pos: OF **Bats:** Right **Ht:** 5'11" **Wt:** 176 **Age:** 23

Yr Team	Lg	G	AB	R	H	2B	3B	HR	RBI	BB	SO	SB	CS	Avg	OBP	Slg
96 Canton-Akrn	AA	131	513	79	169	28	12	14	85	16	74	18	10	.329	.353	.513
97 Buffalo	AAA	119	416	59	119	19	8	11	44	24	95	10	5	.286	.329	.450
5 Minor League Yrs		573	2190	317	637	112	33	67	308	102	426	63	43	.291	.326	.464

Signed out of Venezuela in 1991, Alex Ramirez doesn't get a lot of attention as a prospect, but he did decently in his first Triple-A exposure and is still pretty young. He is something of a "tweener," in that each of his tools is a bit above-average, but none are outstanding. From the Seven Skill standpoint, he makes contact, has some power, runs decently and has adequate defensive skills, but needs to improve his judgment at the plate to maximize his on-base ability. At this point, Ramirez doesn't have a future as a regular, but he should develop into a useful reserve. He might also get buried at the Triple-A level. **Grade C**

Aramis Ramirez   *Pittsburgh Pirates*

Pos: 3B   **Bats:** Right   **Ht:** 6'1"   **Wt:** 176   **Age:** 19

Yr Team	Lg	G	AB	R	H	2B	3B	HR	RBI	BB	SO	SB	CS	Avg	OBP	Slg
96 Erie	A	61	223	37	68	14	4	9	42	31	41	0	0	.305	.403	.525
Augusta	A	6	20	3	4	1	0	1	2	1	7	0	2	.200	.304	.400
97 Lynchburg	A	137	482	85	134	24	2	29	114	80	103	5	3	.278	.390	.517
2 Minor League Yrs		204	725	125	206	39	6	39	158	112	151	5	5	.284	.392	.516

The Pirates have upgraded their Latin American scouting over the last several years, an effort that yielded Jose Guillen, and now Aramis Ramirez. Signed out of the Dominican in 1994, Ramirez is an exceptionally talented young power hitter. While he doesn't hit for a tremendously good average yet, he has excellent command of the strike zone, given his age and power, and projects as a solid 30-homer guy in the majors, with lots of walks. His OPS was +25 percent last year, near the top of the Carolina League, and he was the youngest player in the circuit. He isn't fast, but who cares? With the glove, Ramirez demonstrates above-average range and a very strong arm, but makes his share of errors, primarily due to inexperience. He is young, and is said to be arrogant at times, but he certainly has time to outgrow that. Ramirez needs to refine his fielding, and prove that his attitude isn't a serious problem, but unless he gets injured or suddenly loses the strike zone, I don't see how he can fail to be a star. **Grade A**

Daniel Ramirez   *New York Mets*

Pos: OF   **Bats:** Right   **Ht:** 6'0"   **Wt:** 175   **Age:** 24

Yr Team	Lg	G	AB	R	H	2B	3B	HR	RBI	BB	SO	SB	CS	Avg	OBP	Slg
96 Capital City	A	47	143	20	33	5	0	1	13	11	30	6	4	.231	.290	.287
Pittsfield	A	70	260	28	73	5	5	1	22	14	45	24	9	.281	.325	.350
97 Capital City	A	130	478	82	146	24	4	1	42	44	104	51	25	.305	.367	.379
4 Minor League Yrs		353	1283	186	358	50	13	5	138	95	246	109	53	.279	.334	.350

Daniel Ramirez has quick feet to go with his quick bat. A Dominican, Ramirez needs to improve his command of the strike zone. If he does that, he should continue to hit for average as he moves up, and might develop some power. His defense in center is pretty good, although he isn't likely to win any awards for it. Ramirez was old for the league, and needs to advance quickly to avoid getting submerged as a career minor leaguer. **Grade C**

Julio Ramirez   *Florida Marlins*

Pos: OF   **Bats:** Right   **Ht:** 5'11"   **Wt:** 160   **Age:** 20

Yr Team	Lg	G	AB	R	H	2B	3B	HR	RBI	BB	SO	SB	CS	Avg	OBP	Slg
96 Brevard Cty	A	17	61	11	15	0	1	0	2	4	18	2	3	.246	.288	.279
Marlins	R	42	171	33	49	5	3	0	15	14	34	25	8	.287	.351	.351
97 Kane County	A	99	376	70	96	18	7	14	53	37	122	41	6	.255	.329	.452
3 Minor League Yrs		206	812	149	218	32	15	16	83	68	216	85	23	.268	.331	.404

Julio Ramirez is a youthful raw tools outfielder, signed by the Marlins out of the Dominican Republic in 1994. He showed glimmers of power and speed at Kane County in the Midwest League last year, and his OPS was acceptable at plus-eight percent. To drive his production numbers higher, he needs to be more selective at the plate. It seems like I write that about half the people in the book each year, but that doesn't make it any less true. Ramirez has very good range in center field, and his arm is quite strong. If he learns more about hitting and gets a bit stronger, Ramirez could emerge as a top prospect within the next year or so. **Grade C+**

Scott Randall   *Colorado Rockies*

Pos: P   **Throws:** Right   **Ht:** 6'3"   **Wt:** 178   **Age:** 22

Yr Team	Lg	G	GS	IP	H	R	ER	HR	BB	SO	SV	W	L	Pct.	ERA
96 Asheville	A	24	24	154.1	121	53	47	11	50	136	0	14	4	.778	2.74
97 Salem	A	27	26	176.0	167	93	75	8	66	128	0	9	10	.474	3.84
3 Minor League Yrs		66	65	425.1	364	181	143	21	144	342	0	30	17	.638	3.03

From last year's comment about Scott Randall: "I'm intrigued by Randall, and like his chances to succeed in the future if he stays healthy." I could repeat that verbatim this year (which I guess I just did). Randall does not have an overpowering fastball, but it does have movement, and he isn't afraid to throw it inside. His curve and change are very good, and he is a smart, intense adversary on the mound. He threw a no-hitter in 1996, and six innings of a combined one in 1997. Randall was bothered by a nasty viral illness, which sapped his strength and vitality early last year. He still has projection in his body, and if his velocity picks up a bit, he could surprise. **Grade C+**

Fred Rath   *Minnesota Twins*

Pos: P   **Throws:** Right   **Ht:** 6'3"   **Wt:** 205   **Age:** 25

Yr Team	Lg	G	GS	IP	H	R	ER	HR	BB	SO	SV	W	L	Pct.	ERA
96 Ft. Wayne	A	32	0	41.2	26	12	7	1	10	63	14	1	2	.333	1.51
Ft. Myers	A	22	0	29.0	25	10	9	1	10	29	4	2	5	.286	2.79
97 Ft. Myers	A	17	0	22.0	18	4	4	2	3	22	2	4	0	1.000	1.64
New Britain	AA	33	0	50.1	43	17	15	1	13	33	12	3	3	.500	2.68
Salt Lake	AAA	10	0	11.0	11	2	2	1	2	11	3	0	1	.000	1.64
3 Minor League Yrs		141	0	187.1	143	53	42	8	49	208	47	11	12	.478	2.02

Fred Rath is finally getting some respect. He came into pro ball as an undrafted free agent in 1995, from the University of South Florida. He got a chance to close games in 1996 and excelled, then continued his progress in 1997, pitching well at three levels. He will have a shot at the major league bullpen in 1998. Rath is a big guy who throws hard, unlike most minor league closers. He has a 90-MPH sinking fastball, a pretty decent slider, and good control. His stats were excellent at three levels. Despite his success, some scouts still don't like him very much. I'm not sure why; the numbers are great, and he isn't a soft tosser. I would be willing to take a chance on him in middle relief. **Grade B-**

Gary Rath
Los Angeles Dodgers
Pos: P **Throws:** Left **Ht:** 6'2" **Wt:** 185 **Age:** 25

Yr Team	Lg	G	GS	IP	H	R	ER	HR	BB	SO	SV	W	L	Pct.	ERA
96 Albuquerque	AAA	30	30	180.1	177	97	84	13	89	125	0	10	11	.476	4.19
97 Albuquerque	AAA	24	24	132.1	177	107	89	17	49	100	0	7	11	.389	6.05
4 Minor League Yrs		93	91	531.1	551	303	250	43	229	379	0	38	36	.514	4.23

A year ago, after his good season at Albuquerque, it looked like Gary Rath would be the first lefty to start a game for the Dodgers since Bobby Ojeda. Remember, that's the Pacific Coast League, and a 4.19 ERA there is very, very good. Last year was another story; Rath got his brains beat in, and was left in the prospect dust by fellow farmhand Dennis Reyes. Rath's best pitch is a curveball. He also uses a good change and a mediocre fastball. He is the kind of guy who can get crushed if his command is off, especially in the high-powered hitting environment of the PCL. If Rath is healthy, I think he is a good candidate to rebound, especially if he gets away from the Dodgers organization and can regain his bearings in a less hostile Triple-A environment. **Grade C**

Mark Redman
Minnesota Twins
Pos: P **Throws:** Left **Ht:** 6'5" **Wt:** 220 **Age:** 24

Yr Team	Lg	G	GS	IP	H	R	ER	HR	BB	SO	SV	W	L	Pct.	ERA
96 Ft. Myers	A	13	13	82.2	63	24	17	1	34	75	0	3	4	.429	1.85
Hardware City	AA	16	16	106.1	101	51	45	5	50	96	0	7	7	.500	3.81
Salt Lake	AAA	1	1	4.0	7	4	4	1	2	4	0	0	0	—	9.00
97 Salt Lake	AAA	29	28	158.1	204	123	111	19	80	125	1	8	15	.348	6.31
3 Minor League Yrs		67	63	384.0	403	215	187	30	179	326	1	20	27	.426	4.38

Mark Redman was Minnesota's first-round pick in 1995, from the University of Oklahoma. He entered 1997 with a chance to make the major league rotation midway through the season, but he came down with Pacific Coast League Syndrome, which strikes one out of every three Triple-A pitchers. The effects of this illness on statistics can be devastating. Redman's ERA was high even by PCL standards, and his H/IP and K/BB ratios were below average. His K/IP was slightly above, so the season wasn't a complete washout. According to one scout I talked with, the velocity on Redman's fastball has dropped from average to below average over the last two years. His changeup remains effective, but his curve is inconsistent, and he nibbles too much with the fastball. That's deadly in the PCL, and would get him killed in the majors, too. He does have a good move to first base, and is impressive at holding runners. Redman has a reputation as an intelligent person, so he probably has the ability to adjust to his loss of velocity and his difficult pitching environment, given time. **Grade C**

Jason Regan

Seattle Mariners

Pos: 2B **Bats:** Right **Ht:** 5'10" **Wt:** 170 **Age:** 21

Yr Team	Lg	G	AB	R	H	2B	3B	HR	RBI	BB	SO	SB	CS	Avg	OBP	Slg
96 Everett	A	40	124	17	26	11	0	3	22	25	47	3	3	.210	.355	.371
97 Wisconsin	A	51	177	31	45	14	1	9	23	23	55	2	0	.254	.348	.497
Lancaster	A	69	260	50	73	20	2	22	54	45	79	2	2	.281	.399	.627
2 Minor League Yrs		160	561	98	144	45	3	34	99	93	181	7	5	.257	.373	.529

Regan was a 51st-round pick in 1996, out of Blinn (Texas) Junior College, a good base-ball school. His full-season debut was a stunning success, especially after his promotion to Lancaster. He strikes out a bit too much for an infielder, but he draws a lot of walks, and it looks like he might have a little power. . . just kidding. It looks like he might have *a lot* of power: his OPS was +25 percent in the California League. There is reason for caution; he did much of the damage at hitter-friendly Lancaster, and scouts question how much power he will carry to the higher levels. Regan is a reliable defensive player with a strong arm, but his range, even at second base, is limited. It is hard to argue with 22 homers in half a season, especially from a second baseman, but to be honest, I want to see more. Look closely at what he does in Double-A; if the power production continues, he could arrive quickly. **Grade B-**

Desi Relaford

Philadelphia Phillies

Pos: SS **Bats:** Both **Ht:** 5'8" **Wt:** 155 **Age:** 24

Yr Team	Lg	G	AB	R	H	2B	3B	HR	RBI	BB	SO	SB	CS	Avg	OBP	Slg
96 Tacoma	AAA	93	317	27	65	12	0	4	32	23	58	10	6	.205	.259	.281
Scranton-WB	AAA	21	85	12	20	4	1	1	11	8	19	7	1	.235	.305	.341
Philadelphia	NL	15	40	2	7	2	0	0	1	3	9	1	0	.175	.233	.225
97 Scranton-WB	AAA	131	517	82	138	34	4	9	53	43	77	29	8	.267	.329	.400
Philadelphia	NL	15	38	3	7	1	2	0	6	5	6	3	0	.184	.279	.316
7 Minor League Yrs		810	2981	449	750	141	24	42	299	339	557	172	53	.252	.329	.357

Relaford will get a chance to start in Philadelphia with Kevin Stocker traded, but I'm not wild about him. He does make contact at the plate, and occasionally shows doubles power, but his hitting has been very inconsistent throughout his career. He could hit anywhere from .220 to .280 in a major league season. His glove work is like his hitting: occasionally very good, but erratic. He's flashy, but often boots the easy play. He is still fairly young, and his number could come up, but I myself intend to avoid Relaford Roulette. **Grade C**

Dennis Reyes

Los Angeles Dodgers

Pos: P **Throws:** Left **Ht:** 6'3" **Wt:** 220 **Age:** 20

Yr Team	Lg	G	GS	IP	H	R	ER	HR	BB	SO	SV	W	L	Pct.	ERA
96 San Berndno	A	29	28	166.0	166	106	77	11	77	176	0	11	12	.478	4.17
97 San Antonio	AA	12	12	80.1	79	33	27	6	28	66	0	8	1	.889	3.02
Albuquerque	AAA	10	10	57.1	70	40	36	4	33	45	0	6	3	.667	5.65
Los Angeles	NL	14	5	47.0	51	21	20	4	18	36	0	2	3	.400	3.83
4 Minor League Yrs		77	70	422.0	452	255	201	27	187	391	0	35	21	.625	4.29

When I asked frequent Texas League spectators who the best pitcher they saw in 1997 was, the name literally mentioned every time was "Dennis Reyes," even though he only spent half the season at San Antonio. Reyes looks like a clone of Fernando Valenzuela. . . their facial features are very similar, as is their style of pitching. This is not coincidental; Reyes, a Mexican, idolized Valenzuela as a youngster and patterns his pitching after him, although he doesn't throw a screwball. He works with an 89-90 MPH fastball, an excellent curve, and a changeup that mortifies most hitters when thrown correctly, which it usually is. Reyes was born with one leg shorter than the other, so he has difficulty running, and it will be interesting to see how he handles bunts and infield plays in the majors. His fielding numbers weren't too good last year, although the sample is small. His move to first is passable. Basically, I think Reyes is an excellent prospect, but the Dodgers need to handle him correctly. He might have a better chance to develop as a spot starter/long reliever in the majors, than as rotation fodder in the Pacific Coast League. **Grade B+**

Chris Richard   St. Louis Cardinals

Pos: 1B   **Bats:** Left   **Ht:** 6'2"   **Wt:** 185   **Age:** 23

Yr Team	Lg	G	AB	R	H	2B	3B	HR	RBI	BB	SO	SB	CS	Avg	OBP	Slg
96 St. Pete	A	129	460	65	130	28	6	14	82	57	50	7	3	.283	.369	.461
97 Arkansas	AA	113	390	62	105	24	3	11	58	60	59	6	4	.269	.371	.431
3 Minor League Yrs		317	1134	163	315	66	12	28	183	164	140	19	13	.278	.376	.431

Chris Richard first caught my eye when he played for Oklahoma State; the Cardinals drafted him in the 19th round in 1995. He has very good command of the strike zone and a short, sharp swing, but his OPS at Arkansas was only three percent above average, not acceptable for a corner player. He missed several weeks with a severe groin pull, and that may have hurt his numbers. Richard is an excellent defensive first baseman, for what that is worth. I still think he could break out, but I'm probably prejudiced because I liked him in college. **Grade C**

Brian Richardson   Los Angeles Dodgers

Pos: 3B   **Bats:** Right   **Ht:** 6'2"   **Wt:** 190   **Age:** 22

Yr Team	Lg	G	AB	R	H	2B	3B	HR	RBI	BB	SO	SB	CS	Avg	OBP	Slg
96 San Antonio	AA	19	62	10	20	1	1	0	7	2	10	0	2	.323	.364	.371
Albuquerque	AAA	105	355	52	87	17	2	9	43	32	89	4	1	.245	.310	.380
97 San Antonio	AA	133	484	73	144	23	13	13	90	42	97	3	6	.298	.360	.479
6 Minor League Yrs		564	1981	265	522	91	20	39	273	175	489	43	31	.264	.328	.389

He has no future with the Dodgers behind Paul Konerko and Adrian Beltre, but Brian Richardson should have some value to someone. Drafted in the seventh round in 1992, Richardson, whose father played for the NFL's Raiders, is an excellent athlete who is showing signs of developing baseball skills. His season at San Antonio was decent, with an OPS of plus-eight percent, which isn't too bad in that park. He is developing power, and his command of the strike zone is slowly improving. On the other hand, he played Triple-A in 1996, so he should have done well in the Texas League, but then again, he is still very young, and the improvement could be genuine. His glove is quite good: he led the Texas League in fielding, and he has the quick reactions scouts like in a corner player. I am naturally suspicious of tools players, and Richardson still has work to do, but I am optimistic about his chances to have a career. It won't happen in Los Angeles, though. **Grade B-**

Ray Ricken   New York Yankees

Pos: P   **Throws:** Right   **Ht:** 6'5"   **Wt:** 225   **Age:** 24

Yr Team	Lg	G	GS	IP	H	R	ER	HR	BB	SO	SV	W	L	Pct.	ERA
96 Norwich	AA	8	8	46.1	42	26	23	7	20	42	0	5	2	.714	4.47
Columbus	AAA	20	11	68.0	62	44	36	4	37	58	1	4	5	.444	4.76
97 Norwich	AA	2	2	10.2	12	8	8	0	5	13	0	0	2	.000	6.75
Columbus	AAA	26	26	152.2	172	104	94	12	81	99	0	11	7	.611	5.54
4 Minor League Yrs		100	91	546.0	493	286	244	32	239	464	1	33	29	.532	4.02

Ricken was a great prospect after his rapid advancement following his entry into pro ball in 1994, but he has stalled at Columbus and is more suspect than prospect nowadays. The things that drew attention to him are still there, although in muted form. He still has a 90-MPH fastball, but he has never refined his breaking stuff and when his control totters, he gets beat up. He is durable and stays healthy, but that only gets you so far. I still believe Ricken will turn it around eventually, but to be honest there isn't an objective reason for me to think so. If it does happen, it won't be for the Yankees. **Grade C-**

Adam Riggs   Los Angeles Dodgers

Pos: 2B   **Bats:** Right   **Ht:** 6'0"   **Wt:** 190   **Age:** 25

Yr Team	Lg	G	AB	R	H	2B	3B	HR	RBI	BB	SO	SB	CS	Avg	OBP	Slg
96 San Antonio	AA	134	506	68	143	31	6	14	66	37	82	16	6	.283	.339	.451
97 Albuquerque	AAA	57	227	59	69	8	3	13	28	29	39	12	2	.304	.390	.537
Los Angeles	NL	9	20	3	4	1	0	0	1	4	3	1	0	.200	.333	.250
4 Minor League Yrs		391	1516	294	483	99	17	56	244	156	253	78	26	.319	.389	.517

Wilton Guerrero's failure to turn a double play more than once a week gave Adam Riggs his chance in the Show last year. He lost it when Eric Young was acquired, but Riggs should be back at some point. While he will not be a major offensive force, he is a good offensive player for a middle infielder, with power to the gaps and reasonable strike-zone judgment. His OPS was good at +12 percent, although Albuquerque boosted his stats. Riggs' glove work was a serious question a couple of years ago, but he has worked hard and has developed into a solid defensive player. His range factor was above-average for the Pacific Coast League, he didn't make tons of errors, and he can turn the double play. Riggs is not an outstanding talent, but he is a useful one, and is a better player than most utility infielders. **Grade C+**

Armando Rios

San Francisco Giants

Pos: OF **Bats:** Left **Ht:** 5'9" **Wt:** 178 **Age:** 26

Yr Team	Lg	G	AB	R	H	2B	3B	HR	RBI	BB	SO	SB	CS	Avg	OBP	Slg
96 Shreveport	AA	92	329	62	93	22	2	12	49	44	42	9	9	.283	.365	.471
97 Shreveport	AA	127	461	86	133	30	6	14	79	63	85	17	7	.289	.370	.471
4 Minor League Yrs		466	1685	291	489	109	15	42	263	240	271	93	38	.290	.376	.447

Armando Rios is a potential steal for any team willing to take a chance on a guy that scouts downplay due to his lack of overwhelming physical talent. Sure, he's not Barry Bonds, but he's not Mike Kelly, either. Athleticism does *not* equal baseball success. Rios may not be the best athlete around, but he knows how to play baseball. He has some power, he has some speed, he will take a walk, he hustles his butt off, and he is a good defensive outfielder with a laser-accurate arm. Rios would make an excellent fourth outfielder. Oh, sure, he's never proven himself in Triple-A. . . but he has never had a chance in Triple-A. They gotta save that roster space for Kevin Roberson, you know. **Grade C+**

Danny Rios

New York Yankees

Pos: P **Throws:** Right **Ht:** 6'2" **Wt:** 208 **Age:** 25

Yr Team	Lg	G	GS	IP	H	R	ER	HR	BB	SO	SV	W	L	Pct.	ERA
96 Norwich	AA	38	0	43.0	34	14	10	0	21	38	17	3	1	.750	2.09
Columbus	AAA	24	0	27.2	22	7	6	1	6	22	0	4	1	.800	1.95
97 Columbus	AAA	58	0	84.2	73	37	29	8	31	53	3	7	4	.636	3.08
New York	AL	2	0	2.1	9	5	5	3	2	1	0	0	0	—	19.29
5 Minor League Yrs		247	0	312.2	268	106	79	11	111	261	69	19	13	.594	2.27

Rios established himself as a prospect with an excellent 1996 campaign, and while he wasn't as dominating in his first full Triple-A season, he was still good. Rios works with a 90-MPH fastball and hard slider. He doesn't change speeds that well, but as a reliever he doesn't have to, as long as he throws strikes. Although Rios closed games in the lower minors, he pitched middle relief at Columbus, and that is where his future lies, since he has no chance to close games for the Yankees, unless Mariano Rivera falls out of an airplane or something. Rios needs to sharpen his control a little more, but I like his chances to have a career. **Grade C+**

Luis Rivas

Minnesota Twins

Pos: SS **Bats:** Right **Ht:** 5'10" **Wt:** 155 **Age:** 18

Yr Team	Lg	G	AB	R	H	2B	3B	HR	RBI	BB	SO	SB	CS	Avg	OBP	Slg
96 Twins	R	53	201	29	52	12	1	1	13	18	37	35	10	.259	.320	.343
97 Ft. Wayne	A	121	419	61	100	20	6	1	30	33	90	28	18	.239	.301	.322
2 Minor League Yrs		174	620	90	152	32	7	2	43	51	127	63	28	.245	.307	.329

Venezuelan shortstop Luis Rivas is one of the most interesting prospects in the book. On the one hand, Rivas' statistical performance wasn't hot last year, as he ranked below average in both OPS and SEC. His defense is promising but unrefined. On the other hand, he is incredibly young. His official birth date is August 30th, 1979, which would mean that he played a full season in the Midwest League at age 17. The fact that he didn't look completely foolish playing against guys five or six years older than he is means that he has co-lossal growth potential. Suspicious of his birth certificate? Don't be. There are rumors that the date is wrong, but they are the opposite of the gossip you normally hear: insiders whis-per that Rivas may actually be *younger* than listed, because he wouldn't have been al-lowed to sign if the Twins admitted how old he actually is. I don't know if that is true or not, but I will tell you this: anybody who can play full-season professional baseball even halfway decently before he is old enough to vote is a potential superstar. There are lots of things that can go wrong for Rivas, and lots of things that can go right. Whatever grade I give him risks looking ridiculous in the future. Right now, I will give him a **Grade B**, but keep in mind that that could change dramatically, for good or ill, in the next year or two.

Luis Rivera   *Atlanta Braves*

Pos: P   **Throws:** Right   **Ht:** 6'2"   **Wt:** 145   **Age:** 19

Yr Team	Lg	G	GS	IP	H	R	ER	HR	BB	SO	SV	W	L	Pct.	ERA
96 Braves	R	8	6	24.1	18	9	7	0	7	26	0	1	1	.500	2.59
97 Danville	R	9	9	41.0	28	15	11	2	17	57	0	3	1	.750	2.41
Macon	A	4	4	21.0	13	4	3	1	7	27	0	2	0	1.000	1.29
2 Minor League Yrs		21	19	86.1	59	28	21	3	31	110	0	6	2	.750	2.19

He spent most of his time pitching in the Rookie-level Appalachian League, so I won't give him a letter grade, but Mexican righthander Luis Rivera is someone to watch for in 1998. Look at his terrific K/BB ratios, his yet-to-fill-out frame, and his 93-MPH fastball, and you see a top prospect in the making. Scrutinize this guy attentively; he may be at the top of the prospect lists next year.

Ruben Rivera   *San Diego Padres*

Pos: OF   **Bats:** Right   **Ht:** 6'3"   **Wt:** 190   **Age:** 24

Yr Team	Lg	G	AB	R	H	2B	3B	HR	RBI	BB	SO	SB	CS	Avg	OBP	Slg
96 Columbus	AAA	101	362	59	85	20	4	10	46	40	96	15	10	.235	.324	.395
New York	AL	46	88	17	25	6	1	2	16	13	26	6	2	.284	.381	.443
97 Rancho Cuca	A	6	23	6	4	1	0	1	3	3	9	1	0	.174	.259	.348
Las Vegas	AAA	12	48	6	12	5	1	1	6	1	20	1	0	.250	.280	.458
San Diego	NL	17	20	2	5	1	0	0	1	2	9	2	1	.250	.318	.300
6 Minor League Yrs		485	1790	340	481	95	30	83	297	236	542	121	43	.269	.366	.494

Ruben Rivera was the centerpiece of the trade that sent Hideki Irabu from San Diego to New York. The young Panamanian outfielder spent most of the season recovering from shoulder surgery, so his statistical performance at Vegas and San Diego tells us nothing. Based on what he did in the past, he is still a fine prospect, and the word from San Diego is that he should start every day in 1998. When healthy, Rivera shows excellent power, very good speed, and solid defense. His command of the strike zone is occasionally un-even, especially last year at Las Vegas when he was trying too hard to make up for lost time, but his walk rates have been high in the past, and he should be fine in the long run. If Rivera plays, he could hit anywhere from .260-.290, with 20-30 homers, 15-20 steals, and the potential to get much, much better. **Grade B+**

J.P. Roberge
Los Angeles Dodgers

Pos: OF **Bats:** Right **Ht:** 6'0" **Wt:** 180 **Age:** 25

Yr Team	Lg	G	AB	R	H	2B	3B	HR	RBI	BB	SO	SB	CS	Avg	OBP	Slg
96 San Berndno	A	12	44	8	16	3	1	1	6	3	9	1	2	.364	.420	.545
San Antonio	AA	62	232	28	68	14	2	6	27	14	39	9	3	.293	.336	.448
Albuquerque	AAA	53	156	17	50	6	1	4	17	14	28	3	0	.321	.380	.449
97 San Antonio	AA	134	516	94	166	26	4	17	105	39	70	18	9	.322	.374	.486
4 Minor League Yrs		447	1671	296	514	89	10	46	256	124	235	86	27	.308	.361	.455

J. P. Roberge was a successful college hitter at Southern Cal, but as a righthanded-hitting first baseman, his tools had to be exceptional for him to be a high draft, and since they aren't, he lasted until the 18th round in 1994. He had a prosperous season at San Antonio, with a +11 OPS, while ranking 10th in the league in hitting. He has a nice-looking swing, usually makes contact, and has some punch to all fields. His defense at both first base and the outfield is adequate, though not outstanding. Roberge will never be a regular, but he can hit some, and could help some teams as a bench player. **Grade C**

Grant Roberts
New York Mets

Pos: P **Throws:** Right **Ht:** 6'3" **Wt:** 187 **Age:** 20

Yr Team	Lg	G	GS	IP	H	R	ER	HR	BB	SO	SV	W	L	Pct.	ERA
96 Kingsport	R	13	13	68.2	43	18	16	3	37	92	0	9	1	.900	2.10
97 Capital City	A	22	22	129.2	98	37	34	1	44	122	0	11	3	.786	2.36
3 Minor League Yrs		46	38	227.2	160	68	57	5	95	238	0	22	5	.815	2.25

Roberts was an 11th-round pick in 1995, from a California high school. He was projectable, but no one expected him to develop so rapidly. He is now one of the better pitching prospects in baseball. Roberts works with a 93-MPH fastball, a superb curveball, a decent cut fastball, and has made strides with a change. He can throw strikes with any of his pitches at any point in the count, and is said to be very bright and coachable. There were no holes in his Capital City numbers: K/BB +18 percent, K/IP +10 percent, H/IP +25 percent, all comfortably above league norms, although the K ratios weren't as outstanding as the H/IP number. He is an excellent fielder, and does well for a righthander at holding runners. Roberts needs innings, experience, and health. . . he's already had some elbow problems, resulting in minor surgery. While the Wilson/Pulsipher/Isringhausen catastrophe should teach the Mets not to appoint any young pitcher as a savior, the foundation for a great career is here. **Grade B+**

Kerry Robinson
Tampa Bay Devil Rays

Pos: OF **Bats:** Left **Ht:** 6'0" **Wt:** 175 **Age:** 24

Yr Team	Lg	G	AB	R	H	2B	3B	HR	RBI	BB	SO	SB	CS	Avg	OBP	Slg
96 Peoria	A	123	440	98	158	17	14	2	47	51	51	50	26	.359	.422	.475
97 Arkansas	AA	136	523	80	168	16	3	2	62	54	64	40	23	.321	.386	.375
Louisville	AAA	2	9	0	1	0	0	0	0	0	1	0	0	.111	.111	.111
3 Minor League Yrs		321	1222	222	401	45	25	5	135	121	146	104	59	.328	.388	.418

When I asked Texas League observers who the best hitter they saw all year was, no one mentioned Kerry Robinson right off the bat. Other names, Fernando Tatis, for example, came to mind first, but eventually most people said something like "Oh, yeah, that Kerry Robinson guy looks good, too." Robinson was a 34th-round pick in 1995, an afterthought really, a roster filler. He is more than that now. He has a truly smooth swing, and makes contact against all kinds of pitching with regularity. He does not have great power, however, and may have problems driving the ball in the majors. Robinson has good speed and is very aggressive on the bases, perhaps overly so. He gets caught stealing a lot. His defense isn't special, so he has to keep hitting .330 if he wants to be a regular. It is more likely that he will settle in as a .290-.300 hitter at the higher levels, and since he lacks power and defense, that may relegate him to a reserve role. The Devil Rays got him in the expansion draft. **Grade B-**

Juan Rodriguez   *Anaheim Angels*

Pos: OF   **Bats:** Both   **Ht:** 5'10"   **Wt:** 185   **Age:** 23

Yr Team	Lg	G	AB	R	H	2B	3B	HR	RBI	BB	SO	SB	CS	Avg	OBP	Slg
96 Cedar Rapds	A	8	25	3	6	0	1	0	3	1	6	2	1	.240	.269	.320
Boise	A	52	192	24	57	9	0	2	28	12	52	3	3	.297	.332	.375
97 Cedar Rapds	A	111	416	66	117	18	8	12	55	43	106	11	12	.281	.348	.450
3 Minor League Yrs		225	848	120	244	35	17	15	117	63	213	20	23	.288	.337	.422

Juan Rodriguez is a short Puerto Rican outfielder. He has some pop in his bat and some speed in his legs, but his career has been held back by poor strike-zone judgment. He did decently in his first full-season exposure in 1997, posting an OPS of +11 percent, but he still has quite a bit of work to do learning how to hit, and he isn't that young. Rodriguez does have pretty good range in center. Overall, he is just a name for now, but the Angels system isn't exactly loaded with talent, so if something clicks he could advance rapidly. **Grade C-**

Larry Rodriguez   *Arizona Diamondbacks*

Pos: P   **Throws:** Right   **Ht:** 6'2"   **Wt:** 195   **Age:** 23

Yr Team	Lg	G	GS	IP	H	R	ER	HR	BB	SO	SV	W	L	Pct.	ERA
96 Visalia	A	13	10	56.2	72	49	33	8	19	37	0	2	5	.286	5.24
Lethbridge	R	10	10	54.0	56	31	23	1	9	46	0	7	1	.875	3.83
97 South Bend	A	19	19	104.1	102	56	42	6	37	72	0	4	11	.267	3.62
2 Minor League Yrs		42	39	215.0	230	136	98	15	65	155	0	13	17	.433	4.10

Rodriguez defected from Cuba, along with fellow Diamondback prospect Vladimir Nunez, in 1996. The two are often paired together, but their careers are liable to take different paths. They are pitchers, after all. Rodriguez doesn't throw as hard as Nunez; his fastball hits 90 MPH and he has a good slider, but he doesn't blow the radar guns away. He pitched decently in the Midwest League last year, but wasn't exactly dominant. Rodriguez needs good command within the strike zone to succeed, and is more like Osvaldo Fernandez than Livan Hernandez. **Grade C**

Nerio Rodriguez
Baltimore Orioles

Pos: P Throws: Right Ht: 6'1" Wt: 195 Age: 25

Yr Team	Lg	G	GS	IP	H	R	ER	HR	BB	SO	SV	W	L	Pct.	ERA
96 Frederick	A	24	17	111.1	83	42	28	10	40	114	2	8	7	.533	2.26
Rochester	AAA	2	2	15.0	10	3	3	0	2	6	0	1	0	1.000	1.80
Baltimore	AL	8	1	16.2	18	11	8	2	7	12	0	0	1	.000	4.32
97 Rochester	AAA	27	27	168.1	124	82	73	23	62	160	0	11	10	.524	3.90
Baltimore	AL	6	2	22.0	21	15	12	2	8	11	0	2	1	.667	4.91
3 Minor League Yrs		60	46	304.2	225	129	106	33	111	290	2	20	17	.541	3.13

Nerio Rodriguez began his career as a catcher, but he didn't hit, so the Orioles converted him to the mound in a last-ditch effort to save his career. The results have been spectacular. He was expected to spend 1997 in Double-A, but was so impressive in spring camp that they decided to start him in Triple-A, and he pitched fine. He led the International League in strikeouts, and had an excellent set of ratios: K/BB +34 percent, K/IP +20 percent, H/IP +26 percent, all safely above league norms. Rodriguez works with a 93-MPH moving fastball, a sharp slider, and reliable control. His changeup isn't good yet, but he didn't need it much last year. His mechanics are remarkably smooth given his lack of experience. There is talk that he may convert to bullpen work if he can't develop a better offspeed pitch. Expect him to be a fine pitcher in any role, if he stays healthy. **Grade B+**

Nate Rolison
Florida Marlins

Pos: 1B Bats: Left Ht: 6'5" Wt: 225 Age: 21

Yr Team	Lg	G	AB	R	H	2B	3B	HR	RBI	BB	SO	SB	CS	Avg	OBP	Slg
96 Kane County	A	131	474	63	115	28	1	14	75	66	170	3	3	.243	.345	.395
97 Brevard Cty	A	122	473	59	121	22	0	16	65	38	143	3	1	.256	.313	.404
3 Minor League Yrs		290	1081	144	273	60	3	31	159	119	347	6	4	.253	.336	.400

No one questions Rolison's power potential. He has as much raw strength as any hitter in the minor leagues, but the fact that he is so big means his strike zone is very large, and so far he has had difficulty managing it. He is susceptible to all varieties of breaking pitches, as well as hard stuff inside that doesn't allow him to extend his arms. His OPS was only league average last year, although he was young for the Florida State League. The natural ability is here, but the refinement isn't yet. **Grade C**

Jimmy Rollins
Philadelphia Phillies

Pos: SS Bats: Both Ht: 5'9" Wt: 165 Age: 19

Yr Team	Lg	G	AB	R	H	2B	3B	HR	RBI	BB	SO	SB	CS	Avg	OBP	Slg
96 Martinsvle	R	49	172	22	41	3	1	1	16	28	20	11	5	.238	.351	.285
97 Piedmont	A	139	560	94	151	22	8	6	59	52	80	46	6	.270	.330	.370
2 Minor League Yrs		188	732	116	192	25	9	7	75	80	100	57	11	.262	.335	.350

Rollins was the Phillies' second-round pick in 1996, from a California high school. He is a very small guy, but works the count well, gets on base, and has great speed on the bases. He was one of the youngest regulars in the South Atlantic League last year, and wasn't overshadowed by the older competition; managers named him as the league's No. 10 prospect in the *Baseball America* poll. Rollins' glove is excellent: he led the league in fielding, and had a good range factor. We need to see if he can hit at higher levels; his glove and baserunning look great. **Grade C+**

Damian Rolls

Los Angeles Dodgers

Pos: 3B **Bats:** Right **Ht:** 6'2" **Wt:** 205 **Age:** 20

Yr Team	Lg	G	AB	R	H	2B	3B	HR	RBI	BB	SO	SB	CS	Avg	OBP	Slg
96 Yakima	A	66	257	31	68	11	1	4	27	7	46	8	3	.265	.291	.362
97 Savannah	A	130	475	57	100	17	5	5	47	38	83	11	3	.211	.274	.299
2 Minor League Yrs		196	732	88	168	28	6	9	74	45	129	19	6	.230	.280	.321

Rolls was Los Angeles' first-round pick in 1996, from a high school in Kansas City. He didn't have tons of experience as an amateur, and the Dodgers have pushed him very quickly. He should have been in a short-season league last year; the Sally League was too much for him, as his poor statistics demonstrate. He is still very young, and scouts praise the quickness in his wrists, but he has work to do to avoid being another failed Dodger first-rounder. **Grade C-**

Mel Rosario

Baltimore Orioles

Pos: C **Bats:** Both **Ht:** 6'0" **Wt:** 191 **Age:** 24

Yr Team	Lg	G	AB	R	H	2B	3B	HR	RBI	BB	SO	SB	CS	Avg	OBP	Slg
96 Rancho Cuca	A	10	33	7	9	3	0	3	10	3	8	1	0	.273	.333	.636
High Desert	A	42	163	35	52	9	1	10	34	21	45	4	0	.319	.425	.571
Bowie	AA	47	162	14	34	10	0	2	17	6	43	3	2	.210	.257	.309
Rochester	AAA	3	2	0	0	0	0	0	0	0	1	0	0	.000	.000	.000
97 Bowie	AA	123	430	68	113	26	1	12	60	27	106	4	7	.263	.317	.412
Baltimore	AL	4	3	0	0	0	0	0	0	0	1	0	0	.000	.000	.000
5 Minor League Yrs		482	1722	252	439	102	11	61	252	122	447	25	23	.255	.314	.433

Mel Rosario has very nice bat speed, but his offensive production is very erratic, primarily because of bad strike-zone judgment. He does have intriguing defensive skills, and threw out 40 percent of runners attempting to steal, but unless he gets the strike zone under control and is more consistent at the plate, he will never be more than a backup. **Grade C**

Brian Rose

Boston Red Sox

Pos: P **Throws:** Right **Ht:** 6'3" **Wt:** 215 **Age:** 22

Yr Team	Lg	G	GS	IP	H	R	ER	HR	BB	SO	SV	W	L	Pct.	ERA
96 Trenton	AA	27	27	163.2	157	82	73	21	45	115	0	12	7	.632	4.01
97 Pawtucket	AAA	27	26	190.2	188	74	64	21	46	116	0	17	5	.773	3.02
Boston	AL	1	1	3.0	5	4	4	0	2	3	0	0	0	—	12.00
3 Minor League Yrs		75	73	490.1	472	219	189	47	122	336	0	37	17	.685	3.47

Brian Rose might seem to be Carl Pavano's twin brother. They are both from New England, both are very young, both had great seasons in the International League, and both should take rotation spots in 1998. The similarities are a bit superficial however; Pavano is a pure power pitcher, and while Rose isn't exactly Bob Tewksbury, he relies more on finesse than Pavano does. Rose's fastball is average, right at 90 MPH, but his curve, slider, and change are very advanced, and he is extremely intelligent. He has made great strides learning to change speeds, and he has proven quite durable. Although Rose won 17 games for Pawtucket and led the league in ERA, his K/BB and K/IP marks were weaker than Pavano's, and he may need more adjustment time in the majors than his mound mate. Still, he is a fine, fine prospect. **Grade B+**

Pete Rose Jr.   *Cincinnati Reds*

Pos: 3B **Bats:** Left **Ht:** 6'1" **Wt:** 180 **Age:** 28

Yr Team	Lg	G	AB	R	H	2B	3B	HR	RBI	BB	SO	SB	CS	Avg	OBP	Slg
96 Birmingham	AA	108	399	40	97	13	1	3	44	32	54	1	3	.243	.300	.303
97 Indianapols	AAA	12	40	2	9	2	0	0	1	2	11	0	0	.225	.262	.275
Chattanooga	AA	112	445	75	137	31	0	25	98	34	63	0	1	.308	.359	.546
Cincinnati	NL	11	14	2	2	0	0	0	0	2	9	0	0	.143	.250	.143
9 Minor League Yrs		915	3319	403	844	154	25	55	438	303	413	15	23	.254	.319	.365

There are worse players in the major leagues than Pete Rose Jr., but not very many. Rose did have a good year in Double-A, but it was the first time in his career that he hit really well, and at his age it was very likely his career season. With the glove, he has good range at third base, but still makes too many errors. If Rose continues to hit well, he could earn a job as a utility player, but there are 50 guys just as good trapped in the minors. "The luck of having talent is not enough; one must also have a talent for luck."—*Hector Berlioz.* **Grade C-**

Ted Rose   *Cincinnati Reds*

Pos: P **Throws:** Right **Ht:** 6'1" **Wt:** 180 **Age:** 24

Yr Team	Lg	G	GS	IP	H	R	ER	HR	BB	SO	SV	W	L	Pct.	ERA
96 Princeton	R	11	11	59.1	70	44	41	9	21	53	0	3	5	.375	6.22
97 Chston-WV	A	38	13	129.1	108	44	36	7	27	132	4	11	6	.647	2.51
2 Minor League Yrs		49	24	188.2	178	88	77	16	48	185	4	14	11	.560	3.67

Rose was picked in the 14th round in 1996, from Kent University in Ohio. He was a good college pitcher, but scouts didn't like him much because he didn't throw hard. He still doesn't light up the radar guns, but his command is exceptional, and he carved up the unseasoned hitters of the Sally League quite nicely in 1997. His ratios ranged from wonderful to very good: K/BB +111 percent, K/IP +22 percent, H/IP +18 percent. Like all finesse pitchers, he faces the troublesome transition to Double-A. If he does well there, he could advance rapidly. **Grade C**

John Roskos   *Florida Marlins*

Pos: C-1B **Bats:** Right **Ht:** 5'11" **Wt:** 198 **Age:** 23

Yr Team	Lg	G	AB	R	H	2B	3B	HR	RBI	BB	SO	SB	CS	Avg	OBP	Slg
96 Portland	AA	121	396	53	109	26	3	9	58	67	102	3	4	.275	.385	.424
97 Portland	AA	123	451	66	139	31	1	24	84	50	81	4	6	.308	.373	.541
5 Minor League Yrs		408	1441	210	417	101	7	50	256	191	317	10	12	.289	.373	.473

Roskos moved from catcher to first base in 1996, but shifted back to the backstop post in 1997. That's unusual; guys who move away from catcher seldom move back. He had the best offensive season of his pro career last year, with an OPS of +19 percent, and although it was his second year in Double-A and the park helped him, he is young enough that the improvement is probably real. He has a compact swing for a power hitter and doesn't try to pull every pitch. He is an awful defensive catcher, throwing out just 18 percent of stealing runners in 1997. I really don't understand why the Marlins moved him back there; he'll never make it at catcher, and it's not like they need one. He can hit, though. **Grade B**

Mike Rossiter

San Diego Padres

Pos: P   **Throws:** Right   **Ht:** 6'6"   **Wt:** 230   **Age:** 24

Yr Team	Lg	G	GS	IP	H	R	ER	HR	BB	SO	SV	W	L	Pct.	ERA
96 Huntsville	AA	27	25	145.0	167	92	78	15	44	116	0	8	9	.471	4.84
97 Stockton	A	34	8	86.0	83	31	26	6	27	79	0	8	1	.889	2.72
El Paso	AA	8	0	20.2	22	6	6	0	8	11	0	1	0	1.000	2.61
7 Minor League Yrs		146	93	629.0	646	337	283	60	233	545	0	43	37	.538	4.05

Mike Rossiter was once a prospect as a starter in the Oakland system, but several shoulder injuries knocked his career on the ropes. Released in 1996, he hooked on with the Brewers, who converted him to relief last year. He pitched very well. Rossiter has lost some velocity, but he still gets his fastball around 90 MPH, and his control of it and his slider are very good. If he stays healthy, he could have a future as a middle reliever, though he's now with the Padres after signing as a minor league free agent. Rossiter always reminds me of the movie *This Island Earth.* **Grade C-**

Jay Ryan

Chicago Cubs

Pos: P   **Throws:** Right   **Ht:** 6'2"   **Wt:** 180   **Age:** 22

Yr Team	Lg	G	GS	IP	H	R	ER	HR	BB	SO	SV	W	L	Pct.	ERA
96 Orlando	AA	7	7	34.2	39	30	22	6	24	25	0	2	5	.286	5.71
Daytona	A	17	10	67.0	72	42	39	8	33	49	1	1	8	.111	5.24
97 Daytona	A	27	27	170.1	168	105	84	22	55	140	0	9	8	.529	4.44
4 Minor League Yrs		90	83	476.2	452	261	216	49	184	386	1	28	28	.500	4.08

Ryan was a hot property when drafted out of a New Jersey high school in 1994, but the Cubs pushed him too fast. He ended up having a lousy season in 1996 and hurting his arm. He recovered to have a decent year for Daytona in 1997, but much of the sparkle has left his star. Still, it is too early to give up on him. Ryan has solid stuff: 88-90 MPH fastball, good curve, average change. His control is fine, and he has a reputation as a smart guy. His ratios last year were a mixed bag. His K/BB was very good at +26 percent, but his K/IP was just decent at plus-seven, and his H/IP was league average. Ryan's delivery to home plate is slow, and runners steal on him with ease. He also needs to polish his fielding skills at his position. Ryan still has the ability to develop into a very good pitcher, but he's not there yet. **Grade C**

Donnie Sadler
Boston Red Sox

Pos: 2B-SS   **Bats:** Right   **Ht:** 5'6"   **Wt:** 165   **Age:** 22

Yr Team	Lg	G	AB	R	H	2B	3B	HR	RBI	BB	SO	SB	CS	Avg	OBP	Slg
96 Trenton	AA	115	454	68	121	20	8	6	46	38	75	34	8	.267	.329	.385
97 Pawtucket	AAA	125	481	74	102	18	2	11	36	57	121	20	14	.212	.295	.326
4 Minor League Yrs		411	1579	297	403	71	24	27	153	197	308	127	43	.255	.341	.382

The Red Sox have advanced promising Donnie Sadler extremely rapidly, but the bottom fell out of his game at Pawtucket last year. He had a lot of trouble with Triple-A pitchers, and while his walk rate was still good, his strikeout rate shot dramatically upward. He was anxious at the plate and too easy to overpower. Sadler still showed pop in his bat, and is young enough and smart enough to adjust to high-level pitching eventually, if the Bosox are patient with him. Sadler played shortstop, outfield, and second base in 1996, but settled in at the keystone in 1997, and did well with the glove. His error rate was good, and his range factor was well above average. There is a plausible chance that Sadler will rebound with the bat, but he won't be ready for the majors for at least another year, and he could end up being the Matt Drews of hitters. **Grade C**

Jon Saffer
Montreal Expos

Pos: OF   **Bats:** Left   **Ht:** 6'2"   **Wt:** 200   **Age:** 24

Yr Team	Lg	G	AB	R	H	2B	3B	HR	RBI	BB	SO	SB	CS	Avg	OBP	Slg
96 Harrisburg	AA	134	487	96	146	26	4	10	52	78	77	8	16	.300	.401	.431
97 Ottawa	AAA	134	483	81	129	20	9	15	60	76	74	13	6	.267	.374	.439
6 Minor League Yrs		554	2021	342	580	97	29	32	225	290	335	74	48	.287	.380	.411

Jon Saffer gets less applause than Candice Gingrich at a Christian Coalition convention, but he has played well at every level and is still young. His whole problem is that he isn't flashy. He hit for average at the lower levels, but didn't have much power. At Ottawa last year, he increased his power output, but no one noticed because his average dropped. One thing he does really well is draw walks, but few people except plate-discipline geeks like me pay attention to that. His SEC was high at +24 percent. Saffer doesn't have a good defensive reputation, which is also part of his problem, but he did manage 15 assists last year and his range factor was good for a left fielder. Saffer can play, but whether he gets the chance to show us is an open question. **Grade B-**

Mike Saipe   *Colorado Rockies*

Pos: P   **Throws:** Right   **Ht:** 6'1"   **Wt:** 190   **Age:** 24

Yr Team	Lg	G	GS	IP	H	R	ER	HR	BB	SO	SV	W	L	Pct.	ERA
96 New Haven	AA	32	19	138.0	114	53	47	12	42	126	3	10	7	.588	3.07
97 New Haven	AA	19	19	136.2	127	57	47	18	29	123	0	8	5	.615	3.10
Colo Sprngs	AAA	10	10	60.1	74	42	37	10	24	40	0	4	3	.571	5.52
4 Minor League Yrs		98	73	504.2	456	239	203	54	161	453	6	29	27	.518	3.62

Saipe, a 12th-round pick out of the University of San Diego in 1994, has been very successful for two years in a row in Double-A, and could see significant major league action in 1998. His fastball is only average, 87 MPH at best, but he has a phenomenal curveball and a pretty good changeup. He can throw all of his pitches for strikes, and is a fierce competitor. Saipe is the kind of unheralded pitcher that I normally like, but it remains to be seen if he can adjust to the high altitude of Colorado. He might be able to, but I wouldn't bet the staff on it. If he changes organizations, his stock would rise significantly. **Grade C**

Jim Sak   *San Diego Padres*

Pos: P   **Throws:** Right   **Ht:** 6'1"   **Wt:** 195   **Age:** 24

Yr Team	Lg	G	GS	IP	H	R	ER	HR	BB	SO	SV	W	L	Pct.	ERA
96 Rancho Cuca	A	4	4	15.2	21	13	11	2	12	14	0	0	3	.000	6.32
Clinton	A	21	7	65.2	46	31	26	2	45	72	0	3	4	.429	3.56
97 Rancho Cuca	A	57	3	70.2	42	28	23	5	30	113	27	6	3	.667	2.93
3 Minor League Yrs		102	21	234.2	166	93	77	12	113	291	28	18	12	.600	2.95

That is one nice set of numbers: 113 strikeouts in 71 innings? Those numbers are from a sabermetrician's humid fantasy. The Padres drafted this guy in the 10th round in 1995, from Illinois Benedictine College, not exactly a major baseball school. Sak has a 90-MPH fastball, but what made the difference for him in 1997 was a splitter, taught to him by Dave Smith, the Rancho Cucamonga pitching coach and former Astro relief ace. Sak's control wasn't perfect last year, and he needs to repeat his performance at higher levels before I get overly excited about him. **Grade C**

Benj Sampson   *Minnesota Twins*

Pos: P   **Throws:** Left   **Ht:** 6'0"   **Wt:** 197   **Age:** 22

Yr Team	Lg	G	GS	IP	H	R	ER	HR	BB	SO	SV	W	L	Pct.	ERA
96 Ft. Myers	A	11	11	70.0	55	28	27	5	26	65	0	7	1	.875	3.47
Hardware City	AA	16	16	75.1	108	54	48	8	25	51	0	5	7	.417	5.73
97 New Britain	AA	25	20	118.0	112	56	55	12	49	92	0	10	6	.625	4.19
5 Minor League Yrs		116	105	605.1	605	293	260	47	227	448	1	43	33	.566	3.87

A sixth-round pick in 1993 from an Iowa high school, Benj Sampson has had an undistinguished minor league career, but impressed the Twins with sparkling pitching in exhibition action, and got an invite to the Arizona Fall League. He missed time with a back injury early in 1997, but ended the year healthy and throwing well. His fastball can hit 90 MPH, and his breaking ball is sharp and usually effective. No one is predicting stardom, and his stats at New Britain aren't great, or even good for that matter. He might get a chance, and you never know with pitchers. **Grade C**

Alex Sanchez   *Tampa Bay Devil Rays*

Pos: OF   **Bats:** Left   **Ht:** 5'10"   **Wt:** 179   **Age:** 21

Yr Team	Lg	G	AB	R	H	2B	3B	HR	RBI	BB	SO	SB	CS	Avg	OBP	Slg
96 Devil Rays	R	56	227	36	64	7	6	1	22	10	35	20	12	.282	.328	.379
97 Chston-SC	A	131	537	73	155	15	6	0	34	37	72	92	40	.289	.336	.339
2 Minor League Yrs		187	764	109	219	22	12	1	56	47	107	112	52	.287	.333	.351

Put the words "Cuban defector" in front of a player's name, and he automatically becomes a prospect. At least it seems that way. . . maybe this is a sign of subconscious anti-communism among the baseball intelligentsia. Actually, it's just the Katerina Witt Effect: the fruit is more delicious when forbidden. You can find out everything you need to know about Alex Sanchez from looking at his numbers. He is incredibly fast, but doesn't really know what he is doing on the bases. Remember, you have to steal at around a 70-percent success rate before you really help the team. Sanchez makes contact, but doesn't have power, isn't particularly a patient hitter, and needs improvement on defense. **Grade C**

Jesus Sanchez   *New York Mets*

Pos: P   **Throws:** Left   **Ht:** 5'10"   **Wt:** 153   **Age:** 23

Yr Team	Lg	G	GS	IP	H	R	ER	HR	BB	SO	SV	W	L	Pct.	ERA
96 St. Lucie	A	16	16	92.0	53	22	20	6	24	81	0	9	3	.750	1.96
97 Binghamton	AA	26	26	165.1	146	87	79	25	61	176	0	13	10	.565	4.30
4 Minor League Yrs		82	81	514.1	414	212	177	42	167	505	0	38	24	.613	3.10

Sanchez, a Dominican signed in 1992, has overcome 1995 elbow surgery to reestablish his credentials as a keen prospect. He is quite small, and for that reason draws the suspicion of scouts, but his fastball is very good for such a small guy (90 MPH) and his slider is sharp as a laser scalpel. His ratios at Double-A were uniformly solid: K/BB +56 percent, K/IP +35 percent, H/IP plus-nine percent, all admirable by Eastern League standards. He holds runners exceptionally well; there were only 10 stolen base attempts against him last year, and seven of them failed. The main question for Sanchez is durability, an obvious concern given his stature, but I see no reason to think he won't succeed if he stays healthy. **Grade B**

Anthony Sanders   *Toronto Blue Jays*

Pos: OF   **Bats:** Right   **Ht:** 6'2"   **Wt:** 180   **Age:** 24

Yr Team	Lg	G	AB	R	H	2B	3B	HR	RBI	BB	SO	SB	CS	Avg	OBP	Slg
96 Dunedin	A	102	417	75	108	25	0	17	50	34	93	16	12	.259	.324	.441
Knoxville	AA	38	133	16	36	8	0	1	18	7	33	1	3	.271	.317	.353
97 Dunedin	A	1	5	0	1	1	0	0	1	1	1	0	0	.200	.333	.400
Knoxville	AA	111	429	68	114	20	4	26	69	44	121	20	12	.266	.335	.513
5 Minor League Yrs		522	1979	311	503	108	11	62	264	185	453	77	53	.254	.322	.414

What Anthony Sanders did last year was far more remarkable than just the numbers on the page. While Sanders was in spring camp, his wife was killed in a skiing accident. . . wearing skiis that he gave her for Christmas. Although the Blue Jays told Sanders to take as much time off as he needed, even the whole year if necessary, he went out on the field every day at Knoxville and had the best season of his career. I have trouble concentrating when my cat is sick; I can't imagine the strength of will it would take to do such a thing. Sanders has power, speed, and athletic ability. His strike-zone judgment needs improvement, but it is better than it was two years ago, and he seems to understand the need to be more selective. He is fine defensively and can play any of the outfield positions quite well. I worry about the strike-zone issue, but if he continues to make progress in that direction, he could emerge as a fine power hitter. Even if he doesn't, he contributes enough to earn a bench job. **Grade B-**

Frankie Sanders   *Cleveland Indians*

Pos: P   **Throws:** Right   **Ht:** 5'11"   **Wt:** 165   **Age:** 22

Yr Team	Lg	G	GS	IP	H	R	ER	HR	BB	SO	SV	W	L	Pct.	ERA
96 Columbus	A	22	22	121.1	103	52	34	8	37	109	0	9	3	.750	2.52
97 Kinston	A	25	25	146.1	130	72	66	10	66	127	0	11	5	.688	4.06
3 Minor League Yrs		61	59	346.2	290	158	126	20	139	325	0	24	14	.632	3.27

Frankie Sanders pitched well in 1996, and continued to throw effectively in 1997. Short righthanders, as a rule, are disregarded by scouts, but Sanders breaks the mold and has attracted increasing attention. His fastball exceeds the 90-MPH barrier, and his curveball can be devastating. His command of both pitches is gradually improving, and he did nothing wrong at Kinston last year, ranking slightly above-average in all categories. Sanders needs a bit more poise fielding his position, but he holds runners quite well for a righthander. Overall, I think he's a pretty good prospect, but he probably won't be ready to help for at least a year. **Grade B-**

Chance Sanford   *Pittsburgh Pirates*

Pos: 3B   **Bats:** Left   **Ht:** 5'10"   **Wt:** 165   **Age:** 25

Yr Team	Lg	G	AB	R	H	2B	3B	HR	RBI	BB	SO	SB	CS	Avg	OBP	Slg
96 Carolina	AA	131	470	62	115	16	13	4	56	72	108	11	11	.245	.341	.360
97 Carolina	AA	44	149	30	39	10	2	9	36	20	39	3	1	.262	.349	.537
Calgary	AAA	89	325	58	95	27	9	6	60	39	82	9	7	.292	.368	.486
6 Minor League Yrs		617	2227	340	590	125	39	60	315	272	475	63	42	.265	.344	.437

Sanford is seldom mentioned as a prospect, but he isn't helpless at the plate, and has an adaptable glove. He is a line-drive hitter who will take a walk, but is also vulnerable to the strikeout occasionally. He has some speed, but is not an accomplished stealer. Sanford's glove won't hurt the team at second, third, or shortstop; he isn't spectacular, but he makes most of the plays. He is a fringe prospect, but there are worse guys to have on a bench. **Grade C-**

Rob Sasser

Anaheim Angels

Pos: 3B **Bats:** Right **Ht:** 6'4" **Wt:** 190 **Age:** 23

Yr Team	Lg	G	AB	R	H	2B	3B	HR	RBI	BB	SO	SB	CS	Avg	OBP	Slg
96 Macon	A	135	465	64	122	35	3	8	64	65	108	38	8	.262	.355	.402
97 Cedar Rapds	A	134	497	103	135	26	5	17	77	69	92	37	13	.272	.367	.447
5 Minor League Yrs		429	1557	266	407	85	16	36	213	186	341	109	28	.261	.345	.406

Sasser was originally in the Atlanta system; he came to Anaheim in the minor league Rule 5 Draft last winter, and is now with Texas as part of the Ken Hill trade. He is an excellent secondary average player, with power, walks, and speed. His SEC was very high at +49 percent, manifesting a broad base of offensive skills. Defense is there, too; he had the highest range factor among regular third basemen in the Midwest League, and doesn't make excessive errors. Sasser doesn't get much attention as a prospect, but I liked what he did last year, and I am optimistic about his long-term potential. He'll need to do it at higher levels, of course. **Grade C+**

Luis Saturria

Toronto Blue Jays

Pos: OF **Bats:** Right **Ht:** 6'2" **Wt:** 165 **Age:** 21

Yr Team	Lg	G	AB	R	H	2B	3B	HR	RBI	BB	SO	SB	CS	Avg	OBP	Slg
96 Johnson Cty	R	57	227	43	58	7	1	5	40	24	61	12	1	.256	.345	.361
97 Peoria	A	122	445	81	122	19	5	11	51	44	95	23	10	.274	.341	.413
2 Minor League Yrs		179	672	124	180	26	6	16	91	68	156	35	11	.268	.343	.396

A Dominican outfielder signed in 1994, Luis Saturria has promise as a power/speed guy, and Toronto took him in the 1997 major league Rule 5 draft. His offense isn't completely developed yet, but he has good body strength, occasionally drives the ball for power, and has speed. His command of the strike zone is improving as well, which is a good sign, and I think he may be poised for a breakthrough season in 1998. Saturria has pretty good range in the outfield, but his main defensive attribute is a very strong and accurate arm: he had 24 assists last year, splitting his time between right and left fields. He has a neat name, too. **Grade C+**

Jim Scharrer

Atlanta Braves

Pos: 1B **Bats:** Right **Ht:** 6'4" **Wt:** 220 **Age:** 21

Yr Team	Lg	G	AB	R	H	2B	3B	HR	RBI	BB	SO	SB	CS	Avg	OBP	Slg
96 Danville	R	62	242	31	55	17	2	3	32	22	74	3	4	.227	.289	.351
97 Macon	A	121	444	67	109	19	2	20	57	37	136	0	3	.245	.306	.432
3 Minor League Yrs		231	858	108	195	40	4	25	111	72	253	4	10	.227	.288	.371

Drafted in the second round in 1995, Jim Scharrer is similar to fellow Atlanta farmhand and 1996 teammate Mike Hessman: a big guy with enormous power potential, but too crude at the plate to survive at higher levels unless he makes some adjustments. He needs to learn the strike zone to take full advantage of his power and bat speed. Do you, ladies and gentlemen, get tired of reading that phrase and all the variants thereof? I get tired of writing it sometimes, but hey, you have to call them as you see them. Scharrer is young enough to improve enormously. . . . I guess I write that a lot, too. **Grade C**

Scott Schoeneweis
Anaheim Angels

Pos: P   Throws: Left   Ht: 6'0"   Wt: 180   Age: 24

Yr Team	Lg	G	GS	IP	H	R	ER	HR	BB	SO	SV	W	L	Pct.	ERA
96 Lk Elsinore	A	14	12	93.2	86	47	41	6	27	83	0	8	3	.727	3.94
97 Midland	AA	20	20	113.1	145	84	75	7	39	94	0	7	5	.583	5.96
2 Minor League Yrs		34	32	207.0	231	131	116	13	66	177	0	15	8	.652	5.04

Schoeneweis was a third-round pick in 1996, out of Duke. The middle two seasons of his college career had been ruined by testicular cancer and elbow surgery, but he did enough as a senior to rekindle interest among the scouts. His pro debut went well, and the Angels were confident enough in his ability that they sent him to Double-A for 1997. His performance for Midland was adequate; remember, his stats were hurt by the park and league environment. His K/BB was very good at +37 percent. Schoeneweis has a good fastball clocked at 90 MPH. His slider is sharp, if occasionally erratic, and he has worked to develop the changeup. He has the physical and mental ability to succeed, but there are still questions about his long-term health. **Grade C+**

Marcos Scutaro
Cleveland Indians

Pos: 2B   Bats: Right   Ht: 5'10"   Wt: 170   Age: 22

Yr Team	Lg	G	AB	R	H	2B	3B	HR	RBI	BB	SO	SB	CS	Avg	OBP	Slg
96 Columbus	A	85	315	66	79	12	3	10	45	38	86	6	3	.251	.334	.403
97 Buffalo	AAA	21	57	8	15	3	0	1	6	6	8	0	1	.263	.328	.368
Kinston	A	97	378	58	103	17	6	10	59	35	72	23	7	.272	.346	.429
2 Minor League Yrs		203	750	132	197	32	9	21	110	79	166	29	11	.263	.340	.413

The Indians have position-player prospects leaking out of their hair follicles, and here's another one: Marcos Scutaro. He has very good pop at the plate, which combined with speed on the bases makes him dangerous as an offensive player, at least for an infielder. His glove work is good, too; he has above-average range, doesn't make tons of errors, and turns the double play very well. Scutaro needs games at the upper echelons of the farm system, and given the presence of Omar Vizquel and Enrique Wilson, he should get them. The Indians will be in no hurry to promote this guy, but somebody should be able to use his skills within a couple of years. **Grade C+**

Mark Seaver
Oakland Athletics

Pos: P   Throws: Right   Ht: 6'8"   Wt: 240   Age: 22

Yr Team	Lg	G	GS	IP	H	R	ER	HR	BB	SO	SV	W	L	Pct.	ERA
96 Bluefield	R	3	2	15.0	4	2	2	1	5	18	0	1	0	1.000	1.20
High Desert	A	4	4	23.2	19	12	9	1	10	16	0	2	1	.667	3.42
97 Frederick	A	11	10	62.0	57	29	21	6	17	68	0	3	2	.600	3.05
2 Minor League Yrs		18	16	100.2	80	43	32	8	32	102	0	6	3	.667	2.86

When healthy, Mark Seaver is an excellent pitching prospect. Drafted in the fourth round by the Orioles in 1996 from Wake Forest, Seaver has a 93-MPH fastball, good breaking stuff, and fine control. His stats through 11 games at Frederick in the Carolina League were very good, but there's the problem: 11 games. He had shoulder surgery, then was the player to be named later in the Geronimo Berroa deal. The Athletics are banking that he will come back healthy, and if he does, he could be very good. But who knows? Maybe a higher power does, but I sure don't. **Grade C**

Bobby Seay   Tampa Bay Devil Rays

Pos: P   Throws: Left   Ht: 6'2"   Wt: 190   Age: 19

Yr Team	Lg	G	GS	IP	H	R	ER	HR	BB	SO	SV	W	L	Pct.	ERA
97 Chston-SC	A	13	13	61.1	56	35	31	2	37	64	0	3	4	.429	4.55
1 Minor League Yr		13	13	61.1	56	35	31	2	37	64	0	3	4	.429	4.55

Seay was originally the first-round pick of the Chicago White Sox in 1996, but the infamous contract snafu got him declared a free agent, and he signed with Tampa Bay for $3 million. He has a great arm, as you can imagine, and he's very young. . . in more ways than one. His command is shaky more often than not, he has had discipline problems, and some scouts question his pitching instincts. He has had some aches and pains in his arm as well. Seay flashed ability in the South Atlantic League, but didn't pitch enough for me to give him a legitimate grade. He has the physical gifts to be a great pitcher, but it takes more than that to make it.

Fernando Seguignol   Montreal Expos

Pos: 1B   Bats: Both   Ht: 6'5"   Wt: 179   Age: 23

Yr Team	Lg	G	AB	R	H	2B	3B	HR	RBI	BB	SO	SB	CS	Avg	OBP	Slg
96 Delmarva	A	118	410	59	98	14	5	8	55	48	126	12	13	.239	.327	.356
97 Wst Plm Bch	A	124	456	70	116	27	5	18	83	30	129	5	5	.254	.299	.454
5 Minor League Yrs		481	1750	240	421	80	24	42	256	131	494	35	32	.241	.299	.386

Seguignol came to the Expos from the Yankees in the John Wetteland trade a few years back. Signed by the Yanks out of Panama in 1993, Seguignol has excellent power potential, but at this point potential is all it really is. Eighteen homers in the Florida State League is a fine total, but his command of the strike zone is terrible. Pitchers at the higher levels will exploit this often enough to reduce his production to unacceptable levels. Poor outfield defense moved him to first base last year, so if he doesn't hit he doesn't offer anything else. Eddie Epstein says his name sounds like a stomach remedy. **Grade C-**

Jason Sekany   Boston Red Sox

Pos: P   Throws: Right   Ht: 6'4"   Wt: 215   Age: 22

Yr Team	Lg	G	GS	IP	H	R	ER	HR	BB	SO	SV	W	L	Pct.	ERA
96 Red Sox	R	5	2	11.2	14	3	3	1	3	16	1	0	0	—	2.31
97 Michigan	A	16	16	106.0	92	55	48	5	41	103	0	5	6	.455	4.08
Sarasota	A	10	9	64.2	56	43	40	8	41	32	0	4	4	.500	5.57
2 Minor League Yrs		31	27	182.1	162	101	91	14	85	151	1	9	10	.474	4.49

Sekany was picked out of the University of Virginia in the second round in 1996. He had mixed results in college due to control problems, and that has been the story in professional ball, too. Sekany can overpower people with his fastball and slider, but when he is wild, as he was too often at Sarasota, he can get knocked around. The talent is here, but so far the polish isn't. He might be better off as a reliever. **Grade C**

Dan Serafini   *Minnesota Twins*

Pos: P   Throws: Left   Ht: 6'1"   Wt: 185   Age: 24

Yr Team	Lg	G	GS	IP	H	R	ER	HR	BB	SO	SV	W	L	Pct.	ERA
96 Salt Lake	AAA	25	23	130.2	164	84	81	20	58	109	0	7	7	.500	5.58
Minnesota	AL	1	1	4.1	7	5	5	1	2	1	0	0	1	.000	10.38
97 Salt Lake	AAA	28	24	152.0	166	87	84	18	55	118	0	9	7	.563	4.97
Minnesota	AL	6	4	26.1	27	11	10	1	11	15	0	2	1	.667	3.42
6 Minor League Yrs		139	130	756.1	782	420	368	63	341	664	1	48	40	.545	4.38

Dan Serafini has very quietly developed into one of the better pitching prospects in baseball. The 1992 first-round pick has spent two years in the arduous environment of the Pacific Coast League, hasn't been destroyed by the experience, and is still quite young. When he came out of high school, his fastball was just 84-85 MPH, but he has matured physically and now gets to 90 MPH regularly. His curve, slider, and changeup are all good pitches, too, and his control has improved as well. Serafini's ERA was good by PCL precepts. His H/IP and K/IP marks were around league average, but his K/BB was very good at +19 percent, and he pitched well in his major league time. He has a terrific move to first base and has never come down with a serious arm injury in six years of pro ball. Serafini should be in the Minnesota rotation in 1998, and could win 10-12 games. **Grade B**

Richie Sexson   *Cleveland Indians*

Pos: 1B   Bats: Right   Ht: 6'6"   Wt: 206   Age: 23

Yr Team	Lg	G	AB	R	H	2B	3B	HR	RBI	BB	SO	SB	CS	Avg	OBP	Slg
96 Canton-Akrn	AA	133	518	85	143	33	3	16	76	39	118	2	1	.276	.331	.444
97 Buffalo	AAA	115	434	57	113	20	2	31	88	27	87	5	1	.260	.307	.530
Cleveland	AL	5	11	1	3	0	0	0	0	0	2	0	0	.273	.273	.273
5 Minor League Yrs		549	2031	321	558	115	7	84	331	164	428	19	12	.275	.336	.462

Richie Sexson has outstanding potential as a power hitter, but there are flaws in his game. He is very tall, very strong, and hasn't finished growing, but like most gangly young hitters, his swing gets tied up easily and he struggles to keep it consistent. As it stands, he is very vulnerable to sliders or changeups on the outer half of the plate, as he gets into bad habits and tries to pull too often. Statistically, there was little wrong with his production at Buffalo: OPS +10 percent, SEC +22 percent. His walk rate was low, however—a symptom of his difficulty with the strike zone. Sexson has a very good work ethic, but he can get frustrated. He's still very young, but he probably needs another year of Triple-A. **Grade B**

Chris Sexton
Colorado Rockies

Pos: SS **Bats:** Right **Ht:** 5'11" **Wt:** 180 **Age:** 26

Yr Team	Lg	G	AB	R	H	2B	3B	HR	RBI	BB	SO	SB	CS	Avg	OBP	Slg
96 New Haven	AA	127	444	50	96	12	2	0	28	71	68	8	5	.216	.324	.252
97 New Haven	AA	98	360	65	107	22	4	1	38	62	37	8	16	.297	.400	.389
Colo Sprngs	AAA	33	112	18	30	3	1	1	8	16	21	1	1	.268	.359	.339
5 Minor League Yrs		591	2135	362	593	88	21	16	216	372	275	62	48	.278	.383	.361

What do major league teams look for in a utility infielder? Defensive versatility is paramount, of course. They also look for speed, little-ball skills, and a good work ethic. If I were running a major league team, I would want all those things too, but I would also look for the ability to get on base. Chris Sexton gets little respect, but he would fit the bill for me as a utility guy. He can play the infield positions pretty well, he can do the little-ball stuff, he works hard, and he draws walks. It is unfortunate that the same utility players get recycled from team to team, while guys like Sexton hang around the minors waiting for a break. **Grade C-**

Scott Sheldon
Texas Rangers

Pos: SS **Bats:** Right **Ht:** 6'3" **Wt:** 185 **Age:** 29

Yr Team	Lg	G	AB	R	H	2B	3B	HR	RBI	BB	SO	SB	CS	Avg	OBP	Slg
96 Edmonton	AAA	98	350	61	105	27	3	10	60	43	83	5	3	.300	.379	.480
97 Edmonton	AAA	118	422	89	133	39	6	19	77	59	104	5	2	.315	.404	.571
Oakland	AL	13	24	2	6	0	0	1	2	1	6	0	0	.250	.308	.375
7 Minor League Yrs		688	2339	369	609	141	17	51	307	272	574	48	24	.260	.342	.401

Scott Sheldon never did much in the minors before 1996, but his last two years have been quite successful. Granted, much of the improvement in his stats can be attributed to the Pacific Coast League, but he has shown enough to be considered for a utility job. He has some pop in his bat, some patience, works hard, and is a good glove up the middle. Let's put it this way: there is no reason why any team, expansion or otherwise, should have a poor backup infielder if this guy is available. The Rangers agree and signed him to a Triple-A contract in the offseason. **Grade C**

Alvie Shepherd
Baltimore Orioles

Pos: P **Throws:** Right **Ht:** 6'7" **Wt:** 245 **Age:** 23

Yr Team	Lg	G	GS	IP	H	R	ER	HR	BB	SO	SV	W	L	Pct.	ERA
96 Frederick	A	41	6	96.2	112	67	60	13	47	104	10	6	5	.545	5.59
97 Bowie	AA	22	19	106.1	98	68	63	19	57	80	0	10	6	.625	5.33
2 Minor League Yrs		63	25	203.0	210	135	123	32	104	184	10	16	11	.593	5.45

The Orioles drafted Shepherd in the first round in 1995, out of the University of Nebraska, because they loved his 95-MPH fastball. Command, control and breaking stuff were problems, and they have remained obstacles to his development. Although scouts expect him to become a relief pitcher in the majors, he was used as a starter last year so he could work on his offspeed stuff. The results were not particularly impressive. Because he throws so hard, no one will give up on him quickly. **Grade C**

Jason Shiell
Atlanta Braves

Pos: P **Throws:** Right **Ht:** 6'0" **Wt:** 180 **Age:** 21

Yr Team	Lg	G	GS	IP	H	R	ER	HR	BB	SO	SV	W	L	Pct.	ERA
96 Danville	R	12	12	59.1	44	14	13	1	19	57	0	3	1	.750	1.97
97 Macon	A	27	24	129.0	113	53	41	12	32	101	0	10	5	.667	2.86
3 Minor League Yrs		51	36	210.2	180	83	65	13	61	171	2	14	9	.609	2.78

Shiell was a 48th-round pick in 1995 from a high school in Georgia. Although not a hard thrower, he has pitched very well in pro ball, and was excellent at Macon last year. His ratios show his potential and his flaws: his K/BB at +34 percent and his H/IP at +12 percent are promising, but his K/IP at -10 percent is a signal that his stuff may not hold up at higher levels. We'll see. **Grade C**

Steve Shoemaker
Colorado Rockies

Pos: P **Throws:** Right **Ht:** 6'1" **Wt:** 195 **Age:** 25

Yr Team	Lg	G	GS	IP	H	R	ER	HR	BB	SO	SV	W	L	Pct.	ERA
96 Salem	A	25	13	86.1	63	49	45	6	63	105	1	2	7	.222	4.69
97 Salem	A	9	9	52.0	31	21	16	3	25	76	0	3	3	.500	2.77
New Haven	AA	14	14	95.1	64	36	32	6	53	111	0	6	4	.600	3.02
Colo Sprngs	AAA	5	4	20.1	23	19	19	5	17	27	0	1	1	.500	8.41
4 Minor League Yrs		85	71	410.1	314	195	170	33	251	459	1	19	25	.432	3.73

Shoemaker was originally in the Yankees system, drafted in the fourth round in 1994 from the University of Alabama. He came to the Rockies in the Joe Girardi trade and has emerged as a top prospect. Shoemaker has a strong fastball clocked at 93 MPH, with movement, and has developed a sharp slider to go with it. He doesn't change speeds very well, and his control is still wobbly at times. He overmatched the Carolina and Eastern Leagues with K/IP marks of +78 percent and +62 percent, respectively, but had problems in Triple-A, although he continued to strike people out. He holds runners well for a righthander. Shoemaker will probably see some major league action in 1998, and while I like his arm strength, I am concerned about his control. I don't care how hard you throw; if you walk people in Coors Field, you will get killed. Heck, sometimes you get killed there even if you don't walk people. **Grade B**

Brian Sikorski
Houston Astros

Pos: P **Throws:** Right **Ht:** 6'1" **Wt:** 190 **Age:** 23

Yr Team	Lg	G	GS	IP	H	R	ER	HR	BB	SO	SV	W	L	Pct.	ERA
96 Quad City	A	26	25	166.2	140	79	58	12	70	150	0	11	8	.579	3.13
97 Kissimmee	A	11	11	67.2	64	29	23	2	16	46	0	8	2	.800	3.06
Jackson	AA	17	17	93.1	91	55	48	8	31	74	0	5	5	.500	4.63
3 Minor League Yrs		79	53	365.0	318	172	137	23	131	309	12	26	17	.605	3.38

Brian Sikorski, a product of Western Michigan University, was a fourth-round pick in 1995. He works with an 89-MPH fastball, a good slider, a good curve, and a changeup. Although none of his pitches are overwhelmingly awesome, they can be effective when he throws strikes, which he usually does. His stats aren't hot, but he held his own in Double-A, and scouts like him as a consistent, durable inning-eater. Sikorski isn't going to be an ace starter, but if he stays healthy and doesn't fall into bad habits, he should be a solid fourth or fifth guy in a major league rotation. **Grade C+**

Jose Silva   Pittsburgh Pirates

Pos: P   **Throws:** Right   **Ht:** 6'5"   **Wt:** 210   **Age:** 24

Yr Team	Lg	G	GS	IP	H	R	ER	HR	BB	SO	SV	W	L	Pct.	ERA
96 Knoxville	AA	22	6	44.0	45	27	24	3	22	26	0	2	3	.400	4.91
Toronto	AL	2	0	2.0	5	3	3	1	0	0	0	0	0	—	13.50
97 Calgary	AAA	17	11	66.0	74	27	25	3	22	54	0	5	1	.833	3.41
Pittsburgh	NL	11	4	36.1	52	26	24	4	16	30	0	2	1	.667	5.94
6 Minor League Yrs		102	76	448.1	397	208	166	26	185	433	0	29	23	.558	3.33

Silva was one of the best prospects in the Blue Jays system for several years, but his career was held back by a huge variety of injuries. He was sent to Pittsburgh in the Carlos Garcia/Orlando Merced trade, and actually managed to stay on the mound for most of the 1997 season. More importantly, he showed that he still has a good arm. His fastball runs into the 90s, with movement, and he has a very good breaking ball. He pitched well for Calgary, and although he failed to distinguish himself in major league action, Silva should have a major league role in 1998. The injury jinx may recur, and anybody who tells you they know what Silva will do in 1998 is lying, or on drugs. **Grade C**

Ted Silva   Texas Rangers

Pos: P   **Throws:** Right   **Ht:** 6'0"   **Wt:** 170   **Age:** 23

Yr Team	Lg	G	GS	IP	H	R	ER	HR	BB	SO	SV	W	L	Pct.	ERA
96 Charlotte	A	16	16	113.1	98	39	36	9	27	95	0	10	2	.833	2.86
Tulsa	AA	11	11	75.1	72	27	25	5	16	27	0	7	2	.778	2.99
97 Tulsa	AA	26	25	171.2	178	88	78	21	42	121	0	13	10	.565	4.09
3 Minor League Yrs		64	63	427.0	407	180	164	39	97	309	0	35	18	.660	3.46

Few scouts consider Ted Silva to be a top prospect, and for good reason. His fastball is below average, and while his breaking pitches are very good, he has no margin for error. He must be perfect to avoid getting crushed. So far in both college and the pros, he has been perfect often enough to not only survive, but to prosper. He handled the difficult challenge of the Texas League in 1997, and should move up to Triple-A in 1998. Silva's K/BB ratio is very good, but he doesn't strike people out at an outstanding rate, and he gives up a lot of hits. He is very smart and does all the little things well. Silva might make it, but as much as I like underdogs, I have to admit that the odds are stacked against him. **Grade C**

Brian Simmons

Chicago White Sox

Pos: OF   Bats: Both   Ht: 6'2"   Wt: 191   Age: 24

Yr Team	Lg	G	AB	R	H	2B	3B	HR	RBI	BB	SO	SB	CS	Avg	OBP	Slg
96 South Bend	A	92	356	73	106	29	6	17	58	48	69	14	9	.298	.380	.556
Pr William	A	33	131	17	26	4	3	4	14	9	39	2	0	.198	.250	.366
97 Birmingham	AA	138	546	108	143	28	12	15	72	88	124	15	12	.262	.365	.440
3 Minor League Yrs		309	1213	216	309	68	22	39	160	170	277	35	25	.255	.347	.444

Scouts have loved Brian Simmons' tools since his days at the University of Michigan, and he has done well in the minors since signing as a second-round pick in 1995. His Double-A debut was a success, and he will move up to Triple-A in 1997. A switch-hitter with power and speed, Simmons could develop into a Seven Skill player. His OPS was adequate at plus-four percent, but his SEC was very good at +29 percent, indicating his broad base of skills. He does have some weaknesses; he can be had with a good change of speed, and some observers say his swing is a bit long. He was an Academic All-American in college, so the intelligence to succeed is there; his work ethic and hustle are excellent as well. His defense is ahead of his offense at this point. He has exceptional range in center field and an above-average arm. Simmons probably needs some Triple-A time, but I like his long-term potential. **Grade B**

Randall Simon

Atlanta Braves

Pos: 1B   Bats: Left   Ht: 6'0"   Wt: 180   Age: 22

Yr Team	Lg	G	AB	R	H	2B	3B	HR	RBI	BB	SO	SB	CS	Avg	OBP	Slg
96 Greenville	AA	134	498	74	139	26	2	18	77	37	61	4	9	.279	.331	.448
97 Richmond	AAA	133	519	62	160	45	1	14	102	17	76	1	6	.308	.335	.480
Atlanta	NL	13	14	2	6	1	0	0	1	1	2	0	0	.429	.467	.500
5 Minor League Yrs		556	2027	265	574	129	6	63	343	106	290	19	27	.283	.322	.446

For a couple of days after Fred McGriff was traded to Tampa, it looked like Randall Simon would have a shot at the first-base job. Then the Braves made what might end up being the dumbest free-agent signing since Matt Young. The signing of Andres Galarraga is— how shall I put this?—completely, totally, and incontrovertably insane. It keeps Ryan Klesko in the outfield, it blocks Simon, it blocks A. J. Zapp, who could be ready within two years, and it blocks several other guys in the lower minors. It is contracts like this, and the one Jay Bell got, that kill the small-revenue teams, by inflating the market for players that are actually good. I could understand signing the Big Cat to a one-year contract, if you were afraid to commit to the youngsters, but *three* years???? Simon hit for power and average at Richmond, and some of those doubles he hit could turn into homers as he matures. Simon's main weakness is his strike-zone judgment. His walk ratio was well below decent, which hurts his on-base percentage and inhibits his production. On the other hand, his strikeout rate wasn't bad, so he does make contact and can learn the strike zone if he is encouraged to do so. Simon isn't a great player, but he is young enough to develop substantially, if he gets the right coaching and puts in the effort. **Grade C+**

Benji Simonton
San Francisco Giants

Pos: 1B **Bats:** Right **Ht:** 6'1" **Wt:** 225 **Age:** 25

Yr Team	Lg	G	AB	R	H	2B	3B	HR	RBI	BB	SO	SB	CS	Avg	OBP	Slg
96 Shreveport	AA	137	469	86	117	25	1	23	76	101	144	6	4	.249	.389	.454
Phoenix	AAA	1	4	1	3	0	0	1	2	1	0	0	0	.750	.800	1.500
97 Shreveport	AA	116	387	73	99	15	2	20	79	81	120	7	5	.256	.388	.460
6 Minor League Yrs		656	2224	393	592	122	20	102	415	397	723	50	26	.266	.385	.477

Benji Simonton is the Cecil Fielder of the Texas League. That's actually not fair from a physical standpoint; Simonton isn't as blubbery as Cecil, but his offensive game is similar: low average, lots of power, lots of walks, lots of strikeouts. Scouts say that Simonton's swing is too long to succeed at higher levels, but he hasn't had a chance to prove or disprove that contention. His SECs are always great, +58 percent last year, +62 percent in 1996. That's a function of his power, of course. With J.T. Snow finally playing well, Simonton has no chance to advance in San Francisco, but he might prove useful to another team. **Grade C**

Chris Singleton
New York Yankees

Pos: OF **Bats:** Left **Ht:** 6'2" **Wt:** 195 **Age:** 25

Yr Team	Lg	G	AB	R	H	2B	3B	HR	RBI	BB	SO	SB	CS	Avg	OBP	Slg
96 Shreveport	AA	129	500	68	149	31	9	5	72	24	58	27	12	.298	.333	.426
Phoenix	AAA	9	32	3	4	0	0	0	0	1	2	0	0	.125	.152	.125
97 Shreveport	AA	126	464	85	147	26	10	9	61	22	50	27	11	.317	.343	.474
5 Minor League Yrs		529	2045	301	576	101	33	21	231	109	267	120	45	.282	.320	.394

Singleton, a former wide receiver for the University of Nevada, was possibly the best athlete in the Giants' system, and he did have a good year for Double-A Shreveport. He has bat speed and some punch into the gaps, but his swing won't drive many balls over fences, and his command of the strike zone is weak, despite the fact that he usually makes contact. He was also a league repeater and needs a chance in Triple-A. With the glove, Singleton has developed into a fine defensive outfielder, with superb range in particular. I wouldn't mind having him as a reserve outfielder, but I think Armando Rios has broader skills. Perhaps the Giants agree: they traded Singleton to the Yankees for Charlie Hayes. **Grade C**

Will Skett
Toronto Blue Jays

Pos: OF **Bats:** Right **Ht:** 5'11" **Wt:** 190 **Age:** 23

Yr Team	Lg	G	AB	R	H	2B	3B	HR	RBI	BB	SO	SB	CS	Avg	OBP	Slg
96 St. Cathrns	A	75	272	47	75	13	1	15	52	33	73	13	3	.276	.370	.496
97 Dunedin	A	98	361	63	97	22	3	19	71	45	100	12	7	.269	.374	.504
Knoxville	AA	30	110	18	30	6	1	3	15	4	31	4	4	.273	.302	.427
2 Minor League Yrs		203	743	128	202	41	5	37	138	82	204	29	14	.272	.363	.490

Skett was drafted in the 21st round in 1996, out of Long Beach State University. Unlike most lower-round college selections, Skett has some tools. He has good power for a smaller guy, runs well, and is a good defensive outfielder. His OPS was excellent for the Florida State League at +20 percent. Strike-zone judgment is a weakness, and while he held his own in Double-A, his walk rate went from decent to horrendous. If he makes more consistent contact, Skett could be a surprise in 1998. **Grade C**

Nick Skuse   *Detroit Tigers*

Pos: P   **Throws:** Right   **Ht:** 6'7"   **Wt:** 240   **Age:** 26

Yr Team	Lg	G	GS	IP	H	R	ER	HR	BB	SO	SV	W	L	Pct.	ERA
96 Lk Elsinore	A	6	6	32.0	36	27	23	1	22	18	0	0	3	.000	6.47
Cedar Rapds	A	18	16	94.2	77	47	43	10	58	50	0	5	6	.455	4.09
97 Lk Elsinore	A	17	0	26.2	23	13	6	2	8	40	0	0	0	—	2.03
Midland	AA	30	0	33.0	31	26	23	4	15	30	16	0	0	—	6.27
Vancouver	AAA	1	0	1.0	0	0	0	0	0	2	0	0	0	—	0.00
4 Minor League Yrs		116	55	388.2	389	232	192	32	181	309	16	22	18	.550	4.45

Skuse was an eighth-round pick in 1994, from Sonoma State University. He is a huge pitcher with a good arm, but control problems have obstructed his development. Having failed as a starter, Skuse moved to the pen last year and was very effective at Lake Elsinore, mainly due to improved control. His walk rate moved upward at Midland and his ERA spiked, he still posted 16 saves, wasn't charged with a loss, and still struck people out. This wouldn't be the first time a pitcher with control problems figured out what he was doing after moving to the bullpen. Skuse needs a good season in the high minors to position himself for a middle-relief job. He was traded to Detroit for Phil Nevin and Matt Walbeck in the offseason. **Grade C**

Bobby Smith   *Tampa Bay Devil Rays*

Pos: SS-3B   **Bats:** Right   **Ht:** 6'3"   **Wt:** 190   **Age:** 23

Yr Team	Lg	G	AB	R	H	2B	3B	HR	RBI	BB	SO	SB	CS	Avg	OBP	Slg
96 Richmond	AAA	124	445	49	114	27	0	8	58	32	114	15	9	.256	.310	.371
97 Richmond	AAA	100	357	47	88	10	2	12	47	44	109	6	5	.246	.340	.387
6 Minor League Yrs		643	2325	304	590	116	15	53	300	197	580	68	41	.254	.319	.385

Tool-laden but unrefined, Bobby Smith returned to Richmond for a repeat performance in 1997. He made marginal improvement, upping his walk rate slightly and increasing his home-run output, but his doubles fell off dramatically, and his OPS remained below average. He is one of those guys who is physically strong, but has difficulty translating that strength into power at the plate. On defense, Smith converted full-time from third base to shortstop and did not disgrace himself, although he still needs work with the glove, particularly in turning the double play. I wrote last year that Smith could be an expansion pick, and he went to the Devil Rays in the first round. **Grade C**

Bubba Smith
Texas Rangers
Pos: 1B-DH **Bats:** Right **Ht:** 6'2" **Wt:** 225 **Age:** 28

Yr Team	Lg	G	AB	R	H	2B	3B	HR	RBI	BB	SO	SB	CS	Avg	OBP	Slg
96 Tulsa	AA	134	513	82	150	28	0	32	94	48	121	0	1	.292	.357	.534
97 Okla City	AAA	140	514	60	131	30	1	27	94	53	139	2	2	.255	.327	.475
7 Minor League Yrs		817	2947	397	791	173	5	168	560	270	808	10	22	.268	.333	.502

Do you ever play the game called "If I Were Dictator"? Sometimes when my wife and I are particularly bored, like on a long car trip, we will talk about things we would do if one of us became Dictator of Planet Earth. I would be a benevolent despot, of course. . . anyhow, one thing I would do, in addition to banning sweet potatoes, locking Donald Fehr and Jerry Reinsdorf in a room together, and pouring tons of money into the space program, would be to force a major league team to give Bubba Smith a job. Yeah, he strikes out a lot. He can be overpowered by high fastballs, and will chase sliders away. He will also crush the occasional 450-foot home run, and he batters lefthanded pitching. Smith is a fan favorite for his friendly personality and intense work ethic. He deserves a chance, even if I never achieve world domination. **Grade C-**

Demond Smith
Oakland Athletics
Pos: OF **Bats:** Both **Ht:** 5'11" **Wt:** 170 **Age:** 25

Yr Team	Lg	G	AB	R	H	2B	3B	HR	RBI	BB	SO	SB	CS	Avg	OBP	Slg
96 Huntsville	AA	123	447	75	116	17	14	9	62	55	89	30	15	.260	.351	.421
Edmonton	AAA	2	3	0	1	0	0	0	0	0	2	0	0	.333	.333	.333
97 Edmonton	AAA	42	151	22	33	3	4	5	22	23	31	10	3	.219	.326	.391
Huntsville	AA	87	323	79	90	20	6	8	39	65	76	31	9	.279	.404	.452
8 Minor League Yrs		606	2230	425	618	105	52	46	282	291	469	206	89	.277	.368	.433

Do you ever just decide that you like somebody or something, even though people try to dissuade you from the idea? For example, I like 1970s Charlton Heston apocalypse movies like *Soylent Green* and *The Omega Man*. I also like Demond Smith. Smith is a speed/tools player, and I am usually suspicious of the type, but if I were running a team, I'd get a hold of this guy. I like his walk rate, I like his speed, and I like his defensive ability in the outfield. I also like his work ethic; he had a bad reputation when he was young, but has overcome that and knows he must cultivate his skills to get to the majors. Smith usually struggles during his first exposure at a level, and that is what happened to him in Triple-A last year. He will never be a star, but he could be a useful bench guy given time to adjust. I'd rather run him out there than some of the ungrateful stiffs who have jobs. Smith is the kind of guy that a good manager could get some use out of by saying, "Relax, kid. Just do what got you here. Take some pitches, get on base, field the ball. Work hard, and you'll get a pension. And don't eat the green wafers." **Grade C**

Matt Smith
Kansas City Royals

Pos: 1B **Bats:** Left **Ht:** 6'4" **Wt:** 215 **Age:** 21

Yr Team	Lg	G	AB	R	H	2B	3B	HR	RBI	BB	SO	SB	CS	Avg	OBP	Slg
96 Wilmington	A	125	451	48	112	17	2	5	59	42	110	3	4	.248	.315	.328
97 Wichita	AA	52	176	19	40	7	1	1	15	13	37	1	0	.227	.283	.295
Lansing	A	62	227	33	63	4	3	4	33	21	45	4	2	.278	.336	.374
4 Minor League Yrs		388	1367	162	332	51	10	17	165	112	314	17	11	.243	.302	.332

Matt Smith was Kansas City's first-round pick in 1994 from an Oregon high school. He is an excellent athlete and by all accounts is a smart individual with a fine work ethic. In most sports, a guy with athletic ability, intelligence, and drive makes a fine player, but it doesn't always work that way in baseball. Smith's swing just doesn't render strength into power, and it may never do so. He understands that he has to get better command of the strike zone, but hasn't been able to do it on the field. Smith was a pitcher in high school; if I were the Royals, I would seriously consider moving him back to the mound. I don't think he is going to hit. **Grade C-**

Travis Smith
Milwaukee Brewers

Pos: P **Throws:** Right **Ht:** 5'10" **Wt:** 170 **Age:** 25

Yr Team	Lg	G	GS	IP	H	R	ER	HR	BB	SO	SV	W	L	Pct.	ERA
96 Stockton	A	14	6	58.2	56	17	12	4	21	48	1	6	1	.857	1.84
El Paso	AA	17	17	107.2	119	56	50	6	39	68	0	7	4	.636	4.18
97 El Paso	AA	28	28	184.1	210	106	85	12	58	107	0	16	3	.842	4.15
3 Minor League Yrs		79	58	406.2	426	195	162	26	137	286	6	33	10	.767	3.59

A short righthander drafted in the 19th round in 1995 from Texas Tech, Travis Smith led the Texas League in wins last year and ranked eighth in ERA, a nice achievement in the El Paso pinball machine. He does not throw hard and is very hittable, but prospered last year because he has good control of his breaking stuff and never gives in to the hitter. Because of his extreme lack of velocity and commonplace strikeout rate, I can't predict success for him, but you never know with pitchers. **Grade C-**

Fausto Solano
Toronto Blue Jays

Pos: SS **Bats:** Right **Ht:** 5'9" **Wt:** 144 **Age:** 23

Yr Team	Lg	G	AB	R	H	2B	3B	HR	RBI	BB	SO	SB	CS	Avg	OBP	Slg
96 Hagerstown	A	134	514	89	132	32	5	3	36	89	72	35	25	.257	.371	.356
97 Knoxville	AA	115	378	52	100	24	4	10	56	37	47	8	14	.265	.329	.429
4 Minor League Yrs		431	1575	249	411	94	15	20	152	208	230	81	56	.261	.350	.378

Solano, signed out of the Dominican in 1992, has unusual pop in his bat for a player his size. He is selective—at least compared to most Toronto prospects—which helps him drive the ball into the gaps. On the negative side, his OPS and SEC were both slightly below average. Solano is an average defensive shortstop who would fit best as a utility infielder in the majors. If he continues to show some life with the bat, he could earn that role somewhere. **Grade C-**

Russ Spear

Detroit Tigers

Pos: P   Throws: Right   Ht: 6'3"   Wt: 190   Age: 20

Yr Team	Lg	G	GS	IP	H	R	ER	HR	BB	SO	SV	W	L	Pct.	ERA
96 Clinton	A	11	10	51.2	60	43	35	3	42	44	0	4	3	.571	6.10
Jamestown	A	8	7	34.2	39	24	20	5	15	28	0	2	1	.667	5.19
97 W Michigan	A	23	23	139.2	126	63	46	9	61	112	0	11	6	.647	2.96
3 Minor League Yrs		56	53	292.2	308	195	147	24	154	237	0	20	12	.625	4.52

The Tigers got Spear from the Padres as a throw-in in the Brad Ausmus/John Flaherty trade in 1996. An Australian, Spear has just an average fastball, but his breaking pitches and changeup are highly refined for a young pitcher, and his control is reasonably good. He may not be finished growing, either, and could pick up more velocity. Spear needs to improve his command within the strike zone from good to excellent if he wants to make it at higher levels. He also has a cool name for a pitcher. **Grade C**

Sean Spencer

Seattle Mariners

Pos: P   Throws: Left   Ht: 5'11"   Wt: 185   Age: 22

Yr Team	Lg	G	GS	IP	H	R	ER	HR	BB	SO	SV	W	L	Pct.	ERA
97 Lancaster	A	39	0	60.1	41	12	11	4	15	72	18	2	3	.400	1.64
1 Minor League Yr		39	0	60.1	41	12	11	4	15	72	18	2	3	.400	1.64

Spencer was a 40th-round draft pick in 1996, out of the University of Washington. He doesn't throw hard, but he throws strikes with his breaking stuff and was extremely effective as the closer at Lancaster in 1997. Like all finesse pitchers, especially closers, Double-A will be the true test for Spencer, but it wouldn't surprise me to see him emerge as a middle-relief candidate as soon as 1999. His numbers last year were really good. **Grade C**

Shane Spencer

New York Yankees

Pos: OF   Bats: Right   Ht: 5'11"   Wt: 182   Age: 26

Yr Team	Lg	G	AB	R	H	2B	3B	HR	RBI	BB	SO	SB	CS	Avg	OBP	Slg
96 Norwich	AA	126	450	70	114	19	0	29	89	68	99	4	2	.253	.353	.489
Columbus	AAA	9	31	7	11	4	0	3	6	5	5	0	1	.355	.459	.774
97 Columbus	AAA	125	452	78	109	34	4	30	86	71	105	0	2	.241	.346	.533
8 Minor League Yrs		790	2816	473	760	168	15	101	469	364	472	66	26	.270	.356	.448

Shane Spencer has changed as a hitter over the last two years, making less contact than in the past and posting a lower batting average, but increasing his power output. Despite his sub-.250 average, his OPS was a fine +15 percent and his SEC was near the top of the International League at +56 percent. He can be had by pitchers with very good stuff or exceptional control, but he will hammer anything lackluster. Spencer has an excellent work ethic, and has worked hard to improve his defense, which has gone from poor to mediocre to pretty good in three years. He will never be a star, but Spencer would make a sound fourth outfielder or platoon partner for a lefty bat like Ricky Ledee. **Grade C**

Denny Stark   Seattle Mariners

Pos: P   Throws: Right   Ht: 6'2"   Wt: 210   Age: 23

Yr Team	Lg	G	GS	IP	H	R	ER	HR	BB	SO	SV	W	L	Pct.	ERA
96 Everett	A	12	4	30.1	25	19	15	2	17	49	0	1	3	.250	4.45
97 Wisconsin	A	16	15	91.1	52	27	20	3	33	105	0	6	3	.667	1.97
Lancaster	A	3	3	16.2	13	7	6	1	10	17	0	1	1	.500	3.24
2 Minor League Yrs		31	22	138.1	90	53	41	6	60	171	0	8	7	.533	2.67

University of Toledo product Denny Stark went to Seattle in the fourth round of the 1996 draft. His statistics for Wisconsin in the Midwest League in 1997 were superior: K/BB +42 percent, K/IP +35 percent, H/IP +36 percent. The H/IP mark was the best in the league. He was obviously too good for the competition, so he made his last three starts at Lancaster in the California League and continued to pitch well, although not as well. Stark has three major league pitches: 92-MPH fastball, a splitter, and a cutting slider. He throws strikes, knows how to pitch, and holds runners very well for a righthander, a nice side effect of his quick delivery. Stark should be a fine pitcher if he stays healthy. **Grade B**

T.J. Staton   Pittsburgh Pirates

Pos: OF   Bats: Left   Ht: 6'3"   Wt: 200   Age: 23

Yr Team	Lg	G	AB	R	H	2B	3B	HR	RBI	BB	SO	SB	CS	Avg	OBP	Slg
96 Carolina	AA	112	386	72	119	24	3	15	57	58	99	17	7	.308	.403	.503
97 Calgary	AAA	65	199	30	47	14	0	2	22	22	51	3	3	.236	.317	.337
Carolina	AA	58	207	33	60	11	2	6	33	12	60	8	4	.290	.341	.449
5 Minor League Yrs		439	1507	217	426	91	13	30	197	138	374	76	30	.283	.347	.420

I really liked T. J. Staton last year, but his game came crashing down in Triple-A in 1997, basically because he forgot the lessons he learned in 1996 about controlling the strike zone. Staton has juice in his bat, and when he hangs back and waits for a pitch to drive, he hits for both power and average, as he did in 1996. But last year he went back to the old wild-swinging approach, with a major loss of production. His defense is nothing special, so he has to make his mark with the bat. Will Staton recover his discipline? I wish I knew. The Pirates don't seem to emphasize strike-zone judgment in their instruction; Staton may be better off with a team that does, like Oakland. He is young enough to get it back, if he works hard and gets the right coaching. **Grade C+**

Blake Stein   Oakland Athletics

Pos: P   Throws: Right   Ht: 6'7"   Wt: 210   Age: 24

Yr Team	Lg	G	GS	IP	H	R	ER	HR	BB	SO	SV	W	L	Pct.	ERA
96 St. Pete	A	28	27	172.0	122	48	41	4	54	159	1	16	5	.762	2.15
97 Arkansas	AA	22	22	133.2	128	67	63	17	49	114	0	8	7	.533	4.24
Huntsville	AA	7	7	34.2	36	24	22	3	20	25	0	3	2	.600	5.71
4 Minor League Yrs		97	96	539.2	452	229	204	40	208	500	1	41	21	.661	3.40

A tall pitcher with a good slider but just a mediocre fastball, Blake Stein was part of the haul Oakland received from St. Louis in exchange for Mark McGwire. He was awesome in the Florida State League in 1996, but in 1997 Texas League and Southern League hitters could get a better read on his stuff. When his control is sharp, which it usually is,

Stein can get people out by hitting the corners with the fastball and using his slider as an out pitch. He doesn't project as a major rotation force, but as a fourth or fifth guy, he wouldn't be bad. **Grade C**

Dernell Stenson   *Boston Red Sox*

Pos: OF   **Bats:** Left   **Ht:** 6'1"   **Wt:** 215   **Age:** 19

Yr Team	Lg	G	AB	R	H	2B	3B	HR	RBI	BB	SO	SB	CS	Avg	OBP	Slg
96 Red Sox	R	32	97	16	21	3	1	2	15	16	26	4	3	.216	.358	.330
97 Michigan	A	131	471	79	137	35	2	15	80	72	105	6	4	.291	.400	.469
2 Minor League Yrs		163	568	95	158	38	3	17	95	88	131	10	7	.278	.392	.445

I am occasionally asked why I tend to downgrade "tools" players. I don't think it is a very fair question; I don't downgrade guys with tools, but I want to see some evidence that a player has the skills to use his tools before I go overboard with praise. Dernell Stenson is a "tools" player, for example, but he has the skills to use them, and I am quite high on him. A third-round pick in 1996 from a Georgia high school, Stenson is extremely strong and is fast afoot for his size. His plate discipline is surprisingly good for an inexperienced player, and his power production should only increase as he moves up. His OPS was steadfast at +21 percent. Stenson is raw defensively, but that is less important than his bat at this stage. He needs development time to iron out the rough edges, but I think the Red Sox have a winner here. **Grade B+**

Tom Stepka   *Colorado Rockies*

Pos: P   **Throws:** Right   **Ht:** 6'2"   **Wt:** 185   **Age:** 22

Yr Team	Lg	G	GS	IP	H	R	ER	HR	BB	SO	SV	W	L	Pct.	ERA
96 Portland	A	12	12	68.0	74	42	28	8	10	48	0	5	4	.556	3.71
Asheville	A	2	2	16.0	6	2	1	1	1	16	0	2	0	1.000	0.56
97 Salem	A	28	28	182.1	205	100	84	25	28	120	0	11	14	.440	4.15
2 Minor League Yrs		42	42	266.1	285	144	113	34	39	184	0	18	18	.500	3.82

Stepka, from Le Moyne College in New York, was selected in the 10th round by the Rockies in 1996. He does not throw hard, but he gets his fastball and breaking stuff in the strike zone regularly and hits the corners enough to survive, even though he gives up a lot of hits. His K/BB was outstanding at +124 percent, but his H/IP was poor at -19 percent. Stepka's control must improve from excellent to flawless if he is to endure at higher levels. **Grade C-**

Mike Stoner   *Arizona Diamondbacks*

Pos: OF   **Bats:** Right   **Ht:** 6'0"   **Wt:** 200   **Age:** 24

Yr Team	Lg	G	AB	R	H	2B	3B	HR	RBI	BB	SO	SB	CS	Avg	OBP	Slg
96 Lethbridge	R	24	78	13	25	1	2	1	13	12	13	1	0	.321	.415	.423
Bakersfield	A	36	147	25	43	6	1	6	22	8	18	1	1	.293	.327	.469
97 High Desert	A	136	567	115	203	44	5	33	142	36	91	6	4	.358	.392	.628
2 Minor League Yrs		196	792	153	271	51	8	40	177	56	122	8	5	.342	.383	.578

Stoner was signed as an undrafted free agent out of the University of North Carolina in 1996. He annihilated California League pitching at High Desert last year, with a stunning

OPS of 1.020, +33 percent. His home park helped a great deal: High Desert increases home runs by 71 percent, batting average by 11 percent, and overall runs scored by 24 percent. Stoner's strike-zone judgment is also not to my liking, and his defense in left field is nothing special. Stoner had a great year, but considering league and park factors, he needs to do it again before we get excited about him. **Grade C**

DaRond Stovall
Montreal Expos

Pos: OF **Bats**: Both **Ht**: 6'1" **Wt**: 185 **Age**: 25

Yr Team	Lg	G	AB	R	H	2B	3B	HR	RBI	BB	SO	SB	CS	Avg	OBP	Slg
96 Expos	R	9	34	5	15	3	2	0	7	3	6	3	0	.441	.486	.647
Wst Plm Bch	A	8	31	8	14	4	0	1	8	6	7	2	2	.452	.541	.677
Harrisburg	AA	74	272	38	60	7	1	10	36	32	86	10	5	.221	.307	.364
97 Harrisburg	AA	45	169	29	48	4	1	9	39	23	30	4	0	.284	.364	.479
Ottawa	AAA	98	342	40	83	23	2	4	48	31	114	10	13	.243	.306	.357
7 Minor League Yrs		807	2860	380	669	117	27	70	384	340	858	117	69	.234	.314	.367

Stovall's tools send ripples of pleasure through the souls of scouts, but his numbers just sort of give me a queasy feeling. To each his own. Stovall did play well early in the season at Harrisburg, but after his promotion to Triple-A, he fell back into old habits and lost command of the strike zone. His OPS at Ottawa was five percent below league. Stovall has all the physical talents to succeed: speed, power, athletic ability. He doesn't know how to use his talents, or at least he can't use them consistently. From those to whom much is given, much is expected. **Grade C**

Robert Stratton
New York Mets

Pos: OF **Bats**: Right **Ht**: 6'2" **Wt**: 220 **Age**: 20

Yr Team	Lg	G	AB	R	H	2B	3B	HR	RBI	BB	SO	SB	CS	Avg	OBP	Slg
96 Mets	R	17	59	5	15	2	0	2	9	2	22	3	2	.254	.279	.390
97 Kingsport	R	63	245	51	61	11	5	15	50	19	94	11	6	.249	.319	.518
2 Minor League Yrs		80	304	56	76	13	5	17	59	21	116	14	8	.250	.311	.493

Stratton was the first-round pick of the Mets in 1996, out of a California high school. Like many top Met picks in recent years, he is a power-hitting outfielder with poor strike-zone judgment. He did okay at Kingsport, although his strikeout rate gives hitting coaches nightmares. Stratton is very raw in all phases of the game, and his work ethic has been questioned at times, so it is an open question whether he will live up to his potential. Even if he works hard, it may be a struggle. Learning the strike zone ain't easy.

Eric Stuckenschneider
Los Angeles Dodgers

Pos: OF **Bats**: Right **Ht**: 6'0" **Wt**: 190 **Age**: 26

Yr Team	Lg	G	AB	R	H	2B	3B	HR	RBI	BB	SO	SB	CS	Avg	OBP	Slg
96 Savannah	A	140	470	111	130	28	6	16	63	111	96	50	18	.277	.424	.464
97 Vero Beach	A	131	452	100	126	25	3	6	45	101	79	40	11	.279	.419	.387
4 Minor League Yrs		377	1250	285	355	75	15	29	165	296	250	123	40	.284	.431	.438

Stuckenschneider was elderly to be playing in the Florida State League and scouts have never liked his physical tools, but he has some baseball skills. His secondary offense is incredible: tons of walks, tons of steals, leading to a SEC of +68 percent. He hustles, which combined with his name makes him a crowd favorite. He works hard on defense, but doesn't really have the range for center or the arm for right, although that is where he played in 1997. If he continues this combination of walks and speed in Double-A, then he will have to be taken seriously. If Rupert Murdoch buys the Dodgers, he'll probably release Stuckenschnieder to save money on uniform letters. **Grade C-**

Everett Stull   *Baltimore Orioles*

Pos: P **Throws:** Right **Ht:** 6'3" **Wt:** 195 **Age:** 26

Yr Team	Lg	G	GS	IP	H	R	ER	HR	BB	SO	SV	W	L	Pct.	ERA
96 Harrisburg	AA	14	14	80.0	64	31	28	8	52	81	0	6	3	.667	3.15
Ottawa	AAA	13	13	69.2	87	57	49	7	39	69	0	2	6	.250	6.33
97 Ottawa	AAA	27	27	159.1	166	110	103	25	86	130	0	8	10	.444	5.82
Montreal	NL	3	0	3.1	7	7	6	1	4	2	0	0	1	.000	16.20
6 Minor League Yrs		134	133	728.1	667	439	385	65	454	726	0	36	55	.396	4.76

Stull has a great fastball, timed as high as 96 MPH, although 94 is more usual. It isn't straight, either, which is part of his problem. Batters have difficulty hitting Stull's fastball, but he can't throw it for strikes very often, forcing him to groove pitches, resulting in more hits allowed than a pitcher with his velocity should give up. He also lacks command of his curve, which, like the fastball, has wicked movement. It is puzzling why the Expos didn't try him in relief. He fits the profile of the hard-throwing starter with weak command who occasionally thrives in the bullpen. I continue to believe that Stull will develop into a good pitcher eventually, but it is a matter of faith. I can't prove it scientifically. He went to Baltimore as the player to be named later in the Mike Johnson trade; maybe the change of scenery will help. **Grade C**

Darren Stumberger   *Cleveland Indians*

Pos: 1B **Bats:** Right **Ht:** 6'3" **Wt:** 205 **Age:** 24

Yr Team	Lg	G	AB	R	H	2B	3B	HR	RBI	BB	SO	SB	CS	Avg	OBP	Slg
96 Columbus	A	129	471	77	146	30	3	22	89	53	72	0	1	.310	.385	.527
97 Kinston	A	133	502	72	142	30	0	15	79	60	88	1	0	.283	.360	.432
4 Minor League Yrs		458	1677	258	475	100	4	58	277	204	288	4	4	.283	.364	.451

Stumberger, drafted in the 19th round in 1994 from the University of South Florida, is an "organization player," meaning he hangs around the lower levels of the minor leagues filling rosters, but nobody thinks he is a prospect. One wonders at the injustice of names sometimes; if his name were "Bart Savagewood" or "Dmitri Merrick" or "Preston Wilson" or something, he might get more attention. Stumberger has hit well throughout his career, but he needs to do it in Double-A before anyone will notice. Even if he does that, it will be hard for him to shake the tag of "minor league slugger." Ask Bubba Smith, who even has the advantage of a cool name. **Grade C-**

Marcus Sturdivant
Seattle Mariners

Pos: OF **Bats:** Left **Ht:** 5'10" **Wt:** 150 **Age:** 24

Yr Team	Lg	G	AB	R	H	2B	3B	HR	RBI	BB	SO	SB	CS	Avg	OBP	Slg
96 Lancaster	A	68	292	54	83	19	6	0	31	32	35	23	9	.284	.360	.390
Port City	AA	63	243	34	69	11	4	2	23	26	33	13	7	.284	.351	.387
97 Memphis	AA	112	432	71	117	18	5	2	35	63	61	21	17	.271	.363	.350
6 Minor League Yrs		561	2106	330	573	87	31	11	205	227	255	123	73	.272	.344	.358

Seattle selected Sturdivant in the 28th round in 1992 from a small high school in North Carolina. He is a small guy and does not drive the ball, but he is selective at the plate and generally makes contact. He has very good speed which he can use on the bases or in the field, and has improved his defensive reliability in center field as well. Sturdivant won't start for Seattle, or anyone else, but with his speed, patience, and glove, he would make a good reserve outfielder, which is how the Mariners project him. **Grade C**

Larry Sutton
Kansas City Royals

Pos: 1B **Bats:** Left **Ht:** 5'11" **Wt:** 175 **Age:** 27

Yr Team	Lg	G	AB	R	H	2B	3B	HR	RBI	BB	SO	SB	CS	Avg	OBP	Slg
96 Wichita	AA	125	463	84	137	22	2	22	84	77	66	4	1	.296	.401	.495
97 Omaha	AAA	106	380	61	114	27	1	19	72	61	57	0	0	.300	.395	.526
Kansas City	AL	27	69	9	20	2	0	2	8	5	12	0	0	.290	.338	.406
6 Minor League Yrs		597	2121	380	622	134	9	94	390	390	326	13	15	.293	.405	.498

Larry Sutton had a fine season in his Triple-A debut, and did well enough in the majors to indicate that he can hit, if given the opportunity. Sutton added 10 pounds of muscle over the offseason, and did show a slight increase in pull power over previous seasons, although he will still drive pitches to the opposite field, as in the past. He hits lefties well, his strike-zone judgment is very good, and his on-base percentage spikes his overall production. His OPS was near the top of the American Association at +22 percent. Sutton is also a very fine defensive player at first base. He is too old to be a top prospect, but he does enough things well enough to be a better-than-average regular. Sutton is basically a lefthanded Jeff Conine. **Grade B-**

Mac Suzuki
Seattle Mariners

Pos: P **Throws:** Right **Ht:** 6'4" **Wt:** 195 **Age:** 22

Yr Team	Lg	G	GS	IP	H	R	ER	HR	BB	SO	SV	W	L	Pct.	ERA
96 Port City	AA	16	16	74.1	69	41	39	10	32	66	0	3	6	.333	4.72
Tacoma	AAA	13	2	22.1	31	19	18	3	12	14	0	0	3	.000	7.25
Seattle	AL	1	0	1.1	2	3	3	0	2	1	0	0	0	—	20.25
97 Tacoma	AAA	32	10	83.1	79	60	55	13	64	63	0	4	9	.308	5.94
6 Minor League Yrs		128	32	286.0	268	169	156	33	176	250	13	13	23	.361	4.91

Mac Suzuki still throws hard, and he still has no idea what he is doing. The Mariners have tried him as a starter and as a reliever, but he struggles in both roles. Suzuki still has the 93-MPH fastball, and his curve has good movement, but he can't throw either pitch for strikes. He was a raw thrower when he signed for $750,000 in 1993, and four years later, that's what he still is. Suzuki is the Japanese Bill Bene. **Grade C-**

Fernando Tatis — Texas Rangers

Pos: 3B **Bats:** Both **Ht:** 6'1" **Wt:** 175 **Age:** 23

Yr Team	Lg	G	AB	R	H	2B	3B	HR	RBI	BB	SO	SB	CS	Avg	OBP	Slg
96 Charlotte	A	85	325	46	93	25	0	12	53	30	48	9	3	.286	.353	.474
Okla City	AAA	2	4	0	2	1	0	0	0	0	1	0	0	.500	.500	.750
97 Tulsa	AA	102	382	73	120	26	1	24	61	46	72	17	8	.314	.390	.576
Texas	AL	60	223	29	57	9	0	8	29	14	42	3	0	.256	.297	.404
4 Minor League Yrs		380	1422	227	436	105	7	57	230	146	248	68	34	.307	.376	.511

Technically, I don't have to write about Fernando Tatis, since he played more than 50 games in the majors, but a lot of people ask me about him, so I will oblige with a report. He will be the Rangers' third baseman in 1998, and while he may struggle at times, Tatis will have a fine career. Scouts told me he was clearly the best player in the Texas League last year, and *Baseball America* agreed, naming him the circuit's top prospect at the end of the season. Tatis has a smooth swing that can produce long home runs, line-drive singles, or doubles in the gaps. His command of the strike zone is good, and there was certainly nothing wrong with his Tulsa stats: his OPS was +24 percent. Tatis is still unrefined with the glove, but his range, hands and arm all rate above-average, and he should be fine defensively with more experience. He works very hard and is a bright guy. Tatis was responsible for sending Dean Palmer to Kansas City, and he will be a worthy successor at the hot corner. **Grade A-**

Reggie Taylor — Philadelphia Phillies

Pos: OF **Bats:** Left **Ht:** 6'1" **Wt:** 180 **Age:** 21

Yr Team	Lg	G	AB	R	H	2B	3B	HR	RBI	BB	SO	SB	CS	Avg	OBP	Slg
96 Piedmont	A	128	499	68	131	20	6	0	31	29	136	36	17	.263	.305	.327
97 Clearwater	A	134	545	73	133	18	6	12	47	30	130	40	23	.244	.285	.365
3 Minor League Yrs		326	1283	177	317	42	18	14	110	82	324	94	47	.247	.296	.341

Reggie Taylor started to show some signs of life last year. He began to drive pitches for power, and is making progress learning to use his speed on the bases and in the outfield. On the other hand, his strike-zone judgment remains very poor. The next improvement I want to see is an increase in his walk numbers and a reduction in strikeouts. With the glove, Taylor has made great strides learning outfield defense. His range is excellent, and while he still makes more errors than he should, his strong arm is increasingly accurate. Taylor is still very raw, but he looks better than he did a year ago, and the Phillies are impressed with his work ethic. **Grade C**

Miguel Tejada — Oakland Athletics

Pos: SS **Bats:** Right **Ht:** 5'11" **Wt:** 180 **Age:** 21

Yr Team	Lg	G	AB	R	H	2B	3B	HR	RBI	BB	SO	SB	CS	Avg	OBP	Slg
96 Modesto	A	114	458	97	128	12	5	20	72	51	93	27	16	.279	.352	.459
97 Huntsville	AA	128	502	85	138	20	3	22	97	50	99	15	11	.275	.344	.458
Oakland	AL	26	99	10	20	3	2	2	10	2	22	2	0	.202	.240	.333
3 Minor League Yrs		316	1229	227	332	47	13	50	213	142	246	61	29	.270	.347	.452

Tejada struggled in his major league exposure, primarily because command of the strike zone got away from him, but he is still an outstanding prospect. His offensive promise is obvious to anyone who can read a stat sheet: power in Double-A at age 20 equals top prospect. On the other hand, his OPS was just four percent above league average, basically because his on-base percentage isn't yet what it could be. Tejada's command of the strike zone is good, but not perfect, and major league pitchers exposed this. Still, he has immense offensive potential, especially for a shortstop. With the glove, Tejada is often compared to Ozzie Smith. He made 36 errors at Huntsville, a reduction of eight from his 1996 total, and he led his league in range factor for the second year in a row. Remember, a guy who makes too many errors but has excellent range is a good bet to cut down the error total with experience. Tejada's problems in the majors indicate he may need some Triple-A time, but in the long run I expect him to be a Seven Skill shortstop, and those are very rare. **Grade A-**

Jay Tessmer — New York Yankees

Pos: P **Throws:** Right **Ht:** 6'3" **Wt:** 190 **Age:** 25

Yr Team	Lg	G	GS	IP	H	R	ER	HR	BB	SO	SV	W	L	Pct.	ERA
96 Tampa	A	68	0	97.1	68	18	16	2	19	104	35	12	4	.750	1.48
97 Norwich	AA	55	0	62.2	78	41	37	7	24	51	17	3	6	.333	5.31
3 Minor League Yrs		157	0	198.0	173	67	57	9	55	207	72	17	10	.630	2.59

Jay Tessmer caught a bad case of "Soft-Tossing A-ball Closer Who Gets Clobbered in Double-A" disease. This virus permanently incapacitates the careers of 90 percent of its victims, and the ones it spares from everlasting prospect paralysis, it leaves as middle relievers. Tessmer got outs in A-ball using a submarine motion and a nasty sinker/slider combo, but Double-A hitters, particularly lefties, were tougher competition. He has no future as a closer, but I still think he has a chance as a middle reliever for a team willing to use him in situations where he can show his strengths. **Grade C-**

Evan Thomas

Philadelphia Phillies

Pos: P **Throws:** Right **Ht:** 5'10" **Wt:** 175 **Age:** 23

Yr Team	Lg	G	GS	IP	H	R	ER	HR	BB	SO	SV	W	L	Pct.	ERA
96 Batavia	A	13	13	81.0	60	29	25	3	23	75	0	10	2	.833	2.78
97 Clearwater	A	13	12	84.2	68	30	23	7	23	89	0	5	5	.500	2.44
Reading	AA	15	15	83.0	98	51	38	10	32	83	0	3	6	.333	4.12
2 Minor League Yrs		41	40	248.2	226	110	86	20	78	247	0	18	13	.581	3.11

Evan Thomas is one of my favorites. He was an awesome college pitcher at Florida International; his senior year, he went 10-3, 1.78, with 220 strikeouts in 147 innings. Yet, despite this performance, he was only drafted in the 10th round. "Aha!," you say, "he must be a finesse pitcher!" Well, no, not really. He has a good major league fastball, 89-91 MPH, and a very nice curveball he throws for strikes. The reason he was a late draft was because he's too short to be a prospect, according to traditional scouting doctrine. Thomas nailed his theses to the cathedral door last year, breezing through the Florida State League and holding his own after promotion to Reading. His H/IP went up at the higher level, but his K/IP remained excellent at +30 percent. He may be short, but Thomas is a good pitcher. **Grade B-**

Andy Thompson

Toronto Blue Jays

Pos: 3B **Bats:** Right **Ht:** 6'3" **Wt:** 210 **Age:** 22

Yr Team	Lg	G	AB	R	H	2B	3B	HR	RBI	BB	SO	SB	CS	Avg	OBP	Slg
96 Dunedin	A	129	425	64	120	26	5	11	50	60	108	16	4	.282	.370	.445
97 Knoxville	AA	124	448	75	128	25	3	15	71	63	76	0	5	.286	.378	.455
3 Minor League Yrs		377	1334	187	358	70	10	32	178	152	292	18	12	.268	.347	.408

Scouts have loved Andy Thompson's power potential since his high school days in Wisconsin, but the potential remained dormant until he learned the strike zone. He has raised his walk rate, cut his strikeouts, and while his home-run total still isn't outstanding, it should continue to increase as he matures and develops a more consistent swing. Defense is another matter. He continues to make errors at an unacceptable rate, and while he has a strong arm and reasonable range for a slow guy, the Blue Jays will have a hard time finding him a place to play if he doesn't improve the glove work at third. They have other players available at first base, and Thompson's range in the outfield would be average at best. I do like his offensive potential. **Grade B**

Mike Thurman
Montreal Expos

Pos: P **Throws:** Right **Ht:** 6'5" **Wt:** 190 **Age:** 24

Yr Team	Lg	G	GS	IP	H	R	ER	HR	BB	SO	SV	W	L	Pct.	ERA
96 Wst Plm Bch	A	19	19	113.2	122	53	43	3	23	68	0	6	8	.429	3.40
Harrisburg	AA	4	4	24.2	25	14	14	6	5	14	0	3	1	.750	5.11
97 Harrisburg	AA	20	20	115.2	102	54	49	16	30	85	0	9	6	.600	3.81
Ottawa	AAA	4	4	19.2	17	13	12	1	9	15	0	1	3	.250	5.49
Montreal	NL	5	2	11.2	8	9	7	3	4	8	0	1	0	1.000	5.40
4 Minor League Yrs		71	71	390.2	405	217	189	31	101	262	0	22	27	.449	4.35

Thurman was a supplemental first-round pick in 1994, from Oregon State University. His first two pro seasons were marred by shoulder trouble, but he was healthy in 1997 and revalidated his prospect status. Thurman has an average fastball—88 MPH on a good day—but his curveball and changeup are potential out pitches, and he throws strikes. His K/BB ratio was very good at +39 percent and his H/IP was decent at plus-nine, but his K/IP was slightly below average. He is bright, fields his position well, and does all the little things. Like almost all pitchers, Thurman will need adjustment time in the majors. As a righthanded finesse guy, his margin for error is small, but if he stays healthy there is no real reason for him not to have a career. **Grade C**

Justin Towle
Cincinnati Reds

Pos: C **Bats:** Right **Ht:** 6'3" **Wt:** 210 **Age:** 24

Yr Team	Lg	G	AB	R	H	2B	3B	HR	RBI	BB	SO	SB	CS	Avg	OBP	Slg
96 Winston-Sal	A	116	351	60	90	19	1	16	47	93	96	17	3	.256	.416	.453
97 Chattanooga	AA	119	418	62	129	37	5	11	70	55	77	5	5	.309	.389	.500
6 Minor League Yrs		500	1530	239	404	95	9	44	222	257	386	32	24	.264	.373	.424

Towle doesn't get much attention, but I have always been attracted to his good walk numbers, and he played quite well in Double-A. He is the best catching prospect the Reds have, and one of the better ones in baseball. Towle's numbers were well above average for the Southern League: OPS +15 percent, SEC +18 percent. He is quite patient, and some of the doubles he hit last year should convert to home runs eventually. Towle threw out 44 percent of runners, the league average being 38 percent. It was the second straight year he broke 40 percent. Basically, there is no reason not to think highly of Towle. He hits well, he fields a difficult position more than adequately, and he isn't too old. I don't know why he isn't praised as a prospect more often. **Grade B**

Bubba Trammell
Tampa Bay Devil Rays

Pos: OF **Bats:** Right **Ht:** 6'2" **Wt:** 205 **Age:** 26

Yr Team	Lg	G	AB	R	H	2B	3B	HR	RBI	BB	SO	SB	CS	Avg	OBP	Slg
96 Jacksnville	AA	83	311	63	102	23	2	27	75	32	61	3	2	.328	.403	.675
Toledo	AAA	51	180	32	53	14	1	6	24	22	44	5	1	.294	.369	.483
97 Toledo	AAA	90	319	56	80	15	1	28	75	38	91	2	2	.251	.336	.567
Detroit	AL	44	123	14	28	5	0	4	13	15	35	3	1	.228	.307	.366
4 Minor League Yrs		411	1499	249	434	102	13	82	287	163	308	32	15	.290	.364	.539

I wrote last year that Bubba Trammell reminded me of Bobby Higginson, and that is still true. When he reached the borderline between the high minors and the majors, Higginson went through a period where he had difficulty deciding what kind of hitter he wanted to be. Blending the desire to bash the ball for power with the necessity for contact can be tough, especially for guys who lack wonderful natural skills. Higginson eventually harmonized the two approaches, and emerged as a fine hitter for both power and average. I think the same thing will happen for Bubba Trammell. He was too pull-conscious in the majors and for much of the season at Toledo, but toward the end of the season, he regained his steady stroke. He should still be a productive major league hitter, and the Devil Rays will probably give him a full shot. **Grade B**

Peter Tucci
Toronto Blue Jays

Pos: OF **Bats:** Right **Ht:** 6'2" **Wt:** 205 **Age:** 22

Yr Team	Lg	G	AB	R	H	2B	3B	HR	RBI	BB	SO	SB	CS	Avg	OBP	Slg
96 St. Cathrns	A	54	205	28	52	8	7	7	33	23	58	5	3	.254	.328	.463
97 Hagerstown	A	127	466	60	123	28	5	10	75	35	95	9	5	.264	.318	.410
2 Minor League Yrs		181	671	88	175	36	12	17	108	58	153	14	8	.261	.321	.426

Tucci was Toronto's supplemental first-round pick in 1996, as compensation for losing Roberto Alomar to free agency. From Providence College, where he hit .363 with 16 home runs his junior year, Tucci was drafted for his offensive potential (why else would he be a first-rounder?), but he was outhit at Hagerstown by teammates Tim Giles and Luis Lopez, considered by most scouts to be marginal prospects. Defensively, he has good range, a very strong arm, and tied for the league lead in fielding percentage. It is possible that Tucci is still adjusting to wood bats, but it is also possible he wasn't as good as he looked in college. **Grade C**

Jon Tucker
Los Angeles Dodgers

Pos: 1B **Bats:** Left **Ht:** 6'4" **Wt:** 200 **Age:** 21

Yr Team	Lg	G	AB	R	H	2B	3B	HR	RBI	BB	SO	SB	CS	Avg	OBP	Slg
96 Great Falls	R	48	174	39	60	12	1	12	54	15	30	13	5	.345	.397	.632
Savannah	A	14	47	8	15	2	1	1	12	6	7	1	0	.319	.400	.468
97 Vero Beach	A	121	422	59	123	27	0	13	78	35	85	5	3	.291	.343	.448
3 Minor League Yrs		224	758	112	217	44	2	27	149	69	157	19	8	.286	.345	.456

Tucker was an eighth-round selection in 1995, from a California high school. He showed significant power potential in the Florida State League last year, with an OPS of +12 percent and a respectable home-run total for the circuit. His strike-zone judgment needs improvement, but he's young and has time to pick that up. Glove work is an asset; he led the league in fielding at first base. Tucker looks like he could develop into a pretty good player, but he has a big problem staring him in the face called Paul Konerko. **Grade B-**

Pedro Valdes   *Chicago Cubs*

Pos: OF **Bats:** Left **Ht:** 6'1" **Wt:** 160 **Age:** 24

Yr Team	Lg	G	AB	R	H	2B	3B	HR	RBI	BB	SO	SB	CS	Avg	OBP	Slg
96 Iowa	AAA	103	397	61	117	23	0	15	60	31	57	2	0	.295	.343	.466
Chicago	NL	9	8	2	1	1	0	0	1	1	5	0	0	.125	.222	.250
97 Iowa	AAA	125	464	65	132	30	1	14	60	48	67	9	2	.284	.350	.444
7 Minor League Yrs		732	2639	335	760	150	11	57	370	182	412	30	26	.288	.333	.418

Pedro Valdes had another good year at Iowa in 1997, again hitting for average and moderate power, while showing increasing command of the strike zone. The Cubs don't seem to appreciate him, however, and his chance will probably have to come with another team. Valdes has a short, well-honed line-drive swing that has been good for average at every level. He doesn't have the power teams like in a corner outfielder, which limits his opportunity unless his batting average is *very* high. Glove work is a strength for him. He has a very high range factor for a right fielder, and has a strong and accurate arm. Valdes still has some growth potential, and if the Cubs don't want him somebody should be able to use him. He would make a very fine fourth outfielder at the least. **Grade B-**

Mario Valdez   *Chicago White Sox*

Pos: 1B **Bats:** Left **Ht:** 6'2" **Wt:** 190 **Age:** 23

Yr Team	Lg	G	AB	R	H	2B	3B	HR	RBI	BB	SO	SB	CS	Avg	OBP	Slg
96 South Bend	A	61	202	46	76	19	0	10	43	36	42	2	4	.376	.480	.619
Birmingham	AA	51	168	22	46	10	2	3	28	32	34	0	0	.274	.399	.411
97 Nashville	AAA	81	282	44	79	20	1	15	61	43	77	1	1	.280	.388	.518
Chicago	AL	54	115	11	28	7	0	1	13	17	39	1	0	.243	.350	.330
4 Minor League Yrs		376	1250	197	358	90	10	41	213	208	288	12	18	.286	.396	.473

I've been slow to give this guy his due. Last year I compared him to Willie Montanez, which I really did not intend as an insult, but may have sounded like one. Willie Montanez was not that bad of a player, but Mario Valdez should be better than that. He has above-average power, very good command of the strike zone, and a honey swing. His OPS at Nashville was near the top of the American Association at +19 percent. As a defensive player, he is not amazingly wonderful, but would be an improvement over Frank Thomas. He won't be moving Thomas out of Chicago, of course. . . **Grade B**

Javier Valentin

Pos: C   **Bats:** Both   **Ht:** 5'10"   **Wt:** 191   **Age:** 22

Yr Team	Lg	G	AB	R	H	2B	3B	HR	RBI	BB	SO	SB	CS	Avg	OBP	Slg
96 Ft. Myers	A	87	338	34	89	26	1	7	54	32	65	1	0	.263	.330	.408
Hardware City	AA	48	165	22	39	8	0	3	14	16	35	0	3	.236	.308	.339
97 New Britain	AA	102	370	41	90	17	0	8	50	30	61	2	3	.243	.297	.354
Minnesota	AL	4	7	1	2	0	0	0	0	0	3	0	0	.286	.286	.286
5 Minor League Yrs		444	1593	200	417	89	7	47	232	158	301	3	14	.262	.329	.415

Two years ago, Javier Valentin was one of the best catching prospects in baseball, perhaps the top one. He hit a plateau in 1996, changed his name from Jose to Javier, then struggled quite a bit in 1997. This isn't unusual for young catchers, but it isn't good, either. Valentin didn't have a sound year offensively at New Britain, to say the least. His OPS was -15 percent; his SEC was even worse at -31 percent. No matter how you slice it, that's rotten, maggot-infested bologna. On the other hand, his defense was pretty good. He caught 43 percent of runners attempting to steal. . . the Eastern League average was 39 percent. The Twins still like him, and he remains a good prospect, especially because he is still young. He needs to get the offense back. **Grade C+**

Ramon Valette

Pos: SS   **Bats:** Right   **Ht:** 6'1"   **Wt:** 160   **Age:** 26

Yr Team	Lg	G	AB	R	H	2B	3B	HR	RBI	BB	SO	SB	CS	Avg	OBP	Slg
96 Hardware City	AA	23	71	7	17	2	2	1	6	0	11	6	0	.239	.270	.366
Tri-City	IND	16	41	5	6	4	0	0	2	2	7	0	0	.146	.217	.244
Daytona	A	14	31	5	6	2	1	0	2	3	5	1	0	.194	.257	.323
97 Daytona	A	106	371	54	123	25	2	6	50	20	49	20	6	.332	.372	.458
8 Minor League Yrs		607	1969	247	481	95	8	21	201	114	371	87	23	.244	.291	.333

Dominican shortstop Ramon Valette was originally in the Twins system, but he didn't hit and drew his release in 1995. The Cubs picked him up in 1996, and he had a great year at Daytona in 1997, leading the tough Florida State League in hitting. At this point, I wouldn't get too excited. He was too old for the league, and I won't believe in his bat until he does it at a higher level. He is not a Gold Glove at shortstop, but he has enough range for the position and also has experience at second. If Valette is going to make it, it will be in a utility role. **Grade C-**

Jason Varitek

Pos: C   **Bats:** Both   **Ht:** 6'2"   **Wt:** 210   **Age:** 25

Yr Team	Lg	G	AB	R	H	2B	3B	HR	RBI	BB	SO	SB	CS	Avg	OBP	Slg
96 Port City	AA	134	503	63	132	34	1	12	67	66	93	7	6	.262	.350	.406
97 Tacoma	AAA	87	307	54	78	13	0	15	48	34	71	0	1	.254	.329	.443
Pawtucket	AAA	20	66	6	13	5	0	1	5	8	12	0	0	.197	.284	.318
Boston	AL	1	1	0	1	0	0	0	0	0	0	0	0	1.000	1.000	1.000
3 Minor League Yrs		345	1228	165	302	66	3	38	164	169	302	7	8	.246	.338	.397

Jason Varitek may see considerable action in Fenway Park in 1998. Will he live up to the hype he generated coming out of college? In a word, no. It is pretty clear now that Varitek will not star, but he should be okay. He has some power, and although his command of the strike zone is pretty good, his swing is too slow to allow him to hit for average. Right now, he hits something like a switch-hitting Bill Haselman. Although Varitek has a strong arm, he has never thrown out lots of runners in the pros, nailing 30 percent last year in the Pacific Coast League, a below-average total. He is mobile and reliable behind the plate, however, and handles a pitching staff well. While Varitek won't be a luminary in the Show, his combination of power and defense does have value, provided that expectations aren't too high. **Grade C**

Mike Vavrek
Colorado Rockies

Pos: P   Throws: Left   Ht: 6'2"   Wt: 185   Age: 23

Yr Team	Lg	G	GS	IP	H	R	ER	HR	BB	SO	SV	W	L	Pct.	ERA
96 Salem	A	26	25	149.2	167	92	81	15	59	103	0	10	8	.556	4.87
97 Salem	A	10	9	62.2	55	21	15	3	18	48	0	2	2	.500	2.15
New Haven	AA	17	17	122.2	94	38	35	7	34	101	0	12	3	.800	2.57
3 Minor League Yrs		68	66	425.2	388	175	148	28	139	320	0	29	17	.630	3.13

Vavrek was picked in the fifth round in 1995 from Lewis University in Illinois. He is the standard soft-tossing southpaw. His fastball is usually around 86 MPH, but his slider and changeup are very good, and he throws strikes. He led the Eastern League in ERA, and his K/BB was excellent at +55 percent. Vavrek is bright, and knows how to pitch. He makes adjustments, and understands that he can't survive at the higher levels unless his command is exquisite. I think he has a chance to succeed, and he could do for the Rockies what Tony Saunders did for the Marlins last year, but Vavrek won't be moving into an easy environment by any means. **Grade C+**

Javier Vazquez
Montreal Expos

Pos: P   Throws: Right   Ht: 6'2"   Wt: 175   Age: 21

Yr Team	Lg	G	GS	IP	H	R	ER	HR	BB	SO	SV	W	L	Pct.	ERA
96 Delmarva	A	27	27	164.1	138	64	49	12	57	173	0	14	3	.824	2.68
97 Wst Plm Bch	A	19	19	112.2	98	40	27	8	28	100	0	6	3	.667	2.16
Harrisburg	AA	6	6	42.0	15	5	5	2	12	47	0	4	0	1.000	1.07
4 Minor League Yrs		88	84	489.1	397	201	158	30	159	463	0	35	14	.714	2.91

Javier Vazquez, a Puerto Rican drafted in the fifth round in 1994, has materialized as an outstanding prospect. He was great at Delmarva in 1996, but 1997 was special because he did it again at a higher level. He was nearly unhittable in six Double-A starts. Vazquez's velocity is growing. His fastball, just average in 1996, hits the low 90s now, and his curve, slider, and changeup continue to improve. He throws strikes and knows what he is doing in the box. Nothing wrong with the ratios: K/BB +83 percent, K/IP +24 percent, H/IP +26 percent, all safely above Florida State League standards. There were even better in the Eastern League. The basic question for Vazquez is the same for every young pitcher: will he get hurt? **Grade B+**

Ramon Vazquez

Seattle Mariners

Pos: SS   **Bats:** Left   **Ht:** 5'11"   **Wt:** 170   **Age:** 21

Yr Team	Lg	G	AB	R	H	2B	3B	HR	RBI	BB	SO	SB	CS	Avg	OBP	Slg
96 Everett	A	33	126	25	35	5	2	1	18	26	26	7	2	.278	.392	.373
Tacoma	AAA	18	49	7	11	2	1	0	4	4	12	0	0	.224	.296	.306
Wisconsin	A	3	10	1	3	1	0	0	1	2	2	0	0	.300	.417	.400
97 Wisconsin	A	131	479	79	129	25	5	8	49	78	93	16	10	.269	.373	.392
3 Minor League Yrs		224	805	132	207	36	9	9	83	129	160	27	15	.257	.361	.358

A Puerto Rican who attended Indian Hills Community College in Iowa, Ramon Vazquez was drafted by the Mariners in the 27th round in 1995. The thing I noticed about him was, as you may guess, his high walk rate, plus eight home runs is a good total for a middle infielder in the Midwest League. It remains to be seen if he will hit at higher levels. It also remains to be seen if he will field at higher levels: he made 35 errors, and his range factor at shortstop was below average. It says a lot about the Mariners system that I noticed him; for most teams, he wouldn't merit a comment, but the Mariners have exploited their farms so badly that there isn't much prospect topsoil left. **Grade C-**

Jorge Velandia

Oakland Athletics

Pos: SS   **Bats:** Right   **Ht:** 5'9"   **Wt:** 160   **Age:** 23

Yr Team	Lg	G	AB	R	H	2B	3B	HR	RBI	BB	SO	SB	CS	Avg	OBP	Slg
96 Memphis	AA	122	392	42	94	19	0	9	48	31	65	3	7	.240	.295	.357
97 Las Vegas	AAA	114	405	46	110	15	2	3	35	29	62	13	3	.272	.326	.341
San Diego	NL	14	29	0	3	2	0	0	0	1	7	0	0	.103	.133	.172
6 Minor League Yrs		639	1976	251	463	95	8	21	206	161	346	51	26	.234	.295	.322

Some scouts like Venezuelan shortstop Jorge Velandia, due to his steady glove, his speed, and his ability to make contact from both sides of the plate. However, a .272 average with three home runs at Las Vegas is unimpressive, to say the least. Vegas inflated batting average by eight percent and home runs by 18 percent last year. All three of Velandia's round-trippers came at home. His OPS was 19 percent below the Pacific Coast League. Add it up. He can't hit. Defensively, Velandia is good but not spectacular. Unless he shows more ability with the bat, he will never make it as a regular. He went to Oakland in an offseason trade. **Grade C-**

Edgard Velazquez

Colorado Rockies

Pos: OF   **Bats:** Right   **Ht:** 6'0"   **Wt:** 170   **Age:** 22

Yr Team	Lg	G	AB	R	H	2B	3B	HR	RBI	BB	SO	SB	CS	Avg	OBP	Slg
96 New Haven	AA	132	486	72	141	29	4	19	62	53	114	6	2	.290	.365	.484
97 Colo Sprngs	AAA	120	438	70	123	24	10	17	73	34	119	6	3	.281	.340	.498
5 Minor League Yrs		541	2015	286	555	104	25	62	263	166	490	35	29	.275	.334	.444

A year ago, I had Edgard Velazquez pegged as one of the best prospects in baseball. He always had the tools to succeed, and after an excellent 1996 Double-A season, I expected him to break out with a monster campaign in Triple-A, and challenge for a job in 1998. Well, I was wrong. Velazquez remains a fine prospect, but the Pacific Coast League proved to be a very difficult challenge, mainly due to the fact that he lost command of the strike zone. His walk rate dropped substantially, with a concurrent drop in production across the board. His OPS was only league average, and he did most of his damage in his home park. Basically, he fell back into his old habit of chasing pitches outside the strike zone. Will Velazquez rebound? He remains very young, and with a year in Triple-A under his belt, there is a reasonable chance he will come back and re-establish himself. I still like him, but obviously I can't be as optimistic as I was last year. **Grade B**

Andrew Vessel   *Texas Rangers*

Pos: OF   **Bats:** Right   **Ht:** 6'3"   **Wt:** 205   **Age:** 23

Yr Team	Lg	G	AB	R	H	2B	3B	HR	RBI	BB	SO	SB	CS	Avg	OBP	Slg
96 Charlotte	A	126	484	63	111	25	6	3	67	45	94	1	6	.229	.298	.324
97 Tulsa	AA	138	517	78	135	35	1	12	75	41	87	3	1	.261	.320	.402
5 Minor League Yrs		558	2102	271	519	119	13	33	305	155	386	20	36	.247	.306	.363

The 1996 season was a total disaster for Andrew Vessel, but in 1997 he recovered the ground he lost by playing fairly well for Tulsa. Vessel has exceptional physical attributes and is the best athlete in the Texas farm system, but his 1996 season at Charlotte was ruined by injuries and a bad attitude over not getting promoted. In 1997, he was healthy, and more mature as an individual. Vessel can drive a pitch for a long distance, but his swing is inconsistent and he is prone to slumps. He needs to be more selective, but his bat speed is very good and he doesn't strike out too much. His defense is similar to his offense: promising, but unrefined. Vessel is still young, and having his attitude back on track certainly helps, but even if he works hard, there is no guarantee that his tools will become skills. Texas removed him from the 40-man roster in the offseason. **Grade C+**

Joe Victery   *Seattle Mariners*

Pos: P   **Throws:** Right   **Ht:** 6'2"   **Wt:** 205   **Age:** 22

Yr Team	Lg	G	GS	IP	H	R	ER	HR	BB	SO	SV	W	L	Pct.	ERA
96 Everett	A	13	8	51.2	43	22	18	4	15	45	1	5	4	.556	3.14
97 Lancaster	A	28	14	102.1	98	70	55	9	53	86	0	5	4	.556	4.84
2 Minor League Yrs		41	22	154.0	141	92	73	13	68	131	1	10	8	.556	4.27

Hey, how could I pass up a chance to put someone named "Joe Victery" in the book? It helps that he is a prospect, too, albeit a marginal one right now. Victery was a 12th-round pick in 1996, out of the University of Oklahoma. His 1997 stats aren't a true indicator of his potential, since he was recovering from offseason knee surgery to repair torn cartilage. When healthy, Victery has a low-90s fastball, a nice curve, and good control. His fastball was inconsistent last year, but he should be fully healthy in 1998, and will get a chance to demonstrate whether he can live up to his name or not. **Grade C**

Mike Villano

Florida Marlins

Pos: P **Throws:** Right **Ht:** 6'1" **Wt:** 200 **Age:** 26

Yr Team	Lg	G	GS	IP	H	R	ER	HR	BB	SO	SV	W	L	Pct.	ERA
96 San Jose	A	39	2	88.0	48	12	7	2	33	133	8	7	1	.875	0.72
Shreveport	AA	2	2	12.0	6	4	4	0	8	7	0	2	0	1.000	3.00
97 Shreveport	AA	30	0	34.1	41	25	24	5	20	26	2	3	1	.750	6.29
Phoenix	AAA	13	11	71.1	75	36	33	7	27	41	0	5	3	.625	4.16
3 Minor League Yrs		121	15	263.2	217	96	82	17	120	278	12	20	7	.741	2.80

Mike Villano was outstanding at Class-A San Jose in 1996, but he had a lot of trouble in Double-A in 1997. His control was off, resulting in too many walks, as well as hits off of grooved pitches down the middle. In late July, Villano's ERA stood at 6.29, and his prospect status was starting to fade. Then the Giants did an interesting thing. They promoted him to Triple-A, and converted him to a starter. Interestingly enough, it worked. His control improved, and he ended up with a 4.16 ERA, very nice by Phoenix standards. Villano has a 92-MPH fastball, a good slider, and a respectable changeup. A former catcher, he doesn't have a lot of mound experience. The Giants traded him to Florida in the Robb Nen deal. He should spend at least part of the season in a Marlins uniform, and if his control is sharp, he could be very good. **Grade C+**

Ken Vining

Chicago White Sox

Pos: P **Throws:** Left **Ht:** 5'11" **Wt:** 180 **Age:** 23

Yr Team	Lg	G	GS	IP	H	R	ER	HR	BB	SO	SV	W	L	Pct.	ERA
96 Bellingham	A	12	11	60.1	45	16	14	4	23	69	0	4	2	.667	2.09
97 San Jose	A	23	23	136.2	140	77	64	9	60	142	0	9	6	.600	4.21
Winston-Sal	A	5	5	34.2	36	17	11	2	11	38	0	2	2	.500	2.86
2 Minor League Yrs		40	39	231.2	221	110	89	15	94	249	0	15	10	.600	3.46

The big sleeper in the Roberto Hernandez/Wilson Alvarez trade is Ken Vining. He was a very successful college pitcher at Clemson, going 10-3, 2.97 his junior year, and teaming with 1996 first-round picks Kris Benson and Billy Koch to form a tremendous pitching troika. He went to the Giants in the fourth round, although some observers thought he could have gone as high as the second. Vining, unlike most lefties his size, is *not* a soft tosser: his fastball hits 90, and he has sharp breaking stuff. His ERA in the California League was a bit high, but remember that is a hitters' circuit. Look at his Cal League strikeout ratios: K/BB +25 percent, K/IP +22 percent. His H/IP was a notch below average, and he doesn't hold runners that well. Those are the only negatives I can find in his profile. As pitchers go, Vining is a good bet to emerge. He is one of my favorite unsung prospects. **Grade B**

Shon Walker
Pittsburgh Pirates

Pos: OF Bats: Left Ht: 6'1" Wt: 182 Age: 23

Yr Team	Lg	G	AB	R	H	2B	3B	HR	RBI	BB	SO	SB	CS	Avg	OBP	Slg
96 Lynchburg	A	97	323	61	98	19	3	14	70	49	99	3	4	.303	.394	.511
97 Lynchburg	A	100	303	59	79	15	6	15	48	77	131	2	3	.261	.408	.498
6 Minor League Yrs		531	1726	275	430	84	13	46	245	319	628	58	29	.249	.365	.393

Shon Walker was once a hot prospect, a supplemental first-round pick in 1992 out of high school. Injuries, strikeouts, and defensive problems have conspired to make him little more than an organization player now. I may be alone, but I haven't totally given up on him. He draws walks and hits for power, and is still fairly young. On the other hand, his strikeout rate is frightening, and he doesn't have a position. He will likely spend the next decade filling rosters. **Grade C-**

Daryle Ward
Houston Astros

Pos: 1B Bats: Left Ht: 6'2" Wt: 230 Age: 22

Yr Team	Lg	G	AB	R	H	2B	3B	HR	RBI	BB	SO	SB	CS	Avg	OBP	Slg
96 Toledo	AAA	6	23	1	4	0	0	0	1	0	3	0	0	.174	.174	.174
Lakeland	A	128	464	65	135	29	4	10	68	57	77	1	1	.291	.373	.435
97 Jackson	AA	114	422	72	139	25	0	19	90	46	68	4	2	.329	.398	.524
New Orleans	AAA	14	48	4	18	1	0	2	8	7	7	0	0	.375	.455	.521
4 Minor League Yrs		447	1642	234	488	93	4	50	303	175	299	11	6	.297	.367	.450

Daryle Ward came to the Astros as part of the nine-player trade with the Tigers last winter. I had the pleasure of meeting his father Gary during my Arizona Fall League trip. That was really cool, since Gary Ward was my favorite player when I was young. Daryle was drafted in the 15th round in 1994, from Rancho Santiago Junior College in California. The Tigers didn't have room for him, and with Jeff Bagwell around the Astros really don't either, but he can flat-out bash the ball. He is extremely strong, he can hit for average, he controls the strike zone, and has learned to pull with power. He hit several tape-measure shots for Jackson last year, while compiling a solid OPS of +20 percent, and continued to hit after his promotion to Triple-A. Many scouts think he is ready to succeed in the majors right now. Ward moves well for a big guy at first base; he has good hands and is actually a fine athlete, although he does need some defensive polish. A year ago, I thought Daryle would hit about like his father, who was pretty good, but now it looks like Daryle could be much better than that. **Grade B+**

Jeremy Ware
Montreal Expos

Pos: OF Bats: Right Ht: 6'1" Wt: 190 Age: 22

Yr Team	Lg	G	AB	R	H	2B	3B	HR	RBI	BB	SO	SB	CS	Avg	OBP	Slg
96 Expos	R	15	44	10	16	3	3	0	17	9	4	6	1	.364	.472	.568
Vermont	A	32	94	12	18	2	0	0	6	15	25	5	3	.191	.303	.213
97 Cape Fear	A	138	529	84	139	32	5	16	77	43	114	32	7	.263	.322	.433
3 Minor League Yrs		223	783	124	201	41	10	18	115	85	171	48	15	.257	.334	.404

As most of you know, the Expos grab Canadian talent whenever possible. They prefer guys with a Quebec background, but they snatched Jeremy Ware out of Toronto's backyard in 1994, drafting him out of an Ontario high school in the 25th round. Ware has good tools, but is raw; his numbers at Cape Fear demonstrate this quite clearly. He shows power, but his command of the strike zone is marginal, which helped keep his OPS to plus-seven, good but not great by any means. Defensively, he has a very strong arm and respectable range, but is inexperienced and makes too many mistakes. Ware has received little notice, but he is young and has tools. If he develops some skills to go with them, he could be good. **Grade C**

Jarrod Washburn
Anaheim Angels

Pos: P   Throws: Left   Ht: 6'1"   Wt: 185   Age: 23

Yr Team	Lg	G	GS	IP	H	R	ER	HR	BB	SO	SV	W	L	Pct.	ERA
96 Lk Elsinore	A	14	14	92.2	79	38	34	5	33	93	0	6	3	.667	3.30
Vancouver	AAA	2	2	8.1	12	16	10	1	12	5	0	0	2	.000	10.80
Midland	AA	13	13	88.0	77	44	43	11	25	58	0	5	6	.455	4.40
97 Midland	AA	29	29	189.1	211	115	101	23	65	146	0	15	12	.556	4.80
Vancouver	AAA	1	1	5.0	4	2	2	0	2	6	0	0	0	—	3.60
3 Minor League Yrs		70	70	447.2	435	239	214	42	158	382	0	29	26	.527	4.30

Washburn has a 92-93 MPH fastball, outstanding for a southpaw. The pitch has tremendous movement as well as velocity, and while he can't always hit spots with it, he doesn't always have to. A lot of hitters can't catch up with it. His slider is less refined; he bounces it in the dirt frequently, and it sometimes takes him two or three innings to find the right grip. He has a change but seldom uses it. Washburn had a pretty good season in the difficult Texas League, and in a rough Midland park. His strikeout marks were fine: K/BB +30 percent, K/IP +10 percent. His H/IP was worse than average, but that was mostly because of the park. Washburn does not change speeds well, and needs to refine his slider. The Angels are very high on him, and will promote him as soon as he looks ready. He reminds some scouts of Mark Langston. He had a strong second half. **Grade B**

Dusty Wathan
Seattle Mariners

Pos: C   Bats: Both   Ht: 6'5"   Wt: 215   Age: 24

Yr Team	Lg	G	AB	R	H	2B	3B	HR	RBI	BB	SO	SB	CS	Avg	OBP	Slg
96 Lancaster	A	74	246	41	64	10	1	8	40	26	65	1	1	.260	.344	.407
97 Lancaster	A	56	202	27	60	17	0	4	35	21	51	0	1	.297	.381	.441
Memphis	AA	49	149	20	40	4	1	4	19	19	28	1	1	.268	.368	.389
4 Minor League Yrs		272	875	135	232	42	3	24	129	94	186	4	4	.265	.355	.402

The Mariners signed Dusty Wathan as an undrafted free agent in 1994. The son of John Wathan, Dusty spent a couple of years as a reserve catcher before finally getting a chance to start in 1997. He took advantage of the opportunity, and is now considered a prospect. Wathan is *not* like his father. He is a slow, ponderous power hitter, rather than a quick line-drive guy. Strikeouts are a problem, but when he makes contact he can crush the ball. Wathan is a very good defensive catcher, and nailed 42 percent of runners trying to steal on him in Double-A. His future in the majors is as a defensive sub. **Grade C-**

Pat Watkins

Cincinnati Reds

Pos: OF   **Bats**: Right   **Ht**: 6'2"   **Wt**: 185   **Age**: 25

Yr Team	Lg	G	AB	R	H	2B	3B	HR	RBI	BB	SO	SB	CS	Avg	OBP	Slg
96 Chattanooga	AA	127	492	63	136	31	2	8	59	30	64	15	11	.276	.325	.396
97 Chattanooga	AA	46	177	35	62	15	1	7	30	15	16	9	3	.350	.405	.565
Indianapols	AAA	84	325	46	91	14	7	9	35	24	55	13	9	.280	.330	.449
Cincinnati	NL	17	29	2	6	2	0	0	0	0	5	1	0	.207	.207	.276
5 Minor League Yrs		587	2218	368	630	123	21	73	307	196	340	89	45	.284	.345	.457

Pat Watkins, Cincinnati's supplemental first-round pick in 1993 from East Carolina University, made some progress last year converting his robust physical tools into skills. He was awesome at Chattanooga, and did well enough at Indianapolis to make the Reds optimistic about his chances in 1998. Watkins is quite strong, although his swing still doesn't provide great lift and he will never be a major home-run threat. He runs great, has made progress learning to steal bases, and is a fine defensive outfielder. On the negative end, his command of the strike zone is still a weakness, and he isn't young as prospects go. Watkins may develop into a decent player, but he won't be a star, and may not hit enough to be a legitimate starter. **Grade C**

Neil Weber

Arizona Diamondbacks

Pos: P   **Throws**: Left   **Ht**: 6'5"   **Wt**: 205   **Age**: 25

Yr Team	Lg	G	GS	IP	H	R	ER	HR	BB	SO	SV	W	L	Pct.	ERA
96 Harrisburg	AA	18	18	107.0	90	37	36	8	44	74	0	7	4	.636	3.03
97 Ottawa	AAA	9	9	39.2	46	46	35	7	40	27	0	2	5	.286	7.94
Harrisburg	AA	18	18	112.2	93	56	48	17	51	121	0	7	6	.538	3.83
5 Minor League Yrs		114	113	641.1	583	341	281	59	323	555	0	37	38	.493	3.94

A lefty with a very live arm, Neil Weber throws in the low 90s and possesses a sharp curve. He started the season at Ottawa and was absolutely terrible, giving up hits like a batting-practice machine and walking a batter per inning. Demoted to Double-A, he regained his command and ended the season on an up note, but it doesn't mean much since he already has spent two years at that level. Weber is the classic unpredictable pitching prospect, and there's no way to know how he will do for Arizona next year. **Grade C**

Jason Weekley

Los Angeles Dodgers

Pos: OF   **Bats**: Right   **Ht**: 6'3"   **Wt**: 190   **Age**: 24

Yr Team	Lg	G	AB	R	H	2B	3B	HR	RBI	BB	SO	SB	CS	Avg	OBP	Slg
96 Great Falls	R	64	238	35	87	12	5	7	43	18	63	18	12	.366	.411	.546
Savannah	A	1	4	0	0	0	0	0	0	1	0	0	0	.000	.200	.000
97 San Berndno	A	101	313	58	88	15	5	16	59	41	102	3	6	.281	.365	.514
2 Minor League Yrs		166	555	93	175	27	10	23	102	60	165	21	18	.315	.382	.524

Weekley was a 41st-round pick in 1996. His pro debut in the Pioneer League was stunning, on the surface, but the league leader hit .424. Weekley ranked sixth in the league, which puts .366, as impressive as it is, in context. The Dodgers gave Weekley a chance to show himself as a genuine prospect in 1997 and gave him a job in the California League.

He did well, with an OPS of +15 percent. He is not impressive defensively, so he will have to continue to hit as he moves up, and he just might. **Grade C**

Robb Welch
Boston Red Sox

Pos: P **Throws:** Right **Ht:** 6'4" **Wt:** 190 **Age:** 22

Yr Team	Lg	G	GS	IP	H	R	ER	HR	BB	SO	SV	W	L	Pct.	ERA
96 Lowell	A	14	14	81.1	85	50	46	7	37	63	0	2	7	.222	5.09
97 Michigan	A	26	26	153.2	142	88	72	8	80	158	0	13	10	.565	4.22
4 Minor League Yrs		58	54	314.2	313	188	163	16	163	276	0	21	22	.488	4.66

Welch, from Twin Falls, Idaho, was drafted in the fourth round in 1994. Idaho is not exactly a baseball hotbed, so as one would expect, Welch was rather raw when he signed. When drafted, he was basically a projectable kid with a live arm, but he is making progress and had a good season for Michigan. Welch has the basic four-pitch repertoire, and while none of his pitches are tremendous, they all show promise. His K/BB was only average last year, but his K/IP was nice at +23 percent. He won't be in the majors anytime soon; he must improve his command, stay healthy, and do well at higher levels. Welch is basically a Yada-Yada-Yada Pitching Prospect; his profile is identical to a lot of other guys. **Grade C**

Jake Westbrook
Montreal Expos

Pos: P **Throws:** Right **Ht:** 6'3" **Wt:** 180 **Age:** 20

Yr Team	Lg	G	GS	IP	H	R	ER	HR	BB	SO	SV	W	L	Pct.	ERA
96 Rockies	R	11	11	62.2	66	33	20	0	14	57	0	4	2	.667	2.87
Portland	A	4	4	24.2	22	8	7	1	5	19	0	1	1	.500	2.55
97 Asheville	A	28	27	170.0	176	93	81	16	55	92	0	14	11	.560	4.29
2 Minor League Yrs		43	42	257.1	264	134	108	17	74	168	0	19	14	.576	3.78

The Rockies love drafting high school pitchers, and sent two of their recent draftees, Jake Westbrook and John Nicholson, to Montreal in the Mike Lansing trade. Westbrook has a major league fastball, 88-90 MPH, and his slider and curveball are auspicious. He throws strikes, but at times Westbrook gets too cute: coaches want him to challenge hitters, rather than trying to trick them. He gives up too many hits for a pitcher with good stuff, and his strikeout rate was disappointing at Asheville. Westbrook is intelligent and projectable, and his arm is "loose," meaning that his arm action is free and it doesn't look like he will get hurt easily. If the Expos are patient, he should be a good one, but I want to see his strikeout rate increase. I think it could turn out to be a good trade for Montreal. **Grade B-**

Matt White
Tampa Bay Devil Rays

Pos: P **Throws:** Right **Ht:** 6'5" **Wt:** 215 **Age:** 19

Yr Team	Lg	G	GS	IP	H	R	ER	HR	BB	SO	SV	W	L	Pct.	ERA
97 Hudson Vall	A	15	15	84.0	78	44	38	3	29	82	0	4	6	.400	4.07
1 Minor League Yr		15	15	84.0	78	44	38	3	29	82	0	4	6	.400	4.07

Some scouts say that Matt White was the best high school pitcher they ever saw. He was declared a free agent after the notorious contract-tender saga in 1996, and the Devil Rays signed the big righthander to a record $10.2 million bonus. White missed the early part of the 1997 season with a stress fracture in his back, but took the mound in the second half, and impressed enough people in the New York-Penn League to be named the circuit's top prospect. He has a 95-MPH fastball, a fine curve, a nice changeup, and decent control and composure. With no full-season experience, I can't give him a letter grade. History is replete with examples of highly-touted young moundsmen like White who get hurt, and injuries are probably the only thing that could stop him.

Greg Whiteman   *Philadelphia Phillies*

Pos: P   Throws: Left   Ht: 6'2"   Wt: 185   Age: 24

Yr Team	Lg	G	GS	IP	H	R	ER	HR	BB	SO	SV	W	L	Pct.	ERA
96 Lakeland	A	27	27	150.1	134	66	62	5	89	122	0	11	10	.524	3.71
97 Clearwater	A	11	11	51.0	57	30	26	3	26	32	0	3	3	.500	4.59
Reading	AA	9	9	53.1	57	27	24	6	21	31	0	4	4	.500	4.05
4 Minor League Yrs		89	89	475.1	446	246	218	25	244	417	0	31	32	.492	4.13

Whiteman had been a prospect in the Tigers system for several years; he has a 90-MPH fastball, a sharp breaking pitch, and an annoyingly inconsistent track record. He became a free agent last year due to a waiver error by the Tigers, and the Phillies snatched him up. Basically, his profile is the same as it was before: he has a great arm for a lefty, but doesn't know how to use it. He could figure it out someday, or he could hang around for 10 more years without making any progress. One thing is for sure: as long as he throws hard, he won't have much of a problem finding teams willing to give him a chance. **Grade C-**

Mike Whitlock   *Toronto Blue Jays*

Pos: 1B   Bats: Left   Ht: 6'3"   Wt: 200   Age: 21

Yr Team	Lg	G	AB	R	H	2B	3B	HR	RBI	BB	SO	SB	CS	Avg	OBP	Slg
96 Hagerstown	A	131	424	72	107	22	1	20	91	108	132	1	4	.252	.412	.450
97 Dunedin	A	107	322	41	62	14	0	11	48	69	132	1	1	.193	.346	.339
3 Minor League Yrs		292	914	140	212	46	4	34	161	218	312	7	5	.232	.390	.403

After his fine 1996 season, Mike Whitlock was being compared to Fred McGriff. No more. The Florida State League is a tough environment for a power hitter, but to say that Whitlock really struggled in 1997 is an understatement of colossal proportions. He continued to draw walks, and 11 homers in the FSL isn't that bad, but his strikeout rate was terrible, and he showed no ability at all to hit for contact. Whitlock is still young, and his career isn't ruined yet, but it is hard to remain enthusiastic about his chances at this point. **Grade C-**

Luke Wilcox

Tampa Bay Devil Rays

Pos: OF **Bats:** Left **Ht:** 6'4" **Wt:** 190 **Age:** 24

Yr Team	Lg	G	AB	R	H	2B	3B	HR	RBI	BB	SO	SB	CS	Avg	OBP	Slg
96 Tampa	A	119	470	72	133	32	5	11	76	40	71	14	10	.283	.339	.443
97 Tampa	A	12	40	7	12	4	0	0	4	7	6	1	1	.300	.408	.400
Norwich	AA	74	300	45	83	13	1	6	34	18	36	13	3	.277	.323	.387
3 Minor League Yrs		264	1033	149	301	65	13	18	142	85	141	37	17	.291	.347	.432

Wilcox didn't play extremely well in his first Double-A season. His walk rate dropped substantially, and although he continued to show some spark with the bat and some speed on the bases, it was a disappointing season, even considering that Norwich isn't a great place to hit. He does have a very good glove, and can play left, center or right without difficulty. If Wilcox can do a little better with the strike zone, he would make an adequate reserve outfielder, and being with the Devil Rays may get him an extra chance or two. **Grade C**

Glenn Williams

Atlanta Braves

Pos: SS **Bats:** Both **Ht:** 6'1" **Wt:** 185 **Age:** 20

Yr Team	Lg	G	AB	R	H	2B	3B	HR	RBI	BB	SO	SB	CS	Avg	OBP	Slg
96 Macon	A	51	181	14	35	7	3	3	18	18	47	4	2	.193	.271	.315
97 Macon	A	77	297	52	79	18	2	14	52	24	105	9	6	.266	.327	.481
4 Minor League Yrs		285	1034	137	233	44	9	27	136	96	317	28	18	.225	.298	.364

The Braves finally yielded dividends from their $800,000 investment in Australian prospect Glenn Williams. His power manifested itself in 1997: his OPS was very good at +19 percent, and production like that is rare for a young infielder. On the negative side, his main weakness as a hitter was also clearly apparent: you guessed it, poor strike-zone judgment. It will be difficult for him at higher levels unless he gets a better idea of the area around home plate. Williams' range at shortstop isn't good, and he will likely move to third base soon. He has the tools to be a fine defensive player with more experience. Williams has fought injuries throughout his career, and missed much of last season with shoulder problems. He needs to get a full season in, but he made progress last year and still has youth on his side. **Grade C+**

Jason Williams

Cincinnati Reds

Pos: 2B **Bats:** Right **Ht:** 5'8" **Wt:** 180 **Age:** 24

Yr Team	Lg	G	AB	R	H	2B	3B	HR	RBI	BB	SO	SB	CS	Avg	OBP	Slg
97 Burlington	A	68	256	49	83	17	1	7	41	21	40	9	6	.324	.382	.480
Chattanooga	AA	69	271	38	84	21	1	5	28	18	35	5	5	.310	.349	.450
1 Minor League Yr		137	527	87	167	38	2	12	69	39	75	14	11	.317	.366	.465

Jason Williams was a solid college hitter at LSU, but scouts didn't like his athleticism and were skeptical about his ability to hit with wood. Though he was good enough to start at shortstop for the 1996 U.S. Olympic team, he dropped to the 16th round in that year's draft. Williams proved the bat doubters wrong by hitting quite well in both the Midwest and Southern Leagues in 1997. He is a bit too impatient for my taste, but he makes contact and shows good power into the gaps. He projects as a .270-.290 hitter in the majors. Williams played shortstop for Burlington, but moved over to second in Double-A and was terrific there. His fielding percentage of .988 would have led the league if he had played enough games, and his range factor was well above average. I want to see him in Triple-A before going overboard, but he sure had a nice debut for a 16th-round pick. **Grade B**

Jeff Williams   Los Angeles Dodgers

Pos: P   **Throws:** Left   **Ht:** 6'0"   **Wt:** 185   **Age:** 25

Yr Team	Lg	G	GS	IP	H	R	ER	HR	BB	SO	SV	W	L	Pct.	ERA
97 San Antonio	AA	5	5	28.1	30	17	17	2	7	14	0	2	1	.667	5.40
San Berndno	A	18	18	116.0	101	52	40	8	34	72	0	10	4	.714	3.10
1 Minor League Yr		23	23	144.1	131	69	57	10	41	86	0	12	5	.706	3.55

Jeff Williams, a native of Australia, pitched college ball at Southeastern Louisiana University, and was signed by the Dodgers as a free agent after playing for the Australian team in the 1996 Olympics. His first pro season was a success, as he pitched well in the California League and wasn't terrible in the Texas League. Williams works with an average fastball, but his curve, slider, and changeup are fine, and he isn't afraid to throw strikes. His K/IP rate is too low for me to get excited about him, but pitchers are as predictable as quantum fluctuations. **Grade C**

Keith Williams   San Francisco Giants

Pos: OF   **Bats:** Right   **Ht:** 6'0"   **Wt:** 190   **Age:** 25

Yr Team	Lg	G	AB	R	H	2B	3B	HR	RBI	BB	SO	SB	CS	Avg	OBP	Slg
96 Phoenix	AAA	108	398	63	109	25	3	13	63	52	96	2	2	.274	.354	.450
San Francisco	NL	9	20	0	5	0	0	0	0	0	6	0	0	.250	.250	.250
97 Phoenix	AAA	3	5	0	1	0	0	0	0	0	2	0	0	.200	.200	.200
Shreveport	AA	131	493	83	158	37	7	22	106	46	94	3	0	.320	.377	.558
5 Minor League Yrs		544	2046	340	615	137	25	79	384	234	417	35	15	.301	.371	.508

Man, the Giants system is really giving me a case of deja vu. It seems like I write about the same group of position players every year. . . Dante Powell, Armando Rios, Benji Simonton, Chris Singleton, Keith Williams. It's getting boring. . . they need some more prospects. Well, I guess they had some, but they traded them to the White Sox and the Marlins. Anyhow, Keith Williams has certainly proven that he can hit in the Texas League, so it is pointless to leave him there again. He has power, but he isn't likely to hit for average in the majors. His defense isn't great, either, leaving the power as his only skill. He could probably hit 20 homers in the majors, but a .250 average with 20 homers and mediocre defense isn't exactly going to move Barry Bonds out of town. **Grade C-**

Antone Williamson
Milwaukee Brewers

Pos: 1B **Bats:** Left **Ht:** 6'1" **Wt:** 195 **Age:** 24

Yr Team	Lg	G	AB	R	H	2B	3B	HR	RBI	BB	SO	SB	CS	Avg	OBP	Slg
96 New Orleans	AAA	55	199	23	52	10	1	5	23	19	40	1	0	.261	.326	.397
97 Tucson	AAA	83	304	53	87	20	5	5	41	49	41	3	1	.286	.389	.434
Milwaukee	AL	24	54	2	11	3	0	0	6	4	8	0	1	.204	.254	.259
4 Minor League Yrs		285	1054	157	302	69	13	21	180	131	169	7	3	.287	.366	.436

Most people are certain now that Antone Williamson will *not* be a star; the question that faces us is, will he be adequate? Scouts still like his swing, and he is more patient than he used to be, but he still isn't showing much power, and a .286 average at Tucson isn't impressive. Dreadful defense at third base has moved him to first, where he should be pretty good with the glove given time. Right now, he looks like a .260 hitter with doubles power. That's okay for a shortstop, but for a corner player it sucks like a chest wound. It isn't too late yet for Williamson, especially if he can stop getting injured, but time is running out. **Grade C**

Craig Wilson
Pittsburgh Pirates

Pos: C **Bats:** Right **Ht:** 6'2" **Wt:** 195 **Age:** 21

Yr Team	Lg	G	AB	R	H	2B	3B	HR	RBI	BB	SO	SB	CS	Avg	OBP	Slg
96 Hagerstown	A	131	495	66	129	27	5	11	70	32	120	17	11	.261	.316	.402
97 Lynchburg	A	117	401	54	106	26	1	19	69	39	98	6	5	.264	.350	.476
3 Minor League Yrs		297	1080	153	287	67	7	37	174	95	259	31	18	.266	.338	.444

Wilson was originally in the Blue Jays system, and came to the Pirates as part of the big Carlos Garcia/Orlando Merced trade. He has significant power potential, but his command of the strike zone is borderline, and pitchers at higher levels may exploit this if he doesn't become more patient. Wilson is said to have a strong arm, but he threw out just 26 percent of runners attempting to steal in 1997, after nailing 37 percent in 1996. I want to see if Wilson can hit in Double-A, and he needs to get his throwing back to previous standards. **Grade C**

Enrique Wilson
Cleveland Indians

Pos: SS-2B **Bats:** Both **Ht:** 5'11" **Wt:** 160 **Age:** 22

Yr Team	Lg	G	AB	R	H	2B	3B	HR	RBI	BB	SO	SB	CS	Avg	OBP	Slg
96 Canton-Akrn	AA	117	484	70	147	17	5	5	50	31	46	23	16	.304	.346	.390
Buffalo	AAA	3	8	1	4	1	0	0	0	1	1	0	2	.500	.556	.625
97 Buffalo	AAA	118	451	78	138	20	3	11	39	42	41	9	8	.306	.369	.437
Cleveland	AL	5	15	2	5	0	0	0	1	0	2	0	0	.333	.333	.333
6 Minor League Yrs		559	2160	340	628	99	31	45	271	161	182	79	62	.291	.343	.428

Enrique Wilson should start at second base in Cleveland in 1998, and he will be a candidate for Rookie of the Year. Hitting out of a slightly open stance, Wilson has good pop into the gaps, is reasonably selective, makes contact exceptionally well, and will be a 15-homer threat at his peak. He wasn't intimidated by Triple-A pitching last year, and his OPS of .805, plus-six percent in the American Association, is great for an infielder. Defensively, he is excellent. He has great range, a strong arm, superior instincts, and adapted well to second base after spending his career at shortstop, although he needs to smooth out his actions a bit on the double play. Omar Vizquel is the reason Wilson was moved to second; there wasn't anything wrong with his glove at short. Wilson missed the September stretch run after contracting chicken pox. That's a nasty disease as an adult; I caught it last year and it quite literally could have killed me. Wilson will definitely be a good one; he could be a great one. **Grade A-**

Preston Wilson   *New York Mets*

Pos: OF   **Bats:** Right   **Ht:** 6'2"   **Wt:** 193   **Age:** 23

Yr Team	Lg	G	AB	R	H	2B	3B	HR	RBI	BB	SO	SB	CS	Avg	OBP	Slg
96 St. Lucie	A	23	85	6	15	3	0	1	7	8	21	1	1	.176	.263	.247
97 St. Lucie	A	63	245	32	60	12	1	11	48	8	66	3	4	.245	.267	.437
Binghamton	AA	70	259	37	74	12	1	19	47	21	71	7	1	.286	.340	.560
5 Minor League Yrs		472	1793	250	452	84	12	82	281	102	489	51	24	.252	.298	.450

Midway through last season, I took a glance at Preston Wilson's St. Lucie stats, and saw that horrific K/BB ratio. Eight walks in 245 at-bats, with 66 strikeouts? "Still no prospect," I thought. Then, when the season ended, I looked closely at Wilson's numbers after his promotion to Double-A Binghamton. The strikeout rate was still too high, but his walk rate nearly tripled. Not surprisingly, he hit better than he has done at any time in his career. Will he keep that up? I don't know. Sometimes something just clicks for a player. It is possible that Preston Wilson finally figured out how to be more selective. He is still young enough for it to be authentic refinement. On the other hand, it was only half a season, and many times players who make a dramatic improvement in zone judgment regress the next season. Watch him closely in 1998. My guess is that he will fall back to old habits, but that is just a guess. If the walk rate stays near respectable levels, he could be the power-hitting star projected by scouts. **Grade C**

Scott Winchester   *Cincinnati Reds*

Pos: P   **Throws:** Right   **Ht:** 6'2"   **Wt:** 210   **Age:** 24

Yr Team	Lg	G	GS	IP	H	R	ER	HR	BB	SO	SV	W	L	Pct.	ERA
96 Columbus	A	52	0	61.1	50	27	22	8	16	60	26	7	3	.700	3.23
97 Kinston	A	34	0	36.2	21	6	6	2	11	45	29	2	1	.667	1.47
Akron	AA	6	0	7.0	8	3	3	1	2	8	1	0	0	—	3.86
Chattanooga	AA	9	0	10.2	9	4	2	0	3	3	3	2	1	.667	1.69
Indianapols	AAA	4	0	5.2	2	0	0	0	2	2	0	0	0	—	0.00
Cincinnati	NL	5	0	6.0	9	5	4	1	2	3	0	0	0	—	6.00
3 Minor League Yrs		128	0	150.0	114	50	42	11	40	145	70	14	6	.700	2.52

A 14th-round pick in 1995, Scott Winchester was a prosperous closer at Clemson, and has continued to thrive in that role in the minors. He went from Cleveland to Cincinnati in the John Smiley trade, and will likely have a spot in the Reds' bullpen in 1998. Winchester, unlike many college and minor league relief aces, has a good arm, with a 92-MPH fastball and a hard slider. His control is sharp, and he usually pitches well under pressure. Winchester won't close in the majors right away, but he should do well as a middle reliever once he gets his feet wet. **Grade B-**

Randy Winn
Tampa Bay Devil Rays

Pos: OF Bats: Both Ht: 6'2" Wt: 175 Age: 23

Yr Team	Lg	G	AB	R	H	2B	3B	HR	RBI	BB	SO	SB	CS	Avg	OBP	Slg
96 Kane County	A	130	514	90	139	16	3	0	35	47	115	30	18	.270	.340	.313
97 Brevard Cty	A	36	143	26	45	8	2	0	15	16	28	16	8	.315	.400	.399
Portland	AA	96	384	66	112	15	6	8	36	42	92	35	20	.292	.371	.424
3 Minor League Yrs		313	1254	220	363	46	15	8	108	120	266	100	53	.289	.361	.369

Randy Winn, from the University of Santa Clara, was drafted in the third round in 1995. Speed is his game: he was named Fastest Baserunner in the Eastern League, although he is still learning how to use his swiftness properly. Winn doesn't have much power, and gets in trouble when he tries too hard to hit for distance, resulting in strikeouts and medium-range fly balls. When he stays within himself, as the scouts say, he is a dangerous line-drive hitter. His defense is good enough for center. Winn will never be a starter, but if he can develop his offense a bit more he could be a nice reserve. In my opinion, neither expansion team is as good as they could be. There are a lot of excellent hitters trapped in the minor leagues right now that either team could have picked up in the draft. Winn wasn't one of them. **Grade C**

Jay Witasick
Oakland Athletics

Pos: P Throws: Right Ht: 6'4" Wt: 205 Age: 25

Yr Team	Lg	G	GS	IP	H	R	ER	HR	BB	SO	SV	W	L	Pct.	ERA
96 Huntsville	AA	25	6	66.2	47	21	17	3	26	63	4	0	3	.000	2.30
Edmonton	AAA	6	0	8.2	9	4	4	1	6	9	2	0	0	—	4.15
Oakland	AL	12	0	13.0	12	9	9	5	5	12	0	1	1	.500	6.23
97 Modesto	A	9	2	17.1	16	9	8	1	5	29	1	0	1	.000	4.15
Edmonton	AAA	13	1	27.1	25	13	13	3	15	17	0	3	2	.600	4.28
Oakland	AL	8	0	11.0	14	7	7	2	6	8	0	0	0	—	5.73
5 Minor League Yrs		109	65	445.0	369	196	163	29	167	476	7	27	24	.529	3.30

Jay Witasick has some of the best stuff in the Oakland system, including a 92-MPH fastball and a hard breaking pitch, but most of the 1997 season was spent on the sidelines waiting for his elbow to stop hurting. Surgery was avoided, or at least it has been as I write this. Speculation is vain, but it wouldn't surprise me at all if the elbow problems keep up until he goes under the knife. If that happens, his career is on hold indefinitely. By the way, Witasick is a good pitcher, if healthy, and would make a fine reliever. **Grade C**

Kevin Witt
Toronto Blue Jays

Pos: 1B Bats: Left Ht: 6'4" Wt: 185 Age: 22

Yr Team	Lg	G	AB	R	H	2B	3B	HR	RBI	BB	SO	SB	CS	Avg	OBP	Slg
96 Dunedin	A	124	446	63	121	18	6	13	70	39	96	9	4	.271	.335	.426
97 Knoxville	AA	127	501	76	145	27	4	30	91	44	109	1	0	.289	.349	.539
4 Minor League Yrs		430	1669	234	439	90	15	64	247	126	405	15	10	.263	.319	.450

Kevin Witt, Toronto's first-round pick in 1994 from a Florida high school, is a lanky young hitter who generates great power through bat speed rather than brute strength. If he adds some muscle to his frame, his production could increase even more. Witt's OPS was fine at +15 percent, his SEC quite nice at +19. Both marks were very good for the Southern League, though not in the top echelon. Witt's basic problem, like nearly all Toronto prospects, is strike-zone judgment. In his case it is primarily a function of his long arms, and he has made strides to correct this weakness. His walk rate has increased gradually over the last three years. Witt has played shortstop, third base, outfield, and first at various times, and he isn't that good at any of them. He can hit, although it may be a year before he is ready to contribute. **Grade B+**

Mike Wolff

Anaheim Angels

Pos: OF-DH **Bats:** Right **Ht:** 6'1" **Wt:** 195 **Age:** 27

Yr Team	Lg	G	AB	R	H	2B	3B	HR	RBI	BB	SO	SB	CS	Avg	OBP	Slg
96 Lk Elsinore	A	12	42	12	12	3	0	2	7	9	10	3	0	.286	.412	.500
Vancouver	AAA	71	256	46	64	15	3	10	38	34	69	6	4	.250	.340	.449
97 Vancouver	AAA	91	266	58	75	15	0	21	64	53	75	6	4	.282	.417	.575
6 Minor League Yrs		602	2057	368	567	121	13	88	348	321	492	48	39	.276	.377	.475

Mike Wolff isn't a hot prospect by any means, but you could do worse for a backup outfielder. He lacks physical tools, but plays intelligently and maximizes what he does have. He will take a walk and will bang the occasional tater. Although he does have a strong arm, his defense in the field is no better than adequate. That is part of the reason why he has trouble getting a job, of course. I can understand that, but personally I would rather see Wolff in the majors than some of the people who got playing time last year, like Lee Tinsley or Scott Pose. **Grade C-**

Kerry Wood

Chicago Cubs

Pos: P **Throws:** Right **Ht:** 6'5" **Wt:** 190 **Age:** 20

Yr Team	Lg	G	GS	IP	H	R	ER	HR	BB	SO	SV	W	L	Pct.	ERA
96 Daytona	A	22	22	114.1	72	51	37	6	70	136	0	10	2	.833	2.91
97 Orlando	AA	19	19	94.0	58	49	47	2	79	106	0	6	7	.462	4.50
Iowa	AAA	10	10	57.2	35	35	30	2	52	80	0	4	2	.667	4.68
3 Minor League Yrs		54	54	273.1	170	143	119	10	207	329	0	20	11	.645	3.92

If you ask a scout who the best pitching prospect in baseball is, he likely will say "Kerry Wood." This is understandable. Twenty-year-old pitchers who throw 97 MPH are very rare, and the velocity reports on the fastball are not exaggerated. He also has a really good curveball that he can sometimes throw for strikes. He tries to use a changeup, and although he tips it off occasionally, the situations in which he employs it are appropriate. He has an idea how to pitch and doesn't just try to blow hitters away, though he does overthrow now and then. A peek at his numbers shows his awesome potential, as well as his weaknesses. He led the American Association in K/IP at +84 percent, but his K/BB was terrible at -21 percent. Basically, when Wood throws strikes, he is nearly unhittable, but when he walks people, he gets beat. I have no doubt that Wood has the physical and mental equipment to be a dominant major league pitcher, but I do have concerns. First of all, the Cubs took a big risk by promoting him to Triple-A. His control was bad in Double-A, and I don't understand what Triple-A hitters could teach him about control that Double-A hitters couldn't. Secondly, I can't shake the feeling that he is going to get hurt. He was overused in high school, and has already had elbow trouble in the pros. He was healthy last year, but while his mechanics look smooth from behind home plate, if you watch him from the first base side, it looks like his motion puts some strain on the elbow. Don't get me wrong; this guy is a gem. I don't doubt his ability, but I wonder if he is being handled correctly, and if he will stay healthy. **Grade A-**

Steve Woodard   *Milwaukee Brewers*

Pos: P   **Throws:** Right   **Ht:** 6'4"   **Wt:** 225   **Age:** 22

Yr Team	Lg	G	GS	IP	H	R	ER	HR	BB	SO	SV	W	L	Pct.	ERA
96 Stockton	A	28	28	181.1	201	89	81	14	33	142	0	12	9	.571	4.02
97 El Paso	AA	19	19	136.1	136	56	48	8	25	97	0	14	3	.824	3.17
Tucson	AAA	1	1	7.0	3	0	0	0	1	6	0	1	0	1.000	0.00
Milwaukee	AL	7	7	36.2	39	25	21	5	6	32	0	3	3	.500	5.15
4 Minor League Yrs		84	81	522.1	521	242	209	37	103	424	0	42	16	.724	3.60

Woodard was one of the better stories of 1997, outdueling Roger Clemens in his major league debut. He was a fifth-round pick in 1994, from a high school in Alabama. He is a big, durable, strong-legged pitcher with an average fastball, but good breaking stuff, pinpoint command, and pitching intelligence. Woodard was awesome at El Paso, where he had the second-best K/BB in the league at +125 percent. His best pitches are a curveball and changeup, but he is willing to throw his fastball on the inside corner, and Texas League observers praised his aggressiveness and attention to detail. Woodward's K/BB ratio in the majors was excellent, and if he stays healthy, he has a chance to be a very fine pitcher. **Grade B**

Jay Woolf   *St. Louis Cardinals*

Pos: SS   **Bats:** Both   **Ht:** 6'1"   **Wt:** 170   **Age:** 20

Yr Team	Lg	G	AB	R	H	2B	3B	HR	RBI	BB	SO	SB	CS	Avg	OBP	Slg
96 Peoria	A	108	362	68	93	12	8	1	27	57	87	28	12	.257	.360	.343
97 Pr William	A	70	251	59	62	11	3	6	18	55	75	26	5	.247	.391	.386
3 Minor League Yrs		209	724	143	186	30	12	7	59	120	183	60	20	.257	.366	.360

Although he missed much of the season due to migrane headaches, Jay Woolf is a very interesting prospect. A second-round pick in 1995 from a Florida high school, Woolf's combination of walks and speed is very intriguing, and he has the physical strength to develop some power as he matures. His SEC was very high at +66 percent, showing that he contributes to the offense despite his mediocre batting average. Woolf has the tools to be a good defensive shortstop, but needs more polish; ain't anything unusual about that. Normally, I would see him as a major sleeper for 1998, but serious questions exist about his work ethic and desire to play baseball. **Grade C**

Greg Wooten
Seattle Mariners

Pos: P   **Throws:** Right   **Ht:** 6'7"   **Wt:** 210   **Age:** 24

Yr Team	Lg	G	GS	IP	H	R	ER	HR	BB	SO	SV	W	L	Pct.	ERA
96 Wisconsin	A	13	13	83.2	58	27	23	3	29	68	0	7	1	.875	2.47
Lancaster	A	14	14	97.0	101	47	41	7	25	71	0	8	4	.667	3.80
97 Memphis	AA	26	26	155.0	166	91	77	14	59	98	0	11	10	.524	4.47
2 Minor League Yrs		53	53	335.2	325	165	141	24	113	237	0	26	15	.634	3.78

Wooten was an excellent college pitcher at Portland State, but has had rougher going in the pros since signing as a third-rounder in 1995. Although his velocity is down from his college days, Wooten still has a 90-MPH fastball, a good slider, and a splitter he uses as a changeup. His control is pretty good, and he seldom walks himself into trouble, but his command within the strike zone isn't great, and he doesn't strike a lot of people out. He has had bouts of elbow and shoulder trouble as well. Wooten remains a potentially good pitcher, but I want to see improvement in his K/BB and K/IP ratios before I project sudden success. **Grade C+**

Ron Wright
Pittsburgh Pirates

Pos: 1B   **Bats:** Right   **Ht:** 6'0"   **Wt:** 215   **Age:** 22

Yr Team	Lg	G	AB	R	H	2B	3B	HR	RBI	BB	SO	SB	CS	Avg	OBP	Slg
96 Durham	A	66	240	47	66	15	2	20	62	37	71	1	0	.275	.363	.604
Greenville	AA	63	232	39	59	11	1	16	52	38	73	1	0	.254	.360	.517
Carolina	AA	4	14	1	2	0	0	0	0	2	7	0	1	.143	.250	.143
97 Calgary	AAA	91	336	50	102	31	0	16	63	24	81	0	2	.304	.348	.539
4 Minor League Yrs		404	1518	240	401	89	4	85	297	173	371	5	3	.264	.338	.496

Ron Wright's season was cut short by a broken wrist, but he showed enough to prove that his bat will work at the higher levels. I wrote last year that he would never be a .300 hitter, but he seemed intent on proving me wrong, as he shortened his swing a bit, resulting in a higher average, without losing much power. Some of that was park and league effect, and I still think he won't be much more than a .270 hitter in the majors, but his power production should stifle any criticism of his batting average. He should be good for 30-40 home runs annually, 45 at his peak. Defense isn't his calling card and never will be, but again, if he hits 40 homers, it shouldn't matter if he makes a few errors. Wright could be the leading Harmon Killebrew/Mark McGwire-type hitter of the early 21st century. **Grade B+**

Kelly Wunsch
Milwaukee Brewers

Pos: P   **Throws:** Left   **Ht:** 6'5"   **Wt:** 192   **Age:** 25

Yr Team	Lg	G	GS	IP	H	R	ER	HR	BB	SO	SV	W	L	Pct.	ERA
97 Stockton	A	24	22	143.0	141	65	55	11	62	98	0	7	9	.438	3.46
4 Minor League Yrs		90	87	500.2	518	310	259	45	254	401	0	24	39	.381	4.66

Kelly Wunsch came back from two years of elbow trouble in 1997, and managed to stay in the rotation most of the season at Stockton. His fastball used to be very good, but it is just average now, and his breaking stuff and control aren't sharp enough yet to completely compensate. His K/BB was very poor at -22 percent. Wunsch needs to stay healthy, improve his command, and finish making the transition from power to finesse. That's a tall order. **Grade C-**

Esteban Yan

Tampa Bay Devil Rays

Pos: P   **Throws:** Right   **Ht:** 6'4"   **Wt:** 180   **Age:** 23

Yr Team	Lg	G	GS	IP	H	R	ER	HR	BB	SO	SV	W	L	Pct.	ERA
96 Bowie	AA	9	1	16.0	18	12	10	2	8	16	0	0	2	.000	5.63
Rochester	AAA	22	10	71.2	75	37	34	6	18	61	1	5	4	.556	4.27
Baltimore	AL	4	0	9.1	13	7	6	3	3	7	0	0	0	—	5.79
97 Rochester	AAA	34	12	119.0	107	54	41	13	37	131	2	11	5	.688	3.10
Baltimore	AL	3	2	9.2	20	18	17	3	7	4	0	0	1	.000	15.83
5 Minor League Yrs		131	86	586.1	567	297	218	43	154	468	4	37	38	.493	3.35

Esteban Yan is often ignored as a prospect, but he shouldn't be. He always posts excellent K/BB ratios, +84 percent last year, +72 percent the year before, and he is not a finesse guy. His fastball runs 92 MPH, his breaking stuff is quite sharp, and his strikeout rate is very high. Command and control are obviously strengths for him. The main problem for Yan is durability. He has had shoulder problems, and has yet to settle into one role. Yan didn't do well in his 1997 major league trial, and the Orioles need pitching less than most teams do, so he was left exposed in the expansion draft. Unless his command totally blows up on him, he should spend 1998 in the majors, and could be very good. **Grade B**

Ed Yarnall

New York Mets

Pos: P   **Throws:** Left   **Ht:** 6'4"   **Wt:** 220   **Age:** 22

Yr Team	Lg	G	GS	IP	H	R	ER	HR	BB	SO	SV	W	L	Pct.	ERA
97 St. Lucie	A	18	18	105.1	93	33	29	5	30	114	0	5	8	.385	2.48
Norfolk	AAA	1	1	5.0	11	8	8	1	7	2	0	0	1	.000	14.40
Binghamton	AA	5	5	32.1	20	11	11	2	11	32	0	3	2	.600	3.06
1 Minor League Yr		24	24	142.2	124	52	48	8	48	148	0	8	11	.421	3.03

Yarnall was the ace of the LSU team that won the College World Series in 1996, going 11-1 with a 2.38 ERA. The Mets picked him in the third round, he signed late, and didn't make his pro debut until 1997. He was terrific. Yarnall outmatched the Florida State League (K/BB +90 percent, K/IP +40 percent, H/IP +10 percent), and was just as good in the Double-A Eastern League. He made one start for Norfolk and got pounded, but one game does not a failure make. Yarnall works with a moving 89-91 MPH fastball, a very good curve, a good slider, and a changeup. His control is reliable, and he looks like he knows what he is doing on the mound. I like Yarnall and I think he is going to be quite a pitcher, assuming the Mets don't have him throw 290 innings next year. **Grade B+**

A.J. Zapp

Atlanta Braves

Pos: 1B **Bats:** Left **Ht:** 6'2" **Wt:** 190 **Age:** 19

Yr Team	Lg	G	AB	R	H	2B	3B	HR	RBI	BB	SO	SB	CS	Avg	OBP	Slg
96 Braves	R	47	161	9	24	9	0	0	5	15	58	0	0	.149	.225	.205
97 Danville	R	65	234	34	79	23	2	7	56	35	78	0	1	.338	.437	.543
2 Minor League Yrs		112	395	43	103	32	2	7	61	50	136	0	1	.261	.354	.405

Zapp, Atlanta's first-round pick in 1996, had a terrific season in the Rookie-level Appalachian League last year, and should move to a full-season level in 1998. He hit for an excellent average and very good power, but his strikeout rate was high. Scouts praise Zapp as a pure hitter with a beautiful swing who should excel at all levels, but we need to see him in a full-season league.

Other Prospect Reports

This section contains brief overviews of other guys who may get a chance in the major leagues in 1998. Most of them would be considered Grade C or C– prospects; there are a few exceptions, and they are noted.

Of all the players in this section, the ones most likely to contribute would be the pitchers.

Andy Abad — Boston Red Sox
1997 Statistics **Pos:** 1B-OF **Age:** 25 **B:**L **T:**L

	G	AB	HR	RBI	SB	Avg	OBP	SLG
AAA Pawtucket	68	227	9	32	3	.273	.376	.423
AA Trenton	45	165	8	24	2	.303	.423	.527

First baseman/outfielder with doubles power, some patience. No chance to play in Boston, barring Armageddon.

Sharnol Adriana — Toronto Blue Jays
1997 Statistics **Pos:** 2B **Age:** 27 **B:**R **T:**R

	G	AB	HR	RBI	SB	Avg	OBP	SLG
AA Knoxville	99	314	6	39	9	.236	.341	.334

Good 1996 season in Triple-A, bad 1997 season in Double-A, possibly a result of discouragement. Has some patience, some pop, better than many reserve infielders.

Pat Ahearne — Los Angeles Dodgers
1997 Statistics **Pos:** P **Age:** 28 **B:**R **T:** R

	W	L	ERA	G	GS	Sv	IP	H	BB	SO
AAA Albuquerque	2	4	4.90	20	8	0	60.2	82	20	44
AA San Antonio	4	5	4.50	14	14	0	84.0	109	13	45

Ultimate finesse pitcher, the kind of guy who could learn a splitter or knuckleball and come out of nowhere. Not likely, but it never is, even when it happens.

Israel Alcantara — Montreal Expos
1997 Statistics **Pos:** 3B **Age:** 24 **B:**R **T:**R

	G	AB	HR	RBI	SB	Avg	OBP	SLG
AA Harrisburg	89	301	27	68	4	.282	.348	.595

Double-A third baseman for last two years, has power potential but injuries and poor strike-zone judgment have hurt him. Could break out if healthy and if he learns to lay off the breaking stuff.

Antonio Alfonseca — Florida Marlins
1997 Statistics **Pos:** P **Age:** 25 **B:**R **T:** R

	W	L	ERA	G	GS	Sv	IP	H	BB	SO
AAA Charlotte	7	2	4.32	46	0	7	58.1	58	20	45
NL Florida	1	3	4.91	17	0	0	25.2	36	10	19

Good arm, performance history erratic and prone to injuries. Human interest story due to six digits on each appendage.

Rafael Alvarez — Minnesota Twins
1997 Statistics **Pos:** OF **Age:** 21 **B:**L **T:**L

	G	AB	HR	RBI	SB	Avg	OBP	SLG
AAA Salt Lake	17	48	0	5	5	.271	.352	.333
AA New Britain	16	47	2	7	1	.255	.340	.383
A Ft. Myers	47	122	1	15	6	.270	.357	.385

Venezuelan outfielder, played at three levels, didn't do much at any of them. Very young, needs to stay healthy and have a consolidation season at one level. Grade C+ prospect.

John Ambrose — Chicago White Sox
1997 Statistics **Pos:** P **Age:** 23 **B:**R **T:** R

	W	L	ERA	G	GS	Sv	IP	H	BB	SO
A Winston-Sal	8	13	5.47	27	27	0	149.2	136	117	137

Throws very hard, control is nearly as bad as White Sox owner Jerry Reinsdorf's desire to win.

Kym Ashworth — Detroit Tigers
1997 Statistics **Pos:** P **Age:** 21 **B:**L **T:** L

	W	L	ERA	G	GS	Sv	IP	H	BB	SO
A San Berndno	0	3	6.46	9	5	0	30.2	34	24	26
A Yakima	0	1	3.63	4	4	0	17.1	13	10	15

Young Australian, career on the ropes due to injuries. Example 78,992 why it is a bad idea to have an 18-year-old pitch 127 hard innings in the California League.

Justin Atchley — Cincinnati Reds
1997 Statistics **Pos:** P **Age:** 24 **B:**L **T:** L

	W	L	ERA	G	GS	Sv	IP	H	BB	SO
AA Chattanooga	4	2	4.70	13	13	0	67.0	75	14	48

Live-armed lefty, has injury problems. Put on 40-man roster, could surprise in 1998 if healthy.

Jeff Ball — San Francisco Giants
1997 Statistics **Pos:** 3B **Age:** 28 **B:**R **T:**R

	G	AB	HR	RBI	SB	Avg	OBP	SLG
AAA Phoenix	126	470	18	103	10	.321	.396	.530

Versatile glove, can hit some, but too old to be considered a prospect. A good manager could get something out of him. Beavis and Butt-Head's favorite player.

Brian Barber
St. Louis Cardinals
1997 Statistics **Pos:** P **Age:** 25 **B:**R **T:** R

	W	L	ERA	G	GS	Sv	IP	H	BB	SO
AAA Louisville	4	8	6.90	18	18	0	92.2	111	44	74
AA Arkansas	0	1	10.47	3	3	0	16.1	28	5	15
A Pr William	1	1	4.09	2	2	0	11.0	10	5	13

Injuries and inconsistency have ruined him. The two often go together.

Glen Barker
Detroit Tigers
1997 Statistics **Pos:** OF **Age:** 26 **B:**R **T:**R

	G	AB	HR	RBI	SB	Avg	OBP	SLG
AAA Toledo	21	47	1	3	6	.191	.283	.277
AA Jacksnville	69	257	6	29	17	.280	.361	.412
A Lakeland	13	57	1	11	7	.316	.361	.439

Double-A roster filler, has speed and a touch of power, but strikes out too much.

Kevin Barker
Milwaukee Brewers
1997 Statistics **Pos:** 1B **Age:** 22 **B:**L **T:**L

	G	AB	HR	RBI	SB	Avg	OBP	SLG
AA El Paso	65	238	10	63	3	.277	.352	.517
A Stockton	70	267	13	45	4	.303	.362	.562

Hit well in California League, but production was disappointing at El Paso. Young enough to improve, has a nice swing, worth keeping track of. Grade C+ prospect.

Brian Barkley
Boston Red Sox
1997 Statistics **Pos:** P **Age:** 22 **B:**L **T:** L

	W	L	ERA	G	GS	Sv	IP	H	BB	SO
AA Trenton	12	9	4.94	29	29	0	178.2	208	79	121

Added to 40-man roster in November. Adequate season in Double-A, gives up a lot of hits. No reason to expect immediate success.

Jeff Barry
Colorado Rockies
1997 Statistics **Pos:** OF **Age:** 29 **B:**B **T:**R

	G	AB	HR	RBI	SB	Avg	OBP	SLG
AAA Colo Sprngs	81	273	13	70	5	.300	.375	.513
AA New Haven	40	146	5	12	3	.219	.253	.349

Veteran outfielder hit well at Colorado Springs, which isn't hard.

Blake Barthol
Colorado Rockies
1997 Statistics **Pos:** C **Age:** 24 **B:**R **T:**R

	G	AB	HR	RBI	SB	Avg	OBP	SLG
AA New Haven	109	325	6	39	5	.243	.326	.348

Catcher with offensive and defensive potential, did not have good season at New Haven, but the Rockies sent him to the Arizona Fall League anyway. Couldn't be worse than Manwaring.

Robbie Beckett
Colorado Rockies
1997 Statistics **Pos:** P **Age:** 25 **B:**R **T:** L

	W	L	ERA	G	GS	Sv	IP	H	BB	SO
AAA Colo Sprngs	1	3	6.79	45	1	1	54.1	61	47	67
NL Colorado	0	0	5.40	2	0	0	1.2	1	1	2

Still throws hard, still has no idea how to pitch. At least he is consistent. PhD practicum for Leo Mazzone.

Clay Bellinger
New York Yankees
1997 Statistics **Pos:** 3B **Age:** 29 **B:**R **T:**R

	G	AB	HR	RBI	SB	Avg	OBP	SLG
AAA Columbus	111	416	12	59	10	.274	.338	.450

Making the rounds of Triple-A, looking for a shot at a utility job. Unlikely to get it, although no worse than most backup infielders.

Joel Bennett
Baltimore Orioles
1997 Statistics **Pos:** P **Age:** 28 **B:**R **T:** R

	W	L	ERA	G	GS	Sv	IP	H	BB	SO
AA Bowie	6	8	3.18	44	10	4	113.1	89	40	146

Outstanding curveball, good control, usually pitches well, but is discounted as a prospect due to lack of a good fastball.

Shayne Bennett
Montreal Expos
1997 Statistics **Pos:** P **Age:** 25 **B:**R **T:** R

	W	L	ERA	G	GS	Sv	IP	H	BB	SO
AAA Ottawa	1	2	1.57	25	0	14	34.1	23	21	29
AA Harrisburg	4	2	4.40	23	1	2	47.0	47	20	38
NL Montreal	0	1	3.18	16	0	0	22.2	21	9	8

Australian forkball pitcher looking for a bullpen spot. Effective when he throws strikes, which he doesn't always do. A little voice in my head says he may emerge in

1998, but I have no real evidence that he will.

Tom Bennett — Oakland Athletics

1997 Statistics   **Pos:** P **Age:** 21 **B:**R **T:** R

	W	L	ERA	G	GS	Sv	IP	H	BB	SO
A Modesto	6	9	5.71	25	24	0	112.0	118	73	116

Got banged around in the California League. Live arm, doesn't know how to pitch yet.

Dave Berg — Florida Marlins

1997 Statistics   **Pos:** SS **Age:** 27 **B:**R **T:**R

	G	AB	HR	RBI	SB	Avg	OBP	SLG
AAA Charlotte	117	424	9	47	16	.295	.377	.448

Seeking bench job and wouldn't be bad at it. A little pop, a little speed, will take a walk, not awful with the glove.

Mike Berry — Baltimore Orioles

1997 Statistics   **Pos:** 3B **Age:** 27 **B:**R **T:**R

	G	AB	HR	RBI	SB	Avg	OBP	SLG
AAA Rochester	54	177	1	19	1	.299	.349	.412
AA Bowie	53	204	8	30	1	.230	.318	.397

Veteran minor leaguer, occasionally hits well and has an adequate glove. Definitely with the wrong team.

Randy Betten — Anaheim Angels

1997 Statistics   **Pos:** OF **Age:** 26 **B:**R **T:**R

	G	AB	HR	RBI	SB	Avg	OBP	SLG
AAA Vancouver	23	61	1	12	1	.279	.353	.393
AA Midland	57	220	3	24	7	.291	.357	.418
A Lk Elsinore	35	116	2	27	7	.345	.437	.474

Can play third, first or outfield without embarrassing himself. Could be utility player if everything breaks right for him.

Todd Betts — Cleveland Indians

1997 Statistics   **Pos:** 3B **Age:** 24 **B:**L **T:**R

	G	AB	HR	RBI	SB	Avg	OBP	SLG
AA Akron	128	439	20	69	1	.246	.355	.444

Lefthanded hitter with power and patience, but low batting average and shaky defense at third limit his appeal. Could have value as a bench guy.

Henry Blanco — Los Angeles Dodgers

1997 Statistics   **Pos:** C **Age:** 26 **B:**R **T:**R

	G	AB	HR	RBI	SB	Avg	OBP	SLG
AAA Albuquerque	91	294	6	47	7	.313	.388	.449
NL Los Angeles	3	5	1	1	0	.400	.400	1.000

Looking for spot as Piazza's caddy. Defense good, but an Albuquerque hitter.

Nate Bland — Los Angeles Dodgers

1997 Statistics   **Pos:** P **Age:** 23 **B:**L **T:** L

	W	L	ERA	G	GS	Sv	IP	H	BB	SO
AA San Antonio	3	2	7.02	10	8	0	41.0	47	24	30
A Vero Beach	7	7	3.38	17	14	0	82.2	85	38	67

Occasionally mentioned as a prospect, but marginal. Nibbles too much with middling stuff.

Frank Bolick — Anaheim Angels

1997 Statistics   **Pos:** DH **Age:** 31 **B:**B **T:**R

	G	AB	HR	RBI	SB	Avg	OBP	SLG
AAA Vancouver	102	362	16	66	4	.304	.382	.533
AA Midland	28	97	8	27	0	.330	.476	.649

Switch-hitter with power and patience, too old to be a prospect but usually hits well.

D.J. Boston — Colorado Rockies

1997 Statistics   **Pos:** 1B **Age:** 26 **B:**L **T:**L

	G	AB	HR	RBI	SB	Avg	OBP	SLG
AAA Colo Sprngs	2	6	0	0	0	.333	.333	.333
AA New Haven	83	293	7	49	1	.287	.384	.420
A Visalia	14	49	1	4	0	.224	.309	.347

Mediocre hitter for a first baseman. Streaky, but could get hot and earn some major league at-bats.

Steve Bourgeois — Colorado Rockies

1997 Statistics   **Pos:** P **Age:** 25 **B:**R **T:** R

	W	L	ERA	G	GS	Sv	IP	H	BB	SO
AAA Colo Sprngs	9	7	5.99	33	18	0	121.2	154	66	86

Former Giants prospect I've always sort of liked as a fifth starter/long reliever type, but he is with the wrong team. Could contribute in the right environment.

Brent Bowers — New York Mets

1997 Statistics Pos: OF **Age:** 26 **B:**L **T:**R

	G	AB	HR	RBI	SB	Avg	OBP	SLG
AAA Scranton-WB	39	110	3	7	1	.255	.308	.355

Great athlete, occasionally plays well when he isn't on the disabled list or in a wild-swinging funk.

Doug Brady — Chicago White Sox

1997 Statistics Pos: 2B **Age:** 28 **B:**B **T:**R

	G	AB	HR	RBI	SB	Avg	OBP	SLG
AAA Nashville	106	370	7	36	13	.238	.276	.343

Hasn't played well in two years. Chance for utility job is fading faster than the Spice Girls.

Derek Brandow — Toronto Blue Jays

1997 Statistics Pos: P **Age:** 28 **B:**R **T:** R

	W	L	ERA	G	GS	Sv	IP	H	BB	SO
AAA Syracuse	7	11	5.41	31	25	0	143.0	161	91	120

Syracuse veteran, best attribute is durability. Walks too many people for a pitcher with average stuff.

Melvin Brazoban — Pittsburgh Pirates

1997 Statistics Pos: P **Age:** 21 **B:**R **T:** R

	W	L	ERA	G	GS	Sv	IP	H	BB	SO
R Rangers	1	3	4.20	14	0	2	30.0	28	14	36

Raw righthander, good arm. Major league Rule 5 draft pick.

Kary Bridges — Pittsburgh Pirates

1997 Statistics Pos: 2B **Age:** 26 **B:**L **T:**R

	G	AB	HR	RBI	SB	Avg	OBP	SLG
AAA New Orleans	23	64	0	3	1	.172	.239	.250
AAA Calgary	33	95	0	6	1	.263	.314	.305
AA Carolina	66	283	3	29	9	.336	.354	.435

Contact hitter, no power, defense adequate but not tremendous.

Darryl Brinkley — San Diego Padres

1997 Statistics Pos: OF **Age:** 29 **B:**R **T:**R

	G	AB	HR	RBI	SB	Avg	OBP	SLG
AA Mobile	55	215	5	33	10	.307	.394	.451

Too old to be a real prospect. Can hit a bit, runs well, but has weak glove, and questionable attitude.

Chris Brock — Atlanta Braves

1997 Statistics Pos: P **Age:** 28 **B:**R **T:** R

	W	L	ERA	G	GS	Sv	IP	H	BB	SO
AAA Richmond	10	6	3.34	20	19	0	118.2	97	51	83
NL Atlanta	0	0	5.58	7	6	0	30.2	34	19	16

Decent arm but injury-prone, pitches well at times but mediocre record overall. Looking for long-relief slot.

Jim Brower — Texas Rangers

1997 Statistics Pos: P **Age:** 25 **B:**R **T:** R

	W	L	ERA	G	GS	Sv	IP	H	BB	SO
AAA Okla City	2	1	7.23	4	3	0	18.2	30	8	7
AA Tulsa	5	12	5.21	23	23	0	140.0	156	42	103

Average fastball, decent slider, occasionally has a good game. You never know with pitchers.

Alvin Brown — Los Angeles Dodgers

1997 Statistics Pos: P **Age:** 27 **B:**R **T:** R

	W	L	ERA	G	GS	Sv	IP	H	BB	SO
AAA Albuquerque	4	6	6.13	12	11	0	61.2	74	35	43
AA San Antonio	6	5	3.74	16	16	0	96.1	83	33	67

Good arm, doesn't give the impression that he knows what he is doing on the mound.

Ray Brown — Kansas City Royals

1997 Statistics Pos: 1B-OF **Age:** 25 **B:**L **T:**R

	G	AB	HR	RBI	SB	Avg	OBP	SLG
AAA Las Vegas	41	140	2	15	1	.257	.316	.393
AA Mobile	57	179	4	30	1	.352	.453	.508

Didn't do very well at Vegas, which didn't help his cause. Can hit if given the chance.

Julio Bruno
Detroit Tigers
1997 Statistics   **Pos:** 3B **Age:** 25 **B:** R **T:** R

	G	AB	HR	RBI	SB	Avg	OBP	SLG
AA Jacksnville	120	438	6	57	6	.265	.327	.370

A prospect with the Padres a couple of years ago, but has never hit. No reason to think he will start.

Will Brunson
Los Angeles Dodgers
1997 Statistics   **Pos:** P **Age:** 28 **B:** L **T:** L

	W	L	ERA	G	GS	Sv	IP	H	BB	SO
AAA Albuquerque	1	1	6.49	27	0	0	26.1	39	10	25
AA San Antonio	5	5	3.47	17	11	0	72.2	68	13	71

Fairly live arm, did well as a starter in Double-A but crushed out of the Albuquerque bullpen. Could see some relief work.

Pat Bryant
Boston Red Sox
1997 Statistics   **Pos:** OF **Age:** 25 **B:** R **T:** R

	G	AB	HR	RBI	SB	Avg	OBP	SLG
AAA Pawtucket	9	34	0	4	2	.294	.314	.412
AA Trenton	104	379	19	77	18	.288	.396	.507

Product of the Cleveland system, picked up by Dan Duquette after 1996 injury season. Bryant has fine tools and shows them on the field more often than not. Needs to play well in Triple-A, and I think he will. Grade C+ prospect.

Mel Bunch
Montreal Expos
1997 Statistics   **Pos:** P **Age:** 26 **B:** R **T:** R

	W	L	ERA	G	GS	Sv	IP	H	BB	SO
AAA Ottawa	4	4	6.35	16	14	0	78.0	102	45	58
AA Harrisburg	3	3	4.20	9	9	0	49.1	45	22	50

A prospect a couple of years ago in the Royals system, career deadlocked by injuries and control problems.

Darren Burton
Philadelphia Phillies
1997 Statistics   **Pos:** OF **Age:** 25 **B:** B **T:** R

	G	AB	HR	RBI	SB	Avg	OBP	SLG
AAA Scranton-WB	70	253	8	39	3	.249	.305	.431
AA Reading	45	184	8	34	1	.315	.352	.538

He looks like a baseball player if you watch him play, but the numbers just aren't there.

Mike Busby
St. Louis Cardinals
1997 Statistics   **Pos:** P **Age:** 25 **B:** R **T:** R

	W	L	ERA	G	GS	Sv	IP	H	BB	SO
AAA Louisville	4	8	4.61	15	14	0	93.2	95	30	65
NL St. Louis	0	2	8.79	3	3	0	14.1	24	4	6

Big starter with adequate stuff, effective when command is sharp and arm isn't sore.

Homer Bush
New York Yankees
1997 Statistics   **Pos:** 2B **Age:** 25 **B:** R **T:** R

	G	AB	HR	RBI	SB	Avg	OBP	SLG
AAA Columbus	74	275	2	26	12	.247	.308	.327
AAA Las Vegas	38	155	3	14	5	.277	.310	.413
AL New York	10	11	0	3	0	.364	.364	.364

Small guy, has speed and a glove, but poor strike-zone judgment would keep him off my team, if I had one.

Adam Butler
Atlanta Braves
1997 Statistics   **Pos:** P **Age:** 24 **B:** L **T:** L

	W	L	ERA	G	GS	Sv	IP	H	BB	SO
AA Greenville	5	1	2.57	46	0	22	49.0	40	15	56

Very good year as Double-A closer, throws fairly hard, candidate for relief role.

Tim Byrdak
Kansas City Royals
1997 Statistics   **Pos:** P **Age:** 24 **B:** L **T:** L

	W	L	ERA	G	GS	Sv	IP	H	BB	SO
A Wilmington	4	3	3.51	22	2	3	41.0	34	12	47

"Hello? Acme Company? This is Herk Robinson. I'd like to order your Lefthanded Pitcher Model 433. Yes, the budget model. Please deliver to the Harry S. Truman Sports Complex, COD. Thank you."

Jolbert Cabrera
Montreal Expos
1997 Statistics   **Pos:** 3B **Age:** 25 **B:** R **T:** R

	G	AB	HR	RBI	SB	Avg	OBP	SLG
AAA Ottawa	68	191	0	12	15	.283	.320	.377
AA Harrisburg	48	171	2	11	5	.251	.360	.339

Brother of fellow Expo prospect Orlando Cabrera. Jolbert has some speed, a multi-purpose glove, and a shot at a utility job. Has a cooler name than his brother.

Jose Cabrera — Houston Astros
1997 Statistics   **Pos:** P **Age:** 26 **B:**R **T:** R

	W	L	ERA	G	GS	Sv	IP	H	BB	SO
AAA Buffalo	3	0	1.20	5	0	0	15.0	8	7	11
AAA New Orleans	2	2	2.54	31	0	0	46.0	31	13	48
NL Houston	0	0	1.17	12	0	0	15.1	6	6	18

Former starter, converted to middle relief and did very well. Reasonably good stuff, fine control. Could do well in Astros bullpen, Grade C+.

Miguel Cairo — Tampa Bay Devil Rays
1997 Statistics   **Pos:** 2B **Age:** 23 **B:**R **T:**R

	G	AB	HR	RBI	SB	Avg	OBP	SLG
AAA Iowa	135	569	5	46	40	.279	.314	.381
NL Chicago	16	29	0	1	0	.241	.313	.276

Slick-fielding infielder with a turn of speed and some doubles but will struggle to hit .260 in the majors. Would be valuable in utility role, but probably overmatched as a regular in Devil Rays' infield.

Todd Carey — Boston Red Sox
1997 Statistics   **Pos:** 1B **Age:** 26 **B:**L **T:**R

	G	AB	HR	RBI	SB	Avg	OBP	SLG
AAA Pawtucket	113	380	12	58	1	.216	.281	.353

Has some power, but poor strike-zone judgment and a long swing will keep him out of the majors.

Cesarin Carmona — San Diego Padres
1997 Statistics   **Pos:** SS **Age:** 21 **B:**B **T:**R

	G	AB	HR	RBI	SB	Avg	OBP	SLG
A Clinton	65	234	11	32	15	.252	.299	.440

Raw shortstop, has power and speed, but weak command of the strike zone in the Midwest League. Put on 40-man roster, won't help the Padres soon.

Quincy Carter — Chicago Cubs
1997 Statistics   **Pos:** OF **Age:** 20 **B:**R **T:**R

	G	AB	HR	RBI	SB	Avg	OBP	SLG
A Rockford	105	388	2	34	17	.211	.302	.304

Touted as a hot prospect due to "tools," but horrible year in Midwest League indicates he doesn't have skills.

Jovino Carvajal — Anaheim Angels
1997 Statistics   **Pos:** OF **Age:** 29 **B:**B **T:**R

	G	AB	HR	RBI	SB	Avg	OBP	SLG
AAA Vancouver	131	480	2	51	28	.285	.320	.423

Great speed, gap power, hits enormous numbers of triples. Lack of patience at the plate and erratic glove work limit his usefulness as a reserve.

Marino Castillo — San Diego Padres
1997 Statistics   **Pos:** P **Age:** 27 **B:**R **T:** R

	W	L	ERA	G	GS	Sv	IP	H	BB	SO
AAA Las Vegas	6	5	5.14	30	19	0	126.0	146	43	102
AA Mobile	0	1	4.32	8	0	1	8.1	14	5	10

A 5.14 ERA is respectable at Las Vegas. The Padres take park effect into account more than most teams do, but it won't help him enough.

Nelson Castro — Anaheim Angels
1997 Statistics   **Pos:** SS **Age:** 21 **B:**B **T:**R

	G	AB	HR	RBI	SB	Avg	OBP	SLG
A Boise	69	293	7	37	26	.294	.381	.427

Dominican shortstop, played in short-season Northwest League in 1997, put on 40-man roster to protect him from Rule 5 draft. Has some power, lots of speed, could be very good but needs to play full-season ball.

Silvio Censale — Philadelphia Phillies
1997 Statistics   **Pos:** P **Age:** 26 **B:**L **T:** L

	W	L	ERA	G	GS	Sv	IP	H	BB	SO
AA Reading	9	4	4.36	20	20	0	107.1	88	56	102

Pretty good arm, throws strikes, career has been slowed by a creaky elbow. Could surprise if healthy.

Eddie Christian — *Seattle Mariners*
1997 Statistics **Pos:** OF-DH **Age:** 26 **B:**B **T:**L

	G	AB	HR	RBI	SB	Avg	OBP	SLG
AAA Tacoma	35	135	1	9	3	.319	.383	.393
AA Memphis	68	238	4	39	8	.336	.421	.471

Veteran outfielder, makes contact but lacks power, had good year in Double-A and Triple-A, but not considered a prospect.

Scott Christman — *Chicago White Sox*
1997 Statistics **Pos:** P **Age:** 26 **B:**L **T:** L

	W	L	ERA	G	GS	Sv	IP	H	BB	SO
AA Birmingham	2	7	9.05	15	14	0	63.2	100	38	39

Was a prospect at one time, but injuries have demolished him.

Chris Clapinski — *Florida Marlins*
1997 Statistics **Pos:** 2B **Age:** 26 **B:**B **T:**R

	G	AB	HR	RBI	SB	Avg	OBP	SLG
AAA Charlotte	110	340	12	52	14	.262	.366	.450

Profile similar to Charlotte teammate Dave Berg. Could have use as utility player, but needs a manager willing to take a chance on him.

Trevor Cobb — *Minnesota Twins*
1997 Statistics **Pos:** P **Age:** 24 **B:**L **T:** L

	W	L	ERA	G	GS	Sv	IP	H	BB	SO
AA New Britain	6	4	3.43	19	13	1	94.1	77	39	68
A Ft. Myers	7	0	2.97	15	7	0	60.2	49	16	48

Curveball specialist, has been very effective at times but has a history of injuries. Possible sleeper.

Dan Collier — *Texas Rangers*
1997 Statistics **Pos:** DH-OF **Age:** 27 **B:**R **T:**R

	G	AB	HR	RBI	SB	Avg	OBP	SLG
AA Tulsa	115	389	26	79	1	.257	.351	.509

Veteran outfielder, has real power, but smart pitchers can get him out.

Dennis Colon — *Houston Astros*
1997 Statistics **Pos:** 1B **Age:** 24 **B:**L **T:**R

	G	AB	HR	RBI	SB	Avg	OBP	SLG
AAA New Orleans	129	400	6	64	2	.270	.342	.378

Contact hitter with doubles power. No future in Houston or anywhere else unless he starts hitting .320.

Hayward Cook — *Florida Marlins*
1997 Statistics **Pos:** OF **Age:** 25 **B:**R **T:**R

	G	AB	HR	RBI	SB	Avg	OBP	SLG
AA Portland	69	166	5	21	2	.295	.348	.464

Injury-prone outfielder, can hit pretty well but never healthy enough to put in a full season.

Mike Coolbaugh — *Oakland Athletics*
1997 Statistics **Pos:** 3B **Age:** 25 **B:**R **T:**R

	G	AB	HR	RBI	SB	Avg	OBP	SLG
AA Huntsville	139	559	30	132	8	.308	.369	.542

One of a group of veterans who put up big numbers at Double-A Huntsville, probably the best of the bunch. Can hit enough to be useful, but salary not big enough to draw interest from most teams. Poor man's Todd Zeile.

Kyle Cooney — *Los Angeles Dodgers*
1997 Statistics **Pos:** C **Age:** 24 **B:**R **T:**R

	G	AB	HR	RBI	SB	Avg	OBP	SLG
AA San Antonio	72	252	8	49	4	.290	.339	.464

Good defensive catcher, hits sometimes but poor strike-zone judgment wounds him. Looking for job as Piazza's personal assistant.

Alex Cora — *Los Angeles Dodgers*
1997 Statistics **Pos:** SS **Age:** 22 **B:**L **T:**R

	G	AB	HR	RBI	SB	Avg	OBP	SLG
AA San Antonio	127	448	3	48	12	.234	.279	.317

Joey Cora's brother, a weaker hitter than his brother but a better defensive player. Utility future if offense doesn't improve.

Bryan Corey — Detroit Tigers

1997 Statistics — Pos: P Age: 24 B:R T: R

	W	L	ERA	G	GS	Sv	IP	H	BB	SO
AA Jacksnville	3	8	4.76	52	0	9	68.0	74	21	37

Awesome in 1996, but struggled making Double-A transition in 1997, as many pitchers do. Not a pure finesse guy, but needs to prove himself all over again.

John Cotton — Chicago White Sox

1997 Statistics — Pos: OF Age: 27 B:L T:R

	G	AB	HR	RBI	SB	Avg	OBP	SLG
AAA Nashville	94	323	11	50	8	.269	.318	.433
AA Birmingham	33	124	7	26	1	.290	.346	.573

Has a bit of punch at the plate and some speed, but wears "career minor leaguer" tag.

Rickey Cradle — Seattle Mariners

1997 Statistics — Pos: OF Age: 24 B:R T:R

	G	AB	HR	RBI	SB	Avg	OBP	SLG
AAA Syracuse	11	25	1	3	0	.120	.241	.240
AA Knoxville	84	257	10	34	5	.214	.337	.401

Has tools but no idea how to use them.

Brandon Cromer — Pittsburgh Pirates

1997 Statistics — Pos: SS Age: 24 B:L T:R

	G	AB	HR	RBI	SB	Avg	OBP	SLG
AAA Calgary	68	228	8	36	3	.232	.288	.421
AA Carolina	55	193	4	14	1	.228	.326	.394

Acquired from Blue Jays in Carlos Garcia/Orlando Merced deal. Has pop in bat for infielder, but strikes out and doesn't hit for average. Utility player in a year or two.

D.T. Cromer — Oakland Athletics

1997 Statistics — Pos: 1B Age: 27 B:L T:L

	G	AB	HR	RBI	SB	Avg	OBP	SLG
AA Huntsville	134	545	15	121	12	.323	.389	.501

First-base version of Mike Coolbaugh.

Rich Croushore — St. Louis Cardinals

1997 Statistics — Pos: P Age: 27 B:R T: R

	W	L	ERA	G	GS	Sv	IP	H	BB	SO
AAA Louisville	1	2	2.47	14	6	1	43.2	37	13	41
AA Arkansas	7	5	4.18	17	16	0	92.2	111	37	67

Hard thrower, struggled as starter but did well when shifted to bullpen. Middle-relief candidate.

Fausto Cruz — Anaheim Angels

1997 Statistics — Pos: 2B Age: 26 B:R T:R

	G	AB	HR	RBI	SB	Avg	OBP	SLG
AAA Vancouver	118	413	11	67	5	.288	.323	.441

Good prospect two years ago, but has lost the strike zone.

Ivan Cruz — New York Yankees

1997 Statistics — Pos: 1B Age: 29 B:L T:L

	G	AB	HR	RBI	SB	Avg	OBP	SLG
AAA Columbus	116	417	24	95	4	.300	.404	.561
AL New York	11	20	0	3	0	.250	.318	.300

Continues to smash the ball in Triple-A. Would be a cheap option at first base or DH.

Nelson Cruz — Chicago White Sox

1997 Statistics — Pos: P Age: 25 B:R T: R

	W	L	ERA	G	GS	Sv	IP	H	BB	SO
AAA Nashville	11	7	5.11	21	20	0	123.1	139	31	93
AL Chicago	0	2	6.49	19	0	0	26.1	29	9	23

Soft tosser, great K/BB ratios in the minors, got knocked around in the majors. Could still have a career.

Carl Dale — Oakland Athletics

1997 Statistics — Pos: P Age: 25 B:R T: R

	W	L	ERA	G	GS	Sv	IP	H	BB	SO
AA Huntsville	6	4	5.38	20	16	0	85.1	95	43	57

Big pitcher with good arm, stats better than they look considering context. There are hints of arm trouble.

Mark Dalesandro — Chicago Cubs
1997 Statistics **Pos:** C **Age:** 29 **B:**R **T:**R

	G	AB	HR	RBI	SB	Avg	OBP	SLG
AAA Iowa	115	405	8	48	0	.262	.317	.356

Defensive specialist who won't hit much, will have Rick Wrona-like career.

Brian Daubach — Florida Marlins
1997 Statistics **Pos:** 1B **Age:** 26 **B:**L **T:**R

	G	AB	HR	RBI	SB	Avg	OBP	SLG
AAA Charlotte	136	461	21	93	1	.278	.367	.510

Has major league power, took some time to emerge as a prospect but has played well the last two years. No worse than some guys with jobs. Could hit .260 with 20 homers.

Tom Davey — Toronto Blue Jays
1997 Statistics **Pos:** P **Age:** 24 **B:**R **T:** R

	W	L	ERA	G	GS	Sv	IP	H	BB	SO
AA Knoxville	6	7	5.83	20	16	0	92.2	108	50	72
A Dunedin	1	3	4.31	7	6	0	39.2	44	15	36

Has one of the better arms in the Toronto system, but no polish.

Clint Davis — Texas Rangers
1997 Statistics **Pos:** P **Age:** 28 **B:**R **T:** R

	W	L	ERA	G	GS	Sv	IP	H	BB	SO
AAA Okla City	6	1	3.20	40	1	0	70.1	55	46	53

Successful minor league reliever for several years. Could get some middle-relief innings if he gets on a hot streak, but would lose his job as soon as the streak ended.

Jeff Davis — Texas Rangers
1997 Statistics **Pos:** P **Age:** 25 **B:**R **T:** R

	W	L	ERA	G	GS	Sv	IP	H	BB	SO
AA Tulsa	4	6	3.65	11	11	0	69.0	76	17	25

Extreme finesse pitcher, also extremely fragile. Can get people out when healthy, but never healthy.

Jason Dawsey — Milwaukee Brewers
1997 Statistics **Pos:** P **Age:** 23 **B:**L **T:** L

	W	L	ERA	G	GS	Sv	IP	H	BB	SO
AA El Paso	2	2	6.81	8	7	0	38.1	50	23	14

Soft tosser, great 1996 season but injured in 1997.

Lorenzo de la Cruz — Toronto Blue Jays
1997 Statistics **Pos:** DH **Age:** 26 **B:**R **T:**R

	G	AB	HR	RBI	SB	Avg	OBP	SLG
AAA Syracuse	39	128	5	13	1	.219	.254	.367
AA Knoxville	39	146	7	26	2	.336	.410	.555

Streaky hitter, whacks line drives but never takes a walk. Could stumble into a bench job if he has a well-timed hot streak.

Ynocencio de la Cruz — Diamondbacks
1997 Statistics **Pos:** P **Age:** 26 **B:**R **T:** R

	W	L	ERA	G	GS	Sv	IP	H	BB	SO
R Mets	3	3	1.15	6	5	0	39.0	31	3	42
R Kingsport	2	3	6.61	6	6	0	31.1	46	8	31

Young Dominican had his moments in Gulf Coast League. Taken in major league Rule 5 draft.

Maximo de la Rosa — Cleveland Indians
1997 Statistics **Pos:** P **Age:** 26 **B:**R **T:** R

	W	L	ERA	G	GS	Sv	IP	H	BB	SO
AAA Buffalo	2	2	6.49	15	4	0	43.0	43	33	31
AA Akron	4	9	4.44	17	13	0	97.1	112	32	70

Dominican pitcher with very good fastball, but little else. Struggled in Triple-A. Better upside than his little brother, Minimo.

Rob DeBoer — Oakland Athletics
1997 Statistics **Pos:** DH-C **Age:** 27 **B:**R **T:**R

	G	AB	HR	RBI	SB	Avg	OBP	SLG
AA Huntsville	91	288	18	48	8	.243	.385	.493

Has power, but very low average limits his appeal.

Joey DePastino — Boston Red Sox

1997 Statistics   **Pos:** C **Age:** 24 **B:**R **T:**R

	G	AB	HR	RBI	SB	Avg	OBP	SLG
AA Trenton	79	276	17	55	1	.254	.345	.496

Similar to organization-mate Walt McKeel: has power, looking to win backup job.

Marc Deschenes — Los Angeles Dodgers

1997 Statistics   **Pos:** P **Age:** 25 **B:**R **T:** R

	W	L	ERA	G	GS	Sv	IP	H	BB	SO
A Kinston	2	0	0.81	20	0	10	22.1	9	4	39
A Columbus	2	2	1.90	40	0	19	42.2	31	21	69

Great year as A-ball closer, 20th-round draft pick as a shortstop out of college in 1995. Major league Rule 5 draft pick. Intriguing.

Kris Detmers — St. Louis Cardinals

1997 Statistics   **Pos:** P **Age:** 23 **B:**B **T:**L

	W	L	ERA	G	GS	Sv	IP	H	BB	SO
AAA Louisville	3	3	7.20	10	5	0	35.0	43	17	22
AA Arkansas	5	7	5.77	15	15	0	78.0	99	27	44

Prospect status fading, due to wavering command and nagging injuries.

Eddy Diaz — Milwaukee Brewers

1997 Statistics   **Pos:** 3B **Age:** 26 **B:**R **T:**R

	G	AB	HR	RBI	SB	Avg	OBP	SLG
AAA Tucson	94	356	9	70	0	.329	.381	.489
AL Milwaukee	16	50	0	7	0	.220	.235	.300

Standard Triple-A veteran infielder, searching for a bench job but not likely to get it even though he isn't a bad player.

Lino Diaz — Kansas City Royals

1997 Statistics   **Pos:** 3B **Age:** 27 **B:**R **T:**R

	G	AB	HR	RBI	SB	Avg	OBP	SLG
AA Wichita	92	289	2	51	3	.284	.348	.415

Fan favorite in Wichita, due to hustling attitude, versatility, and perceived clutch ability.

John Dillinger — Pittsburgh Pirates

1997 Statistics   **Pos:** P **Age:** 24 **B:**R **T:** R

	W	L	ERA	G	GS	Sv	IP	H	BB	SO
AA Carolina	6	4	6.00	23	11	0	81.0	88	52	64

Great name, good arm, poor command, sore shoulder.

Travis Driskill — Cleveland Indians

1997 Statistics   **Pos:** P **Age:** 26 **B:**R **T:** R

	W	L	ERA	G	GS	Sv	IP	H	BB	SO
AAA Buffalo	8	7	4.65	29	24	0	147.0	159	60	102

Mediocre season at Buffalo, best pitch is a hard slider. Might be better off in relief.

Mike Duvall — Florida Marlins

1997 Statistics   **Pos:** P **Age:** 23 **B:**R **T:** L

	W	L	ERA	G	GS	Sv	IP	H	BB	SO
AA Portland	4	6	1.84	45	0	18	68.1	63	20	49
A Brevard Cty	1	0	0.73	11	0	6	12.1	7	3	9

Good year as Double-A closer, no future outside of middle-relief, one-out role against lefties.

Steve Eddie — Cincinnati Reds

1997 Statistics   **Pos:** 3B **Age:** 27 **B:**R **T:**R

	G	AB	HR	RBI	SB	Avg	OBP	SLG
AA Chattanooga	118	394	8	49	3	.287	.319	.431

Roster-filler infielder, played decently in Double-A. Could see some major league time if injuries strike, but unlikely to do much with it.

Brian Edmondson — Atlanta Braves

1997 Statistics   **Pos:** P **Age:** 25 **B:**R **T:** R

	W	L	ERA	G	GS	Sv	IP	H	BB	SO
AA Binghamton	2	0	1.23	14	0	3	22.0	17	7	18
AAA Norfolk	4	3	2.90	31	4	1	68.1	62	37	65

Seven-year pro had fine 1997, taken in major league Rule 5 draft.

Robert Eenhoorn — Anaheim Angels

1997 Statistics   **Pos:** SS **Age:** 30 **B:**R **T:**R

	G	AB	HR	RBI	SB	Avg	OBP	SLG
AAA Vancouver	120	455	12	58	1	.308	.350	.473
AL Anaheim	11	20	1	6	0	.350	.333	.550

Dutch infielder, originally in Yankees system. Looking for bench job, might get it.

Darrell Einerston — New York Yankees

1997 Statistics   **Pos:** P **Age:** 25 **B:** R **T:** R

	W	L	ERA	G	GS	Sv	IP	H	BB	SO
A Tampa	5	4	2.15	45	0	6	71.0	63	19	55

Middle-relief candidate, average fastball, pretty good slider, aggressive.

Robert Ellis — Detroit Tigers

1997 Statistics   **Pos:** P **Age:** 27 **B:** R **T:** R

	W	L	ERA	G	GS	Sv	IP	H	BB	SO
AAA Vancouver	9	10	5.92	29	23	0	149.0	185	83	70

Very good arm, hard slider, can't change speeds. No reason to project success, but it isn't impossible.

Jose Espinal — Chicago Cubs

1997 Statistics   **Pos:** P **Age:** 21 **B:** R **T:** R

	W	L	ERA	G	GS	Sv	IP	H	BB	SO
A Rockford	10	10	4.92	24	24	0	120.2	147	41	107

Midwest League pitcher, put on 40-man roster in late November. This was a protection move, to prevent his loss in the Rule 5 draft. Has ability, but raw; unlikely to help anytime soon.

Bart Evans — Kansas City Royals

1997 Statistics   **Pos:** P **Age:** 27 **B:** R **T:** R

	W	L	ERA	G	GS	Sv	IP	H	BB	SO
AA Wichita	1	2	4.59	32	0	6	33.1	45	8	28
A Wilmington	0	1	6.53	16	2	0	20.2	22	15	22

Throws hard, has elbow problems, control is erratic but occasionally very good. Could surprise.

Ethan Faggett — Boston Red Sox

1997 Statistics   **Pos:** OF **Age:** 23 **B:** L **T:** L

	G	AB	HR	RBI	SB	Avg	OBP	SLG
AA Trenton	17	56	2	8	2	.286	.379	.429
A Sarasota	114	410	3	46	23	.293	.366	.405

Fast outfielder with line-drive swing, unlikely to start in the majors, but might earn a bench job for a year or three.

Steve Falteisek — Montreal Expos

1997 Statistics   **Pos:** P **Age:** 26 **B:** R **T:** R

	W	L	ERA	G	GS	Sv	IP	H	BB	SO
AAA Ottawa	6	9	3.96	22	22	0	125.0	135	54	56
NL Montreal	0	0	3.38	5	0	0	8.0	8	3	2

Triple-A starter who doesn't throw hard, has good control but doesn't strike anybody out.

Ramon Fermin — Cincinnati Reds

1997 Statistics   **Pos:** P **Age:** 25 **B:** R **T:** R

	W	L	ERA	G	GS	Sv	IP	H	BB	SO
AAA Toledo	4	2	4.93	41	8	0	80.1	103	33	46

Has a major league arm, and Rookie league command.

Jared Fernandez — Boston Red Sox

1997 Statistics   **Pos:** P **Age:** 26 **B:** R **T:** R

	W	L	ERA	G	GS	Sv	IP	H	BB	SO
AAA Pawtucket	0	3	5.79	11	11	0	62.0	76	28	33
AA Trenton	4	6	5.41	21	16	0	121.1	138	66	73

Knuckleball pitcher, inherently impossible to predict.

Mike Figga — New York Yankees

1997 Statistics   **Pos:** C **Age:** 27 **B:** R **T:** R

	G	AB	HR	RBI	SB	Avg	OBP	SLG
AAA Columbus	110	390	12	54	3	.244	.278	.392
AL New York	2	4	0	0	0	.000	.000	.000

Catcher with power, mediocre glove, terrible plate discipline. Will hang around Triple-A for the next seven years, and get a few at-bats in the Show.

Tony Fiore — Philadelphia Phillies

1997 Statistics   **Pos:** P **Age:** 26 **B:** R **T:** R

	W	L	ERA	G	GS	Sv	IP	H	BB	SO
AAA Scranton-WB	3	5	3.86	9	9	0	60.2	60	26	56
AA Reading	8	3	3.01	17	16	0	104.2	89	40	64

Adequate arm, can get people out when he is sharp. Strikeout rate too low for me to get excited about him.

Tim Florez — San Francisco Giants
1997 Statistics   **Pos:** 2B **Age:** 28 **B:**R **T:**R

	G	AB	HR	RBI	SB	Avg	OBP	SLG
AAA Phoenix	114	402	7	61	6	.301	.363	.433

Contact hitter, not much power. Led Pacific Coast League in fielding percentage; could earn a job for a manager who values defense on the bench.

Pat Flury — Kansas City Royals
1997 Statistics   **Pos:** P **Age:** 25 **B:**R **T:** R

	W	L	ERA	G	GS	Sv	IP	H	BB	SO
AAA Omaha	1	0	6.08	18	0	0	26.2	29	16	24
AA Wichita	8	3	3.56	42	0	5	48.0	47	18	47

"Hello, Acme Company? This is Herk Robinson again. I'd also like to order your Righthanded Double-A Middle-Relief Pitcher Model 500. No, I don't want the fastball option. Thank you."

Ben Ford — Arizona Diamondbacks
1997 Statistics   **Pos:** P **Age:** 22 **B:**R **T:** R

	W	L	ERA	G	GS	Sv	IP	H	BB	SO
AA Norwich	4	3	4.22	28	0	1	42.2	35	19	38
A Tampa	4	0	1.93	32	0	18	37.1	27	14	37

Hard-throwing relief pitcher, selected from the Yankees system in the expansion draft. 92-MPH fastball, good slider, reminds some people of Jeff Nelson. Grade C+ prospect.

Tim Forkner — Houston Astros
1997 Statistics   **Pos:** 3B **Age:** 25 **B:**L **T:**R

	G	AB	HR	RBI	SB	Avg	OBP	SLG
AA Jackson	116	398	7	46	4	.261	.357	.377

Line-drive hitter with patience, seems to be stagnating in Double-A. Useful if he is hitting .300.

Chris Freeman — Toronto Blue Jays
1997 Statistics   **Pos:** P **Age:** 25 **B:**R **T:** R

	W	L	ERA	G	GS	Sv	IP	H	BB	SO
AA Knoxville	3	3	2.48	47	2	8	83.1	71	36	86

Effective Double-A middle reliever with a high strikeout rate. Could surprise and have a Woody Williams-type career.

Ricky Freeman — Chicago Cubs
1997 Statistics   **Pos:** 1B **Age:** 26 **B:**R **T:**R

	G	AB	HR	RBI	SB	Avg	OBP	SLG
AAA Iowa	31	77	1	4	1	.169	.273	.208
AA Orlando	81	308	16	73	8	.312	.378	.542

Reasonably good hitter, but too old to be considered a hot prospect, and no chance in Chicago if Grace is healthy.

Anton French — Seattle Mariners
1997 Statistics   **Pos:** OF **Age:** 22 **B:**B **T:**R

	G	AB	HR	RBI	SB	Avg	OBP	SLG
AA Knoxville	2	6	0	1	0	.333	.333	.667
A Dunedin	78	261	3	17	35	.222	.293	.299

Great tools, poor performance, questionable attitude. Not a good combination.

Aaron Fuller — Boston Red Sox
1997 Statistics   **Pos:** OF **Age:** 26 **B:**B **T:**R

	G	AB	HR	RBI	SB	Avg	OBP	SLG
AA Trenton	128	481	6	46	40	.260	.384	.358

Draws megatons of walks, runs very well, hustles. Has very little power, but no worse a player than Otis Nixon.

Aaron Fultz — San Francisco Giants
1997 Statistics   **Pos:** P **Age:** 24 **B:**L **T:** L

	W	L	ERA	G	GS	Sv	IP	H	BB	SO
AA Shreveport	6	3	2.83	49	0	1	70.0	65	19	60

Former starter, converted to relief last year and did well. Average fastball, good breaking stuff, control fine. Could be a good middle-inning guy.

Bryon Gainey — New York Mets
1997 Statistics   **Pos:** 1B **Age:** 22 **B:**L **T:**R

	G	AB	HR	RBI	SB	Avg	OBP	SLG
A St. Lucie	117	405	13	51	0	.240	.280	.390

Occasionally mentioned as a prospect by rabid Mets fans. Rabid Mets-haters should hope the people who run the team agree.

Steve Gajkowski — Seattle Mariners
1997 Statistics   **Pos:** P **Age:** 28 **B:**R **T:** R

	W	L	ERA	G	GS	Sv	IP	H	BB	SO
AAA Tacoma	5	3	3.87	44	3	2	93.0	100	24	48

Finesse pitcher, throws strikes but very hittable.

Rick Gama — San Diego Padres
1997 Statistics   **Pos:** 2B **Age:** 24 **B:**R **T:**R

	G	AB	HR	RBI	SB	Avg	OBP	SLG
AA Mobile	88	295	6	43	9	.288	.390	.417
A Rancho Cuca	25	115	2	12	4	.252	.289	.383

Infielder who makes contact, draws walks. Steady in the field, but limited range keeps him at second, and hurts his chance for a job.

Gus Gandarillas — Minnesota Twins
1997 Statistics   **Pos:** P **Age:** 26 **B:**R **T:** R

	W	L	ERA	G	GS	Sv	IP	H	BB	SO
AAA Salt Lake	1	0	3.18	11	2	2	22.2	22	6	13
AA New Britain	2	4	4.70	17	7	0	61.1	67	15	29

Looking for middle-relief slot. Good arm, pitches well when healthy, but is rarely healthy.

Webster Garrison — Oakland Athletics
1997 Statistics   **Pos:** 2B **Age:** 32 **B:**R **T:**R

	G	AB	HR	RBI	SB	Avg	OBP	SLG
AAA Edmonton	125	429	15	80	5	.289	.372	.459

One of my favorites, a minor league veteran who has played well for years in Triple-A. Keeping him out of the majors seems to be an article of faith among GMs.

Marty Gazarek — Chicago Cubs
1997 Statistics   **Pos:** OF **Age:** 24 **B:**R **T:**R

	G	AB	HR	RBI	SB	Avg	OBP	SLG
AA Orlando	76	290	10	52	10	.331	.382	.514

Very good year in Double-A, has power and speed, but age and strike-zone problems limit his future.

Ken Giard — Pittsburgh Pirates
1997 Statistics   **Pos:** P **Age:** 24 **B:**R **T:** R

	W	L	ERA	G	GS	Sv	IP	H	BB	SO
AA Greenville	3	0	1.96	25	0	6	36.2	30	11	39
A Durham	2	2	2.33	30	0	12	38.2	28	35	47

Great year for Durham and Greenville. Big, throws hard, had control problems before last year. Candidate for middle relief.

David Gibralter — Boston Red Sox
1997 Statistics   **Pos:** 1B **Age:** 22 **B:**R **T:**R

	G	AB	HR	RBI	SB	Avg	OBP	SLG
AA Trenton	123	478	14	86	3	.274	.344	.418

Has good power potential, but struggles when the strike zone gets away from him, which is too often. Young enough to improve significantly.

Steve Gibralter — Cincinnati Reds
1997 Statistics   **Pos:** OF **Age:** 25 **B:**R **T:**R

	G	AB	HR	RBI	SB	Avg	OBP	SLG
AA Chattanooga	30	97	2	12	0	.258	.348	.412

Once a top prospect, but last two years destroyed by injuries. Could rebound, but don't bet on it.

Shawn Gilbert — New York Mets
1997 Statistics   **Pos:** SS-OF **Age:** 33 **B:**R **T:**R

	G	AB	HR	RBI	SB	Avg	OBP	SLG
AAA Norfolk	78	288	8	33	16	.264	.362	.399
NL New York	29	22	1	1	1	.136	.174	.273

Veteran infielder, hustles, will play any position asked without causing too much embarrassment. Won't hit much.

Ed Giovanola — San Diego Padres
1997 Statistics   **Pos:** 3B **Age:** 29 **B:**L **T:**R

	G	AB	HR	RBI	SB	Avg	OBP	SLG
AAA Richmond	116	395	2	46	2	.291	.385	.390
NL Atlanta	14	8	0	0	0	.250	.400	.250

Can hit some and field some. Would be a very good utility infielder if someone would let him.

Chip Glass
Cleveland Indians
1997 Statistics **Pos:** OF **Age:** 26 **B:**L **T:**L

	G	AB	HR	RBI	SB	Avg	OBP	SLG
AA Akron	113	394	5	37	16	.259	.360	.360

Double-A flycatcher, has some speed and will take a walk but not much of a hitter. Praying for a bench job.

Keith Glauber
Cincinnati Reds
1997 Statistics **Pos:** P **Age:** 26 **B:**R **T:** R

	W	L	ERA	G	GS	Sv	IP	H	BB	SO
AAA Louisville	1	3	5.17	15	0	5	15.2	18	4	14
AA Arkansas	5	7	2.75	50	0	3	59.0	48	25	53

Standard minor league reliever, stuff isn't great but he can get people out, at least in the minors. Major league Rule 5 draft pick.

Gary Glover
Toronto Blue Jays
1997 Statistics **Pos:** P **Age:** 21 **B:**R **T:** R

	W	L	ERA	G	GS	Sv	IP	H	BB	SO
A Hagerstown	6	17	3.73	28	28	0	173.2	165	58	155

Huge thrower, making some progress in learning how to pitch. Won't be ready soon.

Ryan Glynn
Texas Rangers
1997 Statistics **Pos:** P **Age:** 23 **B:**R **T:** R

	W	L	ERA	G	GS	Sv	IP	H	BB	SO
AA Tulsa	1	1	3.38	3	3	0	21.1	21	10	18
A Charlotte	8	7	4.97	23	22	1	134.0	148	44	96

Strong pitcher with good stuff, doesn't know how to pitch.

Jimmy Gonzalez
San Diego Padres
1997 Statistics **Pos:** C **Age:** 25 **B:**R **T:**R

	G	AB	HR	RBI	SB	Avg	OBP	SLG
AA Jackson	97	342	14	58	2	.254	.338	.430
A Kissimmee	12	44	2	6	0	.341	.388	.705

Good defensive catcher with some power. No worse a player than Greg Myers.

Jeff Granger
Pittsburgh Pirates
1997 Statistics **Pos:** P **Age:** 26 **B:**R **T:** L

	W	L	ERA	G	GS	Sv	IP	H	BB	SO
AAA Calgary	1	7	5.55	30	12	1	82.2	111	33	68
NL Pittsburgh	0	0	18.00	9	0	0	5.0	10	8	4

Had a terrible season, prospect status nearly gone. As a lefty, he has 90 lives, and he will need them.

Rick Greene
Milwaukee Brewers
1997 Statistics **Pos:** P **Age:** 27 **B:**R **T:** R

	W	L	ERA	G	GS	Sv	IP	H	BB	SO
AAA Toledo	6	8	2.83	57	0	1	70.0	49	32	51

Once a prospect, now an organization staff filler. Pitched well in middle relief at Toledo. Traded to Brewers.

Tim Grieve
Kansas City Royals
1997 Statistics **Pos:** P **Age:** 26 **B:**R **T:** R

	W	L	ERA	G	GS	Sv	IP	H	BB	SO
AA Wichita	3	1	3.38	17	0	1	37.1	30	21	36
A Wilmington	4	1	1.88	26	0	7	38.1	24	20	34

Ben's brother. Has adequate stuff, successful when he throws strikes. Injury-prone, future is in middle relief.

Craig Griffey
Cincinnati Reds
1997 Statistics **Pos:** OF **Age:** 26 **B:**R **T:**R

	G	AB	HR	RBI	SB	Avg	OBP	SLG
AAA Tacoma	3	3	0	0	0	.333	.333	1.000
AA Memphis	35	120	0	5	6	.217	.289	.258
AA Chattanooga	55	180	0	15	8	.228	.319	.267

Worse case of nepotism than Pete Rose Junior and Billy Ripken combined.

Mike Grzanich
Houston Astros
1997 Statistics **Pos:** P **Age:** 25 **B:**R **T:** R

	W	L	ERA	G	GS	Sv	IP	H	BB	SO
AA Jackson	7	6	4.96	38	13	12	101.2	114	46	73

Double-A starter/reliever/closer, throws fairly hard, effective in any role when his command is on.

Creighton Gubanich *San Diego Padres*

1997 Statistics   **Pos:** C **Age:** 26 **B:**R **T:**R

	G	AB	HR	RBI	SB	Avg	OBP	SLG
AAA Edmonton	43	145	7	34	0	.331	.395	.566
AAA Tucson	24	85	5	17	1	.341	.356	.576
AAA Colo Sprngs	14	47	3	6	0	.191	.255	.404

Product of the Athletics system. Can hit some, defense mediocre.

Mark Guerra *New York Mets*

1997 Statistics   **Pos:** P **Age:** 26 **B:**R **T:** R

	W	L	ERA	G	GS	Sv	IP	H	BB	SO
AA Binghamton	4	8	3.23	48	7	7	94.2	96	30	74

A favorite of mine, although I'm not sure why. Doesn't have great stuff, control good but not terrific. Utility pitcher in Double-A.

Mike Gulan *St. Louis Cardinals*

1997 Statistics   **Pos:** 3B **Age:** 27 **B:**R **T:**R

	G	AB	HR	RBI	SB	Avg	OBP	SLG
AAA Louisville	116	412	14	61	5	.267	.316	.447
NL St. Louis	5	9	0	1	0	.000	.100	.000

Has never learned the strike zone, and it is probably too late for him to do so.

Luther Hackman *Colorado Rockies*

1997 Statistics   **Pos:** P **Age:** 23 **B:**R **T:** R

	W	L	ERA	G	GS	Sv	IP	H	BB	SO
AA New Haven	0	6	7.82	10	10	0	50.2	58	34	34
A Salem	1	4	5.80	15	15	0	80.2	99	37	59

Strong-legged righthanded starter with adequate stuff, command failed him in Double-A.

Mike Halperin *Pittsburgh Pirates*

1997 Statistics   **Pos:** P **Age:** 24 **B:**L **T:** L

	W	L	ERA	G	GS	Sv	IP	H	BB	SO
AAA Calgary	1	0	6.43	15	4	0	28.0	44	24	18
AA Carolina	6	7	3.87	17	17	0	93.0	102	40	66

Doesn't throw hard, effective in Double-A, lousy in Triple-A. Needs adjustment time.

Ryan Hancock *San Diego Padres*

1997 Statistics   **Pos:** P **Age:** 26 **B:**R **T:** R

	W	L	ERA	G	GS	Sv	IP	H	BB	SO
AAA Vancouver	3	3	3.63	39	2	2	74.1	72	36	60
AAA Las Vegas	0	0	12.60	4	0	0	5.0	9	4	3

Part of the Rickey Henderson trade with the Angels. Hancock has adequate arm strength, but his command is unsteady.

Tim Harikkala *Seattle Mariners*

1997 Statistics   **Pos:** P **Age:** 26 **B:**R **T:** R

	W	L	ERA	G	GS	Sv	IP	H	BB	SO
AAA Tacoma	6	8	6.43	21	21	0	113.1	160	50	86
AA Memphis	3	1	3.74	5	5	0	33.2	39	4	26

Acceptable stuff, throws strikes, but lacks command within the strike zone and gets pounded.

Denny Harriger *Detroit Tigers*

1997 Statistics   **Pos:** P **Age:** 28 **B:**R **T:** R

	W	L	ERA	G	GS	Sv	IP	H	BB	SO
AAA Toledo	11	8	3.99	27	27	0	167.0	159	63	109

Successful Triple-A pitcher, but marginal for majors due to lack of velocity.

Jeff Harris *Minnesota Twins*

1997 Statistics   **Pos:** P **Age:** 23 **B:**R **T:** R

	W	L	ERA	G	GS	Sv	IP	H	BB	SO
AA New Britain	2	1	2.34	28	0	3	42.1	30	16	44
A Ft. Myers	2	4	2.14	24	0	1	42.0	30	15	32

Middle-relief candidate, stuff is okay, has good control.

Brian Harrison *Kansas City Royals*

1997 Statistics   **Pos:** P **Age:** 29 **B:**R **T:** R

	W	L	ERA	G	GS	Sv	IP	H	BB	SO
AAA Omaha	10	12	5.05	30	29	0	178.1	208	55	83

Control pitcher, adequate slider but weak fastball. Working on a knuckler.

Tommy Harrison *Atlanta Braves*

1997 Statistics   **Pos:** P **Age:** 26 **B:**R **T:** R

	W	L	ERA	G	GS	Sv	IP	H	BB	SO
AAA Richmond	9	7	4.20	22	22	0	122.0	118	40	92

Pedestrian season at Richmond, could get a shot with a desperate team, or with the Braves if there is a chicken pox outbreak.

Derek Hasselhoff — Chicago White Sox

1997 Statistics Pos: P Age: 24 B:R T: R

	W	L	ERA	G	GS	Sv	IP	H	BB	SO
AAA Nashville	1	1	9.82	6	0	0	7.1	9	7	2
AA Birmingham	5	2	2.41	18	0	3	33.2	35	11	22
A Winston-Sal	3	2	1.56	20	0	3	34.2	22	15	41

Minor league middle-relief pitcher, looking for same job in the majors. Idol of German baseball fans.

Lionel Hastings — Florida Marlins

1997 Statistics Pos: 2B Age: 25 B:R T:R

	G	AB	HR	RBI	SB	Avg	OBP	SLG
AA Portland	93	279	10	35	6	.344	.426	.527

Double-A repeater, had a great year. No shortage of infielders in Marlins system, so he will have to keep playing like that to get a shot.

Ryan Hawblitzel — Philadelphia Phillies

1997 Statistics Pos: P Age: 26 B:R T: R

	W	L	ERA	G	GS	Sv	IP	H	BB	SO
AAA Scranton-WB	6	9	4.99	34	15	2	115.1	132	33	80

Got away from the Rockies system, which increases his chance to have a career from zero to slim.

Rick Heiserman — St. Louis Cardinals

1997 Statistics Pos: P Age: 25 B:R T: R

	W	L	ERA	G	GS	Sv	IP	H	BB	SO
AAA Louisville	0	0	4.50	1	0	0	2.0	2	1	0
AA Arkansas	5	8	4.17	34	20	4	131.2	151	36	90

Tall pitcher with good stuff, throws strikes, but gives up a lot of hits because he grooves pitches down the middle.

Dan Held — Philadelphia Phillies

1997 Statistics Pos: 1B Age: 27 B:R T:R

	G	AB	HR	RBI	SB	Avg	OBP	SLG
AA Reading	138	525	26	86	1	.272	.345	.495

Double-A slugger, has nothing left to prove at that level, but strikeouts and defense are serious concerns. No worse than Pete Incaviglia.

Rodney Henderson — Montreal Expos

1997 Statistics Pos: P Age: 27 B:R T: R

	W	L	ERA	G	GS	Sv	IP	H	BB	SO
AAA Ottawa	5	9	4.95	26	20	1	123.2	136	49	103

Once a hot prospect, still throws fairly hard, but isn't making progress. Needs a change of scenery.

Bob Henley — Montreal Expos

1997 Statistics Pos: C Age: 25 B:R T:R

	G	AB	HR	RBI	SB	Avg	OBP	SLG
AA Harrisburg	79	280	12	49	5	.304	.380	500

Double-A catcher, looks like he can hit some and defense isn't awful. Season ended with August concussion. Might get a chance to play with Fletcher out of the picture. Grade C+ prospect.

Wilson Heredia — Texas Rangers

1997 Statistics Pos: P Age: 26 B:R T: R

	W	L	ERA	G	GS	Sv	IP	H	BB	SO
AAA Okla City	7	12	4.97	27	26	0	168.1	167	70	113
AL Texas	1	0	3.20	10	0	0	19.2	14	16	8

Adequate stuff, but his command is wobbly. Has a chance if it improves.

Carlos Hernandez — Houston Astros

1997 Statistics Pos: 2B Age: 22 B:R T:R

	G	AB	HR	RBI	SB	Avg	OBP	SLG
AA Jackson	92	363	4	33	17	.292	.355	.364

Tiny Venezuelan infielder makes contact but doesn't drive the ball. Quite young, could be very good if he gets stronger. Grade C+ prospect.

Fernando Hernandez — Detroit Tigers

1997 Statistics Pos: P Age: 26 B:R T: R

	W	L	ERA	G	GS	Sv	IP	H	BB	SO
AAA Toledo	6	5	4.11	55	1	4	76.2	71	51	98
AL Detroit	0	0	40.50	2	0	0	1.1	5	3	2

90-MPH fastball with movement, but control is a problem. Converted to relief last year, had a high strikeout rate but still walks too many guys for comfort.

Jason Herrick — Anaheim Angels
1997 Statistics   Pos: OF **Age:** 24 **B:**L **T:**L

	G	AB	HR	RBI	SB	Avg	OBP	SLG
AA Midland	118	416	20	67	9	.252	.311	.481

Has power but swings hard at everything, including sliders in the dirt. Would struggle to break .220 in the majors.

Vee Hightower — Chicago Cubs
1997 Statistics   Pos: OF **Age:** 25 **B:**B **T:**R

	G	AB	HR	RBI	SB	Avg	OBP	SLG
AA Orlando	87	283	6	29	16	.233	.340	.339

Switch-hitter with speed, patience, some power, but keeps getting injured. Time almost out.

Matt Howard — New York Yankees
1997 Statistics   Pos: SS **Age:** 30 **B:**R **T:**R

	G	AB	HR	RBI	SB	Avg	OBP	SLG
AAA Columbus	122	478	6	67	22	.312	.391	.437

Good contact hitter with speed, versatile glove. Deserves a shot at a bench job.

Bobby Howry — Chicago White Sox
1997 Statistics   Pos: P **Age:** 24 **B:**L **T:** R

	W	L	ERA	G	GS	Sv	IP	H	BB	SO
AA Birmingham	0	0	2.84	12	0	2	12.2	16	3	3
AA Shreveport	6	3	4.91	48	0	22	55.0	58	21	43

Acquired from Giants in Roberto Hernandez/Wilson Alvarez betrayal. Sinker-slider type looking for middle-relief job.

Dan Hubbs — Los Angeles Dodgers
1997 Statistics   Pos: P **Age:** 27 **B:**R **T:** R

	W	L	ERA	G	GS	Sv	IP	H	BB	SO
AAA Albuquerque	6	4	3.90	62	3	3	94.2	103	38	87

Good ERA at Albuquerque, nice strikeout rate. Stuff OK, could do well in relief.

Bobby Hughes — Milwaukee Brewers
1997 Statistics   Pos: C **Age:** 27 **B:**R **T:**R

	G	AB	HR	RBI	SB	Avg	OBP	SLG
AAA Tucson	89	290	7	51	0	.310	.376	.497

Has taken a long time to master the high minors, now hoping for a backup role in ma-jors. Offense and defense occasionally good but unreliable.

Torii Hunter — Minnesota Twins
1997 Statistics   Pos: OF **Age:** 22 **B:**R **T:**R

	G	AB	HR	RBI	SB	Avg	OBP	SLG
AA New Britain	127	471	8	56	8	.231	.305	.338
AL Minnesota	1	0	0	0	0	-	-	-

Tools player, first-round pick in 1993. Had terrible year in Double-A. Great defensive outfielder.

Jimmy Hurst — Boston Red Sox
1997 Statistics   Pos: OF **Age:** 26 **B:**R **T:**R

	G	AB	HR	RBI	SB	Avg	OBP	SLG
AAA Toledo	110	377	18	58	14	.271	.348	.459
AA Jacksnville	5	17	2	6	0	.471	.524	.941
AL Detroit	13	17	1	1	0	.176	.263	.412

Great athlete, above-average power and speed, looks like he has made progress with the strike zone. May have turned the corner, just in time to lose his prospect status to age.

Adam Hyzdu — Boston Red Sox
1997 Statistics   Pos: OF **Age:** 26 **B:**R **T:**R

	G	AB	HR	RBI	SB	Avg	OBP	SLG
AAA Pawtucket	119	413	23	84	10	.276	.387	.499

Successful Dan Duquette reclamation project, can hit for power but no room for him in Boston.

Mike Iglesias — Los Angeles Dodgers
1997 Statistics   Pos: P **Age:** 25 **B:**R **T:** R

	W	L	ERA	G	GS	Sv	IP	H	BB	SO
AA San Antonio	6	2	3.64	42	0	8	59.1	51	26	55

Pretty good arm. Not spectacular in Double-A but not awful. Middle-relief candidate in 1999.

Garey Ingram — Los Angeles Dodgers
1997 Statistics   Pos: 2B **Age:** 27 **B:**R **T:**R

	G	AB	HR	RBI	SB	Avg	OBP	SLG
AA San Antonio	92	348	12	52	16	.299	.371	.523
NL Los Angeles	12	9	0	1	1	.444	.500	.444

Veteran minor leaguer, always seems to play well but never gets a chance in the

Show. The kind of guy expansion is supposed to benefit but often doesn't.

Gavin Jackson — Boston Red Sox
1997 Statistics Pos: SS **Age:** 24 **B:**R **T:**R

	G	AB	HR	RBI	SB	Avg	OBP	SLG
AA Trenton	100	301	1	46	2	.272	.381	.322

Contact hitter with little punch, does have some discipline. Has potential as a utility-man because of versatile glove.

Pete Janicki — Anaheim Angels
1997 Statistics Pos: P **Age:** 27 **B:**R **T:** R

	W	L	ERA	G	GS	Sv	IP	H	BB	SO
AAA Vancouver	1	4	7.80	42	0	1	47.1	48	44	43
AA Midland	0	0	0.00	2	0	0	1.2	3	2	2

Injuries have ruined his career.

Manny Jimenez — Atlanta Braves
1997 Statistics Pos: SS **Age:** 26 **B:**R **T:**R

	G	AB	HR	RBI	SB	Avg	OBP	SLG
AA Greenville	115	430	5	45	3	.291	.333	.391

Erratic Dominican shortstop could get a shot as a utility guy if he keeps hitting.

Earl Johnson — Detroit Tigers
1997 Statistics Pos: OF **Age:** 26 **B:**R **T:**R

	G	AB	HR	RBI	SB	Avg	OBP	SLG
AA Mobile	78	307	1	22	35	.254	.300	.319
AA Jacksnville	36	146	2	13	7	.226	.272	.301

Go Speed Racer Go. Go back to Double-A and learn to hit.

J.J. Johnson — Minnesota Twins
1997 Statistics Pos: OF **Age:** 24 **B:**R **T:**R

	G	AB	HR	RBI	SB	Avg	OBP	SLG
AAA Salt Lake	26	82	0	5	2	.146	.195	.183
AA New Britain	103	356	3	42	13	.236	.312	.309

Tools player, did poorly in 1997 after good 1996. Might rebound, might fade further.

Bobby M. Jones — Colorado Rockies
1997 Statistics Pos: P **Age:** 25 **B:**R **T:** L

	W	L	ERA	G	GS	Sv	IP	H	BB	SO
AAA Colo Sprngs	7	11	5.14	25	21	0	133.0	135	71	104
NL Colorado	1	1	8.38	4	4	0	19.1	30	12	5

Live arm for a southpaw, 5.14 ERA at Colorado Springs isn't bad. Won't survive in Coors Field for any length of time.

Randy Jorgensen — Seattle Mariners
1997 Statistics Pos: 1B **Age:** 25 **B:**L **T:**L

	G	AB	HR	RBI	SB	Avg	OBP	SLG
AA Memphis	129	477	11	70	1	.291	.349	.432

Line-drive bat, marginal power, very good glove at first base. Will be hard for him to find a job.

Terry Joseph — Chicago Cubs
1997 Statistics Pos: OF **Age:** 24 **B:**R **T:**R

	G	AB	HR	RBI	SB	Avg	OBP	SLG
AA Orlando	134	452	11	68	17	.277	.374	.447

One of a bushel of Cubs minor league outfielders with some power, some speed and marginal prospect status.

Ryan Karp — Tampa Bay Devil Rays
1997 Statistics Pos: P **Age:** 27 **B:**L **T:** L

	W	L	ERA	G	GS	Sv	IP	H	BB	SO
AAA Scranton-WB	4	3	4.19	32	5	1	73.0	72	42	55
NL Philadelphia	1	1	5.40	15	1	0	15.0	12	9	18

Injury-prone southpaw has a sharp slider. Will be given every chance to contribute and may do so.

Gus Kennedy — Chicago Cubs
1997 Statistics Pos: OF **Age:** 24 **B:**R **T:**R

	G	AB	HR	RBI	SB	Avg	OBP	SLG
A Daytona	113	368	14	57	15	.261	.347	.429

Once in the Braves system. Has power, speed, patience, is prone to strikeouts. Sleeper will need to hit in Double-A.

Bill King
Oakland Athletics

1997 Statistics   Pos: P **Age:** 25 **B:**R **T:** R

	W	L	ERA	G	GS	Sv	IP	H	BB	SO
AA Huntsville	9	7	4.19	28	27	0	176.0	216	28	103

Control pitcher gave up a ton of hits in Double-A but never walks anybody. Decent slider, could surprise.

Eugene Kingsale
Baltimore Orioles

1997 Statistics   Pos: OF **Age:** 21 **B:**B **T:**R

	G	AB	HR	RBI	SB	Avg	OBP	SLG
AA Bowie	13	46	0	4	5	.413	.481	.543
R Orioles	6	17	0	0	1	.294	.400	.294

Extremely fast, young Aruban outfielder has potential as a hitter but is always injured. Keep an eye on him. Grade C+ if healthy.

Chris Kirgan
Colorado Rockies

1997 Statistics   Pos: 1B **Age:** 24 **B:**R **T:**R

	G	AB	HR	RBI	SB	Avg	OBP	SLG
AA Bowie	139	504	19	71	0	.230	.313	.393

Slow slugger, strikes out too much and would have problems hitting .220 in the majors.

Randy Knoll
Philadelphia Phillies

1997 Statistics   Pos: P **Age:** 21 **B:**R **T:** R

	W	L	ERA	G	GS	Sv	IP	H	BB	SO
A Clearwater	1	2	4.45	5	5	0	30.1	33	7	20

Lost 1997 season to shoulder injury. Decent stuff, fine control, needs his health back. If he gets it, he could move quickly.

Brian Koelling
Cincinnati Reds

1997 Statistics   Pos: 2B **Age:** 28 **B:**R **T:**R

	G	AB	HR	RBI	SB	Avg	OBP	SLG
AA Chattanooga	73	279	3	22	18	.280	.348	.366

Minor league vet hoping for expansion job. He won't get it.

David Lamb
Baltimore Orioles

1997 Statistics   Pos: 2B-SS **Age:** 22 **B:**B **T:**R

	G	AB	HR	RBI	SB	Avg	OBP	SLG
AA Bowie	73	269	4	38	0	.331	.408	.465
A Frederick	70	249	2	39	3	.261	.339	.378

Sleeper prospect has good patience at the plate and started to hit last year. It could have been a fluke or it could have been real progress. Grade C+ prospect; watch this guy.

Frank Lankford
Los Angeles Dodgers

1997 Statistics   Pos: P **Age:** 27 **B:**R **T:** R

	W	L	ERA	G	GS	Sv	IP	H	BB	SO
AAA Columbus	7	4	2.69	15	13	0	93.2	84	22	40
AA Norwich	4	2	2.90	11	11	0	68.1	58	15	39

Throws strikes with middling stuff, had a good year as a starter in the high minors after spending career in middle relief. Worth taking a look at if he continues to pitch well. Picked up in the major league Rule 5 draft.

Greg LaRocca
San Diego Padres

1997 Statistics   Pos: 2B **Age:** 25 **B:**R **T:**R

	G	AB	HR	RBI	SB	Avg	OBP	SLG
AA Mobile	76	300	3	31	8	.267	.336	.363

Organization player who can hold down second or short without killing the defense, and he has hit in the past. Needs to get his offense back to have hope for utility job.

Sean Lawrence
Pittsburgh Pirates

1997 Statistics   Pos: P **Age:** 27 **B:**L **T:** L

	W	L	ERA	G	GS	Sv	IP	H	BB	SO
AAA Calgary	8	9	4.21	26	26	0	143.1	154	57	116

Lefty, not a real hard thrower but not exactly a finesse guy. No reason for him to succeed, but no reason for him to fail either.

Jalal Leach
Seattle Mariners

1997 Statistics   Pos: OF **Age:** 29 **B:**L **T:**L

	G	AB	HR	RBI	SB	Avg	OBP	SLG
AAA Tacoma	115	415	9	55	6	.308	.357	.451

Journeyman Triple-A outfielder, somewhat athletic, decent hitter, but too old to get his hopes up.

312

Aaron Ledesma — Tampa Bay Devil Rays
1997 Statistics   Pos: SS **Age:** 26 **B:**R **T:**R

	G	AB	HR	RBI	SB	Avg	OBP	SLG
AAA Rochester	85	326	3	43	12	.325	.388	.439
AL Baltimore	43	88	2	11	1	.352	.437	.500

Not a bad hitter, but he doesn't have the range that teams like in a utility infielder, and he lacks power.

Derek Lee — San Diego Padres
1997 Statistics   Pos: OF **Age:** 31 **B:**L **T:**R

	G	AB	HR	RBI	SB	Avg	OBP	SLG
AAA Las Vegas	75	231	5	35	4	.294	.377	.437

Not to be confused with Derrek Lee, the hot prospect recently traded by the Padres. Derek with one "r" is a minor league vet and not a bad player, but he had trouble getting respect even when he was young. No one pays attention any longer.

Keith Legree — Minnesota Twins
1997 Statistics   Pos: OF **Age:** 26 **B:**L **T:**R

	G	AB	HR	RBI	SB	Avg	OBP	SLG
AA New Britain	113	343	9	58	10	.242	.350	.388

Former college basketball star, drew walks and hit for power in Double-A. Has a chance.

John LeRoy — Tampa Bay Devil Rays
1997 Statistics   Pos: P **Age:** 22 **B:**R **T:** R

	W	L	ERA	G	GS	Sv	IP	H	BB	SO
AA Greenville	5	5	5.03	29	14	1	98.1	105	43	84
NL Atlanta	1	0	0.00	1	0	0	2.0	1	3	3

Pitched very well in A-ball in 1996, very poorly in Double-A in 1997, then very well in the Arizona Fall League. Live arm, does better as a reliever than a starter. Could surprise.

T.R. Lewis — Atlanta Braves
1997 Statistics   Pos: OF **Age:** 26 **B:**R **T:**R

	G	AB	HR	RBI	SB	Avg	OBP	SLG
AAA Richmond	117	363	7	58	8	.295	.362	.435

Has proven he can hit in Triple-A, but doesn't have much power and prone to injuries. Would have use as a reserve outfielder and pinch hitter.

Marcus Logan — St. Louis Cardinals
1997 Statistics   Pos: P **Age:** 25 **B:**R **T:** R

	W	L	ERA	G	GS	Sv	IP	H	BB	SO
AA Arkansas	11	7	4.12	27	25	0	153.0	152	64	101

Staff filler at Arkansas, led team in wins. Could make a major league appearance if his command improves.

Kevin Lomon — San Diego Padres
1997 Statistics   Pos: P **Age:** 26 **B:**R **T:** R

	W	L	ERA	G	GS	Sv	IP	H	BB	SO
AAA Columbus	1	1	6.28	3	3	0	14.1	7	14	
AA Norwich	9	7	3.21	18	18	0	115.0	104	50	117

Product of Braves system, doesn't throw hard. Very effective in Double-A but struggles above that level.

Ryan Long — Kansas City Royals
1997 Statistics   Pos: OF **Age:** 25 **B:**R **T:**R

	G	AB	HR	RBI	SB	Avg	OBP	SLG
AAA Omaha	113	411	19	56	2	.265	.305	.467
AL Kansas City	6	9	0	2	0	.222	.300	.222

Strong power hitter with terrible strike-zone judgment. Not a good fit in Royals Stadium.

Johann Lopez — Houston Astros
1997 Statistics   Pos: P **Age:** 22 **B:**R **T:** R

	W	L	ERA	G	GS	Sv	IP	H	BB	SO
AA Jackson	6	8	4.38	35	19	1	133.2	131	57	109

Venezuelan pitcher with adequate stuff. Could surprise if he picks up more velocity or improves his command from good to terrific.

Mickey Lopez — Milwaukee Brewers
1997 Statistics   Pos: 2B **Age:** 24 **B:**B **T:**R

	G	AB	HR	RBI	SB	Avg	OBP	SLG
AA El Paso	134	483	3	58	20	.300	.366	.404

Good year in Double-A, but everybody had a good year at El Paso. Can field, might hit some.

Andrew Lorraine — Oakland Athletics
1997 Statistics **Pos:** P **Age:** 25 **B:** L **T:** L

	W	L	ERA	G	GS	Sv	IP	H	BB	SO
AAA Edmonton	8	6	4.74	23	20	0	117.2	143	34	75
AL Oakland	3	1	6.37	12	6	0	29.2	45	15	18

Still looking for the magic that made him a top prospect in college.

Billy Lott — Pittsburgh Pirates
1997 Statistics **Pos:** OF **Age:** 27 **B:** R **T:** R

	G	AB	HR	RBI	SB	Avg	OBP	SLG
AAA Ottawa	32	108	2	18	1	.222	.271	.324
AAA Calgary	71	239	15	55	6	.314	.405	.577

Dodgers product, has power, but strikes out a lot and is too old to be a real prospect. He has 80 percent of the value of a Billy Ashley.

Kevin Lovingier — St. Louis Cardinals
1997 Statistics **Pos:** P **Age:** 26 **B:** L **T:** L

	W	L	ERA	G	GS	Sv	IP	H	BB	SO
AA Arkansas	4	3	2.54	59	0	3	74.1	68	26	82

Candidate for middle-relief spot, and a good one. Decent fastball, nice forkball, good control. Grade C+ prospect.

Sean Lowe — St. Louis Cardinals
1997 Statistics **Pos:** P **Age:** 27 **B:** R **T:** R

	W	L	ERA	G	GS	Sv	IP	H	BB	SO
AAA Louisville	6	10	4.37	26	23	1	131.2	142	53	117
NL St. Louis	0	2	9.35	6	4	0	17.1	27	10	8

Good arm, no real evidence he knows how to use it.

Lou Lucca — Florida Marlins
1997 Statistics **Pos:** 3B **Age:** 27 **B:** R **T:** R

	G	AB	HR	RBI	SB	Avg	OBP	SLG
AAA Charlotte	96	292	18	51	5	.284	.335	.551

Can hit some, decent with the glove. No outstanding skills and can't play second or short, which hurts his chances.

Mark Lukasiewicz — Toronto Blue Jays
1997 Statistics **Pos:** P **Age:** 25 **B:** L **T:** L

	W	L	ERA	G	GS	Sv	IP	H	BB	SO
AAA Syracuse	2	3	5.17	30	0	0	31.1	37	13	31
AA Knoxville	2	0	3.65	27	0	7	37.0	26	14	43

Southpaw with live arm, looking for one-out role.

Matt Luke — New York Yankees
1997 Statistics **Pos:** OF **Age:** 27 **B:** L **T:** L

	G	AB	HR	RBI	SB	Avg	OBP	SLG
AAA Columbus	87	337	8	45	0	.228	.296	.374

One-time prospect has power, but strike-zone problems and constant injuries have crippled his career.

Ryan Luzinski — Baltimore Orioles
1997 Statistics **Pos:** C **Age:** 24 **B:** R **T:** R

	G	AB	HR	RBI	SB	Avg	OBP	SLG
AAA Rochester	42	125	2	16	0	.208	.324	.328
AA Bowie	30	81	5	15	3	.284	.363	.519
A Frederick	1	3	0	0	0	.667	.750	.667

Still struggling with strikeouts, injuries and defense.

Chris Macca — Colorado Rockies
1997 Statistics **Pos:** P **Age:** 23 **B:** R **T:** R

	W	L	ERA	G	GS	Sv	IP	H	BB	SO
AA New Haven	0	4	7.77	46	0	9	44.0	47	55	29

Reliever has a solid fastball and a good slider, but command collapsed in Double-A. Had 30 saves in 1996 and 29 strikeouts in 1997.

Fausto Macey — Anaheim Angels
1997 Statistics **Pos:** P **Age:** 22 **B:** R **T:** R

	W	L	ERA	G	GS	Sv	IP	H	BB	SO
AAA Vancouver	1	3	8.10	9	8	0	40.0	47	32	23
AA Midland	6	9	8.03	17	17	0	96.1	141	46	38

Had one of the worst seasons I have ever seen. Young, projectable, looks like a pitcher, but has no idea what he's doing.

Robert Machado — Chicago White Sox
1997 Statistics Pos: C Age: 24 B:R T:R

	G	AB	HR	RBI	SB	Avg	OBP	SLG
AAA Nashville	84	308	8	30	5	.269	.297	.406
AL Chicago	10	15	0	2	0	.200	.250	.333

Venezuelan catcher, good defensive skills with a little power. Could get significant playing time after the loss of Jorge Fabregas in the expansion draft, but a .250 hitter at best.

Alan Mahaffey — Chicago Cubs
1997 Statistics Pos: P Age: 24 B:L T:L

	W	L	ERA	G	GS	Sv	IP	H	BB	SO
A Ft. Myers	1	2	4.10	38	0	1	48.1	46	8	55
AA New Britain	1	2	3.57	13	1	1	22.2	19	10	29

Major league Rule 5 draft pick. Finesse lefty with good control.

Ricky Magdaleno — Cincinnati Reds
1997 Statistics Pos: SS Age: 23 B:R T:R

	G	AB	HR	RBI	SB	Avg	OBP	SLG
AAA Indianapolis	56	155	4	14	0	.206	.277	.355
AA Chattanooga	61	187	8	34	1	.262	.398	.471

Infielder with power, showed patience in Double-A and played well, but hit poorly at Indianapolis. Still young enough to have a career.

Mike Mahoney — Atlanta Braves
1997 Statistics Pos: C Age: 25 B:R T:R

	G	AB	HR	RBI	SB	Avg	OBP	SLG
AA Greenville	87	298	8	46	1	.228	.299	.366

Good handler of pitchers. Scouts like his defense but his bat is a problem. Possible backup in a year or two. Voted best defensive catcher in the Southern League.

Marty Malloy — Atlanta Braves
1997 Statistics Pos: 2B Age: 25 B:L T:R

	G	AB	HR	RBI	SB	Avg	OBP	SLG
AAA Richmond	108	414	2	25	17	.285	.351	.370

Decent lefty stick, decent glove. No reason why he can't have a Mark Lemke-like career if some manager takes a liking to him.

Sean Maloney — Milwaukee Brewers
1997 Statistics Pos: P Age: 26 B:R T:R

	W	L	ERA	G	GS	Sv	IP	H	BB	SO
AAA Tucson	0	2	4.82	15	0	5	18.2	24	3	21
AL Milwaukee	0	0	5.14	3	0	0	7.0	7	2	5

Looked great as relief candidate in 1996, but arm fell off in 1997.

David Manning — Texas Rangers
1997 Statistics Pos: P Age: 26 B:R T:R

	W	L	ERA	G	GS	Sv	IP	H	BB	SO
AAA Okla City	1	3	4.40	5	5	0	28.2	33	9	15
AA Tulsa	4	7	4.88	13	12	0	75.2	77	27	55
A Charlotte	0	0	1.50	1	1	0	6.0	4	4	4

Live arm, but command problems have slowed him down and he ended the season on the disabled list with circulatory problems.

Javier Martinez — Pittsburgh Pirates
1997 Statistics Pos: P Age: 21 B:R T:R

	W	L	ERA	G	GS	Sv	IP	H	BB	SO
A Daytona	2	6	5.79	9	9	0	51.1	65	26	34
A Rockford	1	7	5.70	17	17	0	79.0	85	50	70

Taken from the Cubs as the top pick in the major league Rule 5 draft, then sold to the Pirates. Bad stats, strong arm, good winter in Puerto Rico.

Jesus Martinez — Florida Marlins
1997 Statistics Pos: P Age: 24 B:L T:L

	W	L	ERA	G	GS	Sv	IP	H	BB	SO
AAA Albuquerque	7	1	6.21	26	12	0	84.0	112	52	80

Doesn't have the arm of brothers Pedro and Ramon. Has the pitching instincts of Clancy, my mother's dog.

Manny Martinez — Pittsburgh Pirates
1997 Statistics Pos: OF Age: 27 B:R T:R

	G	AB	HR	RBI	SB	Avg	OBP	SLG
AAA Calgary	109	420	16	66	17	.331	.379	.531

Triple-A outfielder with some speed, some power, not very patient. Looking for reserve role.

Ramon Martinez — *San Francisco Giants*
1997 Statistics **Pos:** SS **Age:** 25 **B:**R **T:**R

	G	AB	HR	RBI	SB	Avg	OBP	SLG
AAA Phoenix	18	57	1	7	1	.281	.333	.368
AA Shreveport	105	404	5	54	4	.319	.382	.455

Product of Royals system. Good glove, contact hitter, hard worker, can play little ball.

Mike Matthews — *Cleveland Indians*
1997 Statistics **Pos:** P **Age:** 24 **B:**L **T:**L

	W	L	ERA	G	GS	Sv	IP	H	BB	SO
AAA Buffalo	0	2	7.71	5	5	0	21.0	32	10	17
AA Akron	6	8	3.82	19	19	0	113.0	116	57	69

Lefty, once threw very hard and still has good velocity, but injuries have stalled him.

Walt McKeel — *Boston Red Sox*
1997 Statistics **Pos:** C **Age:** 26 **B:**R **T:**R

	G	AB	HR	RBI	SB	Avg	OBP	SLG
AAA Pawtucket	66	237	6	30	0	.253	.347	.392
AA Trenton	7	25	0	4	0	.160	.192	.240
AL Boston	5	3	0	0	0	.000	.000	.000

Has some power, glove not so terrible that he doesn't deserve a look.

Adam Melhuse — *Toronto Blue Jays*
1997 Statistics **Pos:** C **Age:** 26 **B:**B **T:**R

	G	AB	HR	RBI	SB	Avg	OBP	SLG
AAA Syracuse	38	118	2	9	1	.237	.311	.347
AA Knoxville	31	87	3	10	0	.230	.364	.368

Has more plate patience than most Blue Jays prospects. Some power, adequate glove, looking for bench spot, like most of the guys in this section.

Carlos Mendez — *Kansas City Royals*
1997 Statistics **Pos:** 1B **Age:** 23 **B:**R **T:**R

	G	AB	HR	RBI	SB	Avg	OBP	SLG
AA Wichita	129	507	12	90	4	.325	.346	.464

Venezuelan can hit some, but defensive problems, strike-zone judgment and questions about his age limit his appeal.

Reynol Mendoza — *Florida Marlins*
1997 Statistics **Pos:** P **Age:** 27 **B:**R **T:** R

	W	L	ERA	G	GS	Sv	IP	H	BB	SO
AAA Charlotte	7	8	5.49	46	17	9	114.2	134	57	93

Soft tosser eventually will see some big-league innings because he stays healthy and is occasionally effective.

Mark Merchant — *Kansas City Royals*
1997 Statistics **Pos:** DH-OF **Age:** 29 **B:**B **T:**R

	G	AB	HR	RBI	SB	Avg	OBP	SLG
AAA Omaha	2	5	0	0	0	.000	.000	.000
AA Wichita	49	147	9	38	0	.340	.431	.585

Has actually hit very well at times, but propensity for injuries and "first-round bust" label have doomed his career. Has done enough to warrant a look, but bad tags die hard.

Lou Merloni — *Boston Red Sox*
1997 Statistics **Pos:** 3B-2B **Age:** 26 **B:**R **T:**R

	G	AB	HR	RBI	SB	Avg	OBP	SLG
AAA Pawtucket	49	165	5	24	0	.297	.368	.448
AA Trenton	69	255	5	37	3	.310	.402	.467

Can play second or third, has a pretty good bat. Worse players are in the majors.

Damian Miller — *Arizona Diamondbacks*
1997 Statistics **Pos:** C **Age:** 28 **B:**R **T:**R

	G	AB	HR	RBI	SB	Avg	OBP	SLG
AAA Salt Lake	85	314	11	82	6	.338	.395	.522
AL Minnesota	25	66	2	13	0	.273	.282	.379

Minor league veteran, a good defensive catcher with an okay bat. Could hang around as a backup for a long time.

Nate Minchey — *Colorado Rockies*
1997 Statistics **Pos:** P **Age:** 28 **B:**R **T:** R

	W	L	ERA	G	GS	Sv	IP	H	BB	SO
AAA Colo Sprngs	15	6	4.51	27	21	0	157.2	172	53	107
NL Colorado	0	0	13.50	2	0	0	2.0	5	1	1

Effective Triple-A starter since the Civil War, deserves a chance somewhere.

Doug Mirabelli — San Francisco Giants
1997 Statistics **Pos:** C **Age:** 27 **B:** R **T:** R

	G	AB	HR	RBI	SB	Avg	OBP	SLG
AAA Phoenix	100	332	8	48	1	.265	.384	.419
NL San Francisco	6	7	0	0	0	.143	.250	.143

Possible 1998 backup catcher for Giants. Occasional pop at the plate, draws walks, defense good enough for the role.

Mike Misuraca — Milwaukee Brewers
1997 Statistics **Pos:** P **Age:** 29 **B:** R **T:** R

	W	L	ERA	G	GS	Sv	IP	H	BB	SO
AAA Tucson	8	7	4.98	33	10	1	108.1	119	39	62
AL Milwaukee	0	0	11.32	5	0	0	10.1	15	7	10

Soft tosser must be absolutely perfect to survive, and that is a tough thing for a human to be.

Donovan Mitchell — Houston Astros
1997 Statistics **Pos:** OF **Age:** 28 **B:** L **T:** R

	G	AB	HR	RBI	SB	Avg	OBP	SLG
AA Jackson	128	477	5	44	22	.256	.344	.348

Has speed, draws walks, doesn't hit much. Might get a few paychecks as an emergency reserve.

Doug Mlicki — Houston Astros
1997 Statistics **Pos:** P **Age:** 26 **B:** R **T:** R

	W	L	ERA	G	GS	Sv	IP	H	BB	SO
AAA New Orleans	4	3	3.60	14	3	0	30.0	27	10	18
AA Jackson	4	4	5.36	9	9	0	48.2	69	20	35
A Kissimmee	0	0	0.00	1	1	0	4.0	4	0	2

Fairly good stuff, good control, lost much of 1997 to injury. Not a bad pitcher if healthy.

Izzy Molina — Oakland Athletics
1997 Statistics **Pos:** C **Age:** 26 **B:** R **T:** R

	G	AB	HR	RBI	SB	Avg	OBP	SLG
AAA Edmonton	61	218	6	34	2	.261	.300	.422
AL Oakland	48	111	3	7	0	.198	.219	.324

Virtually the same outlook at last year: as a Triple-A catcher with a decent glove, he might stumble into a job someday.

Ivan Montane — Seattle Mariners
1997 Statistics **Pos:** P **Age:** 24 **B:** R **T:** R

	W	L	ERA	G	GS	Sv	IP	H	BB	SO
AA Memphis	0	8	7.53	22	12	0	71.2	83	51	63
A Lancaster	1	2	5.29	6	6	0	32.1	40	13	34

Excellent velocity but no command, and he isn't a rocket scientist. Or even a hot-air balloon scientist.

Joel Moore — Colorado Rockies
1997 Statistics **Pos:** P **Age:** 25 **B:** L **T:** R

	W	L	ERA	G	GS	Sv	IP	H	BB	SO
AAA Colo Sprngs	3	1	7.76	5	5	0	26.2	47	12	20
AA New Haven	6	4	3.84	19	12	0	77.1	77	35	47

Injury-plagued starter can be effective when not on the disabled list. Best chance would come with another team.

Ramon Morel — Chicago Cubs
1997 Statistics **Pos:** P **Age:** 23 **B:** R **T:** R

	W	L	ERA	G	GS	Sv	IP	H	BB	SO
AAA Calgary	6	7	5.75	27	18	0	101.2	131	42	72
NL Pittsburgh	0	0	4.70	5	0	0	7.2	11	4	4
NL Chicago	0	0	4.91	3	0	0	3.2	3	3	3

Dominican with decent arm, needs command but too tentative under pressure.

Shea Morenz — New York Yankees
1997 Statistics **Pos:** OF **Age:** 24 **B:** L **T:** R

	G	AB	HR	RBI	SB	Avg	OBP	SLG
A Tampa	117	403	7	44	2	.236	.277	.328

Let's play *Baseball Jeopardy*. The Answer: This University of Texas quarterback was a first-round pick in the baseball draft, and his career failed because of lack of strike-zone judgment.

Mike Moriarty — Minnesota Twins
1997 Statistics **Pos:** SS **Age:** 24 **B:** R **T:** R

	G	AB	HR	RBI	SB	Avg	OBP	SLG
AA New Britain	135	421	6	48	12	.221	.309	.340

Outstanding defensive shortstop, didn't hit in Double-A.

Bobby Morris — Cleveland Indians
1997 Statistics   **Pos:** 2B **Age:** 25 **B:**L **T:**R

	G	AB	HR	RBI	SB	Avg	OBP	SLG
AA Akron	42	119	1	15	1	.252	.375	.370
AA Orlando	4	16	0	1	0	.313	.389	.375
A Kinston	10	32	2	10	0	.156	.282	.375

Product of Cubs system, brother of Hal Morris. Showed ability in A-ball but has struggled at higher levels. Injuries have hurt him.

Mike Moyle — Cleveland Indians
1997 Statistics   **Pos:** C **Age:** 26 **B:**R **T:**R

	G	AB	HR	RBI	SB	Avg	OBP	SLG
AA Akron	104	342	16	53	3	.231	.342	.415

Minor league veteran hit for power in Double-A. Longest of longshots.

Juan Munoz — St. Louis Cardinals
1997 Statistics   **Pos:** OF **Age:** 24 **B:**L **T:**L

	G	AB	HR	RBI	SB	Avg	OBP	SLG
AA Arkansas	58	215	6	31	6	.279	.330	.423
A Pr William	66	256	4	48	3	.313	.355	.477

Did well in Florida State League, mediocre in Double-A. Contact hitter doesn't drive the ball for great power.

Mike Murphy — Texas Rangers
1997 Statistics   **Pos:** OF **Age:** 26 **B:**R **T:**R

	G	AB	HR	RBI	SB	Avg	OBP	SLG
AAA Okla City	73	243	5	25	14	.329	.425	.486
AA Tulsa	46	156	4	19	6	.256	.405	.410

Non-prospect has a quick bat and can hit for average, but power is limited and he strikes out too much.

Calvin Murray — San Francisco Giants
1997 Statistics   **Pos:** OF **Age:** 26 **B:**R **T:**R

	G	AB	HR	RBI	SB	Avg	OBP	SLG
AA Shreveport	122	419	10	56	52	.272	.375	.418

Still hanging around, flashy in the field and on the bases. There's no convincing evidence he'll hit enough to play regularly.

Glenn Murray — Cincinnati Reds
1997 Statistics   **Pos:** OF **Age:** 27 **B:**R **T:**R

	G	AB	HR	RBI	SB	Avg	OBP	SLG
AAA Indianapolis	7	12	0	0	0	.167	.286	.250
AA Chattanooga	94	329	26	73	7	.283	.387	.581

Has substantive power. A .280 hitter in Double-A, a .250 hitter in Triple-A and a .220 hitter in the majors.

Joe Nathan — San Francisco Giants
1997 Statistics   **Pos:** P **Age:** 23 **B:**R **T:** R

	W	L	ERA	G	GS	Sv	IP	H	BB	SO
A Salem-keizr	2	1	2.47	18	5	2	62.0	53	26	44

Northwest League pitcher on the 40-man roster because the Giants have to protect *somebody*.

Mike Neal — Cleveland Indians
1997 Statistics   **Pos:** 2B-SS **Age:** 26 **B:**R **T:**R

	G	AB	HR	RBI	SB	Avg	OBP	SLG
AA Akron	126	457	17	69	8	.282	.372	.455

Double-A infielder can hit some, but no future in Cleveland with Enrique Wilson around.

Mike Neill — Oakland Athletics
1997 Statistics   **Pos:** OF **Age:** 27 **B:**L **T:**L

	G	AB	HR	RBI	SB	Avg	OBP	SLG
AAA Edmonton	7	21	0	3	1	.190	.393	.190
AA Huntsville	122	486	14	80	16	.340	.427	.496

Outfield version of Mike Coolbaugh and D.T. Cromer.

Chris Nelson — Oakland Athletics
1997 Statistics   **Pos:** P **Age:** 25 **B:**B **T:** R

	W	L	ERA	G	GS	Sv	IP	H	BB	SO
AA Huntsville	9	3	4.97	20	15	0	99.2	116	25	71
A Modesto	3	3	3.83	8	8	0	47.0	55	7	53

Curveball pitcher with good control. Fringe prospect, but that's good enough for a hurler these days.

Alan Newman — San Diego Padres
1997 Statistics **Pos:** P **Age:** 28 **B:** L **T:** L

	W	L	ERA	G	GS	Sv	IP	H	BB	SO
AA Birmingham	7	3	2.49	44	0	10	72.1	55	40	64

Once a prospect in the Twins system. Throws very hard, command has been a problem and still is.

Darrell Nicholas — Milwaukee Brewers
1997 Statistics **Pos:** OF **Age:** 25 **B:** R **T:** R

	G	AB	HR	RBI	SB	Avg	OBP	SLG
AA El Paso	127	518	14	68	17	.315	.349	.506

Runs well, but El Paso power and poor command of strike zone are major negatives.

Brad Niedermaier — Minnesota Twins
1997 Statistics **Pos:** P **Age:** 25 **B:** R **T:** R

	W	L	ERA	G	GS	Sv	IP	H	BB	SO
AAA Salt Lake	2	1	5.88	16	0	0	26.0	29	13	20
A Ft. Myers	2	3	1.47	32	0	17	36.2	27	12	47

Throws a decent fastball and a knuckle-curve. Had a good year as a closer in A-ball. Middle-relief candidate.

Jose Nieves — Chicago Cubs
1997 Statistics **Pos:** SS **Age:** 22 **B:** R **T:** R

	G	AB	HR	RBI	SB	Avg	OBP	SLG
A Daytona	85	331	4	42	16	.275	.313	.378

Can field, doesn't look like he'll hit much.

Doug O'Neill — Texas Rangers
1997 Statistics **Pos:** OF **Age:** 27 **B:** R **T:** R

	G	AB	HR	RBI	SB	Avg	OBP	SLG
AAA Okla City	11	31	0	1	1	.194	.265	.290
AA Tulsa	118	412	20	64	12	.277	.356	.473

Has power, some speed, but weak strike-zone judgment and penchant for strikeouts restrict his allure.

Jamie Ogden — Minnesota Twins
1997 Statistics **Pos:** OF **Age:** 26 **B:** L **T:** L

	G	AB	HR	RBI	SB	Avg	OBP	SLG
AAA Salt Lake	97	367	14	53	14	.286	.351	.477

Could hit .240 in the majors with a bit of power, not enough to earn a real job.

Rafael Orellano — Boston Red Sox
1997 Statistics **Pos:** P **Age:** 24 **B:** L **T:** L

	W	L	ERA	G	GS	Sv	IP	H	BB	SO
AAA Pawtucket	3	5	7.14	16	12	0	69.1	65	55	46
AA Trenton	0	1	17.05	2	2	0	6.1	14	7	5
R Red Sox	1	0	1.29	2	1	0	7.0	2	1	9

Career on the ropes after two very poor seasons. Chance for rebound very slim, though not nonexistent.

Willis Otanez — Baltimore Orioles
1997 Statistics **Pos:** 3B **Age:** 24 **B:** R **T:** R

	G	AB	HR	RBI	SB	Avg	OBP	SLG
AAA Rochester	49	168	5	25	0	.208	.269	.351
AA Bowie	19	78	3	13	0	.333	.398	.564
R Orioles	8	25	2	3	0	.320	.393	.640

Season ruined by elbow surgery. Has offensive and defensive potential if healthy.

Alex Pacheco — Seattle Mariners
1997 Statistics **Pos:** P **Age:** 24 **B:** R **T:** R

	W	L	ERA	G	GS	Sv	IP	H	BB	SO
AAA Tacoma	0	2	8.78	15	2	0	27.2	45	15	21
AA Memphis	1	1	3.75	9	0	0	12.0	7	9	13

Good arm, middle-relief candidate when healthy, which he wasn't last year.

Scott Pagano — Philadelphia Phillies
1997 Statistics **Pos:** OF **Age:** 26 **B:** B **T:** R

	G	AB	HR	RBI	SB	Avg	OBP	SLG
AA Reading	117	468	3	44	17	.274	.348	.340

Switch-hitting outfielder has speed, patience. Hoping for a bench job.

Bronswell Patrick — Houston Astros
1997 Statistics **Pos:** P **Age:** 27 **B:** R **T:** R

	W	L	ERA	G	GS	Sv	IP	H	BB	SO
AAA New Orleans	6	5	3.22	30	12	0	100.2	108	30	88

Durable swingman, best pitch is a curveball. I wouldn't be afraid to take a look at him as a long reliever.

Jay Payton — New York Mets
1997 Statistics **Pos:** OF **Age:** 25 **B:** R **T:** R

	G	AB	HR	RBI	SB	Avg	OBP	SLG
Did Not Play-Injured								

Hey, Jay, you're not a pitcher. It's OK to stay healthy, even if you are a Met.

Eddie Pearson — Chicago White Sox

1997 Statistics — **Pos:** 1B **Age:** 24 **B:** B **T:** R

	G	AB	HR	RBI	SB	Avg	OBP	SLG
AAA Nashville	41	148	4	16	1	.223	.252	.331
AA Birmingham	95	382	5	59	1	.327	.366	.458

Finally hit in Double-A, struggled in Triple-A. Has as much of a chance to play in Chicago as Marilyn Manson does of being named Poet Laureate of the United States.

Michael Peeples — Toronto Blue Jays

1997 Statistics — **Pos:** 2B **Age:** 21 **B:** R **T:** R

	G	AB	HR	RBI	SB	Avg	OBP	SLG
A Dunedin	129	477	2	42	26	.256	.331	.338

Added to 40-man roster. Has speed, draws walks, some glove skills. Must show he can hit at higher levels.

William Pennyfeather — Dodgers

1997 Statistics — **Pos:** OF **Age:** 29 **B:** R **T:** R

	G	AB	HR	RBI	SB	Avg	OBP	SLG
AAA Albuquerque	115	402	17	54	11	.254	.299	.453

A prospect seven years ago, hit .254 in Triple-A. Cheaper than Ruben Sierra, but not as good.

Billy Percibal — Baltimore Orioles

1997 Statistics — **Pos:** P **Age:** 24 **B:** R **T:** R

	W	L	ERA	G	GS	Sv	IP	H	BB	SO
AA Bowie	0	1	3.00	1	1	0	6.0	5	1	5
A Frederick	1	3	5.74	7	6	0	26.2	28	18	28
R Orioles	0	0	0.90	4	3	0	10.0	11	2	12

A good prospect two years ago, still recovering from serious elbow surgery.

Dan Perkins — Minnesota Twins

1997 Statistics — **Pos:** P **Age:** 23 **B:** R **T:** R

	W	L	ERA	G	GS	Sv	IP	H	BB	SO
AA New Britain	7	10	4.91	24	24	0	144.2	158	53	114

Has a strong fastball and slider, but regressed in Double-A debut. Has struggled before, could rebound.

Chris Petersen — Chicago Cubs

1997 Statistics — **Pos:** SS **Age:** 27 **B:** B **T:** R

	G	AB	HR	RBI	SB	Avg	OBP	SLG
AAA Iowa	119	391	3	33	1	.240	.306	.315

Good glove at short and second, not much of a bat. Would fit in well with Cubs' "Who needs hitting?" philosophy.

Tom Phelps — Montreal Expos

1997 Statistics — **Pos:** P **Age:** 24 **B:** L **T:** L

	W	L	ERA	G	GS	Sv	IP	H	BB	SO
AA Harrisburg	10	6	4.71	18	18	0	101.1	115	39	86

Sneaky finesse pitcher sometimes referred to as a prospect. Career on hold after August shoulder surgery.

Ricky Pickett — San Francisco Giants

1997 Statistics — **Pos:** P **Age:** 28 **B:** L **T:** L

	W	L	ERA	G	GS	Sv	IP	H	BB	SO
AAA Phoenix	3	3	3.19	61	0	12	67.2	52	49	85

Good arm, strikes people out, but never given a real shot. He may do something that irks managers or he may have just gotten buried.

Bo Porter — Chicago Cubs

1997 Statistics — **Pos:** OF **Age:** 25 **B:** R **T:** R

	G	AB	HR	RBI	SB	Avg	OBP	SLG
AA Orlando	8	31	1	3	0	.258	.281	.387
A Daytona	122	440	17	65	23	.307	.393	.495

Another Cubs outfielder who's a decent hitter but is too old for the levels he has played at. If he does well in Double-A, he might have a future.

Chop Pough — Kansas City Royals

1997 Statistics — **Pos:** 3B **Age:** 28 **B:** R **T:** R

	G	AB	HR	RBI	SB	Avg	OBP	SLG
AAA Omaha	124	433	22	59	0	.252	.335	.455

Fans love him and he could hit .250 with 20 homers in the majors. Nice guy.

Brian Powell — Detroit Tigers
1997 Statistics **Pos: P Age: 24 B:R T: R**

	W	L	ERA	G	GS	Sv	IP	H	BB	SO
A Lakeland	13	9	2.50	27	27	0	183.1	153	35	122

Pitched well in Florida State League, but he was in Double-A in 1996. Average stuff, needs great command to survive.

John Powell — Texas Rangers
1997 Statistics **Pos: P Age: 26 B:R T: R**

	W	L	ERA	G	GS	Sv	IP	H	BB	SO
AAA Okla City	0	0	4.50	1	0	0	4.0	5	1	2
AA Tulsa	4	3	2.56	43	0	5	63.1	54	23	56

Short junkball pitcher, can be impressive when control is sharp. There have been good major league pitchers with similar stuff, but he needs a break and isn't likely to get one.

Chris Prieto — San Diego Padres
1997 Statistics **Pos: OF Age: 25 B:L T:L**

	G	AB	HR	RBI	SB	Avg	OBP	SLG
AA Mobile	109	388	2	58	26	.320	.418	.438
A Rancho Cuca	22	82	4	12	4	.280	.416	.476

Had the best year of his career in Double-A. Line-drive hitter, has speed, looking for bench job.

Chris Pritchett — Anaheim Angels
1997 Statistics **Pos: 1B Age: 28 B:L T:R**

	G	AB	HR	RBI	SB	Avg	OBP	SLG
AAA Vancouver	109	383	7	47	5	.279	.356	.428

Occasionally mentioned as a prospect by people who think first basemen who hit .279 with little power in the Pacific Coast League are prospects.

Dave Pyc — Florida Marlins
1997 Statistics **Pos: P Age: 27 B:L T: L**

	W	L	ERA	G	GS	Sv	IP	H	BB	SO
AAA Albuquerque	12	12	5.33	31	23	1	152.0	181	50	106

Southpaw with adequate stuff, taken by the Florida Marlins in the Triple-A Rule 5 draft.

Angel Ramirez — New York Yankees
1997 Statistics **Pos: OF Age: 25 B:R T:R**

	G	AB	HR	RBI	SB	Avg	OBP	SLG
AAA Syracuse	7	23	0	0	0	.174	.174	.217
AA Norwich	2	1	0	0	0	.000	.000	.000
AA Knoxville	85	369	5	37	11	.309	.331	.453

Similar to fellow Blue Jay Lorenzo de la Cruz: a streaky line-drive hitter with poor strike-zone judgment. Younger than de la Cruz and may have a better future.

Jon Ratliff — Chicago Cubs
1997 Statistics **Pos: P Age: 26 B:R T: R**

	W	L	ERA	G	GS	Sv	IP	H	BB	SO
AAA Iowa	1	3	5.57	9	4	1	32.1	30	7	25
AA Orlando	6	4	4.35	18	15	0	101.1	112	32	68

First-round pick from 1993 can't get over Triple-A hump. Off the map completely, still has good control but little else.

Luis Raven — Chicago White Sox
1997 Statistics **Pos: DH Age: 29 B:R T:R**

	G	AB	HR	RBI	SB	Avg	OBP	SLG
AA Birmingham	117	456	30	112	4	.336	.397	.612

Continues to smash the ball in Double-A. He might hit in the majors, but strikeout rate and weak glove skills limit his chances.

Ken Ray — Kansas City Royals
1997 Statistics **Pos: P Age: 23 B:R T: R**

	W	L	ERA	G	GS	Sv	IP	H	BB	SO
AAA Omaha	5	12	6.37	25	21	0	113.0	131	63	96

93-MPH fastball but no breaking stuff and can't change speeds. I would move him to relief. Bizarro Dave Swartzbaugh.

Brandon Reed — Detroit Tigers
1997 Statistics **Pos: P Age: 23 B:R T: R**

	W	L	ERA	G	GS	Sv	IP	H	BB	SO
AA Jacksnville	11	9	4.55	27	27	0	176.0	190	54	90

Recovered from 1996 injury. Lackluster fastball, tries to get by with breaking stuff and control.

Chris Reed
Cincinnati Reds
1997 Statistics — **Pos:** P **Age:** 24 **B:**R **T:** R

	W	L	ERA	G	GS	Sv	IP	H	BB	SO
AAA Indianapols	0	1	5.79	3	3	0	14.0	19	9	4
AA Chattanooga	6	8	5.34	23	23	0	129.2	140	68	96

Big pitcher with adequate stuff, got beat up in first Double-A exposure. Could rebound if control improves.

Glenn Reeves
Florida Marlins
1997 Statistics — **Pos:** OF **Age:** 24 **B:**R **T:**R

	G	AB	HR	RBI	SB	Avg	OBP	SLG
AA Portland	66	222	6	35	9	.351	.453	.514

Australian outfielder, looks like he can hit but gets hurt a lot. Grade C+ prospect if healthy.

Chris Reitsma
Boston Red Sox
1997 Statistics — **Pos:** P **Age:** 20 **B:**R **T:** R

	W	L	ERA	G	GS	Sv	IP	H	BB	SO
A Michigan	4	1	2.90	9	9	0	49.2	57	13	41

Pitched well in Midwest League, but lost most of season to broken arm. Has velocity, control, intelligence. Solid prospect if healthy.

Mike Rennhack
Milwaukee Brewers
1997 Statistics — **Pos:** OF **Age:** 23 **B:**B **T:**R

	G	AB	HR	RBI	SB	Avg	OBP	SLG
AA El Paso	106	369	9	64	4	.276	.342	.463

Good athlete. But .276 in El Paso is like .216 in the majors.

Al Reyes
Milwaukee Brewers
1997 Statistics — **Pos:** P **Age:** 26 **B:**R **T:** R

	W	L	ERA	G	GS	Sv	IP	H	BB	SO
AAA Tucson	2	4	5.02	38	0	7	57.1	52	34	70
AL Milwaukee	1	2	5.46	19	0	1	29.2	32	9	28

Minor league reliever hoping for major league job in the same role. Good control, middling stuff.

Marquis Riley
Anaheim Angels
1997 Statistics — **Pos:** OF **Age:** 27 **B:**B **T:**R

	G	AB	HR	RBI	SB	Avg	OBP	SLG
AAA Vancouver	65	242	0	8	27	.264	.359	.289

Exceptional speed, less power than Boutros Boutros-Gali at a Michigan Militia meeting.

Todd Rizzo
Chicago White Sox
1997 Statistics — **Pos:** P **Age:** 26 **B:**R **T:** L

	W	L	ERA	G	GS	Sv	IP	H	BB	SO
AAA Nashville	4	5	3.57	54	0	6	70.2	63	33	60

Looking for lefty one-out job. There are worse things he could do.

Chris Roberts
New York Mets
1997 Statistics — **Pos:** P **Age:** 26 **B:**R **T:** L

	W	L	ERA	G	GS	Sv	IP	H	BB	SO
AAA Norfolk	0	4	2.89	7	6	0	37.1	38	17	21
AA Binghamton	5	8	4.96	19	19	0	105.1	103	33	66

Still struggling to overcome arm trouble, has lost some of his velocity and never had much to begin with.

Willis Roberts
Detroit Tigers
1997 Statistics — **Pos:** P **Age:** 22 **B:**R **T:** R

	W	L	ERA	G	GS	Sv	IP	H	BB	SO
AA Jacksnville	6	15	6.28	26	26	0	149.0	181	64	86

Lousy season in Double-A after good 1996 campaign. Live arm, young, should rebound.

Frank Rodriguez
Milwaukee Brewers
1997 Statistics — **Pos:** P **Age:** 25 **B:**R **T:** R

	W	L	ERA	G	GS	Sv	IP	H	BB	SO
AAA Tucson	3	1	4.40	12	6	0	47.0	53	19	41
AA El Paso	2	2	3.40	31	0	4	50.1	46	13	40

No relation to Twins pitcher. Pretty good stuff, held back by command and injury problems. Could surprise.

Dan Rohrmeier
Seattle Mariners
1997 Statistics   **Pos:** OF **Age:** 33 **B:**R **T:**R

	G	AB	HR	RBI	SB	Avg	OBP	SLG
AAA Tacoma	125	471	33	120	1	.297	.354	.616
AL Seattle	7	9	0	2	0	.333	.455	.333

Solid season at Tacoma earned him a few major league swings. No reason why he can't be a good bat off the bench.

Mike Romano
Toronto Blue Jays
1997 Statistics   **Pos:** P **Age:** 26 **B:**R **T:** R

	W	L	ERA	G	GS	Sv	IP	H	BB	SO
AAA Syracuse	2	4	4.25	40	12	0	108.0	100	74	83

Triple-A swingman with adequate stuff, held back by less-than-adequate command.

Mandy Romero
San Diego Padres
1997 Statistics   **Pos:** C **Age:** 30 **B:**B **T:**R

	G	AB	HR	RBI	SB	Avg	OBP	SLG
AAA Las Vegas	33	91	3	13	0	.308	.385	.473
AA Mobile	61	222	13	52	0	.320	.422	.595
NL San Diego	21	48	2	4	1	.208	.240	.333

Older catcher, hit well in Double-A and got a brief shot in the majors. No worse than most reserve catchers.

Aaron Royster
Philadelphia Phillies
1997 Statistics   **Pos:** OF **Age:** 25 **B:**R **T:**R

	G	AB	HR	RBI	SB	Avg	OBP	SLG
AA Reading	112	412	15	62	2	.257	.342	.434

Has some pop in his bat, no speed, unlikely to hit .240 in the majors.

Toby Rumfield
Atlanta Braves
1997 Statistics   **Pos:** 1B **Age:** 25 **B:**R **T:**R

	G	AB	HR	RBI	SB	Avg	OBP	SLG
AA Chattanooga	101	331	5	38	0	.287	.326	.405

Can hit a little, but doesn't have a real position.

Sean Runyan
Detroit Tigers
1997 Statistics   **Pos:** P **Age:** 23 **B:**L **T:** L

	W	L	ERA	G	GS	Sv	IP	H	BB	SO
AA Mobile	5	2	2.34	40	1	1	61.2	54	28	52

Below-average fastball but good breaking stuff, effective against lefties. Could get a bullpen spot eventually. Major league Rule 5 draft pick.

Chad Rupp
Minnesota Twins
1997 Statistics   **Pos:** 1B-DH **Age:** 26 **B:**R **T:**R

	G	AB	HR	RBI	SB	Avg	OBP	SLG
AAA Salt Lake	117	426	32	94	2	.272	.352	.575

Righthanded-hitting first baseman has big-league power but would struggle to clear .230 in the majors.

Al Sadler
Milwaukee Brewers
1997 Statistics   **Pos:** P **Age:** 26 **B:**R **T:** R

	W	L	ERA	G	GS	Sv	IP	H	BB	SO
AAA Tucson	1	0	1.50	1	1	0	6.0	7	4	1
AA El Paso	6	6	6.62	35	9	4	66.2	102	28	58

Good arm, no command. 'Nuff said.

Marc Sagmoen
Texas Rangers
1997 Statistics   **Pos:** OF **Age:** 26 **B:**L **T:**L

	G	AB	HR	RBI	SB	Avg	OBP	SLG
AAA Okla City	111	418	5	44	4	.263	.306	.404
AL Texas	21	43	1	4	0	.140	.174	.256

Line-drive hitter, can whack a double but needs to hit for a better average to have value as a reserve.

Martin Sanchez
Arizona Diamondbacks
1997 Statistics   **Pos:** P **Age:** 21 **B:**R **T:** R

	W	L	ERA	G	GS	Sv	IP	H	BB	SO
A Kane County	3	5	4.50	51	0	22	54.0	40	32	57

You have to like the saves and strikeouts. Dominican went in major league Rule 5 draft.

Tracy Sanders
Pittsburgh Pirates
1997 Statistics   **Pos:** 1B **Age:** 28 **B:**L **T:**R

	G	AB	HR	RBI	SB	Avg	OBP	SLG
AA Carolina	116	376	21	78	7	.271	.397	.505

One-time prospect in Cleveland system, signed by Pirates out of independent league. Had a good power year at Carolina, no worse a player than Mark Johnson.

Francisco Saneaux   Baltimore Orioles
1997 Statistics   **Pos:** P **Age:** 24 **B:**R **T:** R

	W	L	ERA	G	GS	Sv	IP	H	BB	SO
AA Bowie	0	0	8.56	8	0	0	13.2	8	32	13
A Frederick	2	6	4.50	32	5	0	74.0	56	84	89

The Latin Steve Dalkowski.

Jose Santiago   Kansas City Royals
1997 Statistics   **Pos:** P **Age:** 23 **B:**R **T:** R

	W	L	ERA	G	GS	Sv	IP	H	BB	SO
AA Wichita	2	1	4.00	22	0	3	27.0	32	8	12
A Wilmington	1	1	4.91	4	0	2	3.2	3	1	1
A Lansing	1	0	2.08	9	0	1	13.0	10	6	8
AL Kansas City	0	0	1.93	4	0	0	4.2	7	2	1

Puerto Rican reliever throws fairly hard. Despite a surprise midseason call-up in 1997, doesn't have a really good out pitch. Personality a serious question after he was banned from Carolina League after throwing a ball at a fan and hitting an innocent bystander.

Jon Sbrocco   San Francisco Giants
1997 Statistics   **Pos:** 2B **Age:** 27 **B:**L **T:**R

	G	AB	HR	RBI	SB	Avg	OBP	SLG
AA Shreveport	97	271	2	27	7	.262	.361	.362

Draws lots of walks, has doubles power, glove work average at best.

Steve Schrenk   Baltimore Orioles
1997 Statistics   **Pos:** P **Age:** 29 **B:**R **T:** R

	W	L	ERA	G	GS	Sv	IP	H	BB	SO
AAA Rochester	4	7	4.66	25	24	0	125.2	127	36	99

Veteran sinker-slider guy with good control, could sneak into a job if he has a torrid streak when some team needs a pitcher.

Carl Schutz   Atlanta Braves
1997 Statistics   **Pos:** P **Age:** 26 **B:**L **T:** L

	W	L	ERA	G	GS	Sv	IP	H	BB	SO
AAA Richmond	4	6	5.33	27	10	0	79.1	83	51	66

Southpaw swingman with good arm, control problems have hindered his development. Has a chance as long as Leo Mazzone is in the organization.

Tate Seefried   New York Mets
1997 Statistics   **Pos:** 1B **Age:** 25 **B:**L **T:**R

	G	AB	HR	RBI	SB	Avg	OBP	SLG
AAA Norfolk	33	96	3	13	2	.229	.321	.406
AA Binghamton	96	335	29	79	9	.313	.405	.621

Good bat speed, but not good enough to compensate for the fact that he doesn't know how to hit. Triple-A pitchers expose his weaknesses.

Chris Seelbach   Florida Marlins
1997 Statistics   **Pos:** P **Age:** 25 **B:**R **T:** R

	W	L	ERA	G	GS	Sv	IP	H	BB	SO
AAA Charlotte	5	0	6.26	16	6	0	50.1	58	34	50

Good arm, but not good enough to compensate for the fact that he doesn't know how to pitch. Triple-A hitters expose his weaknesses.

Chris Sheff   Florida Marlins
1997 Statistics   **Pos:** OF **Age:** 27 **B:**R **T:**R

	G	AB	HR	RBI	SB	Avg	OBP	SLG
AAA Charlotte	120	322	11	43	16	.255	.341	.435

Roster filler, usually plays decently but not enough to get noticed. Cup-of-coffee candidate.

Al Shirley   Kansas City Royals
1997 Statistics   **Pos:** OF **Age:** 24 **B:**R **T:**R

	G	AB	HR	RBI	SB	Avg	OBP	SLG
AA Wichita	81	240	4	25	9	.271	.332	.371

Tools intact: size, strength, speed. Has made some progress learning to use them, but needs Triple-A success.

Mitch Simons   Minnesota Twins
1997 Statistics   **Pos:** 2B **Age:** 29 **B:**R **T:**R

	G	AB	HR	RBI	SB	Avg	OBP	SLG
AAA Salt Lake	115	462	5	59	26	.299	.366	.448

Has speed, a little pop, hustles. Would be decent utility infielder.

Steve Sinclair — Toronto Blue Jays

1997 Statistics — Pos: P Age: 26 B:L T: L

	W	L	ERA	G	GS	Sv	IP	H	BB	SO
AAA Syracuse	0	0	6.00	6	0	0	9.0	11	3	9
A Dunedin	2	5	2.90	43	0	3	68.1	63	26	66

Being groomed as a middle reliever and probably can do the job. Won't make any All-Star teams, but he could make some money.

Duane Singleton — Anaheim Angels

1997 Statistics — Pos: OF Age: 25 B:L T:R

	G	AB	HR	RBI	SB	Avg	OBP	SLG
AAA Vancouver	108	383	5	36	15	.206	.282	.305
AA Midland	13	55	2	8	4	.309	.371	.545

Looks like a baseball player, runs great, can't hit.

Steve Sisco — Kansas City Royals

1997 Statistics — Pos: 2B Age: 28 B:R T:R

	G	AB	HR	RBI	SB	Avg	OBP	SLG
AAA Omaha	54	188	3	12	2	.261	.289	.351
AA Wichita	55	182	3	24	3	.286	.365	.401

Can play all defensive positions pretty well, hustles, never complains. Offense one step above bad.

J.D. Smart — Montreal Expos

1997 Statistics — Pos: P Age: 24 B:R T: R

	W	L	ERA	G	GS	Sv	IP	H	BB	SO
AA Harrisburg	6	3	3.69	12	12	0	70.2	75	24	43
A Wst Plm Bch	5	4	3.26	17	13	1	102.0	105	21	65

Doesn't throw hard but pitches up to his name. Needs to succeed at higher levels to get a chance, and even then he'll only get one.

Cam Smith — Seattle Mariners

1997 Statistics — Pos: P Age: 24 B:R T: R

	W	L	ERA	G	GS	Sv	IP	H	BB	SO
AA Mobile	3	5	7.03	26	15	1	79.1	85	73	88

Some of the best stuff around, and some of the worst control.

Danny Smith — Texas Rangers

1997 Statistics — Pos: P Age: 28 B:L T: L

	W	L	ERA	G	GS	Sv	IP	H	BB	SO
AAA Okla City	3	14	5.64	23	23	0	129.1	154	42	67
AA Tulsa	1	1	3.64	5	5	0	29.2	25	15	27

First-round pick back in 1990, career has been handicapped by injuries. Most of his velocity is gone.

Scott Smith — Seattle Mariners

1997 Statistics — Pos: OF Age: 26 B:R T:R

	G	AB	HR	RBI	SB	Avg	OBP	SLG
AA Memphis	123	453	14	67	4	.249	.320	.393

Has power potential but struggles against high-level breaking stuff. Probably too old to get much better.

John Snyder — Chicago White Sox

1997 Statistics — Pos: P Age: 23 B:R T: R

	W	L	ERA	G	GS	Sv	IP	H	BB	SO
AA Birmingham	7	8	4.64	20	20	0	114.1	130	43	90

Sinker-slider guy, mediocre in Double-A. You never know with pitchers.

Matt Snyder — Baltimore Orioles

1997 Statistics — Pos: P Age: 23 B:R T: R

	W	L	ERA	G	GS	Sv	IP	H	BB	SO
AA Bowie	7	5	4.16	67	0	19	80.0	89	42	68

Double-A reliever with an adequate fastball and a great curve. Needs to improve control.

Steve Soderstrom — SF Giants

1997 Statistics — Pos: P Age: 25 B:R T: R

	W	L	ERA	G	GS	Sv	IP	H	BB	SO
AAA Phoenix	4	8	6.47	31	15	1	105.2	141	52	78

Trying to make transition from power to finesse after a series of injuries. It isn't working yet.

Justin Speier — Chicago Cubs

1997 Statistics — Pos: P Age: 24 B:R T: R

	W	L	ERA	G	GS	Sv	IP	H	BB	SO
AAA Iowa	2	0	0.00	8	0	1	12.1	5	1	9
AA Orlando	6	5	4.48	50	0	6	78.1	77	23	63

Chris Speier's son has a respectable fastball, decent control. Middle-relief candidate after pitching well in the Arizona Fall League.

Kennie Steenstra — Chicago Cubs
1997 Statistics Pos: P **Age:** 27 **B:**R **T:** R

	W	L	ERA	G	GS	Sv	IP	H	BB	SO
AAA Iowa	5	10	3.92	25	25	0	160.2	161	41	111

Maximum finesse pitcher, okay in Triple-A but hasn't received any major league innings because of lack of rudimentary fastball.

Mike Stefanski — St. Louis Cardinals
1997 Statistics Pos: C **Age:** 28 **B:**R **T:**R

	G	AB	HR	RBI	SB	Avg	OBP	SLG
AAA Louisville	57	197	6	22	0	.305	.346	.447
AA Arkansas	1	4	0	0	0	.250	.250	.750

Veteran catcher had a good year with the bat, looking for job on the bench. Another example of why no team should ever be looking for a backup catcher.

Rod Steph — Baltimore Orioles
1997 Statistics Pos: P **Age:** 28 **B:**R **T:** R

	W	L	ERA	G	GS	Sv	IP	H	BB	SO
AAA Rochester	3	3	4.25	41	0	14	48.2	49	12	51
AA Bowie	1	0	1.32	7	0	0	13.2	6	3	9

Triple-A closer, mediocre stuff but good control and nice K/BB numbers. Middle-relief candidate for a team that needs pitching.

Andy Stewart — Kansas City Royals
1997 Statistics Pos: C **Age:** 27 **B:**R **T:**R

	G	AB	HR	RBI	SB	Avg	OBP	SLG
AAA Omaha	86	288	6	24	1	.274	.335	.378
AL Kansas City	5	8	0	0	0	.250	.250	.375

Defensive catcher with a bit of power, could be an adequate backup for a strong starter.

Pedro Swann — Atlanta Braves
1997 Statistics Pos: OF **Age:** 27 **B:**L **T:**R

	G	AB	HR	RBI	SB	Avg	OBP	SLG
AA Greenville	124	465	24	83	5	.286	.358	.512

Veteran Double-A and Triple-A outfielder, always seems to play pretty well, but never gets a chance. I wouldn't mind having him as a reserve. Needs a new organization.

Dave Swartzbaugh — Chicago Cubs
1997 Statistics Pos: P **Age:** 30 **B:**R **T:** R

	W	L	ERA	G	GS	Sv	IP	H	BB	SO
AAA Iowa	8	7	2.82	24	20	1	134.0	129	48	97
NL Chicago	0	1	9.00	2	2	0	8.0	12	7	4

Another finesse guy, deserves more of a chance than he has received. The new Mickey Weston.

Jeff Tam — New York Mets
1997 Statistics Pos: P **Age:** 27 **B:**R **T:** R

	W	L	ERA	G	GS	Sv	IP	H	BB	SO
AAA Norfolk	7	5	4.67	40	11	6	111.2	137	14	67

Mets farm system staff filler for years. Has great control but nothing else.

Jamie Taylor — Colorado Rockies
1997 Statistics Pos: 3B **Age:** 27 **B:**L **T:**R

	G	AB	HR	RBI	SB	Avg	OBP	SLG
AA New Haven	104	329	8	41	2	.325	.389	.456
A Salem	23	80	1	9	2	.263	.379	.375

Experienced infielder hit well at New Haven. Future restricted, but if he gets hot at Colorado Springs he might get a few days in the Show.

Juan Thomas — Chicago White Sox
1997 Statistics Pos: 1B-DH **Age:** 25 **B:**R **T:**R

	G	AB	HR	RBI	SB	Avg	OBP	SLG
AA Birmingham	80	311	10	55	1	.302	.354	.463
A Winston-Sal	45	164	13	28	1	.262	.335	.543

Righthanded first baseman with genuine power but wrong first name.

Brian Tollberg — San Diego Padres
1997 Statistics Pos: P **Age:** 25 **B:**R **T:** R

	W	L	ERA	G	GS	Sv	IP	H	BB	SO
AA Mobile	6	3	3.72	31	13	0	123.1	123	24	108

Double-A finesse swingman, mediocre stuff but awesome K/BB ratios. I'd rather run him out there than Sean Bergman.

Paul Torres — Seattle Mariners

1997 Statistics Pos: 3B Age: 27 B:R T:R

	G	AB	HR	RBI	SB	Avg	OBP	SLG
AAA Tacoma	59	209	5	22	1	.301	.346	.464
AA Memphis	62	218	6	55	3	.344	.439	.491

So erratic he should be a pitcher. Sometimes hits really well, sometimes an automatic out.

Jody Treadwell — Los Angeles Dodgers

1997 Statistics Pos: P Age: 29 B:R T: R

	W	L	ERA	G	GS	Sv	IP	H	BB	SO
AAA Albuquerque	10	5	5.12	27	21	1	128.1	143	54	108

A 5.12 ERA at Albuquerque isn't bad, but try convincing a scouting director, even a smart one, that it's acceptable.

Chris Turner — Minnesota Twins

1997 Statistics Pos: 1B-C Age: 29 B:R T:R

	G	AB	HR	RBI	SB	Avg	OBP	SLG
AAA Vancouver	37	135	4	22	0	.370	.437	.533
A Lk Elsinore	3	12	0	1	0	.083	.083	.250
AL Anaheim	13	23	1	2	0	.261	.393	.522

Veteran minor league catcher looking for bench job. One of many backstops hurt by the fact that teams don't carry third catchers any longer.

Brad Tweedlie — Boston Red Sox

1997 Statistics Pos: P Age: 26 B:R T: R

	W	L	ERA	G	GS	Sv	IP	H	BB	SO
AA Trenton	4	6	5.77	41	0	5	57.2	62	44	30

One of the better arms in the Bosox system, but has no command.

Brad Tyler — Atlanta Braves

1997 Statistics Pos: OF Age: 29 B:L T:R

	G	AB	HR	RBI	SB	Avg	OBP	SLG
AAA Richmond	129	383	18	77	13	.264	.355	.496

Above-average power, high walk rate, lefty bat would make him valuable as a reserve. Poor glove work and age limit his opportunities.

Tim Unroe — Milwaukee Brewers

1997 Statistics Pos: 3B Age: 27 B:R T:R

	G	AB	HR	RBI	SB	Avg	OBP	SLG
AAA Tucson	63	234	9	46	3	.291	.320	.487
AL Milwaukee	32	16	2	5	2	.250	.333	.688

Has pop in his bat, but too impatient. Not a great defensive player at third base, doesn't hit enough for first.

Ryan VanDeWeg — San Diego Padres

1997 Statistics Pos: P Age: 24 B:R T: R

	W	L	ERA	G	GS	Sv	IP	H	BB	SO
AA Mobile	9	8	5.43	27	27	0	159.0	198	55	81

Has a good arm but failed Double-A debut, stalling his development. No reason to expect a comeback, but no reason why one can't happen either.

Jay Veniard — Toronto Blue Jays

1997 Statistics Pos: P Age: 23 B:L T: L

	W	L	ERA	G	GS	Sv	IP	H	BB	SO
AA Knoxville	3	8	5.85	17	15	0	75.1	97	37	54
A Dunedin	1	3	1.88	10	8	0	52.2	49	35	32

Effective in A-ball, feeble in Double-A. Good arm, could do well if control improves.

Scott Vieira — Chicago Cubs

1997 Statistics Pos: 1B Age: 24 B:R T:R

	G	AB	HR	RBI	SB	Avg	OBP	SLG
A Daytona	134	476	18	80	9	.275	.382	.458

Righthanded-hitting first baseman had a good year in the Florida State League, but his chance to play for the Cubs is remote.

Jeff Wallace — Pittsburgh Pirates

1997 Statistics Pos: P Age: 21 B:L T: L

	W	L	ERA	G	GS	Sv	IP	H	BB	SO
AA Carolina	4	8	5.40	38	0	3	43.1	43	36	39
A Lynchburg	5	0	1.65	9	0	1	16.1	9	10	13
NL Pittsburgh	0	0	0.75	11	0	0	12.0	8	8	14

Hard fastball, command weak. Hyped as a prospect, but his numbers aren't good.

Brett Walters — San Diego Padres
1997 Statistics **Pos:** P **Age:** 23 **B:**R **T:** R

	W	L	ERA	G	GS	Sv	IP	H	BB	SO
AA Mobile	10	7	4.47	31	19	0	145.0	169	30	98

Australian curveball specialist, fine control but gives up too many hits.

Bryan Ward — San Francisco Giants
1997 Statistics **Pos:** P **Age:** 26 **B:**L **T:** L

	W	L	ERA	G	GS	Sv	IP	H	BB	SO
AAA Charlotte	2	9	6.93	15	14	0	75.1	102	30	48
AA Portland	6	3	3.91	12	12	0	76.0	71	19	69

Lefty with decent arm and good control, does well in Double-A but gets pounded in Triple-A. Chances are diminishing.

Mike Warner — Atlanta Braves
1997 Statistics **Pos:** OF **Age:** 26 **B:**L **T:**L

	G	AB	HR	RBI	SB	Avg	OBP	SLG
AA Greenville	91	303	7	35	12	.320	.432	.482

Can hit some, but no star potential due to age. Would have value as a pinch hitter. See Gabe Whatley.

B.J. Waszgis — Boston Red Sox
1997 Statistics **Pos:** C **Age:** 27 **B:**R **T:**R

	G	AB	HR	RBI	SB	Avg	OBP	SLG
AAA Rochester	100	315	13	48	1	.260	.383	.438

Has patience and power, glove good enough to keep him around as a backup for a long time if he hits adequately.

Jim Wawruck — Baltimore Orioles
1997 Statistics **Pos:** OF **Age:** 27 **B:**L **T:**L

	G	AB	HR	RBI	SB	Avg	OBP	SLG
AAA Rochester	94	339	5	35	12	.271	.342	.392

Triple-A Joe Orsulak.

Eric Weaver — Los Angeles Dodgers
1997 Statistics **Pos:** P **Age:** 24 **B:**R **T:** R

	W	L	ERA	G	GS	Sv	IP	H	BB	SO
AAA Albuquerque	0	3	6.42	21	8	0	68.2	101	38	54
AA San Antonio	7	2	3.61	13	13	0	84.2	80	38	60

Good arm, got banged around in the Pacific Coast League. He's the 402,711th pitcher to have his career short-circuited that way.

Mike Welch — Philadelphia Phillies
1997 Statistics **Pos:** P **Age:** 25 **B:**L **T:** R

	W	L	ERA	G	GS	Sv	IP	H	BB	SO
AAA Norfolk	2	2	3.66	46	0	20	51.2	53	16	35

Triple-A closer, has a good arm but not a great one. Middle-relief candidate.

Gabe Whatley — Atlanta Braves
1997 Statistics **Pos:** OF-1B **Age:** 26 **B:**L **T:**R

	G	AB	HR	RBI	SB	Avg	OBP	SLG
AA Greenville	95	310	15	57	5	.303	.403	.535
A Durham	43	154	8	30	9	.273	.390	.532

Solid Double-A season, but a bit too old to get excited about. See Mike Warner.

Derrick White — Anaheim Angels
1997 Statistics **Pos:** OF **Age:** 28 **B:**R **T:**R

	G	AB	HR	RBI	SB	Avg	OBP	SLG
AAA Vancouver	116	414	11	65	11	.324	.396	.498
AA Midland	10	37	0	3	1	.189	.302	.243

Has power, a little speed, becoming more patient recently. Wouldn't be bad as a reserve.

Casey Whitten — Cleveland Indians
1997 Statistics **Pos:** P **Age:** 25 **B:**L **T:** L

	W	L	ERA	G	GS	Sv	IP	H	BB	SO
AAA Buffalo	0	0	0.00	2	0	0	1.0	1	0	0
AA Akron	1	3	5.87	4	4	0	15.1	20	11	14

Injuries may have ruined what was a promising career.

Drew Williams — Milwaukee Brewers
1997 Statistics **Pos:** 1B **Age:** 26 **B:**L **T:**R

	G	AB	HR	RBI	SB	Avg	OBP	SLG
AA El Paso	71	257	9	36	2	.237	.298	.405
A Stockton	48	175	3	23	4	.257	.343	.400

Power-hitting first baseman didn't adjust well to Double-A pitching. Chances slipping fast.

Shad Williams — Anaheim Angels
1997 Statistics　　　Pos: P **Age:** 27 **B:**R **T:** R

	W	L	ERA	G	GS	Sv	IP	H	BB	SO
AAA Vancouver	6	2	3.82	40	10	0	99.0	98	41	52
AL Anaheim	0	0	0.00	1	0	0	1.0	1	1	0

Relies on curveball and control, has survived three seasons in the Pacific Coast League. Deserves a chance.

Todd Williams — Cincinnati Reds
1997 Statistics　　　Pos: P **Age:** 27 **B:**R **T:** R

	W	L	ERA	G	GS	Sv	IP	H	BB	SO
AAA Indianapolis	2	0	2.13	12	0	2	12.2	11	6	11
AA Chattanooga	3	3	2.10	48	0	31	55.2	38	25	45

Product of Dodgers system, submarine pitcher banks on control. Will never close in the majors, but could be okay as a middle reliever.

Craig Wilson — Chicago White Sox
1997 Statistics　　　Pos: SS **Age:** 27 **B:**R **T:**R

	G	AB	HR	RBI	SB	Avg	OBP	SLG
AAA Nashville	137	453	6	42	4	.272	.343	.364

Has some speed and okay glove, could get some infield time with White Sox dumping Ozzie Guillen. Plays in the Cubs organization under the name Chris Wimmer.

Desi Wilson — San Francisco Giants
1997 Statistics　　　Pos: 1B **Age:** 29 **B:**L **T:**L

	G	AB	HR	RBI	SB	Avg	OBP	SLG
AAA Phoenix	121	451	7	53	16	.344	.404	.477

Huge first baseman, lacks power. Valuable when hitting .340, but not when hitting .280.

Tom Wilson — New York Yankees
1997 Statistics　　　Pos: C **Age:** 27 **B:**R **T:**R

	G	AB	HR	RBI	SB	Avg	OBP	SLG
AAA Columbus	1	3	0	0	0	.000	.250	.000
AA Norwich	124	419	21	80	1	.296	.416	.516

Veteran catcher, had a good year in Double-A but too old to have a real career. Might have value as a backup.

Vance Wilson — New York Mets
1997 Statistics　　　Pos: C **Age:** 25 **B:**R **T:**R

	G	AB	HR	RBI	SB	Avg	OBP	SLG
AA Binghamton	92	322	15	40	2	.276	.328	.469

Up and coming catcher had a good year in Double-A and played great in Arizona Fall League. Defense solid, has some power, could see some major league time with Todd Hundley injured. Grade C+ prospect.

Chris Wimmer — Chicago Cubs
1997 Statistics　　　Pos: 2B **Age:** 27 **B:**R **T:**R

	G	AB	HR	RBI	SB	Avg	OBP	SLG
AAA Louisville	5	12	0	1	0	.167	.167	.167
AA Orlando	102	371	2	28	23	.275	.333	.348

Has speed, OK glove, could get some infield time if the Cubs can't find a replacement for Ryne Sandberg. Plays in the White Sox organization under the name Craig Wilson.

Darrin Winston — Philadelphia Phillies
1997 Statistics　　　Pos: P **Age:** 31 **B:**R **T:** L

	W	L	ERA	G	GS	Sv	IP	H	BB	SO
AAA Scranton-WB	7	4	3.43	39	9	0	89.1	74	36	66
NL Philadelphia	2	0	5.25	7	1	0	12.0	8	3	8

Journeyman southpaw earned some major league innings with a nice Triple-A campaign. Could hang around for a while.

Shannon Withem — New York Mets
1997 Statistics　　　Pos: P **Age:** 25 **B:**R **T:** R

	W	L	ERA	G	GS	Sv	IP	H	BB	SO
AAA Norfolk	9	10	4.34	29	27	0	155.2	167	48	109

Still trying to get over the experience of being a pitching prospect in the Tigers system.

Bryan Wolff — San Diego Padres
1997 Statistics　　　Pos: P **Age:** 26 **B:**R **T:** R

	W	L	ERA	G	GS	Sv	IP	H	BB	SO
AA Mobile	1	2	4.80	20	0	0	30.0	34	19	37
AA Wichita	1	1	6.52	12	0	1	9.2	18	5	8
A Rancho Cuca	3	0	1.62	9	2	1	33.1	19	6	39

Minor league reliever has a major league arm, could see big-league action if his command becomes more consistent.

Jason Wood
Oakland Athletics

1997 Statistics   **Pos:** 3B **Age:** 28 **B:**R **T:**R

	G	AB	HR	RBI	SB	Avg	OBP	SLG
AAA Edmonton	130	505	19	87	2	.321	.383	.531

Too old to be a genuine prospect, but hits enough to deserve a brief trial.

Joe Young
Toronto Blue Jays

1997 Statistics   **Pos:** P **Age:** 22 **B:**R **T:** R

	W	L	ERA	G	GS	Sv	IP	H	BB	SO
AA Knoxville	5	4	4.42	19	11	0	59.0	52	40	62

Big, hard-throwing starter, began the year on the disabled list but came off to pitch okay in Double-A. Needs to improve his control, possible sleeper if healthy.

Alan Zinter
Seattle Mariners

1997 Statistics   **Pos:** 1B **Age:** 29 **B:**B **T:**R

	G	AB	HR	RBI	SB	Avg	OBP	SLG
AAA Tacoma	110	404	20	70	3	.287	.388	.502

Has power, but stuck in Triple-A forever because of strikeouts and defensive problems.

John Sickels' Top 50 Prospects

	Player	Pos	Team	Grade
1	Adrian Beltre	3B	Los Angeles Dodgers	A
2	Ben Grieve	RF	Oakland Athletics	A
3	Paul Konerko	3B	Los Angeles Dodgers	A
4	Todd Helton	1B	Colorado Rockies	A
5	Aramis Ramirez	3B	Pittsburgh Pirates	A
6	Travis Lee	1B	Arizona Diamondbacks	A
7	Carl Pavano	RHP	Montreal Expos	A–
8	Miguel Tejada	SS	Oakland Athletics	A–
9	Kerry Wood	RHP	Chicago Cubs	A–
10	Mark Kotsay	CF	Florida Marlins	A–
11	Matt Clement	RHP	San Diego Padres	A–
12	Chad Hermansen	2B	Pittsburgh Pirates	A–
13	Sean Casey	1B	Cleveland Indians	A–
14	Enrique Wilson	2B	Cleveland Indians	A–
15	Scott Elarton	RHP	Houston Astros	A–
16	Fernando Tatis	3B	Texas Rangers	A–
17	Eric Chavez	3B	Oakland Athletics	A–
18	A.J. Hinch	C	Oakland Athletics	B+
19	Ramon Hernandez	C	Oakland Athletics	B+
20	Alex Gonzalez	SS	Florida Marlins	B+
21	Ron Wright	1B	Pittsburgh Pirates	B+
22	Kris Benson	RHP	Pittsburgh Pirates	B+
23	Brad Fullmer	1B	Montreal Expos	B+
24	Nerio Rodriguez	RHP	Baltimore Orioles	B+
25	Brent Butler	SS	St. Louis Cardinals	B+
26	Eric Milton	LHP	New York Yankees	B+
27	Juan Encarnacion	RF	Detroit Tigers	B+
28	Ramon Ortiz	RHP	Anaheim Angels	B+
29	D'Angelo Jimenez	SS	New York Yankees	B+
30	Brian Rose	RHP	Boston Red Sox	B+
31	Russ Branyan	3B	Cleveland Indians	B+
32	Ruben Rivera	CF	San Diego Padres	B+
33	Ken Cloude	RHP	Seattle Mariners	B+
34	Mike Darr	RF	San Diego Padres	B+
35	Javier Vazquez	RHP	Montreal Expos	B+
36	Ben Petrick	C	Colorado Rockies	B+
37	Cesar King	C	Texas Rangers	B+
38	Mike Lowell	3B	New York Yankees	B+
39	Michael Coleman	CF	Boston Red Sox	B+
40	Bruce Chen	LHP	Atlanta Braves	B+
41	Derrek Lee	1B	Florida Marlins	B+
42	Donzell McDonald	CF	New York Yankees	B+
43	Cliff Politte	RHP	St. Louis Cardinals	B+
44	Ruben Mateo	CF	Texas Rangers	B+
45	Magglio Ordonez	CF	Chicago White Sox	B+
46	Daryle Ward	1B	Houston Astros	B+
47	Mike Caruso	SS	Chicago White Sox	B+
48	Ricky Ledee	LF	New York Yankees	B+
49	David Ortiz	1B	Minnesota Twins	B+
50	Gabe Kapler	RF	Detroit Tigers	B+

Appendix

Minor League Team	Organization	League	Level	Minor League Team	Organization	League	Level
Akron Aeros	Indians	EL	AA	Dunedin Blue Jays	Blue Jays	FSL	A+
Albuquerque Dukes	Dodgers	PCL	AAA	Durham Bulls	Braves	CL	A+
Arkansas Travelers	Cardinals	TL	AA	Edmonton Trappers	Athletics	PCL	AAA
Asheville Tourists	Rockies	SAL	A	El Paso Diablos	Brewers	TL	AA
Astros (Kissimmee)	Astros	GCL	R	Elizabethton Twins	Twins	APPY	R+
Athletics (Phoenix)	Athletics	AZL	R	Erie SeaWolves	Pirates	NY-P	A-
Auburn Doubledays	Astros	NY-P	A-	Eugene Emeralds	Braves	NWL	A-
Augusta GreenJackets	Pirates	SAL	A	Everett AquaSox	Mariners	NWL	A-
Bakersfield Blaze	Giants	CAL	A+	Expos (West Palm Beach)	Expos	GCL	R
Batavia Clippers	Phillies	NY-P	A-	Frederick Keys	Orioles	CL	A+
Beloit Snappers	Brewers	MWL	A	Fort Myers Miracle	Twins	FSL	A+
Billings Mustangs	Reds	PIO	R+	Fort Wayne Wizards	Twins	MWL	A
Binghamton Mets	Mets	EL	AA	Great Falls Dodgers	Dodgers	PIO	R+
Birmingham Barons	White Sox	SL	AA	Greensboro Bats	Yankees	SAL	A
Bluefield Orioles	Orioles	APPY	R+	Greenville Braves	Braves	SL	AA
Boise Hawks	Angels	NWL	A-	Hagerstown Suns	Blue Jays	SAL	A
Bowie Baysox	Orioles	EL	AA	Harrisburg Senators	Expos	EL	AA
Braves (Orlando)	Braves	GCL	R	Helena Brewers	Brewers	PIO	R+
Brevard County Manatees	Marlins	FSL	A+	Hickory Crawdads	White Sox	SAL	A
Bristol Sox	White Sox	APPY	R+	High Desert Mavericks	Diamondbacks	CAL	A+
Buffalo Bisons	Indians	AA	AAA	Hudson Valley Renegades	Devil Rays	NY-P	A-
Burlington Bees	Reds	MWL	A	Huntsville Stars	Athletics	SL	AA
Burlington Indians	Indians	APPY	R+	Idaho Falls Braves	Padres	PIO	R+
Butte Copper Kings	Angels	PIO	R+	Indianapolis Indians	Reds	AA	AAA
Calgary Cannons	Pirates	PCL	AAA	Iowa Cubs	Cubs	AA	AAA
Cape Fear Crocs	Expos	SAL	A	Jackson Generals	Astros	TL	AA
Capital City Bombers	Mets	SAL	A	Jacksonville Suns	Tigers	SL	AA
Carolina Mudcats	Pirates	SL	AA	Jamestown Jammers	Tigers	NY-P	A-
Cedar Rapids Kernels	Angels	MWL	A	Johnson City Cardinals	Cardinals	APPY	R+
Charleston (S.C.) River Dogs	Devil Rays	SAL	A	Kane County Cougars	Marlins	MWL	A
Charleston (W.Va.) Alley Cats	Reds	SAL	A	Kingsport Mets	Mets	APPY	R+
Charlotte Knights	Marlins	IL	AAA	Kinston Indians	Indians	CL	A+
Charlotte Rangers	Rangers	FSL	A+	Kissimmee Cobras	Astros	FSL	A+
Chattanooga Lookouts	Reds	SL	AA	Knoxville Smokies	Blue Jays	SL	AA
Clearwater Phillies	Phillies	FSL	A+	Lake Elsinore Storm	Angels	CAL	A+
Clinton Lumber Kings	Padres	MWL	A	Lakeland Tigers	Tigers	FSL	A+
Colorado Springs Sky Sox	Rockies	PCL	AAA	Lancaster Jet Hawks	Mariners	CAL	A+
Columbus Clippers	Yankees	IL	AAA	Lansing Lugnuts	Royals	MWL	A
Columbus RedStixx	Indians	SAL	A	Las Vegas Stars	Padres	PCL	AAA
Cubs (Mesa)	Cubs	AZL	R	Lethbridge Black Diamonds	Diamondbacks	PIO	R+
Danville Braves	Braves	APPY	R+	Louisville Redbirds	Cardinals	AA	AAA
Daytona Cubs	Cubs	FSL	A+	Lowell Spinners	Red Sox	NY-P	A-
Delmarva Shorebirds	Orioles	SAL	A	Lynchburg Hillcats	Pirates	CL	A+
Devil Rays (St. Petersburg)	Devil Rays	GCL	R	Macon Braves	Braves	SAL	A
Diamondbacks (Peoria)	Diamondbacks	AZL	R	Mariners (Peoria)	Mariners	AZL	R

Minor League Team	Organization	League	Level	Minor League Team	Organization	League	Level
Marlins (Melbourne)	Marlins	GCL	R	Salem Avalanche	Rockies	CL	A+
Martinsville Phillies	Phillies	APPY	R+	Salem-Keizer Volcanoes	Giants	NWL	A-
Medicine Hat Blue Jays	Blue Jays	PIO	R+	Salt Lake Buzz	Twins	PCL	AAA
Memphis Chicks	Mariners	SL	AA	San Antonio Missions	Dodgers	TL	AA
Mets (Port St. Lucie)	Mets	GCL	R	San Bernardino Stampede	Dodgers	CAL	A+
Michigan Battle Cats	Red Sox	MWL	A	San Jose Giants	Giants	CAL	A+
Midland Angels	Angels	TL	AA	Sarasota Red Sox	Red Sox	FSL	A+
Mobile BayBears	Padres	SL	AA	Savannah Sand Gnats	Dodgers	SAL	A
Modesto A's	Athletics	CAL	A+	Scranton/Wilkes-Barre Red Barons	Phillies	IL	AAA
Nashville Sounds	White Sox	AA	AAA	Shreveport Captains	Giants	TL	AA
New Britain Rock Cats	Twins	EL	AA	South Bend Silver Hawks	Diamondbacks	MWL	A
New Haven Ravens	Rockies	EL	AA	Southern Oregon Timberjacks	Athletics	NWL	A-
New Jersey Cardinals	Cardinals	NY-P	A-	Spokane Indians	Royals	NWL	A-
New Orleans Zephyrs	Astros	AA	AAA	St. Catharines Stompers	Blue Jays	NY-P	A-
Norfolk Tides	Mets	IL	AAA	St. Lucie Mets	Mets	FSL	A+
Norwich Navigators	Yankees	EL	AA	St. Petersburg Devil Rays	Devil Rays	FSL	A+
Ogden Raptors	Brewers	PIO	R+	Stockton Ports	Brewers	CAL	A+
Oklahoma City 89ers	Rangers	AA	AAA	Syracuse SkyChiefs	Blue Jays	IL	AAA
Omaha Royals	Royals	AA	AAA	Tacoma Rainiers	Mariners	PCL	AAA
Oneonta Yankees	Yankees	NY-P	A-	Tampa Yankees	Yankees	FSL	A+
Orioles (Sarasota)	Orioles	GCL	R	Tigers (Lakeland)	Tigers	GCL	R
Orlando Rays	Cubs	SL	AA	Toledo Mud Hens	Tigers	IL	AAA
Ottawa Lynx	Expos	IL	AAA	Tucson Toros	Brewers	PCL	AAA
Padres (Peoria)	Padres	AZL	R	Trenton Thunder	Red Sox	EL	AA
Pawtucket Red Sox	Red Sox	IL	AAA	Tulsa Drillers	Rangers	TL	AA
Peoria Chiefs	Cardinals	MWL	A	Twins (Fort Myers)	Twins	GCL	R
Phoenix Firebirds	Giants	PCL	AAA	Utica Blue Sox	Marlins	NY-P	A-
Piedmont Boll Weevils	Phillies	SAL	A	Vancouver Canadians	Angels	PCL	AAA
Pirates (Bradenton)	Pirates	GCL	R	Vermont Expos	Expos	NY-P	A-
Pittsfield Mets	Mets	NY-P	A-	Vero Beach Dodgers	Dodgers	FSL	A+
Portland Sea Dogs	Marlins	EL	AA	Visalia Oaks	Athletics	CAL	A+
Portland Rockies	Rockies	NWL	A-	Watertown Indians	Indians	NY-P	A-
Prince William Cannons	Cardinals	CL	A+	West Michigan Whitecaps	Tigers	MWL	A
Princeton Devil Rays	Devil Rays	APPY	R+	West Palm Beach Expos	Expos	FSL	A+
Pulaski Rangers	Rangers	APPY	R+	White Sox (Sarasota)	White Sox	GCL	R
Quad City River Bandits	Astros	MWL	A	Wichita Wranglers	Royals	TL	AA
Rancho Cucamonga Quakes	Padres	CAL	A+	Williamsport Cubs	Cubs	NY-P	A-
Rangers (Port Charlotte)	Rangers	GCL	R	Wilmington Blue Rocks	Royals	CL	A+
Reading Phillies	Phillies	EL	AA	Winston-Salem Warthogs	White Sox	CL	A+
Red Sox (Fort Myers)	Red Sox	GCL	R	Wisconsin Timber Rattlers	Mariners	MWL	A
Richmond Braves	Braves	IL	AAA	Yakima Bears	Dodgers	NWL	A-
Rochester Red Wings	Orioles	IL	AAA	Yankees (Tampa)	Yankees	GCL	R
Rockford Cubbies	Cubs	MWL	A				
Rockies (Chandler)	Rockies	AZL	R				
Royals (Fort Myers)	Royals	GCL	R				

About STATS, Inc.

STATS, Inc. is the nation's leading independent sports information and statistical analysis company, providing detailed sports services for a wide array of commercial clients.

As one of the fastest-growing sports companies—in 1994, we ranked 144th on the "Inc. 500" list of fastest-growing privately held firms—STATS provides the most up-to-the-minute sports information to professional teams, print and broadcast media, software developers and interactive service providers around the country. Some of our major clients are ESPN, the Associated Press, Fox Sports, Electronic Arts, MSNBC, SONY and Topps. Much of the information we provide is available to the public via STATS On-Line. With a computer and a modem, you can follow action in the four major professional sports, as well as NCAA football and basketball. . . as it happens!

STATS Publishing, a division of STATS, Inc., produces 12 annual books, including the *Major League Handbook*, *The Scouting Notebook*, the *Pro Football Handbook*, the *Pro Basketball Handbook* and the *Hockey Handbook* as well as the *STATS Fantasy Insider* magazine. These publications deliver STATS' expertise to fans, scouts, general managers and media around the country.

In addition, STATS offers the most innovative—and fun—fantasy sports games and support products around, from *Bill James Fantasy Baseball* and *Bill James Classic Baseball* to *STATS Fantasy Football* and *STATS Fantasy Hoops*. Check out the latest STATS and Bill James fantasy game, *Stock Market Baseball* and our immensely popular Fantasy Portfolios.

Information technology has grown by leaps and bounds in the last decade, and STATS will continue to be at the forefront as a supplier of the most up-to-date, in-depth sports information available. For those of you on the information superhighway, you can always catch STATS in our area on America Online or at our Internet site.

For more information on our products, or on joining our reporter network, contact us on:

America On-Line — (Keyword: STATS)
Internet — www.stats.com
Toll Free in the USA at 1-800-63-STATS (1-800-637-8287)
Outside the USA at 1-847-676-3383

Or write to:

STATS, Inc.
8131 Monticello Ave.
Skokie, IL 60076-3300

About John Sickels

John Sickels was born and raised in Des Moines, Iowa. He received his B.A. in European History and Philosophy from Northwest Missouri State University in 1990, earned his M.A. in Modern European History from the University of Kansas in 1993, and is currently working on his Ph.D. dissertation. John worked as Bill James' research assistant from 1993 to 1996, helping Mr. James with a variety of projects, particularly the evaluation of major and minor league players. He writes articles about the minor leagues for ESPN's SportsZone website on the Internet. This is his third book.

Glossary

Most of the information in this book is pretty straightforward. But for the sake of completeness, here is a rundown of all the abbreviations and definitions:

For Hitters:

AB=at-bats, Age=player's age on March 29, 1998 (Opening Day), Avg=batting average, BB=walks, CS=caught stealing, H=hits, HR=home runs, Ht=height, G=games, Lg=minor league level, OBP=on-base percentage, R=runs, RBI=runs batted in, SLG=slugging percentage, Pos=position, SB=stolen bases, SO=strikeouts, Wt=weight, Yr=year, 2B=doubles, 3B=triples.

For Pitchers:

Age=player's age on March 29, 1998, BB=walks issued, ER=earned runs allowed, ERA=earned run average, G=games pitched, GS=games started, H=hits allowed, HR=home runs allowed, Ht=height, IP=innings pitched, L=losses, Lg=minor league level, Pct=winning percentage, POS=position, R=runs allowed, Sv=saves, SO=strikeouts, W=wins, Wt= weight, Yr=year.

Definitions:

Slow-A: Otherwise known as "Regular A," these full-season leagues contain less-experienced professional players. The Slow-A leagues are the Midwest League and South Atlantic League (Sally).

Fast-A: Otherwise known as "Advanced A," these A-level leagues are the California League, Carolina League and Florida State League.

Secondary Average: (Total Bases minus Hits plus Walks plus Stolen Bases) divided by At-Bats

The Ultimate Baseball Authorities

Bill James and STATS proudly introduce the ultimate baseball histories, guaranteed to bring your baseball memories to life. From 1876 to today, STATS defines Major League Baseball like no one else.

STATS All-Time Major League Handbook is the ONLY baseball register featuring complete year-by-year career historical statistics for EVERY major league batter, pitcher and fielder. In-depth position-by-position fielding stats and hitting stats for pitchers round out the most detailed player register ever compiled. Available January, 1998.

STATS All-Time Baseball Sourcebook provides complete summaries of every major league season, including standings, league leaders, in-depth team profiles and highlights. This is the ONLY baseball reference with complete postseason info — from pennant races to League Championships to the World Series, you'll be on hand for every triumph and heartbreak since 1876. Franchise sections list clubs' seasonal and all-time record holders, hitting and pitching leaders and more. Available March, 1998.

10th ANNIVERSARY EDITION!

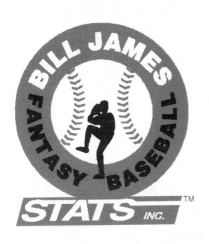

Bill James Fantasy Baseball enters its 10th season of offering baseball fans the most unique, realistic and exciting game that fantasy sports has to offer.

As team owner and GM, you draft a 26-player roster and can expand to as many as 28. Players aren't ranked like in rotisserie leagues—you'll get credit for everything a player does, like hitting homers, driving in runs, turning double plays, pitching quality outings and much more!

The team which scores the most points among all leagues, and wins the World Series, will receive the John McGraw Award, which includes a one-week trip to the Grapefruit League in spring training, a day at the ballpark with Bill James, and a new fantasy league named in his/her honor!

Unique Features Include:

- **Live fantasy experts** — available seven days a week

- **The best weekly reports in the business** — detailing who is in the lead, win-loss records, MVPs, and team strengths and weaknesses

- **On-Line computer system** — a world of information, including daily updates of fantasy standings and stats

- **Over twice as many statistics as rotisserie**

- **Transactions that are effective the very next day!**

"My goal was to develop a fantasy league based on the simplest yet most realistic principles possible. A league in which the values are as nearly as possible what they ought to be, without being distorted by artificial category values or rankings...."

- Bill James

Use Order Form in This Book, or Call 1-800-63-STATS or 847-676-3383 or visit www.stats.com

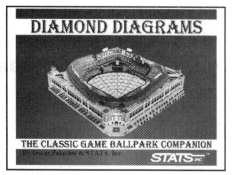

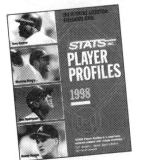

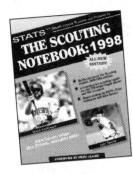
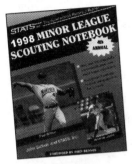
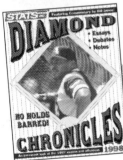
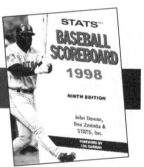

ROUNDING OUT THE STARTING LINEUP...

STATS Pro Football Handbook 1998

- A complete season-by-season register for every active NFL player
- Numerous statistical breakdowns for hundreds of NFL players
- Leader boards in a number of innovative and traditional categories
- Exclusive evaluations of offensive linemen
- **Item #FH98, $19.95, Available 2/1/98**

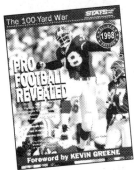

STATS Pro Football Revealed 1998
The 100-Yard War

- Profiles each team, complete with essays, charts and play diagrams
- Detailed statistical breakdowns on players, teams and coaches
- Essays about NFL trends and happenings by leading experts
- Same data as seen on ESPN's *Sunday Night Football* broadcasts
- **Item #PF98, $19.95, Available 7/1/98**

STATS Pro Basketball Handbook 1997-98

- Career stats for every player who logged minutes during 1996-97
- Team game logs with points, rebounds, assists and much more
- Leader boards from points per game to triple doubles
- Essays cover the hottest topics facing the NBA. Foreword by Bill Walton
- **Item #BH98, $19.95, Available Now!**

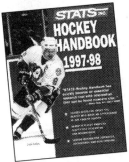

STATS Hockey Handbook 1997-98

- Complete career register for every 1996-97 NHL player and goalie
- Exclusive breakdowns identify player strengths and weaknesses
- Specific coverage for each team, plus league profiles
- Standard and exclusive leader boards
- **Item #HH98, $19.95, Available Now!**

Order from STATS™ Today!

Use Order Form in This Book, or Call 1-800-63-STATS or 847-676-3383 or visit www.stats.com

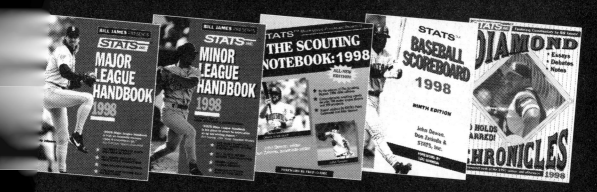

Get Into STATS Fantasy Hoops!

Soar into next season with STATS Fantasy Hoops! SFH lets YOU make the calls. Don't just sit back and watch Grant Hill, Shawn Kemp and Michael Jordan—get in the game and coach your team to the top!

How to Play SFH:
1. Sign up to coach a team
2. You'll receive a full set of rules and a draft form with SFH point values for all eligible players—anyone who played in the NBA last year, plus all NBA draft picks
3. Complete the draft form and return it to STATS
4. You will take part in the draft with nine other owners, and we will send you league rosters
5. You make unlimited weekly transactions including trades, free-agent signings, activations, and benchings
6. Six of the 10 teams in your league advance to postseason play, with two teams ultimately advancing to the Finals

SFH point values are based on actual NBA results, mirroring the real thing. Weekly reports will tell you everything you need to know to lead your team to the SFH Championship!

PLAY STATS Fantasy Football!

STATS Fantasy Football puts YOU in charge! You draft, trade, cut, bench, activate players and even sign free agents each week. SFF pits you head-to-head against 11 other owners.

STATS' scoring system applies realistic values, tested against actual NFL results. Each week, you'll receive a superb in-depth report telling you all about both team and league performances.

How to Play SFF:
1. Sign up today!
2. STATS sends you a draft form listing all eligible NFL players
3. Fill out the draft form and return it to STATS, and you will take part in the draft along with 11 other team owners
4. Go head-to-head against the other owners in your league. You'll make week-by-week roster moves and transactions through STATS' Fantasy Football experts, via phone, fax, or on-line!

STATS Fantasy Football on the Web? Check it out! www.stats.com

Order from STATS INC. Today!

Use Order Form in This Book, or Call 1-800-63-STATS or 847-676-3383 or visit www.stats.com

STATS, Inc. Order Form

Name_____

Address_____

City_____ State_____ Zip_____

Phone_____ Fax_____ E-mail Address_____

Method of Payment (U.S. Funds Only):
❑ Check   ❑ Money Order   ❑ Visa   ❑ MasterCard

Credit Card Information:

Cardholder Name_____

Credit Card Number_____ Exp. Date_____

Signature_____

PUBLICATIONS (STATS books include FREE first class shipping; magazines — add $2)

Qty.	Product Name	Item #	Price	Total
	STATS All-Time Major League Handbook	ATHA	$54.95	
	STATS All-Time Baseball Sourcebook	ATSA	$54.95	
	STATS All-Time Major League COMBO (BOTH books!)	ATCA	$99.95	
	STATS Major League Handbook 1998	HB98	$19.95	
	STATS Major League Handbook 1998 (Comb-bound)	HC98	$21.95	
	STATS Projections Update 1998 (MAGAZINE)	PJUP	$9.95	
	The Scouting Notebook: 1998	SN98	$19.95	
	The Scouting Notebook: 1998 (Comb-bound)	SC98	$21.95	
	STATS Minor League Scouting Notebook 1998	MN98	$19.95	
	STATS Minor League Handbook 1998	MH98	$19.95	
	STATS Minor League Handbook 1998 (Comb-bound)	MC98	$21.95	
	STATS Player Profiles 1998	PP98	$19.95	
	STATS Player Profiles 1998 (Comb-bound)	PC98	$21.95	
	STATS 1998 BVSP Match-Ups!	BP98	$19.95	
	STATS Baseball Scoreboard 1998	SB98	$19.95	
	STATS Diamond Chronicles 1998	CH98	$19.95	
	Pro Football Revealed: The 100 Yard War (1998 Edition)	PF98	$19.95	
	STATS Pro Football Handbook 1998	FH98	$19.95	
	STATS Pro Football Handbook 1998 (Comb-bound)	FC98	$21.95	
	STATS Basketball Handbook 1997-98	BH98	$19.95	
	STATS Hockey Handbook 1997-98	HH98	$19.95	
	STATS Diamond Diagrams 1998	DD98	$19.95	
	STATS Fantasy Insider: 1998 Major League Baseball Edition (MAGAZINE)	IB98	$5.95	
	STATS Fantasy Insider: 1998 Pro Football Edition (MAGAZINE)	IF98	$5.95	
	Prior Editions (Please circle appropriate year)			
	STATS Major League Handbook '90 '91 '92 '93 '94 '95 '96 '97		$9.95	
	The Scouting Report/Notebook '94 '95 '96 '97		$9.95	
	STATS Player Profiles '93 '94 '95 '96 '97		$9.95	
	STATS Minor League Handbook '92 '93 '94 '95 '96 '97		$9.95	
	STATS BVSP Match-Ups! '94 '95 '96 '97		$5.95	
	STATS Baseball Scoreboard '92 '93 '94 '95 '96 '97		$9.95	
	STATS Basketball Scoreboard/Handbook '93-'94 '94-'95 '95-'96 '96-'97		$9.95	
	Pro Football Revealed: The 100 Yard War '94 '95 '96 '97		$9.95	
	STATS Pro Football Handbook '95 '96 '97		$9.95	
	STATS Minor League Scouting Notebook '95 '96 '97		$9.95	
	STATS Hockey Handbook '96-'97		$9.95	

FANTASY GAMES

Qty.	Product Name	Item Number	Price	Total
	Bill James Classic Baseball	BJCB	$129.00	
	STATS Fantasy Hoops	SFH	$79.00	
	STATS Fantasy Football	SFF	$69.00	
	Bill James Fantasy Baseball	BJFB	$89.00	

1st Fantasy Team Name (ex. Colt 45's): _____ _____

   What Fantasy Game is this team for? _____

2nd Fantasy Team Name (ex. Colt 45's): _____ _____

   What Fantasy Game is this team for? _____

NOTE: $1.00/player is charged for all roster moves and transactions.

For Bill James Fantasy Baseball:

Would you like to play in a league drafted by Bill James?   ❏ Yes   ❏ No

MULTIMEDIA PRODUCTS (Prices include shipping & handling charges)

Qty.	Product Name	Item Number	Price	Total
	Bill James Encyclopedia CD-Rom	BJCD	$49.95	

TOTALS

	Price	Total
Product Total (excl. Fantasy Games)		
Canada—all orders—add:	$2.50/book	
Magazines—shipping—add:	$2.00/each	
Order 2 or more books—subtract:	$1.00/book	
(NOT to be combined with other specials)		
Subtotal		
Fantasy Games Total		
IL residents add 8.5% sales tax		
GRAND TOTAL		

For Faster Service, Please Call 800-63-STATS or 847-676-3383
Fax Your Order to 847-676-0821
Visit STATS on the World Wide Web at www.stats.com
or on AOL at Keyword STATS
STATS, Inc • 8131 Monticello Avenue • Skokie, Illinois 60076-3300

NOTE: *Orders for shipments outside of the USA or Canada are Credit Card only.*
Actual shipping charges will be added to the product cost.